Philosophy of Literature

BLACKWELL PHILOSOPHY ANTHOLOGIES

Each volume in this outstanding series provides an authoritative and comprehensive collection of the essential primary readings from philosophy's main fields of study. Designed to complement the *Blackwell Companions to Philosophy* series, each volume represents an unparalleled resource in its own right, and will provide the ideal platform for course use.

1   Cottingham: *Western Philosophy: An Anthology*
2   Cahoone: *From Modernism to Postmodernism: An Anthology* (expanded second edition)
3   LaFollette: *Ethics in Practice: An Anthology* (second edition)
4   Goodin and Pettit: *Contemporary Political Philosophy: An Anthology*
5   Eze: *African Philosophy: An Anthology*
6   McNeill and Feldman: *Continental Philosophy: An Anthology*
7   Kim and Sosa: *Metaphysics: An Anthology*
8   Lycan: *Mind and Cognition: An Anthology* (second edition)
9   Kuhse and Singer: *Bioethics: An Anthology*
10 Cummins and Cummins: *Minds, Brains, and Computers – The Foundations of Cognitive Science: An Anthology*
11 Sosa and Kim: *Epistemology: An Anthology*
12 Kearney and Rasmussen: *Continental Aesthetics – Romanticism to Postmodernism: An Anthology*
13 Martinich and Sosa: *Analytic Philosophy: An Anthology*
14 Jacquette: *Philosophy of Logic: An Anthology*
15 Jacquette: *Philosophy of Mathematics: An Anthology*
16 Harris, Pratt, and Waters: *American Philosophies: An Anthology*
17 Emmanuel and Goold: *Modern Philosophy – From Descartes to Nietzsche: An Anthology*
18 Scharff and Dusek: *Philosophy of Technology – The Technological Condition: An Anthology*
19 Light and Rolston: *Environmental Ethics: An Anthology*
20 Taliaferro and Griffiths: *Philosophy of Religion: An Anthology*
21 Lamarque and Olsen: *Aesthetics and the Philosophy of Art – The Analytic Tradition: An Anthology*
22 John and Lopes: *Philosophy of Literature – Contemporary and Classic Readings: An Anthology*

Philosophy of Literature
Contemporary and Classic Readings
An Anthology

Edited by
Eileen John
and
Dominic McIver Lopes

Blackwell
Publishing

350 Main Street, Malden, MA 02148-5020, USA
108 Cowley Road, Oxford OX4 1JF, UK
550 Swanston Street, Carlton, Victoria 3053, Australia

First published 2004 by Blackwell Publishing Ltd

Library of Congress Cataloging-in-Publication Data

Philosophy of literature : contemporary and classic readings : an
anthology / edited by Eileen John and Dominic McIver Lopes.
    p. cm.— (Blackwell philosophy anthologies ; 22)
Includes bibliographical references and index.
    ISBN 1–4051–1209–3 (hardcover : alk. paper) — ISBN 1–4051–1208–5
(pbk. : alk paper)
 1. Literature—History and criticism. 2. Literature—Philosophy. I.
John, Eileen. II. Lopes, Dominic. III. Series.
    PN501.P54 2004
    801—dc22

                                                                        2003016237

A catalogue record for this title is available from the British Library.

Typeset in 9 on 11pt Ehrhardt
by Kolam Information Services Pvt. Ltd, Pondicherry, India

For further information on
Blackwell Publishing, visit our website:
http://www.blackwellpublishing.com

Contents

Contents

Acknowledgments

The contents of this anthology reflect the advice of Eva Dadlez, Jeff Dean, Berys Gaut, Carol Gould, John A. Fisher, Stacie Friend, James Harold, Matthew Kieran, Peter Lamarque, Derek Matravers, Aaron Meskin, James Shelley, Robert Stecker, and Blackwell's anonymous reviewers. We appreciate the candor and resourcefulness of our advisors. We also thank Lisa Martin and Anastasia Panagopoulos for bibliographic assistance, Nola Semczyszyn for indexing, Sandra Rapheal for copy-editing, Damian Lopes for consultations concerning concrete poetry, and Susan Herrington and Dustin Stokes for editorial acumen. This book is dedicated to our friend and colleague, Phil Alperson.

The editors and publisher gratefully acknowledge the permission granted to reproduce the copyright material in this book:

1 Extracts from Plato, *Republic*, trans. Francis Cornford (Oxford: Oxford University Press, 1941), pp. 68–72, 74–80, 324–40. Reprinted by permission of Oxford University Press.

2 From *The Poetics of Aristotle: Translation and Commentary* by Stephen Halliwell (Chapel Hill: University of North Carolina Press, 1987), chs. 1–11, 13–15, 17, 19. © 1987 by Stephen Halliwell. Used by permission of the publisher.

3 David Hume, "Of Tragedy" from *Essays Moral, Political, and Literary* (London, 1742). Public domain.

4 Friedrich Nietzsche, *Birth of Tragedy and the Case of Wagner*, trans. Walter Kaufmann (New York: Vintage, 1967), pp. 33–8, 56–60, 89–93. Copyright © 1967 by Walter Kaufmann. Used by permission of Random House, Inc.

5 Sigmund Freud, "Creative Writers and Day-Dreaming," trans. I. F. Grant Duff, from *The Standard Edition of the Complete Psychological Works of Sigmund Freud*, ed. James Strachey (London: Hogarth Press, 1953), vol. 9, pp. 143–53. Sigmund Freud copyrights by the Institute of Psychoanalysis and the Hogarth Press. Reprinted by permission of the Random House Group Ltd.

6 Arrigo Lora-Totino, "Spazio" from Emmett Williams (ed.), *Anthology of Concrete Poetry* (New York: Something Else, 1967), n.p. Reprinted by permission of Ultramarine Publishing Ltd.

7 E. D. Hirsch, Jr., "What Isn't Literature?" from Paul Hernadi (ed.), *What Is Literature?* (Bloomington: Indiana University Press, 1978), pp. 24–34. Reprinted by permission of E. D. Hirsch, Jr.

8 Extract from Monroe Beardsley, "The Concept of Literature" from *Literary Theory and Structure* (New Haven: Yale University Press, 1973), pp. 23–39. Reprinted by permission of Yale University Press.

9 Extract from Peter Lamarque and Stein Haugom Olsen, "Literary Practice" from *Truth, Fiction, and Literature* (Oxford: Oxford University Press, 1994), pp. 255–67. Reprinted by permission of Oxford University Press.

10 Extract from Robert Stecker, "What is Literature?" from *Revue Internationale de Philosophie* 50 (1996), pp. 681–94. Reprinted by permission of *Revue Internationale de Philosophie*.

11 Jorge Luis Borges, "Pierre Menard, Author of the *Quixote*" from *Labyrinths*, trans. James E. Irby (New York: New Directions, 1964), pp. 36–44. Copyright © 1962, 1964 by New Directions Publishing Corporation. Reprinted by permission of New Directions Publishing Corporation and Laurence Pollinger Ltd.

12 Extract from Richard Wollheim, "Literary Works as Types" from *Art and Its Objects*, 2nd edn. (Cambridge: Cambridge University Press, 1980), sections 4, 6–8, 35–7. Reprinted by permission of the publisher and author.

13 J. O. Urmson, "Literature" from George Dickie and R. J. Sclafani (eds.), *Aesthetics: A Critical Anthology* (New York: St Martin's Press, 1977), pp. 334–41. Copyright © 1977 by Bedford/St Martin's. Reprinted with permission of Bedford/St Martin's.

14 Nelson Goodman and Catherine Elgin, "Interpretation and Identity: Can the Work Survive the World?" from *Critical Inquiry* 12 (1986), pp. 567–74. Reprinted by permission of the University of Chicago Press and Catherine Elgin.

15 Extract from Gregory Currie, "Work and Text" from *Mind* 100 (1991), pp. 325–6, 328–40. Reprinted by permission of Oxford University Press.

16 Garry Trudeau, *Doonesbury*, strip of April 7, 2002. Reprinted by permission of Universal Press Syndicate.

17 John Searle, "The Logical Status of Fictional Discourse" from *New Literary History* 6 (1975), pp. 319, 321–32. © New Literary History, University of Virginia. Reprinted with permission of the Johns Hopkins University Press.

18 David Lewis, "Truth in Fiction" from *American Philosophical Quarterly* 15 (1978), pp. 37–45.

19 Gregory Currie, "What is Fiction?" from *Journal of Aesthetics and Art Criticism* 43 (1985), pp. 385–92. Reprinted by permission of Blackwell Publishing Ltd.

20 Kendall Walton, "Fiction and Nonfiction" from *Mimesis as Make-Believe: On the Foundations of the Representational Arts* (Cambridge, Mass.: Harvard University Press, 1990), pp. 36–41, 70–3, 77–8, 81–2, 84–9. Copyright © 1990 by the President and Fellows of Harvard College. Reprinted by permission of the publisher.

21 Amie Thomasson, "Fictional Characters as Abstract Artifacts" from *Fiction and Metaphysics* (Cambridge: Cambridge University Press, 1999), pp. 5–23, 155, 156. Reprinted by permission of the publisher and author.

22 Peter Lamarque, "Logic and Criticism" from *Fictional Points of View* (Ithaca, NY: Cornell University Press, 1996), pp. 55–70, originally published in *Argumentation* (Kluwer Academic Press, 1990).

23 Harold Pinter, "Applicant" from *Complete Works* (London: Methuen, 1978), vol. 3, pp. 231–4. Reprinted by permission of Faber and Faber Ltd and Grove/Atlantic, Inc.

24 Colin Radford, "How Can We Be Moved by the Fate of Anna Karenina?" from *Aristotelian Society Supplementary Volume* 49 (1975), pp. 67–80. Reprinted by courtesy of the Editor of the Aristotelian Society: © 1975.

25 Kendall Walton, "Fearing Fictionally" from *Mimesis as Make-Believe* (Cambridge, Mass.: Harvard University Press, 1990), pp. 195–204, 241–5, 249. Copyright © 1990 by the President and Fellows of Harvard College. Reprinted by permission of the publisher.

26 Susan Feagin, "The Pleasures of Tragedy" from *American Philosophical Quarterly* 20 (1983), pp. 95–104. Reprinted by permission of the University of Illinois Press.

27 Flint Schier, "Tragedy and the Community of Sentiment" from Peter Lamarque (ed.), *Philosophy and Fiction* (Aberdeen: Aberdeen University Press, 1983), pp. 73–86, 91.

28 Anne Carson, "Essay on What I Think About Most" from *Men in the Off Hours* (New York: Knopf, 2000), pp. 30–6. Copyright © 2000 by Anne Carson. Used by permission of Alfred A. Knopf, a division of Random House, Inc.

29 Max Black, "Metaphor" from *Proceedings of the Aristotelian Society* 55 (1955), pp. 273, 275–92. Reprinted by courtesy of the Editor of the Aristotelian Society: © 1955.

30 Donald Davidson, "What Metaphors Mean" from *Critical Inquiry* 5 (1978), pp. 31–47. Reprinted by permission of the author.

31 Extract from Ted Cohen, "Metaphor and Feeling" from *Philosophy and Literature* 21 (1997), pp. 223–5, 227–37, 239, and notes. Copyright © The Johns Hopkins University Press.

32 Extract from Kendall Walton, "Metaphor and Prop Oriented Make-Believe" from *European Journal of Philosophy* 1 (1993), pp. 39–42, 45–9, 51–7. Reprinted by permission of Blackwell Publishing Ltd.

33 Extracts from Wayne C. Booth, "Who Is Responsible in Ethical Criticism, and for What?" from *The Company We Keep* (Berkeley: University of California Press, 1988), pp. 125–6, 134–5. Reprinted by permission of the University of California Press.

34 Extracts from Richard Wollheim, "Criticism as Retrieval" from *Art and Its Objects*, 2nd edn. (Cambridge: Cambridge University Press, 1980), pp. 185–96, 199–204. Reprinted by permission of the publisher and author.

35 Alexander Nehamas, "The Postulated Author: Critical Monism as a Regulative Ideal" from *Critical Inquiry* 8 (1981), pp. 133–49. Reprinted by permission of the University of Chicago Press and Alexander Nehamas.

36 Extract from Robert Stecker, "Art Interpretation" from *Journal of Aesthetics and Art Criticism* 52 (1994), pp. 193–9, 205. Reprinted by permission of Blackwell Publishing Ltd.

37 Noël Carroll, "Art, Intention, and Conversation" from Gary Iseminger (ed.), *Intention and Interpretation* (Philadelphia: Temple University Press, 1992), pp. 97–101, 114–26, 129–31. © 1992 by Temple University. All rights reserved. Reprinted by permission of Temple University Press.

38 Jerrold Levinson, "Intention and Interpretation" from Gary Iseminger (ed.), *Intention and Interpretation* (Philadelphia: Temple University Press, 1992), pp. 222–32, 240–4, 252–3, 255. © 1992 by Temple University. All rights reserved. Reprinted by permission of Temple University Press.

39 Jenefer Robinson, "Style and Personality in the Literary Work" from *Philosophical Review* 94 (1985), pp. 227–47. Copyright © 1985 Cornell University. Reprinted by permission of the publisher and author.

40 Edith Wharton, "Xingu" from *Xingu and Other Stories* (New York: Scribner, 1916), pp. 3, 5–11. Public domain.

41 Jerome Stolnitz, "On the Cognitive Triviality of Art" from *British Journal of Aesthetics* 32 (1992), pp. 191–200. Reprinted by permission of Oxford University Press.

42 Catherine Wilson, "Literature and Knowledge" from *Philosophy* 58 (1983), pp. 489–96. Reprinted by permission of the publisher and author.

43 Martha Nussbaum, " 'Finely Aware and Richly Responsible': Literature and the Moral Imagination," (excerpted version of chapter 5) from *Love's Knowledge* (Oxford: Oxford University Press, 1990), pp. 148–65. Reprinted by permission of Oxford University Press and Oxford University Press, Inc.

44 Peter Lamarque and Stein Haugom Olsen, "Literature, Truth, and Philosophy" from *Truth, Fiction, and Literature* (Oxford: Oxford University Press, 1994), pp. 368–94. Reprinted by permission of Oxford University Press.

45 Extracts from Berys Gaut, "The Ethical Criticism of Art" from Jerrold Levinson (ed.), *Aesthetics and Ethics: Essays at the Intersection*

(Cambridge: Cambridge University Press, 1998), pp. 182–97, 199, 201, 202. Reprinted by permission of the publisher and author.

Every effort has been made to trace copyright holders and to obtain their permission for the use of copyright material. The publisher apologizes for any errors or omissions in the above list and would be grateful if notified of any corrections that should be incorporated in future reprints or editions of this book.

Preface

If you are a student of the philosophy of literature then you are likely to care about philosophy or about literature or, ideally, about both. In any case, this anthology has something to offer you.

Literary historians and critics study works of literature as cultural artifacts, investigating the conditions in which particular works are written and received, and formulating generalizations about the corpus of literary works. This investigation can take place at several scales. One might explain the small-scale features of a particular work as symptoms of its author's life, or attribute changing features of a genre to the evolution of a tradition of writing, or link the development of a medium (e.g. the novel) to large-scale formations (e.g. the rise of the middle class). This cluster of enterprises relies on conceptual tools that it is the business of philosophy to analyze: an implicit definition of literature, a sense of the boundaries of individual works, conceptions of fiction and metaphor, and standards of interpretation and evaluation. To be sure, literary scholars do not employ these tools uncritically; contemporary literary scholarship is attentive to theory. But philosophy of literature, in so far as it stresses rigorous and methodical theory-building, has something to offer students of literature who wish to think about their subject from a strictly theoretical perspective.

Students of philosophy need not care deeply about literature in order to find something of interest in the philosophy of literature, for doing philosophy of literature is one way of doing philosophy. This book collects topics in value theory, metaphysics (the definition of literature, theories of fiction, the ontology of literature), and the philosophies of language and mind (theories of fiction, emotional engagement, interpretation, and metaphor). Some of these topics generate problems ranking among the hardest in philosophy, and their solution advances our understanding of many areas of the discipline.

Any selection is also an exclusion. This volume features the best recent efforts of the most influential so-called analytic or Anglo–American philosophers. Largely excluded are examples of the growing body of work by philosophers locating philosophical themes in narrative artworks, though some of the authors included here write insightfully about specific literary works. Also excluded, with the exception of Friedrich Nietzsche's *Birth of Tragedy*, are works in the Franco–Germanic philosophical tradition. These are readily available elsewhere, as are works of literary criticism that advance and defend philosophical claims – a good collection is *Literary Aesthetics*, edited for Blackwell by Alan Singer and Allen Dunn.

While this volume focuses on recent work, it begins with some of the most influential texts on literature from historical sources. This section is followed by seven thematically organized sections. Each of these opens with a short work of literature or literary criticism that serves to introduce, illustrate, and indeed to test the theoretical discussions that follow it. In some cases, the theoretical selections directly refer to the literary or critical selection. In all cases, the testing function of the opening selection is particularly important: an effective heuristic in aesthetics is to seek a reflective equilibrium between theoretical considerations and our experience of literature.

PART I

Classic Sources

Introduction

This volume reflects the fairly recent development of a sustained, focused philosophical conversation about literature in the analytic tradition. But this conversation did not come out of nowhere. The historical sources collected in this section give a sample of influential works, but it is a rich sample and can be read in a number of ways. The readings are interesting in relation to each other: consider how Plato, Aristotle, and Sigmund Freud conceive of the social and psychological dimensions of popular fiction, or how David Hume and Friedrich Nietzsche account for the pleasures of tragedy. And how does each of them engage with questions of reality and illusion, knowledge and deception? Some of these texts are candidates for literary status themselves, and some of them comment explicitly on the relations between philosophy and literature, so they can also be read with those concerns in mind: how can literature be philosophical or philosophy literary?

Collectively these readings display qualities that distinguish them in temperament, as it were, from much recent work: the historical sources are ex-pansive, ambitious, speculative, and evaluatively confident in ways that do not really seem available to us now. Even Hume, writing a nicely focused essay on tragedy, moves freely from the logical consequences of a view to psychological specula-tion to aesthetic evaluation. These qualities are also part of what makes these sources very inter-esting in relation to the thematic sections that follow, as the older works tend to address clumps of thematic issues at once. The connections are too numerous to document here. For instance, along with making the explicit link between Hume's essay and the essays on tragedy in the emotion section, one could read Aristotle at least in relation to the sections on definition, emotion, fiction, and values, and Freud in relation to emotion, fiction, interpretation, and values, and so on and on. Since the historical thinkers are uniformly concerned with the pleasures and values found in experience with literature, these readings make especially deep contributions on the concluding theme of literary values.

1

Republic

Plato

Book II

WHAT is this education to be, then? Perhaps we shall hardly invent a system better than the one which long experience has worked out, with its two branches for the cultivation of the mind and of the body. And I suppose we shall begin with the mind, before we start physical training.

Naturally.

Under that head will come stories; and of these there are two kinds: some are true, others fictitious. Both must come in, but we shall begin our education with the fictitious kind.

I don't understand, he said.

Don't you understand, I replied, that we begin by telling children stories, which, taken as a whole, are fiction, though they contain some truth? Such story-telling begins at an earlier age than physical training; that is why I said we should start with the mind.

You are right.

And the beginning, as you know, is always the most important part, especially in dealing with anything young and tender. That is the time when the character is being moulded and easily takes any impress one may wish to stamp on it.

Quite true.

Then shall we simply allow our children to listen to any stories that anyone happens to make up, and so receive into their minds ideas often the very opposite of those we shall think they ought to have when they are grown up?

No, certainly not.

It seems, then, our first business will be to supervise the making of fables and legends, rejecting all which are unsatisfactory; and we shall induce nurses and mothers to tell their children only those which we have approved, and to think more of moulding their souls with these stories than they now do of rubbing their limbs to make them strong and shapely. Most of the stories now in use must be discarded.

What kind do you mean?

If we take the great ones, we shall see in them the pattern of all the rest, which are bound to be of the same stamp and to have the same effect.

No doubt; but which do you mean by the great ones?

The stories in Hesiod and Homer and the poets in general, who have at all times composed fictitious tales and told them to mankind.

Which kind are you thinking of, and what fault do you find in them?

The worst of all faults, especially if the story is ugly and immoral as well as false – misrepresenting the nature of gods and heroes, like an artist whose picture is utterly unlike the object he sets out to draw.

That is certainly a serious fault; but give me an example.

Extracts from Plato, *Republic*, trans. Francis Cornford (Oxford: Oxford University Press, 1941, pp. 68–72, 74–80, 324–40. Reprinted by permission of Oxford University Press.

A signal instance of false invention about the highest matters is that foul story, which Hesiod repeats, of the deeds of Uranus and the vengeance of Cronos; and then there is the tale of Cronos's doings and of his son's treatment of him. Even if such tales were true, I should not have supposed they should be lightly told to thoughtless young people. If they cannot be altogether suppressed, they should only be revealed in a mystery, to which access should be as far as possible restricted by requiring the sacrifice, not of a pig, but of some victim such as very few could afford.

It is true: those stories are objectionable.

Yes, and not to be repeated in our commonwealth, Adeimantus. We shall not tell a child that, if he commits the foulest crimes or goes to any length in punishing his father's misdeeds, he will be doing nothing out of the way, but only what the first and greatest of the gods have done before him.

I agree; such stories are not fit to be repeated.

Nor yet any tales of warfare and intrigues and battles of gods against gods, which are equally untrue. If our future Guardians are to think it a disgrace to quarrel lightly with one another, we shall not let them embroider robes with the Battle of the Giants or tell them of all the other feuds of gods and heroes with their kith and kin. If by any means we can make them believe that no one has ever had a quarrel with a fellow citizen and it is a sin to have one, that is the sort of thing our old men and women should tell children from the first; and as they grow older, we must make the poets write for them in the same strain. Stories like those of Hera being bound by her son, or of Hephaestus flung from heaven by his father for taking his mother's part when she was beaten, and all those battles of the gods in Homer, must not be admitted into our state, whether they be allegorical or not. A child cannot distinguish the allegorical sense from the literal, and the ideas he takes in at that age are likely to become indelibly fixed; hence the great importance of seeing that the first stories he hears shall be designed to produce the best possible effect on his character.

Yes, that is reasonable. But if we were asked which of these stories in particular are of the right quality, what should we answer?

I replied: You and I, Adeimantus, are not, for the moment, poets, but founders of a commonwealth. As such, it is not our business to invent stories ourselves, but only to be clear as to the main outlines to be followed by the poets in making their stories and the limits beyond which they must not be allowed to go.

True; but what are these outlines for any account they may give of the gods?

Of this sort, said I. A poet, whether he is writing epic, lyric, or drama, surely ought always to represent the divine nature as it really is. And the truth is that that nature is good and must be described as such.

Unquestionably.

Well, nothing that is good can be harmful; and if it cannot do harm, it can do no evil; and so it cannot be responsible for any evil.

I agree. [. . .]

It follows, then, that the divine, being good, is not, as most people say, responsible for everything that happens to mankind, but only for a small part; for the good things in human life are far fewer than the evil, and, whereas the good must be ascribed to heaven only, we must look elsewhere for the cause of evils.

I think that is perfectly true.

So we shall condemn as a foolish error Homer's description of Zeus as the "dispenser of both good and ill." We shall disapprove when Pandarus' violation of oaths and treaties is said to be the work of Zeus and Athena, or when Themis and Zeus are said to have caused strife among the gods. [. . .]

The poet will only be allowed to say that the wicked were miserable because they needed chastisement, and the punishment of heaven did them good. If our commonwealth is to be well-ordered, we must fight to the last against any member of it being suffered to speak of the divine, which is good, being responsible for evil. Neither young nor old must listen to such tales, in prose or verse. Such doctrine would be impious, self-contradictory, and disastrous to our commonwealth. [. . .]

To be deceived about the truth of things and so to be in ignorance and error and to harbour untruth in the soul is a thing no one would consent to. Falsehood in that quarter is abhorred above everything.

It is indeed.

Well then, as I was saying, this ignorance in the soul which entertains untruth is what really deserves to be called the true falsehood; for the spoken falsehood is only the embodiment or image of a previous condition of the soul, not pure unadulterated falsity. Is it not so?

It is.

This real falsehood, then, is hateful to gods and men equally. But is the spoken falsehood always a hateful thing? Is it not sometimes helpful – in war, for instance, or as a sort of medicine to avert some fit of folly or madness that might make a friend attempt some mischief? And in those legends we were discussing just now, we can turn fiction to account; not knowing the facts about the distant past, we can make our fiction as good an embodiment of truth as possible.

Yes, that is so.

Well, in which of these ways would falsehood be useful to a god? We cannot think of him as embodying truth in fiction for lack of information about the past.

No, that would be absurd.

So there is no room in his case for poetical inventions. Would he need to tell untruths because he has enemies to fear?

Of course not.

Or friends who are mad or foolish?

No; a fool or a madman could hardly enjoy the friendship of the gods.

Gods, then, have no motive for lying. There can be no falsehood of any sort in the divine nature.

None.

We conclude, then, that a god is a being of entire simplicity and truthfulness in word and in deed. In himself he does not change, nor does he delude others, either in dreams or in waking moments, by apparitions or oracles or signs.

I agree, after all you have said.

You will assent, then, to this as a second principle to guide all that is to be said or written about the gods: that they do not transform themselves by any magic or mislead us by illusions or lies. [. . .]

Book III

So far, then, as religion is concerned, we have settled what sorts of stories about the gods may, or may not, be told to children who are to hold heaven and their parents in reverence and to value good relations with one another.

Yes, he said; and I believe we have settled right.

We also want them to be brave. So the stories they hear should be such as to make them unafraid of death. A man with that fear in his heart cannot be brave, can he?

Surely not.

And can a man be free from that fear and prefer death in battle to defeat and slavery, if he believes in a world below which is full of terrors?

No.

Here again, then, our supervision will be needed. The poets must be told to speak well of that other world. The gloomy descriptions they now give must be forbidden, not only as untrue, but as injurious to our future warriors. We shall strike out all lines like these:

> I would rather be on earth as the hired
> servant of another, in the house of a landless
> man with little to live on, than be king over
> all the dead;[1]

or these:

> Alack, there is, then, even in the house of
> Death a spirit or a shade; but the wits dwell
> in it no more.[2]

We shall ask Homer and the poets in general not to mind if we cross out all passages of this sort. If most people enjoy them as good poetry, that is all the more reason for keeping them from children or grown men who are to be free, fearing slavery more than death.

I entirely agree.

We must also get rid of all that terrifying language, the very sound of which is enough to make one shiver: "loathsome Styx," "the River of Wailing," "infernal spirits," "anatomies," and so on. For other purposes such language may be well enough; but we are afraid that fever consequent upon such shivering fits may melt down the fine-tempered spirit of our Guardians. So we will have none of it; and we shall encourage writing in the opposite strain.

Clearly.

Another thing we must banish is the wailing and lamentations of the famous heroes. For this reason: if two friends are both men of high character, neither of them will think that death has any terrors for his comrade; and so he will not mourn for his friend's sake, as if something terrible had befallen him.

No. [. . .]

We shall do well, then, to strike out descriptions of the heroes bewailing the dead, and make over such lamentations to women (and not to women of good standing either) and to men of low character, so that the Guardians we are training for our country may disdain to imitate them.

Quite right. [...]

Again, our Guardians ought not to be overmuch given to laughter. Violent laughter tends to provoke an equally violent reaction. We must not allow poets to describe men of worth being overcome by it; still less should Homer speak of the gods giving way to "unquenchable laughter" at the sight of Hephaestus "bustling from room to room." That will be against your principles.

Yes, if you choose to call them mine.

Again, a high value must be set upon truthfulness. If we were right in saying that gods have no use for falsehood and it is useful to mankind only in the way of a medicine, obviously a medicine should be handled by no one but a physician.

Obviously.

If anyone, then, is to practise deception, either on the country's enemies or on its citizens, it must be the Rulers of the commonwealth, acting for its benefit; no one else may meddle with this privilege. For a private person to mislead such Rulers we shall declare to be a worse offence than for a patient to mislead his doctor or an athlete his trainer about his bodily condition, or for a seaman to misinform his captain about the state of the ship or of the crew. So, if anyone else in our commonwealth "of all that practise crafts, physician, seer, or carpenter," is caught not telling the truth, the Rulers will punish him for introducing a practice as fatal and subversive in a state as it would be in a ship. [...]

We have now distinguished the kinds of stories that may and may not be told about gods and demigods, heroes, and the world below. There remains the literature concerned with human life.

Clearly.

We cannot lay down rules for that at our present stage.

Why not?

Because, I suspect, we shall find both poets and prose-writers guilty of the most serious misstatements about human life, making out that wrongdoers are often happy and just men miserable; that injustice pays, if not detected; and that my being just is to another man's advantage, but a loss to myself. We shall have to prohibit such poems and tales and tell them to compose others in the contrary sense. Don't you think so?

I am sure of it.

Well, as soon as you admit that I am right there, may I not claim that we shall have reached agreement on the subject of all this inquiry?

That is a fair assumption.

Then we must postpone any decision as to how the truth is to be told about human life, until we have discovered the real nature of justice and proved that it is intrinsically profitable to its possessor, no matter what reputation he may have in the eyes of the world.

That is certainly true. [...]

Book X

Indeed, I continued, our commonwealth has many features which make me think it was based on very sound principles, especially our rule not on any account to admit the poetry of dramatic representation. Now that we have distinguished the several parts of the soul, it seems to me clearer than ever that such poetry must be firmly excluded.

What makes you say so?

Between ourselves – for you will not denounce me to the tragedians and the other dramatists – poetry of that sort seems to be injurious to minds which do not possess the antidote in a knowledge of its real nature.

What have you in mind?

I must speak out, in spite of a certain affection and reverence I have had from a child for Homer, who seems to have been the original master and guide of all this imposing company of tragic poets. However, no man must be honoured above the truth; so, as I say, I must speak my mind.

Do, by all means.

Listen then, or rather let me ask you a question. Can you tell me what is meant by representation in general? I have no very clear notion myself.

So you expect me to have one!

Why not? It is not always the keenest eye that is the first to see something.

True; but when you are there I should not be very desirous to tell what I saw, however plainly. You must use your own eyes.

Well then, shall we proceed as usual and begin by assuming the existence of a single essential nature or Form for every set of things which we call by the same name? Do you understand?

I do.

Then let us take any set of things you choose. For instance there are any number of beds or of tables, but only two Forms, one of Bed and one of Table.

Yes.

And we are in the habit of saying that the craftsman, when he makes the beds or tables we use or whatever it may be, has before his mind the

Form of one or other of these pieces of furniture. The Form itself is, of course, not the work of any craftsman. How could it be?

It could not.

Now what name would you give to a craftsman who can produce all the things made by every sort of workman?

He would need to have very remarkable powers!

Wait a moment, and you will have even better reason to say so. For, besides producing any kind of artificial thing, this same craftsman can create all plants and animals, himself included, and earth and sky and gods and the heavenly bodies and all the things under the earth in Hades.

That sounds like a miraculous feat of virtuosity.

Are you incredulous? Tell me, do you think there could be no such craftsman at all, or that there might be someone who could create all these things in one sense, though not in another? Do you not see that you could do it yourself, in a way?

In what way, I should like to know.

There is no difficulty; in fact there are several ways in which the thing can be done quite quickly. The quickest perhaps would be to take a mirror and turn it round in all directions. In a very short time you could produce sun and stars and earth and yourself and all the other animals and plants and lifeless objects which we mentioned just now.

Yes, in appearance, but not the actual things.

Quite so: you are helping out my argument. My notion is that a painter is a craftsman of that kind. You may say that the things he produces are not real; but there is a sense in which he too does produce a bed.

Yes, the appearance of one.

And what of the carpenter? Were you not saying just now that he only makes a particular bed, not what we call the Form or essential nature of Bed?

Yes, I was.

If so, what he makes is not the reality, but only something that resembles it. It would not be right to call the work of a carpenter or of any other handicraftsman a perfectly real thing, would it?

Not in the view of people accustomed to thinking on these lines.

We must not be surprised, then, if even an actual bed is a somewhat shadowy thing as compared with reality.

True.

Now shall we make use of this example to throw light on our question as to the true nature of this artist who represents things? We have here three sorts of bed: one which exists in the nature of things

and which, I imagine, we could only describe as a product of divine workmanship; another made by the carpenter; and a third by the painter. So the three kinds of bed belong respectively to the domains of these three: painter, carpenter, and god.

Yes.

Now the god made only one ideal or essential Bed, whether by choice or because he was under some necessity not to make more than one; at any rate two or more were not created, nor could they possibly come into being.

Why not?

Because, if he made even so many as two, then once more a single ideal Bed would make its appearance, whose character those two would share; and that one, not the two, would be the essential Bed. Knowing this, the god, wishing to be the real maker of a real Bed, not a particular manufacturer of one particular bed, created one which is essentially unique.

So it appears.

Shall we call him, then, the author of the true nature of Bed, or something of that sort?

Certainly he deserves the name, since all his works constitute the real nature of things.

And we may call the carpenter the manufacturer of a bed?

Yes.

Can we say the same of the painter?

Certainly not.

Then what is he, with reference to a bed?

I think it would be fairest to describe him as the artist who represents the things which the other two make.

Very well, said I; so the work of the artist is at the third remove from the essential nature of the thing?

Exactly.

The tragic poet, too, is an artist who represents things; so this will apply to him: he and all other artists are, as it were, third in succession from the throne of truth.

Just so.

We are in agreement, then, about the artist. But now tell me about our painter: which do you think he is trying to represent – the reality that exists in the nature of things, or the products of the craftsman?

The products of the craftsman.

As they are, or as they appear? You have still to draw that distinction.

How do you mean?

I mean: you may look at a bed or any other object from straight in front or slantwise or at any angle. Is there then any difference in the bed itself, or does it merely look different?

It only looks different.

Well, that is the point. Does painting aim at reproducing any actual object as it is, or the appearance of it as it looks? In other words, is it a representation of the truth or of a semblance?

Of a semblance.

The art of representation, then, is a long way from reality; and apparently the reason why there is nothing it cannot reproduce is that it grasps only a small part of any object, and that only an image. Your painter, for example, will paint us a shoemaker, a carpenter, or other workman, without understanding any one of their crafts; and yet, if he were a good painter, he might deceive a child or a simple-minded person into thinking his picture was a real carpenter, if he showed it them at some distance.

No doubt.

But I think there is one view we should take in all such cases. Whenever someone announces that he has met with a person who is master of every trade and knows more about every subject than any specialist, we should reply that he is a simple fellow who has apparently fallen in with some illusionist and been tricked into thinking him omniscient, because of his own inability to discriminate between knowledge and ignorance and the representation of appearances.

Quite true.

Then it is now time to consider the tragic poets and their master, Homer, because we are sometimes told that they understand not only all technical matters but also all about human conduct, good or bad, and about religion; for, to write well, a good poet, so they say, must know his subject; otherwise he could not write about it. We must ask whether these people have not been deluded by meeting with artists who can represent appearances, and in contemplating the poets' work have failed to see that it is at the third remove from reality, nothing more than semblances, easy to produce with no knowledge of the truth. Or is there something in what they say? Have the good poets a real mastery of the matters on which the public thinks they discourse so well?

It is a question we ought to look into.

Well then, if a man were able actually to do the things he represents as well as to produce images of them, do you believe he would seriously give himself up to making these images and take that as a completely satisfying object in life? I should imagine that, if he had a real understanding of the actions he represents, he would far sooner devote himself to performing them in fact. The memorials he would try to leave after him would be noble deeds, and he would be more eager to be the hero whose praises are sung than the poet who sings them.

Yes, I agree; he would do more good in that way and win a greater name.

Here is a question, then, that we may fairly put to Homer or to any other poet. We will leave out of account all mere matters of technical skill: we will not ask them to explain, for instance, why it is that, if they have a knowledge of medicine and not merely the art of reproducing the way physicians talk, there is no record of any poet, ancient or modern, curing patients and bequeathing his knowledge to a school of medicine, as Asclepius did. But when Homer undertakes to tell us about matters of the highest importance, such as the conduct of war, statesmanship, or education, we have a right to inquire into his competence. "Dear Homer," we shall say, "we have defined the artist as one who produces images at the third remove from reality. If your knowledge of all that concerns human excellence was really such as to raise you above him to the second rank, and you could tell what courses of conduct will make men better or worse as individuals or as citizens, can you name any country which was better governed thanks to your efforts? Many states, great and small, have owed much to a good lawgiver, such as Lycurgus at Sparta, Charondas in Italy and Sicily, and our own Solon. Can you tell us of any that acknowledges a like debt to you?"

I should say not, Glaucon replied. The most devout admirers of Homer make no such claim.

Well, do we hear of any war in Homer's day being won under his command or thanks to his advice?

No.

Or of a number of ingenious inventions and technical contrivances, which would show that he was a man of practical ability like Thales of Miletus or Anacharsis the Scythian?

Nothing of the sort.

Well, if there is no mention of public services, do we hear of Homer in his own lifetime presiding, like Pythagoras, over a band of intimate disciples who loved him for the inspiration of his society and handed down a Homeric way of life, like the way of life which the Pythagoreans called after their founder and which to this day distinguishes them from the rest of the world?

No; on the contrary, Homer's friend with the absurd name, Creophylus, would look even more absurd when considered as a product of the poet's training, if the story is true that he completely neglected Homer during his lifetime.

Yes, so they say. But what do you think, Glaucon? If Homer had really possessed the knowledge qualifying him to educate people and make them better men, instead of merely giving us a poetical representation of such matters, would he not have attracted a host of disciples to love and revere him? After all, any number of private teachers like Protagoras of Abdera and Prodicus of Ceos have succeeded in convincing their contemporaries that they will never be fit to manage affairs of state or their own households unless these masters superintend their education; and for this wisdom they are so passionately admired that their pupils are all but ready to carry them about on their shoulders. Can we suppose that Homer's contemporaries, or Hesiod's, would have left them to wander about reciting their poems, if they had really been capable of helping their hearers to be better men? Surely they would sooner have parted with their money and tried to make the poets settle down at home; or failing that, they would have danced attendance on them wherever they went, until they had learnt from them all they could.

I believe you are quite right, Socrates.

We may conclude, then, that all poetry, from Homer onwards, consists in representing a semblance of its subject, whatever it may be, including any kind of human excellence, with no grasp of the reality. We were speaking just now of the painter who can produce what looks like a shoemaker to the spectator who, being as ignorant of shoemaking as he is himself, judges only by form and colour. In the same way the poet, knowing nothing more than how to represent appearances, can paint in words his picture of any craftsman so as to impress an audience which is equally ignorant and judges only by the form of expression; the inherent charm of metre, rhythm, and musical setting is enough to make them think he has discoursed admirably about generalship or shoemaking or any other technical subject. Strip what the poet has to say of its poetical colouring, and I think you must have seen what it comes to in plain prose. It is like a face which was never really handsome, when it has lost the fresh bloom of youth.

Quite so.

Here is a further point, then. The artist, we say, this maker of images, knows nothing of the reality, but only the appearance. But that is only half the story. An artist can paint a bit and bridle, while the smith and the leather-worker can make them. Does the painter understand the proper form which bit and bridle ought to have? Is it not rather true that not even the craftsmen who make them know that, but only the horseman who understands their use?

Quite true.

May we not say generally that there are three arts concerned with any object – the art of using it, the art of making it, and the art of representing it?

Yes.

And that the excellence or beauty or rightness of any implement or living creature or action has reference to the use for which it is made or designed by nature?

Yes.

It follows, then, that the user must know most about the performance of the thing he uses and must report on its good or bad points to the maker. The flute-player, for example, will tell the instrument-maker how well his flutes serve the player's purpose, and the other will submit to be instructed about how they should be made. So the man who uses any implement will speak of its merits and defects with knowledge, whereas the maker will take his word and possess no more than a correct belief, which he is obliged to obtain by listening to the man who knows.

Quite so.

But what of the artist? Has he either knowledge or correct belief? Does he know from direct experience of the subjects he portrays whether his representations are good and right or not? Has he even gained a correct belief by being obliged to listen to someone who does know and can tell him how they ought to be represented?

No, he has neither.

If the artist, then, has neither knowledge nor even a correct belief about the soundness of his work, what becomes of the poet's wisdom in respect of the subjects of his poetry?

It will not amount to much.

And yet he will go on with his work, without knowing in what way any of his representations is sound or unsound. He must, apparently, be reproducing only what pleases the taste or wins the approval of the ignorant multitude.

Yes, what else can he do?

We seem, then, so far to be pretty well agreed that the artist knows nothing worth mentioning about the subjects he represents, and that art is a form of play, not to be taken seriously. This description, moreover, applies above all to tragic poetry, whether in epic or dramatic form.

Exactly. [. . .]

But now look here, said I; the content of this poetical representation is something at the third remove from reality, is it not?

Yes.

On what part of our human nature, then, does it produce its effect?

What sort of part do you mean?

Let me explain by an analogy. An object seen at a distance does not, of course, look the same size as when it is close at hand; a straight stick looks bent when part of it is under water; and the same thing appears concave or convex to an eye misled by colours. Every sort of confusion like these is to be found in our minds; and it is this weakness in our nature that is exploited, with a quite magical effect, by many tricks of illusion, like scene-painting and conjuring.

True.

But satisfactory means have been found for dispelling these illusions by measuring, counting, and weighing. We are no longer at the mercy of apparent differences of size and quantity and weight; the faculty which has done the counting and measuring or weighing takes control instead. And this can only be the work of the calculating or reasoning element in the soul.

True.

And when this faculty has done its measuring and announced that one quantity is greater than, or equal to, another, we often find that there is an appearance which contradicts it. Now, as we have said, it is impossible for the same part of the soul to hold two contradictory beliefs at the same time. Hence the part which agrees with the measurements must be a different part from the one which goes against them; and its confidence in measurement and calculation is a proof of its being the highest part; the other which contradicts it must be an inferior one.

It must.

This, then, was the conclusion I had in view when I said that paintings and works of art in general are far removed from reality, and that the element in our nature which is accessible to art and responds to its advances is equally far from wisdom. The offspring of a connexion thus formed on no true or sound basis must be as inferior as the parents. This will be true not only of visual art, but of art addressed to the ear, poetry as we call it.

Naturally.

Then, instead of trusting merely to the analogy from painting, let us directly consider that part of the mind to which the dramatic element in poetry appeals, and see how much claim it has to serious worth. We can put the question in this way. Drama, we say, represents the acts and fortunes of human beings. It is wholly concerned with what they do, voluntarily or against their will, and how they fare, with the consequences which they regard as happy or otherwise, and with their feelings of joy and sorrow in all these experiences. That is all, is it not?

Yes.

And in all these experiences has a man an undivided mind? Is there not an internal conflict which sets him at odds with himself in his conduct, much as we were saying that the conflict of visual impressions leads him to make contradictory judgements? However, I need not ask that question; for, now I come to think of it, we have already agreed that innumerable conflicts of this sort are constantly occurring in the mind. But there is a further point to be considered now. We have said that a man of high character will bear any stroke of fortune, such as the loss of a son or of anything else he holds dear, with more equanimity than most people. We may now ask: will he feel no pain, or is that impossible? Will he not rather observe due measure in his grief?

Yes, that is nearer the truth.

Now tell me: will he be more likely to struggle with his grief and resist it when he is under the eyes of his fellows or when he is alone?

He will be far more restrained in the presence of others.

Yes; when he is by himself he will not be ashamed to do and say much that he would not like anyone to see or hear.

Quite so.

What encourages him to resist his grief is the lawful authority of reason, while the impulse to give way comes from the feeling itself; and, as we said, the presence of contradictory impulses proves that two distinct elements in his nature must be involved. One of them is law-abiding, prepared to listen to the authority which declares that it is best to bear misfortune as quietly as possible without resentment, for several reasons: it is never certain that misfortune may not be a blessing; nothing is gained by chafing at it; nothing human is matter for great concern; and, finally, grief hinders us from calling in the help we most urgently need. By this I mean reflection on what has happened, letting reason decide on the best move in the game of life that the fall of the dice permits. Instead of behaving like a child who goes on shrieking after a fall and hugging the wounded part, we should accustom the mind to set itself at once to raise up the fallen and cure the hurt, banishing lamentation with a healing touch.

Certainly that is the right way to deal with misfortune.

And if, as we think, the part of us which is ready to act upon these reflections is the highest, that other part which impels us to dwell upon our sufferings and can never have enough of grieving over them is unreasonable, craven, and faint-hearted.

Yes.

Now this fretful temper gives scope for a great diversity of dramatic representation; whereas the calm and wise character in its unvarying constancy is not easy to represent, nor when represented is it readily understood, especially by a promiscuous gathering in a theatre, since it is foreign to their own habit of mind. Obviously, then, this steadfast disposition does not naturally attract the dramatic poet, and his skill is not designed to find favour with it. If he is to have a popular success, he must address himself to the fretful type with its rich variety of material for representation.

Obviously.

We have, then, a fair case against the poet and we may set him down as the counterpart of the painter, whom he resembles in two ways: his creations are poor things by the standard of truth and reality, and his appeal is not to the highest part of the soul, but to one which is equally inferior. So we shall be justified in not admitting him into a well-ordered commonwealth, because he stimulates and strengthens an element which threatens to undermine the reason. As a country may be given over into the power of its worst citizens while the better sort are ruined, so, we shall say, the dramatic poet sets up a vicious form of government in the individual soul: he gratifies that senseless part which cannot distinguish great and small, but regards the same things as now one, now the other; and he is an image-maker whose images are phantoms far removed from reality.

Quite true.

But, I continued, the heaviest count in our indict-ment is still to come. Dramatic poetry has a most formidable power of corrupting even men of high character, with a few exceptions.

Formidable indeed, if it can do that.

Let me put the case for you to judge. When we listen to some hero in Homer or on the tragic stage moaning over his sorrows in a long tirade, or to a chorus beating their breasts as they chant a lament, you know how the best of us enjoy giving ourselves up to follow the performance with eager sympathy. The more a poet can move our feelings in this way, the better we think him. And yet when the sorrow is our own, we pride ourselves on being able to bear it quietly like a man, condemning the behav-iour we admired in the theatre as womanish. Can it be right that the spectacle of a man behaving as one would scorn and blush to behave oneself should be admired and enjoyed, instead of filling us with disgust?

No, it really does not seem reasonable.

It does not, if you reflect that the poet ministers to the satisfaction of that very part of our nature whose instinctive hunger to have its fill of tears and lamentations is forcibly restrained in the case of our own misfortunes. Meanwhile the noblest part of us, insufficiently schooled by reason or habit, has relaxed its watch over these querulous feelings, with the excuse that the sufferings we are contemplating are not our own and it is no shame to us to admire and pity a man with some preten-sions to a noble character, though his grief may be excessive. The enjoyment itself seems a clear gain, which we cannot bring ourselves to forfeit by disdaining the whole poem. Few, I believe, are capable of reflecting that to enter into another's feelings must have an effect on our own: the emo-tions of pity our sympathy has strengthened will not be easy to restrain when we are suffering ourselves.

That is very true.

Does not the same principle apply to humour as well as to pathos? You are doing the same thing if, in listening at a comic performance or in ordinary life to buffooneries which you would be ashamed to indulge in yourself, you thoroughly enjoy them instead of being disgusted with their ribaldry. There is in you an impulse to play the clown, which you have held in restraint from a reasonable fear of being set down as a buffoon; but now you have given it rein, and by encouraging its impu-dence at the theatre you may be unconsciously carried away into playing the comedian in your private life. Similar effects are produced by poetic representation of love and anger and all those de-sires and feelings of pleasure or pain which accom-pany our every action. It waters the growth of passions which should be allowed to wither away and sets them up in control, although the goodness and happiness of our lives depend on their being held in subjection.

I cannot but agree with you.

If so, Glaucon, when you meet with admirers of Homer who tell you that he has been the educator of Hellas and that on questions of human conduct and culture he deserves to be constantly studied as a guide by whom to regulate your whole life, it is well to give a friendly hearing to such people, as entirely well-meaning according to their lights, and you may acknowledge Homer to be the first and greatest of the tragic poets; but you must be quite sure that we can admit into our commonwealth only the poetry which celebrates the praises of the gods and of good men. If you go further and admit the honeyed muse in epic or in lyric verse, then pleasure and pain will usurp the sovereignty of law and of the principles always recognized by common consent as the best.

Quite true.

So now, since we have recurred to the subject of poetry, let this be our defence: it stands to reason that we could not but banish such an influence from our commonwealth. But, lest poetry should convict us of being harsh and unmannerly, let us tell her further that there is a long-standing quarrel between poetry and philosophy. There are countless tokens of this old antagonism, such as the lines which speak of "the cur which at his master yelps," or "one mighty in the vain talk of fools" or "the throng of all-too-sapient heads," or "subtle thinkers all in rags."[3] None the less, be it declared that, if the dramatic poetry whose end is to give pleasure can show good reason why it should exist in a well-governed society, we for our part should welcome it back, being ourselves conscious of its charm; only it would be a sin to betray what we believe to be the truth. You too, my friend, must have felt this charm, above all when poetry speaks through Homer's lips.

I have indeed.

It is fair, then, that before returning from exile poetry should publish her defence in lyric verse or some other measure; and I suppose we should allow her champions who love poetry but are not poets to plead for her in prose, that she is no mere source of pleasure but a benefit to society and to human life. We shall listen favourably; for we shall clearly be the gainers, if that can be proved.

Undoubtedly.

But if it cannot, then we must take a lesson from the lover who renounces at any cost a passion which he finds is doing him no good. The love for poetry of this kind, bred in us by our own much admired institutions, will make us kindly disposed to believe in her genuine worth; but so long as she cannot make good her defence we shall, as we listen, rehearse to ourselves the reasons we have just given, as a counter-charm to save us from relapsing into a passion which most people have never outgrown. We shall reiterate that such poetry has no serious claim to be valued as an apprehension of truth. One who lends an ear to it should rather beware of endangering the order established in his soul, and would do well to accept the view of poetry which we have expressed.

I entirely agree.

Yes, Glaucon; for much is at stake, more than most people suppose: it is a choice between becoming a good man or a bad; and poetry, no more than wealth or power or honours, should tempt us to be careless of justice and virtue.

Your argument has convinced me, as I think it would anyone else.

Notes

1 Spoken by the ghost of Achilles, *Od.* xi. 489.
2 Spoken by Achilles when the ghost of Patroclus eludes his embrace, *Iliad* xxiii. 103.
3 The source of these poetical attacks on philosophy is unknown. The earliest philosophers to denounce Homer and Hesiod had been Xenophanes and Heraclitus, about the beginning of the fifth century.

2

Poetics

Aristotle

Chapter 1

To discuss the art of poetry in general, as well as the potential of each of its types; to explain the unity of plot required for successful poetic composition; also to analyse the number and nature of the component parts of poetry; and to deal similarly with the other questions which belong to this same method of enquiry – these are my proposed topics, beginning in the natural way from first principles.

Now, epic and tragic poetry, as well as comedy and dithyramb (and most music for the pipe or lyre), are all, taken as a whole, kinds of mimesis. But they differ from one another in three respects: namely, in the *media* or the *objects* or the *mode* of mimesis. For just as there are people who produce mimetic images of many things in the media of colours and shapes (some relying on a skilled art, some on practice), and others who use the medium of the voice, so in the case of all the arts mentioned above mimesis is effected in the media of rhythm, language and melody.

But these can be employed separately or in combination, as follows:

(a) the arts of the pipe and lyre (and any other arts with a similar potential, such as that of the pan-pipes) use melody and rhythm alone;

(b) the art of dancing presents mimesis in the medium of rhythm without melody (for dancers, through the rhythms which shape their movements, engage in the mimesis of character, emotions and actions);

(c) the art which employs language alone, or language in metrical form (whether in a combination of metres or just one kind), is still without a name. For we have no common name for the mimes of Sophron and Xenarchus and Socratic dialogues, nor for any mimetic work which might be written in iambic trimeters or elegiac couplets or something else of this kind. It is of course true that people attach the verbal idea of "poetry" (*poiein*) to the name of the metre, and so call these writers "elegiac poets" (*elegopoioi*), "epic poets" (*epopoioi*), and so on; but the categories refer not to their status as poets in virtue of mimesis, but to the metre they have in common: since, if a work of medicine or natural philosophy is written in metre, people still use these same descriptions. But Homer and Empedocles have nothing in common except their metre; and so, while one

From *The Poetics of Aristotle: Translation and Commentary* by Stephen Halliwell (Chapel Hill: University of North Carolina Press, 1987. chapters 1–11, 13–15, 17, 19. © 1987 by Stephen Halliwell. Used by permission of the publisher.

must call the former a poet, the latter should be called a natural philosopher rather than a poet. A corollary is that even if someone should produce a mimesis in a mixture of all the metres (as Chairemon did in his mixed rhapsody, *Centaur*), he too must be called a poet. So let distinctions of these kinds be drawn in these matters.

(d)   Finally, there are some poetic arts which employ all the stated media (that is, rhythm, melody and metre), such as dithyramb, nome, tragedy and comedy: they differ, though, in that some use all throughout, some only in parts. These, then, are the distinctions between the arts as regards the media of their mimesis.

Chapter 2

Since mimetic artists portray people in action, and since these people must be either good or bad (for men's characters practically always conform to these categories alone), they can portray people better than ourselves, worse than ourselves, or on the same level. The same is true in painting: Polygnotus portrayed men who are superior, Pauson worse, and Dionysius on the same level. And it is evident that each of the stated types of mimesis will exhibit these differences, and will thus be distinguishable according to the variations in the objects which it represents. For such differences are possible in dancing, and in music for the pipe and lyre, as well as in the arts which use language alone or language in metre: for instance, Homer represented superior men, Cleophon men like us, Hegemon of Thasos (the first writer of parodies) and Nicochares (author of the *Deiliad*) inferior men. The same principle applies in dithyramb and the nome, as one sees . . . and from the possibility of portraying the Cyclopes in the manner of Timotheus and Philoxenus. This very distinction also separates tragedy from comedy: the latter tends to represent men worse than present humanity, the former better.

Chapter 3

Beside the two already cited, there is a third distinction: namely, the mode in which the various objects are represented. For it is possible to use the same media to offer a mimesis of the same objects

in any one of three ways: first, by alternation between narrative and dramatic impersonation (as in Homeric poetry); second, by employing the voice of narrative without variation; third, by a wholly dramatic presentation of the agents.

So then, as indicated at the outset, mimesis can be distinguished in these three respects: by its *media*, its *objects*, and its *modes*. Consequently, in one respect Sophocles uses the same mimesis as Homer, for in both cases the objects are good men; while in another respect, Sophocles and Aristophanes are parallel, since both use the mimetic mode of dramatic enactment. [. . .]

So then, let these remarks suffice to cover the number and nature of the mimetic distinctions.

Chapter 4

Poetry in general can be seen to owe its existence to two causes, and these are rooted in nature. First, there is man's natural propensity, from childhood onwards, to engage in mimetic activity (and this distinguishes man from other creatures, that he is thoroughly mimetic and through mimesis takes his first steps in understanding). Second, there is the pleasure which all men take in mimetic objects.

An indication of the latter can be observed in practice: for we take pleasure in contemplating the most precise images of things whose sight in itself causes us pain – such as the appearance of the basest animals, or of corpses. Here too the explanation lies in the fact that great pleasure is derived from exercising the understanding, not just for philosophers but in the same way for all men, though their capacity for it may be limited. It is for this reason that men enjoy looking at images, because what happens is that, as they contemplate them, they apply their understanding and reasoning to each element (identifying this as an image of such-and-such a man, for instance). Since, if it happens that one has no previous familiarity with the sight, then the object will not give pleasure *qua* mimetic object but because of its craftmanship, or colour, or for some other such reason.

Given, then, that mimetic activity comes naturally to us – together with melody and rhythm (for it is evident that metres are species of rhythm) – it was originally those with a special natural capacity who, through a slow and gradual process, brought poetry into being by their improvisations. And poetry was split into two types according to the poets' own characters: the more dignified made noble actions and noble agents the object of their mimesis; while lighter poets took the actions of base men and began by composing invectives, just as the other group produced hymns and encomia. Now, we cannot cite an invective by any individual poet before Homer's time, though it is likely there were many such poets; their known history starts with Homer, with his *Margites* and other such works. It was appropriate that in these works the iambic metre came to find its place – and this is why it is called "iambic" now, because it was in this metre that they abused one another (in the manner called *iambizein*).

Of the old poets, some composed in epic hexameters, others in iambics. Just as Homer was the supreme poet of serious subjects (for he was unique both in the quality and in the *dramatic* nature of his poetry), similarly he was the first to reveal the form of comedy, by producing dramatic poetry which dealt not with invective but with the ridiculous. For the *Margites* stands in the same relation to later comedies as do the *Iliad* and *Odyssey* to tragedies. And when the possibility of tragedy and comedy had been glimpsed, men aspired to either type of poetry according to their personal capacities; so some became poets of comedy instead of iambic verses, while others abandoned epic for tragedy, because the latter's forms were greater than, and superior to, epic's.

To consider whether tragedy is by now sufficiently developed in its types – judging it both in itself and in relation to audiences – is a separate matter. At any rate, having come into being from an improvisational origin (which is true of both tragedy and comedy, the first starting from the leaders of the dithyramb, the second from the leaders of the phallic songs which are still customary in many cities), tragedy was gradually enhanced as poets made progress with the potential which they could see in the genre. And when it had gone through many changes, tragedy ceased to evolve, since it had attained its natural fulfilment.

It was Aeschylus who first increased the number of actors from one to two, reduced the choral parts, and gave speech the leading role; the third actor and scene-painting came with Sophocles. A further aspect of change concerns scale: after a period of slight plots and humorous diction, it was only at a late stage that tragedy attained dignity by departing from the style of satyr-plays, and that the iambic metre replaced the trochaic tetrameter. To begin with, poets used the tetrameter because the poetry had more of the tone of a satyr-play and of dance; and it was only when speech was brought in that the nature of the genre found its appropriate metre (the iambic is the most colloquial of metres, as we see from the fact that we frequently produce the rhythm of iambic lines in our conversation, while we rarely produce hexameters and only by departing from the register of ordinary speech).

There were further developments concerning the number of episodes, and we shall take as read the other particular elaborations which are said to have been effected, since it would be a large task to give a thorough account of every detail.

Chapter 5

Comedy, as I earlier said, is a mimesis of men who are inferior, but not in a way which involves complete evil: the comic is one species of the shameful. For the comic is constituted by a fault and a mark of shame, but lacking in pain or destruction: to take an obvious example, the comic mask is ugly and misshapen, but does not express pain. Now, while the stages of tragedy's development, and those responsible for them, have been preserved, comedy's have not been, because it was not originally given serious attention: the archon first granted a comic chorus at quite a late date; before that, the performers were volunteers. The first recorded comic poets belong to the era when the genre already possessed some established forms. We are simply ignorant about such matters as who invented masks, or introduced prologues, or increased the number of actors, and other such details. But as for the use of poetic plot-structures, that originally came from Sicily; and of Athenian poets Crates was the first to abandon the iambic concept and to compose generalised stories and plots.

Epic conforms with tragedy insofar as it is a mimesis, in spoken metre, of ethically serious subjects; but it differs by virtue of using *only* spoken verse and of being in the narrative mode. There is also a difference of scale: whereas tragedy strives as far as possible to limit itself to a single day, epic is distinctive by its lack of a temporal limit, although in the early days poets of tragedy were as free in this respect as those of epic. The parts of epic are all common to tragedy, but the latter has some peculiar to itself. Consequently, whoever knows the difference between a good and a bad tragedy knows the same for epic too; for epic's attributes all belong to tragedy as well, though not all of tragedy's are shared by epic.

Chapter 6

I shall discuss epic mimesis and comedy later. But let us deal with tragedy by taking up the definition of its essential nature which arises out of what has so far been said.

Tragedy, then, is a representation of an action which is serious, complete, and of a certain magnitude – in language which is garnished in various forms in its different parts – in the mode of dramatic enactment, not narrative – and through the arousal of pity and fear effecting the *katharsis* of such emotions.

By "garnished" language I mean with rhythm and melody; and by the "various forms" I mean that some parts use spoken metre, and others use lyric song. Since the mimesis is enacted by agents, we can deduce that one element of tragedy must be the adornment of visual spectacle, while others are lyric poetry and verbal style, for it is in these that the mimesis is presented. By "style" I mean the composition of the spoken metres; the meaning of "lyric poetry" is entirely evident.

Since tragedy is a representation of an action, and is enacted by agents, who must be characterised in both their character and their thought (for it is through these that we can also judge the qualities of their actions, and it is in their actions that all men either succeed or fail), we have the plot-structure as the mimesis of the action (for by this term "plot-structure" I mean the organisation of the events) while characterisation is what allows us to judge the nature of the agents, and "thought" represents the parts in which by their speech they put forward arguments or make statements.

So then, tragedy as a whole must have six elements which make it what it is: they are plot-structure, character, style, thought, spectacle, lyric poetry. Two of these are the media, one the mode, and three the objects, of the mimesis – and that embraces everything. Many poets have exploited these parts in order to produce certain types of play [. . .].

The most important of these elements is the structure of events, because tragedy is a representation not of people as such but of actions and life, and both happiness and unhappiness rest on action. The goal is a certain activity, not a qualitative state; and while men do have certain qualities by virtue of their character, it is in their actions that they achieve, or fail to achieve, happiness. It is not, therefore, the function of the agents' actions to allow the portrayal of their characters; it is,

rather, for the sake of their actions that characterisation is included. So, the events and the plot-structure are the goal of tragedy, and the goal is what matters most of all.

Besides, without action you would not have a tragedy, but one without character would be feasible, for the tragedies of most recent poets are lacking in characterisation, and in general there are many such poets. Compare, among painters, the difference between Zeuxis and Polygnotus: while Polygnotus is a fine portrayer of character, Zeuxis' art has no characterisation. Furthermore, if a poet strings together speeches to illustrate character, even allowing he composes them well in style and thought, he will not achieve the stated aim of tragedy. Much more effective will be a play with a plot and structure of events, even if it is deficient in style and thought.

In addition to these considerations, tragedy's greatest means of emotional power are components of the plot-structure: namely, reversals and recognitions. Moreover, it is symptomatic that poetic novices can achieve precision in style and characterisation before they acquire it in plot-construction – as was the case with virtually all the early poets. And so, the plot-structure is the first principle and, so to speak, the soul of tragedy, while characterisation is the element of second importance. (An analogous point holds for painting: a random distribution of the most attractive colours would never yield as much pleasure as a definite image without colour.) Tragedy is a mimesis of action, and only for the sake of this is it mimesis of the agents themselves.

Third in importance is thought: this is the capacity to produce pertinent and appropriate arguments, which is the task in prose speeches of the arts of politics and rhetoric. The older poets used to make their characters speak in a political vein, whereas modern poets do so in a rhetorical vein. Character is the element which reveals the nature of a moral choice, in cases where it is not anyway clear what a person is choosing or avoiding (and so speeches in which the speaker chooses or avoids nothing at all do not possess character); while thought arises in passages where people show that something is or is not the case, or present some universal proposition.

The fourth element is style: as previously said, I mean by this term the verbal expression achieved through the choice of words, which has the same force whether in verse or in prose. Of the remaining elements, lyric poetry is the most important of garnishings, while spectacle is emotionally power-ful but is the least integral of all to the poet's art: for the potential of tragedy does not depend upon public performance and actors; and, besides, the art of the mask-maker carries more weight than the poet's as regards the elaboration of visual effects.

Chapter 7

Given these definitions, my next topic is to pre-scribe the form which the structure of events ought to take, since this is the first and foremost component of tragedy. We have already laid down that tragedy is a representation of an action which is complete, whole and of a certain magnitude (for something can be whole but of no magnitude).

By "whole" I mean possessing a beginning, middle and end. By "beginning" I mean that which does not have a necessary connection with a preceding event, but which can itself give rise nat-urally to some further fact or occurrence. An "end," by contrast, is something which naturally occurs after a preceding event, whether by necessity or as a general rule, but need not be followed by anything else. The "middle" involves causal con-nections with both what precedes and what ensues. Consequently, well designed plot-structures ought not to begin or finish at arbitrary points, but to follow the principles indicated.

Moreover, any beautiful object, whether a living creature or any other structure of parts, must pos-sess not only ordered arrangement but also an ap-propriate scale (for beauty is grounded in both size and order). A creature could not be beautiful if it is either too small – for perception of it is practically instantaneous and so cannot be experienced – or too great, for contemplation of it cannot be a single experience, and it is not possible to derive a sense of unity and wholeness from our perception of it (imagine an animal a thousand miles long). Just, therefore, as a beautiful body or creature must have some size, but one which allows it to be perceived all together, so plot-structures should be of a length which can be easily held in the memory.

An artistic definition of length cannot be related to dramatic competitions and the spectators' con-centration. For if a hundred tragedies had to com-pete, they would measure them by the water-clock (as people say they once did). The limit which accords with the true nature of the matter is this: beauty of size favours as large a structure as pos-sible, provided that coherence is maintained. A concise definition is to say that the sufficient limit of a poem's scale is the scope required for a probable or necessary succession of events which produce a transformation either from affliction to prosperity, or the reverse.

Chapter 8

A plot-structure does not possess unity (as some believe) by virtue of centring on an individual. For just as a particular thing may have many random properties, some of which do not combine to make a single entity, so a particular character may per-form many actions which do not yield a single "action". Consequently, all those poets who have written a *Heracleid* or *Theseid*, or the like, are evi-dently at fault: they believe that because Heracles was a single individual, a plot-structure about him ought thereby to have unity. As in other respects, Homer is exceptional by the fineness of his insight into this point, whether we regard this as an ac-quired ability or a natural endowment of his: al-though composing an *Odyssey*, he did not include everything that happened to the hero (such as his wounding on Parnassus or his pretence of madness at the levy – events which involved no necessary or probable connection with one another). Instead, he constructed the *Odyssey* around a single action of the kind I mean, and likewise with the *Iliad*.

So then, just as in the other mimetic arts a unitary mimesis is a representation of a unitary object, so the plot-structure, as the mimesis of action, should be a representation of a unitary and complete action; and its parts, consisting of the events, should be so constructed that the displace-ment or removal of any one of them will disturb and disjoint the work's wholeness. For anything whose presence or absence has no clear effect cannot be counted an integral part of the whole.

Chapter 9

It is a further clear implication of what has been said that the poet's task is to speak not of events which have occurred, but of the kind of events which *could* occur, and are possible by the standards of probability or necessity. For it is not the use or absence of metre which distin-guishes poet and historian (one could put Herod-otus' work into verse, but it would be no less a sort of history with it than without it): the difference lies in the fact that the one speaks of events which have occurred, the other of the sort of events which could occur.

It is for this reason that poetry is both more philosophical and more serious than history, since poetry speaks more of universals, history of particulars. A "universal" comprises the *kind* of speech or action which belongs by probability or necessity to a certain *kind* of character – something which poetry aims at *despite* its addition of particular names. A "particular," by contrast, is (for example) what Alcibiades did or experienced.

This point has become clear in the case of comedy, where it is only after constructing a plot in terms of probable events that they give the characters ordinary names, so diverging from the iambic poets' practice of writing about individuals. In tragedy, on the other hand, the poets hold to the actual names. (The reason for this is that people are ready to believe in what is possible; and while we may not yet believe in the possibility of things that have not already happened, actual events are evidently possible, otherwise they would not have occurred.) Even so, there are some tragedies in which one or two of the familiar names are kept, while others are due to the poet; and some plays in which all are new, as in Agathon's *Antheus*: for in this play both the events and the names are equally the poet's work, yet the pleasure it gives is just as great. So, fidelity to the traditional plots which are the subject of tragedies is not to be sought at all costs. Indeed, to do this is absurd, since even familiar material is familiar only to a minority, but it can still afford pleasure to all.

It is clear, then, from what has been said that the poet should be a maker of plot-structures rather than of verses, in so far as his status as poet depends on mimesis, and the object of his mimesis is actions. And he is just as much a poet even if the material of his poetry comprises actual events, since there is no reason why *some* historical events should not be in conformity with probability, and it is with respect to probability that the poet can make his poetry from them.

Of simple plot-structures and actions the worst are episodic. I call an "episodic" plot-structure one in which the episodes follow in a succession which is neither probable nor necessary. Such plays are produced by bad poets through their own fault, and by good poets because of their actors: for in composing declamatory set-pieces, and straining the plot-structure to excess, they are often compelled to distort the dramatic sequence.

Since tragic mimesis portrays not just a whole action, but events which are fearful and pitiful, this can best be achieved when things occur contrary to expectation yet still on account of one another. A sense of wonder will be more likely to be aroused in this way than as a result of the arbitrary or fortuitous, since even chance events make the greatest impact of wonder when they *appear* to have a purpose (as in the case where Mitys's statue at Argos fell on Mitys's murderer and killed him, while he was looking at it: such things do not *seem* to happen without reason). So then, plot-structures which embody this principle must be superior.

Chapter 10

Plot-structures can be divided into the simple and the complex, for the actions which they represent consist naturally of these types. By a "simple" action I mean one which is, as earlier defined, continuous and unitary, but whose transformation occurs without reversal or recognition. A "complex" action is one whose transformation involves recognition or reversal, or both. Reversal and recognition should arise from the intrinsic structure of the plot, so that what results follows by either necessity or probability from the preceding events: for it makes a great difference whether things happen because of one another, or only *after* one another.

Chapter 11

Reversal, as indicated, is a complete swing in the direction of the action; but this, as we insist, must conform to probability or necessity. Take, for example, Sophocles' *Oedipus Tyrannus*, where the person comes to bring Oedipus happiness, and intends to free him from his fear about his mother; but he produces the opposite effect, by revealing Oedipus' identity. And in *Lynceus* the one person is led off to die, while Danaus follows to kill him; yet it comes about that the latter's death and the former's rescue result from the chain of events.

Recognition, as the very name shows, is a change from ignorance to knowledge, bringing the characters into either a close bond, or enmity, with one another, and concerning matters which bear on their prosperity or affliction. The finest recognition occurs in direct conjunction with reversal – as with the one in the *Oedipus*. There are, of course, other kinds of recognition, for recognition can relate to inanimate or fortuitous objects, or reveal that someone has, or has not, committed a deed. But the type I have mentioned is the one which is most integral to the plot-structure and its action: for such a combination of recognition and reversal will produce pity or fear (and it is events of this kind that tragedy, on our definition, is a mimesis of), since both affliction and prosperity will hinge on such circumstances. And since recognition involves people, there are cases where one person's recognition by another takes place (when this other's own identity is clear), and cases where the recognition must be reciprocal: for instance, Iphigeneia was recognised by Orestes through the sending of the letter, but another means of recognition was needed for Iphigeneia's identification of *him*.

Well then, reversal and recognition form two components of the plot-structure; the third is suffering. To the definitions of reversal and recognition already given we can add that of suffering: a destructive or painful action, such as visible deaths, torments, woundings, and other things of the same kind. [. . .]

Chapter 13

It follows on from my earlier argument that I should define what ought to be aimed at and avoided in plot-construction, as well as the source of tragedy's effect. Since, then, the structure of the finest tragedy should be complex, not simple, and, moreover, should portray fearful and pitiful events (for this is the distinctive feature of this type of mimesis), it is to begin with clear that:

(a) good men should not be shown passing from prosperity to affliction, for this is neither fearful nor pitiful but repulsive;

(b) wicked men should not be shown passing from affliction to prosperity, for this is the most untragic of all possible cases and is entirely defective (it is neither moving nor pitiful nor fearful);

(c) the extremely evil man should not fall from prosperity to affliction, for such a plot-structure might move us, but would not arouse pity or fear, since pity is felt towards one whose affliction is undeserved, fear towards one who is like ourselves (so what happens in such a case will be neither pitiful nor fearful).

We are left, then, with the figure who falls between these types. Such a man is one who is not preeminent in virtue and justice, and one who falls into affliction not because of evil and wicked-ness, but because of a certain fallibility (*hamartia*). He will belong to the class of those who enjoy great esteem and prosperity, such as Oedipus, Thyestes, and outstanding men from such families.

It is imperative that a fine plot-structure be single and not double (as some assert), and involve a change from prosperity to affliction (rather than the reverse) caused not by wickedness but by a great fallibility on the part of the sort of agent stipulated, or one who is better, not worse, than indicated. Actual practice tends to confirm my thesis. For in the beginning the poets' choice of stories was arbitrary, whereas now the finest tragedies are constructed around a few families – Alcmaeon, for example, Oedipus, Orestes, Meleager, Thyestes, Telephus, and others who have suffered or committed terrible deeds.

This, then, is the plot-pattern for the tragedy which best fulfils the standards of poetic art. Those who fault Euripides for following this, and for ending many of his plays with affliction, make the same mistake as mentioned above. For such an ending is legitimate, as argued, and the greatest confirmation is that such plays make the most tragic impression in acted competition (provided they are staged effectively), and Euripides, whatever other faults of organisation he may have, at least makes the most tragic impression of all poets.

The second-best pattern (which some hold to be the best) is the kind which involves a double structure (like the *Odyssey*) and contrasting outcomes for good and bad characters. It is the weakness of audiences which produces the view of this type's superiority; poets are led to give the spectators what they want. But this is not the proper pleasure to be derived from tragedy – more like that of comedy: for in that genre people who are outright foes in the plot (say, Orestes and Aegisthus) go off as friends at the end, and nobody is killed.

Chapter 14

The effect of fear and pity can arise from theatrical spectacle, but it can also arise from the intrinsic structure of events, and it is this which matters more and is the task of a superior poet. For the plot-structure ought to be so composed that, even without seeing a performance, anyone who hears the events which occur will experience terror and pity as a result of the outcome; this is what someone would feel while hearing the plot of the *Oedipus*. To produce this effect through spectacle is not part of the poet's art, and calls for material resources; while those who use spectacle to produce an effect not of the fearful but only of the sensational fall quite outside the sphere of tragedy: for it is not every pleasure, but the appropriate one, which should be sought from tragedy. And since the poet ought to provide the pleasure which derives from pity and fear by means of mimesis, it is evident that this ought to be embodied in the events of the plot.

Let us, then, take up the question of what sort of circumstances make an impression of terror or pity. These are the only possibilities: such actions must involve dealings between those who are bonded by kinship or friendship; or between enemies; or between those who are neither. Well, if enemy faces enemy, neither the deed nor the prospect of it will be pitiful (except for the intrinsic potential of visible suffering); and the same is true of those whose relations are neutral. What must be sought are cases where suffering befalls bonded relations – when brother kills brother (or is about to, or to do something similar), son kills father, mother kills son, or son kills mother. Now, one cannot alter traditional plots (I mean, Clytemnestra's death at Orestes' hands, or Eriphyle's at Alcmaeon's) but the individual poet should find ways of handling even these to good effect.

I should explain more clearly what I mean by "to good effect". It is possible

(a) for the deed to be done with full knowledge and understanding, as the old poets used to arrange it, and in the way that Euripides too made Medea kill her children;

(b) for the deed to be done, but by agents who do not know the terrible thing they are doing, and who then later recognise their bond-relationship to the other, as with Sophocles' *Oedipus* (that is an instance where the deed occurs outside the drama, but Astydamas' *Alcmaeon*, and Telegonus in *Odysseus Wounded*, supply examples within the play itself);

(c) alternatively, for one who is on the point of committing an incurable deed in ignorance to come to a recognition before he has done it.

These are the only possibilities, for either the deed is done or it is not, and the agents must either know the facts or be ignorant of them. Of these cases, the worst is where the agent, in full knowledge, is on the point of acting, yet fails to do so: for this is repulsive and untragic (as it lacks suffering). Consequently, poets only rarely do this (for instance, Haemon's intention against Creon in *Antigone*). Not much better is for the deed to be executed in such a case. A superior arrangement is where the agent acts in ignorance, and discovers the truth after acting: for here there is nothing repulsive, and the recognition produces a powerful effect. But the best case is the last I have listed – for example, where Merope is about to kill her son in the *Cresphontes*, but does not do so because she recognises him; likewise with sister and brother in *Iphigeneia*, and in the *Helle*, where the son, on the point of handing her over, recognises his mother. Hence, as said before, tragedies concentrate on a few families. Luck not art led poets to find how to achieve such an effect in their plots; so they have to turn to the families in which such sufferings have occurred.

Enough, then, about the structure of events and the required qualities of plots.

Chapter 15

Regarding characterisation, there should be four aims:

(a) first and foremost, that the characters be good. Characterisation will arise, as earlier explained (ch.6), where speech or action exhibits the nature of an ethical choice; and the character will be good when the choice is good. But this depends on each class of person: there can be a good woman and a good slave, even though perhaps the former is an inferior type, and the latter a wholly base one.

(b) that the characters be appropriate. For it is *possible* to have a woman manly in character, but it is not appropriate for a woman to be so manly or clever.

(c) likeness of character – for this is independent of making character good and appropriate, as described.

(d) consistency of character. For even where an inconsistent person is portrayed, and such a character is presupposed, there should still be consistency in the inconsistency.

An illustration of unnecessary wickedness of character is Menelaus in *Orestes*; of unbecoming and inappropriate character, the lament of Odysseus in *Scylla*, or Melanippe's speech; and of inconsistency, *Iphigeneia in Aulis* (for the girl who beseeches bears no resemblance to the later girl). In characterisation just as in plot-construction, one should always seek the principle of necessity or probability, so that a necessary or probable reason exists for a particular character's speech or action, and similarly for the sequence of events.

It is evident that the dénouements of plot-structures should arise from the plot itself, and not, as in *Medea*, from a *deus ex machina*, or in the episode of the departure in the *Iliad*. But the *deus ex machina* should be used for events outside the play, whether earlier events of which a human cannot have knowledge, or future events which call for a prospective narrative; for we attribute to the gods a vision of all things. No irrational element should have a part in the events, unless outside the tragedy (as, for example, in Sophocles' *Oedipus*).

Since tragedy is a mimesis of men better than ourselves, the example set by good portrait-painters should be followed: they, while rendering the individual physique realistically, improve on their subjects' beauty. Similarly, the poet, while portraying men who are irascible or lazy or who have other such faults, ought to give them, despite such traits, goodness of character. An example of this is Homer's presentation of Achilles as good, despite his harshness. In addition to observing these points, the poet must guard against contraventions of the perceptions which necessarily attach to poetic art, since there are many ways of making mistakes in relation to these. But I have discussed these matters adequately in my published writings. [. . .]

Chapter 17

A poet ought to imagine his material to the fullest possible extent while composing his plot-structures and elaborating them in language. By seeing them as vividly as possible in this way – as if present at the very occurrence of the events – he is likely to discover what is appropriate, and least likely to miss contradictions. (One can see this from the criticism brought against Carcinus: for Amphiaraus was returning from the shrine, but the poet missed the point by not visualising it, and the play failed in the theatre on account of the spectators' annoyance.) So far as possible, the poet should even include gestures in the process of composition: for, assuming the same natural talent, the most convincing effect comes from those who actually put themselves in the emotions; and the truest impression of distress or anger is given by the person who experiences these feelings. Consequently, it is the imaginative man, rather than the manic, who is the best composer of poetry: since, of these types, the former can mould their emotions, while the latter are carried away.

Whether it exists already or is his own invention, the poet should lay out the general structure of his story, and then proceed to work out episodes and enlarge it. What I mean by contemplating the general structure can be illustrated from *Iphigeneia*. A girl was sacrificed and mysteriously vanished from her sacrificers; she was planted in another land, where strangers were traditionally sacrificed to the goddess whose priesthood the girl came to hold. Subsequently, it happened that the priestess's brother came to the place (the fact that a god's oracle sent him, and the reason for this, are outside the plot). Captured on his arrival, he was on the point of being sacrificed when he caused his own recognition (whether according to Euripides' version, or, as in Polyidus', by saying – as was plausible – that it was his own as well as his sister's destiny to be sacrificed). The upshot was his rescue.

The next stage is to supply names and work out the episodes. But care must be taken to make the episodes integral – as with the fit of madness which occasions Orestes' capture, and his rescue through the purification-rite. Now, in drama the episodes are concise, while epic gains extra length from them. For the main story of the *Odyssey* is short: a man is abroad for many years, is persecuted by Poseidon, and is left desolate; further, circumstances at home mean that his property is consumed by suitors, and his son is a target for conspiracy; but the man survives shipwreck to reach home again, reveals his identity to certain people, and launches an attack – his own safety is restored, and he destroys his enemies. This much is essential; the rest consists of episodes. [. . .]

Chapter 19

Having discussed the other elements, it remains for me to discuss style and thought. The details of thought can be left to my discourses on rhetoric, since they belong more integrally to that subject.

Thought pertains to all those effects which must be produced by the spoken language; its functions are demonstration, refutation, the arousal of emotions such as pity, fear, anger, and such like, and arguing for the importance or unimportance of things. (It is clear that the same basic principles underlie the achievement of effects of pity, terror, importance, probability, in the dramatic events; but the difference is that these must appear without explicit statement, whereas in the spoken language it is the speaker and his words which produce the effect. For what would be the point of a speaker, if the desired effect were evident even without his words?)

In matters of verbal style, one kind of study concerns figures of speech. Knowledge of these (for instance, the difference between a command, a prayer, a narrative, a threat, a question, an answer, and so on) belongs to the art of rhetorical delivery and to anyone with such expertise. For no serious charge can be brought against poetry on the basis of knowledge or ignorance of these matters. Why should anyone follow Protagoras in finding fault with Homer for purporting to address a prayer, but in fact delivering a command, by saying "Sing, Goddess, of the wrath ..."? According to Protagoras, to enjoin someone to do or avoid something is a command. Let this consideration be left for some other enquiry, not for poetry.

3

Of Tragedy

David Hume

It seems an unaccountable pleasure which the spectators of a well-written tragedy receive from sorrow, terror, anxiety, and other passions, that are in themselves disagreeable and uneasy. The more they are touched and affected, the more are they delighted with the spectacle; and as soon as the uneasy passions cease to operate, the piece is at an end. One scene of full joy and contentment and security is the utmost that any composition of this kind can bear; and it is sure always to be the concluding one. If, in the texture of the piece, there be interwoven any scenes of satisfaction, they afford only faint gleams of pleasure, which are thrown in by way of variety, and in order to plunge the actors into deeper distress by means of that contrast and disappointment. The whole art of the poet is employed in rousing and supporting the compassion and indignation, the anxiety and resentment of his audience. They are pleased in proportion as they are afflicted, and never are so happy as when they employ tears, sobs, and cries to give vent to their sorrow, and relieve their heart, swollen with the tenderest sympathy and compassion.

The few critics who have had some tincture of philosophy have remarked this singular phenomenon, and have endeavoured to account for it.

L'Abbé Dubos, in his reflections on poetry and painting, asserts that nothing is in general so disagreeable to the mind as the languid, listless state of indolence into which it falls upon the removal of all passion and occupation. To get rid of this painful situation, it seeks every amusement and pursuit: business, gaming, shows, executions; whatever will rouse the passions and take its attention from itself. No matter what the passion is: let it be disagreeable, afflicting, melancholy, disordered; it is still better than that insipid languor which arises from perfect tranquillity and repose.

It is impossible not to admit this account as being, at least in part, satisfactory. You may observe, when there are several tables of gaming, that all the company run to those where the deepest play is, even though they find not there the best players. The view or, at least, imagination of high passions, arising from great loss or gain, affects the spectator by sympathy, gives him more touches of the same passions, and serves him for a momentary entertainment. It makes the time pass the easier with him, and is some relief to that oppression under which men commonly labor when left entirely to their own thoughts and meditations.

We find that common liars always magnify, in their narrations, all kinds of danger, pain, distress, sickness, deaths, murders, and cruelties; as well as joy, beauty, mirth, and magnificence. It is an absurd secret which they have for pleasing their company, fixing their attention, and attaching them to such marvellous relations by the passions and emotions which they excite.

From *Essays Moral, Political, and Literary* (London, 1742).

There is, however, a difficulty in applying to the present subject, in its full extent, this solution, however ingenious and satisfactory it may appear. It is certain that the same object of distress which pleases in a tragedy, were it really set before us, would give the most unfeigned uneasiness, though it be then the most effectual cure to languor and indolence. Monsieur Fontenelle seems to have been sensible of this difficulty, and accordingly attempts another solution of the phenomenon; at least makes some addition to the theory above mentioned.

"Pleasure and pain," says he,

"which are two sentiments so different in themselves, differ not so much in their cause. From the instance of tickling, it appears, that the movement of pleasure, pushed a little too far, becomes pain; and that the movement of pain, a little moderated, becomes pleasure. Hence it proceeds that there is such a thing as a sorrow soft and agreeable: it is a pain weakened and diminished. The heart likes naturally to be moved and affected. Melancholy objects suit it, and even disastrous and sorrowful, provided they are softened by some circumstance. It is certain that, on the theatre, the representation has almost the effect of reality; yet it has not altogether that effect. However we may be hurried away by the spectacle; whatever dominion the senses and imagination may usurp over the reason, there still lurks at the bottom a certain idea of falsehood in the whole of what we see. This idea, though weak and disguised, suffices to diminish the pain which we suffer from the misfortunes of those whom we love, and to reduce that affliction to such a pitch as converts it into a pleasure. We weep for the misfortune of a hero to whom we are attached. In the same instant we comfort ourselves by reflecting that it is nothing but a fiction; and it is precisely that mixture of sentiments which composes an agreeable sorrow, and tears that delight us. But as that affliction which is caused by exterior and sensible objects is stronger than the consolation which arises from an internal reflection, they are the effects and symptoms of sorrow that ought to predominate in the composition."

This solution seems just and convincing, but perhaps it wants still some new addition in order to make it answer fully the phenomenon which we here examine. All the passions, excited by eloquence, are agreeable in the highest degree, as well as those which are moved by painting and the theatre. The epilogues of Cicero are, on this account chiefly, the delight of every reader of taste; and it is difficult to read some of them without the deepest sympathy and sorrow. His merit as an orator, no doubt, depends much on his success in this particular. When he had raised tears in his judges and all his audience, they were then the most highly delighted, and expressed the greatest satisfaction with the pleader. The pathetic description of the butchery made by Verres of the Sicilian captains is a masterpiece of this kind; but I believe none will affirm that the being present at a melancholy scene of that nature would afford any entertainment. Neither is the sorrow here softened by fiction, for the audience were convinced of the reality of every circumstance. What is it then which in this case raises a pleasure from the bosom of uneasiness, so to speak; and a pleasure which still retains all the features and outward symptoms of distress and sorrow?

I answer: this extraordinary effect proceeds from that very eloquence with which the melancholy scene is represented. The genius required to paint objects in a lively manner, the art employed in collecting all the pathetic circumstances, the judgment displayed in disposing them: the exercise, I say, of these noble talents, together with the force of expression and beauty of oratorial numbers, diffuse the highest satisfaction on the audience, and excite the most delightful movements. By this means, the uneasiness of the melancholy passions is not only overpowered and effaced by something stronger of an opposite kind, but the whole impulse of those passions is converted into pleasure, and swells the delight which the eloquence raises in us. The same force of oratory, employed on an uninteresting subject, would not please half so much, or rather would appear altogether ridiculous; and the mind, being left in absolute calmness and indifference, would relish none of those beauties of imagination or expression which, if joined to passion, give it such exquisite entertainment. The impulse or vehemence arising from sorrow, compassion, indignation, receives a new direction from the sentiments of beauty. The latter, being the predominant emotion, seizes the whole mind, and convert the former into themselves, at least tincture them so strongly as totally to alter their nature. And the soul being, at the same time, roused by passion and charmed by eloquence, feels on the whole a strong movement which is altogether delightful.

The same principle takes place in tragedy, with this addition, that tragedy is an imitation; and imitation is always of itself agreeable. This circumstance serves still farther to smooth the motions of passion, and convert the whole feeling into one uniform and strong enjoyment. Objects of the greatest terror and distress please in painting, and please more than the most beautiful objects that appear calm and indifferent. The affection, rousing the mind, excites a large stock of spirit and vehemence, which is all transformed into pleasure by the force of the prevailing movement. It is thus the fiction of tragedy softens the passion by an infusion of a new feeling, not merely by weakening or diminishing the sorrow. You may by degrees weaken a real sorrow till it totally disappears; yet in none of its gradations will it ever give pleasure, except perhaps, by accident, to a man sunk under lethargic indolence, whom it rouses from that languid state.

To confirm this theory it will be sufficient to produce other instances where the subordinate movement is converted into the predominant, and gives force to it, though of a different, and even sometimes though of a contrary nature.

Novelty naturally rouses the mind and attracts our attention, and the movements which it causes are always converted into any passion belonging to the object, and join their force to it. Whether an event excite joy or sorrow, pride or shame, anger or good will, it is sure to produce a stronger affection when new or unusual. And though novelty of itself be agreeable, it fortifies the painful, as well as agreeable passions.

Had you any intention to move a person extremely by the narration of any event, the best method of increasing its effect would be artfully to delay informing him of it, and first to excite his curiosity and impatience before you let him into the secret. This is the artifice practiced by Iago in the famous scene of Shakespeare; and every spectator is sensible that Othello's jealousy acquires additional force from his preceding impatience, and that the subordinate passion is here readily transformed into the predominant one.

Difficulties increase passions of every kind; and by rousing our attention, and exciting our active powers, they produce an emotion which nourishes the prevailing affection.

Parents commonly love that child most whose sickly infirm frame of body has occasioned them the greatest pains, trouble, and anxiety in rearing him. The agreeable sentiment of affection here acquires force from sentiments of uneasiness.

Nothing endears so much a friend as sorrow for his death. The pleasure of his company has not so powerful an influence.

Jealousy is a painful passion; yet without some share of it, the agreeable affection of love has difficulty to subsist in its full force and violence. Absence is also a great source of complaint among lovers, and gives them the greatest uneasiness; yet nothing is more favourable to their mutual passion than short intervals of that kind.

And if long intervals often prove fatal, it is only because, through time, men are accustomed to them, and they cease to give uneasiness. Jealousy and absence in love compose the "dolce peccante" of the Italians, which they suppose so essential to all pleasure.

There is a fine observation of the elder Pliny which illustrates the principle here insisted on. "It is very remarkable," says he,

> "that the last works of celebrated artists, which they left imperfect, are always the most prized, such as the Iris of Aristides, the Tyndarides of Nichomachus, the Medea of Timomachus, and the Venus of Apelles. These are valued even above their finished productions: the broken lineaments of the piece, and the half-formed idea of the painter are carefully studied; and our very grief for that curious hand, which had been stopped by death, is an additional increase to our pleasure."

These instances (and many more might be collected) are sufficient to afford us some insight into the analogy of nature, and to show us that the pleasure which poets, orators, and musicians give us by exciting grief, sorrow, indignation, compassion, is not so extraordinary or paradoxical as it may at first sight appear. The force of imagination, the energy of expression, the power of numbers, the charms of imitation: all these are naturally of themselves delightful to the mind; and when the object presented lays also hold of some affection, the pleasure still rises upon us by the conversion of this subordinate movement into that which is predominant. The passion though perhaps naturally, and when excited by the simple appearance of a real object, it may be painful; yet is so smoothed, and softened, and mollified, when raised by the finer arts, that it affords the highest entertainment.

To confirm this reasoning, we may observe that if the movements of the imagination be not predominant above those of the passion, a contrary effect follows; and the former, being now subordinate, is converted into the latter, and still farther increases the pain and affliction of the sufferer.

Who could ever think of it as a good expedient for comforting an afflicted parent to exaggerate, with all the force of elocution, the irreparable loss which he has met with by the death of a favourite child? The more power of imagination and expression you here employ, the more you increase his despair and affliction.

The shame, confusion, and terror of Verres, no doubt, rose in proportion to the noble eloquence and vehemence of Cicero; so also did his pain and uneasiness. These former passions were too strong for the pleasure arising from the beauties of elocution; and operated, though from the same principle, yet in a contrary manner, to the sympathy, compassion, and indignation of the audience.

Lord Clarendon, when he approaches towards the catastrophe of the royal party, supposes that his narration must then become infinitely disagreeable, and he hurries over the King's death without giving us one circumstance of it. He considers it as too horrid a scene to be contemplated with any satisfaction, or even without the utmost pain and aversion. He himself, as well as the reader of that age, were too deeply concerned in the events, and felt a pain from subjects which an historian and a reader of another age would regard as the most pathetic and interesting, and, by consequence, the most agreeable.

An action represented in tragedy may be too bloody and atrocious. It may excite such movements of horror as will not soften into pleasure; and the greatest energy of expression, bestowed on descriptions of that nature, serves only to augment our uneasiness. Such is that action represented in "The Ambitious Stepmother", where a venerable old man, raised to the height of fury and despair, rushes against a pillar, and striking his head upon it besmears it all over with mingled brains and gore. The English theatre abounds too much with such shocking images.

Even the common sentiments of compassion require to be softened by some agreeable affection, in order to give a thorough satisfaction to the audience. The mere suffering of plaintive virtue, under the triumphant tyranny and oppression of vice, forms a disagreeable spectacle, and is carefully avoided by all masters of the drama. In order to dismiss the audience with entire satisfaction and contentment, the virtue must either convert itself into a noble courageous despair, or the vice receive its proper punishment.

Most painters appear in this light to have been very unhappy in their subjects. As they wrought much for churches and convents, they have chiefly represented such horrible subjects as crucifixions and martyrdoms, where nothing appears but tortures, wounds, executions, and passive suffering, without any action or affection. When they turned their pencil from this ghastly mythology, they had commonly recourse to Ovid, whose fictions, though passionate and agreeable, are scarcely natural or probable enough for painting.

The same inversion of that principle which is here insisted on displays itself in common life, as in the effects of oratory and poetry. Raise so the subordinate passion that it becomes the predominant, it swallows up that affection which it before nourished and increased. Too much jealousy extinguishes love; too much difficulty renders us indifferent; too much sickness and infirmity disgusts a selfish and unkind parent.

What so disagreeable as the dismal, gloomy, disastrous stories with which melancholy people entertain their companions? The uneasy passion being there raised alone, unaccompanied with any spirit, genius, or eloquence, conveys a pure uneasiness, and is attended with nothing that can soften it into pleasure or satisfaction.

4

The Birth of Tragedy

Friedrich Nietzsche

1

We shall have gained much for the science of aesthetics, once we perceive not merely by logical inference, but with the immediate certainty of vision, that the continuous development of art is bound up with the *Apollinian* and *Dionysian* duality – just as procreation depends on the duality of the sexes, involving perpetual strife with only periodically intervening reconciliations. The terms Dionysian and Apollinian we borrow from the Greeks, who disclose to the discerning mind the profound mysteries of their view of art, not, to be sure, in concepts, but in the intensely clear figures of their gods. Through Apollo and Dionysus, the two art deities of the Greeks, we come to recognize that in the Greek world there existed a tremendous opposition, in origin and aims,[1] between the Apollinian art of sculpture, and the nonimagistic, Dionysian art of music. These two different tendencies run parallel to each other, for the most part openly at variance; and they continually incite each other to new and more powerful births, which perpetuate an antagonism, only superficially reconciled by the common term "art"; till eventually,[2] by a metaphysical miracle of the Hellenic "will," they appear coupled with each other, and through this coupling ultimately generate an equally Dionysian and Apollinian form of art – Attic tragedy.

In order to grasp these two tendencies, let us first conceive of them as the separate art worlds of *dreams* and *intoxication*. These physiological phenomena present a contrast analogous to that existing between the Apollinian and the Dionysian. It was in dreams, says Lucretius, that the glorious divine figures first appeared to the souls of men; in dreams the great shaper beheld the splendid bodies of superhuman beings; and the Hellenic poet, if questioned about the mysteries of poetic inspiration, would likewise have suggested dreams and he might have given an explanation like that of Hans Sachs in the *Meistersinger*:

> The poet's task is this, my friend,
> to read his dreams and comprehend.
> The truest human fancy seems
> to be revealed to us in dreams:
> all poems and versification
> are but true dreams' interpretation.

The beautiful illusion of the dream worlds, in the creation of which every man is truly an artist, is the prerequisite of all plastic art, and, as we shall see, of an important part of poetry also. In our dreams we delight in the immediate understanding of figures; all forms speak to us; there is nothing unimportant or superfluous. But even when this dream reality is most intense, we still have, glimmering through it, the sensation that it is *mere*

From *Birth of Tragedy and the Case of Wagner*, trans. Walter Kaufmann (New York: Vintage, 1967), pp. 33–8, 59–60, 89–93. Copyright © 1967 by Walter Kaufmann. Used by permission of Random House, Inc.

appearance: at least this is my experience, and for its frequency – indeed, normality – I could adduce many proofs, including the sayings of the poets.

Philosophical men even have a presentiment that the reality in which we live and have our being is also mere appearance, and that another, quite different reality lies beneath it. Schopenhauer actually indicates as the criterion of philosophical ability the occasional ability to view men and things as mere phantoms or dream images. Thus the aesthetically sensitive man stands in the same relation to the reality of dreams as the philosopher does to the reality of existence; he is a close and willing observer, for these images afford him an interpretation of life, and by reflecting on these processes he trains himself for life.

It is not only the agreeable and friendly images that he experiences as something universally intelligible: the serious, the troubled, the sad, the gloomy, the sudden restraints, the tricks of accident, anxious expectations, in short, the whole divine comedy of life, including the inferno, also pass before him, not like mere shadows on a wall – for he lives and suffers with these scenes – and yet not without that fleeting sensation of illusion. And perhaps many will, like myself, recall how amid the dangers and terrors of dreams they have occasionally said to themselves in self-encouragement, and not without success: "It is a dream! I will dream on!" I have likewise heard of people who were able to continue one and the same dream for three and even more successive nights – facts which indicate clearly how our innermost being, our common ground, experiences dreams with profound delight and a joyous necessity.

This joyous necessity of the dream experience has been embodied by the Greeks in their Apollo: Apollo, the god of all plastic energies, is at the same time the soothsaying god. He, who (as the etymology of the name indicates) is the "shining one," the deity of light, is also ruler over the beautiful illusion of the inner world of fantasy. The higher truth, the perfection of these states in contrast to the incompletely intelligible everyday world, this deep consciousness of nature, healing and helping in sleep and dreams, is at the same time the symbolical analogue of the soothsaying faculty and of the arts generally, which make life possible and worth living. But we must also include in our image of Apollo that delicate boundary which the dream image must not overstep lest it have a pathological effect (in which case mere appearance would deceive us as if it were crude

reality). We must keep in mind that measured restraint, that freedom from the wilder emotions, that calm of the sculptor god. His eye must be "sunlike," as befits his origin; even when it is angry and distempered it is still hallowed by beautiful illusion. And so, in one sense, we might apply to Apollo the words of Schopenhauer when he speaks of the man wrapped in the veil of *māyā*[3] (*Welt als Wille und Vorstellung*, I, p. 416[4]): "Just as in a stormy sea that, unbounded in all directions, raises and drops mountainous waves, howling, a sailor sits in a boat and trusts in his frail bark: so in the midst of a world of torments the individual human being sits quietly, supported by and trusting in the *principium individuationis*." In fact, we might say of Apollo that in him the unshaken faith in this *principium* and the calm repose of the man wrapped up in it receive their most sublime expression; and we might call Apollo himself the glorious divine image of the *principium individuationis*, through whose gestures and eyes all the joy and wisdom of "illusion," together with its beauty, speak to us.

In the same work Schopenhauer has depicted for us the tremendous *terror* which seizes man when he is suddenly dumfounded by the cognitive form of phenomena because the principle of sufficient reason, in some one of its manifestations, seems to suffer an exception. If we add to this terror the blissful ecstasy that wells from the innermost depths of man, indeed of nature, at this collapse of the *principium individuationis*, we steal a glimpse into the nature of the *Dionysian*, which is brought home to us most intimately by the analogy of intoxication.

Either under the influence of the narcotic draught, of which the songs of all primitive men and peoples speak, or with the potent coming of spring that penetrates all nature with joy, these Dionysian emotions awake, and as they grow in intensity everything subjective vanishes into complete self-forgetfulness. In the German Middle Ages, too, singing and dancing crowds, ever increasing in number, whirled themselves from place to place under this same Dionysian impulse. In these dancers of St. John and St. Vitus, we rediscover the Bacchic choruses of the Greeks, with their prehistory in Asia Minor, as far back as Babylon and the orgiastic Sacaea. There are some who, from obtuseness or lack of experience, turn away from such phenomena as from "folk-diseases," with contempt or pity born of the consciousness of their own "healthy-mindedness."

But of course such poor wretches have no idea how corpselike and ghostly their so-called "healthy-mindedness" looks when the glowing life of the Dionysian revelers roars past them.

Under the charm of the Dionysian not only is the union between man and man reaffirmed, but nature which has become alienated, hostile, or subjugated, celebrates once more her reconciliation with her lost son, man. Freely, earth proffers her gifts, and peacefully the beasts of prey of the rocks and desert approach. The chariot of Dionysus is covered with flowers and garlands; panthers and tigers walk under its yoke. Transform Beethoven's "Hymn to Joy" into a painting; let your imagination conceive the multitudes bowing to the dust, awestruck – then you will approach the Dionysian. Now the slave is a free man; now all the rigid, hostile barriers that necessity, caprice, or "impudent convention"[5] have fixed between man and man are broken. Now, with the gospel of universal harmony, each one feels himself not only united, reconciled, and fused with his neighbor, but as one with him, as if the veil of *māyā* had been torn aside and were now merely fluttering in tatters before the mysterious primordial unity.

In song and in dance man expresses himself as a member of a higher community; he has forgotten how to walk and speak and is on the way toward flying into the air, dancing. His very gestures express enchantment. Just as the animals now talk, and the earth yields milk and honey, supernatural sounds emanate from him, too: he feels himself a god, he himself now walks about enchanted, in ecstasy, like the gods he saw walking in his dreams. He is no longer an artist, he has become a work of art: in these paroxysms of intoxication the artistic power of all nature reveals itself to the highest gratification of the primordial unity. The noblest clay, the most costly marble, man, is here kneaded and cut, and to the sound of the chisel strokes of the Dionysian world-artist rings out the cry of the Eleusinian mysteries: "Do you prostrate yourselves, millions? Do you sense your Maker, world?"[6] [. . .]

7

We must now avail ourselves of all the principles of art considered so far, in order to find our way through the labyrinth, as we must call it, of *the origin of Greek tragedy*. I do not think I am unreasonable in saying that the problem of this origin has as yet not even been seriously posed, to say nothing of solved, however often the ragged tatters of ancient tradition have been sewn together in various combinations and torn apart again. This tradition tells us quite unequivocally *that tragedy arose from the tragic chorus*, and was originally only chorus and nothing but chorus. Hence we consider it our duty to look into the heart of this tragic chorus as the real proto-drama, without resting satisfied with such arty clichés as that the chorus is the "ideal spectator" or that it represents the people in contrast to the aristocratic region of the scene. This latter explanation has a sublime sound to many a politician – as if the immutable moral law had been embodied by the democratic Athenians in the popular chorus, which always won out over the passionate excesses and extravagances of kings. This theory may be ever so forcibly suggested by one of Aristotle's observations; still, it has no influence on the original formation of tragedy, inasmuch as the whole opposition of prince and people – indeed the whole politico-social sphere – was excluded from the purely religious origins of tragedy. But even regarding the classical form of the chorus in Aeschylus and Sophocles, which is known to us, we should deem it blasphemy to speak here of intimations of "constitutional popular representation." From this blasphemy, however, others have not shrunk. Ancient constitutions knew of no constitutional representation of the people in *praxi*, and it is to be hoped that they did not even "have intimations" of it in tragedy.

Much more famous than this political interpretation of the chorus is the idea of A. W. Schlegel, who advises us to regard the chorus somehow as the essence and extract of the crowd of spectators – as the "ideal spectator." This view, when compared with the historical tradition that originally tragedy was only chorus, reveals itself for what it is – a crude, unscientific, yet brilliant claim that owes its brilliancy only to its concentrated form of expression, to the typically Germanic bias in favor of anything called "ideal," and to our momentary astonishment. For we are certainly astonished the moment we compare our familiar theatrical public with this chorus, and ask ourselves whether it could ever be possible to idealize from such a public something analogous to the Greek tragic chorus. We tacitly deny this, and now wonder as much at the boldness of Schlegel's claim as at the totally different nature of the Greek public. For we had always believed that the right spectator, whoever he might be, must always remain conscious that he was viewing a work of art and not an empirical reality. But the tragic chorus of the Greeks is forced to recognize real beings in the figures on the stage. The chorus of the Oceanides really believes that it sees before it the Titan Prometheus, and it considers itself as real as the god of the scene. But could the highest and purest type of spectator regard Prometheus as bodily present and real, as the Oceanides do? Is it characteristic of the ideal spectator to run onto the stage and free the god from his torments? We had always believed in an aesthetic public and considered the individual spectator the better qualified the more he was capable of viewing a work of art as art, that is, aesthetically. But now Schlegel tells us that the perfect, ideal spectator does not at all allow the world of the drama to act on him aesthetically, but corporally and empirically. Oh, these Greeks! we sigh; they upset all our aesthetics! But once accustomed to this, we repeated Schlegel's saying whenever the chorus came up for discussion.

Now the tradition, which is quite explicit, speaks against Schlegel. The chorus as such, without the stage – the primitive form of tragedy – and the chorus of ideal spectators do not go together. What kind of artistic genre could possibly be extracted from the concept of the spectator, and find its true form in the "spectator as such"? The spectator without the spectacle is an absurd notion. We fear that the birth of tragedy is to be explained neither by any high esteem for the moral intelligence of the masses nor by the concept of the spectator without a spectacle; and we consider the problem too deep to be even touched by such superficial considerations.

An infinitely more valuable insight into the significance of the chorus was displayed by Schiller in the celebrated Preface to his *Bride of Messina*, where he regards the chorus as a living wall that tragedy constructs around itself in order to close itself off from the world of reality and to preserve its ideal domain and its poetical freedom.

With this, his chief weapon, Schiller combats the ordinary conception of the natural, the illusion usually demanded in dramatic poetry. Although the stage day is merely artificial, the architecture only symbolical, and the metrical language ideal in character, nevertheless an erroneous view still prevails in the main, as he points out: it is not sufficient that one merely tolerates as poetic license what is actually the essence of all poetry. The introduction of the chorus, says Schiller, is the

decisive step by which war is declared openly and honorably against all naturalism in art.

It would seem that to denigrate this view of the matter our would-be superior age has coined the disdainful catchword "pseudo-idealism." I fear, however, that we, on the other hand, with our present adoration of the natural and the real, have reached the opposite pole of all idealism, namely, the region of wax-work cabinets. There is an art in these, as there is in certain novels much in vogue at present; but we really should not be plagued with the claim that such art has overcome the "pseudo-idealism" of Goethe and Schiller.

It is indeed an "ideal" domain, as Schiller correctly perceived, in which the Greek satyr chorus, the chorus of primitive tragedy, was wont to dwell. It is a domain raised high above the actual paths of mortals. For this chorus the Greek built up the scaffolding of a fictitious *natural state* and on it placed fictitious *natural beings*. On this foundation tragedy developed and so, of course, it could dispense from the beginning with a painstaking portrayal of reality. Yet it is no arbitrary world placed by whim between heaven and earth; rather it is a world with the same reality and credibility that Olympus with its inhabitants possessed for the believing Hellene. The satyr, as the Dionysian chorist, lives in a religiously acknowledged reality under the sanction of myth and cult. That tragedy should begin with him, that he should be the voice of the Dionysian wisdom of tragedy, is just as strange a phenomenon for us as the general derivation of tragedy from the chorus.

Perhaps we shall have a point of departure for our inquiry if I put forward the proposition that the satyr, the fictitious natural being, bears the same relation to the man of culture that Dionysian music bears to civilization. Concerning the latter, Richard Wagner says that it is nullified by music just as lamplight is nullified by the light of day. Similarly, I believe, the Greek man of culture felt himself nullified in the presence of the satyric chorus; and this is the most immediate effect of the Dionysian tragedy, that the state and society and, quite generally, the gulfs between man and man give way to an overwhelming feeling of unity leading back to the very heart of nature. The metaphysical comfort – with which, I am suggesting even now, every true tragedy leaves us – that life is at the bottom of things, despite all the changes of appearances, indestructibly powerful and pleasurable – this comfort appears in incarnate clarity in the chorus of satyrs, a chorus of natural beings who live ineradicably, as it were, behind all civilization and remain eternally the same, despite the changes of generations and of the history of nations.

With this chorus the profound Hellene, uniquely susceptible to the tenderest and deepest suffering, comforts himself, having looked boldly right into the terrible destructiveness of so-called world history as well as the cruelty of nature, and being in danger of longing for a Buddhistic negation of the will. Art saves him, and through art – life.

For the rapture of the Dionysian state with its annihilation of the ordinary bounds and limits of existence contains, while it lasts, a *lethargic* element in which all personal experiences of the past become immersed. This chasm of oblivion separates the worlds of everyday reality and of Dionysian reality. But as soon as this everyday reality re-enters consciousness, it is experienced as such, with nausea: an ascetic, will-negating mood is the fruit of these states.

In this sense the Dionysian man resembles Hamlet: both have once looked truly into the essence of things, they have *gained knowledge*, and nausea inhibits action; for their action could not change anything in the eternal nature of things; they feel it to be ridiculous or humiliating that they should be asked to set right a world that is out of joint. Knowledge kills action; action requires the veils of illusion: that is the doctrine of Hamlet, not that cheap wisdom of Jack the Dreamer who reflects too much and, as it were, from an excess of possibilities does not get around to action. Not reflection, no – true knowledge, an insight into the horrible truth, outweighs any motive for action, both in Hamlet and in the Dionysian man.

Now no comfort avails any more; longing transcends a world after death, even the gods; existence is negated along with its glittering reflection in the gods or in an immortal beyond. Conscious of the truth he has once seen, man now sees everywhere only the horror or absurdity of existence; now he understands what is symbolic in Ophelia's fate; now he understands the wisdom of the sylvan god, Silenus: he is nauseated.

Here, when the danger to his will is greatest, *art* approaches as a saving sorceress, expert at healing. She alone knows how to turn these nauseous thoughts about the horror or absurdity of existence into notions with which one can live: these are the *sublime* as the artistic taming of the horrible, and the *comic* as the artistic discharge of the nausea of

absurdity. The satyr chorus of the dithyramb is the saving deed of Greek art; faced with the intermediary world of these Dionysian companions, the feelings described here exhausted themselves. [...]

14

Let us now imagine the one great Cyclops eye of Socrates fixed on tragedy, an eye in which the fair frenzy of artistic enthusiasm had never glowed. To this eye was denied the pleasure of gazing into the Dionysian abysses. What, then, did it have to see in the "sublime and greatly lauded" tragic art, as Plato called it? Something rather unreasonable, full of causes apparently without effects, and effects apparently without causes; the whole, moreover, so motley and manifold that it could not but be repugnant to a sober mind, and a dangerous tinder for sensitive and susceptible souls. We know the only kind of poetry he comprehended: the *Aesopian fable*; and this he favored no doubt with the smiling accommodation with which the good honest Gellert sings the praise of poetry in the fable of the bee and the hen:

> *Poems are useful: they can tell*
> *The truth by means of parable*
> *To those who are not very bright.*

But to Socrates it seemed that tragic art did not even "tell the truth"; moreover, it addressed itself to "those who are not very bright," not to the philosopher: a twofold reason for shunning it. Like Plato, he reckoned it among the flattering arts which portray only the agreeable, not the useful; and therefore he required of his disciples abstinence and strict separation from such unphilosophical attractions – with such success that the youthful tragic poet Plato first burned his poems that he might become a student of Socrates. But where unconquerable propensities struggled against the Socratic maxims, their power, together with the impact of his tremendous character, was still great enough to force poetry itself into new and hitherto unknown channels.

An instance of this is Plato, who in condemning tragedy and art in general certainly did not lag behind the naïve cynicism of his master; he was nevertheless constrained by sheer artistic necessity to create an art form that was related to those forms of art which he repudiated. Plato's main objection to the older art – that it is the imitation of a phantom and hence belongs to a sphere even lower than the empirical world – could certainly not be directed against the new art; and so we find Plato endeavoring to transcend reality and to represent the idea which underlies this pseudo-reality. Thus Plato, the thinker, arrived by a detour where he had always been at home as a poet – at the point from which Sophocles and the older art protested solemnly against that objection. If tragedy had absorbed into itself all the earlier types of art, the same might also be said in an eccentric sense of the Platonic dialogue which, a mixture of all extant styles and forms, hovers midway between narrative, lyric, and drama, between prose and poetry, and so has also broken the strict old law of the unity of linguistic form. This tendency was carried still further by the *Cynic* writers, who in the greatest stylistic medley, oscillating between prose and metrical forms, realized also the literary image of the "raving Socrates" whom they represented in real life.

The Platonic dialogue was, as it were, the barge on which the shipwrecked ancient poetry saved herself with all her children: crowded into a narrow space and timidly submitting to the single pilot, Socrates, they now sailed into a new world, which never tired of looking at the fantastic spectacle of this procession. Indeed, Plato has given to all posterity the model of a new art form, the model of the *novel* – which may be described as an infinitely enhanced Aesopian fable, in which poetry holds the same rank in relation to dialectical philosophy as this same philosophy held for many centuries in relation to theology: namely, the rank of *ancilla*. This was the new position into which Plato, under the pressure of the demonic Socrates, forced poetry.

Here *philosophic thought* overgrows art and compels it to cling close to the trunk of dialectic. The *Apollinian* tendency has withdrawn into the cocoon of logical schematism; just as in the case of Euripides we noticed something analogous, as well as a transformation of the *Dionysian* into naturalistic affects. Socrates, the dialectical hero of the Platonic drama, reminds us of the kindred nature of the Euripidean hero who must defend his actions with arguments and counterarguments and in the process often risks the loss of our tragic pity; for who could mistake the *optimistic* element in the nature of dialectic, which celebrates a triumph with every conclusion and can breathe only in cool clarity and consciousness – the optimistic element which, having once penetrated tragedy

must gradually overgrow its Dionysian regions and impel it necessarily to self-destruction – to the death-leap into the bourgeois drama. Consider the consequences of the Socratic maxims: "Virtue is knowledge; man sins only from ignorance; he who is virtuous is happy." In these three basic forms of optimism lies the death of tragedy. For now the virtuous hero must be a dialectician; now there must be a necessary, visible connection between virtue and knowledge, faith and morality; now the transcendental justice of Aeschylus is degraded to the superficial and insolent principle of "poetic justice" with its customary *deus ex machina*.

As it confronts this new Socratic-optimistic stage world, how does the *chorus* appear now, and indeed the whole musical-Dionysian substratum of tragedy? As something accidental, a dispensable vestige of the origin of tragedy; while we have seen that the chorus can be understood only as the *cause* of tragedy, and of the tragic in general. This perplexity in regard to the chorus already manifests itself in Sophocles – an important indication that even with him the Dionysian basis of tragedy is beginning to break down. He no longer dares to entrust to the chorus the main share of the effect, but limits its sphere to such an extent that it now appears almost co-ordinate with the actors, just as if it were elevated from the orchestra into the scene; and thus its character is, of course, completely destroyed, even if Aristotle favors precisely this theory of the chorus. This alteration in the position of the chorus, which Sophocles at any rate recommended by his practice and, according to tradition, even by a treatise, is the first step toward the *destruction* of the chorus, whose phases follow one another with alarming rapidity in Euripides, Agathon, and the New Comedy. Optimistic dialectic drives *music* out of tragedy with the scourge of its syllogisms; that is, it destroys the essence of tragedy, which can be interpreted only as a manifestation and projection into images of Dionysian states, as the visible symbolizing of music, as the dream-world of a Dionysian intoxication.

If we must thus assume an anti-Dionysian tendency operating even prior to Socrates, which merely received in him an unprecedentedly magnificent expression, we must not draw back before the question of what such a phenomenon as that of Socrates indicates; for in view of the Platonic dialogues we are certainly not entitled to regard it as a merely disintegrating, negative force. And though there can be no doubt that the most immediate effect of the Socratic impulse tended to the dissolution of Dionysian tragedy, yet a profound experience in Socrates' own life impels us to ask whether there is *necessarily* only an antipodal relation between Socratism and art, and whether the birth of an "artistic Socrates" is altogether a contradiction in terms.

For with respect to art that despotic logician occasionally had the feeling of a gap, a void, half a reproach, a possibly neglected duty. As he tells his friends in prison, there often came to him one and the same dream apparition, which always said the same thing to him: "Socrates, practice music." Up to his very last days he comforts himself with the view that his philosophizing is the highest of the muses, and he finds it hard to believe that a deity should remind him of the "common, popular music." Finally, in prison, in order that he may thoroughly unburden his conscience, he does consent to practice this music for which he has but little respect. And in this mood he writes a prelude to Apollo and turns a few Aesopian fables into verse. It was something akin to the demonic warning voice that urged him to these practices; it was his Apollinian insight that, like a barbaric king, he did not understand the noble image of a god and was in danger of sinning against a deity – through his lack of understanding. The voice of the Socratic dream vision is the only sign of any

misgivings about the limits of logic: Perhaps – thus he must have asked himself – what is not intelligible to me is not necessarily unintelligent? Perhaps there is a realm of wisdom from which the logician is exiled? Perhaps art is even a necessary correlative of, and supplement for science?

Notes

1 In the first edition: " . . . an opposition of style: two different tendencies run parallel in it, for the most part in conflict; and they . . . " Most of the changes in the revision of 1874 are as slight as this (compare the next note) and therefore not indicated in the following pages. This translation, like the standard German editions, follows Nietzsche's revision.

2 First edition: "till eventually, at the moment of the flowering of the Hellenic 'will,' they appear fused to generate together the art form of Attic tragedy."

3 A Sanskrit word usually translated as illusion.

4 This reference, like subsequent references to the same work, is Nietzsche's own and refers to the edition of 1873 edited by Julius Frauenstädt – still one of the standard editions of Schopenhauer's works.

5 An allusion to Friedrich Schiller's hymn *An die Freude* (to joy), used by Beethoven in the final movement of his Ninth Symphony.

6 Quotation from Schiller's hymn.

5

Creative Writers and Day-Dreaming

Sigmund Freud

WE laymen have always been intensely curious to know – like the Cardinal who put a similar question to Ariosto[1] – from what sources that strange being, the creative writer, draws his material, and how he manages to make such an impression on us with it and to arouse in us emotions of which, perhaps, we had not even thought ourselves capable. Our interest is only heightened the more by the fact that, if we ask him, the writer himself gives us no explanation, or none that is satisfactory; and it is not at all weakened by our knowledge that not even the clearest insight into the determinants of his choice of material and into the nature of the art of creating imaginative form will ever help to make creative writers of *us*.

If we could at least discover in ourselves or in people like ourselves an activity which was in some way akin to creative writing! An examination of it would then give us a hope of obtaining the beginnings of an explanation of the creative work of writers. And, indeed, there is some prospect of this being possible. After all, creative writers themselves like to lessen the distance between their kind and the common run of humanity; they so often assure us that every man is a poet at heart and that the last poet will not perish till the last man does.

Should we not look for the first traces of imaginative activity as early as in childhood? The child's best-loved and most intense occupation is with his play or games. Might we not say that every child at play behaves like a creative writer, in that he creates a world of his own, or, rather, rearranges the things of his world in a new way which pleases him? It would be wrong to think he does not take that world seriously; on the contrary, he takes his play very seriously and he expends large amounts of emotion on it. The opposite of play is not what is serious but what is real. In spite of all the emotion with which he cathects his world of play, the child distinguishes it quite well from reality; and he likes to link his imagined objects and situations to the tangible and visible things of the real world. This linking is all that differentiates the child's "play" from "phantasying".

The creative writer does the same as the child at play. He creates a world of phantasy which he takes very seriously – that is, which he invests with large amounts of emotion – while separating it sharply from reality. Language has preserved this relationship between children's play and poetic creation. It gives [in German] the name of *Spiel* ["play"] to those forms of imaginative writing which require to be linked to tangible objects and which are capable of representation. It speaks of a *Lustspiel* or *Trauerspiel* ["comedy" or "tragedy": literally,

Trans. I. F. Grant Duff, from *The Standard Edition of the Complete Psychological Works of Sigmund Freud*, ed. James Strachey (London: Hogarth Press, 1953), vol. 9, pp. 143–53. Sigmund Freud copyright by the Institute of Psychoanalysis and the Hogarth Press. Reprinted by permission of the Random House Group Ltd.

"pleasure play" or "mourning play"] and describes those who carry out the representation as *Schauspieler* ["players": literally "show-players"]. The unreality of the writer's imaginative world, however, has very important consequences for the technique of his art; for many things which, if they were real, could give no enjoyment, can do so in the play of phantasy, and many excitements which, in themselves, are actually distressing, can become a source of pleasure for the hearers and spectators at the performance of a writer's work.

There is another consideration for the sake of which we will dwell a moment longer on this contrast between reality and play. When the child has grown up and has ceased to play, and after he has been labouring for decades to envisage the realities of life with proper seriousness, he may one day find himself in a mental situation which once more undoes the contrast between play and reality. As an adult he can look back on the intense seriousness with which he once carried on his games in childhood; and, by equating his ostensibly serious occupations of to-day with his childhood games, he can throw off the too heavy burden imposed on him by life and win the high yield of pleasure afforded by *humour*.

As people grow up, then, they cease to play, and they seem to give up the yield of pleasure which they gained from playing. But whoever understands the human mind knows that hardly anything is harder for a man than to give up a pleasure which he has once experienced. Actually, we can never give anything up; we only exchange one thing for another. What appears to be a renunciation is really the formation of a substitute or surrogate. In the same way, the growing child, when he stops playing, gives up nothing but the link with real objects; instead of *playing*, he now *phantasies*. He builds castles in the air and creates what are called *day-dreams*. I believe that most people construct phantasies at times in their lives. This is a fact which has long been overlooked and whose importance has therefore not been sufficiently appreciated.

People's phantasies are less easy to observe than the play of children. The child, it is true, plays by himself or forms a closed psychical system with other children for the purposes of a game; but even though he may not play his game in front of the grown-ups, he does not, on the other hand, conceal it from them. The adult, on the contrary, is ashamed of his phantasies and hides them from other people. He cherishes his phantasies as his most intimate possessions, and as a rule he would rather confess his misdeeds than tell anyone his phantasies. It may come about that for that reason he believes he is the only person who invents such phantasies and has no idea that creations of this kind are widespread among other people. This difference in the behaviour of a person who plays and a person who phantasies is accounted for by the motives of these two activities, which are nevertheless adjuncts to each other.

A child's play is determined by wishes: in point of fact by a single wish – one that helps in his upbringing – the wish to be big and grown up. He is always playing at being "grown up", and in his games he imitates what he knows about the lives of his elders. He has no reason to conceal this wish. With the adult, the case is different. On the one hand, he knows that he is expected not to go on playing or phantasying any longer, but to act in the real world; on the other hand, some of the wishes which give rise to his phantasies are of a kind which it is essential to conceal. Thus he is ashamed of his phantasies as being childish and as being unpermissible.

But, you will ask, if people make such a mystery of their phantasying, how is it that we know such a lot about it? Well, there is a class of human beings upon whom, not a god, indeed, but a stern goddess – Necessity – has allotted the task of telling what they suffer and what things give them happiness. These are the victims of nervous illness, who are obliged to tell their phantasies, among other things, to the doctor by whom they expect to be cured by mental treatment. This is our best source of knowledge, and we have since found good reason to suppose that our patients tell us nothing that we might not also hear from healthy people.

Let us now make ourselves acquainted with a few of the characteristics of phantasying. We may lay it down that a happy person never phantasies, only an unsatisfied one. The motive forces of phantasies are unsatisfied wishes, and every single phantasy is the fulfilment of a wish, a correction of unsatisfying reality. These motivating wishes vary according to the sex, character and circumstances of the person who is having the phantasy; but they fall naturally into two main groups. They are either ambitious wishes, which serve to elevate the subject's personality; or they are erotic ones. In young women the erotic wishes predominate almost exclusively, for their ambition is as a rule absorbed by erotic trends. In young men egoistic and ambitious wishes come to the fore clearly enough alongside of erotic ones. But we will not lay stress on the opposition between the two trends; we would rather emphasize the fact that they are often united. Just as, in many altar-pieces, the portrait of the donor is to be seen in a corner of the picture, so, in the majority of ambitious phantasies, we can discover in some corner or other the lady for whom the creator of the phantasy performs all his heroic deeds and at whose feet all his triumphs are laid. Here, as you see, there are strong enough motives for concealment; the well-brought-up young woman is only allowed a minimum of erotic desire, and the young man has to learn to suppress the excess of self-regard which he brings with him from the spoilt days of his childhood, so that he may find his place in a society which is full of other individuals making equally strong demands.

We must not suppose that the products of this imaginative activity – the various phantasies, castles in the air and day-dreams – are stereotyped or unalterable. On the contrary, they fit themselves in to the subject's shifting impressions of life, change with every change in his situation, and receive from every fresh active impression what might be called a "date-mark". The relation of a phantasy to time is in general very important. We may say that it hovers, as it were, between three times – the three moments of time which our ideation involves. Mental work is linked to some current impression, some provoking occasion in the present which has been able to arouse one of the subject's major wishes. From there it harks back to a memory of an earlier experience (usually an infantile one) in which this wish was fulfilled; and it now creates a situation relating to the future which represents a fulfilment of the wish. What it thus creates is a day-dream or phantasy, which carries about it traces of its origin from the occasion which provoked it and from the memory. Thus past, present and future are strung together, as it were, on the thread of the wish that runs through them.

A very ordinary example may serve to make what I have said clear. Let us take the case of a poor orphan boy to whom you have given the address of some employer where he may perhaps find a job. On his way there he may indulge in a day-dream appropriate to the situation from which it arises. The content of his phantasy will perhaps be something like this. He is given a job, finds favour with his new employer, makes himself indispensable in the business, is taken into his em-

ployer's family, marries the charming young daughter of the house, and then himself becomes a director of the business, first as his employer's partner and then as his successor. In this phantasy, the dreamer has regained what he possessed in his happy childhood – the protecting house, the loving parents and the first objects of his affectionate feelings. You will see from this example the way in which the wish makes use of an occasion in the present to construct, on the pattern of the past, a picture of the future.

There is a great deal more that could be said about phantasies; but I will only allude as briefly as possible to certain points. If phantasies become over-luxuriant and over-powerful, the conditions are laid for an onset of neurosis or psychosis. Phantasies, moreover, are the immediate mental precursors of the distressing symptoms complained of by our patients. Here a broad by-path branches off into pathology.

I cannot pass over the relation of phantasies to dreams. Our dreams at night are nothing else than phantasies like these, as we can demonstrate from the interpretation of dreams. Language, in its unrivalled wisdom, long ago decided the question of the essential nature of dreams by giving the name of "day-dreams" to the airy creations of phantasy. If the meaning of our dreams usually remains obscure to us in spite of this pointer, it is because of the circumstance that at night there also arise in us wishes of which we are ashamed; these we must conceal from ourselves, and they have consequently been repressed, pushed into the unconscious. Repressed wishes of this sort and their derivatives are only allowed to come to expression in a very distorted form. When scientific work had succeeded in elucidating this factor of *dream-distortion*, it was no longer difficult to recognize that night-dreams are wish-fulfilments in just the same way as day-dreams – the phantasies which we all know so well.

So much for phantasies. And now for the creative writer. May we really attempt to compare the imaginative writer with the "dreamer in broad daylight", and his creations with day-dreams? Here we must begin by making an initial distinction. We must separate writers who, like the ancient authors of epics and tragedies, take over their material ready-made, from writers who seem to originate their own material. We will keep to the latter kind, and, for the purposes of our comparison, we will choose not the writers most highly esteemed by the critics, but the less pretentious authors of novels, romances and short stories, who nevertheless have the widest and most eager circle of readers of both sexes. One feature above all cannot fail to strike us about the creations of these story-writers: each of them has a hero who is the centre of interest, for whom the writer tries to win our sympathy by every possible means and whom he seems to place under the protection of a special Providence. If, at the end of one chapter of my story, I leave the hero unconscious and bleeding from severe wounds, I am sure to find him at the beginning of the next being carefully nursed and on the way to recovery; and if the first volume closes with the ship he is in going down in a storm at sea, I am certain, at the opening of the second volume, to read of his miraculous rescue – a rescue without which the story could not proceed. The feeling of security with which I follow the hero through his perilous adventures is the same as the feeling with which a hero in real life throws himself into the water to save a drowning man or exposes himself to the enemy's fire in order to storm a battery. It is the true heroic feeling, which one of our best writers has expressed in an inimitable phrase: "Nothing can happen to *me*!" It seems to me, however, that through this revealing characteristic of invulnerability we can immediately recognize His Majesty the Ego, the hero alike of every day-dream and of every story.

Other typical features of these egocentric stories point to the same kinship. The fact that all the women in the novel invariably fall in love with the hero can hardly be looked on as a portrayal of reality, but it is easily understood as a necessary constituent of a day-dream. The same is true of the fact that the other characters in the story are sharply divided into good and bad, in defiance of the variety of human characters that are to be observed in real life. The "good" ones are the helpers, while the "bad" ones are the enemies and rivals, of the ego which has become the hero of the story.

We are perfectly aware that very many imaginative writings are far removed from the model of the naïve day-dream; and yet I cannot suppress the suspicion that even the most extreme deviations from that model could be linked with it through an uninterrupted series of transitional cases. It has struck me that in many of what are known as "psychological" novels only one person – once again the hero – is described from within. The author sits inside his mind, as it were, and looks at the other characters from outside. The psycho-

logical novel in general no doubt owes its special nature to the inclination of the modern writer to split up his ego, by self-observation, into many part-egos, and, in consequence, to personify the conflicting currents of his own mental life in several heroes. Certain novels, which might be described as "eccentric", seem to stand in quite special contrast to the type of the day-dream. In these, the person who is introduced as the hero plays only a very small active part; he sees the actions and sufferings of other people pass before him like a spectator. Many of Zola's later works belong to this category. But I must point out that the psychological analysis of individuals who are not creative writers, and who diverge in some respects from the so-called norm, has shown us analogous variations of the day-dream, in which the ego contents itself with the role of spectator.

If our comparison of the imaginative writer with the day-dreamer, and of poetical creation with the day-dream, is to be of any value, it must, above all, show itself in some way or other fruitful. Let us, for instance, try to apply to these authors' works the thesis we laid down earlier concerning the relation between phantasy and the three periods of time and the wish which runs through them; and, with its help, let us try to study the connections that exist between the life of the writer and his works. No one has known, as a rule, what expectations to frame in approaching this problem; and often the connection has been thought of in much too simple terms. In the light of the insight we have gained from phantasies, we ought to expect the following state of affairs. A strong experience in the present awakens in the creative writer a memory of an earlier experience (usually belonging to his childhood) from which there now proceeds a wish which finds its fulfilment in the creative work. The work itself exhibits elements of the recent provoking occasion as well as of the old memory.

Do not be alarmed at the complexity of this formula. I suspect that in fact it will prove to be too exiguous a pattern. Nevertheless, it may contain a first approach to the true state of affairs; and, from some experiments I have made, I am inclined to think that this way of looking at creative writings may turn out not unfruitful. You will not forget that the stress it lays on childhood memories in the writer's life – a stress which may perhaps seem puzzling – is ultimately derived from the assumption that a piece of creative writing, like a day-dream, is a continuation of, and a substitute for, what was once the play of childhood.

We must not neglect, however, to go back to the kind of imaginative works which we have to recognize, not as original creations, but as the re-fashioning of ready-made and familiar material. Even here, the writer keeps a certain amount of independence, which can express itself in the choice of material and in changes in it which are often quite extensive. In so far as the material is already at hand, however, it is derived from the popular treasure-house of myths, legends and fairy tales. The study of constructions of folk-psychology such as these is far from being complete, but it is extremely probable that myths, for instance, are distorted vestiges of the wishful phantasies of whole nations, the *secular dreams* of youthful humanity.

You will say that, although I have put the creative writer first in the title of my paper, I have told you far less about him than about phantasies. I am aware of that, and I must try to excuse it by pointing to the present state of our knowledge. All I have been able to do is to throw out some encouragements and suggestions which, starting from the study of phantasies, lead on to the problem of the writer's choice of his literary material. As for the other problem – by what means the creative writer achieves the emotional effects in us that are aroused by his creations – we have as yet not touched on it at all. But I should like at least to point out to you the path that leads from our discussion of phantasies to the problems of poetical effects.

You will remember how I have said that the day-dreamer carefully conceals his phantasies from other people because he feels he has reasons for being ashamed of them. I should now add that even if he were to communicate them to us he could give us no pleasure by his disclosures. Such phantasies, when we learn them, repel us or at least leave us cold. But when a creative writer presents his plays to us or tells us what we are inclined to take to be his personal day-dreams, we experience a great pleasure, and one which probably arises from the confluence of many sources. How the writer accomplishes this is his innermost secret; the essential *ars poetica* lies in the technique of overcoming the feeling of repulsion in us which is undoubtedly connected with the barriers that rise between each single ego and the others. We can guess two of the methods used by this technique. The writer softens the character of his egoistic day-dreams by altering and disguising it, and he bribes us by the purely formal – that is, aesthetic – yield of pleasure which he offers us in the presentation of his phantasies. We give the name of an *incentive bonus*, or a *fore-pleasure*, to a yield of pleasure such as this, which is offered to us so as to make possible the release of still greater pleasure arising from deeper psychical sources. In my opinion, all the aesthetic pleasure which a creative writer affords us has the character of a fore-pleasure of this kind, and our actual enjoyment of an imaginative work proceeds from a liberation of tensions in our minds. It may even be that not a little of this effect is due to the writer's enabling us thenceforward to enjoy our own day-dreams without self-reproach or shame. This brings us to the threshold of new, interesting and complicated enquiries; but also, at least for the moment, to the end of our discussion.

Note

1   Cardinal Ippolito d'Este was Ariosto's first patron, to whom he dedicated the *Orlando Furioso*. The poet's only reward was the question: "Where did you find so many stories, Lodovico?"

PART II

Definition of Literature

Introduction

"Spazio," the first "reading" in this section, looks like something you might expect to find in a museum of modern art. It is made up of text, but so are other avant-garde paintings, and the repetition of the Italian word for space produces a striking optical effect characteristic of the pictorial arts. Yet "Spazio" is reprinted from an *Anthology of Concrete Poetry* and its creator, Arrigo Lora-Totino, calls himself a poet, is known in literary circles as a poet, and has written a great deal of what is obviously poetry. Is "Spazio" a work of literature?

One way to answer this question is to consult a definition of literature. Definitions supply individually necessary and jointly sufficient conditions, so a good definition of literature will enable us, in principle, to list all and only things that are works of literature. It will indicate whether or not "Spazio" is a work of literature or, failing that, make clear exactly why the work straddles the boundary between literature and non-literature.

Some think that any search for necessary and sufficient conditions for being a work of literature is bound to fail because literature comprises a heterogeneous mix of phenomena. In bookstores the literature section houses works of fiction with aesthetic merit. But not all literary works are fictions, if some historical, biographical, scientific, and philosophical works (and all lyric poetry) count as literature. Moreover, some literary works have little aesthetic merit – though we may disagree about which ones these are. Finally, a comic book that is a work of fiction and has aesthetic merit may be a work of art but not a work of literature.

These objections to the possibility of defining literature assume that the purpose of a definition of literature is to *describe* and not to *regulate* our intuitions about how to sort works as literary or non-literary. Imagine that we defined literature as fiction and that we held this definition to be regulative. In that case we would have no choice but to concede that, intuitions to the contrary aside, Thucydides' *History of the Peloponnesian War* is not a work of literature. The lesson is that counter-examples drawn from intuition only refute descriptive definitions. But this is little consolation, for there are reasons to be wary of regulative definitions.

The literary theorist E. D. Hirsch Jr. warns that regulative definitions of literature sometimes cut us off from works that would offer literary rewards if we acknowledged them as literature. In recent years scholars and the reading public have benefited from a broadened arena of literature that embraces work by authors previously denied entry into the canon on such grounds as gender, race and ethnicity, economic and political status, and cultural visibility. Hirsch recommends that we acknowledge that the boundaries of the body of literary works are vague and ever shifting. He suggests that we eschew the task of defining literature.

Few philosophers have given up on the hope of devising a definition of literature that, first, does not conflict with strong intuitions, and second, does not restrict the domain of literature in a way that reproduces parochial biases. A good definition can sometimes bring home to us that our intuitive judgments are mistaken by exposing bias or confusion about borderline cases. Definitions can play a benign regulative role.

The final three chapters in this section propose plausible but incompatible definitions of literature. Monroe Beardsley defines literature in terms of semantic features of literary works: something is a work of literature if and only if its creation involves an imitative use of language. Since many artifacts are defined by their use, an alternative is to define literature in terms of practices of literary reading. This relocates the problem – literature is defined in terms of readerly practices which in turn need definition – and the challenge is to analyze the kinds of expectations, sympathies, evaluations, and patterns of reasoning that make up the practice of reading literature. These elements of response may be normative or non-normative. Peter Lamarque and Stein Haugom Olsen argue that literary practice is necessarily aesthetic, hence normative. To read literature as literature is always to evaluate it. Robert Stecker is skeptical of this strong aestheticism and argues that the kind of reader responses that define literary practice include a hybrid of aesthetic and non-aesthetic elements. For Stecker, characteristically literary modes of engagement need not be evaluative – they can be emotional, for instance.

The viability of any definition of literature depends on its immunity from counterexamples and also its explanatory power. Thus definitions of literature connect to some of the other topics addressed in this volume. If works of literature are necessarily bits of language then we must know more about the interpretation of literature, metaphor, and comprehension of fiction. If literature is defined normatively then we must examine the value of literature and our aesthetic responses to it.

6

Spazio

Arrigo Lora-Totino

From Emmett Williams (ed.), *Anthology of Concrete Poetry* (New York: Something Else, 1967), n.p. Reprinted by permission of Ultramarine Publishing Ltd.

What Isn't Literature?

E. D. Hirsch, Jr.

My title seems to imply a skepticism almost total about the validity of any boundary lines marking off literature from non-literature. Therefore, let me state immediately that such an extreme position, arguing the absence of any distinction between literature and non-literature would be false, demonstrably false, by the following demonstration: I can gather a group of educated persons and set before them a series of texts paired off in groups of two. I can then ask them to write down on each text either the letter L or the letter N, standing for "literature" and "non-literature," I can choose the examples with care to exclude borderline cases, and then look confidently at the results of the experiment. After some trial and error, I can easily devise a list which always produces uniform and unanimous judgments from all educated persons. Armed with these absolutely consistent results, I can state with assurance that among educated speakers of English there is a genuine and demonstrable distinction between literature and non-literature. Though I have never heard of this experiment being performed, and have not troubled to perform it myself, I believe we could all agree that it probably could be performed successfully. If, for instance, the pairs of examples always consisted of poems by Keats, technical reports from *Science* magazine, and sonnets of Shakespeare, the results would be reassuring.

On the other hand, I am equally sure that I could devise an experiment which would produce results that were anything but unanimous and reassuring. I could include letters by Matthew Arnold, and Jane Austen, histories by Macaulay, Hume, and Eugene Genovese, biographies by Boswell and Mary Moorman, political speeches by Burke and Harold Macmillan, legal opinions by Cardozo and Warren Burger, scientific works by Darwin and Heisenberg, and a number of examples of still more doubtful classification by writers who have not yet entered the canon. In this experiment, we can be sure that the results will be extremely varied in a number of respects. We would have to report that our usage panel assigned L to the letters of Jane Austen by a vote of 70 per cent to 30 per cent, but that they withheld the classification from the letters of Jane Carlyle by a majority of 60 to 40. And we would find a further inconsistency in the pattern of voting. Some respondents, who side with the majority in one case, will side with the minority in another. We can predict these results also with some confidence, and perhaps someday an experimenter will decide to confirm this exceedingly obvious prediction. But even with these results before us, we need not suppose that the one experiment somehow negates the other, or calls into doubt the existence of such a thing as literature. No one doubts the reality of chairs, and yet nobody knows where

From Paul Hernadi (ed.), *What Is Literature?* (Bloomington: Indiana University Press, 1978), pp. 24–34. Reprinted by permission of E. D. Hirsch, Jr.

chairs fade off into sofas and ottomans on one side and stools on the other; any similar experiments conducted with chairs would be likely to yield similar results.

So, my aim is not to suggest that the class literature doesn't exist as an understandable and real entity, any less than does the class chair. Moreover, I don't want to suggest that the great variety of borderline cases is an intellectual embarrassment for serious literary study and criticism. The word *science* suffers the same difficulties; so does the word *art*. So, of course, does the word made famous by Wittgenstein, the word *game*. One of the great insights to be gained from reading Wittgenstein is a realization that language and thought require us to use classifications which slip and slide into domains of indispensable vagueness. We get into trouble only when we assume that the classification really *has* a boundary line or means the same thing in different uses. The only embarrassment to be suffered from the amorphousness of words is the attempt to pretend that they are not amorphous. Literary theory gets into trouble only when it pretends that the word *literature* can be satisfactorily defined, and then tries to erect generalizations on such a delusive definition. My skepticism, then, is not aimed at the existence of the class, literature, but at the attempt to falsely constrict its existence through definition. This paper might be considered a defense of literature against literary theory.

I think, though, that justice demands a sympathetic understanding of the dilemma of literary theory and the reasons it should wish to make definitions of *literature*. First of all, literary theorists share with the rest of us a tendency to assume that a word which we all understand *must* have a definable meaning. We know what literature is; let us therefore make that knowledge precise by distinguishing those traits which make a work literature from those which do not. Now, what I tried to show in my two imaginary experiments is that we know what literature is only vaguely, so that any attempt to remove that vagueness in a definition actually falsifies our knowledge of the word, rather than clarifies it. To define is to mark off boundaries distinguishing what is literature from what is not, but our knowledge of literature has no such defining boundaries; there are many cases about which we are not sure – important cases, not just peripheral ones. What the theorist should understand is that his definitions do not create literature, but can only attempt to clarify and make explicit

what is already implicit in our use of the word. The theorist who defines literature is in a position exactly analogous to the linguistic theorist who formulates a grammar. All sophisticated linguists know that their job is to formulate explicit rules for what is implicitly known by every native speaker. The native speaker is the court of last resort; he can never be wrong; only the grammarian can be. If the rules of the grammar do not coincide with or precisely describe the usage of native speakers, then the grammar is defective. So it is with definitions of literature; if they deviate in the least from the usage of educated men, it is the definition that is wrong, and not common usage. The literary theorist is like the grammarian in that he describes and clarifies a reality, but does not create the reality he describes.

It may be that the defining theorist retains an uneasy feeling that his work is not just descriptive, but prescriptive, that he has the job of telling us what we *ought* to conceive literature to be. There are a number of reasons he should wish to take this upon himself, and certainly with theorists like Coleridge, who had a sense of cultural mission, such a reformulation of our concept of literature is at once noble and valid. I shall be dealing with such normative aims a little further along in this paper. But we should be clear that present-day literary theorists of the academy have not for the most part taken on the prophet's robe. Their aim is to follow in the footsteps of Aristotle, and describe that which *is*, to do it better than anyone has before, and then to give a solid intellectual foundation to the great enterprise or industry which is the academic study of literature. The subject exists; the field exists; let us be clear about the essential nature of our subject. Then we will know how to proceed in our work, what problems to tackle, and what methods are particularly appropriate to the subject as we have defined it. The hopes are worthy, and the history of criticism continues to be strewn with the wrecks of these hopes. I concede that even unsuccessful descriptive definitions can be helpfully illuminating, of course. But the hope of success is a false hope, and can be proved to be a false hope. Like many other boys, I tried for years, off and on, to find a method for trisecting an angle with ruler and compass alone. Like the tribe of literary theorists who still attempt to define literature, I refused to give up the challenge, and spent many amusing but fruitless hours devising ever more sophisticated methods with ruler and compass. I was only willing to

E. D. Hirsch, Jr.

stop when a precocious mathematical freshman at college explained to me that I was trying to solve a problem having three unknowns by using only two equations; hence the attempt really was logically fruitless and impossible. I wonder whether such merely logical proofs will ever stop people from trying to trisect angles or define literature.

The reason I want to defend literature against the definitions of literary theory is not just a purely logical and disinterested reason, though that has its own delight and interest. I want to expose the futility of such definitions because they have done and continue to do a certain amount of harm. Besides being misleading, they always confine and constrict the subject in a way that makes the teaching and study of literature more narrow and one-sided than is good for ourselves, our students, and our culture. In particular, the aesthetic orientation of the usual definitions has tended to aestheticize our choice of texts to be studied and our way of teaching those texts. If literature were just a subspecies of the category *art* and if *art* were something that is only properly understood and appreciated under aesthetic principles, then our literary and cultural lives would be much impoverished. For we have not yet escaped from the fact that the only really successful delineation of the aesthetic mode of perception has been achieved by Kant and his successors. And the hallmark of this aesthetic mode is the disinterested contemplation of beauty. This high calling is in no way to be scorned or underestimated, and I wish to avoid even the hint of doing so. Nonetheless, definitions of literature in our time have tended to be oriented to the aesthetic as a guiding assumption of the definition. And to regard literature as primarily and essentially aesthetic is not only a mistake; it is also a very unfortunate narrowing of our responses to literature, and our perceptions of its breadth and possibilities.

Let me therefore return to the reasons for the results of our two experiments. We were able to achieve complete and unanimous agreement about what literature is, in the first experiment, because we chose texts which belong to literature by virtue of fulfilling a number of quite different canonical traits. And the non-literary texts of the experiment were so chosen that they, too, could be excluded from literature on *every* implicit ground that underlies our normal use of the word. In the second experiment, however, the results were uncertain because the works chosen exhibited some traits which qualified them and other traits which

might normally disqualify them. The predictability of our experimental results resided in the variability of the criteria that we use in classifying a text as literature. To explain this point, which we all implicitly know in any case, I will present a few examples of these sometimes conflicting criteria.

The most obvious (and presently the central) criterion we use is that of genre: poems, stories, plays. Now even if these fictional works, which earlier theorists called imitations, were the only works which we happened to call literature, we would find ourselves beset by problems of definition and classification; for the genres themselves merge into hybrid forms which cause just as many problems as the great big genre which we call literature. Take the example of poems, which we now think of as any text in verse, or perhaps as any text exhibiting uneven line lengths on the printed page. But even this tolerant, modern conception, about as broad as any native speaker is likely to conceive in using the word, leads to uncertainty of classification, as may be shown in several instances where prose has been converted into poetry by the simple expedient of transcribing the prose in irregular line lengths. In addition, the question, "Is this text poetry?" suffers still further difficulties and complications when the normative criterion of poetry, also part of our vague conception, is brought to bear. No long poem can be all poetry, asserted Coleridge, and many educated persons refuse to accept as "true" or "genuine" poems certain texts which fail to meet their qualitative standards. The texts are excluded from the class called *poems* as rejects that do not meet the approval of a quality controller. They lack some trait which must be superadded to the mere trait of line-length or form. So powerful is this normative and conceptual principle of classification that some ancients, who stressed imitation or fictionality as the important defining trait of poetry, did not conceive of lyric poems as belonging among the recognized genres.

Let me quickly enumerate some further confusions in the very center of our sense of literature, before moving ahead to the positive conclusion which I intend to draw. My first example is literature by association, on the pattern of guilt by association. Milton is one of our great poets; his work stands at the center of the canon. Because he is a canonical writer, some of his texts, like *Areopagitica* and *The Doctrine and Discipline of Divorce* are included within literature by a large number of persons. Wordsworth is a canonical poet; into literature, therefore, goes his travel book on the Lake Country, along with Dr. Johnson's *Tour of the Hebrides*, under the following principle: literature is anything written by a great literary figure. Another principle is that any text in any genre may be included in literature if it exhibits some excellence of form or style. Nearly everyone would include the Platonic dialogues because they are imitations. On the other hand, are there good reasons for excluding Aristotle's work? Perhaps, but if we exclude his *Poetics*, why should we not exclude Wordsworth's *Prefaces?* And if we include the *Poetics* of Aristotle, on what grounds do we exclude his *Metaphysics*, a far more interesting, imaginative and nontechnical work. Shelley, as we all know, wished to include even some legislative statutes of parliaments under poetry because they created order and harmony out of disorder. Modern usage has not accepted Shelley's comprehensive principle altogether, but we have introduced our own versions of his expansive literary imperialism. We accept Nietzsche and Kierkegaard of course, but also Tacitus and Darwin. I recently asserted that Darwin was a much more interesting figure in 19th-century literature than was Walter Pater, and I mentioned explicitly *The Origin of Species*. This was challenged in subsequent discussion by the late W. K. Wimsatt, who said I should have chosen *The Voyage of the Beagle*, which had more right to be called a literary work. A correspondent wrote me that I was just being eccentric, and that I knew perfectly well that *The Origin of Species* was not a literary work. Yet so various are the criteria by which we actually make such judgments, that I was able to direct him to four expert authorities who had preceded me in print in considering *The Origin of Species* to be literature.

Need I call your attention to the fact that a great many persons consider the Bible to be great literature? But I do not think we would find unanimity in the criteria on which this judgment is based. Some would stress the stylistic magnificence of the Authorized Version. In a large literature course, when I first started teaching, the Bible was conceived to be literature largely because of its poems and stories. But the criterion which many people use in deciding to call the Bible literature is very similar to the Coleridgean principle of bringing the whole soul of man into activity, and this is a principle which has for me a great appeal. Reading the Bible brings the whole soul of man into activity. And this principle can be extended or attenu-

ated to include everything that De Quincey called "The Literature of Power." But it cannot be overstressed that this principle of engaging a reader on more than one level of his being – not just the intellectual or just the emotional, but both – is not and cannot be a truly objective principle of classification. It is in its very essence subjective because the perlocutionary effects of a text are highly variable effects, differently engaging the hearts and minds of various readers. I cannot remember ever reading a book that more engaged my rapt soul than the small volume by Niels Bohr on the relation of atomic structure to the periodic table! Order out of chaos – high poetry in Shelley's sense. For me, that was and is a work of literature, one which altogether obliterates any clear division between the literature of knowledge and the literature of power.

Is it any wonder that no single definition of literature has embraced the whole continuum of uses to which educated persons put the word? Every attempt to make such a definition, without exception, has ended up being a stipulative definition, that is to say, a definition which stipulates how the word literature *ought* to be used, but entirely fails to define how it actually is used by great numbers of educated native speakers. John Ellis recently tried to turn the trick, in an otherwise sensible book called the *Theory of Literary Criticism*, by distinguishing between trait-definitions and use-definitions, the latter being the right way out of the muddle and confusion which surround the word *literature*. That was a sophisticated and intelligent tactic. The only defect in its performance was that his use-definition did not in fact embrace all the uses to which we put the word *literature*. Ellis was forced into the position that uses which fail to correspond to his use-definition are just wrong uses. So we were given yet another stipulative definition of literature: that is, a definition which tries to legislate, but does not actually describe the way competent persons actually use the word.

Now for my positive conclusions. First of all, I have argued that while the word literature embraces an enormous variety, and implies an unsteady, changeable system of criteria, the word is nonetheless meaningful and not entirely arbitrary. While some might include Darwin and Niels Bohr, nobody would include the article "Visual Disturbances after Prolonged Perceptual Isolation" by Heron, Doane, and Scott. The word *literature* has a very great range, but does not embrace all that is written down. Secondly, I believe that the enormous range of the word, embracing as it does both descriptive (that is, generic) criteria, as well as normative criteria, is not at all an accident. The widespread use of the word arose late in the Victorian period in order to fill an important cultural need, and particularly an educational need. Humanistic instruction at the schools and universities had always included a very wide range of texts that were considered important or valuable on a variety of grounds. This remained true so long as the classics formed the basis of humane education in Europe and America. When one read the classics, one read Tacitus and Pliny as well as Vergil and Homer. Nobody then argued whether or not *De Rerum Naturae* by Lucretius was truly literature or truly a poem. To read it was part of a classical education. So, I think it was no accident that, when classical education became displaced by mass education in the local, national languages, that was also the time when the word *literature* in its more or less modern uses began to occur more and more frequently. A word was needed to embrace in the national language the great variety of canonical texts that were required to replace the classical canon. It was the Victorian scholar and educator Edward Dowden who warned against a limitation of the word *literature* to stand only for belletristic writing, to the exclusion of philosophical and other valuable texts.

In recent years, we modern educators have not heeded Dowden's advice. In our eagerness to show that literature was a subject and a substance *sui generis*, with its own special and appropriate methods, we lost sight of the larger educational goals that helped foster the currency of the word itself. We decided to give the word a predominantly aesthetic flavor, and to subsume literature under art. In order to narrow the word in this way, we were hurled into endless attempts to define literature to suit its special claims as a form of art rather than as a canon of texts worthy to be taught, read, and preserved in a culture. My interest in showing that these attempts at definition have resulted in merely stipulative definitions has also had an educational motivation, and I have tried to suggest that the narrowness of a predominantly aesthetic definition can lead, and sometimes has led, to a narrowness of educational goals. In the heyday of the literary study of literature, which meant the aesthetic study of literature, I was once scolded by a class of sophomores for having assigned them Mill's *Essay on Liberty*. Of course, they were right in a sense. It was, contractually, a literary course, and what I was giving them to read did not correspond with what they had been taught to accept as literature. But in a more traditional and still current sense of literature and humane education, they were absolutely wrong. Let me, then, end with my own stipulative definition of literature. Literature includes any text worthy to be taught to students by teachers of literature, when these texts are not being taught to students in other departments of a school or university. That is a stipulative definition for which I claim mainly this virtue: it encourages us to think out our responsibilities in humanistic education, and make curricular choices on the basis of those responsibilities. That seems to me a better and immensely more interesting foundation for the teaching of literature than one derived from a stipulative definition of literature as art.

8

The Concept of Literature

Monroe Beardsley

The uses of the term "literature" are varied, their differences subtle, their lines of connection tangled. We have to deal, evidently, with a cluster of concepts, rather than one. Yet my title is not a misnomer. For an enterprise of conceptual analysis may be constructive as well as descriptive, and I would like not only to sort out some of the current concepts, sharpen distinctions, and trace logical relationships, but also – if possible – to work toward a recommendation. It is often easy to frame a definition that seems sound on the surface, only to find that its adoption brings disturbing gaps or redundancies into our conceptual scheme or requires unacceptable adjustments in other definitions that belong to the same system. On the other hand, it sometimes turns out that alternative sets of concepts are basically equivalent and equally convenient, because they mark, in different terms, the same useful or even indispensable distinctions.

I should confess at the start that in pondering the question, What is literature?, I can't promise to avoid questions of philosophical aesthetics. Those who are concerned with "defending the domain of poetry and poetics from the encircling (if friendly) arm of the general aesthetician," as W. K. Wimsatt has done,[1] may charge me with overprotectiveness. But the marking out of such domains, the rectification of boundaries and the establishment of clear titles, are themselves aesthetic tasks.

One of the less problematic remarks that can be made about the term "literature" is that it is a collective name for literary *works*. True, critics sometimes speak of a "literary quality," and even of degrees of such a quality, and this usage deserves study. But more usually, and intelligibly, "literature" marks off a species of the genus of discourse – i.e. written or spoken pieces of natural language. A discourse is either a literary work or it is not a literary work – or it is a borderline case that balks at classification (which is why we may be tempted to say that it has "literary quality," perhaps meaning that it has some claim, though not a decisive claim, to be called a literary work).

Suppose we agree that literature is the class of literary works. What then? It depends on how much stress we lay on "work." If we make it a mere substitute for "discourse," we get what might be called a *language concept* of literature, and our problem is to discover the marks by which literary discourses are distinguished from nonliterary discourses. If, on the other hand, we take "literary work" as an abbreviation for "literary work of art," we get an *art concept* of literature, and a quite different task confronts us.

The second interpretation may seem the more natural, so let us explore its consequences at once. It entails that we do not know what literature is until we know what art is – i.e. what makes something a work of art, whether verbal or visual or

From *Literary Theory and Structure* (New Haven: Yale University Press, 1973), pp. 23–39. Reprinted by permission of Yale University Press.

Monroe Beardsley

musical. We can tell whether something is a discourse, say a piece of English prose, without knowing anything of its origin; but we cannot tell whether something is a work of art without knowing anything of its origin. For whatever else may be said about this most disputed concept, surely a work of art is at least an artifact, something produced intentionally, and perhaps more specifically with an aesthetic intention. Whatever forms and qualities an object – say, a piece of stone – may feature, we would ordinarily say, I think, that if it can be shown to have acquired those forms and qualities independently of any human acts or purposes, it is not a work of art.

What are we to say, then, of such objects as computer poems? The IBM 7094–7040 DCS at the Yale Computer Center has turned out such stanzas as this:

> The landscape of your clay mitigates me.
> Coldly,
> By your recognizable shape,
> I am wronged.

Is this a literary work (or part of one)? Two answers are open to us. First, we might say that it is indeed literature, but not a literary work of art (since computers have no intentions); it is a literary discourse, and classifiable as such in virtue of certain forms and qualities. Thus we cut the logical link between "literature" and "literary work," and must proceed to define the former independently of the latter. We might go on to say that what we have here is indeed a poem, but not all poems are literary works: a poem is a literary work only if it has been composed by a human poet.

If we take the second terminological path, we do not necessarily deny that "The landscape of your clay" is literature. That depends on how broadly we conceive "compose." We can take the computer as poet; then its work is not, strictly, composed, for no intentions occur. Or we can take the programmer, Professor Marie Borroff, as the poet, and regard the computer as only a rather elaborate mechanism used in composition; then the results can be called literary works of art. This involves some strain on our usual language, since the programmer's instructions, in SNOBOL 3, furnished the computer only with some abstract syntactic constraints plus a vocabulary from which to make random selections. Thus it was intended that an adverb would appear in a certain slot, but not that it would be "coldly." Yet we might say that the

work as a whole was composed, since it did not come into being by accident, and certain features were determined by a human will. And since the final product is a result of Professor Borroff's selection from the various printouts, and also of her arrangement of the text into lines, there may be quite enough design involved to warrant our applying the term "literary work of art."

Thus the art concept of literature may be stretched enough to cover computer poems. It excludes those as yet wholly imaginary masterpieces randomly typed out by assiduous chimpanzees (who have so far done much better in painting than in poetry); of these we may want to say, first, that as long as they remain nonexistent, the problem of classifying them does not arise; and, second, that if they begin to appear, no harm will be done by refusing to call them literature. In the same way, if a chimpanzee happened to put two sticks together that formed the letter T, we would want to say that he did not make a T on purpose, even if he crossed the sticks on purpose. Yet suppose we gradually reduced the role of the programmer in the productions of IBM 7094–7040 DCS, leaving it more and more to its own devices. The odds against its coming up with "The landscape of your clay" would become enormously greater, of course, yet they would not reach impossibility. And if the same discourse were produced entirely, or almost entirely, by chance, we would still call it a poem, just as we called the chimpanzee's stick-work a T. It would not be in a very different category from so-called automatic writing, or a passage dictated in a trance.

There is a point, then, in trying to separate the objective from the psychological elements in our concept of a poem, and of literature in general. We can use two concepts, and both seem to be in operation. The art concept is genetic, since it includes an essential reference to what the maker intended to do, and thought of himself as doing, in creating the discourse. The discourse concept is nongenetic; it is confined to linguistically discernible features. There seems to be a historical development from one to the other. Before detailed and systematic study of the language of literature, it is natural to identify literature by its source or manner of production. It is what a poet sings or what is offered on certain occasions or (later) printed with certain indicators of its kind. But as our understanding increases, the concept becomes less dependent on genetic considerations. We can recognize a poem under all sorts of conditions, without knowing how it came to be written. The broadening of the range of contemporary poetry, and the arrival of the computer, have helped bring us to this freedom.

If we admit the theoretical possibility that one may aim, and try, to compose a literary work and fail – and that one may compose, or cause to be composed, a literary work without aiming to – then we have detached our concept of literature from our concept of its genesis, even if we concede that all the literary works that are of interest to us, or are likely to be of interest to us, are discourses in whose composition human beings have had a hand. So we can ask for an analysis of the concept of literature, understood in this objective fashion: what goes into the class, what is excluded, and how we tell the difference.

One way of marking off a class of literary discourses from other discourses is provided by what I have called the "semantic definition" of "literature": literature consists of those discourses a substantial portion of whose meaning is implicit (or secondary) meaning.[2] This thoroughly nongenetic definition depends on an account of implicit meaning, which was given in terms of the concepts of connotation and suggestion, and of which various species were noted. It is designed to distinguish poems among verses and literary essays among discursive writings. Thus it aims to capture what may be called the *extended* concept of literature, the sense in which the term is applied to some works of history, sermons, speeches, letters – to Bacon's essays and Cicero's orations and parts of the Old Testament.

This proposal has been thoroughly and forcefully criticized by Colin A. Lyas. Though conceding that it accords with what "some critics are prone to do,"[3] Lyas holds that it fails to match the usage of more typical, or sounder, critics, and violates a basic condition that must be satisfied by any acceptable definition of "literature." He makes a number of good points, and throws light on the entire enterprise. Some of his objections bear most heavily on the unfortunate, and indefensible, manner in which the original proposal was framed: "A literary work is a discourse in which an important part of the meaning is implicit." The qualifier "important" was certainly misleading, though not so misleading in its context as in this isolated sentence. Since there are obvious difficulties in speaking of amounts of meaning, the definition was designed to flaunt its vagueness, which it did

all too well. But it does make sense (as Lyas apparently agrees) to say of two discourses that one carries a greater part of its meaning by way of the connotations of its words, the implications of its syntax, the thematic reverberations of its objects and acts.

Lyas has two main lines of argument against the semantic definition. I shall return to the second one later. The first is that the presence of substantial implicit meaning in a discourse is neither a necessary nor a sufficient condition of its being a literary work.

That substantial implicit meaning is not *necessary* is a familiar contention. Famous examples like "The Red Wheelbarrow" crop up as interesting borderline cases, of which we could say that anyone who claims that they are indeed literary works (however minimal) is committed to showing that noteworthy meaning is implicitly present. Lyas offers what "*might* be an example" from Brecht:

When in the white sickroom of the Charité
I awoke towards morning
And heard the blackbird, I knew
Better. For quite a time
I had no longer been afraid of death. Considering
That nothing could be amiss with me, provided
I myself was missing. Now
I succeeded in being glad about
The singing of all blackbirds, even after me.[4]

But when he adds, "Here there does not seem to me to be any more implicit meaning than one could expect to find in any piece of discourse,"[5] I wonder whether the notion of implicit meaning has been communicated. What are we doing as we come to realize that in this poem the blackbird is not a bird of ill omen but the bringer of a new sense of life, if not discovering implicit meaning? And how is the central paradox of the poem – the inseparability of fearing death and affirming life – presented, except implicitly? "The singing of blackbirds" is not just the singing of blackbirds. Substantial implicit meaning seems to be at least one thing that is (by contrast) missing from, say:

When I awoke at Lankenau Hospital at 6:00 A.M.,
And found the nurse giving me another injection,
I asked her at what time breakfast would be served.

Of course, I do not deny that these lines could be embedded in a context in which they would take on a greater significance, but by themselves they do not make a poem, and not literature.

Lyas's argument that substantial implicit meaning in a discourse is not *sufficient* to make it literature consists largely in selecting various types of implicit meaning and showing that none of them, taken individually, is found only in literature. This is true, but it doesn't touch the proposed definition. What does touch it is his contention that implicit meaning can be "a large part" of ordinary discourse.[6] It is true that much of our verbal interchange, beyond the most elementary level, abounds in hints, innuendoes, suppressed premises and conclusions, etc. But I think we have a rough sense of a norm in the relationship between what is conveyed implicitly and what is conveyed explicitly. We recognize discourse that strains toward the side of extra-explicitness as technical and specialized to the needs of a science or a profession; we recognize discourse that leans toward richness in implicit meaning, hypersemantic discourse, as taking on a rather different character. In a business letter there may be implicit promises, hints of personality traits, threats, even wit, but the main information is given in the lines, not between them. A joke, on the other hand, offers very little on its primary level, compared to the point that makes it funny. A metaphor has no literal significance at all, taken as a whole; all of its relevant meaning is implicit. And in a lyric poem, if we can distinguish, say, what the solitary reaper *is* from what she conjures up in the mind of her observer, we find a great deal more of the latter.

It may also be useful to introduce a certain flexibility into the account by acknowledging that norms may be relative to genre. For example, when we read a large number of historical writings, we may form the notion of a norm for this group of discourses, compared to which we would then say that some books on the Civil War, some biographies of Napoleon, are literature, others not. But this norm may be somewhat different from those that hold for discourses on, say, ecology or gastronomy or philosophy.

No doubt these are loose ways of speaking, perhaps too loose to be useful. Since the difference between any two discourses in this respect is a matter of degree, the spectrum practically continuous, and the difficulty of making precise discriminations considerable, some will feel that it is better not to try to introduce the terms that purport to mark a difference in kind. We could speak of degrees of literariness, or intensity of literary quality, as a comparative property, according to the semantic criterion – but not of literary or nonliterary discourses. Yet having gone so far, we may also find it convenient – and sufficiently in accord with at least one strand of familiar usage – to call those discourses that have a marked degree of literariness, decidedly above the norm, literature *tout court*.

Thus I am persuaded that a case can still be made for regarding the possession of an above-normal proportion of implicit meaning as a sufficient condition of being a literary discourse – though not of being a very good one. It is another segment of its border that leaves me least satisfied about this domain. The definition will cover a great deal of prose fiction, including those novels and short stories that are most worthy of attention from a literary point of view. But it will not cover all prose fiction. If we seek a definition that will provide this service – and there are reasons for thinking we should – then we shall have to look further.

A fresh way of regarding literary discourses has emerged in recent years. In involves a concept first advanced by J. L. Austin and later developed by William Alston, John B. Searle, and others.[7] I shall use the term "utterance" as an abbreviation for "act of producing, in speech or writing, a sequence of characters that belong to a language." When an utterance occurs under certain conditions, it may also be an "illocutionary act." For example, if a person with certain qualifications utters certain words on a certain sort of ceremonial occasion, while placing one hand on the Bible, he is taking an oath of office. A mere utterance has semantic and syntactic, and even stylistic, properties. What makes it an illocutionary act is that it conforms to a set of linguistic rules that specify the conditions required for that sort of act to be performed: rules about the nature of the speaker, the hearer, the situation. An utterance does not count as a warning if the event warned against is regarded as desirable by the warnee ("I warn you that you will be kindly treated"); it does not count as a command or request if the act referred to has already been performed ("Please call me yesterday"). Rules of this kind specify the *constitutive conditions* of the illocutionary act. Other rules specify its *purported conditions:* for example, a warning purports that the speaker wishes the hearer to escape the impending harm; if the speaker does not wish this, his warning is insincere, but it is no less a warning, provided the constitutive conditions are satisfied. Again, a request purports that the speaker desires the act requested to be performed, but an insincere request is still a request.

To decide whether an utterance is the performance of an illocutionary act, one inquires whether the constitutive conditions are satisfied; if they are, one can go on to inquire whether the purported conditions are also satisfied. These questions are not always easy to answer, and sometimes they cannot be answered decisively, in which case we have a form of ambiguity – as when, for example, a person in a position of authority asks that something be done, and it is not clear whether he is giving an order or making an unofficial request. If a prescribed form of words is available ("That is an order"), the ambiguity is resolved. Sometimes we are in doubt whether someone is expressing his own opinion or merely passing on, without endorsement, the opinion of another. Sometimes we are quite certain that no illocutionary act has been performed at all: if an actor on the stage utters the constitutional words, "I do solemnly swear that I will faithfully execute the Office of the President of the United States," he is not taking an oath of office, but imitating the taking of an oath of office. He is engaged in make-believe.

While I was working on a series of lectures a few years ago, it occurred to me that the speaker in a poem can be said, on one level of analysis, to be performing a series of illocutionary acts, though in such a way as to fashion them into a single compound act.[8] He pleads, cajoles, deplores, regrets, blesses, curses, beseeches, prays, commemorates, elegizes, resolves, resigns himself. But if we take the speaker to be a fictional entity, then of course these are not genuine illocutionary acts, but make-believe. So I suggested that a poem might be characterized, or even defined, as the imitation of a compound illocutionary act.[9]

"Imitation" must be taken here in what might be called its "depicting" rather than "portrayal" sense.[10] That is, the act imitated need not be anything that has ever occurred; one can imitate a Cookie Monster gobbling cookies, though there is no such thing. This is an old discomfort in the term. In its unguarded use it tends to commit the imitation theorist to too much, so that we want to reply that Prufrock is not imitated but invented or created. It may be safer to call the poem an "imitation illocutionary act"; it may be safest to avoid the term completely and stick to "make-believe."[...]

The application of illocutionary-act theory to the definition of literature has been most carefully worked out by Richard Ohmann, whose proposal is stated in these words:

> *A literary work is a discourse whose sentences lack the illocutionary forces that would normally attach to them. Its illocutionary force is* mimetic. By "mimetic," I mean purportedly imitative. Specifically, a literary work *purportedly imitates* (or reports) a series of speech acts, which in fact have no other existence.[11]

He argues that in all literary works, not only in poems, the constitutive conditions for performing a complete and genuine illocutionary act are not met, so that the utterance is, in Austin's term, "infelicitous"; yet some of the ingredients are there, so that the reader can fill in the imaginary world in which the fictional speaker performs his fictional illocutionary act. To consider one sort of factor (not discussed by Ohmann), an illocutionary act is not completed until there is what Austin calls "uptake" – e.g. X has not warned Y unless Y hears the warning and takes it to be such. When a poem is addressed to a skylark, a waterfowl, a field mouse, a dead athlete, spring, autumn, the west wind, the moon, or Brooklyn Bridge, no uptake is conceivable, and the utterance fails to be an illocutionary act. This is one of the plainest forms of infelicity, but there are many others.

I think it is a mistake to say that in a literary work the "illocutionary force is mimetic," if this means that performing an imitation illocutionary act is performing a kind of illocutionary act (pretending to fall down stairs, or acting out the fall, is not falling down stairs), or to speak of "the illocutionary act of writing a literary work."[12] What we have in, say, Shelley's poem, is a complete verbal utterance that would, given certain conditions (e.g. that a skylark were present, that it could understand English), actually be an illocutionary act.

This proposal seems to me illuminating, and I believe that it in fact provides a sufficient condition for a discourse to be a literary work, though not necessarily a good one (as Ohmann notes). But when proposed as a *necessary* condition, it is open to some objections, which we must consider briefly.

First, as Ohmann explicitly says, the illocutionary-act definition of "literature" will not serve for what I have called the extended concept, which takes in some essays, sermons, etc. The preacher, the polemicist, the philosopher, the historian, is not making-believe, but actually exhorting, pleading, praising, putting down, attacking, arguing, narrating. Ohmann's definition, he says, is designed to mark out the class of "imaginative literature," as distinguished from *belles lettres*: it includes fiction, but not nonfiction. It states the necessary and sufficient conditions for what we may call the *central* concept of literature (poetry and prose fiction). Surely the Ohmann proposal marks an important distinction. And if we follow his lead, we are not debarred from literary criticism of *The Stones of Venice, Of Holy Dying,* "A Free Man's Worship," and "Aes Triplex," even if they are not literary works.[13] On the other hand, if we prefer to cling to the extended concept of literature, we can do so by combining the two definitions we have been discussing. A literary work (in the extended sense) would then be any discourse that is *either* an imitation (compound) illocutionary act *or* distinctly above the norm in its ratio of implicit to explicit meaning.

But does the illocutionary-act definition state a necessary condition for literature, even in the central sense? It seems that one can perform an illocutionary act with a poem. Ohmann's example is Elizabeth Barrett Browning. Surely there are circumstances under which her sending or giving "How do I love thee?" to Robert constitutes a declaration of love. Ohmann's solution is to say that at the time of presentation, the poem was no longer a literary work. I would rather try to distinguish the act of writing the poem (the original utterance) from the act of using it in some way; after all, any woman could perform the same illocutionary act by presenting someone with Elizabeth's poem. It is the act of composing that issues in the poem, and this act, we might argue, is not an illocutionary act – for one thing, because there is no uptake, but also because the process of formalizing a sentiment in verse and rhyme, giving it artistic shape, implies a degree of detachment from the illocutionary role, even if the sentiment is sincerely felt. Then to present the poem is to do something else with it; but to use a literary work for any purpose, as political propaganda, advertising, or inspiration to worship, does not take away its literary status.

I doubt, however, that we can cope in this way with all of the difficult examples. "Avenge O Lord thy slaughter'd saints" responds to an event and, I suppose, automatically secures uptake. There is Kipling and there is Housman on the Golden

Jubilee. Is it really plausible to say that in "Adonais," in "English Bards and Scotch Reviewers," in "Pied Beauty," in "Ode to the Confederate Dead," there is only make-believe? Is there no illocutionary action in Allen Ginsberg's "America" (1956)?

> America when will we end the human war?
> Go fuck yourself with your atom bomb.

Well, perhaps this last is not the best example. When the speaker says, later on,

> America free Tom Mooney
> America save the Spanish Loyalists
> America Sacco & Vanzetti must not die,

we note some infelicities in these imperatives. Perhaps they help to make the whole poem fall short of being an illocutionary act. But not all poems have this feature. When we think of poems read at antiwar gatherings or published in *The Nation* – or even in *Novy Mir*, if Yevgeny F. Markin's two poems of December 1971, "Weightlessness" and "The White Buoy," were really defenses of Alexandr I. Solzhenitsyn – it becomes harder to separate the act of composing from the act of presenting. It is not obvious that any of the conditions for a full illocutionary act are lacking. So perhaps such poems must be placed outside the central class of literary works, though (since they are clearly poems) well within the extended class – an argument for the extended concept of literature.

The only way I can see to avoid this conclusion is to argue, along the lines suggested earlier, that the very possession of certain formal features or other internal marks is in itself a withdrawal of illocutionary force. But though I have tried to defend this position,[14] I am no longer convinced that it can be maintained.

I would make a provisional stop at this point – though conscious that a great many questions remain hanging in the air – if it were not for the challenge presented by Colin Lyas's second objection to the semantic definition of literature – an objection that bears as heavily on the illocutionary-act definition. "Literature," he says, is an "approval term." To apply it to a discourse is to praise, and (more particularly) to praise aesthetically. From this assumption, Lyas draws two conclusions. First, he says that no definition of "literature" is acceptable unless the properties cited in its definiens are such as to "lead us to a favorable evaluation of any work exemplifying the quality in question."[15] This eliminates the semantic definition, apparently, since mere possession of substantial implicit meaning is not in itself an aesthetic merit, and not all aesthetic merits in literature are dependent on substantial implicit meaning. Second, he says that *any* property that is an aesthetic merit in a discourse can be regarded as a criterion of literature – that is, it helps justify our calling that discourse literature. Lyas cites perhaps a score of such properties, among them compactness, sophistication, simplicity, charm, elegance, thrillingness, being well constructed, perceptiveness, sensitivity, psychological penetration, suspense, irony.[16]

This normative concept of literature – the concept of literature as aesthetically praiseworthy discourses – is a recurrent one. Lyas has stated it well, but he hasn't really defended it: he simply "draw[s] attention to the fact" that "literature" is a normative term.[17] His omission is understandable, since we do not really know how to show that a term is or is not normative, per se or in a certain use. The question is much in dispute among philosophers. We can throw light on a particular case by tracing logical connections with other terms. For example, when we want to make an adverse judgment of such a discourse as *Peyton Place*, we may feel a little uneasy about saying that it is "poor literature," and want to say instead that it is "poor as literature" or "poor, considered as literature" – which suggests that we sense an honorific element in the term's meaning. On the other hand, we may find ourselves drawn toward accepting a logical connection between the concept of literature and the concept of literary genres – not that all literature belongs to a genre, but that anything that belongs to a genre is literature. We have a need for a concept of literature for which this principle holds, and I believe we sometimes rely on one. Now we can certainly speak of poor poems and bad poems, in some sense or other, and if (by the genre principle) every poem is a literary work, then "literary work," it would seem, is not honorific. From this argument the alternative conclusion could be drawn that literature is not after all simply the class of literary works – since one of these terms is normative, the other not. But if we reject this escape, then my argument has some weight, I think, against the claim that "literature" is inherently normative.[18] Of course the sentence "X is literature!" can be used to perform the illocutionary act of praising, with the help of a

suitable context or tone of voice. But so can a great many other sentences of a similar logical form whose nouns would not be thought to qualify as normative: "cheesecake," "snow," "a dog," "a bed." As long as we admit the literal possibility of bad cheesecake, "cheesecake" has no built-in approval.

Although I believe that "literature" has not been proved to be a normative term, in its usual applications, Lyas's argument suggests an interesting point. For it still remains to be shown why any particular way of drawing lines among discourses is to be recommended. And this is especially true of the tentative suggestion that "literary discourse" might be defined as "discourse that is either an imitation illocutionary act or distinctly above the norm in its ratio of implicit to explicit meaning." Unless we can demonstrate some connection between the two concepts included in this disjunctive predicate, the definition will seem as arbitrary and capricious as would a definition of "broose" as "anything that is either a broom or a moose."

What I wish to suggest, by way of conclusion, although without anything like an adequate defense, is that there is indeed an underlying relationship between (1) being an imitation illocutionary act and (2) being distinctly above the norm in ratio of implicit to explicit meaning. Though these two properties signify very different sources of literature, or of the literary impulse, their convergence is no accident, and it is understandable why they may belong together in a disjunctive definition of "literature." Both are forms of verbal play that set a discourse notable apart from pragmatic functions – one by deficiency of illocutionary force, the other by excess of semantic display. Both help to make a discourse self-centered and opaque, an object of attention in its own right. Though perhaps not all of the characteristics regarded as aesthetically praiseworthy by Lyas (and I am dubious about some of them) depend specifically on absence of illocutionary force or presence of substantial implicit meaning, nevertheless, it may be that the peculiar value of literature *qua* literature is favored and promoted by both of these properties. It is among discourses marked off from the ordinary run either by withdrawal from the illocutionary sphere or exploitation of linguistic resources that aesthetic goodness is most likely to be found. So it makes sense to mark out the class of literature as that class within which *good* literary discourses are most hopefully to be sought.

Notes

1   See "The Domain of Criticism," in *Aesthetic Inquiry: Essays on Art Criticism and the Philosophy of Art*, ed. Monroe Beardsley and Herbert Schueller (Belmont, Calif., 1967), p. 26.

2   See *Aesthetics: Problems in the Philosophy of Criticism* (New York, 1958), pp. 126–8.

3   "The Semantic Definition of Literature," *Journal of Philosophy* 66 (1969), 90.

4   Ibid., pp. 91–2.

5   Ibid., p. 92.

6   Ibid., pp. 89, 90. Richard Ohmann has raised the same objection in "Speech Acts and the Definition of Literature," *Philosophy and Rhetoric* 4 (1971), 6–7.

7   J. L. Austin, *How to Do Things with Words* (Cambridge, Mass., 1962): William P. Alston, *Philosophy of Language* (Englewood Cliffs, NJ, 1964); John R. Searle, *Speech Acts* (Cambridge, 1969).

8   I had forgotten Austin's suggestion that poetry is one of the "etiolations" of language (see pp. 22, 92*n*) and his remark (p. 104) that "Walt Whitman does not seriously incite the eagle of liberty to soar."

9   See *The Possibility of Criticism* (Detroit, 1970), pp. 57–61.

10   For these terms, as applied to visual representation, see *Aesthetics*, pp. 269–78.

11   "Speech Acts," p. 14; cf. Ohmann's "Speech, Action, and Style," in *Literary Style: A Symposium*, ed. Seymour Chatman (London and New York, 1971).

12   Ibid., p. 13.

13   An interesting borderline case is classical oratory of the epidictic genre, discussed by Chaim Perelman and L. Olbrechts-Tyteca, *The New Rhetoric*, trans. John Wilkinson and Purcell Weaver (Notre Dame, 1969), pp. 47–51. Since it was abstracted from legal and political contexts, it "seemed to have more connection with literature than with argumentation" (p. 48). But Perelman and Olbrechts-Tyteca are no doubt correct in concluding that "epidictic oratory forms a central part of the art of persuasion" (p. 49), in that it serves to "increase the intensity of adherence to certain values" (p. 51). This is its *perlocutionary* force, which, however, depends on its being genuine argument, rather than make-believe argument.

14   See *The Possibility of Criticism*, pp. 58–61, and the discussion of fiction in *Aesthetics*, pp. 411–14, 420–3.

15   Lyas, p. 83.

16   Ibid., pp. 82, 86, 92, 93, 95.

17   Ibid., p. 83.

18   Ohmann recognizes a "non-honorific sense" of the term, "which is a common one in actual use" (see "Speech Acts," p. 1).

9

Literary Practice

Peter Lamarque and
Stein Haugom Olsen

The Concept of Literature

In this respect there is a parallel between the concept of fiction and the concept of literature. For it may be argued that the concept of literature too is an institutional concept, a concept that is defined within a practice involving authors (as producers), texts, and readers. There are no syntactic, semantic, or even more loosely "rhetorical" features of a text that define it as a literary work. A text is identified as a literary work by recognizing the author's intention that the text is produced and meant to be read within the framework of conventions defining the practice (constituting the institution) of literature.[1] With a formulation parallel to that used in our discussion of fiction we can say that this intention is *the intention to invoke the literary response*. In this case, too, we must add the further (Gricean) intention that there be a mutual belief that the response is to be brought about partly at least by means of the recognition of the primary intention. And again with a formulation parallel to that used in our treatment of fiction, we may call this whole complex of attitudes the *literary stance*. Adopting the literary stance towards a text is to identify it as a literary work and apprehend it in accordance with the conventions of the literary practice.[2] The mode of appre-

hension which the practice defines is one of *appreciation*.[3] The literary stance is defined by the expectation of (and consequently the attempt to identify) a certain type of value, i.e. literary aesthetic value, in the text in question.

An institutional practice, as we understand it, is *constituted* by a set of conventions and concepts which both regulate and *define* the actions and products involved in the practice.[4] We have already introduced the basic conception of a social practice in relation to story-telling. The idea of an institutional practice is an extension of this, the difference being largely one of complexity. An institution, in the relevant sense, is a rule-governed practice which makes possible certain (institutional) actions which are defined by the rules of the practice and which could not exist as such without those rules. Often the actions and objects so defined are characterized by (institutional) concepts which again are given meaning only in terms of the rules governing the practice. One example of an institution in this sense would be the legal system which is constituted both by formal procedures for the administration of the law, on the one hand, and, on the other, by powers invested in individuals through clearly defined offices and roles. Take the simple example of an arrest and detention. The action of arresting and detaining someone, described in purely physical

From *Truth, Fiction, and Literature* (Oxford: Oxford University Press, 1994), pp. 255–67. Reprinted by permission of Oxford University Press.

Peter Lamarque and Stein Haugom Olsen

terms, has no inherent features that would set it apart from any other forcible apprehension of an individual, such as, say, kidnapping. The very possibility of a legally sanctioned arrest is dependent on a system that confers powers on individuals to undertake such an action, defining conditions under which such actions may be undertaken, and so on. Apart from such a system the very action of *arresting* someone ceases to exist though the action of forcible apprehension would still remain. The point directly parallels our claim about literary works that they too have no inherent formal features that constitute them as literary works; certain kinds of texts become literary works only by fulfilling a role in, and being subject to the conventions of, an institution.

Literary practice is part of a family of social practices, including that of fictive story-telling, which can be characterized through their constitutive concepts and conventions. The concept of literature itself as well as the literary stance can be characterized and explained only with reference to this framework. The literary stance is an attitude made possible by the defining concepts and conventions of literary practice in the approach to a text. Only by using these concepts and conventions can the reader identify the features of a literary work construed *as a literary work* within the practice. To explore the differences between the concepts of fiction and literature, it is therefore necessary to look at the concepts and conventions which define literary practice.

The Concepts of Literary Practice

Consider the following example:

A sudden blow: the great wings beating still
Above the staggering girl, her thighs caressed
By the dark webs, her nape caught in his bill,
He holds her helpless breast upon his breast.
How can those terrified vague fingers push
The feathered glory from her loosening
                                        thighs?
And how can body, laid in that white rush,
But feel the strange heart beating where it lies?

A shudder in the loins engenders there
The broken wall, the burning roof and tower
And Agamemnon dead.
                        Being so caught up,
So mastered by the brute blood of the air,
Did she put on his knowledge with his power

Before the indifferent beak could let her drop?
(William Butler Yeats, "Leda and the Swan")

The concepts used to identify the literary features of this poem can be roughly divided into three classes or levels. There is first a descriptive level which to a large extent is technical in nature and whose main, though not only, function is to identify formal structures and formal elements. Identifying this poem as a sonnet, and as an Italian rather than an English sonnet, is identifying the way in which the poem is organized. Knowing that an Italian sonnet normally is organized into an octet and a sestet, and that it conventionally has a turning-point or a *volta* after the octet, makes the immediate identification of the two main stages of *this* poem easy: the octet describes a scene of seduction, the sestet the consequences of that seduction. Equally, knowledge of the convention that the octet of a sonnet divides into two quatrains and the sestet into two tercets opens up the clear recognition of the difference in content and function between the two quatrains of the octet and the difference in content and function between the two tercets of the sestets, as well as the clear recognition of the parallels between the first quatrain and the first tercet, and between the second quatrain and the second tercet. However, none of these conventions is a constitutive convention (individually, they are not essential within the practice). Insight into the structure of the poem is possible without knowing what a sonnet is, but knowledge of the conventions and of the term "sonnet" eases literary appreciation. This vocabulary of technical concepts can be found in any dictionary of literary terms and it covers all the special needs of description created by literary works. There are concepts characterizing diction and rhetorical features, concepts characterizing structural features, concepts characterizing elements of content, i.e. through such terms as "plot", "character", and "setting", concepts of genres, periods of literary history, etc. This vocabulary is *not by itself* constitutive of the appreciation of a literary work but it is of great help in promoting this appreciation. It is constitutive of appreciation only in conjunction with the other levels of the conceptual scheme of the practice.

The concepts at the second level of the conceptual scheme constitutive of literary practice are unproblematic in the sense that they are wholly taken over from the conceptual scheme any reader would use in everyday life to characterize objects and actions. These concepts are used to characterize what one may call the *subject* of the literary work, its settings and scenes, its characters, the actions of its characters. To a great extent the reader will draw the terms in which to describe the subject from the text of the work itself. In the first quatrain of "Leda and the Swan" Leda staggers as the great wings of the swan beat above her. However, the reader will supplement these concepts with whatever further concepts he feels are needed to grasp the subject of the work. Thus a reader may say that the first stanza of "Leda and the Swan" describes how Zeus in the shape of a swan forces himself on Leda sexually. He arrives suddenly and surprisingly. Leda is almost (literally) swept off her feet. He assails her with a mixture of sensual caress and violence that overpowers Leda, who is helpless and terrified. In this description the subject is categorized in such a way that the nature of the events and actions are fixed for the reader.

If the vocabulary used to describe the subject is unproblematic in its nature because it is our everyday vocabulary, it may be problematic in its application since that may require interpretation. This interpretation will not always be controversial, and it may indeed look much like unchallengeable description. But since the function of this part of the interpretative vocabulary is that it should bring the subject of the work under descriptions that clarify it by categorizing it for the reader, alternative descriptions are in principle always possible. For example, the above description of the first stanza of "Leda and the Swan" stressed the mixture of sensual caress and violence that overpowers Leda. However, a number of critics tend to construe Zeus' action more strongly. The poem, the reader is told by these critics, is "on the adventures of God as a rapist".[5] To characterize the action described in the octet as a rape would mean that one would emphasize the violence rather than the sensual caress, perhaps pointing out that the caress is presented as passive ("her thighs caressed | By the dark webs") whereas the violence is active. Against this it could be argued that the vocabulary of the second quatrain makes the application of the word "rape" with its entirely negative connotations problematic; nor is it obvious that so specifically human a concept, rooted in human moral behaviour, is applicable to something un-human like a god or a swan. Even at the level of subject, interpretation is not necessarily unproblematic or uncontroversial.

An apprehension of subject is necessary to the appreciation of a literary work. The work exists for the reader only through the subject and the way in which it is presented. However, an apprehension of "Leda and the Swan" which did not move beyond an apprehension of subject would be rudimentary and unsatisfactory. It would not capture the qualities that make the poem a valuable work of art. In order to appreciate a literary work, one must attempt to construe the subject under a perspective, and as being in some way the bearer of a theme. The theme is grasped through the application in interpretation of a third level of concepts: *thematic concepts*. These have attained currency in other than literary contexts, and are used to generalize about human concerns and practices. In their literary application they are used to identify the point and purpose of the subject and the way in which the subject is presented.

In the case of this poem the sensual moment is the point in history where God interferes, with momentous consequences. It is the inception of a new social and ethical order parallel to that brought about through the immaculate conception. The octet presents the moment of divine intervention imagined by the speaker in the poem as both familiar in its sensuality and strange in its revelation of an irresistible force. The first tercet presents elliptically the consequences of the intervention: the destruction, through the twin sisters Helen and Clytemnestra, of the old social and moral order based on revenge and relying on blood feud as a social institution, and the inception of a new order which vests the authority to judge and punish in the state. The fall of the old order is symbolized by the destruction of Troy and the subsequent destruction of the Greek fleet on its way home (as a punishment for having violated the holy shrines in Troy); also by the death of Agamemnon at the hands of his wife as revenge for having sacrificed their daughter Iphigenia to obtain wind for the Greek fleet on its way to Troy. The new social and moral order is symbolized by the establishment of the Areopagite court to judge in cases which previously were seen as calling for blood revenge (the outcome of the *Oresteia* trilogy where Orestes is in the impossible position of being duty bound to kill his mother for having killed his father, Agamemnon, at the same time as being forbidden to commit matricide by the most deep-rooted of Greek moral conventions). Construed like this, the subject as it is presented comes to represent the origin of Western civilization in passion, blood, and violence. It is only when "Leda and the Swan" is apprehended in some such terms as these, that the poem is appreciated as a literary work.

The Conventions of Literary Practice

The constitutive conventions of literary practice are those that make a work of literature what it is: i.e. a work with aesthetic value. Roughly speaking this value is assumed to reside in two principal dimensions of the literary work: the imaginative and the mimetic. In the remainder of this chapter we will offer some preliminary reflections on these.

First of all, literary works have always been recognized as important products of human imagination, as a manifestation of the ability to create worlds imaginatively. This *creative-imaginative aspect* of literature has always been held to be one of its most central qualities. Even when viewed as pernicious and dangerous, by those stressing the negative side of the imagination, it has been recognized as powerful and ineliminable. "[T]he power which poetry has of harming even the good (and there are very few who are not harmed), is surely an awful thing?" Socrates asks an assenting Glaucon in *The Republic* (i. 605 c), when they discuss the poet's ability to move the passions by producing invented imaginings. However, the creative-imaginative aspect of literature has, in general, been recognized as positive, as a quality which makes literature culturally and humanly significant. This creative-imaginative aspect is not a contingent feature, as it is of works of fiction. To recognize something as a literary work is to recognize it as a creative-imaginative effort. That literature should be so is part of the very concept of literature that came into being through the writing and appreciation of the epics, poems, and dramas in ancient Greece in the fifth century and which has been operative in Western culture ever since.

The creative-imaginative aspect manifests itself in two ways. A literary work can give form to a subject or a story which need not itself be invented by the author. Literary works, major and minor, often deal with historical events, or rewrite stories already well known to the audience, as does Milton's *Paradise Lost*, Goethe's *Faust* or, indeed, Yeats's "Leda and the Swan". And different literary works can deal with the *same* story. The Greek tragedians rewrote the old mythical stories in their own way over and over again. Aeschylus, Sophocles, and Euripides all deal with the return of Orestes to the waiting Electra and the consequent murder of Clytemnestra. They each give the story a different treatment, but they do not invent the story itself. What they invent is a perspective, a way of seeing the story which endows it with significance, and to define this perspective, they invent dialogue, minor incident, and character. They also modify the form of the drama in the process: Sophocles increases the number of speaking characters from two to three; Euripides changes the role of the chorus. In their case, creative imagination showed itself not in the invention of story or major incident, but in the *conception* of the stories they rewrote and in the "embellishment" through which they defined this conception. In a wide sense of that vague but much used word, they created the *form* of the story in order to bring out a theme which they believed to be important. Perhaps this is nowhere more obvious than in the kind of highly formalized poem which Yeats uses to make the story of Leda and Zeus the vehicle for his vision.

Secondly, many literary works do, wholly or to some extent, consist of descriptions and stories which are made up or constructed. Literature is *poesis* also in the sense that it is invention rather than report, story rather than history. Authors do not merely retell old stories or provide particular perspectives on historical situations. They invent new stories, new conflicts, new plots and, indeed, if their imagination is sufficiently powerful, new worlds, as do Shakespeare, Dickens, or Scott. In other words, they do not merely create form (a perspective, embellishment) but they also create subject. The distinction between creating form and creating subject is worth insisting on, since most prominent literary theories this century have assumed that the distinction is somehow naïve and theoretically invalid.

The formalist theories of the New Criticism, structuralism, and post-structuralism have had as a central tenet that in creating form, the author creates content. There is one obvious sense in which this is true: the Orestes/Electra story as presented by Aeschylus, Sophocles, and Euripides, are really different narratives with different characters and different visions of the world.[6] However, in another obvious sense it is also false: there is no doubt that the three tragedians and their various audiences (among whom are we ourselves) recognize that they deal with the *same* story. These audiences have also recognized that it is possible to capture the differences between the three plays by seeing them as presenting *different conceptions* of the *same story*. And the point could be made with reference to any author who makes use of an already known story, whether it be history, myth or fiction. Shakespeare deals in his

English history plays with the Wars of the Roses; it would be absurd to deny that this same subject was dealt with in Holinshed and has been extensively treated in subsequent historical monographs. And this is true even if the Shakespearian plays, the historical chronicle, and the modern historical monograph give the subject not merely a different form but also present it under different logical constraints which define different types of discourse. There is therefore a sound logical basis for the distinction between form and subject even though the one cannot exist without the other.

There is also a good theoretical reason to insist on this distinction, namely that it is possible to raise as separate questions what contribution subject and what contribution form makes to aesthetic value. For example, Aristotle devotes chapter 13 of the *Poetics* to arguing that "the finest tragedies are always on the story of some few houses, on that of Alcmeon, Oedipus, Orestes, Meleager, Thyestes, Telephus, or any others that may have been involved, as either agents or sufferers in some deed of horror" (1453 *a*). And though one may disagree with Aristotle on this point, the question itself whether tragedy is best restricted to known subjects is still intelligible and important.

It is possible to argue that the creation of form (or, on the reader's part, the recognition of form) and thus a conception of a subject, may confer on the subject (invented or not) literary value. Any comparison between Shakespeare's historical plays and his sources will illustrate this point. Here is a passage from Sir Thomas North's *Plutarch's Lives of the Noble Grecians and Romans* (1579) juxtaposed with a passage from *Antony and Cleopatra* with a critical comment pointing out some of the differences between the two passages:

Her ladies and gentlewomen also, the fairest of them were apparelled like the nymphes Nereids (which are the mermaides of the waters) and like the Graces, some stearing the helme, others tending the tackle and ropes of the barge, out of the which there came a wonderfull passing sweete savor of perfumes, that perfumed the wharfes side, pestered with innumerable multitudes of people.[7]

At the helm
A seeming mermaid steers: the silken tackle
Swell with the touches of those flower-soft hands,
That yarely frame the office. (II. ii. 212–15)

Leavis points out that the tactual imagery of the second sentence gains its strength from the contrast between the hard and energetic associations of "tackle" and the sensuous adjective "silken" – "hands take hold of the cordage, and it seems impossible to dissociate 'swell' from the tactual effect". One could go further than this and say that all the phrases are linked up and indeed subsumed in a sexual metaphor – the "tackle" is at first limp and silken, but swells under the touch of the "flower-soft" hands: in little, a recapitulation of what happens to Antony under the enchantment of Cleopatra.

In comparison, North and Plutarch give us facts devoid of meaning – one gentlewoman did this, another did that – with no cohesion among those facts and no organic relationship with the rest of the action.[8]

The creation of form here imposes on the subject a coherence it has not possessed beforehand. And the coherence is defined through a thematic construal: the "facts" point beyond themselves and can reasonably be seen as contributing to a general characterization of Cleopatra and her relationship to Antony. The form is "found" rather than "invented" by the reader in this sense: the embellishment consists in the invention of extra detail, the swelling of the sails, and the use of the four words "silken", "swell", "flower-soft", "yarely" which are transferred from other areas of experience to that of sailing a barge. The reader *construes* the swelling of the sails and the application of these words: they do not in themselves hold any theme. But the construal must identify properties which, *under that construal*, can be said to be *of* the passage under interpretation. It is the possibility of this kind of construal which confers on the passage literary value, and it is the assumption that *Antony and Cleopatra* is intended to yield to this kind of construal which constitutes it as a literary work.

Using the distinction between form and subject, we can say that the aesthetic value defined by the creative-imaginative aspect of the concept of literature is constituted by the imposition of form on a subject. Imposing form on a subject is to impose coherence on a complexity of elements: a manifold of elements is in construal both identified and recognized as forming a unity. An *expectation* of a complex and coherent form is thus one central element in the literary stance; and appreciation, the mode of apprehension defined by the literary stance, aims at identifying the complex and coherent form of a literary work of art. Coherence and complexity are not, however, values *sui generis* but acquire value through contributing, with the subject, to the definition of a *humanly interesting content*.

For the creative-imaginative aspect of literature is only one of two basic aspects which define it as an evaluative concept. Let us turn to this second aspect. The concept of literature has always been recognized as having what, for the sake of tradition and convenience, may be called a *mimetic* aspect. The interest which literature has for human beings, it has because it possesses a humanly interesting content, because what literature presents or says concerns readers as human beings. As with the creative-imaginative aspect, the mimetic aspect is both a central and an ineliminable facet of the concept of literature. To recognize something as a literary work is to recognize it as being intended to convey a humanly interesting content. And a humanly interesting content has always been recognized as one of the most important qualities of literature, a quality which gives literature its cultural prominence. Aristotle's claim that "poetry is something more philosophic and of graver import than history" (*Poetics*, 1451^b), is not only partially definitive of the *nature* of literature, but also places literature between two intellectual practices of recognized importance: history and philosophy. Aristotle uses the point that poetry concerns universals rather than particulars – a point integral to our own account of fiction – as part of his defence of literary value, an attempt to meet the charge that literary fiction is frivolous and a threat to knowledge and truth. An *expectation* of a humanly interesting content is thus the other central element in the literary stance, and the other central aim of appreciation is to identify such a content in a literary work.

Again roughly speaking, it may be said that the mimetic aspect of literature manifests itself in two ways, in the rendering of subject and the presentation of theme. Literary works describe individual objects, places, characters, situations, events, actions, and the interaction between these. One prominent tradition in poetics holds that what creates the humanly interesting content of literature is, in some sense, the *truth* of these descriptions. But it is also a characteristic feature of the literary stance that literary works are expected to have a *theme*. Readers assume, in taking up the literary stance, that the descriptions of particular objects, places, characters, situations, events, actions, etc. that one finds in a literary work are

there to contribute to the definition and development of theme. From literature at its best it is expected that this descriptive detail will constitute a context for the presentation of universal human concerns, or, in the words of Thomas Nagel, "mortal questions", "mortal life: how to understand it and how to live it".[9] This literary representation is closely linked with the creation of form: form is imposed on subject thereby yielding a representation of general human interest.

However, literary representation raises problems that have nothing to do with form. It raises problems about the cognitive status of literary works, about the relationship between literature and other intellectual and cultural practices such as religion, philosophy, and science, and about *how* literature does represent "universal human concerns". Again there is a tradition in poetics that takes this area of enquiry to be the important element in literary *mimesis*, arguing that it is through its definition and development of theme that literature acquires human interest.

Notes

1 The introduction of intention within the characterization of a literary work should not be taken as begging any questions about an "intentional fallacy" in literary criticism for this characterization has no implications for the author's privileged position with regard to specific meanings assignable to elements in the work.

2 For an attempt to formulate the conventions defining and structuring the literary stance, see Stein Haugom Olsen, *The Structure of Literary Understanding* (Cambridge, 1978, 1985), chs. 4 and 5.

3 For a discussion of the concept of literary appreciation see "Criticism and Appreciation" in Olsen, *The End of Literary Theory*, 121–37.

4 For further discussion of the distinction between rules that regulate and rules that define a practice, see H. L. A. Hart, *The Concept of Law* (Oxford, 1961), ch. 5; John Rawls in "Two Concepts of Rules," *Philosophical Review*, 64 (1955), 3–32 and reprinted in Philippa Foot (ed.), *Theories of Ethics* (Oxford, 1967); and Searle, in *Speech Acts*, 33–42.

5 Harold Bloom, *Yeats* (New York, 1970), 363.

6 The point is well made in John Jones, *On Aristotle and Greek Tragedy* (London, 1962), a large part of which is taken up by showing how these plays differ.

7 "Extracts from North's *Plutarch*", Appendix V, *Antony and Cleopatra, The Arden Shakespeare* (9th edn.; London, 1954), 246.

8 Philip Hobsbaum, *A Theory of Communication* (London, 1970), 214–15.

9 Nagel, *Mortal Questions*, p. ix.

What is Literature?

Robert Stecker

"Literature" has a use in which it refers to any piece of writing (or any piece of publicly available writing) as in: "the literature on black holes is rapidly growing." However, "literature" has another sense in which it refers to a proper subclass of writings.[1] This is the sense in which Henry James's novel, *The Ambassadors*, is literature while the most recent article on black holes probably is not. It is the latter sense of "literature" in which we are interested here.

In this paper, I will be concerned with the problem of specifying the principle, or principles, by which we classify some works as literature (in the relevant sense), others as non-literature. I will argue for a traditional view which, among many literary theorists and philosophers, is currently out of favor: that literature is the body of works of art produced in linguistic media, and that this body is to be defined in terms of the possession of certain artistic values. Before proposing such a definition, however, I will briefly consider some alternatives currently more in favor.

The definition proposed here is an application to literature of a definition of art I have proposed elsewhere.[2] To simplify somewhat, that definition claims that something is a work of art if and only it is made in a central artform and is intended to fulfill a function of art, or (whether or not it is in a central artform), it fulfills such a function with excellence. One way of applying this definition to literature would simply be to substitute "literature" for "art" in stating the definition. I will try to apply the definition in a more interesting and ambitious way by identifying the functions that must be intended or fulfilled with excellence for an item to be literature. In doing this, I am self-consciously identifying what is literature according to the standards of a period that includes the latter third of the twentieth century. As we will see, it is part of my view that the functions used to identify literature can change over time.

1 Literature as a Procedure

Traditionally, literature is taken to be a body of writings. This will also be the view taken in this essay. However, one popular current way of defining literature takes it to refer to a way of treating texts rather than a body of writings.[3] Following Charles Altieri, I shall call such definitions procedural definitions of literature.

According to Altieri, when we take a text to be a literary one, "one of the things we learn to do when we read is alter certain authorial intentions and at times to impose features like coherence on texts which do not clearly possess it."[4] Another thing we characteristically learn to do is look for some general significance in the particulars of the text. These two procedures are members of the set

From *Revue Internationale de Philosophie* 50 (1996), pp. 681–94. Reprinted by permission of Revue Internationale de Philosophie.

of procedures that define literature for Altieri. Acquaintance with these two will suffice to give an idea of the sort of thing proceduralists take to be definitive of literature.

The first thing to note about procedural definitions, whatever their details, is that they do not solve the problem of classification with which we are concerned. They don't define the sense in which *The Ambassadors* is literature, and an article about black holes is not. As proceduralists themselves sometimes note, whatever procedure we define, we could apply it to both the novel and the article.

However, even if we disregard the fact that procedural definitions do not solve *our* problem, there is a flaw in the procedural approach. Proceduralists try to define a way of reading or interpreting a text and claim this way to be distinctively literary. However, literary critics interpret works in a great variety of ways. I mean by this, not simply that they give many different interpretations of the same work, but that they interpret with many different aims following many different procedures. For example, while some interpretations alter or ignore intentions and impose features like coherence, others carefully try to retrieve an author's intention and avoid imposing features on a text. Both styles of interpretation are equally characteristic of the interpretation of canonical works of literature. The procedural definition of literature rests on a false presupposition; there is no single procedure of reading and interpreting that characterizes the literary.

2 Linguistic Definitions

Some people think that what distinguishes literature from other writing is that, in literature, language is used in a special way. This approach can take a number of forms. I shall consider two here.

A. Since so much of literature is fiction, it is tempting to suppose that literature can be equated with fiction. A literary work is a work that uses language to create a fiction. Unfortunately, it is evident that being fiction is neither necessary nor sufficient for being literature. Fiction pervades everyday life. We are bombarded with it by advertising agencies. We constantly create little fictions when thinking about such things as what to do. If being verbal fiction were sufficient for being literature, then, not only advertising and all our home-

made fictions, but pulp novels, comic books, jokes, and philosophers' imaginary examples would all be literature. You may think that some of these things are literature, but I doubt that you think all of them are. If so, you agree that being fiction does not suffice for being literature.

Nor is it plausible to suppose that being fiction is necessary for being literature. From ancient times (Plutarch's *Lives*, Lucretius's *The Nature of Things*) to the present day (Mailer's *Armies of the Night*, Capote's *In Cold Blood*) nonfictional works are, without controversy, accepted as literature.

Evidently, the distinction between fiction and nonfiction will not provide the principle for distinguishing literature from non-literature that we are looking for. However, it is not an accident that, when we think of paradigmatic works of literature, we usually think of fictions. Works of fiction constitute the heart of literature. An adequate account of the nature of literature will explain why this is so.

B. The idea behind the first proposal is that, in creating literature, writers use words to do something special: create a fiction. The idea behind the second proposal is that, in creating literature, writers can do almost anything, but they must do it by writing in a special way. The difficulty comes in specifying the way one must write for one's writing to be literature.

Many literary works are richly descriptive, or replete with metaphors and other figures of speech, or ironic or ambiguous. Since these characteristics are often associated with literary language, one might hope to use them to specify the way one must write to create literature. Unfortunately, this hope is unfounded. Here are two reasons why it is.

First, many, if not all the properties on the list indicate characteristics of style. This, of course, is not surprising since we are trying to define literature in terms of the way it is written. However, literary styles tend to create counter styles. If one finds richly descriptive prose in some literary works, one also finds writing that self-consciously avoids such prose. The same goes for all the characteristics on the list. This does not show that we need a longer list. If different literary styles are characterized by complementary properties – the property of being F and the property of being non-F – then we obviously cannot expect to define literature in terms of such properties. If we did, everything would be literature.

Second, all the properties on the list are found in ordinary, non-literary speech and writing. They may have become associated with literary language, but they are hardly peculiar to it. Ordinary speech and writing can be ambiguous, ironic, full of metaphors. It can also be descriptive, even highly descriptive.

The present approach attempts to define literature in terms of its perceptible properties, i.e., in terms of characteristic surface features. Because of the considerations just cited, such an approach is unpromising.

3   Literature as an Institution

A more promising and more recent proposal thinks of literature as an informal institution or practice. "A text is identified as a literary work by recognizing the author's intention that the text is produced and meant to be read within a framework of conventions defining the practice . . . of literature."[5] According to Lamarque and Olsen, the basic intention here is the intention that the reader adopt a certain stance toward the work: the expectation of "literary, aesthetic value."[6] For Lamarque and Olsen, literary aesthetic value has two components. The "creative-imaginative" component consists in imposing form or unity on a subject. Thus, Aeschylus, Sophocles, and Euripides each take the same subject, the Orestes/Electra story, and by imposing different forms on this story, present different versions of it. They also present different conceptions of its significance. The "mimetic" component of literary aesthetic value requires that literature have a humanly interesting content embodied in a perennial theme or themes expressed in a work which is responsible for the significance of a version of a story. It might be thought that the mimetic component of literary value implies that literature has a cognitive as well as aesthetic value, but Lamarque and Olsen do not see it that way. They do not deny that a given work of literature can have cognitive value, but this would not be, for them, a distinctively literary value and is not guaranteed by the possession of a work of perennial theme expressed in a complex but unified form. That form presents an imaginary universe to be appreciated for its own sake though in humanly meaningful terms. To see life in terms of this imaginary universe is "an optional extra."[7]

This view contains a wonderful mixture of truth and falsehood. The claim that literature is to be defined in terms of literary value should be endorsed. However, Lamarque and Olsen's conception of literary value should not be endorsed. It is correct that an intention to create such value, and an intention to create in readers an expectation of such value, plays an important role in identifying literary works. However, it is not correct that only works made with such intention are works of literature. Finally, there is such a thing as the practice of literature, but Lamarque and Olsen make two mistakes with regard to it. First, while they seem to regard it as essentially unchanged since ancient Greek times, it has instead evolved a great deal over the course of time (I would question whether the concept of literature extends back to ancient Greece). Second, it is not true that, for a work to be literature, it must be part of the practice in the sense of being written with the sort of intentions mentioned above.

Since in presenting my own view, reasons will be offered for the views asserted in the last paragraph, I will not at this point argue for them now. Rather, I turn to the presentation of my own conception of the nature of literature.

4   Literature as Imaginative Writing

A number of writers concur that it was sometime in the 19th century that the body of writings to be collected under the label "literature" came to be identified with writing that could properly be considered art, and this, in turn, came to be conceived of as imaginative writing.[8] Though many current theorists, including some of the proponents of views we have thus far considered, believe that for one reason or another this conception should be rejected, there is considerable agreement that it is this conception that has shaped our present canon[9] of literary works.

If this admission is correct, it seems to me that proposals that we replace this conception of literature as imaginative writing with some other conception have to be regarded as revisionary, as proposals that we ought to classify in different ways than the way we in fact do. However, if we want to understand how we in fact do classify, we must understand the conception of literature as imaginative writing.

The key term is "imaginative." This is sometimes taken to refer to a class of genres – the novel, the tale, the drama – all of which share the property of being fiction. However, we have already seen that this could not be right. "Imaginative" also does not refer to something a writer must do to create a work of literature. Rather, it refers to a range of values for which works of literature have characteristically been appreciated.

Literary value is often identified as aesthetic value, the value of the experience of a literary work. We saw above that this is how Lamarque and Olsen characterize literary value, and they are certainly not alone in doing so.[10] I deny that this approach provides an adequate characterization of literary value and claim the range of values characteristic of imaginative writing falls under several basic categories. Aesthetic value is certainly one of these, but so is a distinctive sort of cognitive value, and interpretation–centered value.

I do not have space here to explain adequately what it is for a work to possess these valuable properties.[11] In barest outline, I take the aesthetic value of a piece of writing to consist in the pleasure it is capable of giving to those who imaginatively experience or contemplate the world of the work. This can be fleshed out further, as Lamarque and Olsen do, in terms of the appreciation of forms and themes, but that, it seems to me, is just one approach among several viable ones. The imaginative experience of literary works is far more multifaceted than Lamarque and Olsen suggest. If I were to reduce it to a simple idea, it would be this: the core aesthetic experience of a literary work consists of contemplating the conceptions it presents to the imagination for the sake of the enjoyment one gets from doing so. This certainly permits the enjoyment of these conceptions in the manner suggested by Lamarque and Olsen, but also permits other ways of enjoying these conceptions – as conveying a richly and concretely imagined time, place, person or experience, as the rendering of the equivocality or ambiguity of language, experience, or the interpretations we place on these, as presenting events full of internal contradictions, or ones full of coherence and unity.

I take the distinctive sort of cognitive value (henceforth to be called simply "cognitive value") to consist of two things; (1) vivid conceptions we derive from the work (e.g., conceptions of types, of practices, of ideals, values, and moral codes, of theories and their consequences, etc.); (2) what we learn about ourselves, and more speculatively, of other people, when we see how we react to these conceptions. Notice how (1) derives directly from our aesthetic enjoyment of literature. It is nevertheless to be distinguished from it, because the em-

phasis here is in what we take away from the work for the purpose being able to think better about the actual world. The cognitive value of (1) consists in the provision of new ways of thinking (new conceptions) about potentially any aspect of human experience, in such a way that we do not merely entertain such ideas in the abstract, but we concretely imagine what one does and feels when one thinks of the world in this way. We can, for example, define utilitarianism and discuss its pros and cons in abstract ethical theory but in a novel we can watch a utilitarian in action and are confronted by what it means to act and evaluate actions according to this theory. (2) specifies a further cognitive benefit of the imaginative engagement that literature provides. It is the knowledge of ourselves when we see how we react to the conceptions presented to the imagination. To the extent that others are like us, we gain knowledge not only of ourselves but of them.

Finally, there is interpretation-centered value. We have come to value literature because it invites or requires interpretation. The basic idea here is that literature, like other forms of writing, not only invites us to figure out what someone else (the author) is doing in a work, but, unlike other forms of writing, it invites us to *give* a work significance. It invites us to be creative, to participate in creating something. Part of the value of doing this is in the creation of *new* aesthetic and cognitive value. For this reason, interpretation-centered value is not entirely distinct from these other kinds of value. However, part of its value lies in providing an opportunity to exercise our capacity for creativity, and this aspect of its value is distinct from the other three kinds of value.

According to our construal of imaginative writing, then, a piece of writing is to be classified as literature in terms of some relation it bears to the three categories of value just discussed. There are a number of candidates for the appropriate relation. The simplest would be possession of value in one or the other category. This won't work. There are examples of writing that possess cognitive value which are not works of literature. Among these are the imaginary examples we commonly find in philosophical writing. I believe the same is true of the other categories. It is equally unsatisfactory to identify the relation in terms of the intention to create works possessing these values. The counter-examples against the first view also apply to this one. Even joint possession of these values is not sufficient to make something literature. A piece of private correspondence, which possesses all of them but to a tiny degree, does not have much claim to be literature.

Unfortunately, the relation we need is a complicated one. In fact, two distinct relations need to be specified to cover two classes of literary works. Certain genres of writing are regarded by almost everybody as providing the central works of literature. These genres are the novel, the short story and the tale, the drama, and poetry of all kinds. For a work in any of these genres to be a work of literature it is sufficient that the writer intended it to be valuable in any of the categories, and the writer has sufficient technical skill for it to be possible to take that intention seriously. Outside these genres, there are many other works that belong to literature: these include some essays, some works of history, philosophy, social and natural science, some travel books, some nature writing, some diaries and journals, some collections of maxims and epigrams, some collections of letters, some memoirs, biographies and autobiographies. Ignoring for now various qualifications to be stated below, these works belong to literature if they possess a significant degree of one of the values.

5 Objections

I will now consider some objections to the idea of literature as imaginative writing in general, and to my principle of classification in particular. Some, but not all, of these objections will require us to further qualify the principle.

First let me note a common objection to the general approach taken here which is *not* an objection to my particular version of it. The identification of literature with art has commonly involved defining literature solely in terms of aesthetic value. As Robert Scholes claims, "once this notion of art is allowed into the picture, all those aspects of literature which are cognitive or instructive are found to be impurities."[12] This objection might well be mounted against Lamarque and Olsen's conception of literature as a practice. I agree with Scholes that *this* notion of art gives us a distorted conception of literary value. However, since I believe that this notion of art gives us a distorted conception of artistic value in general, it is in good conscience that I state a principle which clearly does not suffer from this defect.

What is an objection to my definition is the claim, made by a number of writers, that there is no single set of properties for which literature has always been valued. According to Terry Eagleton, though literature is to be defined in terms of value, the writing we value as literature is historically variable, and so cannot be pinned down in the way my principle suggests.[13] Eagleton identifies literature simply with writing we value or think good. This obviously won't do since we value certain pieces of writing, an article in *Nature* or in *Consumer Reports* say, without that making them literature. One common way of trying to save a claim like Eagleton's is to distinguish between writing we value for itself and writing we value for some function it performs, and claim that literature is writing in the former category. Eagleton, however, rejects the claim that we value literary works for themselves, and I am sympathetic with this rejection. This is one source of the distorted view of artistic value alluded to just now. It has seemed obvious to many theorists that the cognitive value of literature is a form of instrumental value, while valuing works for their aesthetic value is valuing works for themselves. Unfortunately, it is *not* obvious that aesthetic value is non-instrumental. Many of those who claim this define aesthetic value in terms of a capacity to give aesthetic experience and giving aesthetic experience is a function if ever there was one.

If we are to define literature in terms of value, it is more plausibly to be defined in terms of the possession of particular valuable properties. It is not to be defined simply as writing we value but as writing we value for being F, G, or H. We could then reinterpret Eagleton's claim as the claim that at different times literature is defined in terms of different valuable properties. However, this leads to a new problem. If literature is to be *defined* in terms of valuable properties, say F, G and H, then, if at some time a set of writings is defined in terms of a different set of valuable properties, these writings could not constitute literature, at least, not literature in the same sense. This implies that we *cannot* say, without equivocation, that literature is defined in terms of different properties at different times.

Eagleton's response to this is to acknowledge that there is a problem but claim that it demonstrates the incoherence of our concept of literature. I think it more reasonable to try to avoid the problem and believe we can do so while acknowledging a grain of truth in Eagleton's position. First, remember that our present conception of literature defines a range of values. Not all these

Robert Stecker

values are preeminently associated with literature at all times since the emergence of the concept in the 19th century. At different times, different values are at the forefront of consciousness. An example of this is the value placed on literature's susceptibility to multiple interpretations. This is highly valued in our own century and virtually ignored in previous centuries. Hence different values can be *associated with* literature at different times even though different values do not *define* literature at these times.

Second, it should be recognized that our present conception of literature has historical predecessors. The most immediate predecessor is the 18th-century conception of belles lettres or fine writing. It is in the 18th century that considerations that came to dominate our present conception of literature – that of the aesthetic and of the importance of the imagination – became objects of theoretical inquiry both in epistemology and in a new subject that came to be known as aesthetics. It is not surprising, then, that criteria we use to decide whether something is literature overlap with, rather than coincide with, criteria for deciding whether something is a piece of fine writing.

Historical predecessors to our conception of literature not only helped to shape our conception. They still have a role in determining the extension of "literature." Recognition of this role requires the first qualification that needs to be made to our principle of classification. The qualification concerns only works written when the predecessor concepts held sway. Unlike contemporary works, what determines whether an 18th-century work is literature is a disjunctive condition. It is literature if it bears the right relation to aesthetic, cognitive or interpretation-centered value *or* if it falls under the category fine writing. Similarly, a piece of writing from ancient Greece or Rome belongs to literature if it bears the right relation to A or C *or* falls under the category (ancient) classic. The reason for this is that we tend to incorporate into literature writing already recognized by predecessor concepts.

Eagleton's objection to our principle was that no historically stable set of values is associated with literature. E. D. Hirsch proposes that no definition of literature can capture the continuum of uses with which educated people use the word *now*.[14] Hirsch is no doubt right here but it is not clear that this poses a serious problem for our principle of classification. Not every use of "literature" which diverges from our principle constitutes a counter example to

it. Some uses simply derive from different senses of "literature," as in the "literature on black holes." Other usage is simply loose as with the identification of literature and fiction. Only uses which play a serious role in collecting a body of works together for special consideration are relevant uses. Here, if there are indeed a great variety of such uses, Hirsch does not mention very many of them. However, he does mention one that requires one further qualification to our principle. Hirsch calls this "literature by association." On this use, "literature is anything written by a great literary figure."[15] This way of putting the matter is not exactly right since not every scrap of paper found in the desk of a great writer automatically gets classified as literature. However, it does happen that, in the case of great writers, letters and journals, for example, of little literary interest in themselves, can be included in a writer's complete works and be considered literature. We can admit that writing can be classified as literature in this way while recognizing the sense in saying that such works have little claim to be considered literature in their own right.

The final objection to our principle that I will consider here is that it makes the classification of literature a subjective, or culturally relative, matter. This objection might be based on the claim that all value judgments are subjective or culturally relative, but, since that is, to put it mildly, a controversial claim, it provides a very weak basis for the objection. A different basis for the objection is that the ascription of the particular values in question – aesthetic, cognitive, interpretation-centered – is a subjective or culturally relative matter. This claim too is controversial, but if (for simplicity) we confine the claim to aesthetic value, it does find some support in various traditional ways of defining this value. These define aesthetic value in terms of aesthetic experience, i.e., in terms of an effect a work has on its readers. This makes aesthetic value subjective, in the sense of "subjective" in which it means something like "mind-dependent." On the other hand, it may be an objective matter whether a work has a greater or lesser capacity to produce the experience. If so, the criterion of possessing aesthetic value is capable of providing an intersubjective principle of classification. It is beyond the scope of this essay to *settle* this question. For this reason, the objection cannot be said to stand refuted. It can at least be said, however, that it is an open question just how objective, subjective or culture-relative is the ascription of value to literary works.

6 Conclusion

I have argued that:

A work *w* is a work of literature if and only if *w* is produced in a linguistic medium, and,

1 *w* is a novel, short story, tale, drama, or poem, and the writer of *w* intended that it possess aesthetic, cognitive or interpretation–centered value, and the work is written with sufficient technical skill for it to be possible to take that intention seriously, or

2 *w* possesses aesthetic, cognitive or interpretation–centered value to a significant degree, or

3 *w* falls under a predecessor concept to our concept of literature and was written while the predecessor concept held sway, or

4 *w* belongs to the work of a great writer.

A final remark is needed to avoid misunderstanding. The definition has many gray areas. When does a work possess *sufficient* technical skill to enable readers to take its intention seriously? *Who* are those who must take it seriously? What is a *significant* degree of the values in question? Exactly *when* does a predecessor concept to our concept of literature *begin* and *cease* to hold sway? Which are the *works* of a great writer? *Who* are the great writers? At the very least, these gray areas will make borderline cases inevitable. I do not regard this as an objection to the definition, however. The definition is not intended to make the extension of "literature" precise. It is intended to articulate classificatory practice which does result in borderline cases.

Notes

1 It is a convenient simplification to identify literature with a subclass of *writings*, but it should be remembered that there is such a thing as oral literature.

2 Most recently in "Historical Functionalism or The Four Factor Theory," *British Journal of Aesthetics*, 34, 1994, 255–65, and in *Artworks: Definition, Meaning, Value* (University Park: Penn State Press, 1996), chapter 3.

3 Charles Altieri, "A Procedural Definition of Literature," Norman Holland, "Literature as Transaction," Robert Scholes, "Towards a Semiotics of Literature," all of which are found in *What is Literature?* ed. Paul Hernadi (Bloomington: Indiana University Press, 1978) present rival procedural definitions of literature. One of the most elaborate procedural definitions is found in Jonathan Culler, *Structuralist Poetics: Structuralism, Linguistics, and the Study of Literature* (Ithaca: Cornell University Press, 1975), chapters 6–9.

4 Altieri, p. 69.

5 Peter Lamarque and S. H. Olsen, *Truth, Fiction, and Literature* (Oxford: Oxford University Press, 1994), 255–6.

6 Ibid., 256.

7 Ibid., 455.

8 See Rene Wellek, "What is Literature," E. D. Hirsch, "What Isn't Literature" in Hernadi, *What is Literature?* Also see Terry Eagleton, *Literary Theory: An Introduction* (Minneapolis: University of Minnesota Press, 1983), chapter 2.

9 The use of "canon" here might raise concerns (not to mention passions) regarding the fixing of the extension of literature in the works of a distinctly European/American white male tradition. I, however, think of the canon of literary works, first of all as a constantly expanding group of exemplary writings which by now should include items from all over the world, written by members of all races (if there be such) and genders and many ethnic groups. Second, since works in the (or a) canon are exemplary items, they would not include all the works of literature in any case.

10 Among the recent and most sophisticated variants of this view is Malcolm Budd's in *Values of Art: Pictures, Poetry, Music* (London: Allen Lane, 1995).

11 These values are more fully discussed in my *Artworks: Definition, Meaning, Value* (University Park: Penn State Press, 1996), chapter 13.

12 Scholes, "Towards a Semiotics of Literature," p. 235.

13 Eagleton, *Literary Theory*, chapter 1.

14 Hirsch, "What Isn't Literature?"

15 Ibid., p. 30.

PART III

Ontology of Literature

Introduction

Literary works are preserved by copying – by memorization, printing, or hand copying. In Jorge Luis Borges's story, Pierre Menard writes a text that is word-for-word identical to parts of Cervantes's novel *Don Quixote*. The story's narrator comments that "Cervantes' text and Menard's are verbally identical, but the second is almost infinitely richer." Is Menard's text a copy of *Don Quixote* or is it a new work entirely?

Definitions of literature mark the boundaries of the body of literature, attempting to enumerate the features that works of literature share in common and that distinguish them from other kinds of works. Ontologies of literature mark the boundaries of individual works. They attempt to spell out what *individuates* works from each other and what *identifies* works as persisting over time.

Contrast works of literature with paintings. Paintings are physical objects and their criteria of individuation and identity are criteria that apply to physical objects. Picasso's *Guernica* and a perfect forgery of it are different works because they are different bits of painted canvas. *Guernica*, the painting exhibited in New York in 1958, and *Guernica*, the painting exhibited in Madrid in 2002, are the same work because they are the same painted canvas (which was moved to Madrid in 1981). But "Tintern Abbey" is not a physical object. Although printed copies of Wordsworth's poem are physical objects, the work is not identical to any printed copy of it. Criteria for individuating and identifying works are governed by Leibniz's Law, which states that a is identical to b if and only

if a and b have all the same properties. Since destroying a copy of "Tintern Abbey" does not destroy the poem, the poem and the copy of it have different properties, so the work is not identical to its copy. What, then, is the work and what is its relation to its copies?

A literary work is a generic entity that has multiple instances. Philosophers have catalogued several varieties of generic entities according to their relationship to their instances. Some think that literary works are classes – collections of objects sharing a property. Perhaps a literary work is the class of physical objects having the same word-sequence. However, properties of members of a class are generally not properties of the class itself. Copies of "Tintern Abbey" are written in English, as is the work, but no class is written in English, and as a result the work cannot be a class.

Richard Wollheim suggests that literary works are types whose instances are tokens. A biological species is an example of a type; its tokens are the individual animals or plants belonging to it. A type shares some, not all, of its properties with its tokens – the wolf species ranges from Wyoming to the Arctic but no wolf ranges that distance. But if tokens have a property necessarily, then that property is a property of the type: since nothing is a wolf unless it is a mammal, being a mammal is a property of the species. If literary works are types and copies of them are tokens, then the properties works have are those essential to their copies. Being written by William S. Burroughs is a property of the work *Naked Lunch* only if it is an essential feature of its copies that Burroughs is their author.

Properties of a work determine properties of its copies. Of course, the only way to know the properties of a work is by inspecting its copies. We cannot know how *Anna Karenina* begins by inspecting the work itself, for it is an abstract object. We can only look at printed copies. However, we should not confuse epistemic questions (of how we know things about works) with ontological questions (of what works are and how they relate to their instances). We *know* that a novel begins as it does by inspecting a copy of it – this is a fact about how to know things about works. But properties of *Anna Karenina determine* that none of its copies begin "Stately, plump Buck Mulligan came from the stairhead" – this is a fact about how things are. The route from copy to work is epistemic and the route from work to copy is ontological.

What kinds of properties do literary works have? Chapters 13 to 15 address this question. J. O. Urmson argues that literary works are like musical scores – they are instructions for performance and literature is a performing art. Although this idea is counterintuitive, it has some advantages and is echoed in recent theories of fiction (see Parts IV and V). A more popular view is textualism, which identifies literary works with linguistic entities. For Nelson Goodman and Catherine Elgin, works of literature are word sequences belonging to a language. Gregory Currie exposes some difficulties with textualism and proposes that literary works cannot be reduced to linguistic entities. Interpreting a text is different from interpreting a work, so to know what a work is we must consider what is involved in interpreting it.

These proposals deliver different verdicts on the puzzle of "Pierre Menard" and beget some new puzzles. Works of literature persist even when some of their copies are destroyed, but is a literary work destroyed when every last copy of it is destroyed? When is a literary work created? Does creating one require creating a copy of it? How are copies generated from works? Is a word-for-word replica of *Naked Lunch* accidentally produced by a monkey typist a copy of *Naked Lunch*? Literary works can be accessed through physical objects with quite different properties – anyone who has read "Pierre Menard" in Borges's *Labyrinths* may reread it via the reprint in this volume. How different may copies of the same work be? Why are copies of "Pierre Menard" in the original Portuguese and in the English translation copies of the same work?

Pierre Menard, Author of the *Quixote*

Jorge Luis Borges

The *visible* work left by this novelist is easily and briefly enumerated. Impardonable, therefore, are the omissions and additions perpetrated by Madame Henri Bachelier in a fallacious catalogue which a certain daily, whose *Protestant* tendency is no secret, has had the inconsideration to inflict upon its deplorable readers – though these be few and Calvinist, if not Masonic and circumcised. The true friends of Menard have viewed this catalogue with alarm and even with a certain melancholy. One might say that only yesterday we gathered before his final monument, amidst the lugubrious cypresses, and already Error tries to tarnish his Memory... Decidedly, a brief rectification is unavoidable.

I am aware that it is quite easy to challenge my slight authority. I hope, however, that I shall not be prohibited from mentioning two eminent testimonies. The Baroness de Bacourt (at whose unforgettable *vendredis* I had the honor of meeting the lamented poet) has seen fit to approve the pages which follow. The Countess de Bagnoregio, one of the most delicate spirits of the Principality of Monaco (and now of Pittsburgh, Pennsylvania, following her recent marriage to the international philanthropist Simon Kautzsch, who has been so inconsiderately slandered, alas! by the victims of his disinterested maneuvers) has sacrificed "to veracity and to death" (such were her words) the stately reserve which is her distinction, and, in an open letter published in the magazine *Luxe*, concedes me her approval as well. These authorizations, I think, are not entirely insufficient.

I have said that Menard's visible work can be easily enumerated. Having examined with care his personal files, I find that they contain the following items:

a) A Symbolist sonnet which appeared twice (with variants) in the review *La conque* (issues of March and October 1899).

b) A monograph on the possibility of constructing a poetic vocabulary of concepts which would not be synonyms or periphrases of those which make up our everyday language, "but rather ideal objects created according to convention and essentially designed to satisfy poetic needs" (Nîmes, 1901).

c) A monograph on "certain connections or affinities" between the thought of Descartes, Leibniz and John Wilkins (Nîmes, 1903).

d) A monograph on Leibniz's *Characteristica universalis* (Nîmes, 1904).

e) A technical article on the possibility of improving the game of chess, eliminat-

From *Labyrinths*, trans. James E. Irby (New York: New Directions, 1964), pp. 36–44. Copyright © 1962, 1964 by New Directions Publishing Corporation. Reprinted by permission of New Directions Publishing Corporation and Laurence Pollinger Ltd.

ing one of the rook's pawns. Menard proposes, recommends, discusses and finally rejects this innovation.

f) A monograph on Raymond Lully's *Ars magna generalis* (Nîmes, 1906).

g) A translation, with prologue and notes, of Ruy López de Segura's *Libro de la invención liberal y arte del juego del axedrez* (Paris, 1907).

h) The work sheets of a monograph on George Boole's symbolic logic.

i) An examination of the essential metric laws of French prose, illustrated with examples taken from Saint-Simon (*Revue des langues romanes*, Montpellier, October 1909).

j) A reply to Luc Durtain (who had denied the existence of such laws), illustrated with examples from Luc Durtain (*Revue des langues romanes*, Montpellier, December 1909).

k) A manuscript translation of the *Aguja de navegar cultos* of Quevedo, entitled *La boussole des précieux*.

l) A preface to the Catalogue of an exposition of lithographs by Carolus Hourcade (Nîmes, 1914).

m) The work *Les problèmes d'un problème* (Paris, 1917), which discusses, in chronological order, the different solutions given to the illustrous problem of Achilles and the tortoise. Two editions of this book have appeared so far; the second bears as an epigraph Leibniz's recommendation *"Ne craignez point, monsieur, la tortue"* and revises the chapters dedicated to Russell and Descartes.

n) A determined analysis of the "syntactical customs" of Toulet (*N.R.F.*, March 1921). Menard – I recall – declared that censure and praise are sentimental operations which have nothing to do with literary criticism.

o) A transposition into alexandrines of Paul Valéry's *Le cimetière marin* (*N. R. F.*, January 1928).

p) An invective against Paul Valéry, in the *Papers for the Suppression of Reality* of Jacques Reboul. (This invective, we might say parenthetically, is the exact opposite of his true opinion of Valéry. The latter understood it as such and their old friendship was not endangered.)

q) A "definition" of the Countess de Bagnoregio, in the "victorious volume" – the locution is Gabriele d'Annunzio's, another of its collaborators – published annually by this lady to rectify the inevitable falsifications of journalists and to present "to the world and to Italy" an authentic image of her person, so often exposed (by very reason of her beauty and her activities) to erroneous or hasty interpretations.

r) A cycle of admirable sonnets for the Baroness de Bacourt (1934).

s) A manuscript list of verses which owe their efficacy to their punctuation.[1]

This, then, is the *visible* work of Menard, in chronological order (with no omission other than a few vague sonnets of circumstance written for the hospitable, or avid, album of Madame Henri Bachelier). I turn now to his other work: the subterranean, the interminably heroic, the peerless. And – such are the capacities of man! – the unfinished. This work, perhaps the most significant of our time, consists of the ninth and thirty-eighth chapters of the first part of *Don Quixote* and a fragment of chapter twenty-two. I know such an affirmation seems an absurdity; to justify this "absurdity" is the primordial object of this note.[2]

Two texts of unequal value inspired this undertaking. One is that philological fragment by Novalis – the one numbered 2005 in the Dresden edition – which outlines the theme of a *total* identification with a given author. The other is one of those parasitic books which situate Christ on a boulevard, Hamlet on La Cannebière or Don Quixote on Wall Street. Like all men of good taste, Menard abhorred these useless carnivals, fit only – as he would say – to produce the plebeian pleasure of anachronism or (what is worse) to enthrall us with the elementary idea that all epochs are the same or are different. More interesting, though contradictory and superficial of execution, seemed to him the famous plan of Daudet: to conjoin the Ingenious Gentleman and his squire in *one* figure, which was Tartarin... Those who have insinuated that Menard dedicated his life to writing a contemporary *Quixote* calumniate his illustrious memory.

He did not want to compose another *Quixote* – which is easy – but the *Quixote* itself. Needless to say, he never contemplated a mechanical transcription of the original; he did not propose to copy it. His admirable intention was to produce a few pages which would coincide – word for word and line for line – with those of Miguel de Cervantes.

"My intent is no more than astonishing," he wrote me the 30th of September, 1934, from Bayonne. "The final term in a theological or metaphysical demonstration – the objective world, God, causality, the forms of the universe – is no less previous and common than my famed novel. The only difference is that the philosophers publish the intermediary stages of their labor in pleasant volumes and I have resolved to do away with those stages." In truth, not one worksheet remains to bear witness to his years of effort.

The first method he conceived was relatively simple. Know Spanish well, recover the Catholic faith, fight against the Moors or the Turk, forget the history of Europe between the years 1602 and 1918, *be* Miguel de Cervantes. Pierre Menard studied this procedure (I know he attained a fairly accurate command of seventeenth-century Spanish) but discarded it as too easy. Rather as impossible! my reader will say. Granted, but the undertaking was impossible from the very beginning and of all the impossible ways of carrying it out, this was the least interesting. To be, in the twentieth century, a popular novelist of the seventeenth seemed to him a diminution. To be, in some way, Cervantes and reach the *Quixote* seemed less arduous to him – and, consequently, less interesting – than to go on being Pierre Menard and reach the *Quixote* through the experiences of Pierre Menard. (This conviction, we might say in passing, made him omit the autobiographical prologue to the second part of *Don Quixote*. To include that prologue would have been to create another character – Cervantes – but it would also have meant presenting the *Quixote* in terms of that character and not of Menard. The latter, naturally, declined that facility.) "My undertaking is not difficult, essentially," I read in another part of his letter. "I should only have to be immortal to carry it out." Shall I confess that I often imagine he did finish it and that I read the *Quixote* – all of it – as if Menard had conceived it? Some nights past, while leafing through chapter XXVI – never essayed by him – I recognized our friend's style and something of his voice in this exceptional phrase: "the river nymphs and the dolorous and humid Echo." This happy conjunction of a spiritual and a physical adjective brought to my mind a verse by Shakespeare which we discussed one afternoon:

Where a malignant and a turbaned Turk . . .

But why precisely the *Quixote?* our reader will ask. Such a preference, in a Spaniard, would not have been inexplicable; but it is, no doubt, in a Symbolist from Nîmes, essentially a devoté of Poe, who engendered Baudelaire, who engendered Mallarmé, who engendered Valéry, who engendered Edmond Teste. The aforementioned letter illuminates this point. "The *Quixote*," clarifies Menard, "interests me deeply, but it does not seem – how shall I say it? – inevitable. I cannot imagine the universe without Edgar Allan Poe's exclamation:

Ah, bear in mind this garden was enchanted!

or without the *Bateau ivre* or the *Ancient Mariner*, but I am quite capable of imagining it without the *Quixote*. (I speak, naturally, of my personal capacity and not of those works' historical resonance.) The *Quixote* is a contingent book; the *Quixote* is unnecessary. I can premeditate writing it, I can write it, without falling into a tautology. When I was ten or twelve years old, I read it, perhaps in its entirety. Later, I have reread closely certain chapters, those which I shall not attempt for the time being. I have also gone through the interludes, the plays, the *Galatea*, the exemplary novels, the undoubtedly laborious tribulations of Persiles and Segismunda and the *Viaje del Parnaso* . . . My general recollection of the *Quixote*, simplified by forgetfulness and indifference, can well equal the imprecise and prior image of a book not yet written. Once that image (which no one can legitimately deny me) is postulated, it is certain that my problem is a good bit more difficult than Cervantes' was. My obliging predecessor did not refuse the collaboration of chance: he composed his immortal work somewhat *à la diable*, carried along by the inertias of language and invention. I have taken on the mysterious duty of reconstructing literally his spontaneous work. My solitary game is governed by two polar laws. The first permits me to essay variations of a formal or psychological type; the second obliges me to sacrifice these variations to the "original" text and reason out this annihilation in an irrefutable manner . . . To these artificial hindrances, another – of a congenital kind – must be added. To compose the *Quixote* at the beginning of the seventeenth century was a reasonable undertaking, necessary and perhaps even unavoidable; at the beginning of the twentieth, it is almost impossible. It is not in vain that three hundred years have gone by, filled with exceedingly complex events. Amongst them, to mention only one, is the *Quixote* itself."

In spite of these three obstacles, Menard's fragmentary *Quixote* is more subtle than Cervantes'. The latter, in a clumsy fashion, opposes to the fictions of chivalry the tawdry provincial reality of his country; Menard selects as his "reality" the land of Carmen during the century of Lepanto and Lope de Vega. What a series of *espagnolades* that selection would have suggested to Maurice Barrès or Dr. Rodríguez Larreta! Menard eludes them with complete naturalness. In his work there are no gypsy flourishes or conquistadors or mystics or Philip the Seconds or *autos da fé*. He neglects or eliminates local color. This disdain points to a new conception of the historical novel. This disdain condemns *Salammbô*, with no possibility of appeal.

It is no less astounding to consider isolated chapters. For example, let us examine Chapter XXXVIII of the first part, "which treats of the curious discourse of Don Quixote on arms and letters." It is well known that Don Quixote (like Quevedo in an analogous and later passage in *La hora de todos*) decided the debate against letters and in favor of arms. Cervantes was a former soldier: his verdict is understandable. But that Pierre Menard's Don Quixote – a contemporary of *La trahison des clercs* and Bertrand Russell – should fall prey to such nebulous sophistries! Madame Bachelier has seen here an admirable and typical subordination on the part of the author to the hero's psychology; others (not at all perspicaciously), a *transcription* of the *Quixote*; the Baroness de Bacourt, the influence of Nietzsche. To this third interpretation (which I judge to be irrefutable) I am not sure I dare to add a fourth, which concords very well with the almost divine modesty of Pierre Menard: his resigned or ironical habit of propagating ideas which were the strict reverse of those he preferred. (Let us recall once more his diatribe against Paul Valéry in Jacques Reboul's ephemeral Surrealist sheet.) Cervantes' text and Menard's are verbally identical, but the second is almost infinitely richer. (More ambiguous, his detractors will say, but ambiguity is richness.)

It is a revelation to compare Menard's *Don Quixote* with Cervantes'. The latter, for example, wrote (part one, chapter nine):

> ... truth, whose mother is history, rival of time, depository of deeds, witness of the

past, exemplar and adviser to the present, and the future's counselor.

Written in the seventeenth century, written by the "lay genius" Cervantes, this enumeration is a mere rhetorical praise of history. Menard, on the other hand, writes:

> ... truth, whose mother is history, rival of time, depository of deeds, witness of the past, exemplar and adviser to the present, and the future's counselor.

History, the *mother* of truth: the idea is astounding. Menard, a contemporary of William James, does not define history as an inquiry into reality but as its origin. Historical truth, for him, is not what has happened; it is what we judge to have happened. The final phrases – *exemplar and adviser to the present, and the future's counselor* – are brazenly pragmatic.

The contrast in style is also vivid. The archaic style of Menard – quite foreign, after all – suffers from a certain affectation. Not so that of his forerunner, who handles with ease the current Spanish of his time.

There is no exercise of the intellect which is not, in the final analysis, useless. A philosophical doctrine begins as a plausible description of the universe; with the passage of the years it becomes a mere chapter – if not a paragraph or a name – in the history of philosophy. In literature, this eventual caducity is even more notorious. The *Quixote* – Menard told me – was, above all, an entertaining book; now it is the occasion for patriotic toasts, grammatical insolence and obscene de luxe editions. Fame is a form of incomprehension, perhaps the worst.

There is nothing new in these nihilistic verifications; what is singular is the determination Menard derived from them. He decided to anticipate the vanity awaiting all man's efforts; he set himself to an undertaking which was exceedingly complex and, from the very beginning, futile. He dedicated his scruples and his sleepless nights to repeating an already extant book in an alien tongue. He multiplied draft upon draft, revised tenaciously and tore up thousands of manuscript pages.[3] He did not let anyone examine these drafts and took care they should not survive him. In vain have I tried to reconstruct them.

I have reflected that it is permissible to see in this "final" *Quixote* a kind of palimpsest, through which the traces – tenuous but not indecipherable – of our friend's "previous" writing should be translucently visible. Unfortunately, only a second Pierre Menard, inverting the other's work, would be able to exhume and revive those lost Troys...

"Thinking, analyzing, inventing (he also wrote me) are not anomalous acts; they are the normal respiration of the intelligence. To glorify the occasional performance of that function, to hoard ancient and alien thoughts, to recall with incredulous stupor that the *doctor universalis* thought, is to confess our laziness or our barbarity. Every man should be capable of all ideas and I understand that in the future this will be the case."

Menard (perhaps without wanting to) has enriched, by means of a new technique, the halting and rudimentary art of reading: this new technique is that of the deliberate anachronism and the erroneous attribution. This technique, whose applications are infinite, prompts us to go through the *Odyssey* as if it were posterior to the *Aeneid* and the book *Le jardin du Centaure* of Madame Henri Bachelier as if it were by Madame Henri Bachelier. This technique fills the most placid works with adventure. To attribute the *Imitatio Christi* to Louis Ferdinand Céline or to James Joyce, is this not a sufficient renovation of its tenuous spiritual indications?

For Silvina Ocampo   *Translated by J. E. I.*

Notes

1 Madame Henri Bachelier also lists a literal translation of Quevedo's literal translation of the *Introduction à la vie dévote* of St. Francis of Sales. There are no traces of such a work in Menard's library. It must have been a jest of our friend, misunderstood by the lady.
2 I also had the secondary intention of sketching a personal portrait of Pierre Menard. But how could I dare to compete with the golden pages which, I am told, the Baroness de Bacourt is preparing or with the delicate and punctual pencil of Carolus Hourcade?
3 I remember his quadricular notebooks, his black crossed-out passages, his peculiar typographical symbols and his insect-like handwriting. In the afternoons he liked to go out for a walk around the outskirts of Nîmes; he would take a notebook with him and make a merry bonfire.

Literary Works as Types

Richard Wollheim

4

Let us begin with the hypothesis that works of art are physical objects. I shall call this for the sake of brevity the "physical-object hypothesis". Such a hypothesis is a natural starting point: if only for the reason that it is plausible to assume that things are physical objects unless they obviously aren't. Certain things very obviously aren't physical objects. Now though it may not be obvious that works of art are physical objects, they don't seem to belong among these other things. They don't, that is, immediately group themselves along with thoughts, or periods of history, or numbers, or mirages. Furthermore, and more substantively, this hypothesis accords with many traditional conceptions of Art and its objects and what they are. [...]

6

That there is a physical object that can be identified as *Ulysses* or *Der Rosenkavalier* is not a view that can long survive the demand that we should pick out or point to that object. There is, of course, the copy of *Ulysses* that is on my table before me now, there is the performance of *Der Rosenkavalier* that I will go to tonight, and both these two things may (with some latitude, it is true, in the case of the performance) be regarded as physical objects.

Furthermore, a common way of referring to these objects is by saying things like "*Ulysses* is on my table". "I shall see *Rosenkavalier* tonight": from which it would be tempting (but erroneous) to conclude that *Ulysses* just is my copy of it, *Rosenkavalier* just is tonight's performance.

Tempting, but erroneous; and there are a number of very succinct ways of bringing out the error involved. For instance, it would follow that if I lost my copy of *Ulysses*, *Ulysses* would become a lost work. Again, it would follow that if the critics disliked tonight's performance of *Rosenkavalier*, then they dislike *Rosenkavalier*. Clearly neither of these inferences is acceptable.

We have here two locutions or ways of describing the facts: one in terms of works of art, the other in terms of copies, performances, etc. of works of art. Just because there are contexts in which these two locutions are interchangeable, this does not mean that there are no contexts, moreover no contexts of a substantive kind, in which they are not interchangeable. There very evidently are such contexts, and the physical-object hypothesis would seem to overlook them to its utter detriment.

7

But, it might now be maintained, of course it is absurd to identify *Ulysses* with my copy of it or *Der*

From *Art and its Objects*, 2nd edn. (Cambridge: Cambridge University Press, 1980), sections 4, 6–8, 35–7. Reprinted by permission of the publisher and author.

Rosenkavalier with tonight's performance, but nothing follows from this of a general character about the wrongness of identifying works of art with physical objects. For what was wrong in these two cases was the actual physical object that was picked out and with which the identification was then made. The validity of the physical-object hypothesis, like that of any other hypothesis, is quite unaffected by the consequences of misapplying it.

For instance, it is obviously wrong to say that *Ulysses* is my copy of it. Nevertheless, there is a physical object, of precisely the same order of being as my copy, though significantly not called a "copy", with which such an identification would be quite correct. This object is the author's manuscript: that, in other words, which Joyce wrote when he wrote *Ulysses*.

On the intimate connexion, which undoubtedly does exist, between a novel or a poem on the one hand and the author's manuscript on the other, I shall have something to add later. But the connexion does not justify us in asserting that one just is the other. Indeed, to do so seems open to objections not all that dissimilar from those we have just been considering. The critic, for instance, who admires *Ulysses* does not necessarily admire the manuscript. Nor is the critic who has seen or handled the manuscript in a privileged position as such when it comes to judgement on the novel. And – here we have come to an objection directly parallel to that which seemed fatal to identifying *Ulysses* with my copy of it – it would be possible for the manuscript to be lost and *Ulysses* to survive. None of this can be admitted by the person who thinks that *Ulysses* and the manuscript are one and the same thing.

To this last objection someone might retort that there are cases (e.g., *Love's Labour Won*, Kleist's *Robert Guiscard*) where the manuscript is lost and the work is lost, and moreover the work is lost because the manuscript is lost. Of course there is no real argument here, since nothing more is claimed than that there are *some* cases like this. Nevertheless the retort is worth pursuing, for the significance of such cases is precisely the opposite of that intended. Instead of reinforcing, they actually diminish the status of the manuscript. For if we now ask, When is the work lost when the manuscript is lost?, the answer is, When and only when the manuscript is unique: but then this would be true for any copy of the work were it unique. [...]

8

A final and desperate expedient to save the physical-object hypothesis is to suggest that all those works of art which cannot plausibly be identified with physical objects are identical with classes of such objects. A novel, of which there are copies, is not my or your copy but is the class of all its copies. An opera, of which there are performances, is not tonight's or last night's performance, nor even the ideal performance, but is the class of all its performances. (Of course, strictly speaking, this suggestion doesn't save the hypothesis at all: since a class of physical objects isn't necessarily, indeed is most unlikely to be, a physical object itself. But it saves something like the spirit of the hypothesis.)

However, it is not difficult to think of objections to this suggestion. Ordinarily we conceive of a novelist as writing a novel, or a composer as finishing an opera. But both these ideas imply some moment in time at which the work is complete. Now suppose (which is not unlikely) that the copies of a novel or the performances of an opera go on being produced for an indefinite period: then, on the present suggestion, there is no such moment, let alone one in their creator's lifetime. So we cannot say that *Ulysses* was written by Joyce, or that Strauss composed *Der Rosenkavalier*. Or, again, there is the problem of the unperformed symphony, or the poem of which there is not even a manuscript: in what sense can we now say that these things even *exist*?

But perhaps a more serious, certainly a more interesting, objection is that in this suggestion what is totally unexplained is why the various copies of *Ulysses* are all said to be copies of *Ulysses* and nothing else, why all the performances of *Der Rosenkavalier* are reckoned performances of that one opera. For the ordinary explanation of how we come to group copies or performances as being of this book or of that opera is by reference to something else, something other than themselves, to which they stand in some special relation. (Exactly what this other thing is, or what is the special relation in which they stand to it is, of course, something we are as yet totally unable to say.) But the effect, indeed precisely the point, of the present suggestion is to eliminate the possibility of any such reference: if a novel or opera just is its copies or its performances, then we cannot, for purposes of identification, refer from the latter to the former.

The possibility that remains is that the various particular objects, the copies or performances, are grouped as they are, not by reference to some other thing to which they are related, but in virtue of some relation that holds between them: more specifically, in virtue of resemblance.

But, in the first place, all copies of *Ulysses*, and certainly all performances of *Der Rosenkavalier*, are not perfect matches. And if it is now said that the differences do not matter, either because the various copies or performances resemble each other in all relevant respects, or because they resemble each other more than they resemble the copies or performances of any other novel or opera, neither answer is adequate. The first answer begs the issue, in that to talk of relevant respects presupposes that we know how, say, copies of *Ulysses* are grouped together: the second answer evades the issue, in that though it may tell us why we do not, say, reckon any of the performances of *Der Rosenkavalier* as performances of *Arabella*, it gives us no indication why we do not set some of them up separately, as performances of some third opera.

Secondly, it seems strange to refer to the resemblance between the copies of *Ulysses* or the performances of *Rosenkavalier* as though this were a brute fact: a fact, moreover, which could be used to explain why they were copies or performances of what they are. It would be more natural to think of this so-called "fact" as something that itself stood in need of explanation: and, moreover, as finding its explanation in just that which it is here invoked to explain. In other words, to say that certain copies or performances are of *Ulysses* or *Rosenkavalier* because they resemble one another seems precisely to reverse the natural order of thought: the resemblance, we would think, follows from, or is to be understood in terms of, the fact that they are of the same novel or opera. [. . .]

35

. . . Once it is conceded that certain works of art are not physical *objects*, the subsequent problem that arises, which can be put by asking. What sort of thing are they?, is essentially a logical problem. It is that of determining the criteria of identity and individuation appropriate to, say, a piece of music or a novel. I shall characterize the status of such things by saying that they are (to employ a term introduced by Peirce) *types*. Correlative to the term "type" is the term "token". Those physical

objects which (as we have seen) can out of desperation be thought to be works of art in cases where there are no physical objects that can plausibly be thought of in this way, are *tokens*. In other words, *Ulysses* and *Der Rosenkavalier* are types, my copy of *Ulysses* and tonight's performance of *Rosenkavalier* are tokens of those types. The question now arises, What is a type?

The question is very difficult, and unfortunately, to treat it with the care and attention to detail that it deserves is beyond the scope of this essay.

We might begin by contrasting a type with other sorts of thing that it is not. Most obviously we could contrast a type with a *particular*: this I shall take as done. Then we could contrast it with other various kinds of non-particulars: with a *class* (of which we say that it has *members*), and a *universal* (of which we say that it has *instances*). An example of a class would be the class of red things: an example of a universal would be redness: and examples of a type would be the word "red" and the Red Flag – where this latter phrase is taken to mean not this or that piece of material, kept in a chest or taken out and flown at a masthead, but the flag of revolution, raised for the first time in 1830 and that which many would willingly follow to their death.

Let us introduce as a blanket expression for types, classes, universals, the term *generic entity*, and, as a blanket expression for those things which fall under them, the term *element*. Now we can say that the various generic entities can be distinguished according to the different ways or relationships in which they stand to their elements. These relationships can be arranged on a scale of intimacy or intrinsicality. At one end of the scale we find classes, where the relationship is at its most external or extrinsic: for a class is merely made of, or constituted by, its members which are extensionally conjoined to form it. The class of red things is simply a construct out of all those things which are (timelessly) red. In the case of universals the relation is more intimate: in that a universal is present in all its instances. Redness is in all red things. With types we find the relationship between the generic entity and its elements at its most intimate: for not merely is the type present in all its tokens like the universal in all its instances, but for much of the time we think and talk of the type as though it were itself a kind of token, though a peculiarly important or pre-eminent one. In many ways we treat the Red

Flag as though it were a red flag (cf. "We'll keep the Red Flag flying high").

These varying relations in which the different generic entities stand to their elements are also reflected (if, that is, this is *another* fact) in the degree to which both the generic entities and their elements can satisfy the same predicates. Here we need to make a distinction between sharing properties and properties being transmitted. I shall say that when A and B are both *f*, *f* is shared by A and B. I shall further say that when A is *f* because B is *f*, or B is *f* because A is *f*, *f* is transmitted between A and B. (I shall ignore the sense or direction of the transmission, i.e. I shall not trouble, even where it is possible, to discriminate between the two sorts of situation I have mentioned as instances of transmission.)

First, we must obviously exclude from consideration properties that can pertain only to tokens (e.g. properties of location in space and time) and equally those which pertain only to types (e.g. "was invented by"). When we have done this, the situation looks roughly as follows: Classes can share properties with their members (e.g. the class of big things is big), but this is very rare: moreover, where it occurs it will be a purely contingent or fortuitous affair, i.e. there will be no transmitted properties. In the cases of both universals and types, there will be shared properties. Red things may be said to be exhilarating, and so also redness. Every red flag is rectangular, and so is the Red Flag itself. Moreover, many, if not all, of the shared properties will be transmitted.

Let us now confine our attention to transmitted properties because it is only they which are relevant to the difference in relationship between, on the one hand, universals and types and, on the other hand, their elements. Now there would seem to be two differences in respect of transmitted properties which distinguish universals from types. In the first place, there is likely to be a far larger range of transmitted properties in the case of types than there is with universals. The second difference is this: that in the case of universals no property that an instance of a certain universal has necessarily, i.e. that it has in virtue of being an instance of that universal, can be transmitted to the universal. In the case of types, on the other hand, all and only those properties that a token of a certain type has necessarily, i.e. that it has in virtue of being a token of that type, will be transmitted to the type. Examples would be: Redness, as we have seen, may be exhilarating, and, if it is, it is so for

the same reason that its instances are, i.e. the property is transmitted. But redness cannot be red or coloured, which its instances are necessarily. On the other hand, the Union Jack is coloured and rectangular, properties which all its tokens have necessarily: but even if all its tokens happened to be made of linen, this would not mean that the Union Jack itself was made of linen.

To this somewhat negative account of a type – concentrated largely on what a type is not – we now need to append something of a more positive kind, which would say what it is for various particulars to be gathered together as tokens of the same type. For it will be appreciated that there corresponds to every universal and to every type a class: to redness the class of red things, to the Red Flag the class of red flags. But the converse is not true. The question therefore arises. What are the characteristic circumstances in which we postulate a type? The question, we must appreciate, is entirely conceptual: it is a question about the structure of our language.

A very important set of circumstances in which we postulate types – perhaps a central set, in the sense that it may be possible to explain the remaining circumstances by reference to them – is where we can correlate a class of particulars with a piece of human invention: these particulars may then be regarded as tokens of a certain type. This characterization is vague, and deliberately so: for it is intended to comprehend a considerable spectrum of cases. At one end we have the case where a particular is produced, and is then copied: at the other end, we have the case where a set of instructions is drawn up which, if followed, give rise to an indefinite number of particulars. An example of the former would be the Brigitte Bardot looks: an example of the latter would be the Minuet. Intervening cases are constituted by the production of a particular which was made in order to be copied, e.g. the Boeing 707, or the construction of a mould or matrix which generates further particulars, e.g. the Penny Black. There are many ways of arranging the cases – according, say, to the degree of human intention that enters into the proliferation of the type, or according to the degree of match that exists between the original piece of invention and the tokens that flow from it. But there are certain resemblances between all the cases: and with ingenuity one can see a natural extension of the original characterization to cover cases where the invention is more classificatory than constructive in nature, e.g. the Red Admiral.

36

It will be clear that the preceding characterization of a type and its tokens offers us a framework within which we can (at any rate roughly) understand the logical status of things like operas, ballets, poems, etchings, etc.: that is to say, account for their principles of identity and individuation. To show exactly where these various kinds of things lie within this framework would involve a great deal of detailed analysis, more than can be attempted here, and probably of little intrinsic interest. I shall touch very briefly upon two general sets of problems, both of which concern the feasibility of the project. In this section I shall deal with the question of how the type is identified or (what is much the same thing) how the tokens of a given type are generated. In the next section I shall deal with the question of what properties we are entitled to ascribe to a type. These two sets of questions are not entirely distinct: as we can see from the fact that there is a third set of questions intermediate between the other two, concerning how we determine whether two particulars are or are not tokens of the same type. These latter questions, which arise for instance sharply in connexion with translation, I shall pass over. I mention them solely to place those which I shall deal with in perspective.

First, then, as to how the type is identified. In the case of any work of art that it is plausible to think of as a type, there is what I have called a piece of human invention: and these pieces of invention fall along the whole spectrum of cases as I characterized it. At one end of the scale, there is the case of a poem, which comes into being when certain words are set down on paper or perhaps, earlier still, when they are said over in the poet's head (cf. the Croce–Collingwood theory). At the other end of the scale is an opera which comes into being when a certain set of instructions, i.e. the score, is written down, in accordance with which performances can be produced. As an intervening case we might note a film, of which different copies are made: or an etching or engraving, where different sheets are pulled from the same matrix, i.e. the plate.

There is little difficulty in all this, so long as we bear in mind from the beginning the variety of ways in which the different types can be identified, or (to put it another way) in which the tokens can be generated from the initial piece of invention. It

is if we begin with too limited a range of examples that distortions can occur. For instance, it might be argued that, if the tokens of a certain poem are the many different inscriptions that occur in books reproducing the word order of the poet's manuscript, then "strictly speaking" the tokens of an opera must be the various pieces of sheet music or printed scores that reproduce the marks on the composer's holograph. Alternatively, if we insist that it is the performances of the opera that are the tokens, then, it is argued, it must be the many readings or "voicings" of the poem that are *its* tokens.

Such arguments might seem to be unduly barren or pedantic, if it were not that they revealed something about the divergent media of art: moreover, if they did not bear upon the issues to be discussed in the next section.

37

It is, we have seen, a feature of types and their tokens, not merely that they may share properties, but that when they do, these properties may be transmitted. The question we have now to ask is whether a limit can be set upon the properties that may be transmitted: more specifically, since it is the type that is the work of art and therefore that with which we are expressly concerned, whether there are any properties – always of course excluding those properties which can be predicated only of particulars – that belong to tokens and cannot be said *ipso facto* to belong to their types.

It might be thought that we have an answer, or at least a partial answer, to this question in the suggestion already made, that the properties transmitted between token and type are only those which the tokens possess necessarily. But a moment's reflection will show that any answer along these lines is bound to be trivial. For there is no way of determining the properties that a token of a given type has necessarily, independently of determining the properties of that type: accordingly, we cannot use the former in order to ascertain the latter. We cannot hope to discover what the properties of the Red Flag are by finding out what properties the various red flags have necessarily: for how can we come to know that, e.g. this red flag is necessarily red, prior to knowing that the Red Flag itself is red?

There are, however, three observations that can be made here on the basis of our most general intuitions. The first is that there are no properties or sets of properties that cannot pass from token to type. With the usual reservations, there is nothing that can be predicated of a performance of a piece of music that could not also be predicated of that piece of music itself. This point is vital. For it is this that ensures what I have called the harmlessness of denying the physical-object hypothesis in the domain of those arts where the denial consists in saying that works of art are not physical *objects*. For though they may not be objects but types, this does not prevent them from having physical properties. There is nothing that prevents us from saying that Donne's *Satires* are harsh on the ear, or that Dürer's engraving of St Anthony has a very differentiated texture, or that the conclusion of "Celeste Aida" is *pianissimo*.

The second observation is that, though any single property may be transmitted from token to type, it does not follow that all will be: or to put it another way, a token will have some of its properties necessarily, but it need not have all of them necessarily. The full significance of this point will emerge later.

Thirdly, in the case of *some* arts it is necessary that not all properties should be transmitted from token to type: though it remains true that for any single property it might be transmitted. The reference here is, of course, to the performing arts – to operas, plays, symphonies, ballet. It follows from what was said above that anything that can be predicated of a performance of a piece of music can also be predicated of the piece of music itself: to this we must now add that not every property that can be predicated of the former *ipso facto* belongs to the latter. This point is generally covered by saying that in such cases there is essentially an element of *interpretation*, where for these purposes interpretation may be regarded as the production of a token that has properties in excess of those of the type.

Literature

J. O. Urmson

I wish, in this essay, to raise and suggest answers to two questions about literature. First is the question of the ontological status of a literary work – the question what sort of thing is a poem, a novel, a history. Second is whether or not, when we read a literary work, it is analogous to anything that anybody does in relation to other major arts forms. To pursue these questions I must first make some remarks about these other major art forms, excluding literature, for, since my problem is about what seems, at first sight, to be anomalous features of literature, I must indicate what I take to be normality.

Leaving literature, for the present then, I think that most of the major art forms, in their most common manifestations in Western culture, can be divided into two groups. The reader is asked to note that this is a historical generalization, not a statement of logical or conceptual necessities. First there is the group, which includes painting and sculpture, where the creative artist himself normally fashions the object which is the work of art. We are all, no doubt, aware of imaginative fantasies to the contrary, such as Collingwood's view that all art works are in some way mental, but I assume in this paper that such an art work as a painting or a sculpture is a physical object which can be stolen, or defaced, or stored in a bank and can need to be preserved and restored. This is the common sense view which can be rejected only at the expense of conceptual innovation. Thus it is the work of art as both conceived and made by its creator that spectators typically contemplate in the case of such arts as painting and sculpture. This is no doubt an oversimplified story. There may, for example, be foundry workers involved in the production of a bronze statue, but rightly or wrongly we think of them as living tools of the sculptor, with whom, from beginning to end, all artistic decisions rest.

Then a second group of arts exists, including music, theater, ballet, and opera in their standard forms, in which the audience or spectators do not witness, without any intermediaries, the work made by the creative artist. There is a need for executant artists, with a serious aesthetic role as interpreters. We see and listen to dancers, instrumentalists, and actors, not to choreographers, composers, and playwrights. That the creative artist may from time to time be his own interpreter in performance does not in any way invalidate this distinction.

Now it is only in the case of the performing arts that serious doubts about the identity of the work of art arises, at least at the common sense level. It requires philosophical sophistication even to understand the suggestion that the *Mona Lisa* is not something that usually can be found hanging

From George Dickie and R. J. Sclafani (eds.), *Aesthetics: A Critical Anthology* (New York: St Martin's Press, 1977), pp. 334–41. Copyright © 1977 by Bedford/St Martin's. Reprinted by permission of Bedford/St Martin's.

on a wall of the Louvre. But the case is quite different with regard to the performing arts. It is plain common sense to see that a symphony, a ballet, or a play cannot be simply identified with any physical object, such as a book or manuscript, or with any event, such as a performance. We can, indeed, speak of hearing Beethoven's Fifth Symphony, as we can speak of seeing Michaelangelo's *David*, but, if we hear the Fifth Symphony, it is equally correct to say that we hear a performance of it, whereas there is nothing even analogous to a performance of the *David* that we could witness.

I have argued in a paper entitled "The Performing Arts" (in *Contemporary British Philosophy*, 4) that the best account to give of the contribution of the creative artist in the case of those arts, or works of art, which require also a performer or executant is that he provides a recipe or set of performing instructions for the executant-artist. A similar opinion has, of course, been put forward by others. Thus, when Beethoven composed the Fifth Symphony, he thought out and wrote down a set of instructions for an orchestra. Similarly, the playwright provides a set of instructions for the actors and the creator of a ballet a set of instructions for the dancers. This view seems more plausible than others that are current. Thus, to say that a musical work is a class of performances requires one to say that the composer created such a class – a view which becomes especially uncomfortable if we consider an unperformed work. The suggestion of Wollheim and others that the creative artist creates a type, and Stevenson's view that he creates a megatype, also cause discomfort. It is hard to see how there can be a type or a megatype before there are any tokens.

What may be called a set of performing instructions in the case of temporal arts such as music and ballet, where what the audience witnesses is a set of events that take time, is more naturally called a recipe in the case of such nontemporal arts as require an executant artist. Such nontemporal arts as painting and sculpture, which typically require no artist beyond the creator, comprise works which, as we have seen, are physical objects. Such art works take time to make, and we may spend time contemplating them, but they do not themselves take time. But, if we may consider cooking as an art, it is one which requires an executant artist, the cook, who may be, but need not be, the creator of the recipe he follows. The pecan pie or the hamburger has a status problematic in the same way as that of a symphony or

ballet. In my view, to create *the* pecan pie is to provide a recipe which, if followed by the executant cook, will result in *a* pecan pie.

So I say that a creative artist may do one of two things. He may himself produce the work of art which the spectator witnesses and which will be a physical object, or he may produce a set of instructions for execution by others. It is rather obvious why, if one wishes to have permanent works of art in the temporal arts, such as music, the creative artist should produce only a set of instructions. There do not have to be permanent works of music; one could have a music which consisted entirely of free improvisation and in which there were no permanent works. It would also be theoretically possible to devise a painting notation so that a creative artist could give a set of instructions for executant painters to follow and produce a set of equally valid interpretations of the painting, analogous to musical performances. It is not difficult to see why we in fact do not do this, except in the case of some rudimentary children's painting games. I have neither claimed that any art form must include performing artists as well as creators nor claimed that any art form cannot do so. I merely observe that the standard classics of painting and sculpture conform to one type and that the standard classics of music, theater, and ballet to the other, and I note that one can see good practical reasons why, with traditional techniques, highly organized art works do fall into these two categories. One would not wish to hear a group improvisation of an opera.

Not all arts fit readily into this twofold classification, more particularly not all applied arts, as is clear from the case of architecture. It is quite interesting to consider such cases, though I do not think that they raise very serious philosophical problems. I think it is largely a matter of loose fit to accounts produced for the paradigm cases. There are also novel variations within the arts discussed: What, for example, are we to say of musical composition directly onto tape in an electronic laboratory, and will the account of live theater readily cover the cinematograph? Still, it is not our present task to examine these problems, but to ask whether or not we can give an adequate account of literature in the light of the characterization of the other arts put forward in this paper.

We have distinguished two categories of works of art. First, there are those directly created by the creative artist when there is no executant artist and the identity of the work is unproblematic; second, there are those where the creative artist produces a recipe or set of instructions for performing or for executant artists and where the identity of the work of art is problematic. Now literature appears, at least at first sight, to be anomalous with respect to this classification. On the one hand, there seem to be no executant artists or performers here: who could such artists be? When one, say, reads a novel to oneself, there seems to be only oneself and the novelist involved. Is the reader in fact the executant artist with himself as audience as the pianist who can play to himself as audience and the dancer who can dance for his own satisfaction? But I do not seem to myself to be exhibiting any technical or interpretative skills when I read to myself, and there are other grave objections to this suggestion which we must notice later. Yet, if there is no performing or executant artist, how can I myself be the audience or spectator?

On the other hand, we cannot readily assimilate literature to sculpture and painting. For one thing, the identity of the novel or other literary work seems to be problematic in the same way as that of the musical balletic or theatrical work. In the case of these other arts, we have attempted to explain their problematic status in terms of a recipe or set of instructions for executant artists. But, how can the literary work be a set of instructions for executant artists if there are none such?

So literature seems to be a counterexample to my theory, for, if the theory will not work when applied to literature, that certainly casts doubt upon its acceptability. We surely need a theory which will account equally for all cases in which the identity of the work of art is problematic, for it would be an act of desperation to claim that the status of, say, *Pride and Prejudice* was radically different from that of the *Sleeping Beauty* ballet or Beethoven's Fifth Symphony.

That then is my problem. For those who find my view of the other arts unacceptable, in any case the problem does not exist in the specific form in which I see it, but there will still be the old traditional problem of the identity of a literary work.

Now I am not sure how this problem is to be answered, but I am going to suggest an answer in accordance with my general theory. I am going to suggest that, contrary to first appearances, literature is in principle a performing art.

If we are to make this claim, the most natural thing is first to revive the view that, in reading a literary work to oneself, one is simultaneously performer and audience, just as when one plays a piece of music to oneself. I have already raised the objection to this view that one does not seem to oneself, when so reading, to be utilizing any technical or interpretative skills, but this appeal to subjective feelings is, no doubt, of little weight, so we must notice a more serious objection to it.

If we consider a musical score as a set of instructions to the performer, then, for example, the musical notation of the first bar of the first violin's line in the score of Beethoven's Fifth Symphony must be regarded as a shorthand instruction to the players to play three consecutive G naturals, each a quarter of the total time of a bar, the total duration of which is indicated by the metronome mark at the top of the page. Similarly, if in his script an actor reads

> Tom (*looking out of the window*): It is beginning to rain.

He will, if he is playing the part of Tom, take it as an instruction to look out of the window of the stage set and say "It is beginning to rain." Thus we can distinguish quite clearly the performer's reading of the instructions from his action in accordance with them, and it is in his act of complying with the instructions, not the reading of them, that he shows his technical and interpretative skill. That I can read and understand the instruction to the violinist just as well as he can gives me neither his skill nor his interpretative insight.

But, in the case of the solitary novel reader, the situation is not similar. Not only do we have to make him simultaneously performer and audience, we have to collapse into one act his reading of the instructions and his compliance with them. This explains one's initial uneasiness at the suggestion and is surely too implausible in itself. This horse will not run.

If we are to separate the reading of instructions from the act of complying with them, we must claim, I think, that literature is essentially an oral act. Moreover, this move is not made simply in an attempt to save a theory, for with regard to some literature it has an immediate plausibility. If we consider such a work as the *Iliad*, there is good reason to believe that before writing was known to the Greeks there were bards who had learned the poem by heart and who went around giving performances of it, or of excerpts from it. They, the performers, were taught it orally, that is, by example, just as performers in other arts may still be taught their parts other than by studying the score. It is not implausible to think of the *Iliad* as having been written down, probably in the seventh century B.C., as a set of instructions, as a score, for bards. It is fairly certain that Herodotus wrote his *Histories* as a score and that people first got to know them by hearing public performances. No doubt the first performances, *epideixis*, as the Greeks called them, were given by Herodotus himself, but the distinction of creator and performer is not obliterated by the same man's undertaking both roles. Further, in cultures less generously supplied with printing presses than we are, the tradition of purely oral poetry still survives.

It is clear also that even in Western civilization many poets today think of poetry as essentially an oral art; poetry for them is essentially something to be listened to, and so a performer is required. If you now read it aloud to yourself, attempting to equal the skills of the professional poetry reader, this, rather than silent novel reading, would be like playing the piano to oneself as a performance. Also, we must not forget that Dickens gave readings from his novels in public and that reading aloud within the family group is an activity once common and not yet dead.

But this account will certainly not cover the bulk of modern literature. If much ancient and some modern literature was designed by its creators primarily to be heard, the written word being primarily a score for the performer, this is certainly not true of the great bulk of modern literature. While much of the best literature of all ages can with advantage be read aloud, it is more than doubtful that Dickens's novels, let alone *The Decline and Fall of the Roman Empire*, were ever intended primarily for oral performance.

Faced with this difficulty, let us go back to the case of music. Music is essentially sound; the performer produces sounds in accordance with the instructions of the composer. But there is such a thing as the skill of silent score reading, a skill which some very proficient performers have only to a slight extent. But a reasonably musical person can, after instruction and practice, look at a simple melodic line in a score and recognize what it would sound like if it were performed; he knows what musical sounds would be heard if the instructions were obeyed. Very gifted musicians, after elaborate training, can acquire the same facility in reading complex scores with transposed parts, unusual clefs, and the like. Musical score reading of

this kind is neither original creation nor performance, the two factors we originally considered, nor even the sort of reading required of the performer. It is the reading of a recipe or set of instructions with the ability to recognize what would result from following them. I am reliably informed that experienced cooks may acquire the same skill; they may be able to read the recipe and recognize what the confection would taste like.

It would be implausible to say that musical score readers are giving a performance to themselves or that readers of cookery recipes are preparing a private and immaterial feast. Apart from the fact that they need hear no sound (they may or may not hum to themselves), considered, absurdly, as performances, what the best score readers normally do would be intolerably bad. They habitually read through the slower bits far faster than they perfectly well know that the music should go, and, for many reasons, nobody can read a fast complex piece at a speed that he recognizes to be that of the music. Score reading is something quite distinct from composition or performance. The music critic, Ernest Newman, who went blind in old age, expressed the wish that he had become deaf instead, since he preferred to read a score and imagine an ideal performance than to hear what he usually heard. And some music is probably intended primarily for score readers. Some of the puzzle canons at the beginning of Bach's *Musical Offering* were surely intended primarily for the score reader, and it has been known for composers to attempt to make the notes they wrote visual representations of the cross or some other symbol.

Now I suggest that learning to read an ordinary language is like learning to read a score silently to oneself. It is probably easier, and more of us get a thorough training in it and, consequently, mastery of it. There is therefore a large potential market of verbal score readers.

My claim is that the vast literature primarily intended for private reading in silence should be regarded as analogous to a set of musical scores intended primarily for score reading rather than for performance. So reading *Hamlet* to oneself will not be so unlike reading *War and Peace*. But, whereas the text of *Hamlet* was certainly primarily a score or set of instructions for actors and, thus, like a normal musical score, *War and Peace*, like some vast poetic dramas, is left to the score reader. Reading the text of *Hamlet* is surely not a performance, yet it is equally surely not very unlike reading the text of *War and Peace*.

So my claim is that literature is in logical character a performing art, but one in which in practice we frequently, though far from invariably, confine ourselves to score reading. We read to find out how the performance will go and are then content. This view is, I believe, somewhat confirmed by some of the critical remarks we make about literary style. Even in the case of works which would not normally be read aloud it is a commonplace to speak of assonance, dissonance, sonority, rhythm; we reject as unstylish conjunctions of consonants which would be awkward to say aloud, though we easily read them. We criticize the writing in terms of how it would sound, if it were spoken. Contrast the case of logical notation which is not literature and for which we have only a makeshift oral rendering: who would think of criticizing a piece of writing in formal logic as unstylish because our conventional oral reading of it was awkward in sound?

It is certainly not the case that all literature can be covered without remainder by this account. Sometimes its character as written is important, and not merely in the way that we prefer elegantly printed literature as we like elegantly printed musical scores. The poems of E. E. Cummings are a very clear case. Again, it is essential that Lewis Carroll's mouse's tale should be printed in the shape of a mouse's tail in the way it regularly is unless we are to miss a pun which could not be brought out orally. At a level of, no doubt, very lightweight literary art, but still literary art, we have such poems as

> While cycling downhill Lord Fermanagh
> Broke his bike, and he hadn't a spanagh,
> But the pieces Lord Crichton
> Was able to tichton
> In quite a professional managh.

Whatever interest this jingle has, the aberrational spelling no doubt is an important part of it.

I cannot account for these cases within my theory, but I do not think they need disturb me, any more than that the notation of Schumann's music is full of cryptograms that need to be accounted for in a general discussion of music and its notation. I think that the simple fact is that the notation of a piece of music may also be a code, that a jingle with audible rhyme may be written in a way which is a jest about English spelling, and that, in the case of E. E. Cummings, typography may be used, rather like dynamic marks in a musical score, as a hint to a correct reading.

So I can now formally give answers to the two questions with which I started. I resolve the problem of the ontological status of a literary work by saying that for a literary work to exist it is a necessary and sufficient condition that a set of instructions should exist such that any oral performance which complies with that set of instructions is a performance of the work in question. I resolve the problem of the relation of reading a literary work to what we find in other art forms by saying that is analogous to reading the score of a musical work, of a play, or of a ballet. In each of these cases we neither create the work nor perform the work when we read the score, but we become aware of what we would witness if we were to witness a performance.

That there are other questions about literature than those I have attempted to answer is obvious. That one can find problems about my answers is also obvious. It is possible to write at length about the notion of compliance with a set of instructions of which I have made unelucidated use. But one thing at a time is usually enough, so attempting even a sketch of answers to two questions is, for me, sufficiently ambitious.

Interpretation and Identity: Can the Work Survive the World?

Nelson Goodman and Catherine Elgin

However the work is identified, this much is clear: the various interpretations in question are interpretations of a single text. And that text can be identified syntactically, without appealing to any of the semantic or literary interpretations it bears. But there is no way to individuate a world except by means of a version; hence no way to identify a common subject to which conflicting versions refer.[1] We can make sense of the claim that conflicting interpretations concern the same text, but not of the claim that conflicting versions concern the same world. But the question remains: Is a work to be identified with the text or with an interpretation of it? Is *Ulysses* its text or are there as many works as right interpretations of that text?

The question need not bother us if there is only one right interpretation of any text; for then the work can be identified indifferently with the text or with the right interpretation – there is just the one text, the one right interpretation, the one work. That a text has a single right interpretation that is determined by and entirely in accord with the author's intentions has been, and perhaps still is, like absolute realism, the most popular view. But like absolute realism, it is untenable. Even where an author's intentions are to some extent discoverable, they do not determine correctness of interpretation; for the significance of a work often diverges from, and may transcend or fall short of, what the author had in mind. Where information about the author's intentions is available, it may suggest interpretations of his work. But the importance of such information varies from one work to the next. For works do not always realize their authors' intentions. And even when they do, the realization of those intentions is not always central to the effectiveness or even the identity of a literary work. Understanding a work may be quite different from understanding what the author intended by it.

Whether or not the author's intention yields an interpretation, it certainly does not yield *the* interpretation of a text. For literary texts are susceptible to multiple interpretations. Multiplicity of meaning, subtle and complex ambiguity, is frequently a positive and vital feature of literary, as opposed to scientific, discourse. We disparage *Ulysses*, or even "Ozymandias", if we suppose that it can be correctly construed in just one way.

Thus we are back to the question whether the work is to be identified with the text or with a right interpretation. If the latter, then *Ulysses* becomes many different works, with the interpreter at least as responsible for the work as the author is. The passionate pluralist and resolute relativist may welcome this, arguing that opposing interpretations can no more hold for the same work than opposing

From *Critical Inquiry* 12 (1986), pp. 567–74. Reprinted by permission of the University of Chicago Press and Catherine Elgin.

versions can hold for the same world, and that dissolution of the work into works is hardly shocking after the dissolution of the world into worlds.

But here there is cause for pause. First, the analogy between works and worlds neglects an important difference we have already noted: that while conflicting versions cannot describe the same world, conflicting interpretations may interpret the same text. The text, unlike the world, does not dissolve under opposing accounts. Moreover, no matter where the identity of a literary work is located, disagreement among interpretations differs significantly from disagreement among versions. Opposing interpretations concern a single text, whereas opposing versions have no common ground. Accordingly, nothing is gained by assigning conflicting interpretations to different works as we assign conflicting versions to different worlds. For the question of how correct but conflicting interpretations can concern a single text is no less problematic than the question of how they can concern a single work.

Second, if each right interpretation counts as a distinct work, what makes the difference between interpretations that, in ordinary parlance, are of the same work and interpretations that are of different works? Does what we call an interpretation of *Ulysses* no more belong to the same work as another interpretation of *Ulysses* than to the same work as an interpretation of "Ozymandias"? That the first two are interpretations of the same text makes the difference.

Third, much of the rich multiplicity of meaning that is characteristic of many literary works seems to be not in any single interpretation, but in the very multiplicity of right interpretations, and this feature is not captured if each interpretation is taken to constitute a separate work. But can we perhaps consider the work to be the collection of all right interpretations of the text? In that case, works and texts will be correlated one-to-one, and the work can alternatively be identified with the text. Moreover, since the collection of right interpretations of a text may be countless and ever-growing, we cannot identify the work by identifying the entire collection, but only by identifying the text. The text, unlike "the world" which vanishes behind our various versions, is at least as palpable and accessible as any interpretation. Diverse interpretations are grouped together by the text they interpret; and that text remains impervious to contentions among and changes in them.

But can the text actually bear the weight? What is a text? Are texts always readily distinguishable and identifiable? And is there always just one work for each text and one text for each work?

The question whether there may be more than one text for a single work is acutely raised by translations. If a translation from English into French preserves work-identity, then that work has more than one text. Obviously no translation retains all that is significant in the original. Even if the two are coextensive, reporting exactly the same events in as closely as possible the same way, they will differ somewhat in meaning. For their secondary extensions – the extensions of compounds of the texts and of parallel parts of them[2] – will not be the same. Moreover, they will inevitably differ, usually appreciably, in what they exemplify and express.[3] Indeed, the translator of a poem typically has to decide the relative importance of preserving denotation (what the poem says), exemplification (what rhythmic, melodic, and other formal properties it shows forth), and expression (what feelings and other metaphorical properties it conveys).

In view of this, shall we consider even the best translations of a given work to be different works? Not too hastily; for we must bear in mind that right interpretations may differ as drastically as do good translations. We found reason to consider different interpretations to be interpretations *of* the same work, and good translations might be regarded along with right interpretations as belonging to a collection that is determined by the work. What brings them together as being *of* the work is that they translate or interpret the original text. And the identity of the work rests on this text.

Interpretations and translations are themselves works. But they are not identical with the works they interpret or translate. Neither Harry Levin's critical study, *The Question of Hamlet*, nor August von Schlegel's German translation of the play is the work *Hamlet*. They are distinct works whose texts differ from the text of *Hamlet* and whose rightness depends on (among other things) the access they afford to the play and the understanding they yield concerning it. Moreover, the texts that constitute Levin's and Schlegel's works are themselves subject to interpretation and translation.

But while there is only one text for each work, is there only one work for each text? To answer that we must first be clear about what constitutes *identity of text*. That identity is a matter pertaining solely to the syntax of a language – to the permissible configurations of letters, spaces, and punctuation marks – quite apart from what the text says or otherwise refers to.

Texts, of course, can be of any length, and for convenience we shall concentrate on very short examples. Take the word "cape". It refers ambiguously – sometimes to articles of clothing, sometimes to bodies of land. But it normally does not refer to whatever is either such an article of clothing or such a body of land. Although ambiguous, "cape" is a single word. Inscriptions that refer to land masses are spelled the same as inscriptions that refer to outerwear. Moreover, they can be combined with exactly the same additional characters to yield syntactically significant strings. In the word "cape", then, we have a single short text. Its ambiguity renders it susceptible of two correct literal interpretations.

But now consider another equally brief example: "chat". This also has two alternative applications: to conversations and to cats. This duplicity may at first glance seem no more inimical to identity of text than is the ambiguity of "cape". But this case is different; for "chat" is not even the same word in French as in English. The difference in pronunciation is not a negligible feature; for a word has as instances or replicas not only written and printed inscriptions but also spoken utterances. And French utterances of "chat" are not syntactically interchangeable with English utterances of it. "Chat" in English and in French then does not consist of just the same group of replicas or instances, even though the classes of inscriptions coincide. What is more important, "chat" functions differently in the two language schemes. It differs, for example, in the combinations it enters to make compound terms and sentences: "chat" is an English word in "some chats", but a French word in "quelques chats". It is *a different word, a different text*, in the two languages. All this is purely a matter of syntax; the distinction is independent of what the words mean or refer to. It obtains even where, as with "permission", the two words have the same reference. And it obtains even where a single inscription functions in both languages at once. A note on the bulletin board saying "chat" might remind a forgetful Frenchman to feed the cat and a reticent Englishman to be more sociable.

A text is an inscription in a language. So its identity depends on the language to which it belongs. Usually the identification of the language of a text is unproblematic. But not always. Some sequences of marks – "chat", for instance – occur in more than one language. Others occur in none.

A configuration of marks might be a design or an inscription; and if an inscription, it might belong to any of several languages. We would do well then to consider the basis for identifying inscriptions and the languages they belong to.

The intention of the producer is not decisive on this matter. The scribbles of a three-year-old are not linguistic tokens despite his intention to produce written words. An inscription of "chat" reminds Marie of her obligations as a cat owner, despite its having been penned to remind Maggie of her obligations as a hostess. And a bilingual's inscription of "permission" might be produced without any specific intention concerning the language in which it is to be understood.

Nor can the assignment of inscriptions to languages be strictly a matter of configuration, for the shapes and sizes of letters vary widely and independently of the languages in which their inscriptions occur. And as we have seen, the same configuration can occur in different languages.

Rather, marks are inscriptions in a language when they function as such. To accord a mark the status of an English inscription is then to treat it as having a certain syntactic role. Often there is only one language in which a configuration of marks can plausibly be thought to function. In some cases, though, there is more than one such language. In others, none. Since the text of *Hamlet* is unlikely to function in any other language as well as it does in English, its status as an exclusively English text seems secure. Since "chat" functions equally well in English and in French, its inscriptions might belong to either language. An inscription that serves as an English word when Maggie reads it, serves as a French one when Marie does. And since the child's scribble cannot be differentiated into permissible sequences of letters, spaces, and punctuation marks of any known language, it does not function linguistically. It is not a text. Nor is there any real problem about how inscriptions that are spelled the same, or how even a single concrete inscription, can be two different words, two different texts. For almost anything may likewise function in various ways: the same chunk of bronze may be a sculpture, a doorstop, a weapon.

Thus a case like "chat" (and in principle there is no reason why a much longer string of marks might not constitute different texts in different languages) is not a case of two works having the same text but of two works with different texts. But are there, perhaps, other cases in which we have two works with but one text?

Identical twins, having lived closely together for many years, were sent for the summer to separate but similar camps in New England. Afterward each was asked to write a brief report of his experiences. Although the twins were reporting on numerically distinct people, places, and events, their reports turned out to be exactly the same string of words. Is this a plain case of two works with the same text?

Unmistakably, we have only one text here. Unlike "chat", which functions as different texts in two different languages, this string of words is functioning in a single language. That the twins wrote down numerically distinct inscriptions and reported numerically distinct events in no way affects the identity of the text. The two inscriptions, even if in different handwritings, are replicas of each other. They consist of exactly the same syntactic elements of English in exactly the same combination. And the identity of text between them is a purely syntactic relation. But where writers and subject matters are thus completely distinct, can there be only one work, or must there be two? If two, then identity of work does not always follow upon identity of text.

Here we are in danger of being misled by decorations. The remarkable twins and the improbable coincidence of text divert our attention so that we fail to notice that this case is basically the same as that of words like "cape". The common text has two different applications or interpretations. It does not matter that in the case of the twins the two applications are those of identifiable individuals who wrote down different inscriptions of the text, while the two different applications of "cape" are anonymous; nor does it matter that the twins' case is unlikely to occur while the "cape" case happens often. In both cases, we have a single text with two interpretations. If we treat different interpretations as distinct works, we can take "cape" to be two words, and the twins to have written two reports. But then we lose the distinction between a single work with multiple interpretations and a multiplicity of works – the distinction, roughly, between *Ulysses* and the complete works of Agatha Christie. Since works with few right readings tend to be superficial, and works with many tend not to be, it seems unwise to sacrifice the basis for distinguishing between the two cases.

By now you will have recognized that the point of the twins example is much the same as that raised in a famous case devised by Borges.[4] Suppose, he says, that some centuries after Cervantes,

a certain Pierre Menard writes a novel with the same text as *Don Quixote*. Menard's novel, however, tells a different story and is even, Borges says, in a different style from Cervantes', for in Menard's time the text is archaic whereas in Cervantes' time it was not. This case is widely taken to show conclusively that a work cannot be identical with a text – that Cervantes and Menard produced separate works with the same text. We contend, however, that the supposed two works are actually one. Menard can, perhaps, be credited with two achievements: having produced a replica of the text without copying it; and having formulated or inspired a new interpretation of the work – a way of reading it as a contemporary story in an archaic style with a different plot. But neither singly nor jointly do these amount to creating a new work.

What Menard wrote is simply another inscription of the text. Any of us can do the same, as can printing presses and photocopiers. Indeed, we are told, if infinitely many monkeys were to type for an infinitely long time, one would eventually produce a replica of the text. That replica, we maintain, would be as much an instance of the work, *Don Quixote*, as Cervantes' manuscript, Menard's manuscript, and each copy of the book that ever has been or will be printed.[5] That the monkey may be supposed to have produced his copy randomly makes no difference. It is the same text and is open to all the same interpretations as the instances consciously inscribed by Cervantes, Menard, and the various unknown copyists, printers, and typesetters who produced instances of the work. Questions of the intention or intelligence of the producer of a particular inscription are irrelevant to the identity of the work. Any inscription of the text, no matter who or what produced it, bears all the same interpretations as any other.

Menard may in some way have proposed or inspired a new interpretation of the text. But no more than any other admissible interpretation offered before or since or by others, does the Menard reading count as *the* work *Don Quixote*, or even as *a* work *Don Quixote*. All are merely interpretations of the work. Moreover, all and only right interpretations of Cervantes' text are right inscriptions of Menard's. If it is incorrect for a contemporary reader to interpret Cervantes' text as archaic, it is equally incorrect to so interpret Menard's. For the "two" texts are one. Just as we found that "cape", despite its two applications, is one word not two, so *Don Quixote*, despite its multiple admissible interpretations, is one work not many.

Who then is the author of a literary work? Since the work is the text, it seems reasonable to credit the individual who produced the first inscription of the text. Alternatively, we might take the author to be the individual who produced the first inscription that functioned as the text. Either way, Cervantes wins out over Menard by virtue of having produced the first inscription (or utterance) of *Don Quixote*. Both rules accord with our ordinary practice of attributing authorship. But they have implications that need to be acknowledged. The identity of a literary work is located in the text, and texts can be randomly produced. So the policy of attributing authorship to the first producer of a text might require recognizing a monkey or a machine as the author of a literary work. This seems absurd; for monkeys and machines cannot even understand literary works, much less create them. But the absurdity is only apparent. It is not unusual for a work to have correct interpretations that its author cannot understand. (Consider, for example, Freudian interpretations of *Hamlet*.) Works whose authors are monkeys or machines are simply limiting cases of this phenomenon. The authors of these works cannot understand any interpretations of them.[6]

Who is the author of the work the twins inscribed? If the inscriptions were produced simultaneously, neither twin has a greater claim to authorship than his brother. But they did not work together, so it would be wrong to consider them collaborators. The case is like that of simultaneous discovery in science, where investigators working independently arrive at the same result. In science, both are credited with the discovery. It seems best to do likewise in literature. Both twins then are authors of the report. We can distinguish between joint authorship and multiple authorship. A work is jointly authored if several authors collaborate to produce a single inscription of an original text. A work is multiply-authored if several authors, working independently, produce separate inscriptions of a single original text. Multiply-authored works are unusual, but they present no theoretical difficulty.

Notes

1 See Goodman, *Ways of Worldmaking* (Indianapolis, 1978), pp. 109–14, and *Of Mind and Other Matters* (Cambridge, Mass., 1984), pp. 33–4.
2 See Goodman, "On Likeness of Meaning," *Problems and Projects* (Indianapolis, 1972), pp. 221–30.
3 See Goodman, *Languages of Art: An Approach to a Theory of Symbols* (Indianapolis, 1976), pp. 45–89.
4 See Jorge Luis Borges, "Pierre Menard, Author of the *Quixote*," *Labyrinths: Selected Stories and Other Writings*, ed. Donald A. Yates and James E. Irby (New York, 1962), pp. 36–44.
5 See Goodman, *Languages of Art*, pp. 199–211, and Elgin, *With Reference to Reference* (Indianapolis, 1983), pp. 113–20.
6 Although extreme, such limiting cases are not altogether fanciful. Computers are already credited with proving theorems when their input includes the axioms of a system and their output has the logical form of a valid deduction. At first, attempts were made to attribute the proofs to their programmers rather than to the machines. But these were conceded to have failed when it became evident that the programmers did not know how to prove the theorems in question and often did not even suspect that the formulas were theorems until the computers produced their proofs. If the inability to interpret their own results does not prevent computers from proving theorems, it is hard to see why that inability should be thought to preclude the production, by monkeys or machines, of other types of works.

Work and Text

Gregory Currie

Sometimes we speak indifferently of interpreting texts, and of interpreting literary works. But it is not a matter of indifference how we speak, for text and work are not the same. Nor do interpreting texts and interpreting works differ only with respect to their objects. They are different kinds of activities, and it is a source of error and confusion that we use the same word for both. Interpreting works is the common practice of literary specialists and lay readers, though it can be approached with different degrees of skill and sensitivity. Interpreting texts is an uncommon enterprise which most of us have neither the occasion nor the skill to engage in.

The view that work and text are one I shall call "textualism", and those who hold it I call "textualists". I shall try to sort out the good antitextualist arguments from the bad ones, and assess some textualist responses to the good ones. These responses either miss the point, or involve heavy costs in plausibility. Finally, I consider what we might put in place of textualism.

1 Individuating Texts and Identifying Them

Much will be said further on about distinct works which have the same text. But what decides whether we are dealing with one text or two? Equivalently, what decides whether these two text-tokens are

tokens of the same text-type? I offer as a sufficient condition that the two tokens have the same semantic and syntactic properties. (Roughly, they should consist of words, in the same order, that mean the same thing and are spelled the same way).[1] Whether these conditions are also necessary for textual sameness need not worry us, as the examples I shall use will satisfy the conditions offered as sufficient. Trouble might arise if those conditions are not, in fact, sufficient – if other factors need to be taken into account in settling questions about textual identity.

We now know how to individuate texts, but we may still be uncertain about how to identify a text as the text of a particular work. What makes this text and no other the text of (and so, according to the textualist, identical with) *Emma*? The definitive text of *Emma*, if there is one, is the text intended by Jane Austen: the sequence of words she intended, spelt as she intended them.[2] Incorrect spelling in the autograph may require correction, but whether it does depends on authorial intention. When a deviant spelling is intended as deviant it must stand in any copy that gives the true text. When a deviant spelling arises from mistaken belief about what the correct spelling is we have an error, which needs correcting on any copy that gives the true text. But the correction conforms to (what we take to be) the dominant one of two conflicting intentions. The author intends to spell correctly, and intends to spell this way because she believes

From *Mind* 100 (1991), pp. 325–6, 328–40. Reprinted by permission of Oxford University Press.

this way is correct. So the intention to spell correctly is dominant, and we respect her intention by correcting. Whether or not intentions conflict, it is intention that determines the text.[3]

There might be cases of conflicting intentions without domination. That's one way the author's intentions can fail to determine a precise word sequence as text for the work. Other ways would be through indeterminacy or vagueness of authorial intention. This may already be enough to unsettle the identification of work and text. Undominated conflict among, or indeterminacy of, authorial intention creates a multiplicity of textual candidates for the title of work, with nothing to choose between them. Vagueness of intention blurs the edges of the set, translating as it does into vagueness about the conditions of candidacy. The best we can say is that works are identical with the sets of their candidate texts (which in favorable cases will be a unit class). But this modification is no significant retreat from the identification of work and text. It lends no support to the view that interpreting the work is something different from interpreting the text; for what in a class of texts could there be to interpret but texts? The arguments I shall consider that are aimed against the identification of the work and its text serve as well or as badly against the identification of the work and the class of its texts. And no generality will be lost if we assume we are dealing with determinate works, those for which there is a unique text. So it will be a harmless simplification if I continue to take textualism to be the doctrine that the work is identical with its unique text. [...]

3 Two Works, One Text?

Borges' story "Pierre Menard, Author of the Quixote" has suggested a powerful anti-textualist argument.[4] As we shall see, the argument requires some development so as to block off inviting ways out the textualist might take. But Borges' tale involves certain complexities of plot made much of by recent writers intent on showing that the story presents no counterexample to textualism (see e.g. Tilghman 1982, and Wreen 1990). So as to shut out the noise generated by these complexities, I shall develop the argument by reference to a simpler example of my own.

Jane Austen wrote *Northanger Abbey* in 1803 as a burlesque on the Gothic novel. Imagine that a hitherto unknown manuscript by Anne Radcliffe, entitled "Northanger Abbey" (circa 1793), and

word for word the same as Austen's, turns up in the attic, that we conclude (never mind on what evidence) that this is in fact a coincidence, that Austen had no knowledge of Radcliffe's work, and that, far from being a satire, Radcliffe's *Abbey* was meant as a serious contribution to the genre. There is only ten years separating these two works (if indeed they are two) and we can plausibly assume that linguistic change had not proceeded so far during the time between them as to produce any changes in the conventions governing the use of the words contained in them.[5] In that case there's a word-for-word match between them for semantics as well as for syntax, and these are works with the same text, by my criterion. But, so the argument goes, it is not plausible to say they are the same work; there are so many judgements appropriate to the one but not to the other. There are implicit references in Austen's *Abbey* to certain other works in the genre (works by Radcliffe among them). But it would be anachronistic to see implicit references in Radcliffe to these other works, since, in my fantasy, she did her writing before those other works were composed. Austen's work is suffused with an irony not to be found in Radcliffe's.[6] And so, the argument concludes, there are two works here, with but a single text between them. [...]

5 The Plurality of Interpretation

Those who answer yes to my question – I've called them textualists – need an explanation of the Radcliffe/Austen case and its variants. Here is one.

That a work contains implicit reference to something, that it is in a certain way ironic, these are, in the broadest sense, interpretive remarks about the work. But a work can tolerate being interpreted in more than one way, not just in the sense that conflicting interpretations of it can be offered, but in the sense that conflicting interpretations can be admissible. There might be equally good readings of the one literary work, one ironic and the other not. That's not to say that literary works possess contradictory properties, like being ironic in a certain way, and being not ironic in that way. Perhaps interpretive remarks are not of the fact stating kind. Perhaps they are invitations to see the work in a certain way. The admissibility of an interpretation may not depend upon it being true, and I'll assume, for the sake of the argument, that it does not so depend (see my 1991). Yet for ease of exposition I should still like to talk of works

Gregory Currie

having interpretive properties. We can arrange for this in the following way. When I say that the work is ironic I mean it has the property of *being amenable to an interpretation which attributes irony to it*. So in my sense, to say that the work is ironic is not automatically to exclude the possibility that it is nonironic, for a work that is amenable to an ironic reading may also be amenable to a nonironic one. But with this granted my antitextualist argument looks doubtful; we have the option of explaining the intuition of a plurality in the Radcliffe/Austen case as a plurality of interpretations. There is one work, composed independently by Radcliffe and by Austen, and Austen's later act of composition had the effect merely of suggesting to us new interpretations of that one work: interpretations incompatible with those inspired by Radcliffe's act of composition, which may in turn be incompatible with one another. That, more or less, is the line taken by Catherine Elgin and Nelson Goodman.[7] How plausible is it?

6 Critical Pluralism and Critical Anachronism

I agree with Elgin and Goodman that some works admit of conflicting interpretations, and I grant that Radcliffe's (hypothetical) tale is one of them. But I deny that it admits of the kinds of interpretations inspired by Austen's act of rewriting. To say that a work has many interpretations (I sometimes omit the word "admissible" in what follows, but it is to be added in thought) is not to say how many, or to what extent these interpretations may vary one from another. There are degrees of pluralism, and some degrees of it are more plausible than others. I say it is *not* admissible, given what we know about the circumstances of Radcliffe's writing, to interpret her novel as ironic, or implicitly referring to novels written after her act of composition was completed. I say these interpretive claims are unacceptably anachronistic. But if Radcliffe's novel and the novel rewritten by Austen are identical, any interpretation of the one is an interpretation of the other, and it seems we have to say that the ironic reading of Radcliffe is acceptable. If the choice is between that view and the view that distinct works can share the same text, I prefer the latter.

So far this is just name-calling. We need to see what is wrong with anachronistic interpretation. The argument depends on seeing a connection between the interpretation and the evaluation of

works, a connection to be sketched rather briefly in the next section.

7 Interpretation and the Work's History

We value works of art, in a way not separable from any purely "aesthetic" valuing, because they manifest a range of qualities – skill, originality, and sensitivity among them – of the artists and writers who gave us these works, and we could not value the works properly if we knew nothing about their histories of production. This point was missed by those who argued that the value of a work depends on its "displayed" or "surface" features alone: its visible or audible features for painting and music, and, in the case of literature, the semantic and syntactic properties of its text. Certainly, a property that makes no contribution to the experience of seeing, hearing or reading the work is irrelevant to its value as a work of art:[8] that's why the surface properties of the work are among the most significant determinants of its value. But the experiences that works can give us depend also on sometimes tacit assumptions we make about the work's history of production: assumptions that invest the work's surface features with a significance they would not otherwise have. A painted canvas visibly indistinguishable from Ingres' *Bather* but created by a hurricane in the painter's studio would not exhibit skill or any similar quality of making. Brahms' symphonies, for all their excellence, lack the originality of Beethoven's. If Beethoven had never lived, but Brahms had still composed those, now marvelously original, symphonies, their sonic properties (unchanged in this counterfactual situation) would affect us in ways quite different from the ways they actually do.[9] Those typing monkeys may yet produce intelligible texts, but their texts will not manifest the tight plot construction and sensitive characterization of textually congruent works produced in the conventional way. (See Walton 1987, Dutton 1983, and Currie 1989, Chapter 2. See also Savile 1982, and Juhl 1980.)

If this is right, our judgements about a literary work depend for their acceptability, not only on assumptions about its textual features, but also on assumptions about its history of production. Evaluation is, as I shall say, historically sensitive. But interpretation plays a role in evaluation that makes it historically sensitive also. Evaluation depends on interpretation, in the sense that many of the features we would appeal to in defending an evaluation of the work are interpretive features. We might say that Austen's novel is good partly because of the brilliant handling of the ironic references to the works of Radcliffe and other writers of the Gothic; if historical discoveries revealed that ironic reading as inadmissible we would have to rethink our judgement that the novel was good – good in quite the way we had previously thought, that is. But if Austen's novel and Radcliffe's are identical, and the ironic reading of Austen's novel makes it good, we must say that Radcliffe's novel is good for the same reason. Anachronistic interpretation makes for anachronistic evaluation, and anachronistic evaluation is misevaluation. That is why it is wrong to interpret Radcliffe's novel as ironic: wrong in the same way, if not to the same degree, as interpreting *Bather* as an accidental collocation of pigments.

8 Other Ways Out

Elgin and Goodman might agree that the Austen-inspired interpretations are inadmissible interpretations of Radcliffe's novel. The grounds for thinking otherwise are that these interpretations are admissible of Austen's novel, and Austen's novel and Radcliffe's are identical. But Elgin and Goodman could say that, in the case described, there is no such thing as Austen's novel, and the question of what is an admissible interpretation of it does not arise. They hold that Austen did not write any novel; she merely rewrote Radcliffe's, and the fact that she did this independently of Radcliffe rather than simply by copying has no tendency to make her an author. Authorship goes to the first writer.[10] So there is no such thing as Austen's novel, and the question of what is an admissible interpretation of it does not arise.

In that case, when Radcliffe's manuscript finally turns up we shall have to say that all the interpretive labour provoked by Austen's act of writing has been in vain, that Austen did not, after all, write any novel, that what we took to be interesting interpretations of it are, in fact, anachronistic interpretations of something written ten years before. I cannot imagine that we should say any such things, and to insist that we should seems unmotivated by anything other than the desire to preserve a favoured theory.

The friend of textualism might at this point agree that there is such a thing as Austen's work,

interpretable in various ways. Of course this work is identical with Radcliffe's, and so Austen's is interpretable in the same way. But the case of Radcliffe and Austen is a peculiar one, and it should be no surprise that it leads to peculiar results about interpretation. In normal cases, where there is no second act of composition – and all the cases we actually have are normal in this sense – anachronistic interpretations need not be regarded as admissible.

But the textualist cannot limit the damage in this way: the acceptance of anachronistic interpretations in peculiar cases leads naturally to their acceptance in other cases as well. According to the Elgin-Goodman story, Austen's act of composition had the effect of inspiring a new, admissible, interpretation of Radcliffe's novel. If this interpretation is genuinely admissible, that must be because it makes good sense of the work; it enables us to appreciate the work in ways we otherwise would not. That is what makes an interpretation admissible. If this interpretation is worth having, it is worth having whatever its source. Austen might have proposed it, had she known about Radcliffe's autograph, in the conventional way, by writing a scholarly article saying it would be a good idea to interpret Radcliffe's novel as a pastiche on Gothic conventions. And what Austen can do in this respect can be done by you, me or anyone else. In that case the acceptability of the new interpretation of Radcliffe's novel does not depend on the case being a peculiar one; it does not depend on the contingency of Austen having engaged in this later act of rewriting. And the same holds, of course, for any other work of literature. I conclude that the textualist must either say that the Austen-inspired interpretations of Radcliffe's novel are inadmissible (holding, implausibly, that Austen wrote no novel) or he must endorse a general policy of accepting anachronistic interpretations for all works.

I said that Radcliffe's and Austen's works are distinct because they are differently interpretable, and I cited some interpretive remarks admissible of the one and not of the other. One textualist's response to this argument would be to say that the sorts of interpretive remarks that appear to distinguish these as works are really remarks about the author's act of composition.[11] "The novel is ironic" is, on this view, a piece of metanomic transfer from action to work, properly understood as attributing irony to Austen's act of writing. In that case what needs to be distinguished are not the works (in fact there is just the one) but the acts of composition, which on anybody's account are distinct. So the accusation that textualism leads to the endorsement of flagrantly anachronistic interpretations collapses.

Irony is one of those qualities we sometimes cite in defending the claim that a work is excellent. That seems a good reason for saying that irony is attributed to the work itself. But the textualist might agree that irony is a feature relevant to an appraisal of the work, without agreeing that it is a feature we attribute, or should attribute, to the work itself. After all, the merit of a work may be partly a matter of its originality, and originality depends on features of other works that form a relevant comparison class. For the sake of the argument, let us grant the textualist the assumption that irony and like features, while relevant to a judgement of the work's quality, are not attributable to the work itself.[12] This still leaves the textualist open to the charge that he endorses anachronistic judgements about the work. If we say that Austen's work is, say, excellent, partly on account of the irony displayed in Austen's act of composition, and if we hold, with the textualist, that Austen's work and Radcliffe's are one, then we shall have to say that Radcliffe's work is excellent for the same reason. But the view that the excellence of Radcliffe's work is partly due to the irony of Austen's compositional act, is no less objectionable than the view that Radcliffe's work is ironic because it is identical with Austen's ironic work. So the troubles of textualism are not eased by excluding problematic features like irony from the work and attributing them to something else.

One other textualist solution would be to relativize: to say that Radcliffe's *Abbey* and Austen's, being the same works, have the same properties, and that their interpretive properties are implicitly relational. On this view it's not that Austen's work is ironic and Radcliffe's work isn't. Rather, the one work/text we have in this case is ironic-relative-to-Austen's composition, and not ironic-relative-to-Radcliffe's. The same relativization can then be made for evaluative properties, and we can say that the work is good (in a certain way and to a certain degree) relative to Austen's composition, and not good (in that way and to that degree) relative to Radcliffe's.

This proposal has the advantage over an earlier one that it allows interpretive properties to be properties of the work. And it respects the historical sensitivity of interpretation and of evaluation, by building history into the interpretive and evaluative predicates themselves. Yet the proposal seems an artificial and unsatisfactory one. I know what it is for something to be ironic; I don't know what it is for something to be ironic relative to something somebody did.[13] If it is proposed as a model for this relativity that a sentence can be ironic relative to a particular utterance of it, I reply that it is the utterance, and not properly speaking the sentence at all, which is ironic. Further, the proposal looks suspiciously *ad hoc*; we could use the same manœuvre to protect a whole range of otherwise falsified criteria of identity. Consider the view that psychological continuity is the mark of personal identity. The following well known objection is put: that we can imagine that Jones' brain is split into two halves, with each half taking on the functions of the other. Each half, now a working brain, is placed in and connected to a well tended but brainless body, which starts to function as an independent "person". These two "persons", A and B, diverge psychologically over time, and we can soon say that A believes something that B does not. But the excellent psychological continuity with Jones enjoyed by each renders them identical by the stated criterion. Whatever the solution to this problem is, we would hardly favour the suggestion that there is in fact one person here, occupying two different bodies, and that the real lesson of the case is that psychological attributions are "body relative" – that Jones believes P relative to one body but not relative to the other. But if that manœuvre is so transparently *ad hoc*, why not say the same thing about the structurally similar proposal for saving textualism by relativizing interpretive judgements?

9 Motives

Perhaps there are other versions of textualism, and other arguments the textualist can mount in favour of the work/text identification. Why bother? Textualism might seem attractive if you thought it the only straw floating. There is some evidence that Elgin and Goodman see it that way. Besides their identification of work and text, the only theory of work identity they consider is the view that the work is an *interpretation of* the text; a view they reject on the excellent grounds that to identify works with interpretations is to miss something important about literature: that great works are great partly because they are variously interpretable.[14] But why suppose that the work is either the text or an interpretation of it? Elgin and Goodman offer no argument for the exhaustive nature of these two options. (As we shall see presently see, there are others.)

I suspect that textualism is attractive for Elgin and Goodman, not because of any intrinsic plausibility, but because it is required for the defense of Goodman's distinction between autographic and allographic arts, to which their article is explicitly committed (see Elgin and Goodman 1988, p. 65). Autographic arts are those for which work identification depends on history of production; allographic arts are those for which work identification does not. According to Goodman's taxonomy, while painting and sculpture are autographic, literature and music are allographic, because for them work identification goes by identification of the text or score alone (see Goodman 1968). To deny that text alone can identify a literary work is to allow that historical factors are relevant, as I have argued they are in the case of Radcliffe and Austen, and so literary works will be autographic. Indeed, since much the same line of reasoning holds for musical works, the autographic/allographic distinction is threatened with redundancy; it's hard to think of any works that would turn out to be allographic. In that case I say: So much the worse for the distinction.

Seeing no obvious gain from the identification of work and text, and seeing much difficulty in it, I won't consider here what further moves the textualist might make. Instead I shall assume that a case has been made out for rejecting the identification, and consider what we might put in its place.

10 Locating the Work

If the literary work is not the text, what is it? I want to consider two rather different proposals.

Suppose we identify the work with the author's act of textual composition. This proposal meshes nicely with some of the points made earlier about works. It counts works correctly: two acts, so two works, in the Radcliffe/Austen case. It establishes an appropriately close connection (identity in fact) between work and act, as dictated by the theory of evaluation outlined in §7. It maintains a close connection between works and their texts: by the argument of §1, a specification of the act entails a specification of the text, so act/work and text are logically connected. It also gives answers – in one case a somewhat surprising answer – to the ques-

tions raised in §2 but there left undecided: (i) Is the work's text counterfactually stable? (ii) What is the author's relation to the work – discovery or creation?

The answer to (i) depends on how we transworld identify (or transworld associate) acts. Let us see what answer we get when we plug in the theory of act-identification I regard as most plausible. Could my insulting Albert have occurred at a different time and place, employed a different form of words, had different causes and effects? The answer seems to be that it depends on how different all or any of these things are presumed to be. When we seek to identify that act in counterfactual circumstances we are looking for something very much like that act, and something more like it than anything else available in those circumstances. We are looking, in other words, for counterparts.[15] Acts of composition can be counterparts when they are similar in ways that fall short of requiring them to be acts of composition of the same text. (Just as they can be counterparts incongruent in other respects: e.g. spatio-temporal location.) In that case the same work (act) can have different texts in different worlds, but not texts that are very different, on pain of violating the counterpartness condition. The answer to (ii) is more straightforward. The author does not create the work, nor does he discover it; rather he enacts it.[16]

There are objections that can be brought against the proposal. One is that if work and act are identical, then all properties of the work are properties of the act. But in fact much that we ascribe to the work could not be straightforwardly ascribed to the act. We say the work has an archaic style, but it is not easy to reinterpret this as a remark about the author's act. Acts have styles, but to write in an archaic style is not necessarily to perform an act that has an archaic style. Perhaps this and other problems can be overcome, but it would be prudent to look for another strategy.

To identify the work with a text is to identify it with an entity that has some independent claim to a place in our ontology. Any community of speakers surely has need of the concept of a text, whether or not it has the concept of a literary work. Rejecting textualism, it is tempting, as with the proposal just outlined, to find some other, independently acknowledged entity with which to identify the work. But why play the textualist's game? Why insist on a *reductive* identification of works? Why not simply say that there are works, and that they are distinct from texts? This would not, after all, be an unprecedented move, particularly as applied to cultural entities. We recognize the existence of social institutions like banks and governments, but I do not know of any very attractive theory that identifies these things with entities antecedently acknowledged ("reduction to individuals" seems a particularly discredited programme). We can now signal our commitment to works by saying there are things with the properties we take works to have: things which stand in certain relations to texts, are capable of being (multiply) interpreted, stand in certain other relations to acts of textual composition and to the cultural contexts in which those acts are embedded, etc.

Conceivably, there are no things that have these properties; that is the hostage that anti-reductionism about works gives to fortune. In that case there are no such things as literary works. It is interesting to speculate as to how our literary practices would be reconstructed by an alien sceptical about the existence of literary works. Would she write us off as another benighted community of false believers, on a par with believers in witchcraft and the healing power of the royal touch? Perhaps not. The alien might see a purpose and a value in our practice independent of the existence of its putative objects. That we read, that some of us write, that others of us interpret: these things seem to be ends in themselves, or at least instruments that generate intrinsically worthwhile states of mind. And if *we* become convinced that there are no such things as works, our interpretive practice can retain its value for us undiminished, so long as we reconstrue our talk of literary works as part of an elaborate game of make-believe. No one thinks the less of Dickens' novels because his characters don't exist. It is enough that we make-believe they do. To widen the make-believe so as to include the works themselves should not threaten the literary enterprise. In that case it doesn't matter whether there are such things as works of literature. What matters is only what works are not, for by mislocating them (among the texts, for example) we distort their features, or at least the features which our elaborate game of make-believe requires us to imagine they have.

11   Interpreting Works, Interpreting Texts

I said at the beginning that interpreting texts and interpreting works are very different things. We now see, at least, that they are different, for they are activities directed at different objects. To see how different, we must see what each activity consists in.

Interpreting a work involves many things: the explication of plot, the limning of characters, the analysis of narrative structure, style and genre, together with the application of a whole range of aesthetic and evaluative descriptions. Nor is it an activity with a single correct outcome, since works admit of many interpretations. Arriving at an admissible interpretation for a work of any significance and cultural distance requires sensitivity, skill, and arcane knowledge, though this rarely prevents those of us less well qualified from trying our hands.

But the text, once distinguished from the work, does not offer any such interesting range of interpretive possibilities. Plot, character, narrative structure, style and genre are not features of the text, but of the work, since works with the same text can differ along all these dimensions of variation. The text is just a sequence of words, and the only kind of interpreting that one can do of a text is to expound the meaning of its constituent words and sentences as they are given by the conventions of the language. A text may be ambiguous, in the sense that the conventions of the language assign to some of its constituents more than one meaning. But disambiguation is not to be had at the level of the text itself, for ambiguity is a feature of the text. Disambiguation is a subject of concern for work-interpreters.

This is not to deny, of course, the importance of the text and its meaning for the interpretation of the work. To interpret the work we must know the meaning of the text. But that meaning is not usually got by any act of interpretation. Discovering the meaning(s) of the text is, for a competent speaker of the language, no achievement. Being a competent speaker is a matter of knowing the meanings of words and sentences, so textual meaning is transparent to the competent speaker. There is nothing here that deserves the name "interpretation".[17] When we confront a text belonging to an unknown language, we may embark on the project of discovering the meaning of the text from contextual clues, thereby coming to know some fragment of the rules of the language to which it belongs. This is interpretation – radical interpretation in fact – but it is not the kind of interpretation we think of in connection with literary works. Interpreting works and interpreting texts, where there is the opportunity for it, are quite different kinds of activities.[18]

Notes

1 Thus "die" is one word in English, another in German, by my reckoning. Is "museum" one word in English, another (disregarding capitalization) in German? They have the same spelling and, I assume, the same meaning. Perhaps they differ in their *relational* semantic properties, in which case we can count them different. A similar problem arises when a word has more than one meaning in a given language. Are my tokens of "bank" and yours tokens of the same word-type? These are book-keeping decisions that shouldn't affect any substantive argument. Certainly, the argument I shall consider further on is insensitive to how we decide them, so we may leave them undecided, or decide them in our own, different ways.

2 This view is relatively common amongst those most closely concerned with the editing and reconstruction of texts. Commenting on a remark by Harold Bloom ("I do not know *Lycidas* when I recite it to myself, in the sense that I know *the Lycidas* by *the* Milton") G. Thomas Tanselle says: "A primary reason for not knowing Lycidas in this sense is that he cannot be sure how close his text is to the one Milton intended" (Tanselle 1990, p. 5). But it wants an argument, which Tanselle does not give, to get from here to the conclusion that "the text of the work, or versions of it, ... is always the product of our critical judgement" (1990, p. 10).

3 For more on this point see my 1990, chapter 3.

4 In Borges (1964). For comment see e.g. Danto (1981).

5 But assume it anyway, whether it's historically plausible or not!

6 I am aware, of course, that there are passages in *Northanger Abbey* that would be incredible if they were not meant satirically. To make the example a plausible one, we may have to imagine Austen's text to be somewhat different from the text she actually wrote.

7 Elgin and Goodman (1988). The example they discuss is Borges' Cervantes/Menard story: "Menard may in some way have proposed or inspired a new interpretation of the text. But no more than any other admissible interpretation offered before or since or by others does the Menard reading count as *the* work *Don Quixote*, or even *a* work *Don Quixote*. All are merely interpretations of the work" (1988, p. 63).

8 I mean experience in the broadest sense, which includes cognitive states as well as feelings and sensations.

9 A point well made in Levinson (1980).

10 Elgin and Goodman (1988, pp. 63–4). But notice that Elgin and Goodman describe the Menard-inspired interpretations of Cervantes' work as "admissible" (see note 7 above).

11 In §10 I canvass the possibility that the authors' act and the work are one and the same.

12 *Only* for the sake of argument and not because there is anything intrinsically plausible about the assumption.

13 There is one way to understand predications like *is ironic* as relativized: that is, as relativized to a certain comparison class, as in "ironic for a work of that genre". But that is not the kind of relativity required by the proposal.

14 See Elgin and Goodman (1988, p. 56) for this and other objections to identification of the work with admissible interpretations.

15 On counterparts see Lewis (1973, pp. 39–43; 1986, chapter 4). My comments above about events are not meant as a general endorsement of counterpart theory. Things are otherwise, I claim, with individuals.

16 For a more detailed exposition of this view see my 1990, chapter 3.

17 Certain literary theorists, such as Stanley Fish, have argued that there is no such thing as literal meaning, and no distinction, therefore, between textual identification and interpretation. On this see my (1992).

18 Previous versions of this paper were read at The Australian National University, Massey University, and Otago University. I am grateful to David Braddon-Mitchell, David Lewis, Philip Pettit, Pavel Tichy, and especially Jerrold Levinson for their comments on earlier versions of this paper.

References

Borges, J. L. 1964. *Ficciones*. New York: New Directions.

Currie, G. 1989. *An Ontology of Art*. London: Macmillan.

Currie, G. 1990. *The Nature of Fiction*. Cambridge: Cambridge University Press.

Currie, G. 1991. "Interpreting Fiction". In *Literary Theory and Philosophy*, ed. R. Freedman and L. Reinhardt. London: Macmillan.

Currie, G. 1991. "Text Without Context: Some Errors of Stanley Fish". *Philosophy and Literature*, 15, 212–28.

Danto, A. 1981. *The Transfiguration of the Commonplace*. Cambridge, Mass.: Harvard University Press.

Dutton, D. 1983. "Artistic Crimes". In *The Forger's Art*, ed. D. Dutton, Berkeley and Los Angeles: University of California Press.

Elgin, C. and Goodman, N. 1988. "Interpretations and Identity: Can the Work Survive the World?". In *Reconceptions in Philosophy*, N. Goodman and

C. Elgin. London: Routledge. See pp. 93–7 in this book.

Goodman, N. 1968. *Languages of Art*. Indianapolis, Ind: Hackett.

Ingarden, R. 1973. *The Literary Work of Art*. Evanston, Ill.: Northwestern University Press.

Juhl, P. D. 1990. *Interpretation*. Princeton, NJ: Princeton University Press.

Kivy, P. 1987. "Platonism in Music: Another Kind of Defence". *American Philosophical Quarterly* 24, 245–57.

Kripke, S. 1971. "Identity and Necessity". In *Identity and Individuation*, ed. M. Munitz. New York, NY: New York University Press.

Levinson, J. 1980. "What a Musical Work Is". *Journal of Philosophy* 77, 5–28.

Lewis, D. K. 1973. *Counterfactuals*. Cambridge, Mass.: Harvard University Press.

Lewis, D. K. 1986. *On the Plurality of Worlds*. Oxford: Basil Blackwell.

Prior, E., Pargetter, R. and Jackson, F. 1982. "Functionalism and Type-Type Identity Theories". *Philosophical Studies* 42, 209–25.

Savile, A. 1982. *The Test of Time*. Oxford: Clarendon Press.

Tanselle, T. 1990. "Textual Criticism and Deconstruction". *Studies in Bibliography* 44, 1–33.

Tilghman, B. R. 1982. "Danto and the Ontology of Literature". *Journal of Aesthetics and Art Criticism* 4, 293–9.

Tolhurst, W. E. 1979. "On What a Text is and How it Means". *British Journal of Aesthetics* 19, 3–14.

Tolhurst, W. E. and Wheeler, S. C. 1979: "On Textual Individuation". *Philosophical Studies* 35, 187–97.

Walton, K. 1987. "Style and the Products and Processes of Art". In *The Concept of Style*, ed. B. Lang. Ithaca, NY: Cornell University Press.

Wreen, M. 1990. "Once is not Enough?" *British Journal of Aesthetics* 30, 149–58.

PART IV

Fiction

Introduction

Fiction is both the dominant category within literature and a category frequently studied with nonliterary concerns in mind. Although works of nonfiction are readily accepted and taught as literature, they are more of a rarity, and works of fiction have a more central status as literary paradigms. It is not clear why nonfiction has a more marginal status, but it does. Fiction, on the other hand, takes in much more than works of literature, because fiction can be nonverbal in form (e.g. stories depicted in painting) and because it need not meet even minimal standards for literary value (e.g. Batman stories made up to please a Batman-fixated child are fiction but not literature). Furthermore, from the philosopher's perspective, fiction is a highly provocative phenomenon, but not necessarily for reasons of interest to the lover of literature. The readings selected here give a sense of the wide range of concerns driving the philosophical study of fiction; they also show philosophers who, while they may not be interested in literary aesthetics, do want to reflect the concrete reality of human experience with fiction.

Why is fiction philosophically provocative? Works of verbal fiction appear to contain well-regulated, well-understood discourse that can evoke powerful responses and be highly valued. Yet typically these works are not tethered to actual contexts of speech and thought or to practical purposes of communication, in the ways that seem necessary for giving a discourse discipline, meaning, power, and value. On this basis, philosophers approach fiction as a source of hard ques-

tions for philosophy of language, philosophy of mind, and metaphysics. How should we analyze the thought and speech involved in the production and reception of verbal fiction? What makes a given set of sentences count as fiction rather than nonfiction? Do fictional characters and events exist?

Several authors take up the question of what makes something a work of fiction. As the readings make plain, it is neither necessary nor sufficient, for instance, that the sentences contained in the work be false. In general, the analysis of fiction cannot depend on the most obvious semantic and stylistic features of fiction, but must consider how fiction is defined by human intention or use. One natural place to start is with the intentions and activity of the fiction-maker or author. John Searle and Gregory Currie both take fiction to be defined primarily by the author's intentional actions. In Searle's view, the author of fiction pretends to assert the sentences contained within the work, and this pretence allows the normal conventions governing "serious" assertion to be set aside. In contrast, Currie thinks there is no pretence in what the author does, but there is rather a distinctive speech act of storytelling, in which the author intends the audience to make-believe what is presented in the work. One larger issue raised by the contrast between these views concerns whether the intentions and conventions operative in fiction form what we could call a language-game within the broad category of communicative speech acts and linguistic practices, or whether fiction is not really a language-game at all, but is best categorized in other terms, such as pretence.

Kendall Walton, while sharing Searle's general impulse to define fiction in nonlinguistic terms, shifts the focus away from authorial intentions altogether. For Walton, fitting into the category of fiction does not require being a work of fiction, in the sense of being an artifact dependent on the intentions of a maker, but rather requires only being an object serving the function characteristic of fiction. That function is to be a prop in a game of make-believe, where a prop prescribes what is to be imagined and thus determines fictional truths. As competent readers of fiction, we have learned how to move from the prop offered by the text to the complex imaginings that fill out a fictional "world."

One of the most intuitively puzzling questions about fiction concerns the nature of fictional characters. We seem to know some of them intimately and even care about them, and yet we are often willing to say that they are not real. Amie Thomasson affirms the existence of fictional characters and the host of other entities populating fictional worlds. On her view they exist as abstract artifacts that come into existence through the efforts of storytellers and are capable of going out of existence as well. Thomasson hopes to dispel the mysteriousness of fictional characters, by putting them on a par with other abstract, culturally and institutionally realized artifacts, such as money and government, the existence of which is usually not called into question.

David Lewis takes on the notion of truth at work in claims about what is true in fiction, as in the truth of "Wilbur is a pig, in *Charlotte's Web*." Of course no real-life pig sustains the truth of this sentence. Lewis approaches this problem by an appeal to what would be true in possible worlds in which the story is told as known fact, sticking as closely as possible to some constraining set of background conditions. Lewis's view opens up many lines of inquiry, from the broad question of whether possible worlds can be used in this context, to the perplexities of this kind of counterfactual reasoning. What background conditions do we assume in inferring truths about a world in which a pig talks to a spider who writes in English in her web?

Peter Lamarque returns us to the tension between literary and nonliterary concerns sketched above. Taking Lewis's view as a problematic case, Lamarque argues that the view does not just set aside literary concerns, but is ultimately inapplicable to literary fiction because it ignores basic interpretive features of literary practice. Lamarque thus calls for a study of the interpretation and criticism of specifically literary fiction.

16

Doonesbury

Garry Trudeau

The Logical Status of Fictional Discourse

John Searle

I

I believe that speaking or writing in a language consists in performing speech acts of a quite specific kind called "illocutionary acts." These include making statements, asking questions, giving orders, making promises, apologizing, thanking, and so on. I also believe that there is a systematic set of relationships between the meanings of the words and sentences we utter and the illocutionary acts we perform in the utterance of those words and sentences.

Now for anybody who holds such a view the existence of fictional discourse poses a difficult problem. We might put the problem in the form of a paradox: how can it be both the case that words and other elements in a fictional story have their ordinary meanings and yet the rules that attach to those words and other elements and determine their meanings are not complied with: how can it be the case in "Little Red Riding Hood" both that "red" means red and yet that the rules correlating "red" with red are not in force? This is only a preliminary formulation of our question and we shall have to attack the question more vigorously before we can even get a careful formulation of it. [...]

II

Let us begin by comparing two passages chosen at random to illustrate the distinction between fiction and nonfiction. The first, nonfiction, is from the *New York Times* (15 December 1972), written by Eileen Shanahan:

> Washington, Dec. 14 – A group of federal, state, and local government officials rejected today President Nixon's idea that the federal government provide the financial aid that would permit local governments to reduce property taxes.

The second is from a novel by Iris Murdoch entitled *The Red and the Green*, which begins,

> Ten more glorious days without horses! So thought Second Lieutenant Andrew Chase-White recently commissioned in the distinguished regiment of King Edwards Horse, as he pottered contentedly in a garden on the outskirts of Dublin on a sunny Sunday afternoon in April nineteen-sixteen.[1]

From *New Literary History* 6 (1975), pp. 319, 321–32. © New Literary History, University of Virginia. Reprinted with permission of the Johns Hopkins University Press.

The first thing to notice about both passages is that, with the possible exception of the one word *pottered* in Miss Murdoch's novel, all of the occurrences of the words are quite literal. Both authors are speaking (writing) literally. What then are the differences? Let us begin by considering the passage from the *New York Times*. Miss Shanahan is making an assertion. An assertion is a type of illocutionary act that conforms to certain quite specific semantic and pragmatic rules. These are:

(1) The essential rule: the maker of an assertion commits himself to the truth of the expressed proposition.

(2) The preparatory rules: the speaker must be in a position to provide evidence or reasons for the truth of the expressed proposition.

(3) The expressed proposition must not be obviously true to both the speaker and the hearer in the context of utterance.

(4) The sincerity rule: the speaker commits himself to a belief in the truth of the expressed proposition.

Notice that Miss Shanahan is held responsible for complying with all these rules. If she fails to comply with any of them, we shall say that her assertion is defective. If she fails to meet the conditions specified by the rules, we will say that what she said is false or mistaken or wrong, or that she didn't have enough evidence for what she said, or that it was pointless because we all knew it anyhow, or that she was lying because she didn't really believe it. Such are the ways that assertions can characteristically go wrong, when the speaker fails to live up to the standards set by the rules. The rules establish the internal canons of criticism of the utterance.

But now notice that none of these rules apply to the passage from Miss Murdoch. Her utterance is not a commitment to the truth of the proposition that on a sunny Sunday afternoon in April of nineteen-sixteen a recently commissioned lieutenant of an outfit called the King Edwards Horse named Andrew Chase-White pottered in his garden and thought that he was going to have ten more glorious days without horses. Such a proposition may or may not be true, but Miss Murdoch has no commitment whatever as regards its truth. Furthermore, as she is not committed to its truth, she is not committed to being able to provide

evidence for its truth. Again, there may or may not be evidence for the truth of such a proposition, and she may or may not have evidence. But all of that is quite irrelevant to her speech act, which does not commit her to the possession of evidence. Again, since there is no commitment to the truth of the proposition there is no question as to whether we are or are not already apprised of its truth, and she is not held to be insincere if in fact she does not believe for one moment that there actually was such a character thinking about horses that day in Dublin.

Now we come to the crux of our problem: Miss Shanahan is making an assertion, and assertions are defined by the constitutive rules of the activity of asserting; but what kind of illocutionary act can Miss Murdoch be performing? In particular, how can it be an assertion since it complies with none of the rules peculiar to assertions? If, as I have claimed, the meaning of the sentence uttered by Miss Murdoch is determined by the linguistic rules that attach to the elements of the sentence, and if those rules determine that the literal utterance of the sentence is an assertion, and if, as I have been insisting, she is making a literal utterance of the sentence, then surely it must be an assertion; but it can't be an assertion since it does not comply with those rules that are specific to and constitutive of assertions.

Let us begin by considering one wrong answer to our question, an answer which some authors have in fact proposed. According to this answer, Miss Murdoch or any other writer of novels is not performing the illocutionary act of making an assertion but the illocutionary act of telling a story or writing a novel. On this theory, newspaper accounts contain one class of illocutionary acts (statements, assertions, descriptions, explanations) and fictional literature contains another class of illocutionary acts (writing stories, novels, poems, plays, etc.). The writer or speaker of fiction has his own repertoire of illocutionary acts which are on all fours with, but in addition to, the standard illocutionary acts of asking questions, making requests, making promises, giving descriptions, and so on. I believe that this analysis is incorrect; I shall not devote a great deal of space to demonstrating that it is incorrect because I prefer to spend the space on presenting an alternative account, but by way of illustrating its incorrectness I want to mention a serious difficulty which anyone who wished to present such an account would face. In general the illocutionary act (or acts) performed in the utterance of the sentence is a function of the meaning of the sentence. We know, for example, that an utterance of the sentence "John can run the mile" is a performance of one kind of illocutionary act, and that an utterance of the sentence "Can John run the mile?" is a performance of another kind of illocutionary act, because we know that the indicative sentence form means something different from the interrogative sentence form. But now if the sentences in a work of fiction were used to perform some completely different speech acts from those determined by their literal meaning, they would have to have some other meaning. Anyone therefore who wishes to claim that fiction contains different illocutionary acts from nonfiction is committed to the view that words do not have their normal meanings in works of fiction. That view is at least *prima facie* an impossible view since if it were true it would be impossible for anyone to understand a work of fiction without learning a new set of meanings for all the words and other elements contained in the work of fiction, and since any sentence whatever can occur in a work of fiction, in order to have the ability to read any work of fiction, a speaker of the language would have to learn the language all over again, since every sentence in the language would have both a fictional and a nonfictional meaning. I can think of various ways that a defender of the view under consideration might meet these objections, but as they are all as unplausible as the original thesis that fiction contains some wholly new category of illocutionary acts, I shall not pursue them here.

Back to Miss Murdoch. If she is not performing the illocutionary act of writing a novel because there is no such illocutionary act, what exactly is she doing in the quoted passage? The answer seems to me obvious, though not easy to state precisely. She is pretending, one could say, to make an assertion, or acting as if she were making an assertion, or going through the motions of making an assertion, or imitating the making of an assertion. I place no great store by any of these verb phrases, but let us go to work on "pretend," as it is as good as any. When I say that Miss Murdoch is pretending to make an assertion, it is crucial to distinguish two quite different senses of "pretend." In one sense of "pretend," to pretend to be or to do something that one is not doing is to engage in a form of deception, but in the second sense of "pretend," to pretend to do or be something is to engage in a performance which is *as if* one were doing or being the thing and is without

any intent to deceive. If I pretend to be Nixon in order to fool the Secret Service into letting me into the White House, I am pretending in the first sense; if I pretend to be Nixon as part of a game of charades, it is pretending in the second sense. Now in the fictional use of words, it is pretending in the second sense which is in question. Miss Murdoch is engaging in a nondeceptive pseudo-performance which constitutes pretending to recount to us a series of events. So my first conclusion is this: the author of a work of fiction pretends to perform a series of illocutionary acts, normally of the representative type.[2]

Now *pretend* is an intentional verb: that is, it is one of those verbs which contain the concept of intention built into it. One cannot truly be said to have pretended to do something unless one intended to pretend to do it. So our first conclusion leads immediately to our second conclusion: the identifying criterion for whether or not a text is a work of fiction must of necessity lie in the illocutionary intentions of the author. There is no textual property, syntactical or semantic, that will identify a text as a work of fiction. What makes it a work of fiction is, so to speak, the illocutionary stance that the author takes toward it, and that stance is a matter of the complex illocutionary intentions that the author has when he writes or otherwise composes it.

There used to be a school of literary critics who thought one should not consider the intentions of the author when examining a work of fiction. Perhaps there is some level of intention at which this extraordinary view is plausible; perhaps one should not consider an author's ulterior motives when analyzing his work, but at the most basic level it is absurd to suppose a critic can completely ignore the intentions of the author, since even so much as to identify a text as a novel, a poem, or even as a text is already to make a claim about the author's intentions.

So far I have pointed out that an author of fiction pretends to perform illocutionary acts which he is not in fact performing. But now the question forces itself upon us as to what makes this peculiar form of pretense possible. It is after all an odd, peculiar, and amazing fact about human language that it allows the possibility of fiction at all. Yet we all have no difficulty in recognizing and understanding works of fiction. How is such a thing possible?

In our discussion of Miss Shanahan's passage in the *New York Times*, we specified a set of rules, compliance with which makes her utterance a (sincere and nondefective) assertion. I find it useful to think of these rules as rules correlating words (or sentences) to the world. Think of them as vertical rules that establish connections between language and reality. Now what makes fiction possible, I suggest, is a set of extralinguistic, nonsemantic conventions that break the connection between words and the world established by the rules mentioned earlier. Think of the conventions of fictional discourse as a set of horizontal conventions that break the connections established by the vertical rules. They suspend the normal requirements established by these rules. Such horizontal conventions are not meaning rules; they are not part of the speaker's semantic competence. Accordingly, they do not alter or change the meanings of any of the words or other elements of the language. What they do rather is enable the speaker to use words with their literal meanings without undertaking the commitments that are normally required by those meanings. My third conclusion then is this: the pretended illocutions which constitute a work of fiction are made possible by the existence of a set of conventions which suspend the normal operation of the rules relating illocutionary acts and the world. In this sense, to use Wittgenstein's jargon, telling stories really is a separate language game; to be played it requires a separate set of conventions, though these conventions are not meaning rules; and the language game is not on all fours with illocutionary language games, but is parasitic on them.

This point will perhaps be clearer if we contrast fiction with lies. I think Wittgenstein was wrong when he said that lying is a language game that has to be learned like any other.[3] I think this is mistaken because lying consists in violating one of the regulative rules on the performance of speech acts, and any regulative rule at all contains within it the notion of a violation. Since the rule defines what constitutes a violation, it is not first necessary to learn to follow the rule and then learn a separate practice of breaking the rule. But in contrast, fiction is much more sophisticated than lying. To someone who did not understand the separate conventions of fiction, it would seem that fiction is merely lying. What distinguishes fiction from lies is the existence of a separate set of conventions which enables the author to go through the motions of making statements which he knows to be not true even though he has no intention to deceive.

We have discussed the question of what makes it possible for an author to use words literally and yet not be committed in accordance with the rules that attach to the literal meaning of those words. Any answer to that question forces the next question upon us: what are the mechanisms by which the author invokes the horizontal conventions – what procedures does he follow? If, as I have said, the author does not actually perform illocutionary acts but only pretends to, how is the pretense performed? It is a general feature of the concept of pretending that one can pretend to perform a higher order or complex action by *actually* performing lower order or less complex actions which are constitutive parts of the higher order or complex action. Thus, for example, one can pretend to hit someone by actually making the arm and fist movements that are characteristic of hitting someone. The hitting is pretended, but the movement of the arm and fist is real. Similarly, children pretend to drive a stationary car by actually sitting in the driver's seat, moving the steering wheel, pushing the gear shift lever, and so on. The same principle applies to the writing of fiction. The author pretends to perform illocutionary acts by way of actually uttering (writing) sentences. In the terminology of *Speech Acts*, the *illocutionary act* is pretended, but the *utterance act* is real. In Austin's terminology, the author pretends to perform *illocutionary acts* by way of actually performing *phonetic* and *phatic* acts. The utterance acts in fiction are indistinguishable from the utterance acts of serious discourse, and it is for that reason that there is no textual property that will identify a stretch of discourse as a work of fiction. It is the performance of the utterance act with the intention of invoking the horizontal conventions that constitutes the pretended performance of the illocutionary act.

The fourth conclusion of this section, then, is a development of the third: the pretended performances of illocutionary acts which constitute the writing of a work of fiction consist in actually performing utterance acts with the intention of invoking the horizontal conventions that suspend the normal illocutionary commitments of the utterances.

These points will be clearer if we consider two special cases of fiction, first-person narratives and theatrical plays. I have said that in the standard third-person narrative of the type exemplified by Miss Murdoch's novel, the author pretends to perform illocutionary acts. But now consider the following passage from Sherlock Holmes:

It was in the year '95 that a combination of events, into which I need not enter, caused Mr. Sherlock Holmes and myself to spend some weeks in one of our great university towns, and it was during this time that the small but instructive adventure which I am about to relate befell us.[4]

In this passage Sir Arthur is not simply pretending to make assertions, but he is *pretending to be* John Watson, M.D., retired officer of the Afghan campaign making assertions about his friend Sherlock Holmes. That is, in first-person narratives, the author often pretends to be someone else making assertions.

Dramatic texts provide us with an interesting special case of the thesis I have been arguing in this paper. Here it is not so much the author who is doing the pretending but the characters in the actual performance. That is, the text of the play will consist of some pseudo–assertions, but it will for the most part consist of a series of serious directions to the actors as to how they are to pretend to make assertions and to perform other actions. The actor pretends to be someone other than he actually is, and he pretends to perform the speech acts and other acts of that character. The playwright represents the actual and pretended actions and the speeches of the actors, but the playwright's performance in writing the text of the play is rather like writing a recipe for pretense than engaging in a form of pretense itself. A fictional story is a pretended representation of a state of affairs; but a play, that is, a play as performed, is not a pretended *representation* of a state of affairs but the pretended state of affairs itself, the actors pretend *to be* the characters. In that sense the author of the play is not in general pretending to make assertions; he is giving directions as to how to enact a pretense which the actors then follow. [. . .]

III

The analysis of the preceding section, if it is correct, should help us to solve some of the traditional puzzles about the ontology of a work of fiction. Suppose I say: "There never existed a Mrs. Sherlock Holmes because Holmes never got married, but there did exist a Mrs. Watson because Watson did get married, though Mrs. Watson died not long after their marriage." Is what I have said true or

false, or lacking in truth value, or what? In order to answer we need to distinguish not only between serious discourse and fictional discourse, as I have been doing, but also to distinguish both of these from serious discourse about fiction. Taken as a piece of serious discourse, the above passage is certainly not true because none of these people (Watson, Holmes, Mrs. Watson) ever existed. But taken as a piece of discourse *about* fiction, the above statement is true because it accurately reports the marital histories of the two fictional characters Holmes and Watson. It is not itself a piece of fiction because I am not the author of the works of fiction in question. Holmes and Watson never existed at all, which is not of course to deny that they exist in fiction and can be talked about as such.

Taken as a statement about fiction, the above utterance conforms to the constitutive rules of statement-making. Notice, for example, that I can verify the above statement by reference to the works of Conan Doyle. But there is no question of Conan Doyle being able to verify what he says about Sherlock Holmes and Watson when he writes the stories, because he does not make any statements about them, he only pretends to. Because the author has created these fictional characters, we on the other hand can make true statements about them as fictional characters.

But how is it possible for an author to "create" fictional characters out of thin air, as it were? To answer this let us go back to the passage from Iris Murdoch. The second sentence begins, "So thought Second Lieutenant Andrew Chase-White." Now in this passage Murdoch uses a proper name, a paradigm–referring expression. Just as in the whole sentence she pretends to make an assertion, in this passage she pretends to refer (another speech act). One of the conditions on the successful performance of the speech act of reference is that there must exist an object that the speaker is referring to. Thus by pretending to refer she pretends that there is an object to be referred to. To the extent that we share in the pretense, we will also pretend that there is a lieutenant named Andrew Chase-White living in Dublin in 1916. It is the pretended reference which creates the fictional character and the shared pretense which enables us to talk about the character in the manner of the passage about Sherlock Holmes quoted above. The logical structure of all this is complicated, but it is not opaque. By pretending to refer to (and recount the adventures of) a person,

Miss Murdoch creates a fictional character. Notice that she does not really refer to a fictional character because there was no such antecedently existing character; rather, by pretending to refer to a person she creates a fictional person. Now once that fictional character has been created, we who are standing outside the fictional story can really refer to a fictional person. Notice that in the passage about Sherlock Holmes above, I really referred to a fictional character (e.g., my utterance satisfies the rules of reference). I did not *pretend* to refer to a real Sherlock Holmes; I *really referred* to the fictional Sherlock Holmes. [. . .]

Theorists of literature are prone to make vague remarks about how the author creates a fictional world, a world of the novel, or some such. I think we are now in a position to make sense of those remarks. By pretending to refer to people and to recount events about them, the author creates fictional characters and events. In the case of realistic or naturalistic fiction, the author will refer to real places and events intermingling these references with the fictional references, thus making it possible to treat the fictional story as an extension of our existing knowledge. The author will establish with the reader a set of understandings about how far the horizontal conventions of fiction break the vertical connections of serious speech. To the extent that the author is consistent with the conventions he has invoked or (in the case of revolutionary forms of literature) the conventions he has established, he will remain within the conventions. As far as the *possibility* of the ontology is concerned, anything goes: the author can create any character or event he likes. As far as the *acceptability* of the ontology is concerned, coherence is a crucial consideration. However, there is no universal criterion for coherence: what counts as coherence in a work of science fiction will not count as coherence in a work of naturalism. What counts as coherence will be in part a function of the contract between author and reader about the horizontal conventions.

Sometimes the author of a fictional story will insert utterances in the story which are not fictional and not part of the story. To take a famous example, Tolstoy begins *Anna Karenina* with the sentence "Happy families are all happy in the same way, unhappy families unhappy in their separate, different ways." That, I take it, is not a fictional but a serious utterance. It is a genuine assertion. It is part of the novel but not part of the fictional story. When Nabokov at the beginning of *Ada* deliberately misquotes Tolstoy, saying, "All happy families are more or less dissimilar; all unhappy ones more or less alike," he is indirectly contradicting (and poking fun at) Tolstoy. Both of these are genuine assertions, though Nabokov's is made by an ironic misquotation of Tolstoy. Such examples compel us to make a final distinction, that between a work of fiction and fictional discourse. A work of fiction need not consist entirely of, and in general will not consist entirely of, fictional discourse.

IV

The preceding analysis leaves one crucial question unanswered: why bother? That is, why do we attach such importance and effort to texts which contain largely pretended speech acts? The reader who has followed my argument this far will not be surprised to hear that I do not think there is any simple or even single answer to that question. Part of the answer would have to do with the crucial role, usually underestimated, that imagination plays in human life, and the equally crucial role that shared products of the imagination play in human social life. And one aspect of the role that such products play derives from the fact that serious (i.e., nonfictional) speech acts can be conveyed by fictional texts, even though the conveyed speech act is not represented in the text. Almost any important work of fiction conveys a "message" or "messages" which are conveyed *by* the text but are not *in* the text. Only in such children's stories as contain the concluding "and the moral of the story is . . ." or in tiresomely didactic authors such as Tolstoy do we get an explicit representation of the serious speech acts which it is the point (or the main point) of the fictional text to convey. Literary critics have explained on an ad hoc and particularistic basis how the author conveys a serious speech act through the performance of the pretended speech acts which constitute the work of fiction, but there is as yet no general theory of the mechanisms by which such serious illocutionary intentions are conveyed by pretended illocutions.

John Searle

Notes

1 Iris Murdoch, *The Red and the Green* (New York, 1965), p. 3.
2 The representative class of illocutions includes statements, assertions, descriptions, characteriza-tions, identifications, explanations, and numerous others.
3 Wittgenstein, *Philosophical Investigations* (Oxford, 1953), par. 249.
4 A. Conan Doyle, *The Complete Sherlock Holmes* (Garden City, NY, 1932), II, 596.

18

Truth in Fiction

David Lewis

We can truly say that Sherlock Holmes lived in Baker Street, and that he liked to show off his mental powers. We cannot truly say that he was a devoted family man, or that he worked in close cooperation with the police.

It would be nice if we could take such descriptions of fictional characters at their face value, ascribing to them the same subject-predicate form as parallel descriptions of real-life characters. Then the sentences "Holmes wears a silk top hat" and "Nixon wears a silk top hat" would both be false because the referent of the subject term – fictional Holmes or real-life Nixon, as the case may be – lacks the property, expressed by the predicate, of wearing a silk top hat. The only difference would be that the subject terms "Holmes" and "Nixon" have referents of radically different sorts: one a fictional character, the other a real-life person of flesh and blood.

I dont't question that a treatment along these Meinongian lines could be made to work. Terence Parsons has done it.[1] But it is no simple matter to overcome the difficulties that arise. For one thing, is there not some perfectly good sense in which Holmes, like Nixon, *is* a real-life person of flesh and blood? There are stories about the exploits of super-heroes from other planets, hobbits, fires and storms, vaporous intelligences, and other nonpersons. But what a mistake it would be to class the Holmes stories with these! Unlike Clark Kent et al., Sherlock Holmes is just a person – a person of flesh and blood, a being in the very same category as Nixon.

Consider also the problem of the chorus. We can truly say that Sir Joseph Porter, K. C. B., is attended by a chorus of his sisters and his cousins and his aunts. To make this true, it seems that the domain of fictional characters must contain not only Sir Joseph himself, but also plenty of fictional sisters and cousins and aunts. But how many – five dozen, perhaps? No, for we cannot truly say that the chorus numbers five dozen exactly. We cannot truly say anything exact about its size. Then do we perhaps have a fictional chorus, but no fictional members of this chorus and hence no number of members? No, for we can truly say some things about the size. We are told that the sisters and cousins, even without the aunts, number in dozens.

The Meinongian should not suppose that the quantifiers in descriptions of fictional characters range over all the things he thinks there are, both fictional and nonfictional; but he may not find it easy to say just how the ranges of quantification are to be restricted. Consider whether we can truly say that Holmes was more intelligent than anyone else, before or since. It is certainly appropriate to compare him with some fictional characters, such as Mycroft and Watson; but not with others, such as Poirot or "Slipstick" Libby. It may be appropriate to compare him with some nonfictional characters, such as Newton and Darwin; but probably not with others, such as Conan Doyle or Frank Ramsey.

From *American Philosophical Quarterly* 15 (1978), pp. 37–45.

"More intelligent than anyone else" meant something like "more intelligent than anyone else in the world of Sherlock Holmes." The inhabitants of this "world" are drawn partly from the fictional side of the Meinongian domain and partly from the non-fictional side, exhausting neither.

Finally, the Meinongian must tell us why truths about fictional characters are cut off, sometimes though not always, from the consequences they ought to imply. We can truly say that Holmes lived at 221B Baker Street. I have been told that the only building at 221B Baker Street, then or now, was a bank. It does not follow, and certainly is not true, that Holmes lived in a bank.

The way of the Meinongian is hard, and in this paper I shall explore a simpler alternative. Let us not take our descriptions of fictional characters at face value, but instead let us regard them as abbreviations for longer sentences beginning with an operator "In such-and-such fiction...". Such a phrase is an intensional operator that may be prefixed to a sentence ϕ to form a new sentence. But then the prefixed operator may be dropped by way of abbreviation, leaving us with what sounds like the original sentence ϕ but differs from it in sense.

Thus if I say that Holmes liked to show off, you will take it that I have asserted an abbreviated version of the true sentence "In the Sherlock Holmes stories, Holmes liked to show off." As for the embedded sentence "Holmes liked to show off," taken by itself with the prefixed operator neither explicitly present nor tacitly understood, we may abandon it to the common fate of subject–predicate sentences with denotationless subject terms: automatic falsity or lack of truth value, according to taste.

Many things we might say about Holmes are potentially ambiguous. They may or may not be taken as abbreviations for sentences carrying the prefix "In the Sherlock Holmes stories...". Context, content, and common sense will usually resolve the ambiguity in practice. Consider these sentences:

Holmes lived in Baker Street.
Holmes lived nearer to Paddington Station than to Waterloo Station.
Holmes was just a person – a person of flesh and blood.
Holmes really existed.
Someone lived for many years at 221B Baker Street.
London's greatest detective in 1900 used cocaine.

All of them are false if taken as unprefixed, simply because Holmes did not actually exist. (Or perhaps at least some of them lack truth value.) All are true if taken as abbreviations for prefixed sentences. The first three would probably be taken in the latter way, hence they seem true. The rest would probably be taken in the former way, hence they seem false. The sentence

No detective ever solved almost all his cases.

would probably be taken as unprefixed and hence true, though it would be false if taken as prefixed. The sentence

Holmes and Watson are identical.

is sure to be taken as prefixed and hence false, but that is no refutation of systems of free logic[2] which would count it as true if taken as unprefixed.

(I hasten to concede that some truths about Holmes are not abbreviations of prefixed sentences, and also are not true just because "Holmes" is denotationless. For instance these:

Holmes is a fictional character.
Holmes was killed off by Conan Doyle, but later resurrected.
Holmes has acquired a cultish following.
Holmes symbolizes mankind's ceaseless striving for truth.
Holmes would not have needed tapes to get the goods on Nixon.
Holmes could have solved the A.B.C. murders sooner than Poirot.

I shall have nothing to say here about the proper treatment of these sentences. If the Meinongian can handle them with no special dodges, that is an advantage of his approach over mine.)

The ambiguity of prefixing explains why truths about fictional characters are sometimes cut off from their seeming consequences. Suppose we have an argument (with zero or more premises) which is valid in the modal sense that it is impossible for the premises all to be true and the conclusion false.

$$\frac{\psi_1, \ldots, \psi_n}{\therefore \phi}$$

Then it seems clear that we obtain another valid argument if we prefix an operator "In the fiction $f...$" uniformly to each premise and to the conclusion of the original argument. Truth in a given fiction is closed under implication.

$$\frac{\text{In } f, \ \psi_1, \ldots, \ \text{In } f, \ \psi_n}{\therefore \text{In } f, \ \phi}$$

But if we prefix the operator "In the fiction f..." to some of the original premisses and not to others, or if we take some but not all of the premisses as tacitly prefixed, then in general neither the original conclusion ϕ nor the prefixed conclusion "In the fiction f, ϕ" will follow. In the inference we considered earlier there were two premisses. The premiss that Holmes lived at 221B Baker Street was true only if taken as prefixed. The premiss that the only building at 221B Baker Street was a bank, on the other hand, was true only if taken as unprefixed; for in the stories there was no bank there but rather a rooming house. Taking the premisses as we naturally would in the ways that make them true, nothing follows: neither the unprefixed conclusion that Holmes lived in a bank nor the prefixed conclusion that in the stories he lived in a bank. Taking both premisses as unprefixed, the unprefixed conclusion follows but the first premiss is false. Taking both premisses as prefixed, the prefixed conclusion follows but the second premiss is false.[3]

Our remaining task is to see what may be said about the analysis of the operators "In such-and-such fiction . . .". I have already noted that truth in a given fiction is closed under implication. Such closure is the earmark of an operator of relative necessity, an intensional operator that may be analyzed as a restricted universal quantifier over possible worlds. So we might proceed as follows: a prefixed sentence "In fiction f, ϕ" is true (or, as we shall also say, ϕ is true in the fiction f) iff ϕ is true at every possible world in a certain set, this set being somehow determined by the fiction f.

As a first approximation, we might consider exactly those worlds where the plot of the fiction is enacted, where a course of events takes place that matches the story. What is true in the Sherlock Holmes stories would then be what is true at all of those possible worlds where there are characters who have the attributes, stand in the relations, and do the deeds that are ascribed in the stories to Holmes, Watson, and the rest. (Whether these characters would then *be* Holmes, Watson, and the rest is a vexed question that we must soon consider.)

I think this proposal is not quite right. For one thing, there is a threat of circularity. Even the Holmes stories, not to mention fiction written in less explicit styles, are by no means in the form of straightforward chronicles. An intelligent and informed reader can indeed discover the plot, and could write it down in the form of a fully explicit chronicle if he liked. But this extraction of plot from text is no trivial or automatic task. Perhaps the reader accomplishes it only by figuring out what is true in the stories – that is, only by exercising his tacit mastery of the very concept of truth in fiction that we are now investigating. If so, then an analysis that starts by making uncritical use of the concept of the plot of a fiction might be rather uninformative, even if correct so far as it goes.

A second problem arises out of an observation by Saul Kripke.[4] Let us assume that Conan Doyle indeed wrote the stories as pure fiction. He just made them up. He had no knowledge of anyone who did the deeds he ascribed to Holmes, nor had he even picked up any garbled information originating in any such person. It may nevertheless be, purely by coincidence, that our own world is one of the worlds where the plot of the stories is enacted. Maybe there was a man whom Conan Doyle never heard of whose actual adventures chanced to fit the stories in every detail. Maybe he even was named "Sherlock Holmes." Improbable, incredible, but surely possible! Now consider the name "Sherlock Holmes," *as used in the stories*. Does the name, so used, refer to the man whom Conan Doyle never heard of? Surely not! It is irrelevant that a homonymous name is used by some people, not including Conan Doyle, to refer to this man. We must distinguish between the homonyms, just as we would distinguish the name of London (England) from the homonymous name of London (Ontario). It is false at our world that the name "Sherlock Holmes," as used in the stories, refers to someone. Yet it is true in the stories that this name, as used in the stories, refers to someone. So we have found something that is true in the stories but false (under our improbable supposition) at one of the worlds where the plot of the stories is enacted.

In order to avoid this difficulty, it will be helpful if we do not think of a fiction in the abstract, as a string of sentences or something of that sort. Rather, a fiction is a story told by a storyteller on a particular occasion. He may tell his tales around the campfire or he may type a manuscript and send it to his publisher, but in either case there is an act of storytelling. Different acts of storytelling, different fictions. When Pierre Menard re-tells *Don Quixote*, that is not the same fiction as Cervantes' *Don Quixote* – not even if they are in the same

David Lewis

language and match word for word.[5] (It would have been different if Menard had copied Cervantes' fiction from memory, however; that would not have been what I call an act of storytelling at all.) One act of storytelling might, however, be the telling of two different fictions: one a harmless fantasy told to the children and the censors, the other a subversive allegory simultaneously told to the *cognoscenti*.

Storytelling is pretence. The storyteller purports to be telling the truth about matters whereof he has knowledge. He purports to be talking about characters who are known to him, and whom he refers to, typically, by means of their ordinary proper names. But if his story is fiction, he is not really doing these things. Usually his pretence has not the slightest tendency to deceive anyone, nor has he the slightest intent to deceive. Nevertheless he plays a false part, goes through a form of telling known fact when he is not doing so. This is most apparent when the fiction is told in the first person. Conan Doyle pretended to be a doctor named Watson, engaged in publishing truthful memoirs of events he himself had witnessed. But the case of third-person narrative is not essentially different. The author purports to be telling the truth about matters he has somehow come to know about, though how he has found out about them is left unsaid. That is why there is a pragmatic paradox akin to contradiction in a third-person narrative that ends "... and so none were left to tell the tale."

The worlds we should consider, I suggest, are the worlds where the fiction is told, but as known fact rather than fiction. The act of storytelling occurs, just as it does here at our world; but there it *is* what here it falsely purports to be: truth-telling about matters whereof the teller has knowledge. Our own world cannot be such a world; for if it is really a fiction that we are dealing with, then the act of storytelling at our world was not what it purported to be. It does not matter if, unbeknownst to the author, our world is one where his plot is enacted. The real-life Sherlock Holmes would not have made Conan Doyle any less of a pretender, if Conan Doyle had never heard of him. (This real-life Holmes might have had his real-life Watson who told true stories about the adventures he had witnessed. But even if his memoirs matched Conan Doyle's fiction word for word they would not be the same stories, any more than Cervantes' *Don Quixote* is the same story as Menard's. So our world would still not be one where the Holmes

stories – the *same* Holmes stories that Conan Doyle told as fiction – were told as known fact.) On the other hand, any world where the story is told as known fact rather than fiction must be among the worlds where the plot of the story is enacted. Else its enactment could be neither known nor truly told of.

I rely on a notion of trans-world identity for stories; this is partly a matter of word-for-word match and partly a matter of trans-world identity (or perhaps a counterpart relation) for acts of storytelling. Here at our world we have a fiction f, told in an act a of storytelling; at some other world we have an act a' of telling the truth about known matters of fact; the stories told in a and a' match word for word, and the words have the same meaning. Does that mean that the other world is one where f is told as known fact rather than fiction? Not necessarily, as the case of Menard shows. It is also required that a and a' be the same act of storytelling (or at least counterparts). How bad is this? Surely you would like to know more about the criteria of trans-world identity (or the counterpart relation) for acts of storytelling, and so indeed would I. But I think we have enough of a grip to make it worthwhile going on. I see no threat of circularity here, since I see no way of using the concept of truth in fiction to help with the analysis of trans-world identity of acts of storytelling.

Suppose a fiction employs such names as "Sherlock Holmes." At those worlds where the same story is told as known fact rather than fiction, those names really are what they here purport to be: ordinary proper names of existing characters known to the storyteller. Here at our world, the storyteller only pretends that "Sherlock Holmes" has the semantic character of an ordinary proper name. We have no reason at all to suppose that the name, as used here at our world, really does have that character. As we use it, it may be very unlike an ordinary proper name. Indeed, it may have a highly non-rigid sense, governed largely by the descriptions of Holmes and his deeds that are found in the stories. That is what I suggest: the sense of "Sherlock Holmes" as we use it is such that, for any world w where the Holmes stories are told as known fact rather than fiction, the name denotes at w whichever inhabitant of w it is who there plays the role of Holmes. Part of that role, of course, is to bear the ordinary proper name "Sherlock Holmes". But that only goes to show that "Sherlock Holmes" is used at w as an ordinary proper name, not that it is so used here.

I also suggest, less confidently, that whenever a world w is not one of the worlds just considered, the sense of "Sherlock Holmes" as we use it is such as to assign it no denotation at w. That is so even if the plot of the fiction is enacted by inhabitants of w. If we are right that Conan Doyle told the Holmes stories as fiction, then it follows that "Sherlock Holmes" is denotationless here at our world. It does not denote the real-life Sherlock Holmes whom Conan Doyle never heard of, if such there be.

We have reached a proposal I shall call ANALYSIS 0: *A sentence of the form "In fiction* f, ϕ" *is true iff* ϕ *is true at every world where* f *is told as known fact rather than fiction.*

Is that right? There are some who never tire of telling us not to read anything into a fiction that is not there explicitly, and Analysis 0 will serve to capture the usage of those who hold this view in its most extreme form. I do not believe, however, that such a usage is at all common. Most of us are content to read a fiction against a background of well-known fact, "reading into" the fiction content that is not there explicitly but that comes jointly from the explicit content and the factual background. Analysis 0 disregards the background. Thereby it brings too many possible worlds into consideration, so not enough comes out true in the fiction.

For example, I claim that in the Holmes stories, Holmes lives nearer to Paddington Station than to Waterloo Station. A glance at the map will show you that his address in Baker Street is much nearer to Paddington. Yet the map is not part of the stories; and so far as I know it is never stated or implied in the stories themselves that Holmes lives nearer to Paddington. There are possible worlds where the Holmes stories are told as known fact rather than fiction which differ in all sorts of ways from ours. Among these are worlds where Holmes lives in a London arranged very differently from the London of our world, a London where Holmes's address in Baker Street is much closer to Waterloo Station than to Paddington.

(I do not suppose that such a distortion of geography need prevent the otherworldly places there called "London," "Paddington Station," ... from being the same as, or counterparts of, their actual namesakes. But if I am wrong, that still does not challenge my claim that there are worlds where the stories are told as known fact but where it is true that Holmes lives closer to Waterloo than to Paddington. For it is open to us to regard the place-names, as used in the stories, as fictional names with non-rigid senses like the non-rigid sense I have already ascribed to "Sherlock Holmes." That would mean, incidentally, that "Paddington Station," as used in the stories, does not denote the actual station of that name.)

Similarly, I claim that it is true, though not explicit, in the stories that Holmes does not have a third nostril; that he never had a case in which the murderer turned out to be a purple gnome; that he solved his cases without the aid of divine revelation; that he never visited the moons of Saturn; and that he wears underpants. There are bizarre worlds where the Holmes stories are told as known fact but where all of these things are false.

Strictly speaking, it is fallacious to reason from a mixture of truth in fact and truth in fiction to conclusions about truth in fiction. From a mixture of prefixed and unprefixed premises, nothing follows. But in practice the fallacy is often not so bad. The factual premises in mixed reasoning may be part of the background against which we read the fiction. They may carry over into the fiction, not because there is anything explicit in the fiction to make them true, but rather because there is nothing to make them false. There is nothing in the Holmes stories, for instance, that gives us any reason to bracket our background knowledge of the broad outlines of London geography. Only a few details need changing – principally details having to do with 221B Baker Street. To move the stations around, or even to regard their locations as an open question, would be uncalled for. What's true in fact about their locations is true also in the stories. Then it is no error to reason from such facts to conclusions about what else is true in the stories.

You've heard it all before. Reasoning about truth in fiction is very like counterfactual reasoning. We make a supposition contrary to fact – what if this match had been struck? In reasoning about what would have happened in that counterfactual situation, we use factual premises. The match was dry, there was oxygen about, and so forth. But we do not use factual premises altogether freely, since some of them would fall victim to the change that takes us from actuality to the envisaged counterfactual situation. We do not use the factual premiss that the match was inside the matchbox at the time in question, or that it was at room temperature a second later. We depart from actuality as far as we must to reach a possible world where the counterfactual supposition comes true (and that might be quite far if the supposition is a fantastic one). But we do not make gratuitous changes. We hold fixed the features of actuality that do not have to be changed as part of the least disruptive way of making the supposition true. We can safely reason from the part of our factual background that is thus held fixed.

By now, several authors have treated counterfactual conditionals along the lines just sketched. Differences of detail between these treatments are unimportant for our present purposes. My own version[6] runs as follows. A counterfactual of the form "If it were that ϕ, then it would be that ψ" is non-vacuously true iff some possible world where both ϕ and ψ are true differs less from our actual world, on balance, than does any world where ϕ is true but ψ is not true. It is vacuously true iff ϕ is true at no possible worlds. (I omit accessibility restrictions for simplicity.)

Getting back to truth in fiction, recall that the trouble with Analysis 0 was that it ignored background, and thereby brought into consideration bizarre worlds that differed gratuitously from our actual world. A fiction will in general require some departures from actuality, the more so if it is a fantastic fiction. But we need to keep the departures from actuality under control. It is wrong, or at least eccentric, to read the Holmes stories as if they might for all we know be taking place at a world where three-nostrilled detectives pursue purple gnomes. The remedy is, roughly speaking, to analyze statements of truth in fiction as counterfactuals. What is true in the Sherlock Holmes stories is what would be true if those stories were told as known fact rather than fiction.

Spelling this out according to my treatment of counterfactuals, we have ANALYSIS 1: *A sentence of the form "In the fiction f, ϕ" is non-vacuously true iff some world where f is told as known fact and ϕ is true differs less from our actual world, on balance, than does any world where f is told as known fact and ϕ is not true. It is vacuously true iff there are no possible worlds where f is told as known fact.* (I postpone consideration of the vacuous case.)

We sometimes speak of *the* world of a fiction. What is true in the Holmes stories is what is true, as we say, "in the world of Sherlock Holmes." That we speak this way should suggest that it is right to consider less than all the worlds where the plot of the stories is enacted, and less even than all

the worlds where the stories are told as known fact. "In the world of Sherlock Holmes," as in actuality, Baker Street is closer to Paddington Station than to Waterloo Station and there are no purple gnomes. But it will not do to follow ordinary language to the extent of supposing that we can somehow single out a single one of the worlds where the stories are told as known fact. Is the world of Sherlock Holmes a world where Holmes has an even or an odd number of hairs on his head at the moment when he first meets Watson? What is Inspector Lestrade's blood type? It is absurd to suppose that these questions about the world of Sherlock Holmes have answers. The best explanation of that is that the worlds of Sherlock Holmes are plural, and the questions have different answers at different ones. If we may assume that some of the worlds where the stories are told as known fact differ least from our world, then these are the worlds of Sherlock Holmes. What is true throughout them is true in the stories; what is false throughout them is false in the stories; what is true at some and false at others is neither true nor false in the stories. Any answer to the silly questions just asked would doubtless fall in the last category. It is for the same reason that the chorus of Sir Joseph Porter's sisters and cousins and aunts has no determinate size: it has different sizes at different ones of the worlds of *H.M.S. Pinafore.*

Under Analysis 1, truth in a given fiction depends on matters of contingent fact. I am not thinking of the remote possibility that accidental properties of the fiction might somehow enter into determining which are the worlds where that fiction is told as known fact. Rather, it is a contingent matter which of those worlds differ more from ours and which less, and which (if any) differ least. That is because it is a contingent fact – indeed it is *the* contingent fact on which all others depend – which possible world is our actual world. To the extent that the character of our world carries over into the worlds of Sherlock Holmes, what is true in the stories depends on what our world is like. If the stations of London had been differently located, it might have been true in the stories (and not because the stories would then have been different) that Holmes lived nearer to Waterloo Station than to Paddington Station.

This contingency is all very well when truth in fiction depends on well-known contingent facts about our world, as it does in the examples I have so far given to motivate Analysis 1. It is more disturbing if truth in fiction turns out to depend on contingent facts that are not well known. In an article setting forth little-known facts about the movement of snakes, Carl Gans has argued as follows:

> In "The Adventure of the Speckled Band" Sherlock Holmes solves a murder mystery by showing that the victim has been killed by a Russell's viper that has climbed up a bell rope. What Holmes did not realize was that Russell's viper is not a constrictor. The snake is therefore incapable of concertina movement and could not have climbed the rope. Either the snake reached its victim some other way or the case remains open.[7]

We may well look askance at this reasoning. But if Analysis 1 is correct then so is Gans's argument. The story never quite says that Holmes was right that the snake climbed the rope. Hence there are worlds where the Holmes stories are told as known fact, where the snake reached the victim some other way, and where Holmes therefore bungled. Presumably some of these worlds differ less from ours than their rivals where Holmes was right and where Russell's viper is capable of concertina movement up a rope. Holmes's infallibility, of course, is not a countervailing resemblance to actuality; our world contains no infallible Holmes.

Psychoanalysis of fictional characters provides a more important example. The critic uses (what he believes to be) little-known facts of human psychology as premises, and reasons to conclusions that are far from obvious about the childhood or the adult mental state of the fictional chacter. Under Analysis 1 his procedure is justified. Unless countervailing considerations can be found, to consider worlds where the little-known fact of psychology does not hold would be to depart gratuitously from actuality.

The psychoanalysis of fictional characters has aroused vigorous objections. So would Gans's argument, if anyone cared. I shall keep neutral in these quarrels, and try to provide for the needs of both sides. Analysis 1, or something close to it, should capture the usage of Gans and the literary psychoanalysts. Let us find an alternative analysis to capture the conflicting usage of their opponents. I shall not try to say which usage is more conducive to appreciation of fiction and critical insight.

Suppose we decide, *contra* Gans and the literary psychoanalysts, that little-known or unknown facts about our world are irrelevant to truth in fiction.

But let us not fall back to Analysis 0; it is not our only alternative. Let us still recognize that it is perfectly legitimate to reason to truth in fiction from a background of well-known facts.

Must they really be facts? It seems that if little-known or unknown facts are irrelevant, then so are little-known or unknown errors in the body of shared opinion that is generally taken for fact. We think we all know that there are no purple gnomes, but what if there really are a few, unknown to anyone except themselves, living in a secluded cabin near Loch Ness? Once we set aside the usage given by Analysis 1, it seems clear that whatever purple gnomes may be hidden in odd corners of our actual world, there are still none of them in the worlds of Sherlock Holmes. We have shifted to viewing truth in fiction as the joint product of explicit content and a background of generally prevalent beliefs.

Our own beliefs? I think not. That would mean that what is true in a fiction is constantly changing. Gans might not be right yet, but he would eventually become right about Holmes's error if enough people read his article and learned that Russell's viper could not climb a rope. When the map of Victorian London was finally forgotten, it would cease to be true that Holmes lived nearer to Paddington than to Waterloo. Strange to say, the historical scholar would be in no better position to know what was true in the fictions of his period than the ignorant layman. That cannot be right. What was true in a fiction when it was first told is true in it forevermore. It is our knowledge of what is true in the fiction that may wax or wane.

The proper background, then, consists of the beliefs that generally prevailed in the community where the fiction originated: the beliefs of the author and his intended audience. And indeed the factual premises that seemed to us acceptable in reasoning about Sherlock Holmes were generally believed in the community of origin of the stories. Everyone knew roughly where the principal stations of London were, everyone disbelieved in purple gnomes, and so forth.

One last complication. Suppose Conan Doyle was a secret believer in purple gnomes; thinking that his belief in them was not shared by anyone else he kept it carefully to himself for fear of ridicule. In particular, he left no trace of this belief in his stories. Suppose also that some of his original readers likewise were secret believers in purple gnomes. Suppose, in fact, that everyone alive at the time was a secret believer in purple gnomes, each thinking that his own belief was not shared by anyone else. Then it is clear (to the extent that anything is clear about such a strange situation), that the belief in purple gnomes does not "generally prevail" in quite the right way, and there are still no purple gnomes in the worlds of Sherlock Holmes. Call a belief *overt* in a community at a time iff more or less everyone shares it, more or less everyone thinks that more or less everyone else shares it, and so on. The proper background, we may conclude, comprises the beliefs that are overt in the community of origin of the fiction.

Assume, by way of idealization, that the beliefs overt in the community are each possible and jointly compossible. Then we can assign to the community a set of possible worlds, called the *collective belief worlds* of the community, comprising exactly those worlds where the overt beliefs all come true. Only if the community is uncommonly lucky will the actual world belong to this set. Indeed, the actual world determines the collective belief worlds of the community of origin of the fiction and then drops out of the analysis. (It is of course a contingent matter what that community is and what is overtly believed there.) We are left with two sets of worlds: the worlds where the fiction is told as known fact, and the collective belief worlds of the community of origin. The first set gives the content of the fiction; the second gives the background of prevalent beliefs.

It would be a mistake simply to consider the worlds that belong to both sets. Fictions usually contravene at least some of the community's overt beliefs. I can certainly tell a story in which there are purple gnomes, though there are none at our collective belief worlds. Further, it will usually be overtly believed in the community of origin of a fiction that the story is not told as known fact – storytellers seldom deceive – so none of the worlds where the fiction is told as known fact can be a collective belief world of the community. Even if the two sets do overlap (the fiction is plausible and the author palms it off as fact) the worlds that belong to both sets are apt to be special in ways having nothing to do with what is true in the fiction. Suppose the story tells of a bungled burglary in recent times, and suppose it ends just as the police reach the scene. Any collective belief world of ours where this story is told as known fact is a world where the burglary was successfully covered up; for it is an overt belief among us that no such burglary ever hit the news. That does not make it true in the story that the burglary was covered up.

What we need is something like Analysis 1, but applied from the standpoint of the collective belief worlds rather than the actual world. What is true in the Sherlock Holmes stories is what would be true, according to the overt beliefs of the community of origin, if those stories were told as known fact rather than fiction.

Spelling this out, we have ANALYSIS 2: *A sentence of the form "In the fiction f, ϕ" is non-vacuously true iff, whenever w is one of the collective belief worlds of the community of origin of f, then some world where f is told as known fact and ϕ is true differs less from the world w, on balance, than does any world where f is told as known fact and ϕ is not true. It is vacuously true iff there are no possible worlds where f is told as known fact.* It is Analysis 2, or something close to it, that I offer to opponents of Gans and the literary psychoanalysts.

I shall briefly consider two remaining areas of difficulty and sketch strategies for dealing with them. I shall not propose improved analyses, however; partly because I am not quite sure what changes to make, and partly because Analysis 2 is quite complicated enough already.

I have said that truth in fiction is the joint product of two sources: the explicit content of the fiction, and a background consisting either of the facts about our world (Analysis 1) or of the beliefs overt in the community of origin (Analysis 2). Perhaps there is a third source which also contributes: carry-over from other truth in fiction. There are two cases: intra-fictional and inter-fictional.

In the *Threepenny Opera*, the principal characters are a treacherous crew. They constantly betray one another, for gain or to escape danger. There is also a streetsinger. He shows up, sings the ballad of Mack the Knife, and goes about his business without betraying anyone. Is he also a treacherous fellow? The explicit content does not make him so. Real people are not so very treacherous, and even in Weimar Germany it was not overtly believed that they were, so background does not make him so either. Yet there is a moderately good reason to say that he is treacherous: in the *Threepenny Opera*, that's how people are. In the worlds of the *Threepenny Opera*, everyone put to the test proves treacherous, the streetsinger is there along with the rest, so doubtless he too would turn out to be treacherous if we saw more of him. His treacherous nature is an intra-fictional carry-over from the treacherous natures in the story of Macheath, Polly, Tiger Brown, and the rest.

Suppose I write a story about the dragon Scrulch, a beautiful princess, a bold knight, and what not. It is a perfectly typical instance of its stylized genre, except that I never say that Scrulch breathes fire. Does he nevertheless breathe fire in my story? Perhaps so, because dragons in that sort of story do breathe fire. But the explicit content does not make him breathe fire. Neither does background, since in actuality and according to our beliefs there are no animals that breathe fire. (It just might be analytic that nothing is a dragon unless it breathes fire. But suppose I never *called* Scrulch a dragon; I merely endowed him with all the standard dragonly attributes except fire-breathing.) If Scrulch does breathe fire in my story, it is by inter-fictional carry-over from what is true of dragons in other stories.

I have spoken of Conan Doyle's Holmes stories; but many other authors also have written Holmes stories. These would have little point without inter-fictional carry-over. Surely many things are true in these satellite stories not because of the explicit content of the satellite story itself, and not because they are part of the background, but rather because they carry over from Conan Doyle's original Holmes stories. Similarly, if instead of asking what is true in the entire corpus of Conan Doyle's Holmes stories we ask what is true in "The Hound of the Baskervilles", we will doubt-less find many things that are true in that story only by virtue of carry-over from Conan Doyle's other Holmes stories. [. . .]

Notes

1 In "A Prolegomenon to Meinongian Semantics," *Journal of Philosophy* 71 (1974), 561–80, and in "A Meinongian Analysis of Fictional Objects," *Grazer Philosophische Studien* 1 (1975), 73–86.

2 For instance, the system given in Dana Scott, "Existence and Description in Formal Logic" in *Bertrand Russell: Philosopher of the Century*, ed. Ralph Schoenman (London, 1967).

3 Thus far, the account I have given closely follows that of John Heintz, "Reference and Inference in Fiction," *Poetics*, 8 (1979), 85–99.

4 Briefly stated in his addenda to "Naming and Necessity" in *Semantics of Natural Language*, ed. Gilbert Harman and Donald Davidson (Dordrecht, 1972); and discussed at greater length in an unpublished lecture given at a conference held at the University of Western Ontario in 1973 and on other occasions.

5 Jorge Luis Borges, "Pierre Menard, Author of the *Quixote*" in *Ficciones* (Buenos Aires, 1944: English translation, New York, 1962). See pp. 77–81 in this book.

6 Given in *Counterfactuals* (Oxford, 1973).

7 Carl Gans, "How Snakes Move," *Scientific American* 222 (1970), p. 93.

19

What is Fiction?

Gregory Currie

I

What distinguishes fiction from nonfiction? Seeking an answer, literary theorists have analysed the stylistic features characteristic of fiction and the genres into which works of fiction may fall. But while stylistic or generic features may certainly count as evidence that a work is fiction rather than nonfiction, they cannot be definitive of fiction. For the author of nonfiction may adopt the conventions of fictional writing; and it is agreed on all hands that there are certain works of fiction which, considered merely as texts, might well be nonfiction.

In order to understand what distinguishes fiction from other kinds of discourse it may be helpful to enquire into the conditions which must prevail in order for a successful act of fictional communication to take place. Such an approach suggests a "speech act" analysis of fiction, and it is a version of this theory that I will offer here. Such analyses of fiction are relatively common in the current literature, but the prevailing tendency is to regard fictional utterance (in a generalized sense of utterance which includes writing) as a "pseudo-performance" which is not constitutive of a fully fledged illocutionary act.[1] I want to resist this tendency. My strategy is to treat the utterance of fiction as the performance of an illocutionary act on a par with assertion. I shall then attempt a

definition of fiction in terms of this illocutionary act (together with a causal condition). Before I come to the details of the proposal let us take a critical look at the reasoning which has led speech act theorists to reject this approach.

II

The idea that fiction is associated with a distinctive illocutionary act is considered and rejected by John Searle in his influential study of our topic.[2] He reasons as follows. There are a number of illocutionary acts which one can perform in uttering sentences. One may assert something, make a promise or a request, ask a question, etc. A principle which Searle adheres to is this:

> In general the illocutionary act (or acts) performed in the utterance of a sentence is a function of the meaning of the sentence. We know, for example, that an utterance of the sentence "John can run the mile" is a performance of one kind of illocutionary act, and that an utterance of the sentence "Can John run the mile?" is a performance of another kind of illocutionary act, because we know that the indicative sentence form means something different from the interrogative sentence form. (p. 64)

From *Journal of Aesthetics and Art Criticism* 43 (1985), pp. 385–92. Reprinted by permission of Blackwell Publishing Ltd.

Talk of a sentence form "meaning" something is admittedly obscure, but Searle's point is clear from the first sentence quoted: the meaning of a sentence determines the kind of illocutionary act it is used to perform. I shall call this the *determination principle*.

Searle applies this principle to the idea that the difference between fiction and nonfiction is a difference between kinds of illocutionary acts performed. On this view the writer of nonfiction is performing the illocutionary act of asserting (when using the indicative sentence form), while the writer of fiction is performing the illocutionary act of "telling a story" (p. 63).

Searle rejects this theory because the writer of fiction may use the same indicative sentences as the writer of nonfiction. And this is inconsistent with the determination principle; we would have sameness of meaning and distinctness of illocutionary act: asserting and storytelling.

I want to make two observations about this argument. First, the argument depends entirely upon the determination principle. But the principle seems obviously false. The same sentence may, given the right context, be used to make an assertion, ask a question, or give a command (e.g. "You are going to the concert").

Secondly, it turns out that Searle's own theory of fiction offends against the determination principle. On Searle's view the author of fiction engages "in a nondeceptive pseudo-performance which constitutes pretending to recount to us a series of events" (p. 65). In doing so "an author of fiction pretends to perform illocutionary acts which he is not in fact performing" (p. 66). Instead of engaging in an illocutionary act of any kind the author is pretending to engage in the illocutionary act of asserting when he writes an indicative sentence.

What Searle is saying is that the same sentence with the same meaning can occur in nonfiction as the result of the illocutionary act of assertion, and again in fiction as the result of an act which is not an illocutionary act at all. So sentence meaning does not determine the illocutionary act performed. To put the matter slightly more formally, Searle's determination principle says that there is a function f from sentence meanings to illocutionary acts where $f(P)$ is the act performed in uttering P. But on his own further account there is no such function, because the value of f for a given argument is sometimes an illocutionary act and sometimes (as in the case of fictional utterance) the value is undefined (since the associated act is not

an illocutionary act). And a function cannot be both defined and undefined for a given argument.

Searle might respond by saying that sentence meaning determines illocutionary force in the following modified sense. If we know the meaning of a given sentence *and* know that it is being used to perform an illocutionary act then, we know what kind of illocutionary act it is being used to perform. On this view illocutionary force is a function of two arguments rather than of one. The first argument would be the sentence meaning in question, the second some conventionally chosen object indicating whether the sentence is being used to perform an illocutionary act. If it is, let that object be 1; if not, let it be 0. Let P be an indicative sentence. Then $f(P,1)$ = assertion, and $f(P,0)$ = undefined. This is a way of modifying the determination principle so as to restore consistency with Searle's account of fiction. Notice, however, that the argument I set out earlier against the determination principle is also an argument against this modification of it. Further, if the illocutionary act is taken to be a function of two arguments, only one of which is sentence meaning, then the theory that fiction is the product of an illocutionary act may be presented in a way which is formally parallel to the modified Searlean account. Let f be a function of two arguments – the first a sentence meaning, the second a conventionally chosen object indicating whether the context is fiction or nonfiction. If it is non-fiction, let that object be 1; if fiction, let it be 0. Then $f(P,1)$ = assertion and $f(P,0)$ = telling a story. I do not believe that Searle has given us any reason to prefer one of these accounts to the other, and so he has given us no reason to think that fiction is the product of a merely pretended illocutionary act. Let us take a closer look at the idea that it is.

Monroe Beardsley adopts the "pretended assertion" theory (as we may call it) on grounds rather similar to Searle's:

> . . . if certain words are generally used in performing an illocutionary act of one kind, then to utter those words without fulfilling all the conditions for that illocutionary act is to present something that is like – not quite – that illocutionary act. Thus deception becomes possible – and also harmless pretending. It is only necessary to make it clear that one or more of the requisite conditions are lacking, while at the same time inviting the receiver (the hearer or reader) to make-

believe that they are present, in order to convert a genuine illocutionary action into a fictive one. So fictive discourse, on this view, is discourse in which there is make-believe illocutionary action, but in fact no such action is performed.[3]

I think Beardsley is right to say that the author of fiction invites the receiver to engage in a kind of make-believe. The question is whether, in doing so, the author *himself* engages in make-believe; whether, as Beardsley says, the author performs a make-believe illocutionary act rather than a genuine one. (Notice that Beardsley is not careful to distinguish these two alternatives.) It is true that the author of fiction utters sentences which normally have the illocutionary force of assertion, without their doing so in his mouth. But this is not conclusive evidence that no illocutionary act is being performed. For, as I remarked against Searle, we are clearly capable of transposing utterances from one illocutionary key to another. So it is not true, as Beardsley suggests, that to utter a sentence generally used to perform one illocution without fulfilling the conditions appropriate for that act is always merely to perform a pretence of that act. Suppose that a speaker who utters an indicative sentence, "It's hot in here," is actually giving the command "Open the window." We would not describe such an action as a pretence. The speaker intends his utterance to be understood as a command, and believes that the context will enable his hearer to divine his intention. So too with the author of fiction. He relies upon the audience being aware that they are confronting a work of fiction, and assumes that they will not take utterances which have the indicative form to be assertions. He is thus not pretending anything. He is inviting us to pretend, or rather, to make-believe something. For to read a work as fiction is to play a kind of internalized game of make-believe. Kendall Walton has given an illuminating account of the role of make-believe in fiction and the visual arts, and I shall make relatively uncritical use of the idea in what follows.[4] (Let me apologize here to the reader for the use I make of the barbaric expressions "make-belief," "make-believing," and "make-believed.")

If, as I have suggested, we think of fiction in communicative terms, then I think we see that the hypothesis of authorial pretence plays no role in the explanation of how such communication takes place. What is required is that the reader understands which attitude towards the statements of the text the author intends him to adopt. In the case of fiction the intended attitude is one of make-believe. So the author of fiction intends not merely that the reader will make-believe the text, but that he will do so partly as a result of his recognition of that very intention. Recognition of that intention secures "illocutionary uptake." So while it is essential that the author have a certain complex intention it is not required that he engage in any kind of pretence.

III

These last remarks serve to introduce the strategy I shall adopt here. For I shall take up the suggestion of Strawson and others that the illocutionary act is a function of the speaker's intention. There are, of course, difficulties about implementing this idea in a general way; there are arguments for thinking that speech acts of a purely conventional kind are not amenable to analysis in terms of any mechanism based on a speaker's intentions. But for many cases the intentional approach seems right, and I believe it is right for the case of fiction. After I have filled in some details we shall see one important advantage of this account over Searle's: that it enables us to distinguish the action of the author of fiction from that of the one who merely recites or acts out a fictional work.

We now have the elements for an account of the illocutionary act performed by an author of fiction. The author of fiction intends that the reader make-believe P, where P is the sentence or string of sentences he utters. And he intends that the reader shall come to make-believe P partly as a result of his recognition that the author intends him to do this. The author intends that the reader will read the work *as* fiction because he perceives the work to *be* fiction; that is, because he realizes it to be the product of a certain intention. The reader may recognize this intention in a number of ways; through his perception in the work of certain familiar elements of fictional style, or simply by noting that the work is presented and advertised as fiction. The author may even make an explicit avowal of his intentions, commonly done by prefixing the formula "once upon a time" to the text. Of course the reader may misperceive the author's intentions: he may think that the work is fiction when it is not, as readers of Defoe's *The Apparition of Mrs. Veal* used to misperceive that work as fiction. In that case we have the familiar case where "illocutionary uptake" is not secured.

With this in mind we may present the following "zero-definition" of fictional utterance, where U is the utterer, ø a variable ranging over characteristics of persons, and P a proposition.

(F)
U performs the illocutionary act of uttering fiction in uttering P if and only if
There exists ø such that U utters P intending that anyone who were to have ø
(1)   would make-believe P;
(2)   would recognize U's intention of (1);
(3)   would have (2) as a reason for doing (1).

ø may be any characteristic or group of characteristics (perhaps vague) the author would acknowledge as sufficient to ensure that anyone possessing them would, under normal circumstances, grasp his illocutionary intentions. It may be as general as "member of the author's speech community." On this definition it is of course possible for someone to write fiction without intending that anyone shall actually read it. I call this a "zero definition" because I leave open the possibility that it may require refinement of some kind. But my aim here is to present the outlines of a program, not to pursue any one aspect of it in great depth. I shall therefore leave the question of definition here.

IV

In characterizing fictional communication in this way do we arrive at a satisfactory definition of fiction itself? Not immediately. That is, if we say that a discourse is fictional if and only if it is the product of the illocutionary intention defined by the scheme F, then we are faced with some problem cases. For example, an author may concoct a story which he intends the audience to believe rather than to make-believe. It has been suggested to me that this was Defoe's intention in writing *Robinson Crusoe*. I do not know whether this is the case, but it certainly might have been. If we were to discover that it was we would surely not cease to regard *Robinson Crusoe* as fiction. Conversely, there may be cases where the author had a fictional intention but where we do not want to grant the fictional status to the resulting text. Someone may write a strictly autobiographical account of his or her life (perhaps a life full of highly unlikely events), adopting as he or she does certain stylistic devices usually indicative of fictional discourse.

The author might intend that the audience make-believe the story, and reasonably expect that the audience will understand that this is the intention. But it is doubtful whether such a work is genuinely fiction. These are difficulties for my theory. They are also difficulties for a position like Beardsley's and Searle's.

What examples like the first suggest is the existence of some capacity on the part of the literary public to confer the status of fiction on works which are not fiction merely in virtue of the intentions of their authors. If Defoe really did intend the reading public to be taken in by *Robinson Crusoe* what he produced was not fiction but deceptive assertion. (This is as much a consequence of the Searle–Beardsley theory as of mine, and I think it is intuitively correct.) But it is also true that *Robinson Crusoe* is today too firmly in the fiction category to be shifted by discoveries about the author's intentions. I think we should say that a "core" category of fiction is defined by the author's illocutionary intentions, and then allow for a category of "secondary" fiction defined in terms of a prevailing tendency in the community to adopt the make-believe attitude towards the texts in question. (The case of the Bible tends to confirm this hypothesis. Some people certainly read biblical stories "as fiction," but there are sufficiently many who don't to prevent the fictional attitude from prevailing. And I think we would not comfortably say, whatever our theological standpoint, that the Bible *is* fiction.)

The case of the apparently fictional autobiography presents another kind of difficulty. It is not that the community may intervene to revoke the work's fictional status; intuitively the work never was fiction at all. Is it because the story is true? No; merely being true would not be enough for us to say that the work was not fiction. Someone may write an historical novel, staying with the known facts and inventing incidents only where historical knowledge is lacking. Suppose it then turns out that these events described in the novel exactly correspond to what actually happened. I want to say that the work is fiction, even though it is entirely true.

It may be thought that the trouble arises because the author is engaging in a kind of deception; encouraging the audience, by indirect means, to assume that what he is saying is true. But this does not reach the heart of the matter; there are counterexamples to the proposal which do not depend upon such a deceptive intent as this.

Here are the counterexamples:

1 Jones finds a manuscript *m* which he takes to be fictional and which he determines to plagiarize. He produces his own text, exactly recounting the events in *m*, but written in a somewhat different way. But *m* was, unknown to Jones, nonfiction. Surely Jones's text is nonfiction; but on my theory it is fiction.

2 Jones experiences certain events which he represses. He then writes a story, recounting those events, but which he takes to be a fiction invented by himself. Again, Jones's text is surely nonfiction; on my theory it is fiction.

In these counterexamples, and the many variants of them that we can imagine, the trouble seems to be caused by what we may call an "information-preserving chain" from certain obtaining events to the text in question. That is, in these cases Jones's production of his text depends (causally) upon him processing information which correctly describes certain events. (In 2 the processing is subliminal.)

Much more could be said in explication of the notion of an information-preserving chain, and many difficulties might be encountered on the way. But for present purposes I think we may rest content with the intuitive idea I hope that I have conveyed so far. Let us say, then, that a work is fiction (in the "core" sense) if and only if it is the product of an intention of the kind specified in the schema (F), *and* the resulting text is not related by an information-preserving chain to a sequence of actually occurring events. This allows us to avoid counterexamples 1 and 2, and the deceptive intent counterexample, for in that example there clearly is an information-preserving chain from author to text. It also explains, incidentally, why the accidentally true historical novel is fiction – there is no information-preserving chain between event and text.

David Lewis has drawn my attention to the following interesting case. Kingsley Amis has a short story, entitled "Who or what was it?" in which he begins by saying that he is going to recount certain events which happened to him and to Elizabeth Jane Howard, his wife.[5] At first one is inclined to believe that this is a piece of autobiography, but it becomes increasingly clear that what we are being offered is a fictional story of the supernatural. Amis is playing with his audience; revealing his fictional intent only late in the piece. He apparently does not intend that we make-believe all the propositions of the story (at least on the first reading). But surely the *whole* piece is fiction. What am I to say about this?

Now while it is true that Amis intends us, on a first reading, to believe the earlier part of the story, it seems to me that, for the intended effect to be achieved, Amis must also intend us *retroactively* to make-believe the early part. That is, the effect is achieved, not merely by getting us to switch over from belief to make-belief at some stage, but by getting us to recognize, later, that we have misread the earlier part, and should now revise our understanding of the author's intention. Thus Amis intends that the whole story is to be make-believed; it is just that he does not make this intention clear until late in the piece.

The example raises another question. Amis, sorrowing at the world's credulity, reports that a number of people were wholly taken in by the story, despite the fantastical nature of the events depicted.[6] Suppose he had intended his deception to be seamless, to be carried through to the end. On my account the story would then be nonfiction. Is this correct? I believe it is. The feeling that it is not is due, I believe, to the conflation of the fiction/nonfiction distinction with a distinction between serious and nonserious intention to deceive. Hold on for a moment to the supposition that Amis's deceptive intent was global, and ask about the possible reasons he might have for this deception. Probably the reason would be a desire simply to see how much he could get away with; how much gullibility he could draw on. This would be nonserious deception. But suppose (and I mean no actual imputation of unworthy motive) the reason were a desire to make a name for himself as one in contact with the occult, or perhaps to provide false evidence for an irrationally favored theory about the supernatural. This would be serious deception; and in that case none of us would want to call the work fiction. Those who claim that the work would be fiction even if the deceptive intent were global must really, then, be claiming that the work would be fiction as long as the deceptive intent were global *and* nonserious. In that case the boundary between serious and nonserious deceptive assertion would be part of the boundary between fiction and nonfiction. But I do not think that this can be right. First of all, the boundary between nonserious and serious intention to deceive is vague, perhaps very vague. But the distinction between fiction and nonfiction is, intuitively, a rather sharp one. (That is, as sharp as any such distinction can be prior to explication.) But more importantly, it is clear that if Amis's intention were to deceive us then, regardless of whether that intention was serious or nonserious, he would be lying, and to say that a work is fiction is surely to absolve the author from any accusation that he is telling a lie.

I suggest, then, that the claim that the story would be fiction even on the supposition of a global intention to deceive stems from a desire to avoid classing the story, if it were deceptively intended, with misrepresentations of personal achievement or of scientific evidence, or similarly mischievous activities. But this can be done by distinguishing serious from nonserious deception, and leaving all deception outside the boundary of fiction.

V

I turn now to a distinct advantage of this theory over Searle's. It enables us to distinguish the activity of the author of fiction from that of the speaker of fiction, the actor, or the reciter of poetry. It seems intuitively clear that the author and the speaker are engaged in quite different kinds of linguistic actions. From an illocutionary point of view, the performance of the actor or one who merely reads aloud from a given text is a lower grade activity than that of the author writing (or dictating, as it may be) his work. But Searle tends to assimilate the one to the other. He tells us that "The actor pretends . . . to perform the speech acts and other acts of [the] character [he portrays]."[7] Thus both author and actor are engaging in the same kind of pretence. They are both pretending to perform illocutionary acts which they do not in fact perform.

On the theory presented here we can clearly see the difference between the actions of the author and the actor. The author is performing a genuine illocutionary act determined by his intentions. But the actor on the stage is not performing any illocutionary acts. This is evident from the fact that what he is doing when he utters his lines is quite independent of any illocutionary intentions he may have. What determines that he is acting is the fact that his utterances and other actions are intended by him to conform to the script and to the directions of the play, together with the fact that he is

doing these things in the right institutional setting. Now "acting" is an intentional verb, as my account of it in the previous sentence makes clear. To be acting the actor must have various intentions. But he does not need to have any of those intentions which would make his utterance an illocutionary act.

This explains our intuition that the actor's linguistic performance is a pseudo-performance in the sense that it is not the performance of an illocutionary act. But this is not true of the author of fiction, who performs a genuine illocutionary act.

VI

There are some complications in the notion of make-believe that we need to take note of. I have spoken as if we always make-believe those propositions contained in the text of a fictional work. This is not so.

The author of fiction frequently uses words and sentences nonliterally. What happens in such a case? Suppose that an author of fiction uses words ironically or metaphorically or in some other nonliteral way. Then he is uttering the proposition P but not with the intention of getting us to make-believe P. He intends that we should make-believe Q, where Q is a proposition distinct from P. He does this by invoking the same mechanism of conversational implicature, described by Grice, which we invoke when we speak nonliterally in ordinary conversation.[8] Thus if the author says P at some point in his text, and if the previous course of his text makes it seem inappropriate that we should make-believe P at that point, then we cast about for some other proposition that it would be appropriate for us to make-believe. And our choice of an appropriate proposition is guided by the same rules of quality, quantity, etc., which govern the progress of a well-conducted conversation.

Make-believe is complicated in another direction. There are things that we are called upon to make-believe in a work of fiction that are neither stated nor conversationally implicated by the text itself. If Holmes leaves London and arrives in Edinburgh without his mode of transport being described we are clearly called upon to make-believe that he travelled there by some conventional means of transport available in the late nineteenth century, presumably by railway. We are not to make-believe that he travelled by a teleportation device of his own invention, for it is surely false "in the fiction" that he used such a device.

David Lewis has given a complex and ingenious account of the conditions under which a proposition is true in a given fiction.[9] His account seems to be able to deal with a large class of cases where the text fails explicitly to determine the truth-value of some relevant state of affairs. Counter-examples of one kind or another are to be expected however. As with the characterization of fictive illocutionary intentions given earlier, I shall simply assume that Lewis's account is on the right lines, and help myself to the idea of truth in fiction with a reasonably clear conscience.

The question is, how do we mesh the idea of a proposition being true in a fiction with our account of make-believe? Must the reader make-believe all and only those propositions true in the fiction? It will certainly not generally be the case that the author intends the reader to make-believe all and only all the propositions true in the fiction. It is probably true in the Sherlock Holmes stories that Holmes, for all his amazing powers, is a human being in the biological sense. But it would have been a philosophically very self-conscious Conan Doyle who intended his audience to make-believe that proposition. To answer the question of whether readers of Sherlock Holmes stories do even ideally make-believe that proposition we would have to have a sharper concept of make-belief than we do. Perhaps we can use the vagueness of the concept of make-belief here to our own advantage, simply articulating it further in the way that suits us best. Thus it is perhaps convenient to say that the wholly successful act of fictional communication involves make-believing exactly those propositions true in the fiction. (We must be careful to leave room for greater and lesser degrees of success here. Success in fictional communication cannot be an all or nothing affair.)

If we pursue this line, or any line similar to it, we start to complicate matters by separating the intended act of fictional communication from the reader's act of make-believe. There will be cases of successful fictional communication where the reader is required (ideally) to make-believe propositions which the author does not intend him to make-believe. But this is not an unacceptable consequence. We merely have to understand that fiction involves a two-levelled structure of make-believe. To be fiction the text must be such that what it contains is intended by its author to be make-believed. But in picking up the invitation, the reader also picks up an obligation (ideally) to make-believe certain things not explicitly stated in (or conversationally implicated by) the text.

Let us note also that works of fiction may contain sentences which are nonfiction. The author of fiction may make statements which he does not intend the reader to make-believe, but rather to believe. Thus Walter Scott breaks off the narrative of *Guy Mannering* in order to tell us something about the condition of Scottish gypsies. And it is pretty clear that what he is saying he is asserting. This is an obvious point. But there is a related and less obvious point. It should be clear by now that the distinction, within a text, between fictional and nonfictional statements is not the same as the distinction between false and true statements. Nor is it the distinction between what authors (and readers) acknowledge as factual and what they do not so acknowledge. Thus consider a statement within a fictional text, the truth of which is common knowledge between the author and the intended readership – for instance, a fact about London geography. Such a statement may be offered as an integral part of the narrative, as vital to our understanding of how certain events in the novel take place. The offering of such information is, it seems to me, very different in status from the clearly nonfictional utterances which constitute Scott's remarks on gypsy life. We are not intended to bracket out the geographical information from the rest of the story; we are intended, I think, to adopt the make-believe attitude towards it as much as towards the description of fictive characters and their doings. Thus it may be that we are asked to make-believe not only what is true, but also what is common knowledge between author and reader. A statement may be both fictional *and* common knowledge.

VII

I shall conclude by making a point of clarification about my main thesis.

The answer I have given to the question "What constitutes fictional communication?" is not an answer to any question about the aesthetic value of fictional works. That fictional communication takes place between author and reader does not entail that the reader finds the work satisfying, or that there is anything satisfying in it to be found. To use again the terminology of speech act theory, success in the aesthetic sense is a matter of perlocutionary effect, not of illocutionary uptake. The author may intend the reader to be moved by the work, to draw from it conclusions about the nature of human existence, and so on. But these are not his illocutionary intentions, and the work's being fiction is not dependent upon his having intentions such as these. That the work's aesthetic value is a matter of its being apt to produce certain perlocutionary effects is – the "affective fallacy" to the contrary – a proposition I adhere to, but this is not the place to argue for it. I am concerned here only with what is constitutive of the very notion of fiction.

Notes

1   *See* John Searle, "The Logical Status of Fictional Discourse," *New Literary History* 6 (1975), 319–22. See pp. 112–18 in this book.

2   *See* Searle, ibid. Page references are to the reprint of this article in Searle's *Expression and Meaning* (Cambridge University Press, 1979).

3   M. Beardsley, "Aesthetic Intentions and Fictive Illocutions," in P. Hernadi (ed.), *What is Literature?* (Indiana University Press, 1978), pp. 161–77, at p. 170.

4   *See* Kendall Walton, "Fearing Fictions," *Journal of Philosophy*, 75 (1978), 5–27 and "Pictures and Make Believe," *Philosophical Review* 82 (1973), 283–319.

5   In *Collected Short Stories* (Harmondsworth and New York, 1983). The story was originally given as a radio broadcast by the author.

6   *See* his "Introduction" to *Collected Short Stories*, pp. 11–13.

7   Searle, *Expression and Meaning*, p. 69.

8   *See* H. P. Grice, "Logic and Conversation," in P. Cole and J. L. Morgan (eds.), *Syntax and Semantics*, volume 3: *Speech Acts* (New York, 1975), pp. 41–58. For an application of these ideas to literature see Mary Louise Pratt, *Towards a Speech Act Theory of Literature* (Indiana University Press, 1975), chapter 5.

9   Lewis, "Truth in Fiction." See pp. 119–27 in this book.

20

Fiction and Nonfiction

Kendall Walton

What is fictionality? We understand intuitively what it is for something to be "true in a fictional world"; if we didn't, criticism as we know it would be impossible. But how is fictionality to be analyzed? The first step toward an analysis is to investigate the relation between fictionality and the imagination. In doing so we shall see, finally, what props are and how they are important.

Being fictional and being imagined are characteristics that many propositions share. Readers of *Gulliver's Travels* imagine that there is a society of six-inch-tall people. Fred imagines that he is rich and famous. But it would be a serious mistake simply to identify the fictional with what is imagined. What is fictional need not be imagined, and perhaps what is imagined need not be fictional.

"Let's say that stumps are bears," Eric proposes. Gregory agrees, and a game of make-believe is begun, one in which stumps – all stumps, not just one or a specified few – "count as" bears. Coming upon a stump in the forest, Eric and Gregory imagine a bear. Part of what they imagine is that there is a bear at a certain spot – the spot actually occupied by the stump. "Hey, there's a bear over there!" Gregory yells to Eric. Susan, who is not in on the game but overhears, is alarmed. So Eric reassures her that it is only "in the game" that there is a bear at the place indicated. The proposition that there is a bear there is fictional in the game.

Or so Eric and Gregory think. They approach the bear cautiously, but only to discover that the stump is not a stump at all but a moss-covered boulder. "False alarm. There isn't a bear there after all," Gregory observes with surprise and relief. And for the benefit of outsiders, "We were mistaken in thinking that, in the world of the game, there was a bear there." Eric and Gregory did imagine that a bear was there, but this did not make it fictional in their game. They do not say that fictionally there was a bear which evaporated when they approached, nor that it is *no longer* fictional that a bear was there at the earlier time. Gregory takes back his previous claim that fictionally a bear was in the place indicated, and he is right to do so.

Meanwhile, however, unbeknownst to anyone, there is an actual stump buried in a thicket not twenty feet behind Eric. Fictionally a bear is lurking in the thicket, although neither Eric nor Gregory realizes the danger. No one imagines a bear in the thicket; it is not fictional that a bear is there because somebody imagines that there is. But it is fictional. What makes it fictional? The stump. Thus does the stump generate a fictional truth. It is a prop. Props are generators of fictional truths, things which, by virtue of their nature or existence, make propositions fictional. A snow fort is a prop. It is responsible for the fictionality of the proposition that there is a (real) fort with turrets and a moat. A doll makes it fictional in a child's game that there is a blonde baby girl.

Representational works of art are props also. What makes it fictional in *La Grande Jatte* that a couple is strolling in a park is the painting itself, the pattern of paint splotches on the surface of the canvas. It is because of the words constituting *Gulliver's Travels* that fictionally there is a society of six-inch-tall people who go to war over how eggs are to be broken.

Props generate fictional truths independently of what anyone does or does not imagine. But they do not do so entirely on their own, apart from any (actual or potential) imaginers. Props function only in a social, or at least human, setting. The stump in the thicket makes it fictional that a bear is there only because there is a certain convention, understanding, agreement in the game of make-believe, one to the effect that wherever there is a stump, fictionally there is a bear. I will call this a *principle of generation*. This principle was established by explicit stipulation: "Let's say that stumps are bears." But not all principles are established thus. Some, including most involving works of art, are never explicitly agreed on or even formulated, and imaginers may be unaware of them, at least in the sense of being unable to spell them out. I do not assume that principles of generation are, in general or even normally, "conventional" or "arbitrary," nor that they must be learned. Nevertheless, what principles of generation there are depends on which ones people accept in various contexts. The principles that are in force are those that are understood, at least implicitly, to be in force.

Props are often prompters or objects of imagining also; even all three. Any stumps Eric and Gregory discover during their game have all three roles; they prompt Eric and Gregory to imagine certain things, and among the imaginings they prompt are imaginings about themselves (imaginings, of the stumps, that they are bears). But the three functions are distinct. It is clear already that props need not be prompters or objects of any imaginings. An undiscovered stump prompts no imaginings and is not imagined about, although it is a prop. Nor must prompters or objects be props. Suppose Eric associates raspberries with poison ivy; it was after picking raspberries that he suffered his worst outbreak of poison ivy, and he hasn't forgotten. He sees raspberry bushes in the forest and imagines poison ivy. Let's say that he also imagines of the raspberry bushes that they are poison ivy plants.

This does not make it fictional in his game that poison ivy is growing in the forest, for there is as yet no principle of generation in effect, no even implicit understanding, whereby the raspberry bushes "count as" poison ivy. No such principle need be in force even if it happens that Gregory too associates raspberry bushes with poison ivy for some reason and is prompted to imagine as Eric does. Without the relevant understanding, Eric's and Gregory's imaginations simply wander – in similar directions, as it happens. They interrupt the game to engage in their own personal fantasies.

We are still lacking a positive account of fictionality. We know that being fictional is not the same as being imagined, and we have seen how some fictional truths are established – by props working in conjunction with principles of generation. But what is thus established? The answer will emerge when we consider what connections do obtain between fictionality and imagination.

Imagining is easily thought of as a free, unregulated activity, subject to no constraints save whim, happenstance, and the obscure demands of the unconscious. The imagination is meant to explore, to wander at will through our conceptual universes. In this respect imagination appears to contrast sharply with belief. Beliefs, unlike imaginings, are correct or incorrect. Belief aims at truth. What is true and only what is true is to be believed. We are not free to believe as we please. We are free to imagine as we please.

So it may seem, but it isn't quite so. Imaginings are constrained also; some are proper, appropriate in certain contexts, and others not. Herein lies the key to the notion of fictional truth. Briefly, a fictional truth consists in there being a prescription or mandate in some context to imagine something. Fictional propositions are propositions that are *to be* imagined – whether or not they are in fact imagined.

The agreements which participants in a collective daydream make about what to imagine can be thought of as rules prescribing certain imaginings. It is a rule of a certain joint fantasy that participants are to imagine traveling to Saturn in a rocket, or that they are to imagine of a particular stump that it is a bear. True, the agreements are made, the rules established voluntarily, and their prescriptions are relative to one's role as a participant in the imaginative activity in question. But they do prescribe. Anyone who refuses to imagine what was agreed on refuses to "play the game" or plays it improperly. He breaks a rule.

These rules are categorical. But I shall be interested mostly in conditional rules, ones to the effect that *if* certain circumstances obtain, certain things are to be imagined. The principle of generation in Eric's and Gregory's game is a conditional rule – the rule that if there is a stump at a certain place, one is to imagine that there is a bear there. Given that a stump does occupy a certain spot, imagining that a bear occupies that spot is mandated. Of course if participants in the game are unaware of a particular stump – because it is buried in a thicket, for example – their failure to imagine as prescribed is understandable; one can only do one's best to follow the rule. But to refuse to imagine that there is a bear where there is a stump in full view would be to flout the rule, to refuse to play the game.

The fictionality of the proposition that there is a bear at a certain place consists in the fact that imagining it is prescribed by a rule of the game. The rule is conditional, its prescription dependent on the presence of a stump. Thus does the stump generate the fictional truth.... Fictionality has turned out to be analogous to truth in some ways; the relation between fictionality and imagining parallels that between truth and belief. Imagining aims at the fictional as belief aims at the true. What is true is to be believed; what is fictional is to be imagined. [...]

Nonfiction

Where are we to place Darwin's *Origin of Species*, Prescott's *History of the Conquest of Peru*, and Sandburg's biography of Abraham Lincoln, not to mention philosophical treatises, mathematics textbooks, instruction manuals, recipes, legal documents, and requests to pass the salt? How do such "works of nonfiction" compare with novels and other works of fiction?

Postponing for the moment certain qualifications and refinements, we can say this: It is not the function of biographies, textbooks, and newspaper articles, as such, to serve as props in games of make-believe. They are used to claim truth for certain propositions rather than to make propositions fictional. Instead of establishing fictional worlds, they purport to describe the real world. We read the *New York Times* to find out what actually happened in Washington or Walla Walla, not what happened "in the world of the *Times*." Works of nonfiction do not, in general, qualify as representations in our special sense.

Here is an objection: Darwin's *Origin of Species*, for example, is designed to elicit beliefs. It is arguable that believing something involves imagining it (or at least that occurrent believing involves imagining, and perhaps Darwin's work is designed to induce occurrent beliefs). So doesn't *The Origin of Species* prescribe imaginings, and thus generate fictional truths?

No. In writing his book Darwin no doubt intended to get readers to believe certain things. But there is no understanding to the effect that readers are to believe whatever the book says just because it says it. If we are to believe the theory of evolution, it is because that theory is true, or because there is good evidence for it, not because it is expressed in *The Origin of Species* – although of course *The Origin of Species* might convince us of the theory's truth or inform us of evidence for it. Darwin's book itself does not prescribe believings. So we cannot conclude that it prescribes imaginings, even if believing involves imagining.

Perhaps the reader of *The Origin of Species*, qua reader of that work, is obliged at least to consider, understand, attend to, entertain the propositions expressed in it, regardless of their truth or falsity. If he does not do so, perhaps he is not "playing the game" of reading the book properly. But considering or entertaining propositions falls short of imagining them.

An important symptom of the difference between *The Origin of Species* and works like *Gulliver's Travels* which I count as representational is that what is said in *The Origin of Species* does not of itself warrant assertions like "Species evolved by means of natural selection." It justifies such assertions only insofar as it provides good reason to think they are true. But the sentences in *Gulliver's Travels* warrant the assertive utterance "A war was fought over how to break eggs," quite apart from whether they give us reason to think such a war actually was fought.

Of course it is possible to *read* histories or biographies or treatises or committee reports as novels. One can resolve to imagine whatever propositions Sandburg's biography of Lincoln expresses; one can adopt a principle that one is to do so. (This may but need not involve ignoring whether the propositions are true or false.) One thus plays a game of make-believe in which the biography is a prop of the kind novels usually are. If one does, we might allow that the biography is a representation *for that reader*. But we might deny that it is a representation *simpliciter* (in our sense), on the ground that its *function*, in the relevant sense, is not to be a prop in games of make-believe, no matter how anyone chooses to use it.

Some works straddle the fence. Many historical novels, for instance, are best understood as prescribing the imagining of the propositions they express and *also* seeking to elicit the reader's belief in many of them. (It is usually understood, however, that the reader is not to believe propositions about details of conversations between historical figures which the novelist could not possibly be in a position to know, for example.) Some histories are written in such a vivid, novelistic style that they almost inevitably induce the reader to imagine what is said, regardless of whether or not he believes it. (Indeed this may be true of Prescott's *History of the Conquest of Peru.*) If we think of the work as prescribing such a reaction, it serves as a prop in a game of make-believe. We might even allow that its function is partly to serve as a prop, although this function may be subordinate to that of attempting to inform the reader. There are differences of degree along several dimensions here.

We thus find ourselves with a way of distinguishing *fiction* from *nonfiction*. Works of fiction are simply representations in our special sense, works whose function is to serve as props in games of make-believe. Except for the fact that representations need not be *works*, human artifacts – an important fact, as we shall see – we could use "representation" and "work of fiction" interchangeably.

This notion of fiction is a natural descendant of the one used by booksellers and librarians in separating fairy tales, short stories, novels, and Superman comic books from newspaper articles, instruction manuals, geography textbooks, biographies, and histories. This is not to say that we should expect to draw the line just where they do, however; the rough everyday classification needs refining in order to serve our theoretical purposes. Berkeley's *Dialogues between Hylas and Philonous*, for example, containing those two fictional characters as they do, will fall in our category of fiction.

Berkeley's *Dialogues* constitute a serious attempt to illuminate the reader about the real world, and the manner in which he pursues this objective is similar in many respects to the way Hume, for example, pursues it in *The Treatise of Human Nature*, notwithstanding Berkeley's use of fictional characters. We can understand why the *Dialogues* are commonly classified as "nonfiction." But this

classification, together with an understanding of "fiction" in the spirit of ours, raises the disconcerting specter of an overlap between "fiction" and "nonfiction." We might find ourselves counting the *Dialogues*, and also certain histories and historical novels, as *both*. Better to find a more perspicuous way of characterizing the complexities of these works. For the sake of clarity I will mean by "nonfiction" simply "not fiction." Any work with the function of serving as a prop in games of make-believe, however minor or peripheral or instrumental this function might be, qualifies as "fiction"; only what lacks this function entirely will be called nonfiction.

I have not drawn a precise line around the category of fiction. Nor is it desirable to do so; that would obscure some of the most interesting features of the many complex and subtle works in the border area. But one of the aims of my theory is to develop tools for understanding works that resist classification, works that are in one way or another mixed or marginal or indeterminate or ambiguous.

It is important to consider this way of understanding "fiction" against the background of alternatives. In the following several sections we will examine a selection of more standard accounts. Their shortcomings will point all the more strongly to my own rather unorthodox one, and will reinforce the make-believe approach as a whole. In particular, we will note important advantages that the make-believe theory enjoys over certain linguistically based ones. [. . .]

Fiction and Assertion

Whether a literary work is fiction or nonfiction does not necessarily show in its words. The very same sequence of words, the same sentences, might constitute either a biography or a novel. Nor does the essential difference lie in the relation of the words to the world. We have already seen that it is not a matter of being about real or fictious entities, and that it does not consist in the truth values of a work's sentences, in whether or not they correspond to the facts.

Perhaps what is crucial is not whether what the author writes is true but whether he *claims* truth for it, whether he *asserts* the sentences (the declarative ones anyway) he inscribes.[1] Are literary works of fiction to be understood as texts that are unasserted, and that are not vehicles of other (ordinary) illocutionary actions? This proposal has the advantage of putting some distance between the notion of works of fiction and that of "fiction" as contrasted to reality, fact, and truth. It is obviously much too crude as stated. But its difficulties run deeper than might first appear.

It is true that in writing fiction an author typically does not perform the illocutionary acts that a person using the same words in a nonfictional setting is likely to be performing. In writing (the original German version of) "I have completed the construction of my burrow and it seems to be successful,"[2] Kafka was not asserting, claiming that he had actually finished making a burrow. But this simple observation leaves us far from the heart of the notion of fiction.

It is immediately obvious that to inscribe a series of declarative sentences without asserting them (or performing any other standard illocutionary action) is not necessarily to produce a work of fiction. One might compile a list of sentences for purposes of a grammar lesson or to test a microphone. Fiction is not just language stripped of some of its normal functions; it is something positive, something special.

Is the absence of normal illocutionary force at least a necessary condition of a work's being fiction? Writing fiction has often been said to be somehow incompatible with writing assertively. But it certainly is not. Assertions can be made in any number of ways: by producing a declarative sentence while delivering a lecture, by raising a flag, by honking a horn, by wearing a rose, by extending one's arm through a car window. There is no reason why, in appropriate circumstances, one should not be able to make an assertion by writing fiction. Indeed there is a long tradition of doing just that. There is what we call *didactic* fiction – fiction used for instruction, advertising, propaganda, and so on. There is the not uncommon practice, even in ordinary conversation, of making a point by telling a story, of speaking in parables. (Perhaps writing fiction is more often a means of performing other illocutionary actions – suggesting, asking, raising an issue, reminding, encouraging to act – than a means of making assertions.) [...]

Although writing fiction is not incompatible with making assertons or performing other illocutionary acts, there is a simple but important truth which probably underlines the words of those who seem to say that it is: Works of fiction are not *necessarily* vehicles of assertions or of any other illocutionary acts; to produce a work of fiction is not in itself to perform an illocutionary act. On this point I disagree markedly with many who claim to derive an account of fiction from speech-act theory in other ways.

Pretended and Represented Illocutionary Actions

Some theorists construe storytelling as an act of *pretending* to assert or pretending to perform other illocutionary acts, and works of fiction as vehicles or products of such acts of pretense. John Searle is among those who have taken this line.[3] Iris Murdoch, he says, uses sentences in her novel *The Red and the Green* which would ordinarily be used to make assertions about the thoughts and actions of a certain Second Lieutenant Andrew Chase-White. But this is not what Murdoch does with them. Instead she pretends to make such assertions. In general, Searle claims, "An author of fiction pretends to perform illocutionary acts which he is not in fact performing" (p. 325).

Searle is quick to point out that Murdoch's pretense is not a form of deception. She is not trying to fool anyone. The sense in which she is pretending is one in which "to pretend to . . . do something is to engage in a performance which is *as if* one were doing . . . the thing and is without any intent to deceive" (p. 324).

This won't do as an account of pretending, not even with the qualification Searle adds later that "one cannot truly be said to have pretended to do something unless one intended to pretend to do it" (p. 325). A harpsichordist who plays his instrument as though he were playing a piano, using pianistic techniques, is not necessarily pretending to play the piano, not even if his pianistic style of playing is intentional. We can improve the account by adding that to pretend to do something one must imagine oneself to be doing it. (Eventually I will explain pretense in terms of make-believe, but this can wait.)

I will ignore Searle's contention that the author of fiction is not actually performing the illocutionary acts in question. As we have seen, he might be doing so. But one might devise an appropriate sense of "pretense" in which one can pretend to do something which one is also actually doing. In any case, there are more serious objections to Searle's way of understanding fiction.

I suppose that creators of literary fictions do sometimes pretend to assert what they say or write. A storyteller, an old man spinning yarns about his youthful exploits, may be pretending to claim that he made a fortune in the Yukon gold rush and lost it in a poker game. It is possible that when Murdoch wrote *The Red and the Green* she was pretending to make assertions about a certain Andrew Chase-White. But she may not have been so pretending. Whether or not she was is of no particular significance, and has nothing to do with what makes her work a work of fiction.

The quickest way to see what is wrong with this pretense account of fiction is to remind ourselves that *literary* fictions are not the only ones, and that a crucial test of the adequacy of any account of what makes fictional literature fictional is whether it can plausibly be extended to other media. The pretense theory fails this test resoundingly.

Pierre-Auguste Renoir's painting *Bathers* and Jacques Lipchitz's sculpture *Guitar Player* surely belong in the fiction category. But I very much doubt that in creating them Renoir and Lipchitz were pretending to make assertions (or to perform other illocutionary acts). Painting and sculpting are less standard or obvious ways of asserting than uttering declarative sentences. So it is not clear that painting *Bathers* or sculpting *Guitar Player* should count as behaving as if one were making an assertion. And it is unlikely that either artist imagined himself to be asserting anything. [. . .]

It is essential to see that the ills of the theories of fiction as pretended and as represented illocutionary actions are not superficial ones that might respond to topical treatment. Tinkering with the notion of pretense or that of a narrator will not help. The theories are wrong to the core. The core of both of them is the idea that fiction is parasitic on "serious" discourse, that fictional uses of language, pictures, or anything else are to be understood in terms of their use in making assertions, asking questions, issuing orders, or engaging in other activities characteristic of nonfictional language. These "serious" uses are primary, it is thought, and fictional uses are based on or derived from them in one way or another. What is crucial, according to the core of the theories, is that fiction necessarily involves the use of tools designed primarily for "serious" discourse, and that it is their primary "serious" function that makes possible their use in fiction.

We have seen that works of fiction – pictorial and sculptural ones at least – are not things of sorts which need have any "serious" uses. Indeed, I see no reason to suppose that there must be any such thing as "serious" discourse, involving language or

pictures or anything else, or that anyone must have any conception of such, in order for pictures and sculptures to be fictional. The notion of fiction is not parasitic on that of "serious" discourse.

Why has anyone thought otherwise? Mainly, it seems to me, because of a narrow concentration on literature coupled with the naive assumption that whatever works for literature will work for the other arts as well. Fictional *literature* may be parasitic on "serious" discourse. Literature, fictional or otherwise, necessarily involves the use of language, and perhaps nothing counts as language unless it is sometimes used for "serious" discourse. If so, fictional literature is to be explained partly in terms of "serious" discourse – but because it is literature, not because it is fiction.

Even this is open to challenge. Consider a society in which there is no "serious" discourse, but in which people construct works of fiction out of what look like English sentences. Their works are not vehicles of pretended illocutionary actions. Nor do they represent illocutionary actions; like pictures and sculptures, they have no narrators. Shall we say that they are composed of *language*, and that they are works of *literature?* If so, we will have to grant that even the notion of literary fiction is independent of that of "serious" discourse.

Fiction Making as an Illocutionary Action?

Let us consider one final way in which speech-act theory has been thought to illuminate the nature of fiction. Fiction making is sometimes said to be not one of the standard varieties of illocutionary actions that constitute "serious" discourse, nor an action of pretending to perform such illocutionary actions or one of representing them, but rather a special, sui generis sort of illocutionary action itself. Works of fiction are thought of as essentially vehicles of the illocutionary action of fiction making.[4] It is incumbent on propounders of this view to spell out what kind of illocutionary act fiction making is, of course. But they face a difficulty more serious than this, one infecting the very idea that fiction making is an illocutionary action and that works of fiction are essentially vehicles of such an action.

Speech-act theories attempt to understand language fundamentally in terms of actions that speakers perform rather than properties of words or sentences. Linguistic expressions are regarded as essentially vehicles of speakers' actions; their salient properties, such as their having certain meanings, are explained in terms of their roles in such actions.

Kendall Walton

If the action of fiction making is to be regarded fruitfully as an illocutionary action, as analogous to asserting, questioning, and promising, it must be similarly fundamental. Works of fiction must be understood primarily as vehicles of acts of fiction making, just as sentences are vehicles of acts of asserting, questioning, and promising.

Although we can describe sentences as "assertions," the notion of assertion applies primarily to human actions. No doubt this is because it is the actions, not the sentences, that are fundamental. Assertive sentences are important as means whereby people assert. Sentences are assertions in a merely derivative or parasitic sense. A sentence is an "assertion" if it is a sentence of a kind people ordinarily or typically or normally use to make assertions. Likewise, it is argued, fictionally representing is fundamentally a human action, something people do.[5] They do it by producing texts or pictures or other artifacts; hence we can, if we like, speak in a derivative sense of texts or pictures as fictional representations. But it is the action that is primary – an action that can be classified along with asserting, promising, and requesting as an illocutionary action in its own right.

This analogy fails dramatically. The action of fiction making does not have a place in the institution of fiction similar to that which illocutionary actions have in ordinary conversation.

Consider a naturally occurring inscription of an assertive sentence: cracks in a rock, for example, which by pure coincidence spell out "Mount Merapi is erupting." And suppose we know for sure, somehow, that the cracks were formed naturally, that nobody inscribed (or used) them to assert anything. This inscription will not serve anything like the purposes vehicles of people's assertions typically serve. It will not convince us that Mount Merapi is erupting, or that there is reason to believe it is, or that someone thinks it is or wants us to think so. Ordinarily we are interested in vehicles of a person's assertions precisely because they are just that; an assertive inscription or utterance gets its importance from the fact that someone asserted something in producing it. Our ultimate interest may be in the truth of what is said; but if the words convince us of this truth, they do so, typically, because we take the speaker to have uttered them assertively. Likewise for other illocutionary actions. The *action* of promising, requesting, apologizing, or threatening is crucial. Sentences are important as vehicles of such actions. A naturally occurring inscription of a sentence of a kind nor-

mally used to promise or request or apologize or threaten would be no more than a curiosity.

Contrast a naturally occurring story: cracks in a rock spelling out "Once upon a time there were three bears ... " The realization that the inscription was not made or used by anyone need not prevent us from reading and enjoying the story in much the way we would if it had been. It may be entrancing, suspenseful, spellbinding, comforting; we may laugh and cry. Some dimensions of our experiences of authored stories will be absent, but the differences are not ones that would justify denying that it functions and is understood as a full-fledged *story*. We will not achieve insight into the author or her society if there is no author, nor will we admire her skill as a storyteller or marvel at the perceptiveness of her vision of the human condition. Neither will we acknowledge her affirmations or protestations or receive her promises or apologies. But these opportunities, when we have them, are *consequences* of the author's having told a story, having produced an object whose function is to serve as a prop of a certain sort in games of make-believe. It is because she did this that we achieve insights about her or marvel at her perceptiveness or whatever. This make-believe function needs to be recognized apart from the interests in fiction makers which things possessing it often serve. To restrict "fiction" in its primary sense to actions of fiction making would be to obscure what is special about stories that does not depend on their being authored, on their being vehicles of persons' story-tellings. The basic concept of a *story* and the basic concept of *fiction* attach most perspicuously to objects rather than actions.

Stories do not often occur in nature, but fictional pictures do. We see faces, figures, animals in rock patterns and clouds. The patterns or clouds are not vehicles of anyone's acts of picturing, of fiction making. But to rule that this automatically disqualifies them as pictures or that it makes them such only in a secondary sense would be to slight their role as props. This is a role they share with painted pictures, but it need not involve thinking of them as things of a kind normally produced in acts of picture making (or things of a kind normally presented or displayed as pictures). Naturally occurring designs are best regarded as pictures, full-fledged ones, when it is understood to be their function to serve as props in games of a specifically visual sort.

The fundamental disanalogy between illocutionary actions and acts of fiction making comes out in differences in the roles of agents' intentions. A crucial question for a person on the receiving end of an illocutionary action is almost always, Did he mean it? Did he intend to assert this, to promise that, to issue such and such an order or apology? But one may well read a story or contemplate a (fictional) picture without wondering which fictional truths the author or artist meant to generate. Photographers, especially, can easily be unaware of fictional truths generated by their works. Authors and other artists may be surprised at where extrapolation from the fictional truths they intentionally generated leads. This need not make any particular difference to the appreciator – unless he is concerned with what the artist might be asserting in producing the fiction, what illocutionary actions she might be performing in the process of, and in addition to, producing it. And it does not justify a judgment that the action of fiction making was defective or did not come off at all. The notion of accidental fiction making is not problematic in the way that that of accidental assertion is.

Fiction making is not reasonably classified as an illocutionary action, and works of fiction are not essentially vehicles of acts of fiction making. It may be that *language* is centered on the actions of speakers. The institution of fiction centers not on the activity of fiction makers but on objects – works of fiction or natural objects – and their role in appreciators' activities, objects whose function is to serve as props in games of make-believe. Fiction making is merely the activity of constructing such props.

The fiction maker does come into play insofar as function is understood to depend on her intentions. But it need not be understood to depend on them. Our theory of fiction applies across the board independently of any particular means of fixing functions. In our society the function of a text or picture, how it is to be used, may be determined partly by its maker's intentions. But another society might give less weight to this consideration or none at all, and even we determine the functions of natural objects differently.

Functions are cultural constructs in any case, however, and nothing is fiction independent of a social (or at least human) context or setting. The naturally occurring story of the Three Bears is fiction only by virtue of people's understandings about how to treat certain kinds of texts. Such understandings need not involve anything like someone's making – or presenting or displaying – an inscription for a certain purpose, or meaning something by it, or doing something with it. It may be understood that *any* textual inscription beginning "Once upon a time" is to serve as a prop, including any that no one even knows about.

Along with the act of fiction making (and that of presenting or displaying a fiction) we must exclude *communication* in any sense involving human communicators from the essence of fiction. Language may be essentially a means whereby people communicate with one another; hence the plausibility of basing a theory of language on actions of communicators, language users. To suppose that fiction is essentially a means of communication is no more plausible than to suppose it incapable of serving this purpose.

People do communicate by means of fictions, and we are often interested in what their makers or users do with them or mean by them. Nothing I have said should detract from the role fictions often play as vehicles of action. What I insist on is separate recognition of the primary function of being a prop in games of make-believe, whether or not someone's producing or displaying something with this function is also of interest, and whether or not that function is conferred on it by the maker or displayer.

In addition to being independent of language – of its "serious" uses in particular – the basic notion of fiction has turned out to be strikingly disanalogous to it.

Notes

1 This, with some qualifications, is Monroe Beardsley's proposal (*Aesthetics*, 2nd edn. (New York: Harcourt Brace Jovanovich, 1980), pp. 419–23). See also Richard Ohmann, "Speech Acts and the Definition of Literature," *Philosophy and Rhetoric* 4 (1971), 1–19, esp. pp. 13–14.
2 "The Burrow."
3 Searle, "Logical Status of Fictional Discourse," *New Literary History* 6 (1975) pp. 319–32. A similar theory was advanced by Richard Gale, "The Fictive Use of Language," *Philosophy* 46 (1971), 324–39. See also Lewis, "Truth in Fiction," p. 266 ("Storytelling is pretense. The storyteller purports to be telling the truth about matters whereof he had knowledge"). See pp. 112–18 and 119–27 in this volume.
4 Nicholas Wolterstorff, *Works and Worlds of Art* (New York: Oxford University Press, 1980), pp. 219–34. See also Gale, "Fictive Use of Language"; Marcia Eaton, "Liars, Ranters, and Dramatic Speakers". in *Art and Philosophy*, ed. William Kennick, 2nd edn. (New York: St Martin's, 1979); and Currie, "What Is Fiction?" (see pp. 128–35 in this book).
5 Wolterstorff, *Works and Worlds*, pp. 198–200.

21

Fictional Characters as Abstract Artifacts

Amie Thomasson

If we are to postulate fictional characters at all, it seems advisable to postulate them as entities that can satisfy or at least make sense of our most important beliefs and practices concerning them. Often theories of fiction are driven not by an independent sense of what is needed to understand talk and practices regarding fiction, but rather by a desire to show how fictional characters may find their place in a preconceived ontology of possible, nonexistent, or abstract objects – to demonstrate one more useful application of the ontology under discussion, or to provide catchy and familiar examples. Instead of starting from a ready-made ontology and seeing how we can fit fictional characters into it, I suggest that we begin by paying careful attention to our literary practices so that we can see what sorts of things would most closely correspond to them. I thus begin by discussing what sorts of entities our practices in reading and discussing works of fiction seem to commit us to, and I draw out the *artifactual theory* of fiction as a way of characterizing the sort of entity that seems best suited to do the job of fictional characters.

What Fictional Characters Seem to Be

Fictional objects as I discuss them here include such characters as Emma Woodhouse, Sherlock Holmes, Hamlet, and Tom Sawyer – characters who appear in works of literature and whose fortunes we follow in reading those works. In our everyday discussions of literature we treat fictional characters as created entities brought into existence at a certain time through the acts of an author. If someone contended that George Washington was a great fan of Sherlock Holmes, we might object that in Washington's time there was no Sherlock Holmes – the Holmes character was not created until 1887. The term "fiction" derives from the Latin *fingere* meaning "to form," and this linguistic root is still evident in our practices in treating fictional characters as entities formed by the work of an author or authors in composing a work of fiction. We do not describe authors of fictional works as discovering their characters or selecting them from an ever-present set of abstract, nonexistent, or possible objects. Instead, we describe authors as inventing their characters, making them up, or creating them, so that before being written about by an author, there is no fictional object. Taking authors to be genuinely creative as they make up fictional characters is central to our ordinary understanding of fiction. One of the things we admire about certain authors is their ability to make up sympathetic, multidimensional characters rather than cardboard cutouts, and at times we count our good luck that certain characters like Sherlock Holmes were created when, given a busier medical practice,

From *Fiction and Metaphysics* (Cambridge: Cambridge University Press, 1999), pp. 5–23, 155, 156. Reprinted by permission of the publisher and author.

Arthur Conan Doyle might never have created him.

Thus, if we are to postulate fictional characters that satisfy our apparent practices regarding them, it seems that we should consider them to be entities that can come into existence only through the mental and physical acts of an author – as essentially created entities. Once we begin to treat fictional characters as created entities, a further issue arises. Do they simply need to be created at some time, by someone, or is the identity of a fictional character somehow tied to its particular origin in the work of a particular author or authors taking part in a particular literary tradition? Unexamined intuitions may provide no clear answer to this question, but our goal is to draw out a view of fictional characters that corresponds as closely as possible to our practices in studying fictional characters. Such critical practices provide grounds for taking the latter view, that a particular fictional character not only has to be created but is necessarily tied to its particular origin.

Suppose that a student happens on two literary figures remarkably similar to each other; both, for example, are said to be maids, warding off attempts at seduction, and so on. Under what conditions would we say that these are works about one and the same fictional character? It seems that we would say that the two works are about the same character only if we have reason to believe that the works derived from a common origin – if, for example, one work is the sequel to the other, or if both are developments of the same original myth. Literary scholars mark this difference by distinguishing "sources" drawn on by an author in composing a work from coincidentally similar characters or works, mere "analogs." If one can show that the author of the latter work had close acquaintance with the earlier work, it seems we have good support for the claim that the works are about the same character (as for example in the Pamela Andrews of Richardson's and Fielding's tales). But if someone can prove that the authors of the two works bore no relation to each other or to a common source but were working from distinct traditions and sources, it seems that the student has at best uncovered a coincidence – that different individuals and cultures generated remarkably similar analogous characters.

So it seems that if we wish to postulate fictional objects that correspond to our ordinary practices about identifying them, fictional characters should be considered entities that depend on the particular acts of their author or authors to bring them into existence. Naturally the process of creating a particular character may be diffuse: It may be created by more than one author, over a lengthy period of time, involving many participants in a story-telling tradition, and so on. But the fact that the process of creating a fictional character may be diffuse does not disrupt the general point that, whatever the process of creation for a given character may be, for coming into existence it depends on those particular creative acts. Such a requirement not only is consistent with critical practices in identifying characters but also is crucial to treating characters as identical across different sequels, parodies, and other literary developments.

Once created, clearly a fictional character can go on existing without its author or his or her creative acts, for it is preserved in literary works that may long outlive their author. If we treat fictional characters as creations invented by authors in creating works of literature, and existing because of their appearance in such works, then it seems that for a fictional character to be preserved, some literary work about it must remain in existence. And so we have uncovered a second dependency: Characters depend on the creative acts of their authors in order to come into existence and depend on literary works in order to remain in existence. Here again the question arises: Does a fictional character depend on one particular literary work for its preservation, or does a fictional character need only to appear in some literary work or other to remain in existence? It certainly seems that a character may survive as long as some work in which it appears remains. If we could not allow that the same character may appear in more than one literary work, or even slightly different editions of a work, then we would be unable to account for literary critical discourse about the development of a character across different works, and we would even be unable to admit that readers of different editions of *The Great Gatsby* are discussing one and the same Jay Gatsby. In short, we would be left postulating many characters in cases in which there seems to be but one. So it seems we should allow that one character may appear in more than one work, and if it can appear in more than one work, it must remain in existence as long as one literary work about it does. Thus even if "A Scandal in Bohemia" should exist no longer, the character Sherlock Holmes can go on existing provided that one or more of the other works in which he appears remains in existence. So, although a fictional character depends on a literary work for its continued existence, it depends only on the maintenance of some work in which it appears.

The dependence of a character on a literary work forces us to address a second question: If a character depends on a work of literature, what does a work of literature depend on? When can we say that a literary work exists? Because characters depend on literary works, anything on which literary works depend is also, ultimately, something on which characters depend. As ordinarily treated in critical discourse, a literary work is not an abstract sequence of words or concepts waiting to be discovered but instead is the creation of a particular individual or group at a particular time in particular social and historical circumstances. Thus, as with characters, it seems that literary works must be created by an author or authors at a certain time in order to come into existence.

Like a character, it also seems that a work of literature depends rigidly on the acts of its particular author to exist, so that, even if two authors coincidentally composed the same words in the same order, they would not thereby have composed the same work of literature. One way to see the essentiality of a work's origin to its identity is by observing that literary works take on different properties based on the time and circumstances of their creation and creator. By virtue of originating in a different place in literary, social, and political history, at the hands of a different author, or in a different place in an author's *oeuvre*, one and the same sequence of words can provide the basis for two very different works of literature with different aesthetic and artistic properties. The same sequence of words appearing in *Animal Farm* could have been written in 1905, but that literary work could not have had the property of being a satire of the Stalinist state, a central property of Orwell's tale. If the same words of *Portrait of the Artist as a Young Man* were written by James Joyce not in 1916, but instead after *Ulysses* came out in 1922, that work would lack the property of exhibiting a highly original use of language, which *Portrait of the Artist* has. Two mysteries based on the same sequence of words written in 1816 and today, both ending with "the butler did it," might have the property of having a surprise ending in the former but not the latter case. A screenplay with the same sequence of words as Oliver Stone's *Nixon*, if written in 1913, could have the properties neither of being about (the real) Richard Nixon, nor of being a sympathetic portrayal of

the main character, nor of being revisionary and speculative. Similar cases could be brought to bear to show that a wide variety of aesthetic and artistic properties central to discussions of works of literature – being a work of high modernism, a parody, horrifying, reactionary, exquisitely detailed, an updated retelling of an old story – depend on the context and circumstances of creation, so that literary works may be based on the same series of words but have different aesthetic and artistic properties. In at least some cases, these properties seem essential to the literary work, e.g., being a satire seems essential to *Animal Farm* considered as a work of literature. For that reason, it seems that a literary work is best conceived not as an abstract sequence of words but as an artifact that had to be created in those original circumstances in which it was created.

Like fictional characters, literary works, once created, can clearly survive the death of their author; indeed the great majority of literary works we have today persist despite the deaths of their authors. But does a literary work, once created, always exist, or can a work once again cease to exist even after it is created? If we take seriously the view that literary works are artifacts created at a certain time, it seems natural to allow that, like other artifacts from umbrellas to unions to universities, they can also be destroyed. It would surely seem bizarre to claim that all of the lost stories of past cultures still exist as much as ever. On the contrary, one of the things that is often lamented about the destruction of cultures, be they ancient Greek or Native American, is the loss of the stories and fictional worlds they created. We treat literary tales as entities that can cease to exist, that at times take special efforts and government projects to preserve (e.g., by recording the oral folktales of Appalachia), or that may be destroyed by a temperamental author burning unpublished manuscripts. Treating works of literature as entities that may be destroyed – at least if all copies and memories of them are destroyed – seems a natural consequence of considering them to be cultural artifacts rather than Platonistic abstracta.

Yet certainly there are many who do not share the intuition that literary works may cease to exist after being created. The idea that literary works, if they exist, must exist eternally (once created) seems to me to be a hangover of a Platonism that assimilates all abstract entities to the realm of the changeless and timeless, and in particular a consequence of viewing literary works roughly as series of words or concepts that can survive the destruction of any collection of copies of them. To the extent that it is a hangover of Platonism, this position should lose its appeal if one accepts the earlier arguments that literary works are, instead, artifacts individuated in part by the particular circumstances of their creation.

Apart from a lingering Platonism, one feature of our language might incline some to the view that literary works cannot cease to exist: We often speak not of *destroyed* or *past* works, but rather of *lost* works, as if all that were missing was our ability to find these (still existing) works of ancient, careless, or temperamental authors. This language practice, however, is easily explained without adopting the odd view that works of literature, once created, exist eternally despite even the destruction of the whole real world. The explanation is simply that, because a literary work does not require any *particular* copy to remain in existence, it is hard to be certain that there is not some copy of the work, somewhere, that has survived, and with it the work of literature. Who knows what may be lurking in the basement corridors of the Bodleian Library? A formerly lost sonnet of Shakespeare's was discovered there not so long ago. Unlike in the case of a unique painting, of which we can find the ashes, we can always hold out hope in the case of a literary work that a copy of it remains in some library, attic room, or perfect memory, so that the literary work might be "found" again. (This is reinforced by noting that, although we ordinarily speak of old or ancient works as lost, in the case of a modern manuscript burned by its author, we are more prone to count the work "destroyed" than merely lost.) But none of this speaks against the idea that, provided all copies and memories of a literary work are destroyed, never to be recovered, the literary work is gone as well – or, to put it another way, the literary work is then lost not in the sense in which sets of keys are lost, but in the sense in which an exploded battleship is lost, or a doctor can lose a patient.

If we consider characters to be creations owing their continued existence to the literary works in which they appear, then if all of the works regarding a character can fall out of existence, so can that character. Thus it is a consequence of this view that if all copies of all of the works regarding some ancient Greek heroine have been destroyed, never to be recovered or recalled, then she has fallen out of existence with those works and become a "past" fictional object in much the same way as a person can become a dead, past, concrete object. If we take seriously the idea of fictional characters as artifacts, it seems equally natural to treat them as able to be destroyed just as other artifacts are. Thus fictional characters as well as the literary works in which they appear may fall out of existence with the literature of a culture.

One objection that might be raised to the idea that both fictional characters and literary works may fall out of existence is that it seems we can still think of them, refer to them, and so on, even after their founding texts have all been destroyed. But this is no different than in the case of other perishable objects and artifacts: We may still think of and refer to people after they have died, buildings long since destroyed, civilizations long gone by. If fictional characters and literary works cease to exist, I am not suggesting that they then enter a peculiar realm of Meinongian nonexistence or that it is as if such objects never were, but rather that they become past objects just like the other contingent objects around us. The problem of how we can think of and refer to past objects is no small one but is not unique to fiction.

Ordinarily, a literary work is maintained in existence by the presence of some copy or other of the relevant text (whether on paper, film, tape, or CD-ROM). It is in this way that the literature of past ages has been handed down to our present day. But even if printed words on a page survive, that is not enough to guarantee the ongoing existence of the work. A literary work is not a mere bunch of marks on a page but instead is an intersubjectively accessible recounting of a story by means of a public language. Just as a language dies out without the continued acceptance and understanding of a group of individuals, so do linguistically based literary works. A literary work as such can exist only as long as there are some individuals who have the language capacities and background assumptions they need to read and understand it. If all conscious agents are destroyed, then nothing is left of fictional works or the characters represented in them but some ink on paper. Similarly, if all speakers of a language die out, with the language never to be rediscovered, then the literary works peculiar to that tongue die out as well. Thus preserving some printed or recorded document is not enough to preserve a literary work – some competent readers are also required. If competent readers and a printed text survive, however, that is enough to preserve a literary work.

In other cases, however, we speak of a work of literature as being preserved even if there are no printed copies of the text. In oral traditions, for example, the work is preserved in memory even if it is not being spoken or heard, and (as in *Fahrenheit 451*) it seems that a work could be preserved in memories during times of censorship, even if all printed copies of it were destroyed. So even if a literary work is typically maintained by a printed, comprehensible text, it seems that such is not necessary. A latent memory of the work (disposed to produce an oral or written copy of the work, given the appropriate circumstances) may be enough to maintain it in existence. Thus we can say that, for its maintenance, a character depends generically on the existence of some literary work about it; a literary work, in turn, may be maintained either in a copy of the text and a readership capable of understanding it or in memory.

In sum, it looks as if, if we are to postulate entities that would correspond to our ordinary beliefs and practices about fictional characters, these should be entities that depend on the creative acts of authors to bring them into existence and on some concrete individuals such as copies of texts and a capable audience in order to remain in existence. Thus fictional objects, in this conception, are not the inhabitants of a disjoint ontological realm but instead are closely connected to ordinary entities by their dependencies on both concrete, spatiotemporal objects and intentionality. Moreover, they are not a strange and unique type of entity: Similar dependencies are shared with objects from tables and chairs to social institutions and works of art.

Artifacts of all kinds, from tables and chairs to tools and machines, share with fictional characters the feature of requiring creation by intelligent beings. But it might be thought that the way in which fictional characters are created does make them strange, for although one cannot simply create a table, toaster, or automobile by describing such an object, fictional characters are created merely with words that posit them as being a certain way. For example, because characters are created by being written about by their authors, Jane Austen creates the fictional character Emma Woodhouse and brings her into existence (assuming she did not exist before) in writing the sentence:

> Emma Woodhouse, handsome, clever, and
> rich, with a comfortable home and happy

disposition, seemed to unite some of the best blessings of existence, and had lived nearly twenty-one years in the world with very little to distress or vex her.

But the fact that a character can be created merely through such linguistic acts should cause no peculiar difficulties for a theory of fiction. It has long been noticed that a common feature of so-called conventional or effective illocutionary acts such as appointing, resigning, adjourning, and marrying is that they bring into existence the state of affairs under discussion. Thus, for example, the celebrant of a marriage pronounces a couple husband and wife, a pronouncement that itself creates the couple's new status as husband and wife. More recently, it has been noticed that it is a common feature of many cultural and institutional entities that they can be brought into existence merely by being represented as existing. Searle discusses this general feature using money as the example. A dollar bill may read:

> "This note is legal tender for all debts public and private." But that representation is now, at least in part, a declaration: It creates the institutional status by representing it as existing. It does not represent some prelinguistic natural phenomenon.[1]

A contract, similarly, may be created simply by the utterance of words such as "I hereby promise to." Searle even cites as a general feature of institutional reality that institutional facts can be brought into existence by being represented as existing and can exist only if they are represented as existing (62–3).

What I am suggesting is a parallel with fictional characters: Just as marriages, contracts, and promises may be created through the performance of linguistic acts that represent them as existing, a fictional character is created by being represented in a work of literature. If there is no preexistent object to whom Austen was referring in writing the words above, writing those words brings into existence the object therein described: The fictional character Emma Woodhouse. Thus even the feature that fictional characters may be created not through hard labor on physical materials but through the utterance of words, rather than placing them in a peculiarly awkward situation, points again to their being at home among other cultural entities. Human consciousness is creative.

It is that creativity that enables us to increase our chances of survival by formulating plans and examining scenarios not physically before us. It is also that creativity that enables the human world of governments, social institutions, works of art, and even fictional characters to be constructed on top of the independent physical world by means of our intentional representations.

Nor are fictional characters alone in requiring certain forms of human understanding and practice for their ongoing preservation as well as creation. It has often been argued that works of art in general are not mere physical objects but instead depend both on some instantiation in physical form (in a performance, on canvas, in a printed copy), and – for their intentional properties such as expressiveness and meaning – on the intentional acts of humans.[2] Similarly, cultural and institutional facts regarding money, contracts, and property are plausibly characterized as depending not only on certain physical objects like pieces of paper with a certain history, but also on maintaining forms of human agreement. For something to be money, it is not enough that it be a piece of paper with a certain history, it must also, both initially and continually, be accepted as what people collectively agree to count as money in a particular society.

In short, on this view fictional characters are a particular kind of cultural artifact. Like other cultural objects, fictional characters depend on human intentionality for their existence. Like other artifacts, they must be created in order to exist, and they can cease to exist, becoming past objects. It is primarily in its treatment of fictional characters as ordinary cultural artifacts rather than as the odd inhabitants of a different realm that the artifactual theory differs most markedly from other ways of characterizing fictional objects. It is also their place as cultural artifacts that makes fictional objects of broader philosophical interest, for the ontology of fiction can thus serve as a model for the ontology of other social and cultural objects in the everyday world.

It may help to locate the artifactual theory in conceptual space by briefly contrasting it with other views of what fictional objects are. Some of its advantages vis-à-vis these other theories only show up when we attempt to overcome the problems of developing identity conditions for fictional objects and handling reference to and discourse about them. Nonetheless, a brief comparison should help elucidate the differences between this theory and other treatments of fiction.

Meinongian Theories of Fiction

The most popular and well-developed theories of fiction that have been available are those broadly construable as Meinongian theories, including those that take fictional characters to be either nonexistent or abstract entities, such as those developed by Parsons, Zalta, and Rapaport. Neither Meinong's theory nor contemporary Meinongian theories are devised specifically as theories of fiction; they concern the wider realm of nonexistent objects generally. Nonetheless, much of the motivation for and many of the applications of Meinongian theories of nonexistent objects concern fictional objects. Many different theories have been devised that may roughly be labeled Meinongian; despite their differences, they typically share certain fundamental characteristics captured by the following principles:

1 There is at least one object correlated with every combination of properties.
2 Some of these objects (among them fictional objects) have no existence whatsoever.
3 Although they do not exist, they (in some sense) have the properties with which they are correlated.

The first principle is sometimes known as a "comprehension principle," ensuring a multitude of nonexistent objects. Meinongian theories differ with respect to which properties count in principle one. Parsons's theory, for example, limits properties to simple, nuclear properties such as "is blue" or "is tall"; Zalta's theory permits so-called extranuclear properties (such as "is possible" and "is thought about") and complex properties. Meinongians also vary with respect to how nonexistent objects "have" their properties according to the third principle; for views like Parsons's, there are two kinds of property (nuclear and extranuclear), but only one kind of predication, enabling "have" to be read straightforwardly, as (in this theory) nonexistents have their properties in the same way as real objects do. For views like Zalta's or Rapaport's, there are two modes of predication; nonexistent objects have properties in a different way than their real counterparts. Although ordinary objects exemplify their properties, nonexistent objects "encode" the properties with which they are correlated (Zalta) or have them as "constituents" (Rapaport).

Meinongian theories of fiction resemble the artifactual theory in that both allow that there are fictional objects, that we can refer to them, that they play an important role in experience, and so on. Moreover, Meinongians are largely to be credited with showing that consistent theories of fiction can be developed and with undermining the paradigm according to which there are only real entities (a paradigm Parsons refers to as the "Russellian rut").

But there are also important differences between the artifactual theory and any such Meinongian theory of fiction. First, the theories differ with respect to where they apply the word "exists"; I am willing to claim that fictional characters exist; the Meinongian (by principle two) grants them no existence whatsoever. But because the Meinongian famously maintains that there are such objects, that we can think of them, refer to them, and so on, this difference is largely linguistic.

A deeper difference between the theories regards how many objects they say there are. Unlike the Meinongian, I do not employ any kind of comprehension principle and so do not claim that there is an infinite, ever-present range of nonexistent (or abstract) objects. In the artifactual theory, the only fictional objects there are those that are created. This points to a further difference between this view and that of the Meinongian: In the artifactual view, fictional objects are created at a certain point in time, not merely discovered or picked out. According to the Meinongian, fictional characters are merely some of the infinite range of ever-present nonexistent or abstract objects – namely, those that are described in some story. Accordingly, if an author writes of a character, she or he is merely picking out or referring to an object that was already available for reference. Authors can then be said to discover their characters or pick them out from the broad range of objects available, but not to bring these objects into existence. They *can* be said to make these objects *fictional*, for an abstract or nonexistent object does not become fictional until it is written about. Nonetheless, the object remains the same; it simply bears a new relation to contingent acts of authoring. As Parsons writes:

I have said that, in a popular sense, an author *creates* characters, but this too is hard to analyze. It does not mean, for example, that the author brings those characters into existence, for they do not exist. Nor does he or she make them objects, for they were objects

before they appeared in stories. We might say, I suppose, that the author makes them *fictional* objects, and that they were not fictional objects before the creative act.[3]

In short, the only kind of creation permitted in Meinongian accounts is the author's taking an available object and making it fictional (by writing about it in a story). This, it seems to me, is not robust enough to satisfy the ordinary view that authors are genuinely creative in the sense of creating new objects, not merely picking out old objects and thereby making them fictional. By contrast, in the artifactual theory, authors genuinely bring new characters into being that were not around before – they invent their characters rather than discovering them. In short, the Meinongian might be said to offer a top-down approach to fiction that begins by positing an infinite range of nonexistent or abstract objects and then carves out a portion of those (those described in works of literature) to serve as the fictional characters. In contrast, the artifactual theory attempts to take a bottom-up approach to fictional characters by treating them as constructed entities created by authors and depending on ordinary objects such as stories and a competent audience.

There are also many differences between Meinongian theories and the artifactual theory regarding identity conditions for fictional objects and how reference to and discourse about fictional objects are handled. Some shortcomings of the Meinongian view include an inability to genuinely treat fictional characters as created entities and consequent difficulties in offering adequate identity conditions for fictional characters (especially identity conditions across texts). Other problems arise for Meinongian treatments of fictional discourse, notably in handling fictional discourse about real individuals. Thus, despite the merits of Meinongian theories in offering a consistent and well-developed view of fictional characters, I argue that the artifactual theory provides a better conception of them overall. The main difference underlying the two theories and responsible for the advantages I claim for the artifactual theory lies in a fundamental difference in approach, as the Meinongian sees fictional characters as part of a separate realm of abstract or nonexistent objects, disjoint from and dissimilar to that of ordinary objects, and in the artifactual theory their similarities and connections to entities in the ordinary world are taken as fundamental. [...]

Fictional Characters as Objects of Reference

Other views of fiction consider fictional objects mere objects of reference that we must postulate to make sense of a certain kind of literary discourse. Such views are developed by Crittenden, who treats fictional objects as "grammatical objects," and by van Inwagen, who considers fictional objects to be the "theoretical entities" referred to in works of literary criticism. These views parallel the artifactual view in many important respects, and the differences between such theories and the artifactual theory lie less in direct conflicts than simply in the artifactual theory's filling in areas left blank by the other theories. Nonetheless, there are also important differences of approach between these theories and the artifactual theory.

Working within a broadly Wittgensteinian view of language, Crittenden postulates fictional objects as (mere) objects of reference, or grammatical objects. Although he takes fictional names as referring to certain objects, he repeatedly emphasizes that the status of these objects is merely that of objects of reference, available to be referred to by readers, critics, and other practitioners of the relevant language games of fiction, although they do not exist and are "not to be understood as having any sort of reality whatever."[4]

Although Crittenden denies that fictional characters exist, many of the features he assigns to fictional characters (based on the commitments of language practices) conform to those assigned by the artifactual theory. He too takes fictional objects to be entities created by authors through writing stories, and entities that are dependent on certain kinds of intentionality and practices involving language. But he seems to take dependence as marking a sort of honorary nonexistence and is keenest to point out that fictional objects have no *independent* existence when he is trying to emphasize that they have no "sort of reality whatever." Our later investigations into dependence should give pause to those inclined to equate an entity's existing as dependent with its not (really) existing, or having no metaphysical status. [...]

Among current analytic treatments of fiction, that closest to the artifactual theory is perhaps that which van Inwagen develops, according to which fictional characters are "theoretical entities of literary criticism."[5] In treating fictional charac-

ters as the entities described in literary criticism, van Inwagen rightly emphasizes the importance of postulating fictional characters to make sense of critical discourse about them. The two positions coincide at many points, first and foremost in the claim that fictional characters exist.

The most important difference between the artifactual theory and van Inwagen's, like that between it and Crittenden's, lies in the fact that van Inwagen does little to describe the ontological status of the creatures of fiction he postulates. He describes fictional characters as "theoretical entities"; theoretical entities in general he describes only as those referred to by the special vocabularies of theoretical disciplines, and which make some of those sentences true. So, in the case of creatures of fiction:

> [S]ometimes, if what is said in a piece of literary criticism is to be true, then there must be entities of a certain type, entities that are never the subjects of nonliterary discourse, and which make up the extensions of the theoretical general terms of literary criticism. It is these that I call "theoretical entities of literary criticism."[6]

This, however, does not tell us what fictional characters are like, but only that they are the things that make at least some (which?) of the sentences of literary criticism true. He does not discuss, for example, whether or not they are created, whether they can appear in more than one text, or how they relate to readers, and so we have no way of offering identity conditions for them or of evaluating the truth-value of critical sentences apparently about them. We also have little way of knowing how these creatures of fiction compare with other sorts of entities. Van Inwagen places them in the same category as other entities discussed in literary criticism such as plots, novels, rhyme schemes, and imagery, but it is not clear how they compare with other types of entities such as works of music, copies of texts, and universals. Thus we are left with no means of fitting fictional characters into a general ontological picture or of determining the relative parsimony of theories that do and do not postulate them.

I suspect that the omission of such aspects of a genuine metaphysical theory of fiction is no accident, for both theories attempt to hold a largely deflationary account of fictional characters as entities we must postulate merely to make sense of certain odd types of (theoretical or fictional) discourse; Crittenden at least would see asking such metaphysical questions as going astray in taking these mere objects of reference too ontologically seriously. Both such accounts thus still treat fiction (and for van Inwagen, theoretic discourse generally) as presenting a special case in which we must posit theoretic objects or mere objects of reference to make sense of our discourse. In this respect both theories differ importantly from the artifactual theory because, in this view, fictional characters are not to be considered theoretic entities or mere objects of reference any more than tables and chairs, committee meetings, and works of art are. Instead they are a certain type of object referred to, and indeed not a peculiar type of object but a type of object relevantly similar to stories, governments, and other everyday objects.

Fictional Characters as Imaginary Objects

One view that has a certain similarity in spirit to the artifactual theory, although the two differ in substance, is the view that treats fictional characters as imaginary objects – entities created and sustained by imaginative acts. It is a view developed, for example, by Sartre in his work on the imagination, which he takes to apply not only to imagined objects but also to objects represented in works of art, and even to works of art themselves. An imagined object, in this view, is an entity created in an imaginative act of consciousness and that exists only as long as it is being imagined. As Sartre writes:

> We have seen that the act of imagination is a magical one. It is an incantation destined to produce the object of one's thought, the thing one desires. . . . The faint breath of life we breathe into [imaginary objects] comes from us, from our spontaneity. If we turn away from them they are destroyed.[7]

Such a view is similar in spirit to the artifactual theory in that both insist that fictional characters are created objects, indeed objects created by the intentional acts of their authors. They are likewise similar in that both take fictional characters to remain dependent even after they are created.

But Sartre's view, and similar views of imaginary objects, treat them as existing only as long as

someone is thinking of them. As a result two large problems confront this view *qua* theory of fiction. First, the idea that these objects exist only as long as they are being thought of runs counter to our usual practices in treating Holmes, Hamlet, and the rest as enduring through those periods of time in which no one is imagining them. It seems to have the odd consequence that such characters "flit in and out of existence."[8] Second, if, as Sartre has it, a fictional character is not only created by the author's imaginative acts but (re)created afresh by the imaginative acts of each reader, it is difficult to see how we can legitimately say that two or more readers are each reading about or experiencing one and the same fictional character.

It was Ingarden who first suggested how to avoid these problems and still conceive of fictional characters as, in some sense, dependent on intentionality. In Ingarden's view, a fictional character is a "purely intentional object," an object created by consciousness and having "the source of its existence and total essence" in intentionality.[9] More precisely, a fictional character is created by an author who constructs sentences about it, but it is maintained in its existence thereafter not by the imagination of individuals, but by the words and sentences themselves. Words and sentences have what Ingarden calls "borrowed intentionality," a representational ability derived from intentional acts that confer meaning on phonetic (and typographic) formations. Thus, although fictional characters remain mediately dependent on intentionality, the immediate dependence of fictional characters on words and sentences gives them a relative independence from any particular act of consciousness:

> Both isolated words and entire sentences possess a borrowed intentionality, one that is conferred on them by acts of consciousness. It allows the purely intentional objects to free themselves, so to speak, from immediate contact with the acts of consciousness in the process of execution and thus to acquire a relative independence from the latter. (125–6)

Because these pieces of language are public and enduring, different people may all think of one and the same fictional character, and the character may survive even if no one is thinking of it provided its representation in such pieces of language remains. In sum, Ingarden showed the way to acknowledge the consciousness–dependence of fictional characters without losing their status as lasting, publicly accessible entities; his work provides the true historical predecessor of the theory here defended.

The artifactual theory similarly avoids the problems of Sartre's view by noting that, although the intentional acts of an author are required to bring a fictional character into existence, it is not the case that it exists only for as long as someone imagines it. On the contrary, fictional characters are ordinarily maintained in existence by the existence of some copy or copies of the literary work concerning them. Although that literary work requires the ongoing existence of a community capable of reading and understanding the text, it does not require that someone constantly be reading it or thinking of it in order to remain in existence, just as the ongoing existence of money requires a community willing to accept it as money although it does not constantly require that someone be explicitly thinking "this is money." Thus literary characters on this model do not flit in and out of existence depending on whether people are thinking of them; they exist as long as literary works regarding them remain. Moreover, fictional characters on this view are not created afresh with each person's thinking of them; on the contrary, by reading the same work many different readers may all access one and the same fictional object.

Notes

1 John Searle, *The Construction of Social Reality* (New York: Free Press, 1995), 74.
2 See, e.g., Joseph Margolis, "The Ontological Peculiarity of Works of Art," in *Philosophy Looks at the Arts* 3rd edn., ed. Margolis (Philadelphia: Temple University Press, 1987), 257–9. Other arguments that at least some works of art are not physical entities may be found in Richard Wollheim, *Art and Its Objects* (New York: Harper and Row, 1968), sections 4–10; Roman Ingarden, *The Literary Work of Art*, trans. George Grabowicz (Evanston, Ill.: Northeastern University Press, 1973), sections 2–5; and Nicholas Wolterstorff, *Works and Worlds of Art* (Oxford: Clarendon Press, 1980), 42.
3 Terence Parsons, *Nonexistent Objects* (New Haven: Yale University Press, 1980), 188.
4 Charles Crittenden, *Unreality: The Metaphysics of Fictional Objects* (Ithaca, NY: Cornell University Press, 1991), 69.
5 Peter van Inwagen, "Creatures of Fiction," *American Philosophical Quarterly* 14 (1977), 299–308.
6 van Inwagen, "Creatures of Fiction," 303.
7 Jean-Paul Sartre, *The Psychology of Imagination* (New York: Carol, 1991), 177–8.
8 This phrase is borrowed from Wolterstorff, who advances similar criticisms against R. G. Collingwood's treatment of works of art as imaginary entities (Wolterstorff, *Works and Worlds*, 43).
9 Ingarden, *Literary Work of Art*, 117.

22

Logic and Criticism

Peter Lamarque

We may classify a sentence containing empty singular terms as bet-sensitive if a bet, that so-and-so did such-and-such, can be won or lost according as the sentence "so-and-so did such and such" or a contrary of it is rightly assented to, yet not lost even given that "So-and-so does not exist" is rightly assented to. "Sherlock Holmes lived in Baker Street" is bet-sensitive; "The present King of France is bald" is not.

— *John Woods,* **The Logic of Fiction**

The relation of Elizabeth Bennet to Darcy [in Jane Austen's *Pride and Prejudice*]...expresses itself as a conflict and reconciliation of styles: a formal rhetoric, traditional and rigorous, must find a way to accommodate a female vivacity, which in turn must recognize the principled demands of the strict male syntax. The high moral import of the novel lies in the fact that the union of styles is accomplished without injury to either lover.

— *Lionel Trilling,* **The Opposing Self**

I

It is not always easy to reconcile the requirements of a logic of fiction with the requirements of an aesthetics of fiction. What a logician has to say about fiction per se is often remote from what a literary critic has to say about particular works of fiction. A logician, for example, will inquire about the reference of names in a fictional context or the truth–value of fictional propositions or the ontology of fictional objects. This logical inquiry is indifferent to literary or aesthetic value. A critic, on the other hand, will inquire about the meaning and value of particular works or their themes and characterizations or their truth from the point of view of perceptiveness or verisimilitude.

It might be argued that the difference is simply one of *level* or of *generality*, such that the relation between logic and aesthetics (or literary criticism) is something like the relation between philosophy of science and science itself. But this cannot be right. The difference is more complex and more interesting, for in certain respects the inquiries are incommensurable. When a logician, for example, speaks of a fictional object simply as the referent of a fictional name, virtually no common ground exists with a critic who speaks of a fictional character as performing a certain function in a literary narrative. Or when a logician, in the context of semantic theory, assesses the truth conditions of fictive sentences and a critic, in the context of literary interpretation, assesses the thematic contribution of fictive descriptions, the judgments barely share even a common subject matter.

In this chapter I will explore one instance of this tension between logic and literary criticism: the idea of *reasoning to what is true in fiction*. Ostensibly, this topic is one in which logicians and literary critics have a common interest. Both can agree on one sense of "true in fiction" where it means simply

From *Fictional Points of View* (Ithaca, NY: Cornell University Press, 1996), pp. 55–70, originally published in *Argumentation* (Kluwer Academic Press, 1990).

truth about a fictional world. In this chapter that sense will be the focus of attention; its connection with other senses of "true in fiction" will be examined in Chapter 6. Every reader of fiction is concerned with what happens in a fictional narrative, what the "facts" are, as it were, about the fictional world. Of course, we must not assume that this concern will always be uppermost. Whether it is will depend to a large extent on the type of fiction. The assumption that all fictional narrative depicts a coherent, ordered, "realistic" world is not acceptable to the literary critic, even though it often seems to underlie discussions of the logic of fiction. Some modern theories of narrative even encourage the working assumption that narrative is not descriptive of a "world" except in particular, clearly defined genres. Nevertheless, we should not be deflected from the obvious truth that all narratives to some degree invite readers to form beliefs about their content. Questions about the principles governing this grasp of content exercise both logicians and critics. These principles we can think of as relating to *reasoning to what is true in fiction*.

II

Nowhere does the tension between logic and criticism emerge more strikingly than in the well-known and subtle analysis of "truth in fiction" offered by the philosopher David Lewis.[1] Lewis bases his analysis on the identification of *fictional worlds* with the *possible worlds* of modal logic. But for all its ingenuity, even plausibility, from a logical point of view, it fails radically, as I will argue, to address the concerns of literary critics even though, so it seems, common issues are at stake. Exploring exactly why that is so will yield important lessons for the very enterprise of applying analytical (logical) methods to theoretical problems of literary criticism.

Lewis takes us through a progression of three analyses which are increasingly sensitive to intuitions based on the common experience of reading fiction. The analyses are as follows:

ANALYSIS 0: A sentence of the form "In fiction *f*, φ" is true iff φ is true at every world where *f* is told as known fact rather than fiction. (p. 41)

ANALYSIS 1: A sentence of the form "In fiction *f*, φ" is non-vacuously true iff some

world where *f* is told as known fact and φ is true differs less from our actual world, on balance, than does any world where *f* is told as known fact and φ is not true. It is vacuously true iff there are no possible worlds where *f* is told as known fact. (p. 42)

ANALYSIS 2: A sentence of the form "In fiction *f*, φ" is non-vacuously true iff, whenever *w* is one of the collective belief worlds of the community of origin of *f*, then some world where *f* is told as known fact and φ is true differs less from the world *w*, on balance, than does any world where *f* is told as known fact and φ is not true. It is vacuously true if there are no possible worlds where *f* is told as known fact. (p. 45)

Analysis 0 rules out any reasoning to what is true in a work of fiction beyond what is explicitly given in the content of the sentences in the work. Lewis is right to reject this analysis as too restricted. Both literary critics and ordinary readers take it for granted that inferences beyond what is explicit are not just permissible but indispensable in understanding fiction. Analyses 1 and 2 are offered as genuine alternatives, though the latter, Lewis thinks, conforms better to intuitions arising from literary criticism. What they have in common is the idea that truth in fiction is a product of two sources: the explicit content of sentences in the relevant text and a background against which we reason beyond that content. In Analysis 1 this background consists of facts about the actual world. In Analysis 2 it consists of beliefs overt in the community of origin of the fiction. Analysis 2 is offered as a way of eliminating the use of esoteric facts about the actual world (unknown perhaps to the author and readers of the text) to reason to what is true in the fiction.

Lewis's counterfactual basis for explaining our reasoning about fiction is in many ways highly attractive. It is easy to think of fictional narratives as describing what *would be the case if*. They speak, for the most part, of the possible, not the actual. They describe worlds, often similar, but not identical, to our own world. We can reason about what we are to take as true in a fiction beyond its explicit content, because we read fiction against a presupposed background. All this is nicely captured by Lewis's account.

Yet I see a fundamental flaw in the account (in any version), which makes it unacceptable as a contribution to the aesthetics of fiction (and also to literary criticism). The flaw is that it excludes entirely the *intentionality* of fictional content and the *interpretive* nature of our reasoning about that content. It fails as an account of *literary* reasoning. By referring only to what is *true at such and such a world*, Lewis introduces a realist assumption into the reasoning – that is, an assumption that there are "facts" about the fictional worlds waiting to be discovered – and thus a certain kind of determinacy, which is not warranted in literary criticism. Ultimately, the critic is not so much exploring *facts* as uncovering *meanings*: not chronicling a *world* so much as constructing an *interpretation*. Nowhere is the critic more at odds with the logician. Let us pursue these objections.

III

Lewis explains our reasoning to what is true in fiction in terms of a balance between the world (or worlds) explicitly presented in the text of a fiction and some background world. I will look in more detail at what he says about both components, for his characterization of both, I suggest, is unacceptable to the demands of the literary critic.

Let us begin with his basic conception of the world(s) of a fiction. Lewis argues that the worlds explicitly presented are those where the fictional story is "told as known fact." This eliminates the actual world, because in the actual world, the story is told *as fiction*. So even if, by massive coincidence, all the events and characters depicted in a fiction turn out to have exact counterparts in the real world, the fictional world would still not be identical with the real world, as the acts of storytelling in the two worlds would be different. Lewis's condition, quite rightly, gives precedence in determining fictionality to what a storyteller intends rather than to how things are in the world. In other words it is not literal truth or falsity that makes a narrative factual or fictional but only the mode under which the narrative is presented, how it is told.

But there are problems with the requirement that in the fictional world the story is "told as known fact." First, by covertly introducing the notion of truth via that of knowledge, it threatens the account with circularity. The worlds that we are invited to consider when assessing what is true in a particular fiction are those which contain only what is known to be true by the storyteller. Therefore, to discover what the storyteller knows to be true, we need to know what is true ourselves. Second, this becomes a difficulty in precisely those stories in which the storyteller is depicted as unreliable or in which occur narrative strategies, shifting points of view, a preponderance of dialogue, and so forth. Lewis's account requires that the narrator tells the truth in a pretty straightforward way, recounting only what he knows and doing most of the talking himself. But this is an unwarranted assumption, at least as far as literary criticism is concerned. For one thing the device of the unreliable narrator is common enough in fiction: in Agatha Christie's *The Murder of Roger Ackroyd*, for example, the narrator conceals until the very end the fact that he himself is the murderer, and in three of Iris Murdoch's first-person novels, *Under the Net, The Black Prince*, and *The Sea, The Sea*, the narrators are depicted as self-deceived in varying degrees. Lewis recognizes such cases in which "the storyteller purports to be uttering a mixture of truth and lies" and suggests that the way to deal with them is to "consider those worlds where the act of storytelling really is whatever it purports to be ... here at our world" (p. 40). This suggestion merely highlights the general problem of determining what those worlds are: specifically, which are the truths and which are the lies.

Other features of narrative content, such as irony, hyperbole, metaphoric or symbolic construction, or changing points of view, also threaten Lewis's requirement that a narrator tell only what he *knows*. At the root of the problem is an underlying assumption throughout Lewis's analyses that, as far as truth in fiction is concerned, a sharp distinction is to be made between what is presented explicitly and thus can be accepted as true and what is not explicitly presented and thus requires some construction by the reader against an assumed background. But discovering what is true in a fictional world is not characteristically as clearcut as that. An adequate account of reasoning to what is true in fiction needs to capture the fact that at nearly every level, the reconstruction of fictional worlds needs to invoke a variety of background data, including recognition of genre, ironical or satirical intent, symbolic or allusive frame, narrative mode, historical context, and implicit or connotative meanings.

It is a peculiarity of fictional narrative that it depicts not merely a world but a world-under-a-description. Acts of storytelling generate intentionality in fictional content; there are not just facts reported but facts-as-told as well. Lewis rightly emphasizes the importance of the act of storytelling in identifying fictions: "Different acts of storytelling, different fictions. When Pierre Menard retells *Don Quixote*, that is not the same fiction as Cervantes' *Don Quixote* – even if they are in the same language and match word for word" (p. 39). But this does not go far enough. Acts of storytelling are individuated by storytellers and by the very mode of telling. If Cervantes had retold his story with slight variations, he would have generated a different fiction (and world). The predicates in fictive sentences are not externally but internally related to the situations they characterize in the sense that the particular aspects, attitudes, and values embodied in the predicates help to constitute the situations (events, characters, and so on) depicted. In Borges's story, what makes Menard's *Quixote* a different fiction from Cervantes' is not merely that they are told by different people but also that the implied meanings and attitudes conveyed *by the very same words* differ in the two tellings.

What we discover about a fictional world derives from both *what is said*, where truth conditions alone are at issue, and *how it is said*, where fine-grained meaning, nuance, tone, and point of view must also be taken into account. In short, a fictional world itself is, as I will put it, constitutively aspectual; the complex network of aspects and values characterized by the precise narrative mode of presentation in a work of fiction constitutes the world of the work.

A reader's task is to reconstruct this world by identifying and weighing the aspectual (connotative, evaluative, and so on) qualities in the fictive descriptions. This involves much more than simply accepting as true, or as known fact, what is explicitly reported. Information about fictional worlds is presented through a series of narrative filters. Even at the level of explicit content, readers must determine not only what sentences to accept at face value (recognizing unreliable narration, irony, hyperbole, speaker's point of view) but also what paraphrases of the content of those sentences are licensed (recognizing connotative features, tone, figurative usage, satire, allusion). Fictional worlds given under a description place severe constraints on which *redescriptions* of fictional content accurately record the "facts." We can only discover what is true in a fictional world through a clear grasp of the manner in which the world is presented. One cannot escape the introduction of an interpretive element right at the start of our reasoning about fiction.

It might be possible to accommodate this complexity within the terms of Lewis's analysis by broadening the initial characterization of the worlds of a fiction. What is explicitly presented, the narrative content, might be thought of not just as "known fact" but as *linguistic data* out of which the facts must be *(re)constructed*. Readers, somewhat like scientists or historians, frame and modify hypotheses about fictional content, assessing the quality and connectedness of the data, attempting to construct (fictional) states of affairs such that they render maximally coherent the evidence available. The transparency of fictive descriptions should never be taken for granted.

One problem with this proposed revision of Lewis's analysis is that it introduces an element of indeterminacy even in the overt descriptive content of a fiction. If all the "facts" about a fictional world are subject to a particular way of construing a fictional text, then we might seem to have lost the idea of "facts" altogether and thus a "world." But bearing in mind that fictional worlds (like characters) are constituted by the (senses of) descriptions in a fictional narrative and accepting that the construal of such descriptions need not itself be indeterminate, we have still retained a recognizable conception of "truth in fiction." Of course we do need constraints on the interpretations we place on the textual data. Familiar literary critical constraints – which we might call *principles for the evaluation of content* – operate at the finer level of judgments about tone, irony, point of view, and narratorial reliability. At the broader level at which we judge global features of the fictional world, more general principles seem to apply: a *presumption of verisimilitude*, for example, which assumes the fictional world to be similar to the real world in the absence of clear indications of respects in which they differ, and a *presumption of truthfulness*, which enjoins us to accept as true what we are directly told about the fictional world unless there is specific evidence to doubt this. In the end it is probable that these constraints will yield much the same set of truths as Lewis recognizes at the basic level. But the principles of reasoning are fundamentally different moving from the concept of a storyteller reporting "known facts" to the concept of a reader constructing a world by construing (the meaning of) a text.

IV

Let us move to a consideration of the background world that, according to Lewis's analysis, will serve as a basis for our reasoning to what is true beyond what is explicit in a narrative. For Lewis, this background is either the actual world itself (Analysis 1) or "one of the collective belief worlds of the community of origin" (Analysis 2).

It is helpful to draw a rough distinction between, on the one hand, facts about the physical setting in which a fiction takes place and, on the other hand, more "theory-laden" facts about the actions, motives, intentions, and attitudes of the characters in the fiction (narrator included). More often than not the focus of our interest – and disagreements – in reading a novel will be on the latter, whereas we take the former for granted.

Lewis's account of the background world is more readily applicable to the physical than the psychological inferences we are inclined to draw in reading fiction. It would be natural to appeal to generally prevalent beliefs about the physical world at the time the fiction was created as a source for factual information of a physical kind not made explicit in narrative content. Thus, for example, current skepticism about the influence of the supernatural should not lead us to reason that the witches in *Macbeth* could not have been witches after all. And in Lewis's example, we should not conclude from our knowledge that Russell's vipers cannot climb ropes that in the Sherlock Holmes story "The Adventure of the Speckled Band," either the snake reached its victim in some way other than climbing the rope or Holmes bungled the case.

The psychological inferences we make over and above what is explicit in a narrative are more complicated than the physical inferences. But they do not differ in principle from the point of view of relying on some construal of textual data. I suggest that two different kinds of indeterminacy affect our reasoning about characters, neither of which can be accommodated on Lewis's account but both of which are of significance to the literary critic. One is a general indeterminacy in characterizing human action, and the other, an indeterminacy in literary interpretation. Neither indeterminacy can be explained in terms of possible worlds.

First, Lewis's appeal to the "collective belief worlds of the community of origin" of a fiction to guide us in our inferences to what is true in the fiction puts undue restrictions on our understanding of fictional characters or the appropriate (invited) responses to them. One obvious difficulty is that of determining the relevant community. Those beliefs common to an entire society will be so few or so general as to license only the most mundane inferences. But how could the community be

narrowed except in an ad hoc way? Lewis might simply concede these points and conclude that the only supplementation that is licensed on human or psychological assessments in a fiction will necessarily be of a low-level kind; after all, he proposes his analysis precisely to rule out psychoanalytic speculation. But this runs counter to our intuitions. The inferences we draw in a fiction are not limited to physical descriptions and very general psychological facts. Nor are they limited only to beliefs common to the majority in a community. We feel this especially when we consider innovative works of literature. We want to acknowledge at least the possibility that an author might transcend commonly accepted attitudes and invite us to perceive human characteristics in a way not embodied in the collective beliefs. A simple example might be Thomas Hardy's *Jude the Obscure*. An ordinary reader of the time who shared the collective beliefs about how young ladies should behave and what attitudes were appropriate to marriage might well have attributed selfish and unreasonable motives to Sue Bridehead. We are not explicitly told that she was selfish or inconsiderate or that she deserved her fate (in fact, the opposite is strongly implied), but it seems that whether or not she was or did should not be decided merely by appeal to a general moral consensus in Hardy's Britain. It also seems clear that what we say about her intentions and motives is going to be determined, in part at least, by some overall perspective we as readers take on the novel.

It might be objected that the kinds of detailed inferences we are inclined to draw about the psychological attitudes of fictional characters should not be counted among the *truths* in a fiction but at best considered only as *hypotheses*. Lewis's criterion is strictly for what is true in fiction. My reply is twofold. First, a great deal of our reasoning to what is true in fiction is hypothetical in nature. This is partly a consequence of the idea developed earlier that we should treat a given text not as a report of known facts about a (fictional) world but as a set of linguistically-based data awaiting construal according to general interpretive principles. In that sense hypothesizing (about meaning) occurs at the most fundamental level. Second, the hypotheses we advance about fictional characters and actions often share just the kind of indeterminacy or relativity that we find in our judgments about the actual world (or actual people). They cannot be dismissed simply as "truth-value gaps." There is a difference between the kind of indeterminacy that afflicts fiction qua fiction, like the unspecified number of Lady Macbeth's children, and the kind of indeterminacy that directly reflects an indeterminacy in the actual world, for example concerning attitudes, beliefs, desires, and values, as expressed in a fiction. Lewis's account has to run these together.

Let me develop this last difficulty in more detail. According to Lewis we have a truth–value gap wherever some proposition is true in some worlds of a fiction and false in others, given that these worlds all differ least from the background world. While I would agree that propositions for which we have no evidence at all, either from the text or from the background, might best be considered as lacking a truth–value, I do not think we should automatically dismiss in the same way all propositions about a character's (or narrator's) attitudes and beliefs over which there is some indeterminacy. I am inclined to say, at least of some propositions of this kind, that they are true on some readings of the text and false on others or that they are true *relative to an interpretation*.

To say that a proposition is true relative to an interpretation is to say something more than just that it is true in some worlds and false in others. The former might entail the latter, but it is not equivalent to it. An interpretation is not a world, though it might help determine a world. This is again where the interests of the literary critic diverge from those of the logician. We form hypotheses about characters from the evidence before us, and we take the hypotheses as true in relation to the fictional world (or worlds) determined by them. But many such hypotheses – for example, about the reliability or point of view of a narrator – will determine in an all-embracing way what we take the specified truths to be. Here we find something like a hermeneutic circle. A general interpretive scheme will determine many of the truths within a fictional world, but these truths will in turn give support to the interpretation. There is no neutral ground from which to judge the truth of such propositions.

The hypothetical nature of some of our inferences about fictional characters reflects an indeterminacy in the explanation of action. To explain a person's actions is at least partly to show them to be consistent with propositional attitudes held by the agent. We say that agents have acted rationally precisely in case their beliefs and desires provide them with a reason for doing as they did. Unfortunately, we can discover their propositional attitudes only by observing their actions (including

what they say); having beliefs and desires is (at least partly) being disposed to act in certain ways. But, in turn, to understand actions, to call them intentional or rational, we need to know something about propositional attitudes. We can break into this hermeneutic-like circle only by making some initial suppositions about agents, for example, that they act consistently for the most part.

On one level, rational action is not something we discover but something we assume. The concept of a person is conceptually linked with that of rationality. Here I follow Donald Davidson: "Crediting people with a large degree of consistency cannot be counted mere charity. ... To the extent that we fail to discover a coherent and plausible pattern in the attitudes and actions of others we simply forego the chance of treating them as persons."[2] But there need not be any one coherent pattern, any single or correct theory or explanation, that alone captures and makes sense of the evidence available.

Exactly parallel observations, I believe, apply also to the interpretation of fiction. We need to make initial assumptions about the coherence of a work of fiction before we are able to reason to what is true in that work. And we would not expect any one interpretation to accommodate uniquely the evidence that the text provides for our reasoning. How far can we press the parallel between our reasoning about human motivation and our reasoning to what is true in fiction? At one level, of course, the parallel is close because much of our interest in fiction – at least literary fiction – will precisely involve issues about human moral and psychological motivation. Making sense of a fictional character calls for many of the same kinds of judgments as are required in explaining any (real) human action.

But a further, more interesting parallel sheds light on the literary critical nature of some of our reasoning about fiction. It also highlights the second source of indeterminacy in that reasoning, as mentioned earlier. The parallel is between making sense of human action and offering a literary interpretation. Literary interpretation applied to fiction is quite unlike the kind of reasoning described by Lewis. It is not a matter of discovering truths about a world so much as assigning thematic significance to component parts of a work. It is a search for coherence and sense. It involves making connections by subsuming more and more elements in a work under a network of thematic concepts. Part of this literary interpretation will involve making sense of the actions and thoughts of characters. But interpretation goes well beyond that. It is also concerned with general themes or symbolic structures that bind together all the elements in a work, not just psychological factors. Again there is no a priori reason why any one interpretation should capture all the possible or interesting connections.

Peter Jones has suggested various respects in which "understanding a novel" is comparable to "understanding a person." "To understand a person," he writes, "involves not only judging his behaviour to consist of actions that are purposeful and pointful, but grasping their point, and perhaps seeing grounds for their appropriateness in the context."[3] Similarly, to understand a novel we must assume that "the work is purposive," though "this does not commit us to search for the actual purposes that informed the work."[4] Jones's account of what he calls "creative interpretation" allows for the possibility that different readers will postulate different purposes for different elements in a work; they might "take" the text in different ways, find different significance in it. We could say that on this view literary interpretation is radically underdetermined by the evidence supplied by the text of a literary work.

A similar view has been developed, in a different context, by Ronald Dworkin, who compares literary interpretation and interpretation in law. Dworkin characterizes interpretation as follows:

> Interpretation of works of art and social practices... is indeed essentially concerned with purpose not cause. But the purposes in play are not (fundamentally) those of some author but of the interpreter. Roughly, constructive interpretation is a matter of imposing purpose on an object or practice in order to make of it the best possible example of the form or genre to which it is taken to belong. It does not follow, even from that rough account, that an interpreter can make of a practice or work of art anything he would have wanted it to be.... For the history or shape of a practice or object constrains the available interpretations of it.... Creative interpretation, on the constructive view, is a matter of interaction between purpose and object.[5]

According to this view, common to Jones and Dworkin, interpretation by its very nature is "constructive" or "creative" in that it involves the postulation of purpose or significance. It is concerned with projected meanings rather than given facts. Lewis's model of fictions as possible worlds makes radically different assumptions about what it is to understand fictional content. Although Lewis sees reasoning to what is true in fiction as a quasi-factual investigation about objectively given worlds, the Jones/Dworkin view emphasizes the interpreter and the search for sense and connectedness. Truth is relativized to interpretation. This hermeneutic view introduces an indeterminacy quite different from that of the "truth-value gap."

Interpretation in the Jones/Dworkin sense provides a framework within which we can reason to particular fictional truths. A good example of this "creative interpretation" and the truths it generates can be found in Jones's reading of *Middlemarch*. Jones sees George Eliot's novel as presenting a complex theory of the imagination. Here is one part of his argument:

> The third role of imagination is in the sympathetic understanding of other men; such understanding cannot be reached by those exclusively concerned with themselves, but it rests upon the use of imagination to interpret the outward signs of men's inner lives. Lydgate and Casaubon differed entirely on the uses to which they put their constructive imagination in their professional work; but they both failed to see that such imagination is also essential in their social lives. The mental world of the imagination is quite separate from the actual world in which we live; to connect the two demands a disciplined exercise of will-power.[6]

In this and in the rest of his discussion, Jones offers a number of philosophical concepts and hypotheses as a framework for finding significance and connectedness in the novel: concepts such as "constructive imagination," "sympathetic understanding," "disciplined exercise of will-power," and so on. Within this framework, judgments can be made about what is "true in the fiction," for example, about the characters and their attitudes: hence Jones's judgment that "Lydgate and Casaubon... failed to see that such imagination is... essential in their social lives." This judgment is made possible only by the interpretive framework within which it is set.

It is hard to see what status such a judgment could be given on Lewis's account. Because it might be true in some possible worlds derived from the novel and false in others, Lewis would have to categorize it as "neither true nor false." But that does no justice to its peculiar status as part of a literary (and philosophical) interpretation. The kind of reasoning that Jones undertakes to arrive at such a judgment is not a reasoning about "facts" in a possible world. It makes no appeal to "collect-ive belief worlds." Rather it involves its own im-aginative reconstruction of the text; it proposes a new "way of looking" at the textual data, a new conception of the novel's thematic coherence. A large number of critical judgments are of this kind and are familiar to literary critics. We must, I suggest, assess these judgments as *truths relative to an interpretation*. Needless to say, we must not suppose that any judgment whatsoever can acquire the title of truth in this way. The judgments cor-rectly deemed to be truths will need to be well supported by a plausible and consistent interpret-ation, subject at least to the constraining principles mentioned earlier for evaluating narrative content.

I have suggested a parallel between literary in-terpretation and Davidson's view of human action, conceived as a search for coherence on the assump-tion of rationality. The parallel is supported by the view of "creative interpretation" developed by Jones and Dworkin. But it would be a mistake to suppose that literary interpretation is entirely as-similable to the ways we make sense of human action (Jones) or social practices (Dworkin). There is much that is sui generis in literary inter-pretation. The conventions for making sense of a literary work and for exploring connections within a work, as well as the concepts we apply in inter-pretation, are all rooted in a distinctive practice of literary criticism. Critical reasoning in support of hypotheses such as Jones's on *Middlemarch* is sub-ject to specific principles of evidence and argu-ment. Although I have not looked in detail at these principles, it should at least be clear from the conclusions we have drawn, and the examples themselves, that the principles go well beyond those embodied in Lewis's Analyses 1 and 2. The possible-world model is not adequate to explain the kind of reasoning that is an indispensable part of literary interpretation.

V

We have come a long way from Lewis's original analyses. It has certainly not been my intention to

reject the entire enterprise in which Lewis is en-gaged. My concern has been to identify points of tension between the logician's approach to "truth in fiction" and the requirements of the literary critic. According to Lewis, our reasoning to what is true in fiction is counterfactual; we make infer-ences about what would be the case in worlds where the story is told as known fact, setting the data directly presented in the narrative against a wider background world. There is no objection to the idea that at a basic level we sometimes reason counterfactually about fiction in order to fill out a fictional world. But from the point of view of the literary critic, this can at best be only part of the procedure for determining what is true of such a world.

The details that Lewis provides, both about the direct data in a narrative and the background world by which we generate inferences, are not adequate to the complexities recognized by literary critics. First, treating explicit narrative content as constituting worlds in which the story is "told as known fact" fails to take into account the many different kinds of narrative strategy familiar in literary fictions, such as unreliable narration, shifting points of view, and ironic or symbolic representation. I have proposed instead that we treat narrative sentences not as reporting facts but as embodying meanings that require the reader not just to accept what is given but to construe what is given. This is still within the spirit of Lewis's account. I suggested that certain prin-ciples (or working assumptions) operate in our initial sorting of fictional truths: principles of co-herence, verisimilitude, and trustworthiness, as well as specific critical principles about textual meaning.

Second, Lewis's account of the background world as "the collective belief worlds of the com-munity of origin" of the fiction, to which we appeal in making inferences beyond what is expli-citly presented, is also inadequate for literary criti-cism. The account might be sufficient for reasoning about facts in the physical world, but it is too limited to do justice to literary critical hy-potheses about character and theme. On such matters we need some concept of *interpretation*. At one level we have the kind of interpretation that Davidson introduces in understanding human action. At another level we have more distinctively literary interpretation that identifies thematic development in a fictional narrative. With the concept of interpretation comes the idea of indeterminacy. Rather than supposing there are determinate *facts* to be discovered about the worlds of a literary fiction, we must work with the idea of *truths relative to interpretive frameworks*. But this indeterminacy or relativity is not reducible to "truth-value gaps."

In effect I have introduced, on behalf of the literary critic, complexities at every stage of Lewis's analysis. It might be that a separate formal analysis could be offered for the revised conception of "truth relative to an interpretation." But it is far from clear that any simple formalized principle could capture the kind of reasoning that a critic undertakes to arrive at – and support – an interpretation. The value of any very general principle would be questionable. It might be argued that my objections to Lewis apply only to *literary* fictions and that his aim is to produce a principle applicable to *all* fiction, or fiction per se. Certainly not all fiction is literature, and maybe not all literature is fiction. But I think that our response to literary fiction is on a continuum with our response to any fiction. Rudimentary inter- pretive procedures apply at the most basic level of reading, certainly at the level Lewis is concerned with, where we make reasoned inferences about narrative content. The imposition of meaning in a fictional narrative, over and above the discovery of facts in a possible world, is an indispensable part of our reasoning to what is true in fiction.

Notes

1 David Lewis, "Truth in Fiction," *American Philosophical Quarterly* 15 (1978), 37–46. Page references are given in the text. See also pp. 119–27 in this book.
2 Donald Davidson, "Mental Events," in *Essays on Actions and Events* (Oxford, 1980), pp. 221–2.
3 Peter Jones, *Philosophy and the Novel* (Oxford, 1975), p. 196.
4 Ibid., p. 197.
5 Ronald Dworkin, *Law's Empire* (London, 1986), p. 52.
6 Jones, *Philosophy and the Novel*, p. 48.

PART V

Emotion

Introduction

In the recent past, emotion has not been at the center of definitions of literature or of art in general, as it was, for instance, in Leo Tolstoy's view of art as communication of feeling and R. G. Collingwood's view of art as expression of emotion. And probably emotion, or the capacities to express and elicit emotion, should not have definitional or criterial status in regard to literature. It seems there can be works of literature that pursue other literary goals without expressing or eliciting emotion (perhaps nonfiction essays and conceptually challenging works of fiction, such as the Borges story in Part III, are examples). However, even if not exactly essential to literature, emotional expressiveness and power loom very large in our ordinary sense of what makes literature distinctive, interesting, and important. The mingling of thought and feeling is one of the paradigms of literary experience, often cited, for instance, in articulating the difference between literary and philosophical discourse.

In the readings in this section, the fact that works of literature can prompt powerful felt experiences is taken as a shared starting point. But some of these experiences are presented as philosophically problematic, as both their nature and coherence are called into question. The first problem focuses on emotional response to fiction. Emotion seems to require having certain cognitive elements in place, including at least a belief in the existence of the cause or the object of one's emotion. In our felt responses to fiction, we appear to violate this requirement. We cry over characters that do not exist in the relevant sense, as people capable of suffering, and, in Kendall Walton's example, we claim to be terrified by the giant slime in a movie, while knowing there is no such slime. What is the best way to understand or interpret these common human experiences?

One alternative, developed by Walton, takes genuine emotion to involve a motivating belief–desire complex, and hence deny that these felt responses really constitute emotions: the response to the slime involves experiences associated with fear, but it is what Walton calls "quasi-fear," not fear. My quasi-fear helps make it true that, within the game of make-believe I play with the work of fiction, I am afraid. But that does not imply that I am genuinely afraid.

Colin Radford, meanwhile, grants that these felt responses differ in some ways from the responses we would have to a comparable real situation. But he sees the similarities in how we are "moved" by fiction and by real life as too strong to motivate setting up two separate categories of response. Instead of seeing the lack of belief as putting pressure on the genuineness of the emotion, Radford sees it as undermining its coherence or rationality. Philosophers frequently seek out the "best explanation," but in this case Radford argues that there just is no good explanation to be had. As he says, these feelings may come naturally to us, but that does not mean they have to make sense. Neither Walton's nor Radford's account is immediately appealing, since we either lose some feelings we thought were genuine or we gain some incoherence; their views pose a challenge to anyone who wants to avoid those consequences.

Susan Feagin and Flint Schier address the question posed by David Hume in "Of Tragedy" (see Part I, p. 25). We take pleasure in tragic art, despite the fact that it prompts unpleasant emotions. We normally go out of our way to avoid sorrow, pity, anxiety, and fear, so why do we willingly seek these feelings out in the experience of tragic art? Here it is not just responses to tragic fiction that can be problematic, as Hume notes that it is possible to enjoy an eloquent account of a real-life tragedy, albeit presumably one remote from our lives. One might perhaps say that this is another case of irrationality; do we really take pleasure in tragic art or do we inexplicably seek it out to inflict pain on ourselves?

Hume's own answer strikes many as unsatisfactory. He suggests that the pleasure taken in the artistic virtues of a work, such as the eloquence of its language, in some way appropriates and transforms the painful responses. Thus on Hume's view it is not clear that we do experience the negative emotions, since they are affected "so strongly as totally to alter their nature." Feagin and Schier want to account for the pleasures of tragedy in a way that maintains the tragic nature of our feelings. Feagin appeals to two levels of response: a direct felt response to the tragic events and a meta-response to those feelings. That is, we have a response to the way we respond to the tragedy, and her view is that we rightly take pleasure in having appropriate human feelings when confronting the portrayal of tragic events. Schier thinks there is a desire for a kind of unflinching recognition of tragic realities at work in our appreciation of tragic art. He furthermore argues for the advantages of seeking this recognition through art rather than through witnessing tragic events in real life.

This section begins with Harold Pinter's brief sketch, "Applicant," in which Mr. Lamb is interviewed for a job by Miss Piffs. Despite its brevity, it can summon up some rather complex feelings and remind us of how fluid, incongruous, and interpretive our emotional responses to fiction can be. Is this a tragedy or a comedy? Could there be a comedy that is also an unflinching recognition of tragic reality? What would count as appropriate human responses to Lamb, Piffs, and their story?

23

Applicant

Harold Pinter

An office. LAMB, *a young man, eager, cheerful, enthusiastic, is striding nervously, alone. The door opens.* MISS PIFFS *comes in. She is the essence of efficiency.*

PIFFS:	Ah, good morning.
LAMB:	Oh, good morning, miss.
PIFFS:	Are you Mr. Lamb?
LAMB:	That's right.
PIFFS [*studying a sheet of paper*]:	Yes, You're applying for this vacant post, aren't you?
LAMB:	I am actually, yes.
PIFFS:	Are you a physicist?
LAMB:	Oh yes, indeed. It's my whole life.
PIFFS [*languidly*]:	Good. Now our procedure is, that before we discuss the applicant's qualifications we like to subject him to a little test to determine his psychological suitability. You've no objection?
LAMB:	Oh, good heavens, no.
PIFFS:	Jolly good.

MISS PIFFS *has taken some objects out of a drawer and goes to* LAMB. *She places a chair for him.*

PIFFS:	Please sit down. [*He sits.*] Can I fit these to your palms?
LAMB [*affably*]:	What are they?
PIFFS:	Electrodes.
LAMB:	Oh yes, of course. Funny little things.

She attaches them to his palms.

PIFFS:	Now the earphones.

She attaches earphones to his head.

LAMB:	I say how amusing.
PIFFS:	Now I plug in.

She plugs in to the wall.

LAMB [*a trifle nervously*]:	Plug in, do you? Oh yes, of course. Yes, you'd have to, wouldn't you?

MISS PIFFS *perches on a high stool and looks down on* LAMB.

This help to determine my . . . my suitability does it?

From *Complete Works* (London: Methuen, 1978), vol. 3, pp. 231–4. Reprinted by permission of Faber and Faber Ltd and Grove/Atlantic, Inc.

PIFFS: Unquestionably. Now relax. Just relax. Don't think about a thing.

LAMB: No.

PIFFS: Relax completely. Rela-a-a-x. Quite relaxed?

LAMB nods. MISS PIFFS presses a button on the side of her stool. A piercing high pitched buzz-hum is heard. LAMB jolts rigid. His hands go to his earphones. He is propelled from the chair. He tries to crawl under the chair. MISS PIFFS watches, impassive. The noise stops. LAMB peeps out from under the chair, crawls out, stands, twitches, emits a short chuckle and collapses in the chair.

PIFFS: Would you say you were an excitable person?

LAMB: Not – not unduly, no. Of course, I—

PIFFS: Would you say you were a moody person?

LAMB: Moody? No, I wouldn't say I was moody – well, sometimes occasionally I—

PIFFS: Do you ever get fits of depression?

LAMB: Well, I wouldn't call them depression exactly—

PIFFS: Do you often do things you regret in the morning?

LAMB: Regret? Things I regret? Well, it depends what you mean by often, really – I mean when you say often—

PIFFS: Are you often puzzled by women?

LAMB: Women?

PIFFS: Men.

LAMB: Men? Well, I was just going to answer the question about women—

PIFFS: Do you often feel puzzled?

LAMB: Puzzled?

PIFFS: By women.

LAMB: Women?

PIFFS: Men.

LAMB: Oh, now just a minute, I ... Look, do you want separate answers or a joint answer?

PIFFS: After your day's work do you ever feel tired? Edgy? Fretty?

Irritable? At a loose end? Morose? Frustrated? Morbid? Unable to concentrate? Unable to sleep? Unable to eat? Unable to remain seated? Unable to remain upright? Lustful? Indolent? On heat? Randy? Full of desire? Full of energy? Full of dread? Drained? of energy, of dread? of desire?

Pause.

LAMB [*thinking*]: Well, it's difficult to say really ...

PIFFS: Are you a good mixer?

LAMB: Well, you've touched on quite an interesting point there —

PIFFS: Do you suffer from eczema, listlessness, or falling coat?

LAMB: Er ...

PIFFS: Are you virgo intacta?

LAMB: I beg your pardon?

PIFFS: Are you virgo intacta?

LAMB: Oh, I say, that's rather embarrassing. I mean – in front of a lady—

PIFFS: Are you virgo intacta?

LAMB: Yes, I am, actually. I'll make no secret of it.

PIFFS: Have you always been virgo intacta?

LAMB: Oh yes, always. Always.

PIFFS: From the word go?

LAMB: Go? Oh yes, from the word go.

PIFFS: Do women frighten you?

She presses a button on the other side of her stool. The stage is plunged into redness, which flashes on and off in time with her questions.

PIFFS [*building*]: Their clothes? Their shoes? Their voices? Their laughter? Their stares? Their way of walking? Their way of sitting? Their way of smiling? Their way of talking? Their mouths? Their hands? Their feet? Their shins? Their thighs? Their knees? Their eyes? Their [*Drumbeat*]. Their [*Drumbeat*]. Their [*Cymbal bang*]. Their [*Trombone chord*]. Their [*Bass note*].

LAMB
[*in a high voice*]:   Well it depends what you mean really—

The light still flashes. She presses the other button and the piercing buzz–hum is heard again. LAMB*'s*

hands go to his earphones. He is propelled from the chair, falls, rolls, crawls, totters and collapses.

Silence.

He lies face upwards. MISS PIFFS *looks at him then walks to* LAMB *and bends over him.*

PIFFS: Thank you very much, Mr. Lamb. We'll let you know.

24

How Can We Be Moved by the Fate of Anna Karenina?

Colin Radford

> *"What's Hecuba to him, or he to Hecuba,*
> *That he should weep for her?"*
>
> **Hamlet** *Act II Scene ii.*

1. That men feel concern for the fate of others, that they have some interest, and a warm and benevolent one in what happens to at least some other men, may be simply a brute fact about men, though a happy one. By this I mean that we can conceive that men might have been different in this respect, and so it is possible for us to be puzzled by the fact that they are not different. In a situation where men did not feel concern for others, children might be nurtured only because mothers could not stand the pain of not feeding them, or because it gave them pleasure to do this and to play with them, or because they were a source of pride. So that if a child died, a mother might have the kind of feeling the owner of a car has if his car is stolen and wrecked. He doesn't feel anything for the car, unless he is a sentimentalist, and yet he is sorry and depressed when it happens.

Of course there may be good biological reasons why men should have concern for each other, or at least some other men, but that is not to the point. The present point, a conceptual one, is that we can conceive that all men might have been as some men are, viz., devoid of any feeling for anyone but themselves, whereas we cannot conceive, e.g., that all men might be what some men are, chronic liars.

2. So concern and related feelings are in this sense brute. But what are they? What is it to be moved by something's happening to someone?

Anything like a complete story here is a very long one, and in any case I have a particular interest. Suppose then that you read an account of the terrible sufferings of a group of people. If you are at all humane, you are unlikely to be unmoved by what you read. The account is likely to awaken or reawaken feelings of anger, horror, dismay or outrage and, if you are tender-hearted, you may well be moved to tears. You may even grieve.

But now suppose you discover that the account is false. If the account had caused you to grieve, you could not continue to grieve. If as the account sank in, you were told and believed that it was false this would make tears impossible, unless they were tears of rage. If you learned later that the account was false, you would feel that in being moved to tears you had been fooled, duped.

It would seem then that I can only be moved by someone's plight if I believe that something terrible has happened to him. If I do not believe that he has not and is not suffering or whatever, I cannot grieve or be moved to tears.

It is not only seeing a man's torment that torments us, it is also, as we say, the thought of his torment which torments, or upsets or moves us. But here thought implies belief. We have to

From *Aristotelian Society Supplementary Volume* 49 (1975), pp. 67–80. Reprinted by courtesy of the Editor of the Aristotelian Society: © 1975.

believe in his torment to be tormented by it. When we say that the thought of his plight moves us to tears or grieves us, it is thinking of or contemplating suffering which we believe to be actual or likely that does it.

3. The direction of my argument should now be fairly clear. Moving closer to its goal: suppose that you have a drink with a man who proceeds to tell you a harrowing story about his sister and you are harrowed. After enjoying your reaction he then tells you that he doesn't have a sister, that he has invented the story. In his case, unlike the previous one, we might say that the "heroine" of the account is fictitious. Nonetheless, and again, once you have been told this you can no longer feel harrowed. Indeed it is possible that you may be embarrassed by your reaction precisely because it so clearly indicates that you were taken in – and you may also feel embarrassed for the storyteller that he could behave in such a way. But the possibility of your being harrowed again seems to require that you believe that someone suffered.

Of course, if the man tells you in advance that he is going to tell you a story, you may reach for your hat, but you may stay and be moved. But this is too quick.

Moving closer still: an actor friend invites you to watch him simulate extreme pain, agony. He writhes about and moans. Knowing that he is only acting, could you be moved to tears? Surely not. Of course you may be embarrassed, and after some time you may even get faintly worried, "Is he really acting, or is he really in pain? Is he off his head?" But as long as you are convinced that he is only acting and is not really suffering, you cannot be moved by his suffering, and it seems unlikely as well as – as it were – unintelligible that you might be moved to tears by his portrayal of agony. It seems that you could only perhaps applaud it if it were realistic or convincing, and criticise if it were not.

But now suppose, horribly, that he acts or re-enacts the death agonies of a friend, or a Vietcong that he killed and tells you this. Then you might be horrified.

4. If this account is correct, there is no problem about being moved by historical novels or plays, documentary films, etc. For these works depict and forcibly remind us of the real plight and of the real sufferings of real people, and it is for these persons that we feel.

What seems unintelligible is how we could have a similar reaction to the fate of Anna Karenina, the plight of Madame Bovary or the death of Mercutio. Yet we do. We weep, we pity Anna Karenina, we blink hard when Mercutio is dying and absurdly wish that he had not been so impetuous.

5. Or do we? If we are seized by this problem, it is tempting for us to argue that, since we cannot be anguished or moved by what happens to Anna Karenina, since we cannot pity Madame Bovary and since we cannot grieve at the marvellous Mercutio's death, we do not do so.

This is a tempting thesis especially because, having arrived at it, we have then to think more carefully about our reactions to and feelings about e.g., the death of Mercutio, and these investigations reveal – how could they do otherwise? – that our response to Mercutio's death differs massively from our response to the untimely death of someone we know. As we watch Mercutio die the tears run down our cheeks, but as O. K. Bouwsma has pointed out,[1] the cigarettes and chocolates go in our mouths too, and we may mutter, if not to each other, then to ourselves, "How marvellous! How sublime!" and even "How moving!"

"Now," one might say, "if one really is *moved*, one surely cannot comment on this and in admiring tones? Surely being moved to tears is a massive response which tends to interfere with saying much, even to oneself? And surely the nature of the response is such that any comments made that do not advert to what gives rise to the feeling but to the person experiencing it tend to suggest that the response isn't really felt? Compare this with leaning over to a friend in a theatre and saying 'I am completely absorbed (enchanted, spellbound) by this!' "

But although we cannot truly grieve for Mercutio, we can be moved by his death, and are. If and when one says "How moving" in an admiring tone, one can be moved at the theatre. One's admiration is for the play or the performance, and one can admire or be impressed by this and avow this while being moved by it.

6. So we cannot say that we do not feel for fictional characters, that we are not sometimes moved by what happens to them. We shed real tears for Mercutio. They are not crocodile tears, they are dragged from us and they are not the sort of tears that are produced by cigarette smoke in the theatre. There is a lump in our throats, and it's not the sort of lump that is produced by swallowing a fishbone. We are appalled when we realise what may happen, and are horrified when it does. Indeed, we may be so appalled at the prospect of

what we think is going to happen to a character in a novel or a play that some of us can't go on. We avert the impending tragedy in the only way we can, by closing the book, or leaving the theatre.

This may be an inadequate response, and we may also feel silly or shamefaced at our tears. But this is not because they are always inappropriate and sentimental, as, e.g., is giving one's dog a birthday party, but rather because we feel them to be unmanly. They may be excusable though still embarrassing on the occasion of a real death, but should be contained for anything less.

Of course we are not only moved by fictional tragedies but impressed and even delighted by them. But I have tried to explain this, and that we are other things does not seem to the point. What is worrying is that we are moved by the death of Mercutio and we weep while knowing that no one has really died, that no young man has been cut off in the flower of his youth.

7. So if we can be and if some of us are indeed moved to tears at Mercutio's untimely death, feel pity for Anna Karenina and so on, how can this be explained? How can the seeming incongruity of our doing this be explained and explained away?

First solution

When we read the book, or better when we watch the play and it works, we are "caught up" and respond and we "forget" or are no longer aware that we are only reading a book or watching a play. In particular, we forget that Anna Karenina, Madame Bovary, Mercutio and so on are not real persons.

But this won't do. It turns adults into children. It is true that, e.g., when children are first taken to pantomimes they are unclear about what is going on. The young ones are genuinely and unambiguously terrified when the giant comes to kill Jack. The bolder ones shout "Look out!" and even try to get on the stage to interfere.

But do we do this? Do we shout and try to get on the stage when, watching *Romeo and Juliet*, we see that Tybalt is going to kill Mercutio? We do not. Or if we do, this is extravagant and unnecessary for our being moved. If we really did think someone was really being slain, either a person called Mercutio or the actor playing that rôle, we would try to do something or think that we should. We would, if you like, be genuinely appalled.

So we are not unaware that we are "only" watching a play involving fictional characters, and the problem remains.

Second solution

Of course we don't ever forget that Mercutio is only a character in a play, but we "suspend our disbelief" in his reality. The theatre management and the producer connive at this. They dim the lights and try to find good actors. They, and we, frown on other members of the audience who draw attention to themselves and distract us by coughing, and if, during a scene, say a stage hand steals on, picks up a chair that should have been removed and sheepishly departs, our response is destroyed. The "illusion" is shattered.

All this is true but the paradox remains. When we watch a play we do not direct our thoughts to its only being a play. We don't continually remind ourselves of this – unless we are trying to reduce the effect of the work on us. Nonetheless, and as we have seen, we are never unaware that we are watching a play, and one about fictional characters even at the most exciting and moving moments. So the paradox is not solved by invoking "suspension of disbelief", though it occurs and is connived at.

Third solution

It's just another brute fact about human beings that they can be moved by stories about fictional characters and events, i.e., human beings might not have been like this (and a lot of them are not. A lot of people do not read books or go to the theatre, and are bored if they do).

But our problem is that people *can* be moved by fictional suffering given their brute behaviour in other contexts where belief in the reality of the suffering described or witnessed is necessary for the response.

Fourth solution

But this thesis about behaviour in nonfictional contexts is too strong. The paradox arises only because my examples are handpicked ones in which there is this requirement. But there are plenty of situations in which we can be moved to tears or feel a lump in the throat without thinking that anyone will, or that anyone is even likely to suffer or die an untimely death, or whatever.

But are there? A mother hears that one of her friend's children has been killed in a street accident. When her own children return from school she grabs them in relief and hugs them, almost with a kind of anger. (Is it because they have frightened her?) Their reaction is "What's wrong with you?" They won't get a coherent answer perhaps, but surely the explanation is obvious. The death of the friend's child "brings home", "makes real", and perhaps strengthens the mother's awareness of the likelihood of her own children being maimed or killed. We must try another case. A man's attention wanders from the paper he is reading in his study. He thinks of his sister and, with a jolt, realises that she will soon be flying to the States. Perhaps because he is terrified of flying he thinks of her flying and of her plane crashing and shudders. He imagines how this would affect their mother. She would be desolated, inconsolable. Tears prick his eyes. His wife enters and wants to know what's up. He looks upset. Our man is embarrassed but says truthfully, "I was thinking about Jean's flying to the States and, well, I thought how awful it would be if there were an accident – how awful it would be for my mother." Wife: "Don't be silly! How maudlin! And had you nearly reduced yourself to tears thinking about all this? Really, I don't know what's got into you, etc., etc."

In this case the man's response to his thoughts, his being appalled at the thought of his sister's crashing, *is* silly and maudlin, but it is intelligible and non-problematic. For it would be neither silly nor maudlin if flying were a more dangerous business than we are prone to think it is. Proof: change the example and suppose that the sister is seriously ill. She is not suffering yet, but she had cancer and her brother thinks about her dying and how her death will affect their mother. If that were the situation his wife would do well to offer comfort as well as advice.

So a man can be moved not only by what has happened to someone, by actual suffering and death, but by their prospect and the greater the probability of the awful thing's happening, the more likely are we to sympathise, i.e., to understand his response and even share it. The lesser the probability the more likely we are not to feel this way. And if what moves a man to tears is the contemplation of something that is most unlikely to happen, e.g., the shooting of his sister, the more likely are we to find his behaviour worrying and puzzling. However, we can explain his divergent behaviour, and in various ways. We can do this in terms of his having false beliefs. He thinks a plane crash or a shooting is more likely than it is, which itself needs and can have an explanation. Or his threshold for worry is lower than average, and again this is non-problematic, i.e.,

we understand what's going on. Or lastly, we may decide he gets some kind of pleasure from dwelling on such contingencies and appalling himself. Now this is, logically, puzzling, for how can a man get pleasure from pain? But if only because traces of masochism are present in many of us, we are more likely to find it simply offensive.

The point is that our man's behaviour is only more or less psychologically odd or morally worrying. There is no logical difficulty here, and the reason for this is that the suffering and anguish that he contemplates, however unlikely, is pain that some real person may really experience.

Testing this, let us suppose first that our man when asked "What's up" says, "I was thinking how awful it would have been if Jean had been unable to have children – she wanted them so much." Wife: "But she's got them. Six!" Man: "Yes, I know, but suppose she hadn't?" "My God! Yes it would have been but it didn't happen. How can you sit there and weep over the dreadful thing that didn't happen, and now cannot happen." (She's getting philosophical. Sneeringly) "What are you doing? Grieving for her? Feeling sorry for her?" Man: "All right! But thinking about it, it was so vivid I could imagine just how it would have been." Wife: "You began to snivel!" Man: "Yes."

It is by making the man a sort of Walter Mitty, a man whose imagination is so powerful and vivid that, for a moment anyway, what he imagines seems real, that his tears are made intelligible, though of course not excusable.

So now suppose that the man thinks not of his sister but of a woman ... that is, he makes up a story about a woman who flies to the States and is killed and whose mother grieves, and so on, and that this gives him a lump in his throat. It might appear that, if my thesis is correct, the man's response to the story he invents should be even more puzzling than his being moved by the thought of his sister's not having children. "Yet," one who was not seized by the philosophical problem might say, "this case is really not puzzling. After all, he might be a writer who first gets some of his stories in this manner!"

But that is precisely why this example does not help. It is too close, too like what gives rise to the problem.

Fifth solution

A solution suggested by an earlier remark: if and when we weep for Anna Karenina, we weep for the

Colin Radford

pain and anguish that a real person might suffer and which real persons have suffered, and if her situation were not of that sort we should not be moved.

There is something in this, but not enough to make it a solution. For we do not really weep for the pain that a real person might suffer, and which real persons have suffered, when we weep for Anna Karenina, even if we should not be moved by her story if it were not of that sort. We weep for *her*. We are moved by what happens to her, by the situation she gets into, and which is a pitiful one, but we do not feel pity for her state or fate, or her history or her situation, or even for others, i.e., for real persons who might have or even have had such a history. We pity her, feel for her and our tears are shed for her. This thesis is even more compelling, perhaps, if we think about the death of Mercutio.

But all over again, how can we do this knowing that neither she nor Mercutio ever existed, that all their sufferings do not add one bit to the sufferings of the world?

Sixth solution

Perhaps there really is no problem. In nonfictional situations it may be necessary that in order for a person to be moved, he must believe in the reality of what he sees or is told, or at least he must believe that such a thing may indeed happen to someone. But, as I concede, being moved when reading a novel or watching a play is not exactly like being moved by what one believes happens in real life and, indeed, it is very different. So there are two sorts of being moved and, perhaps, two senses of "being moved". There is being moved (Sense 1) in real life and "being moved" (Sense 2) by what happens to fictional characters. But since there are these two sorts and senses, it does not follow from the necessity of belief in the reality of the agony or whatever it is, for being moved (S. 1), that belief in its reality is, or ought to be necessary for "being moved" (S. 2). So I have not shown that there is a genuine problem, which perhaps explains why I can find no solution.

But although being moved by what one believes is really happening is not exactly the same as being moved by what one believes is happening to fictional characters, it is not wholly different. And it is what is common to being moved in either situation which makes problematic one of the differences, viz., the fact that belief is not necessary in

the fictional situation. As for the hesitant claim that there is a different sense here, this clearly does not follow from the fact that being moved by what happens in real life is different from being moved in the theatre or cinema or when reading a novel, and I find it counterintuitive. But even if the phrase did have different senses for the different cases, it would not follow that there was no problem. It may be that "being moved" (S. 2) is an incoherent notion so that we and our behaviour are incoherent, when we are "moved" (S. 2).

When, as we say, Mercutio's death moves us, it appears to do so in very much the same way as the unnecessary death of a young man moves us and for the same reason. We see the death as a waste, though of course it is really only a waste in the real case, and as a "tragedy", and we are, unambiguously – though problematically as I see it in the case of fiction – saddened by the death. As we watch the play and realise that Mercutio may die or, knowing the play, that he is about to die, we may nonetheless and in either case say to ourselves "Oh! No! Don't let it happen!" (It seems *absurd* to say this, especially when we know the play, and yet we do. This is part of what I see as the problem.) When he is run through we wince and gasp and catch our breath, and as he dies the more labile of us weep.

How would our behaviour differ if we believed that we were watching the death of a real young man, perhaps of the actor playing the part of Mercutio? First, seeing or fearing that the actor playing the part of Tybalt is bent on killing the other actor, we might try to intervene or, if we did not, we might reproach ourselves for not doing so. When he has been run through we might try to get help. But if we are convinced that we can do nothing, as we are when we watch the death of Mercutio or read about Anna, and if we thought that our watching was not improper, these irrelevant differences in our behaviour would disappear. Once again, we would say to ourselves – and, in this case also to each other since there is no question of aesthetic pleasure – "My God! How terrible!" And as the actor lay dying, perhaps delivering Mercutio's lines, either because he felt them to be appropriate or because, unaware that he was actually dying, he felt that the show must go on, we should again weep for the dying man and the pity of it. Secondly, but this is not irrelevant, our response to the real death is likely to be more massive, more intense and longer in duration for, after all, a real young man has been killed, and it will not be alloyed – or allayed – by aesthetic pleasure. But such differences do not destroy the similarity of the response and may even be said to require it.

So a similarity exists, and the essential similarity seems to be that we are saddened. But this is my difficulty. For we are saddened, but how can we be? What are we sad *about*? How can we feel genuinely and involuntarily sad, and weep, as we do, knowing as we do that no one has suffered or died?

To insist that there is this similarity between being moved and "being moved" is not to deny that there are other differences between them besides the necessary presence of belief in the one case and its puzzling absence in the other. Yet, as I have already indicated, some of the peculiar features of "being moved" add to the problem it presents. Not *any* difference between being moved and "being moved", over and above the difference in belief, has the effect of reducing the conceptual problem presented by the latter, as is suggested by this sixth solution. E.g., when we hope that Mercutio will not get killed, we may realise, knowing the play, that he must be killed, unless the play is altered or the performance is interrupted and we may not wish for that. So not only is our hope vain, for he must die and we know this, but it exists alongside a wish that he will die. After the death, in retrospect, our behaviour differs. In the case of the real man, we should continue to be moved and to regret what happened. With Mercutio we are unlikely to do this and, in talking about his death later, we might only be moved to say "How moving it was!" For we are no longer at the performance or responding directly to it. We do not so much realise later as appropriately remind ourselves later that Mercutio is only a character and that, being a character, he will, as it were, be born again to die again at the next performance. Mercutio is not lost to us, when he dies, as the actor is when he dies.

Our response to Mercutio's death is, then, different from our response to the death of the actor. We do not entirely or simply hope that it will not happen, our response is partly aesthetic, the anguish at his death is not perhaps as intense, and it tends not to survive the performance.

Perhaps we are and can be moved by the death of Mercutio only to the extent that, at the time of the performance, we are "caught up" in the play, and see the characters as persons, real persons, though to see them as real persons is not to believe that they are real persons. If we wholly believe, our response is indistinguishable from our response to the real thing, for we believe it to be the real thing. If we are always and fully aware that these are only actors mouthing rehearsed lines, we are not caught up in the play at all and can only respond to the beauty and tragedy of the poetry and not to the death of the character. The difficulty is, however – and it remains – that the belief, to say the least, is never complete. Or, better, even when we are caught up, we are still aware that we are watching a play and that Mercutio is "only" a character. We may become like children, but this is not necessary for our tears.

So the problem remains. The strength of our response may be proportionate to, *inter alia*, our "belief" in Mercutio. But we do not and need not at any time believe that he is a real person to weep for him. So that what is necessary in other contexts, viz., belief, for being moved, is not necessary here and, all over again, how can we be saddened by and cry over Mercutio's death knowing as we do that when he dies no one really dies?

8. I am left with the conclusion that our being moved in certain ways by works of art, though very "natural" to us and in that way only too intelligible, involves us in inconsistency and so incoherence.

It may be some sort of comfort, as well as support for my thesis, to realise that there are other sorts of situation in which we are similarly inconsistent, i.e., in which, while knowing that something is or is not so, we spontaneously behave, or even may be unable to stop ourselves behaving, as if we believed the contrary. Thus, a tennis player who sees his shot going into the net will often give a little involuntary jump to lift it over. Because he knows that this can have no effect it is tempting to say that the jump is purely expressive. But almost anyone who has played tennis will know that this is not true. Or again, though men have increasingly come to think of death as a dreamless sleep, it was pointed out long ago – was it by Dr. Johnson or David Hume?[2] – that they still fear it. Some may say that this fear is not incoherent, for what appals such men is not their also thinking of death as an unpleasant state, but the prospect of their nonexistence. But how can this appal? There is, literally, nothing to fear. The incoherence of fearing the sleep of death for all that it will cause one to miss is even clearer. We do not participate in life when we are dead, but we are not then endlessly wishing to do so. Nonetheless, men fear the endless, dreamless sleep of death and fear it for all that they will miss.

Colin Radford

References

1 In "The Expression Theory of Art," collected in his *Philosophical Essays* (Lincoln: University of Nebraska Press, 1965). Cf. p. 29.

2 Either could have made such an observation, though Hume regarded death with phlegm, Johnson with horror. But in fact it was a contemporary, Miss Seward, "There is one mode of the fear of death which is certainly absurd; and that is the dread of annihilation, which is only a pleasing sleep without a dream." Boswell, *Life of Johnson*, for 1778.

25

Fearing Fictionally

Kendall Walton

> The plot [of a tragedy] must be structured
> ...that the one who is hearing the events
> unroll shudders with fear and feels pity at
> what happens.
>
> *Aristotle,* Poetics

If the gulf separating fictional worlds physically from the real world is as unbridgeable as it seems, it may be hard to make room for psychological interaction across worlds, for the apparent fact that real people fear Frankenstein monsters, pity Willy Loman, admire Superman, and so on. We feel a psychological bond to fictions, an intimacy with them, of a kind we ordinarily feel only toward things we take to be actual, things that are not (or are not thought to be) isolated physically from us. To allow that mere fictions are objects of our psychological attitudes while disallowing the possibility of physical interaction severs the normal links between the physical and the psychological. What is pity or anger which is never to be acted on? What is love that cannot be expressed to its object and is logically or metaphysically incapable of consummation? We cannot even try to rescue Robinson Crusoe from his island, no matter how deep our concern for him. Our fear of the Frankenstein monster is peculiarly unfounded if we are destined to survive no matter what – even if the monster ravishes the entire world!

Let's reconsider. *Do* we have psychological attitudes toward characters and other mere fictions? We do indeed get "caught up" in stories; we frequently become "emotionally involved" when we read novels or watch plays or films. But to construe this involvement as consisting of our having psychological attitudes toward fictional entities is to tolerate mystery and court confusion.

Here is an example of the most tempting kind: Charles is watching a horror movie about a terrible green slime. He cringes in his seat as the slime oozes slowly but relentlessly over the earth, destroying everything in its path. Soon a greasy head emerges from the undulating mass, and two beady eyes fix on the camera. The slime, picking up speed, oozes on a new course straight toward the viewers. Charles emits a shriek and clutches desperately at his chair. Afterwards, still shaken, he confesses that he was "terrified" of the slime.

Was he terrified of it? I think not. Granted, Charles's condition is similar in certain obvious respects to that of a person frightened of a pending real-world disaster. His muscles are tensed, he clutches his chair, his pulse quickens, his adrenaline flows. Let us call this physiological-psychological state *quasi-fear*. But it alone does not constitute genuine fear.

The fact that Charles describes himself as "terrified" of the slime and that others do as well proves nothing, not even if we assume that they are being truthful and, indeed, expressing a truth. We need to know whether this description is to be taken literally. We do not take Charles literally when he says, "There was a ferocious slime on the loose. I saw it coming." Why must we when he adds, "Boy, was I scared!"? Charles might try (seriously or otherwise) to convince us of the genuineness of his fear by shuddering and declaring dramatically that he was "really terrified." This emphasizes the intensity of his experience, but that is not the issue. Our question is whether his experience, however intense, was one of fear of the slime. It may have been a genuinely emotional experience. He may even have been genuinely frightened, as we shall see. But he was not afraid of the slime.

It is conceivable (barely) that a naive moviegoer should take the film to be a live documentary, a news flash portraying a real slime really threatening him and all of us. Such a viewer would be afraid, naturally. But Charles is not naive. He knows perfectly well that the slime is not real and that he is in no danger. How then can he fear it? It would not be far wrong to argue simply as follows: to fear something is in part to think oneself endangered by it. Charles does not think he is endangered by the slime. So he does not fear it.[1]

That fear necessarily involves a belief or judgment that the feared object poses a threat is a natural supposition which many standard theories of emotion endorse.[2] There are dissenting opinions, however, which need to be taken seriously. I will argue that being afraid is in certain respects similar to having such a belief, in any case, and that Charles's state is not relevantly similar to that of believing that the slime endangers him; hence he does not fear it.

But let us assume, temporarily, that to fear something is, in part, to think oneself endangered by it. There will be objections even so. Could it be that Charles *does* think he is in danger from the slime, that he believes it to be real and thus a real threat? Even if he is fully aware that it is purely fictitious, he might also, in a different way or on a different "level," believe the contrary. It has been said that in cases like this, one "suspends one's disbelief," or that "part" of a person believes something that the rest of him disbelieves, or that one finds oneself accepting what one nevertheless knows to be false.

One possibility is that Charles *half* believes that there is a real danger and that he is at least half afraid.[3] To half believe something is to be not quite sure that it is true, but also not sure that it is not true. If a child is told that his house is haunted but is uncertain whether the remark is meant seriously or in jest, he may half believe that it is haunted. If he does, he will be half afraid of the ghosts that may or may not inhabit it.

But Charles has *no* doubts about whether he is in the presence of an actual slime. If he half believed and were half afraid, we would expect him to have *some* inclination to act on his fear in the normal ways. Even a hesitant belief, a mere suspicion, that the slime is real would induce any normal person seriously to consider calling the police and warning his family, just in case. Charles gives no thought whatever to such courses of action. He is not *uncertain* whether the slime is real; he is perfectly sure it is not. Moreover, the fear symptoms that Charles does exhibit are not symptoms of a mere suspicion that the slime is real and a queasy feeling of half fear. They are symptoms of the certainty of grave and immediate danger and sheer terror. Charles's heart pounds violently; he gasps for breath; he grasps the chair until his knuckles are white. This is not the behavior of a man who basically realizes that he is safe but suffers flickers of doubt. If it indicates fear at all, it indicates acute and overwhelming terror. To compromise, to say that Charles half believes he is in danger and is half afraid, does less than justice to the intensity of his reaction.

One who claims that Charles believes he is in danger might argue not that this is a hesitant or weak or half belief but rather that it is a belief of a special kind – a "gut" feeling as opposed to an "intellectual" one. Compare a person who hates flying. In one sense Aaron realizes that airplanes are (relatively) safe. He says, honestly, that they are, and he can quote statistics to prove it. Yet he avoids traveling by air as much as possible. He is brilliant at devising excuses. If he must board a plane, he becomes nervous and upset. Perhaps Aaron believes, at a "gut" level, that flying is dangerous, despite his "intellectual" opinion to the contrary. And he may really be afraid of flying.

But Charles is different. Aaron performs *deliberate* actions that one would expect of someone who thinks flying is dangerous, or at least he is strongly inclined to perform such actions. If he does not actually decide against traveling by air, he has a strong inclination to do so, and once aboard the airplane he must fight a temptation to get off. But Charles does not have even an inclination to leave the theater or call the police. The only signs that he might really believe he is endangered are his more or less automatic, nondeliberate reactions: his throbbing pulse, his sweaty palms, his knotted stomach, a spontaneous shriek. This justifies treating the two cases differently.

Here is one way of characterizing the difference: Deliberate actions are done for reasons; they are done because of what the agent wants and what he thinks will bring about what he wants. There is a presumption that such actions are reasonable in light of the agent's beliefs and desires (however unreasonable the beliefs and desires may be). So we postulate beliefs or desires to make sense of them. People also have reasons for doing things they are inclined to do but, for other reasons, refrain from doing. If Aaron thinks flying is dangerous, then, assuming that he wants to live, his actions or tendencies thereto are reasonable. Otherwise they probably are not. So we legitimately infer that he does believe, at least on a "gut" level, that flying is dangerous. But we do not have to make the same kind of sense of Charles's automatic responses. One doesn't have reasons for things one doesn't *do*, like sweating, increasing one's pulse rate, involuntarily knotting one's stomach. So there is no need to attribute beliefs (or desires) to Charles that will render these responses reasonable. Thus, we can justifiably infer Aaron's ("gut") belief in the danger of flying from his deliberate behavior or inclinations and yet refuse to infer from Charles's automatic responses that he thinks he is in danger.

Could it be that at moments of special crisis during the movie – when the slime first spots Charles, for instance – Charles "loses hold of reality" and *momentarily* takes the slime to be real and really fears it? These moments are too short for Charles to think about doing anything; so (one might claim) it is not surprising that his belief and fear are not accompanied by the normal inclinations to act. This move is unconvincing. In the first place, Charles's quasi-fear responses are not merely momentary; he may have his heart in his throat throughout most of the movie, yet without experiencing the slightest inclination to flee or call the police. These long-term responses and Charles's propensity to describe them afterwards in terms of "fear" would need to be understood even if it were allowed that moments of real fear are interspersed among them. Furthermore, however tempting the momentary-fear idea might be,

comparable views of other psychological states are much less appealing. When we say that someone "pities" Willy Loman or "admires" Superman, it is unlikely that we have in mind special moments during her experience of the work when she forgets, momentarily, that she is dealing with mere fiction and feels flashes of actual pity or admiration. Her "sense of reality" may be robust and healthy throughout the experience, uninterrupted by anything like the special moments of crisis Charles experiences during the horror movie. Indeed, it may be appropriate to say that someone "pities" Willy or "admires" Superman even when she is not watching the play or reading the cartoon. The momentary-fear theory, even if it were plausible, would not help us with cases in which one apparently has other psychological attitudes toward fictions.

Let's look at challenges to the supposition that fear necessarily involves a judgment of danger and that emotions in general have cognitive dimensions. Is it possible that Charles fears the slime even without taking himself to be endangered by it?

Charles's case and others like it are themselves thought by some to show the independence of fear and other emotions from beliefs, but the treatment of these cases is often distressingly question begging. Charles *is* afraid, it is assumed, and he does not think he is in danger. So fear does not require such a belief. One then cooks up a weaker requirement so as to protect the initial assumption: Fear requires only imagining danger, it is said, or the idea of danger vividly presented. (The fuzziness of the line between imagining and believing adds to the confusion.)

The question begging rests implicitly, no doubt, on an assumption that taking Charles to fear the slime, as he says he does, is the natural or ordinary or commonsense or pretheoretically more plausible position, and that it wins by default or at least is to be preferred in the absence of substantial reasons to the contrary. This assumption is unwarranted. One will understandably hesitate to second-guess Charles's assessment of his own psychological condition. But the nature of his assessment is by no means self-evident, and is itself part of what is at issue. To take him literally and straightforwardly when he testifies to being afraid of the slime is dangerously presumptive. His saying this no more establishes that he thinks he is afraid than the fact that children playing a game of make-believe say "There is a monster in the basement!" shows them to believe that a monster is in the basement. If asked whether he has had any really terrifying experiences in the last decade, Charles might well omit mention of his confrontation with the slime. Or he might cite it in a parenthetical spirit, as though it does not really count. ("Well, only in watching a movie.") Initial intuitions are not all on one side, and neither side bears disproportionately the burden of proof.

Patricia Greenspan has undertaken a more substantial reconsideration of standard views about links between emotions and beliefs.[4] Frances, let's suppose, was once attacked by a rabid dog. As a result of this traumatic experience she "exhibit[s] fear in the presence of all dogs," including lovable old Fido, "even though she knows full well that Fido has had his rabies shots and is practically toothless anyway." Frances genuinely fears Fido, Greenspan suggests, as Aaron fears flying, and she avoids the dog when she can. But it is awkward to attribute to her the belief that Fido is dangerous. For one thing, she is perfectly happy to allow friends and loved ones to play with him. (Does she judge Fido to be dangerous to her but not to anyone else?)

Part of the problem is that the notion of *belief* (or *judgment*) is far from clear. It may even be that beliefs do not constitute a natural kind, that no refinement of the ordinary notion has a legitimate place in a sophisticated theory of mind. If so, the question of whether emotions require beliefs will be ill formed. But we do not have to settle these larger issues in order to diagnose Charles's condition. Even if Frances fears in the absence of a belief in danger, this hardly suggests that Charles does. Frances exhibits deliberate behavior characteristic of fear while Charles, we saw, not only does not but has not even the slightest tendency to. Frances "give[s] in to [her] immediate urge to sidestep any unnecessary encounters with Fido"; she flees "when [Fido] approaches, out of fear."[5] Fear is *motivating* in distinctive ways, whether or not its motivational force is attributed to cognitive elements in it. It puts pressure on one's behavior (even if one resists). (If sky divers and mountain climbers *enjoy* fear – not just danger – they nevertheless have *inclinations* to avoid the danger.) To deny this, to insist on considering Charles's non-motivating state to be one of fear of the slime, would be radically to reconceive the notion of fear. Fear emasculated by subtracting its distinctive motivational force is not fear at all.

The issue is not just one of fidelity to a deeply ingrained pretheoretical conception of fear. The

perspicuity of our understanding of human nature is at stake. The "fear" experienced by Charles, whose munching of popcorn is interrupted by a wave of quasi-fear sensations, and that experienced by Frances, who flees from Fido, or Aaron, who, with his teeth gritted in determination, manages to go through with an airplane flight, are animals of different kinds. To assimilate them would be to emphasize superficial similarities at the expense of fundamental differences. A creditor might as well accept payment in fool's gold. We will do better to assimilate genuine fear and genuine emotions generally to belief–desire complexes. (This does not imply that emotions are not "feelings.") If fear does not consist partly in a belief that one is in danger, it is nevertheless similar to such a belief (combined with a desire not to be harmed) in its motivational force, and perhaps in other ways as well.

My claim is not that Charles experiences no genuine fear. He does not fear the slime, but the movie might induce in him fear of something else. If Charles is a child, he may wonder whether there might not be real slimes or other exotic horrors *like* the one in the movie, even though he fully realizes that the movie slime itself is not real. He may genuinely fear these suspected actual dangers; he may have nightmares about them for days afterwards. And he may take steps to avoid them. *Jaws* caused a lot of people to fear sharks, ones they thought might really exist, and to avoid swimming in the ocean. But this does not mean they were afraid of the fictional sharks in the movie. If Charles is an older moviegoer with a heart condition, he may be afraid of the movie itself or of experiencing it. Perhaps he knows that excitement could trigger a heart attack and fears that the movie will cause excitement – by depicting the slime as being especially aggressive or threatening. This is real fear. But it is fear of the depiction of the slime, not of the slime depicted.

Several commentators willing to agree that Charles does not fear the slime have tried to understand his experience as one of actual fear with a different object. Peter Lamarque takes him to fear the *thought* of the slime (or the "sense" of a description of it).[6] That he *might* fear this thought, or the experience of thinking it, is evident; the Charles with a heart condition does. But Lamarque does not have in mind such special circumstances. What we call "fear of the slime" by ordinary appreciators fully aware of its fictitiousness is in general, he thinks, fear of the thought. I see no advantage in this suggestion. The reasons for denying that Charles fears the slime apply equally to the thought. Apart from special circumstances, as when he has a heart condition, he does not consider the thought dangerous or treat it as such, nor does he experience even an inclination to escape from it. Moreover, his experience simply does not feel like fear of a thought; characterizing it as such flies in the face of its phenomenology. And it is the *slime*, not a thought, that Charles so inevitably and unabashedly describes himself as afraid of. The original intuition, for what it's worth, is that the slime is the object of Charles's fear. Lamarque's proposal abandons that intuition and *also* fails to recognize our reasons for denying it. In §7.1 [see pp. 181–3] we will understand Charles's experience in a way that does full justice to its phenomenology and accommodates easily the normal ways of describing it, yet does not have him (literally) fearing the slime or, necessarily, anything at all.

If I am right about Charles, skepticism concerning other psychological attitudes purportedly aimed at fictitious objects is in order as well. We should be wary of the idea that people literally pity Willy Loman or grieve for Anna Karenina or admire Superman while being fully aware that these characters and their sufferings or exploits are purely fictitious. It is not implausible that pity involves a belief (or judgment, or attitude) that what one pities actually suffers misfortune, and admiration a belief that the admired object is admirable, but the normal appreciator does not think it is actually the case that Willy suffers or that Superman is admirable. Perhaps it is more reasonable to think of these emotions as merely *akin* to such beliefs (together with appropriate desires), in particular in their motivational force. But the spectator who "pities" Willy, especially, would seem not to feel the motivational force in question; she feels no inclination to commiserate with him or to try to help him. It is less clear what one must believe about someone in order to grieve for him or what motivational force may be intrinsic to grief. But grief, as well as pity and admiration, would seem to require at the very least awareness of the existence of their objects. It is arguable that for this reason alone appreciators cannot be said actually to pity Willy or grieve for Anna or admire Superman.

Like the slime movie, *Death of a Salesman*, *Anna Karenina*, and Superman comics may induce in appreciators genuine emotions of the *kind* in ques-

tion. *Anna Karenina* fosters genuine sympathy for real people in unfortunate situations like Anna's; this is part of what is important about Tolstoy's novel. But to consider the experience commonly characterized as "pity for Anna" to be merely pity for real people "like" her (or a determination or inclination conditionally to feel pity toward people in like situations) does not do it justice.[7] It is no accident that we speak of sympathizing with or grieving for *Anna*. [. . .]

> I put my face close to the thick glass-plate in front of a puff-adder in the Zoological Gardens, with the firm determination of not starting back if the snake struck at me; but, as soon as the blow was struck, my resolution went for nothing, and I jumped a yard or two backwards with astonishing rapidity. My will and reason were powerless against the imagination of a danger which had never been experienced.
>
> (Charles Darwin)

It is high time we looked in again on Charles, whom we left in the theater quaking with quasi fear as the green slime bore down on him from the screen. We know that he is not really in danger. He knows this too, and he is not really afraid (not of the slime, anyway). His condition needs attention nevertheless. What *is* the nature of his experience? We must account for it in a way that will explain why it seems so natural, so nearly obligatory, for him and others to describe it as fear of the slime. Our account must do justice to the important connections that surely obtain between his experience and an experience of actual fear.

The main component of the answer has been anticipated: Charles is participating psychologically in his game of make-believe. It is not true but fictional that he fears the slime. So of course he speaks of himself as being afraid of it. His speaking thus may itself constitute participation – verbal participation – in his game. It is fictional that he is afraid, and it is fictional that he says he is.

In many ways Charles is like a child, Timmy, playing a game of make-believe with his father. The father pretends to be a ferocious monster who cunningly stalks him and, at a crucial moment, lunges "viciously" at him. Timmy flees screaming to the next room. The scream is more or less involuntary, and so is the flight. But Timmy has a delighted grin on his face even as he runs, and he unhesitatingly comes back for more. He is perfectly aware that his father is only playing, that the whole thing is just a game, and that only fictionally is there a vicious monster after him. He is not really afraid. But it is fictional that he is afraid. Fictionally the monster attacks; fictionally Timmy is in mortal danger and knows that he is; and when he screams and runs, it is fictional that he is terrified. Likewise, when the slime raises its head, spies the camera, and begins oozing toward it, it is fictional in Charles's game that he is threatened. And when as a result Charles gasps and grips his chair, fictionally he is afraid.

What makes it fictional that Charles is afraid? Facts about Charles himself. He is an actor, of a sort, in his game, as well as an object; he is a reflexive prop generating fictional truths about himself. In this respect Charles, and Timmy also, are like actors portraying themselves in ordinary theatrical events, like Ronald Reagan playing Ronald Reagan in a stage play.

But there are crucial differences. Charles represents himself *as* himself, and Reagan does not. This goes with the fact that Charles can hardly fail to realize that the person he represents is himself, whereas Reagan might conceivably think he is playing the part of someone else who shares his name. The fact that it is *Charles* who is quivering in the theater is what makes it fictional that it is *he* who fears the slime. But it is not Reagan's identity that makes it Reagan whom he is impersonating.

Another difference concerns what it is about Charles and Reagan that does the generating. Fictional truths about Charles are generated partly by what he thinks and feels, by his actual mental state. It is partly the fact that he experiences quasi fear, the fact that he feels his heart pounding, his muscles tensed, and so on, that makes it fictional that he is afraid; it would not be appropriate to describe him as afraid if he were not in some such state. This is not true of Reagan playing Reagan. Ordinary onstage actors, whether self-impersonating or not, generate fictional truths by virtue of their acting, their behavior. Whether it is fictional that the character portrayed is afraid depends just on what the actor says and does and how he contorts his face, regardless of what he actually thinks or feels. It makes no difference whether his actual emotional state is anything like one of fear. An actor may find that putting himself into a certain frame of mind makes it easier to act in the required manner. Nonetheless, it is how he acts, not his state of mind, that is responsible for gener-

ating fictional truths. If it is fictional that Reagan is afraid, that is so because of his demeanor on stage, regardless of his actual emotional state.

This is how our conventions for (traditional) theater work, and it is entirely reasonable that they should work this way. Theatrical events are put on for audiences. Audiences cannot be expected to have a clear idea of an actor's personal thoughts and feelings while he is performing. That would require being intimately acquainted with his off-stage personality and taking into account recent events that may have affected his mood (an argument with his director or his wife, a death in the family). If fictional truths depended on actors' private thoughts and feelings, it would be awkward and unreasonably difficult for spectators to ascertain what is going on in the fictional world. It is not surprising that the fictional truths for which actors onstage are responsible are understood to be generated by just what is visible from the galleries. Acting involves dissembling; actors take pains to hide their actual mental states from the audience.

Charles is not performing for an audience. It is not his job to get across to anyone else what fictionally is true of himself. Probably no one but he much cares whether or not it is fictional that he is afraid. So there is no reason why his actual state of mind should not have a role in generating fictional truths about himself.

It is less clear what makes it fictional in the monster game that Timmy is afraid. He might be performing for the benefit of an audience; he might be *showing* someone – an onlooker or just his father – that fictionally he is afraid. If so, perhaps he is like an onstage actor; perhaps his observable behavior is responsible for the fact that fictionally he is afraid. But there is room for doubt. Timmy behaves as though he is afraid, as an actor would, but he also experiences quasi-fear sensations, as does Charles. And his audience probably has much surer access to his mental state than theater audiences have to those of actors. The audience may know him well, and Timmy probably does not try as hard or as skillfully as actors do to hide his actual mental state. It may be perfectly evident to the audience that he suffers from quasi fear as a result of his realization that fictionally a monster is after him. So it is not unreasonable to regard Timmy's mental state as helping to generate fictional truths.

A more definite account of the situation is possible if Timmy is participating in the game solely for his own amusement, with no thought of an audience. In this case he himself, at least, almost certainly understands his fictional fear to depend on his mental state rather than (just) his behavior. (It is possible that at the same time observers understand his behavior alone to be responsible for his fictional fear. The child and the observers may recognize different principles of generation.) Suppose Timmy is an undemonstrative sort who does not scream or run or betray his "fear" in any other especially overt way. His participation in the game is passive. Nevertheless he does experience quasi fear when fictionally the monster attacks, and he still would describe himself as being afraid (although he knows full well that there is no danger and that his "fear" is not real). Certainly in this case it is (partly) his quasi fear which generates the fictional truth he expresses when he says that he is afraid.

My proposal is to construe Charles on the model of this undemonstrative child. Charles may, of course, exhibit his "fear" in certain observable ways. But his observable behavior is not meant to show anyone else that fictionally he is afraid. It is likely to go unnoticed by others, and even Charles himself may be unaware of it. No one, least of all Charles, regards his observable behavior as responsible for the fact that fictionally he is afraid.

Charles's quasi fear is not responsible for the fact that fictionally it is the *slime* that he fears (not by itself anyway), nor even for the fact that fictionally he is afraid rather than angry or excited or merely upset. What is? The details will probably depend on what one takes actual fear to consist in. But Charles's realization that fictionally the slime is bearing down on him is likely to be central.

Recall the familiar and not implausible accounts of fear that go approximately like this: To be (really) afraid of a tornado, for instance, is to have certain phenomenological experiences (quasi fear) as a result of knowing or believing that one is endangered by the tornado. What makes the state one of *fear* rather than anger or excitement is the belief that one is in danger, and what makes the tornado its object is the fact that it is the tornado that one takes to be dangerous.

It is clear enough what to say about Charles if this is what fear is: He experiences quasi fear as a result of realizing that fictionally the slime threatens him. This makes it fictional that his quasi fear is caused by a belief that the slime poses a danger, and hence that he fears the slime.

Fear may not *require* a belief that one is in danger. In §5.2 [see pp. 180–1] I treated sympathetically the suggestion that Frances fears poor

old Fido without judging him to be dangerous. If she does, the account of fear I have just sketched will not do as a *definition*. But many instances of fear may still consist partly in a belief in danger. Quasi fear caused by a belief that one is threatened by a tornado may constitute fear of the tornado, even if it is possible to fear a tornado without so believing. It is fictional that Charles, as we understand him, believes that the slime poses a danger; the fear that, fictionally, he has for the slime is thus unlike Frances' fear of poor old Fido. So we can still say that the fact that Charles is quasi-afraid as a result of realizing that fictionally the slime threatens him is what generates the truth that fictionally he is afraid of the slime, while allowing that this fictional truth *could* be generated in other ways. [. . .]

Now that we have a reasonably clear positive picture of the character of Charles's experience, we can reaffirm with renewed confidence our denial that he fears the slime. The fact that it is fictional that he fears it does not automatically rule out his actually doing so, since fictionality and truth are not incompatible. But that fictional truth, generated in approximately the manner I suggested, preempts the phenomenological and verbal data which might be explained by taking his fear to be actual. It leaves little incentive to so take it, even if we ignore the absence both of a belief that the slime endangers him and of an inclination to escape. This point is strengthened by the fact that our reasons for considering it fictional that Charles fears the slime do not depend on denying that he actually does. It is not just that we can manage to fill the gap left by that denial. What fills the gap is something we have on hand anyway.

Must we declare Aristotle wrong in decreeing that tragedies should evoke fear and pity? Not unless we naively insist on a literal-minded reading of his words. They are better construed in a spirit not entirely detached from that in which we are to understand Charles's exclamation, "Boy, was I scared!"

Notes

1 Our question is whether Charles fears for himself. Fear for someone else plausibly involves the belief that that other person is in danger.

2 On some accounts fear *is* in part a belief or judgment of danger. Others take it to be a feeling caused by

such a belief, or merely accompanied by it. See Daniel Farrell, "Recent Work on the Emotions," *Analyse und Kritik* 10 (1988), 71–102.

3 All "stage presentations are to produce a sort of temporary half-faith" (Coleridge, *Selected Poetry and Prose*, ed. Elizabeth Schneider (New York: Holt, Rinehart and Winston, 1951), p. 396).

4 Patricia Greenspan "Emotions as Evaluations," *Pacific Philosophical Quarterly* 62 (1981), 158–69.

5 Ibid., pp. 164 and 162. Kraut, who argues that emotions do not require beliefs, appears also to

allow action a role in their analyses ("Feelings in Context," *Journal of Philosophy* 83 (1986), 642–52, esp. p. 645).

6 Peter Lamarque, "How Can We Fear and Pity Fictions?" *British Journal of Aesthetics* 21 (1981), 291–304).

7 See William Charlton, "Feeling for the Fictitious," *British Journal of Aesthetics* 24 (1984), 206–16; Ralph W. Clark, "Fictional Entities." *Philosophical Studies* 38 (1980), 341–9.

26

The Pleasures of Tragedy

Susan Feagin

David Hume begins his little essay "Of Tragedy" with the observation: "It seems an unaccountable pleasure which the spectators of a well-written tragedy receive from sorrow, terror, anxiety, and other passions that are in themselves disagreeable and uneasy."[1] Here Hume addresses a paradox that has puzzled philosophers of art since Aristotle: tragedies produce, and are designed to produce, pleasure for the audience, without supposing any special callousness or insensitivity on its part (in fact, quite the opposite). I will introduce a distinction which enables us to understand how we can feel pleasure in response to tragedy, and which also sheds some light on the complexity of such responses. The virtues of this approach lie in its straightforward solution to the paradox of tragedy as well as the bridges the approach builds between this and some other traditional problems in aesthetics, and the promising ways in which we are helped to see their relationships. In particular, we are helped to understand the feeling many have had about the greatness of tragedy in comparison to comedy, and provided a new perspective from which to view the relationship between art and morality. The very close connection which is seen to hold here between pleasures from tragedy and moral feelings also gives rise to a potential problem, which is examined in the last three sections of the paper.

Hume himself alleged that imagination, imitation, and expression are all "naturally" pleasurable to the mind, and argued that when they "predominate" over the unpleasant feelings the latter are "converted" into the former. But it is not clear how the "dominance" of imagination and expression is to be achieved. It is not insured by the fact that what is depicted is fictional, or even by our knowledge that it is fictional, since Hume discusses a play where the events depicted (even though fictional) are so gory that no amount of expression can "soften" them into pleasure. More puzzling, however, is the process of "conversion" which imagination performs on the unpleasant feelings (and which those feelings, when dominant, perform on the natural pleasantness of the imagination). Pains are not merely mitigated by the pleasure, but converted or transformed into something different. The mechanics of this conversion are never explained, and as long as they remain obscure, even if we accept other features of Hume's view, many of which are quite insightful, we have merely substituted one puzzle for another.[2]

I Preliminaries

The paradox of tragedy presupposes a position on the more general problem of how we can (not irrationally or absurdly) respond emotionally to a work of art at all, given that we do not really believe the events or characters depicted in it are

From *American Philosophical Quarterly* 20 (1983), pp. 95–104. Reprinted by permission of the University of Illinois Press.

real. I shall adopt the perspective of Ralph Clark who suggests a way of handling this more general problem which is ingenious for its simplicity.[3] Emotional responses to art are the result of entertaining various counterfactual conditionals: what would it be like if... (Iago were real, a 300-story building caught fire and all the elevators went out, someone had the characteristics and experiences of Anna Karenina).[4] Though this perspective is not essential to my view on the pleasures of tragedy, it does coincide nicely with some points I wish to make later. There are, moreover, some works of art for which Clark's approach will not do. But these tend to be parodies or other sorts of works within the comic genre, rather than tragedies. That is, such works make us laugh because there is no, or little temptation to entertain the supposition that that might really happen (*Godzilla Eats Toledo*, etc.). Even in those cases, however, we can imagine what it would be like to be a person about to suffer (and hence such works can excite fear) even as a result of something deliberately far-fetched. One could even argue that it is just the juxtaposition of such seemingly incompatible responses which often produces delight, or pleasure. But I am interested here in how to explain pleasure deriving from tragedy, rather than the problems of how we can respond emotionally to manifestly unrealistic works, or to any works of art at all. Clearly, my problem presupposes an answer to the more general problem, but in addition requires the resolution of a seeming incongruity between the pleasures produced and the feelings the tragic subject matter seems, morally, to call for.

It would not be surprising to find someone claiming that aesthetically developed persons do not feel pleasure or enjoyment from tragedy at all, and that the appropriate response to such works of art is to be unnerved, disturbed, depressed, or even horrified. If this were true *and* this were all there was to say about the matter, then it would be very difficult indeed to understand why tragedies are so revered. People who pursue them would seem to be morbidly fixated on achieving their own unhappiness, which is more a sign of mental imbalance than aesthetic sophistication. The paradox of pleasure from tragedy would be replaced, then, by a different paradox: why we seek out things that displease us so.

Further, it would be difficult to accept that tragedy produces pleasure if pleasure were thought to be merely a kind of gaiety involving smiles or laughter, or purely sensuous, of short term inter-

est and limited duration. But pleasures come in many shapes and sizes. Not all are highly spirited. Some are serene and calm, and may as well involve profound feelings of satisfaction. Pleasures from tragedy are of these latter sorts. Tragedy provides worthwhile experiences because it answers to important human interests, not superficial ones. These experiences include, as I shall argue, some of the most gratifying feelings human beings recognize themselves to possess. If this is so, and it is still claimed that these experiences are not pleasurable, then it seems we have embarked upon a merely terminological dispute.

Traditionally, the puzzle which is my topic has been posed as how we can derive pleasure from tragedy, and I shall follow suit. But I am using "tragedy" in a broad sense, including under this rubric the appropriate works in film, literature, dance, as well as theater (operas and plays). My remarks here could even be extended, with appropriate modifications, to apply to paintings and sculpture – even though "tragedy" is not used to categorize works in those mediums. What this shows is that certain conclusions about the pleasurableness of tragedies are also seen to hold for other works as well, since the pleasures derive from comparable features of tragedies on the one hand and certain paintings and sculpture on the other. Naturally, then, my remarks do not apply merely to the narrow, Aristotelian sense of tragedy, in which sense there is question about whether such works as, e.g., Arthur Miller's *Death of a Salesman* or Eugene O'Neill's *A Long Day's Journey Into Night* are tragedies. I am concerned here with, to put it bluntly, the class of works of art with unhappy endings (even though the unhappiness of the endings is often punctuated with something we would judge to be felicitous – such as Othello's knowledge of Desdemona's faithfulness, or Alfredo's discovery of Violetta's love in *La Traviata* – in fact, one could argue that the "felicitous" discoveries are more poignant precisely because of the accompanying grief). To extend the concept to paintings and sculpture one would have to change this to "works with unpleasant subject matter." "Unhappy endings" and "unpleasant subject matter" are neither of them technically precise, but they do capture the feature of tragedy which leads to the puzzle. The unhappiness of endings and unpleasantness of subject matter are the aspects of works of art which give rise to the perplexity about how such works can give pleasure to anyone who is not an unfeeling brute, malicious, or unbalanced. It is unfortunate that Hume himself was not very clear on this, as he writes, "One scene full of joy and contentment and security is the utmost that any composition of this kind can bear; and it is sure always to be the concluding one."[5] Quite the contrary, scenes of joy are generally the opening ones, and tales with happy endings are not likely, in anyone's vocabulary, to be called tragedies.

Though my own discussion of the pleasures of tragedy does not utilize such notions as imagination and passion on which Hume depended, it does have its own special presuppositions. I shall speak of two kinds of responses to art: a direct response and a meta-response. A direct response is a response to the qualities and content of the work. A meta-response is a response to the direct response. The distinction is not one of epistemological or ontological status; I presuppose no view about sense data, epistemologically "primitive" experiences, or incorrigibility of mental status. A direct response is direct only in the sense that it is a response to the qualities and content of the work of art. Of course, there are complex questions about what is "in the work" and what constitutes the "work itself," but those need not be resolved for the purposes of this discussion. The important contrast is not between a direct response to the work as opposed to a direct response to what is not really in the work. The important contrast is between a direct response and a meta-response which is a response to the direct response: it is how one feels about and what one thinks about one's responding (directly) in the way one does to the qualities and content of the work. The meta-response is what Ryle called a "higher order" operation: it depends on (and is partly a function of) another mental phenomenon, i.e., a direct response. Ideally, my remarks will be independent of any specific view of the "logical category" of pleasure itself, and I fear perhaps the term "response" may cause some unwarranted discomfort in that sphere. Let me therefore make the following caveats: (1) by calling pleasure a response I do not imply that it is not essentially connected to its source (what one finds pleasurable), i.e., it is not distinguishable as a response independently of what the pleasure is a pleasure in; (2) a response is not necessarily a mental episode or occurrence (a fortiori it is not necessarily a private mental episode) but it may turn out to be a mood or even a disposition or a change of disposition, or some other type of thing.

Both direct and meta-responses exist in ordinary life as well as in artistic contexts. For example, the remains of a spectacular car crash may titillate our curiosity, and we may feel disgusted with ourselves for being so morbid. On the other hand, we may enjoy the enticement of hawkers outside seamy strip joints, and be pleased with ourselves for having overcome a puritanical upbringing. We can be depressed at our failure to meet a challenge, impressed with our ability to rise to an occasion, disgusted with our lack of sympathy for a friend's bereavement, or pleased with the commitment we are inclined to make to help a neighbor. It should be noted that in ordinary as well as aesthetic contexts the two kinds of responses cannot be distinguished merely by what words are used to describe them. "Pleasure," "shock," "melancholy," and "delight" may all describe direct or meta-responses, and the two are not always clearly distinguishable from each other. A blush of embarrassment may be intensified by embarrassment over the blush. That two things being distinguished cannot be infallibly distinguished, and that there are unclear cases of how and even whether the two are distinguishable, does not necessarily undermine the utility of the distinction.

II   A Solution

Direct responses to tragedy are responses to the unpleasantness of the work, and they are hence unpleasant experiences we would expect to have from works having unpleasant subject matter and/or unhappy endings. Direct responses draw on our feelings and sympathies: tear-jerkers jerk tears because of our sympathy with persons who are ill-treated or the victims of misfortune. Many people, in fact, dislike attending depressing plays and violent movies, or reading weighty books and poetry, precisely because these experiences are unpleasant and consequently depress and sadden them, making them too well aware of the evil of people and the perils of existence. These works of art, rather than being uplifting and inspiring, often instead produce feelings of torpor and futility as one is overwhelmed by the amount and variety of viciousness in the world. A dose of direct response unpleasantness is a good antidote to creeping misanthropy, as it feeds off of our concern for others. It is also, as John Stuart Mill discovered, a cure for ennui. Mill reported in his *Autobiography* (Sec. V) that it was his crying over the distressed condition of Marmontel as related in his memoirs that initially jogged Mill out of his "mental crisis" by showing him that he did have feelings, concerns, and cares, and that he was not just "a logic machine."

It is the nature of these direct responses to tragedy which we expect and in fact receive which gives rise to the question in the first place, how do we derive pleasure from tragedy? Certainly the typical person who appreciates and enjoys such works of art doesn't feel the direct response any less poignantly than those described above who don't enjoy these works. Lovers of Dostoyevsky, Verdi, and Shakespeare, let us hope, are no more callous than those who find them too hard to take. But whence the pleasure? It is, I suggest, a meta-response, arising from our awareness of, and in response to, the fact that we do have unpleasant direct responses to unpleasant events as they occur in the performing and literary arts. We find ourselves to be the kind of people who respond negatively to villainy, treachery, and injustice. This discovery, or reminder, is something which, quite justly, yields satisfaction. In a way it shows what we care for, and in showing us we care for the welfare of human beings and that we deplore the immoral forces that defeat them, it reminds us of our common humanity. It reduces one's sense of aloneness in the world, and soothes, psychologically, the pain of solipsism. Perhaps this is something like what Kant had in mind when he spoke in the *Critique of Judgment* of a "common sense." We derive pleasure from the communicability or "shareability" of a response to a work of art: it is something which unites us with other people through feeling something which could, in principle, be felt by anyone.

These meta-pleasures should not be confused with the pleasures from crying or other kinds of emotional release. The pleasure from giving vent or expression to one's pent-up feelings of anger, frustration, or sadness is different from the pleasure from being aware of the fact that you are the kind of person who feels those emotions in response to particular situations as represented in tragic works of art. The emotional release, stressed with a somewhat different emphasis by Aristotle, may in fact be pleasant, leaving one feeling refreshed and renewed. But these external expressions need not accompany one's feelings in any obvious way; many feel embarrassed about them and hence strive to avoid them (or, what is more unfortunate, to avoid the works of art which pro-

duce them). This may lead to a kind of frustration or it may not, I do not feel qualified to undertake any such "psychoanalysis." Nevertheless, one *need* not engage in overt expressions of feelings in order to *have* them, and hence one need not engage in the expression of the feelings (i.e., expressions of the direct responses) in order to feel the pleasures from tragedy. If so, we can conclude that the pleasures from tragedy are not derived merely from the *expression* of grief, sadness, etc. but must have some other source.

III Tragedy and Comedy

The observation is often made that tragedies are much more important or significant artworks than comedies. The great works of Shakespeare are *Hamlet*, *King Lear*, and *Macbeth*, notwithstanding the brilliance of *Twelfth Night* and *As You Like It*. The greatest plays of antiquity are the Oedipus trilogy and the *Oresteia*, despite the cunning wit of Aristophanes. The greatness of Voltaire's *Candide* is due more to his portrayal of the fate of humankind than his avowedly clever humor. There are great comedies, but the significance of the greatest is not thought to reach the significance of even less great tragedies. Why?

It is not due, as one might suppose on first blush, to some essential morbidity in the outlook of those who defend this judgment. If it were, the greatness of tragedy would be due to the simple truth of the basic picture drawn by tragedy of the nature of man's lot: doomed to suffer injustice, wage war, suffer defeat, and be overcome by conniving women, conniving men, mistakes in judgment, accidents of birth, ignorance, and foolish advice. Tragedy then would be taken to confirm, or at least to echo, one's solemn conviction in the nastiness of human life. The pleasure from tragedy would then also be a morbid one, like the evil-doer who, in his every act, enjoys providing more evidence against the existence of a benevolent god. Whether or not one does believe in the existence of such a god, the pleasure taken in providing evidence against its existence by performing acts of evil is undoubtedly a morbid one.

But the greatness of tragedy is not due to any supposed truth of "profound" pictures such as these, and our pleasure in it is not therefore in recognizing this unpleasant truth. Tragedy is anything but morbid, for if people did not feel sympathy with their fellow human beings we would not have the initial negative responses we do to the tragic situation, the unpleasant direct responses. At the foundation of the aesthetic pleasure from tragedy is the same feeling which makes possible moral action: sympathy with, and a concern for, the welfare of human beings *qua* human beings, feelings which are increased if those human beings bear any special relationship to oneself such as friends or family, with an attendant increase in moral commitment to them. I do not wish to argue about the basis of morality, but I do wish to suggest that the basis for our judgments of the aesthetic *significance* of tragedy (as opposed to the lesser significance of comedy) can plausibly be its calling forth feelings which are also at the basis of morality. Judgments about tragedy's greatness derive from a recognition of the importance of morality to human life.

In comedy there must be a "butt" of the joke. The pleasure from comedy, then, is generally a direct response to the failures, defects, or absurd-ities of whomever (or whatever) is the object of ridicule or fun. Of course not all laughing is laughing *at* people – there is also laughing *with* people – and the two kinds of responses also pro-vide a means for explaining what this means. One laughs *with* people when one is among those being laughed at. Depending on the joke, one's own emotional reactions to parts of the work may be the object of fun, or perhaps what one remembers having done or imagines one would have done under circumstances presented in the work. The response has then become more complex, requir-ing a kind of self-awareness, much like the meta-response that pleasure from tragedy requires.

Moreover, responses to comedy are to failures or defects judged to be insignificant. This judgment is important because if the imperfections were thought to be of great significance, the work would then take on the air of tragedy rather than comedy, it would be saddening rather than amusing that people were subject to such flaws. The arro-gance and pomposity of Trissotin in Molière's *The Learned Ladies* is comic because he is a parochial poet with little influence outside of an equally insignificant small circle of dotty old ladies. But the arrogance of Jason is of cosmic proportions: it ruins Medea, and she in turn destroys his children, his bride, his future father-in-law, and by that act unstabilizes the very order of society. Human foibles may be minor or major, and it is precisely the latter ones which tear at (rather than tickle) the hearts of an audience. Comedy, one might say, is

skin deep: it generally goes no further than direct response, and requires that one's responses be to things which do not play major roles in maintaining the happiness and security of human life. Presum-ing an imperfection to be insignificant makes it possible to laugh at it, but believing it to be import-ant makes one cry. The person who laughs at tra-gedy may justifiably be called "callous," and one might sensibly harbor serious doubts about that person's morality.

IV   Immoral Art

This excursion into the importance of tragedy as opposed to comedy has opened the back door to another issue concerning aesthetic value, one which has been infusing the discussion: the nature of the relationship between aesthetic and moral value. I have described the importance or signifi-cance of tragedy in comparison to comedy as due to an appreciation of the pleasure from tragedy being derived from feelings of sympathy with other human beings, which provide for the direct response, and the sympathy itself can plausibly be argued to be the basis also of moral feeling. The greatness of tragedy reflects the importance of morality in human life, and the aesthetic judgment of a particular work's greatness, therefore, would be an aesthetic judgment which reflects one's own particular moral commitments. Hume says at the end of his essay "Of the Standard of Taste" (in what seems to be a reluctant confession) that we cannot admit a work of art to have value unless we approve of its morality.[6] That is, a necessary con-dition of judging a work of art to be good is that it does not conflict with one's own ethical views. This is necessary in order to feel the direct re-sponse, and consequently to feel the pleasure of the meta-response which is dependent on it. Hume illustrates this with some of his own moral judgments, but they of course involve cases where evaluators may differ.

I imagine that a work which conflicts with one's own ethical views would be called an immoral work, though both the conflict and the immorality of the work are hard to pin down. This is because a judgment that a work is immoral is a relational judgment, a judgment of the relationship between one's own ethical convictions and something about the work – what it expresses, says, shows, or approves. Judgments of immorality of a work will then vary according to different ethical convictions

Susan Feagin

as well as different interpretations of the work. A work's supporting multiple interpretations even further complicates any judgment of its immorality.

Nevertheless, assuming good grounds can be given for a given interpretation of a work and, therefore, for the legitimacy of a given direct response, an immoral work would be one which manipulates our responses in a way which has us responding favorably towards something which we would in fact judge as evil, and unfavorably toward something we would in fact judge as good (to put the matter in black-and-white terms). Hypothetically, one might rewrite *Othello* so that one is led to feel pleasure at the victory of Iago, for example, though note there might be some doubt then about whether such a work should be called a tragedy (and *if* called a tragedy, it would be so called for quite a different reason – because of the eventual capture of Iago, not because of Desdemona's death). Some contemporary American horror films could also serve as examples. I am thinking specifically of a number of spin-offs of the well-reviewed film *Halloween* from a couple of years back. The morally horrifying thing about these films is that they are told through the eyes of the rapist/killer, as if to say "you, too, can feel what it is like to be a homicidal maniac," as if there is something worthwhile in having that experience. We don't learn about their psychopathology, nor are we encouraged to identify with the victims since their characters are not developed enough to do so (but only enough to present them as victims). The thrill of the movie is, so to speak, the thrill of the chase. The point is that one finds a work morally disturbing when there is a conflict between the (immoral) feelings it produces (or attempts to produce?) in us and our (ordinary) judgments of morality. It is certainly a conflict which can occur, and which in general leads us to shun the work ourselves and, most likely, to arm our children against it.

The charge of a work's being immoral identifies the work's fault as influencing us immorally, or, if we have the strength of character to resist, attempting to do so. An immoral work, then, is one which encourages a direct response to which we have an unfavorable meta-response. The direct response, as manipulated by the author, if successful, would be pleasurable (exciting, enticing, etc.) but, given the state of one's ordinary moral feeling, one's meta-response would be *displeasure* at finding that one is capable of such callousness. (The

work may be so successful as to prevent all of one's moral feelings, but notice that then the *problem* disappears, at least in one's own mind, for one no longer judges the work to be immoral.) That is, in an immoral work one could not have the meta-pleasure characteristic of pleasure from tragedy, and hence one would certainly not judge it as good on the basis of that pleasure.

I have advanced this characterization of immoral art intending only to capture the possible immorality of tragedy. The meta-pleasure we feel in response to tragic situations is absent in immoral works, and this absence leads to a negative judgment of the work's aesthetic value. This characterization of immoral art could also be applied in obvious ways to comedy and even pornography. One may think it inhumane to laugh at people slipping on banana peels, or base to enjoy explicit depictions of sexual activity. In these one may also recognize the talent (if it takes talent) of the artist in producing the appropriate direct responses, but ultimately reach a negative verdict of its value because one disapproves of people having those sorts of responses to that sort of subject matter.

V A Potential Problem

Given that, on this analysis, the same feelings are at the base of both morality and aesthetic pleasure from tragedy, it is necessary to explain how, consistently with this, one might respond aesthetically and be, for all intents and purposes, an immoral person, and also how one might be morally very upright but aesthetically insensitive. The first is what John Ruskin calls somewhere the "selfish sentimentalist." One can weep, groan, and cringe over a novel or in the theater, but remain blasé if the fictional events were to occur in reality. The pride one feels in one's theater tears is a selfish pride, and has actually very little to do with any concern for human welfare, or, consequently, one's virtue (though it may have a lot to do with one's supposed virtue). Wouldn't such an account as mine have to suppose that the moral feelings exist when one is in the theater, but that they dissolve when one walks outside?

In *The Concept of Mind*, Gilbert Ryle says, "Sentimentalists are people who indulge in induced feelings without acknowledging the fictitiousness of their agitations."[7] Their agitations are not real since their concern is not: without a genuine desire for people's welfare there is no opposition between that desire and the fate that eventually befalls them. They pretend a concern for the poor devils, and then feel real distress when they suffer only because their pretense has been so effective. But then one wonders how people can feel real distress over pretended concerns.

There should be another way of explaining the situation which does not involve so much self-delusion. Indeed, there is. One might genuinely care for others but not nearly so much as for oneself. Hence, when there is no risk to oneself all the tears come pouring forth out of compassion: as a casual reader or theater-goer one is merely a witness to, and cannot be a participant in, the proceedings. That is one of the delights of fiction (even tragedy): one is free to feel as one wishes at no risk to oneself, incurring no obligation, requiring no money, time, or dirty fingernails. But once one gets outside, the situation changes, and one's concern for others may just not be strong enough to overcome self-interest. Concern for others does not miraculously disappear when one travels from the theater to the marketplace – it is overpowered by concern for self. And there is still another way to view the phenomenon, consistently with what I have said about sympathetic responses and meta-responses. Perhaps one identifies with the character in the novel, film, or play, and hence one's concern is self-interested in the sense that it exists *only* because of that identification. What one may never have learned to do is to be concerned about others even when one does *not* feel at one with them. In this case there is a genuine sympathetic response, but one's capacity for sympathy is limited. I, at least, would expect such individuals to show rather pronounced patterns of likes and dislikes with respect to fictional material: only characters with certain salient properties (divorced women, perhaps, or aristocrats, or characters plagued by self-doubt, etc.) would excite their compassion, while others (bachelors, immigrants, or the chronically self-assured, etc.) leave them cold. One of the things we generally expect from a good work of art is a capacity to evoke sympathetic feelings in us for some of its characters, and it is a measure of its goodness that it can melt the hearts even of those not disposed to any concern for others. Of course, there are "cheap" ways of doing this which we all recognize: there are tools for manipulating an audience that practically no one can resist. One such tool is to introduce someone who is young, intelligent, and good, but dies an untimely death (*Love Story*, *Death Be Not Proud*), and another is to capitalize on adorable youngsters who have been wronged in all their innocence and goodness (Cio-Cio-San's child, Trouble, in *Madame Butterfly*). Both are effective in disturbing even the weakest sense of injustice.

The other side of the potential problem is the unimaginative moralist, whose behavior is always exemplary but who cannot get worked up over a fictional creation. Isn't it even more difficult to explain how such a person will not respond sympathetically to fiction although he or she will do so in reality? We certainly do not have a case here of one's sympathy being overpowered by self-interest. The key to the solution is that this moralist is unimaginative, for it takes *more* effort of imagination to respond to a work of art than it does to respond to real life. In art one has to overcome the conventions of the medium, contemplate counterfactuals, and make the appropriate inferences and elaborations on the basis of them. Perhaps this is why some have thought that developing an appreciation of appropriate works of art is a good ingredient of moral education: if one can learn to respond morally in the imagined case, then it will be even easier to do so in reality. Too little, it seems to me, has been written on the role of imagination in art appreciation. The discussion has instead focused on the role of belief, and how we can respond emotionally without believing (or suspending disbelief) in the reality of the characters and events. If we pursue the suggestion mentioned earlier that our responses to art are from entertaining counterfactuals, which, *qua* counterfactuals are *imagined* characters and events (not believed ones), then the way is opened for examining traits of imagination which are involved in doing this. It seems we *are* at last, led back to Hume and imagination, in a way which has more potential for understanding our responses to art than his notion of imagination did. But this is a matter for separate study. For these purposes, we can explain the unimaginative moralist's failure to respond to art by virtue of that person's being unimaginative in a way which is required in the aesthetic context but not required in the actual moral one.

VI Meta-Responses to Art and to Life

Given the nature of pleasure from tragedy as analyzed here, it is not surprising to find philosophers alleging the existence of special "aesthetic emotions," unlike those which exist in real life. Indeed, we don't generally feel pleasure from our sympathetic responses to real tragedies, and there needs to be some explanation of why the pleasurable response is appropriate to fiction and not to reality. The fact about fiction which makes this so is that in it no one *really* suffers; the suffering is fictional, but the fact that perceivers feel genuine sympathy for this imagined suffering enables perceivers to examine their own feelings without regard for other people. In real life, the importance of human compassion is easily overshadowed by the pain of human suffering. It is not possible in real life to respond to the importance of human sympathy as a distinct phenomenon, since that sympathy depends on, one might even say "feeds on," human misery. It is not, in life, an unequivocal good. In art, however, one experiences real sympathy without there having been real suffering, and this is why it is appropriate to feel pleasure at our sympathetic responses to a work of art, whereas it is not appropriate to feel pleasure at our sympathetic responses in reality. There the sympathy comes at too great a cost.

In real life, it is more appropriate to feel satisfaction, pride, or even pleasure with what one has done rather than with what one has felt. Though one should have some caution in how one feels about what one has done (because of unforeseen consequences), "caution" isn't the right word to describe the hesitation one should have in responding to how one felt. Actions can be completed so that one can respond to them in themselves in a way inappropriate with feelings. One can go to a funeral, and be glad, looking back on it, that one had the courage to do so, but sadness over the person's death has no determinate end. Feelings are not the sorts of things which can be completed; they are not tasks to be performed. Feelings reveal one's sensitivities, which can be revealed not only in firsthand experience but also when one simply thinks about or remembers a situation. In real life, to be pleased with the feelings one had reveals a smugness, self-satisfaction, and complacency with what one has already felt. To be pleased that one once was sensitive (though now insensitive), is to be (properly) pleased very little, because one is at best pleased that one *once* was a feeling person (and, as explained above, one is pleased – because one's sympathy exists – at the expense of other people's misfortune). One should be more displeased that one has lost the sensitivity one once had. Pleasurable meta-responses in real life are

foreclosed by the continued call for direct (unpleasant) responses, even when one is confronted with just the idea or memory of the event.

But such is not the case with a work of art. The direct response is to the work of art as experienced in its totality, in the integration of all its sensuous elements. The direct response is possible only in the presence of the work; take away the work and one is left merely to memories and meta-responses. In this sense, a direct response to art has "closure" (unlike feelings in real life and somewhat like actions) so that those responses can, without smugness, self-satisfaction, and complacency, themselves be singled out and responded to.

Though a meta-response of pleasure to sympathy felt in real life would reveal smugness and self-satisfaction, a meta-response of displeasure to one's lack of sympathy is appropriate and even laudable. This shows that it is not the case that meta-responses are always inappropriate (or impossible) in real life, but that it depends on the nature of the situation. Discomfort, disgust, or dissatisfaction with oneself is desirable because it shows that we are aware of defects in our character, which is a first step to self-improvement. It is courting temptation to concentrate on how well one has done, for this makes us inattentive to the ways in which we might do better. It is also true that when one doesn't "reap the benefits" of, i.e., gain pleasure from, one's sympathy, we can be reasonably sure that it is genuine.

The differences between responses and meta-responses to real situations and to art have to do both with (1) the important role actions play in morality but not in our responses to art, and (2) the differing roles which emotions themselves play in the two cases. This latter, at least, turns out to be a very complicated matter, a complete examination of which would require an analysis of the importance of a first person, direct experience of a work of art for an appreciation of it (a phenomenon which I have suggested allows for "closure" of feelings in response to art which is not present in real life). But, most fundamentally, the meta-response of pleasure to the sympathy we feel for other people is appropriate to art but not in life because in the former there is no real suffering to continue to weigh on our feelings. In the latter case, real suffering easily commands our attention, so that any desirability of sympathy is of minuscule importance in comparison with the perniciousness of the conditions which gave rise to it.

In summary, pleasures from tragedy are meta-responses. They are responses to direct responses to works of art, which are themselves painful or unpleasant. But given the basis for the direct response, sympathy, it gives us pleasure to find ourselves responding in such a manner. That is, it is a recognition that there can be a unity of feeling among members of humanity, that we are not alone, and that these feelings are at the heart of morality itself. The judgment that tragedy is a great art form, much greater than comedy or farce, is based on the fact that our pleasures in it derive from feelings which are essential to the existence and maintenance of human society. Further, one's judgment of the goodness of a tragic work of art is dependent upon one's moral approval of it, since disapproval (or indifference) would not generate the pleasurable meta-responses on which judgments of a work's value are based. It is, of course, possible to respond appropriately to art, even when those responses require sympathy, and not with the appropriate sympathy in life, as it is also possible to be morally upstanding in life but insensitive to art. Explanations of these phenomena involve intricacies of their own, but they reinforce rather than resist the analysis given of pleasure from tragedy as a meta-response. The fact that pleasurable meta-responses to our sympathetic responses to tragedy are appropriate to art but not in life suggests one respect in which aesthetic emotions are different from emotions of life, and also has to do with the importance of direct experience of a work for an appreciation of it. The peculiarity of the responses hinges on the fact that what one initially responds to is *not* real, thus making continued sympathy idle, and allowing one to reflect on the sympathy one previously felt.

Notes

1 David Hume, "Of Tragedy" in *Of the Standard of Taste and Other Essays* (Indianapolis: Bobbs–Merrill, 1965), p. 29. See pp. 25–8 in this book.

2 Ibid., pp. 35–6. The words in quotation marks are Hume's.

3 Ralph W. Clark, "Fictional Entities: Talking About Them and Having Feelings About Them," *Philosophical Studies* 38 (1980), p. 347. For an elaboration of such a view see B. J. Rosebury, "Fiction, Emotion, and 'Belief': A Reply to Eva Schaper," *British Journal of Aesthetics* 19 (1979), 120–30.

4 Cf. Barrie Paskins, "On Being Moved by Anna Karenina and *Anna Karenina*," *Philosophy* 52 (1977), 345–6.

5 Hume, "Of Tragedy," p. 29.

6 David Hume, "Of the Standard of Taste" in *Of the Standard of Taste and Other Essays* (Indianapolis: Bobbs–Merrill, 1965), p. 22.

7 Gilbert Ryle, *The Concept of Mind* (New York: Barnes & Noble, 1949), p. 107.

27

Tragedy and the Community of Sentiment

Flint Schier

I

It is a truth universally acknowledged that fictional characters and their predicaments can have a claim on our sentimental regard. Certainly it cannot be doubted that fictions often stake such a claim. It is equally true that we evaluate our emotional responses to fictions, finding some responses generous, fair and mature while seeing others as miserly, unfair, or sentimental. These two data – for such I take them to be – are obviously two sides of the same coin. A work's claim to an emotional response is justified just when that response is justified.

Simple as this last proposition is, it rules out certain views of when an emotional response to a fiction is legitimate. For example, one might suppose that if a certain emotion would be justified *vis-à-vis* a real situation *p*, then that emotion would be justified *vis-à-vis* a fictive representation of *p*. This is obviously wrong: it might be right for me to pity a homeless orphan, but not every fictive orphan has the right to my pity. Obviously, whether or not a character in a story is entitled to engage our emotional response depends not just upon what happens to him in the story, but on the text's mode of presenting the character and his predicament, upon its style, moral vision and so on. (Nothing hangs here on distinguishing our emotional reactions to the character and our reactions to the story, though I should include the former in the latter but not vice versa.)

By contrast, of course, the style with which an actual event is reported seems to have but little to do with whether a certain emotional reaction to it is appropriate. No matter how feeble and schematic someone's expression of grief or tale of woe, an emotionally generous person will respond to his misery. So we have a *prima facie* distinction between fictive and factive emotion (if I may so label the responses to fiction and fact). The appropriateness of factive emotion depends upon what happened, upon the content of the representation. The appropriateness of fictive emotion depends upon more than the content of the story. One doesn't have to be very wide awake to see that what is at issue here is not so much a distinction between fictive and factive emotions as a distinction between our emotions in an aesthetic context and our emotions in "real life" contexts. Distinguishing these contexts will depend at least upon pragmatic considerations. For example, if a report of grief has no particular claim upon our interest of the usual sort (it involves no one we know or care about particularly) we will be inclined to make certain "aesthetic" demands of the story (search for "aesthetic" motives for telling it to us).

From Peter Lamarque (ed.), *Philosophy and Fiction* (Aberdeen: Aberdeen University Press, 1983), pp. 73–86, 91.

In any case, none but the most frigid aesthete would refuse an emotional response to someone in misery simply because his misery was poorly turned out. Yet this is precisely what we do in the case of fiction. If fictive woe wears a shabby suit we feel justified in shutting it out altogether.

This is, I think, just the reverse side of what we might dub Hume's paradox of tragedy. Hume in his small but characteristically penetrating essay "Of Tragedy"[1] poses the question of why we enjoy tragedy precisely when it elicits strong emotions that would, in other contexts, be very painful. In Hume's words

> It seems an unaccountable pleasure which the spectators of a well-written tragedy receive from sorrow, terror, anxiety and other passions that are in themselves disagreeable and uneasy. (p. 221)

Hume is clear that the tragedies we most value and enjoy are precisely those which provoke the strongest emotions:

> The more they (the spectators) are touched and affected the more are they delighted with the spectacle; and as soon as the uneasy passions cease to operate, the piece is at an end. One scene of full joy and contentment and security is the utmost that any composition of this kind can bear ... (p. 221)

It might be thought that the answer to Hume's puzzle is quite straightforward: we are able to find the emotions of pity and terror agreeable because we don't really believe in what is transpiring on stage. Thus the stoic hopes to avoid all emotional commitment to the world by regarding it all as a play. Hume considers this option but dismisses it. For, he justly remarks, we may enjoy a tragedy even when we suppose that the represented events actually took place. He remarks of the epilogues of Cicero:

> The pathetic description of the butchery made by Verres of the Sicilian captains is a masterpiece. ... (T)he sorrow here (is not) softened by fiction; for the audience were convinced of the reality of every circumstance. (p. 224)

Inter alia, Hume rebuffs the idea that we enjoy such spectacles *simply* because they arouse emotions in us, for as he says "being at a melancholy scene of that nature" would afford little entertainment.

Here the proponent of what we might call the doxastic solution to Hume's puzzle will naturally feel that Hume has misunderstood the force of his reply and is trading on an ambiguity. The relevant belief, the absence of which allows us to enjoy terror and pity, is not the belief that what is enacted before us took place once upon a time. Rather, it is the belief that what we are *now* seeing is the real article. It is proposed that one could then explain the lack of pain involved in watching a tragedy merely by adverting to the fact that people do not believe that what they are watching is the real thing. Disbelief is what takes the sting out of terror and pity.

However, such a response to Hume's puzzle would be obtuse for at least two reasons. First, this response simply does not answer Hume's question. Hume wanted to know why we enjoy tragedy. This response claims to do no more than explain why we don't regard the prospect of an evening at *King Lear* with fear and loathing. The question remains of why we find the excitation of normally painful emotions enjoyable or, to use Hume's word, "delightful". Indeed, given that normally unpleasant emotions are excited, it is hard to see how the doxastic solution to the puzzle can even explain the absence of pain in the audience. For surely, if the normally painful emotions are present, it has yet to be explained how they could fail to be painful in the theatre. If belief is relevant at all, it might explain why certain emotions are not aroused. (Hence the stoic's refusal to believe in the world: it frees him of emotional fetters; it doesn't merely take away the pain of wearing them.) But given that tragedy does arouse these painful emotions, in spite of our disbelief (empirically disconfirming the stoic's hope that disbelieving the world's existence would free us from emotion) it is very hard to see how mere disbelief in the spectacle could prevent the emotions it arouses from being painful ones.

There is a second, deeply systematic reason, why *Hume* could not help himself to the doxastic solution to his puzzle. For Hume, believing that p amounts to a particularly vivid idea or impression of p. And it could hardly be doubted that those tragedies we most enjoy are precisely those which come closest to giving us a lively picture of the events they relate. Hence there is a positive correlation between a tragedy's tendency to promote a belief in (or vivid idea of) what it relates and its tendency to promote our enjoyment. Such a positive correlation is, of course, the reverse of what the doxastic solution would predict.

Indeed, given Hume's equation of belief with lively ideas, it is very difficult to see how he can avoid the conclusion that we actually believe that what we see in the theatre is the real McCoy. Given that we are obviously aware that what we are seeing is not the genuine article, the best Hume could do would be to postulate a conflict among our beliefs. We would have, so his story might go, a lively idea of (and hence belief in) the fictive events but also a lively idea of (and hence belief in) the art and skill of the actors, costumiers, etc. These beliefs obviously conflict, but so what?

At any rate, the doxastic solution seems to be a poisoned pawn for Hume. Of course, in an age which piques itself on its sophisticated awareness of the agreeable possibilities of pain (thanks to von Sacher-Masoch) it might well be replied that Hume is just wrong to think that we do not feel pain when we witness a tragic spectacle. Perhaps we go there precisely in order to make ourselves feel pain. Perhaps tragedy is merely the sublimation of *le vice anglais*. Alternatively, perhaps it is just plain fun to watch suffering – perhaps we are all sadists *au fond*.

This reply contains an important truth, but it manifestly fails to solve Hume's puzzle, for even if it is true, as I think it is, that we feel, in some sense, pained by tragic spectacles, Hume is undoubtedly right that we find satisfaction in watching such spectacles. The fact that the experience is painful makes it more paradoxical, not less, that we find satisfaction in it. For let's face it, however much we preen ourselves on our open mindedness towards sado-masochism, there are few who would find satisfaction in watching a man running around with his eyes out (like Gloucester and Oedipus). So if we seek such experiences in the theatre, and we are neither unusually sadistic nor masochistic, this is something which invites an explanation.

Nor will it cut much ice simply to deny Hume's premise that we enjoy tragedy, for if we do not, the puzzle becomes curiouser and curiouser. If we don't even enjoy the thing, why on earth do we all flock to see it? Furthermore, it cannot be doubted that we spontaneously accord the experience of high tragedy – painful and disturbing as it is – an intrinsic value. We don't need to be dragged to the theatre, after all. Of course, as a matter of social history, it is perhaps true that people in the eighteenth century had more stom-ach for gruesome entertainments than we have, and one might instance not only the pleasure taken by many in watching executions – akin perhaps to the frisson we experience in watching horror movies – but one might also instance the fashion for wearing one's hair *à la victime* (in imitation of the short cropped hair of the victims of the guillotine) that became the fashion in Directoire Paris. But I think we cannot dismiss Hume's puzzle as the relic of an age that enjoyed gore but refused to admit this to itself. The fact remains that *we* value and spontaneously seek the experience of watching in the theatre representations of what we would elsewhere avoid like the plague. And once we acknowledge this fact about ourselves, how can we help wanting to explain it to ourselves?

What was Hume's answer to his puzzle? Hume thought that the pleasure we take in the quality of the spectacle – the eloquent diction, the power of the acting, the beauty of the performers and their costume, the intrigue of the plot, and so on – simply overruled the pain we would normally feel in such situations. Indeed, on Hume's view the painful emotions are transformed into pleasurable ones, apparently without loss of identity. Terror is no longer painful at all, but pleasurable.

Hume also saw what was wrong with this answer, though I think he did not see why he had to give the wrong answer – for seeing this would have shaken the foundations of Hume's account of reasons for action and value. Hume notes that if we are told of a real event, the sort of event a daily tabloid might call tragic, perhaps an event close to home, we would feel more pain and not less if the event were related to us in eloquent and moving free verse by someone dressed up like a messenger in a Greek play. This of course brings us right back to our starting point: we don't expect real woe to be tricked out in fancy dress and – what's more – we don't want it to be. Our taste in woe is, if you like, neo-classical; we like our woe neat. But then the problem is: why does eloquence counteract pain in the theatre but aggravate it in real life?

Hume tries to explain the asymmetry between the real and the theatrical emotions by claiming that in the theatre the aesthetic pleasure in the artifice is dominant and this pleasure transposes, as it were, the darker feelings into its key, while in the event of a real woe, the painful feelings toward the event are dominant and so would transform any pleasure in the style of presenting the grief into feelings of yet deeper pain. In each case, the dominant emotion is imperious, spreading itself onto the other emotions and harnessing them to its cause. However, Hume has signally failed to explain the asymmetry between the theatrical and real situations. *Why* is the aesthetic pleasure dominant in the theatre but subdued in the real life case? Surely this is virtually the same problem as the one with which we began.

But it is not *quite* the same problem, and this fact suggests a modest proposal. Namely, that the asymmetry be explained in terms of belief. The dominant emotions are those directed at states of affairs we take to be real. In the theatre, we know that our emotions are not excited by the real McCoy. The style of acting and eloquence of diction are quite real. So aesthetic pleasure gains the upper hand and the other emotions are transposed into the dominant key of aesthetic joy. In the event of a real woe, things are the other way around. The thing really happened and we believe it. Of course, if this event is eloquently related, we note this aesthetic fact. However, the reality of the woe simply overwhelms any aesthetic pleasure we might take and transforms it into grief. Perhaps we might say that in the case of the actual grief, the vividness of our idea of the grief (which becomes, in Hume's account, grief) *absorbs* the vividness of our idea of the eloquence of the report, and so becomes a stronger grief. By contrast, in the fictive case, our *disbelief* in the event dampens our sympathetic grief but this sympathetic grief retains enough of its force to add a certain degree of liveliness to our idea of the theatrical representation.

Unfortunately, this solution is unavailable either to Hume or to ourselves. For one thing, most of us would reject the associationist theory of mental activity upon which Hume's answer is based (upon which the Humean component in the contrived answer is based). Hume's idea seems to be that the close proximity or temporal coincidence of the aesthetic feelings with emotions of, for example, terror and pity simply transforms the latter emotions into the pleasurable character of the former emotions. Yet both the explanantia – and perhaps most important of all – the explanandum seem wrong. The associationist framework is wholly discredited and the facts Hume here invokes it to explain would seem to admit of less tortured explanations. For example, it does seem right that thinking of something beautiful when you are in misery can make you more miserable. But mightn't this be explained in terms of the *contrast* between that beautiful possibility and your present predica-

ment? Doesn't this contrast serve at once to heighten the beauty of the object and the misery of your current state? And if an eloquent recital of the death of a loved one would be deeply mortifying, isn't this because we would feel such a recital to be both insincere and somehow an obstacle to a full absorption in our grief? Perhaps we resent anything which claims our attention when we are absorbed in some intense emotion. Indeed, we might find an eloquent recital of pleasant news equally irritating; it would not necessarily find favour with us thanks to its association with the good news. This, of course, heightens the mystery: why should the contrast be so little damaging to our satisfaction with tragedy, but so very disturbing to us in real life? The contrast between the beauty of the play, the acting and the actors on the one hand, and the misery of the characters represented on the other, does not seem to destroy our satisfaction in watching the play. Why should it do so in real life?

Yet, even if Hume's associationist framework were alright, and even if he were right that our terror in the theatre is anodyne (an assumption I will question shortly), he could not just tack on the doxastic solution to his own. I have already said that Hume could not easily accept any suggestion that we don't believe in the fictive events we see on stage. Given Hume's almost affective conception of what a belief consists in, what could be more a belief than our lively idea of Oedipus's fate? Indeed, Hume's account of sympathy would almost seem to commit him to the view that belief is present in the case of our experience of Oedipus's fate. For according to Hume, sympathy is to be explained in the following way: we have a lively idea or impression of someone's expression, this in turn leads to a lively idea of the feeling expressed and this finally *becomes* something like the very emotion. Thus, our lively idea of Oedipus's pain and grief and horror tends to become those very emotions (obviously there are oddities here: we can have a conjunctive idea of pain, horror and happiness, but we can't have an experience which is at once all of these things). In any case, since we sympathise with Oedipus, we must have a lively enough idea of his fate to count as having a belief in its presence before us.

It might be suggested that this affective conception of belief is merely peculiar to Hume. I think not. I believe that we are dealing with an eighteenth-century conception of what belief is. The manuals of rhetoric and poetic composition suggest that it is one of the chief obligations of orator and poet to induce in his audience a lively image of the events he, as it were, depicts. If the eighteenth century notion of belief is, as I think, precisely that of a lively image, then we can understand Coleridge's notion of "willing suspension of disbelief" as neither metaphor nor nonsense, but (in intention at least) the literal truth. Furthermore, given this notion of belief as a kind of affect (a conception Hume clearly has and one which shows that it cannot be right to attribute to Hume, as John McDowell does, the separation of mind into cognitive and affective compartments) we can understand why it is so important for Diderot that naturalistic art astonish, move and touch him. We might almost say that such feelings are criterial for belief. A spectacle that induces these strong emotions is therein judged by the spectator to be realistic (this is a thought to which I shall return).

In any case, given this conception of belief, which as it were dictates the form of the problem of tragedy for Hume and the eighteenth century, it is wholly ahistorical to insinuate a quite different notion of belief into the Humean solution. For us the problem is one of how we can attach value to tragedy given that (indeed because) it arouses unpleasant feelings in us. We will have to start from scratch if we want an answer to that question. Hume's associationist answer is no longer available to us.

It might appear that there is something in Hume's observation that the puzzle is to be solved by noting that in the theatre there are, as it were, two objects of attention: what is (fictively) happening and what is (really) happening (viz., how what is fictively happening is being represented). It might be said that in the theatre our pleasure stems from attending to how events are represented, not the events themselves. We do of course attend to those events, and they excite painful emotions in us. But we are able to enjoy the experience of tragedy *despite* these painful emotions because (a) we enjoy attending to the style of the drama and the skill of the actors and (b) because we do not believe that what is represented as happening is happening. (We still need (b) to explain the asymmetry between the way style affects us in the theatre and the way it might affect us if we were told in rhyming couplets that our lover had just been killed.)

We might call this the mannerist solution. It suggests that we divide our attention between what is happening and how that is represented and

that our pleasure in the tragic spectacle stems only from the latter and fortunately overcomes the pain which attends our response to the former. This solution fails to find a place either for the pleasure we take in the content of the tragedy or for the value we attach to our emotional responses to that content. It is not simply an incidental fact that fictional characters and their muddles excite our emotions. Rather, as Hume himself understood, this is the essence of tragedy: we attach value to the experience of tragedy precisely because of the emotions that it arouses in us. It is because these emotions are painful that there is, *prima facie*, a puzzle. Furthermore, this solution fails to take into account a possibility which disturbed some eighteenth-century writers, such as Diderot: namely that too much attention to the representational vehicle might destroy the value the experience of tragedy has for us. Far from being a source of pleasure, obtrusive artifice can destroy the very value tragedy has for us. But on this proposed solution to Hume's puzzle – as indeed on Hume's solution – the artifice is the sole ground of the pleasure we take in tragedy; and if that is so, it is hard to see how one could get too much of it. There may be some things you can get too much of, but something which is supremely valuable isn't one of them.

Furthermore, Hume got the explanandum wrong. It seems just wrong to suggest that our reactions to fictive terrors do not retain their painful or disturbing character. Indeed, there is something almost nonsensical about the notion of a pain-free terror, even if it is an enjoyable one. It may be the very awfulness, terribleness, of the terror which we require for our satisfaction in the experience. In any case, it is just this type of logical connection, between painfulness and terror, which Hume's atomism ill equips him to appreciate. Indeed, I think the problem with Hume's view goes deeper than this. It is not just that he is wrong to suppose that terror and anxiety don't retain their painfulness in the theatre. He is even wrong to suppose that we always enjoy or find delight in the experience of tragedies. There may, of course, be some fictions which arouse terror in a way we find enjoyable – ghost stories, monster films, films of violence. Here the experience seems to be of a kind with the frisson of pleasure felt by the audience at an execution. The terror is the product of the thought "There but for the grace of God go I" whereas the pleasure stems from the fact that we are not in fact ourselves in the predicament. We congratulate ourselves on the contrast between ourselves and the victim (we experience what Hobbes called "sudden glory"). I think we can see that such experiences have a quality and value quite different from the quality and value attaching to the experience of tragedy. The emotions involved – basically, terror tinged with self-congratulation – are not admirable in themselves. Furthermore, the experience is enjoyed. By contrast, when we contemplate the fate of Lear and Cordelia, the emotions aroused are of a kind which we value, even though they are painful emotions. We value the empathetic terror and the sympathetic pity an audience spontaneously feels in the contemplation of the fate of the characters in a tragedy.

Hume, of course, could hardly acknowledge this possibility. *How* could we accord value to such emotions, and therefore to the experience of tragedy which induces such emotions, given that they are painful? Of course, Hume could have given a reply of sorts here. He could have argued that the fact that human beings harbour such emotions as pity and empathetic terror is a fact which conduces to the benefit of mankind, since it tends to lead to actions of succouring the distressed. In short, Hume might have appealed to a kind of motive utilitarianism for help in dealing with this *prima facie* objection to his hedonistic account of motivation and value. However, I think all one can say is that the value accorded to the experience of tragedy seems not to be of this utilitarian sort. Nor, indeed, could this provide an answer to Hume's paradox, since we seem to seek in the theatre precisely those emotionally disturbing experiences we elsewhere avoid. We do not take account of the consequences of theatrical experience before valuing it – we just value it. At the very least, that suggests that we are not, consciously at least, utilitarian agents; we appear to ascribe an *intrinsic* value to disturbing experiences. We *spontaneously* seek – without utilitarian forethought – experiences painful in themselves which we nonetheless value. Now from the standpoint of any hedonistic theory of value that must make our behaviour seem at best recklessly irrational – at worst wicked. In any case, I believe this allows us to reformulate our problem in a slightly crisper way. The experience of tragedy is valued, and valued intrinsically, precisely insofar as it arouses certain emotions (pity and empathetic terror) which are disturbing. Furthermore, this experience is sought spontaneously. Our seeking it is not irrational, not sadistic, not masochistic and not hypocritical. *By contrast*, although we value our sympathetic responses to *actual* suffering and

woe, we do not seek to witness such suffering. Why not?

The question has now become why do we *seek* the experience of tragedy? This remains paradoxical, even after we drop Hume's hedonistic conception of value, because we seek in the theatre just those experiences which we elsewhere do not seek. Now how are we to resolve this puzzle? It appears that the solution must do *one or both* of two things. (1) One might attempt to locate a value *peculiar* to tragedy, which does not attach to the witnessing of *actual* suffering, and which therefore explains why we seek the experience of tragedy but not the experience of watching real grief and suffering. (2) One might attempt to show that there is something particularly *bad* about seeking to witness actual suffering, but that there is nothing particularly bad about witnessing fictive or imaginatively represented suffering.

Before going further, we must take the opportunity to stamp out a couple of ambiguities. The first concerns the relation of the audience to the characters. Here, we must take care to compare like with like. For example, it won't do to contrast the fictive representation of a grief befalling someone unknown to the spectator with the experience of hearing about or witnessing a grief befalling someone near and dear to the spectator. Concerning someone near to the spectator, it is unlikely he would seek the experience either of hearing a play about or of witnessing a grief befalling him. However, the asymmetry remains concerning people to whom the spectator is not particularly related by any bonds of kinship or attachment: namely, that one would be willing to see a good play about his grief and suffering, but one would be reluctant in the extreme actually to witness his suffering.

Second, we must be clear that we are talking about *witnessing* a real sorrow, not simply hearing about it. That is, if someone is no relation to us, we are unlikely to feel particularly awful about hearing of his grief, though we should definitely not wish to witness it. Hume is of course correct that if someone is close to us, we should be vastly more pained by an eloquent recital of the news of his death than by a simple but sympathetic statement of the bare fact. However, if someone is not particularly close to us, an eloquent recital of their fate might be indistinguishable from a tragedy. What remains true, however, is that we should have no wish to witness their demise. But then, it would appear, Hume's objection to his own account simply vanishes. There *is* an asymmetry between a theatrical representation of suffering and the witnessing of it: for there is art in the former but no possibility of art in the latter. But we cannot let matters rest there, for as we have seen it is not only the presence of art in the theatrical representation which accounts for its value. It is the fact that something momentously awful is represented. Now if "art" gives this representation value, we have yet to see why and in what sense this is so. Equally, in saying that the difference of import is that between seeing a theatrical representation of and actually witnessing grief and suffering, one is conceding that belief has some role to play in explaining why we freely go to theatrical tragedies but avoid actual suffering like the plague. However, it is as yet unclear *what* role the notion of belief plays in the overall resolution of the puzzle. The following roles are denied to it: disbelief does not prevent pity and terror, for we do react to the fate of tragic characters; nor does it transform painful emotions into pleasurable ones, for the experience of tragedy is far from being always delightful. Nor will it do to say that it is simply a primitive fact that we don't mind going to see disturbing fictive representations but we do mind witnessing events we believe to be occurring before us. For accepting this as primitive is just to give up the hope of deeper explanation. To be sure there is an asymmetry – of belief – and this seems to correlate with our choices: we seek the fictive emotions and avoid the factive one. But one feels that there ought to be more to it than that. *Why* should belief make this difference? And here, it is important to remember Hume's reminder that tragedies can be about real people. We can't, therefore, simply say that we permit ourselves to go to tragedies because it doesn't matter what happens in possible or fictive worlds, it only matters what happens here in the actual world. This can't be right, since tragedies are about the real world and can be about real people. What appears to matter is not the possible world involved, but our *point of view* on it. What matters is whether the event is before us, here, now. The belief that matters is, in David Lewis's jargon, a *de se* belief. It is not a belief that p, but a belief that "I'm now seeing p", that is necessarily absent in the case of a theatrical representation of p. And in any case, the response that watching fictional characters suffer is alright because fictional characters are fictional and they don't matter is belied by the strong emotional response we give to them.

II

Now the very way we have formulated the puzzle seems to exclude a consequentialist solution. We do not typically value the tragic experience as a means to anything else, but rather accord it an intrinsic value. Since it is painful, and not necessarily at all pleasurable or delightful, it seems to present a counterexample to hedonistic theories of value – certainly to hedonistic theories of aesthetic value (such as those of Hume and indeed Kant). This cannot, as we have seen, be made good by adverting to the pleasurable consequences arising from these painful experiences. If there are any such consequences, they have little to do with why we value the experience. More to the point, such character utilitarianism signally fails to solve the puzzle. For if we were to explain tragedy in terms of the hedonistic value to the human race of having the character of one who is compassionate and sympathetic, and even if we were to believe that going to tragedies could somehow develop such a character – rather than pre-supposing that one has such a sympathetic character – even after all these assumptions are granted in favour of the hedonistic response, two objections remain. The first is that if the consequentialist answer were correct, we would stop going to tragedies once we were satisfied with the character of our emotional dispositions (sensibilities). Yet it seems to me that there is nothing odd or irrational about someone of irreproachable sensibility attending a tragedy. Second, the consequentialist answer appears to me to offer no solution to the puzzle. For, if one had it in one's power to witness various *real* tragedies, one would not choose to do so, even on the off chance that it might be character-improving to do so. It should be stressed that these two problems would appear to arise for any consequentialist theory of our motivation in seeking the experience of tragedy. More generally, it must be conceded that consequentialism has nothing to offer a theory of aesthetic value.

The value of the experience of tragedy must be located *in* the experience of it. It is not something external to the experience. Therefore, we must look to that experience and ask what is valuable about it. The feature we hit upon must be a feature of those experiences of tragedy which we spontaneously seek. It must also be a feature which is precisely lacking in those experiences of witnessing real suffering and grief which we do not seek.

The traditional answer is that in tragedy, grief, suffering and other evils of human existence are made intelligible to us. They are seen as part of a natural order, a necessary and inevitable part. Tragedies end on a note of resolution. The natural order has been disturbed, and the tragedy moves ineluctably towards the restoration of that natural order. Sometimes – as with the crucifixion, the death of Socrates, the end of the *Oresteia*, the appearance of Fortinbras at the end of *Hamlet* – there is a hint of the advent of a *new* order. Of course, the moment of resolution is often the most horrible moment in the whole story, the moment at once most devoutly sought and devoutly feared. The Isenheim altarpiece makes the moment of the passion vividly real – yet it is not merely a moment of deep, bodily agony, it is also the moment which sees the birth of a new order among men, when the human race is left with the responsibility for setting its own house in order. We may now start from scratch, the world has been cleansed of the sin of Adam. Likewise, Hamlet – like a kind of Samson – carries the whole court of Denmark with him to the grave. Fortinbras arrives to assert a new order. What matters here is the belief in a universe that inevitably operates according to moral laws – the moral laws are treated as if they were natural laws (and it can be no accident that the tragic vision flourished in classical Greece and in the Renaissance at precisely those times when a notion of natural law informed men's expectations and hopes). Given this belief, the tragedy is bearable. Indeed, can it plausibly be maintained that the devout Christian does not wish to witness the central event in the Church's history? The appropriate belief – in a kind of impersonal providence – would make the actual witnessing of the event bearable. For one with a belief in this world view, there could be no asymmetry between actually witnessing the tragic event and seeing it represented.

For those in command of the tragic view of life, there is no paradox of tragedy. There is no special question of why we witness in the theatre what we would elsewhere avoid. The tragic world view makes the sight of evil bearable, be it in the flesh or in the theatre. But we are not consoled by such a world view. There are bleak tragedies, tragedies that end on a note of wintry quiet, where the only consolation seems to be that life is finite, suffering must have an end – the story is almost over. This

is the atmosphere of Schubert's song cycle *Die Winterreise*. The power of this cycle, its command of our rapt attention, cannot lie in any consoling vision of the world. On the contrary, winter has occupied the haunts of summer, and all that is left is reflection on the winter within the poet's soul – reflection, wandering, madness and death. The power of such an experience must reside in the intimacy of it. We do not witness the suffering from without, but rather from within the very soul of the sufferer. The value we attach to this experience and the reason we seek it is undoubtedly just this: that it gives us an imaginative sense of what it is like to feel, see and live in a certain way. No mere perception of grief from without could give us so strong a sense of the subjective reality of grief.

Yet, in some ways this must make it seem more paradoxical, not less, that we seek the experience of such wintry epiphanies. For, if I am right, they bring us closer to the vivid soul of grief, they offer no consoling promise of anything more than a release from the grip of grief in the metamorphosis from being someone into being nothing. The *loss* of subjectivity – in madness or death – seems to be the only escape from pain. This appears to be the bad news in *King Lear*, and in the *Winter Journey*. But why do we seek such news? Because, I think, many people feel that that is how things are and that it is better to know how things are than not to know. (An intuition that Nozick makes vividly clear to us with his experience machine.) In the experience of a work of art, we are allowed to witness this fate, our fate, from within the experience of another. It is this quality which calls forth our empathetic emotions – emotions of pity and terror. And this is emphatically not like watching someone else suffer – it is an experience in which we realise that when the character speaks of his experience, he is speaking with the "universal voice". We are reminded vividly that men are not islands – it is one of the bonds uniting us that we imaginatively share in fates that are not yet ours, but may be soon.

What is the difference, then, between the experience of such high tragic art and watching a real person go mad? The difference is in the intimacy of the experience – by imaginatively realising his character, the author has made an experience available to us as it were from within, on the most intimate footing.

I think we can provide something like an argument for the intuition that it is the *reality* of this

Flint Schier

suffering that commands us to witness it. I think we often feel that we are justified in watching certain films because – *but only because* – things are actually like that. There would be no justification in watching *fantasies* of torture and mass murder. But because these moral enormities are a fact of our lives we allow – we force – ourselves to witness them in films and photographs.

It might be objected that this is a consequentialist theory of the value of tragedy. We see it as adding to our store of knowledge of the world, and this is valuable to us for various reasons. But the fact is that there appears to be little of value in these revelations over and above the experience of them. Very often, there is nothing we can do about the "facts" they force us to witness. True, it may be argued that watching a film about Auschwitz may have an effect on an audience – it may make them resolve that "never again" shall such things happen. But the value we attach to the experience does not seem to reside solely in this possible upshot – it appears to reside in the revelation of atrocity, the revelation itself and nothing else.

It might be asked: if it is the revelation you seek, and nothing else, why not seek out experiences of actual suffering? The answer seems to be that such experiences cannot be as intimate as theatrical experience (unless of course we know the sufferer – but we have excluded this possibility). The theatre allows us an intimate contact with the suffering of another. Such contact would be impossible in real life, since sufferers are too absorbed in grief to give a running commentary – and if they do provide such a commentary, such an "expression" in Collingwood's sense, then perhaps we might say that in some sense they are artists with a claim on our attention.

In any case, someone truly absorbed in grief cannot make the experience of that grief available to us (he may do so after the fact in a work of art, of course). This impossibility is overcome in the theatre – there we are allowed to see into the grief and other extreme emotions of others. The characters and their experiences are present to us but we are not present to them (we do not interfere with their grief). Of course, I am not merely adverting to the fact that the characters are *not aware* of us (though various devices in the theatre and painting are used to underline this fact). Rather, their expressions and actions have been conceived by a controlling intelligence that would not be available to an ordinary mortal in extreme states of emotion.

I have suggested that tragedy makes possible for us something which is not possible outside of imaginative experience: the vivid, powerful realisation of what it is like to suffer (and of course art makes available more positive emotions to us as well). This knowledge is apparently of a very peculiar kind – it is an end in itself (although it may also be valuable for other purposes). Nor does it seem to be cumulative. We do not ever get the feeling, "Now I know enough about human suffering, about what it is like to suffer. I shall no longer go to see tragedies." Real suffering cannot be expressed by the sufferer in a way that makes a vivid and powerful impact on our understanding – precisely because anyone who is really in the throes of a powerful emotion hasn't got the necessary control over himself to make his experience available to us (also because our presence would necessarily alter the state of anyone aware of it). The artist, of course, possesses the controlling intelligence which allows his characters to act before us and speak to us in a way which makes their suffering unforgettable. This, of course, brings us back to the starting point of the essay: our reaction to fictional characters is not just a reaction to fictional people, it is a reaction to them *as represented* in the text (on stage, in the movie, etc.). Therefore, our reaction is necessarily governed by *how* they are represented, and the kind of emotion that it is appropriate to feel is determined by the quality of the representation. Where little controlling intelligence has been exercised, where the people are treated virtually as found objects, then we may feel that it is inappropriate to respond emotionally to them (as represented). One of the *pleasures* (and here I think this is the right word) of seeing a tragedy, however bleak, stems from our interaction with the controlling intelligence of the artist. The characters to whom we react or fail to respond are the product of that intelligence and our reactions constitute a kind of judgment of his work – of him insofar as he manifests himself in his work. Thus, we are reacting to characters as vividly seen and realised by a controlling intelligence and we respond to the work as an expression of that achieved vision of the characters. It is an important fact about our reaction to the suffering of actual people that our emotional reaction to their suffering does not constitute, even in part, a judgment on their expression of suffering. We simply cannot expect real suffering to permit this kind of control over expression. There is a natural feeling that if such control was exercised, the expression could not be quite sincere. Far from making the suffering more real, such control would make it seem less real. Paradoxically, the opposite is the case in the theatre. Suffering is made more real by artifice. There is no real paradox, though, since the artifice is that of the artist and not the character. [...]

Note

1 David Hume, *Essays, Moral, Political and Literary* (Oxford, 1963). All page references in the text are to this edition. See also pp. 25–8 in this book.

PART VI

Metaphor

Introduction

Certain linguistic devices found outside literary contexts are especially prominent in literature. Fiction is one; metaphor is another. Even so, some philosophers who have written on metaphor are troubled by nonliterary metaphor and their agitation has shaped philosophical thinking about metaphor, in and out of literature.

Philosophers ask three groups of questions about metaphor. First, how do we recognize metaphors in passages of speech or text? What distinguishes metaphors from other figures of speech? What is the relationship between metaphorical and literal speech? Can metaphors be captured in literal paraphrases? These questions ask what metaphors are.

Questions in the second group get at the mechanisms of metaphor – about how metaphors work to communicate. Once recognized, how are they interpreted? Do they have a special kind of meaning – metaphorical meaning?

A third line of inquiry touches upon the point of metaphors. Answering it explains why one would prefer to employ a metaphor rather than literal language or another figure of speech. It is also the key to understanding the value of metaphorical language and its contribution to the value of literature.

Answers to some of these questions may be thought to recommend or even entail answers to the others. For example, the similarity theory of metaphor, which probably originated with Aristotle and which Anne Carson toys with, asserts that a metaphor points to an unexpected similarity between two terms. "His replies to my objections are a smoke screen" says that his replies are similar to a smoke screen in that they obscure my objections. This theory proposes to explain the mechanism of metaphor (to understand a metaphor, discover the similarity) and it also says what a metaphor is (a figure of speech that draws an unexpected comparison). But it also suggests a thesis about the point of metaphor: since plain, literal talk can be substituted for any metaphor without a loss in the message communicated, metaphor is merely ornamental. For this reason Thomas Hobbes condemned metaphor, along with ambiguity, deception, and insult, as one of four cardinal abuses of language that hamper clear philosophy and good science.

Cognitivists, who hold that metaphors have a special cognitive content not borne by other kinds of language, oppose emotivists, who hold that metaphors do nothing but ornament in pretty prose what can be stated plainly. Arguments for each view depend on interwoven conceptions of the mechanism of metaphor, its point, and its definition. The student must disentangle these conceptions in their different combinations.

Max Black spearheaded recent cognitivist defenses of metaphor. He rejects any substitution view which holds that a metaphor can be replaced without loss by some literal paraphrase that gives the meaning of the metaphor. Instead, every metaphorical utterance has two components that interact to produce a metaphorical meaning. In "Mussolini is a utensil" the word "utensil" is used nonliterally; it is the "focus" of the metaphor. The rest of the sentence, which comprises words used literally, is the "frame" of the metaphor. Both the frame and the focus have systems of associated commonplaces or stereotypes. The metaphor leads us to think of the frame in terms of the systems of stereotypes associated with the focus. As Black says, it "organizes our conception of its subject." At the same time, however, stereotypes associated with the frame can organize our conception of the focus. This two-way interaction between the two systems of stereotypes ensures that the meaning of a metaphor never runs out – it is "pregnant." The power of metaphor lies in its powerful semantic charge.

Donald Davidson repudiates Black's assumption that a defense of cognitivism requires attributing a distinctive kind of meaning to metaphors. He argues that the meaning of a metaphorical expression is its literal meaning. It follows that metaphors are either patently false (Mussolini was not a utensil) or uninformatively true (read literally, "life is no picnic" tells us nothing new). Davidson proposes that metaphors are expressions used to prompt us to see one thing as another. What we learn through seeing as cannot be stated in so many words, so the use of a metaphor is irreplaceable.

Another option, one explored by Ted Cohen, is to reject the assumption that a defense of metaphor requires a defense of cognitivism and to develop an alternative that upholds the importance of metaphor as more than pretty prose. Cohen's idea is that the use of the right metaphor shapes our feelings even while it introduces no new cognitive content. Shaping feelings is valuable in so far as it establishes intimate communities of art appreciators.

Kendall Walton advances a more expansive cognitivism than is envisaged by Black or Davidson. For Walton, a metaphor is a fiction, a prop in a game that prescribes certain imaginings. "Argument is war" prescribes imaginings about combat, strategy, victory, and defeat. But, unlike the complex imaginings prescribed by *Solaris* or *Doonesbury*, these imaginings are hardly interesting in themselves. Their interest rather lies in what they tell us about the prop that generates them – the statement "argument is war." In other words, we are sometimes less interested in the imaginings a prop prescribes than in what we can learn about the prop from the imaginings it prescribes. In "argument is war" we attend to features of argument that emerge when it is imagined to be war.

Running throughout the debate between cognitivists and emotivists are differing ideas about the value of literary language in relation to nonliterary language. A Hobbesian may think that a vice in scientific or philosophical writing is a virtue in literary writing, but only if literature is mere pretty figuration. Cognitivists like Black, who claim that metaphors empower both literary and nonliterary language in much the same way, can see literature as drawing some of its value from the same source as science and philosophy. The science of metaphor occasions the study of literary value.

28

Essay on What I Think About Most

Anne Carson

Error.
And its emotions.
On the brink of error is a condition of fear.
In the midst of error is a state of folly and
                                    [defeat.
Realizing you've made an error brings shame
and remorse.
Or does it?

Let's look into this.
Lots of people including Aristotle think error
an interesting and valuable mental event.
In his discussion of metaphor in the *Rhetoric*
Aristotle says there are 3 kinds of words.
Strange, ordinary and metaphorical.

"Strange words simply puzzle us;
ordinary words convey what we know already;
it is from metaphor that we can get hold of
                        [something new & fresh"
(*Rhetoric*, 1410b10–13).
In what does the freshness of metaphor consist?
Aristotle says that metaphor causes the mind to
                                    [experience itself

in the act of making a mistake.
He pictures the mind moving along a plane
                                    [surface
of ordinary language
when suddenly

that surface breaks or complicates.
Unexpectedness emerges.

At first it looks odd, contradictory or wrong.
Then it makes sense.
And at this moment, according to Aristotle,
the mind turns to itself and says:
"How true, and yet I mistook it!"
From the true mistakes of metaphor a lesson
                                    [can be learned.

Not only that things are other than they seem,
and so we mistake them,
but that such mistakenness is valuable.
Hold onto it, Aristotle says,
there is much to be seen and felt here.
Metaphors teach the mind

to enjoy error
and to learn
from the juxtaposition of *what is* and *what is not*
                                    [the case.
There is a Chinese proverb that says,
Brush cannot write two characters with the
                                    [same stroke.
And yet

that is exactly what a good mistake does.
Here is an example.
It is a fragment of ancient Greek lyric

that contains an error of arithmetic.
The poet does not seem to know
that $2 + 2 = 4$.

Alkman fragment 20:
  [?] made three seasons, summer
  and winter and autumn third
  and fourth spring when
  there is blooming but to eat enough
  is not.

Alkman lived in Sparta in the 7th century B.C.
Now Sparta was a poor country
and it is unlikely
that Alkman led a wealthy or well-fed life there.
This fact forms the background of his remarks
which end in hunger.

Hunger always feels
like a mistake.
Alkman makes us experience this mistake
with him
by an effective use of computational error.
For a poor Spartan poet with nothing

left in his cupboard
at the end of winter –
along comes spring
like an afterthought of the natural economy,
fourth in a series of three,
unbalancing his arithmetic

and enjambing his verse.
Alkman's poem breaks off midway through an
                                    [iambic metron
with no explanation
of where spring came from
or why numbers don't help us
control reality better.

There are three things I like about Alkman's
                                    [poem.
First that it is small,
light
and more than perfectly economical.
Second that it seems to suggest colors like pale
                                    [green
without ever naming them.

Third that it manages to put into play
some major metaphysical questions
(like Who made the world)
without overt analysis.

You notice the verb "made" in the first verse
has no subject: [?]

It is very unusual in Greek
for a verb to have no subject, in fact
it is a grammatical mistake.
Strict philologists will tell you
that this mistake is just an accident of
                                    [transmission,
that the poem as we have it

is surely a fragment broken off
some longer text
and that Alkman almost certainly did
name the agent of creation
in the verses preceding what we have here.
Well that may be so.

But as you know the chief aim of philology
is to reduce all textual delight
to an accident of history.
And I am uneasy with any claim to know exactly
what a poet means to say.
So let's leave the question mark there

at the beginning of the poem
and admire Alkman's courage
in confronting what it brackets.
The fourth thing I like
about Alkman's poem
is the impression it gives

of blurting out the truth in spite of itself.
Many a poet aspires
to this tone of inadvertent lucidity
but few realize it so simply as Alkman.
Of course his simplicity is a fake.
Alkman is not simple at all,

he is a master contriver—
or what Aristotle would call an "imitator"
of reality.
Imitation (*mimesis* in Greek)
is Aristotle's collective term for the true
                                    [mistakes of poetry.
What I like about this term

is the ease with which it accepts
that what we are engaged in when we do poetry
                                    [is error,
the willful creation of error,
the deliberate break and complication of
                                    [mistakes

out of which may arise
unexpectedness.

So a poet like Alkman
sidesteps fear, anxiety, shame, remorse
and all the other silly emotions associated with
[making mistakes
in order to engage
the fact of the matter.
The fact of the matter for humans is
[imperfection.

Alkman breaks the rules of arithmetic
and jeopardizes grammar

and messes up the metrical form of his verse
in order to draw us into this fact.
At the end of the poem the fact remains
and Alkman is probably no less hungry.

Yet something has changed in the quotient of
[our expectations.
For in mistaking them,
Alkman has perfected something.
Indeed he has
more than perfected something.
Using a single brushstroke.

29

Metaphor

Max Black

> "Metaphors are no arguments, my pretty maiden."
>
> (*The Fortunes of Nigel*, *Book 2, Ch. 2.*)

To draw attention to a philosopher's metaphors is to belittle him – like praising a logician for his beautiful handwriting. Addiction to metaphor is held to be illicit, on the principle that whereof one can speak only metaphorically, thereof one ought not to speak at all. Yet the nature of the offence is unclear. I should like to do something to dispel the mystery that invests the topic; but since philosophers (for all their notorious interest in language) have so neglected the subject, I must get what help I can from the literary critics. They, at least, do not accept the commandment, "Thou shalt not commit metaphor," or assume that metaphor is incompatible with serious thought. [...]

2

"The chairman ploughed through the discussion." In calling this sentence a case of metaphor, we are implying that at least one word (here, the word "ploughed") is being used metaphorically in the sentence, and that at least one of the remaining words is being used literally. Let us call the word "ploughed" the *focus* of the metaphor, and the remainder of the sentence in which that word occurs the *frame*. (Are *we* now using metaphors – and mixed ones at that? Does it matter?) One notion that needs to be clarified is that of the "metaphorical use" of the focus of a metaphor. Among other things, it would be good to understand how the presence of one frame can result in metaphorical use of the complementary word, while the presence of a different frame for the same word fails to result in metaphor.

If the sentence about the chairman's behaviour is translated word for word into any foreign language for which this is possible, we shall of course want to say that the translated sentence is a case of the *very same* metaphor. So, to call a sentence an instance of metaphor is to say something about its *meaning*, not about its orthography, its phonetic pattern, or its grammatical form.[1] (To use a well-known distinction, "metaphor" must be classified as a term belonging to "semantics" and not to "syntax" – or to any *physical* inquiry about language.)

Suppose somebody says, "I like to plough my memories regularly." Shall we say he is using the same metaphor as in the case already discussed, or not? Our answer will depend upon the degree of similarity we are prepared to affirm on comparing the two "frames" (for we have the same "focus" each time). Differences in the two frames will produce *some* differences in the interplay[2] between focus and frame in the two cases. Whether we regard the differences as sufficiently striking to

From *Proceedings of the Aristotelian Society* 55 (1955), pp. 273, 275–92. Reprinted by courtesy of the Editor of the Aristotelian Society: © 1955.

warrant calling the sentences *two* metaphors is a matter for arbitrary decision. "Metaphor" is a loose word, at best, and we must beware of attributing to it stricter rules of usage than are actually found in practice.

So far, I have been treating "metaphor" as a predicate properly applicable to certain expressions, without attention to any occasions on which the expressions are used, or to the thoughts, acts, feelings, and intentions of speakers upon such occasions. And this is surely correct for *some* expressions. We recognize that to call a man a "cesspool" is to use a metaphor, without needing to know who uses the expression, or on what occasions, or with what intention. The rules of our language determine that some expressions must count as metaphors; and a speaker can no more change this than he can legislate that "cow" shall mean the same as "sheep". But we must also recognize that the established rules of language leave wide latitude for individual variation, initiative, and creation. There are indefinitely many contexts (including nearly all the interesting ones) where the meaning of a metaphorical expression has to be reconstructed from the speaker's intentions (and other clues) because the broad rules of standard usage are too general to supply the information needed. When Churchill, in a famous phrase, called Mussolini "that *utensil*", the tone of voice, the verbal setting, the historical background, helped to make clear *what* metaphor was being used. (Yet, even here, it is hard to see how the phrase "that utensil" could ever be applied to a man except as an insult. Here, as elsewhere, the general rules of usage function as limitations upon the speaker's freedom to mean whatever he pleases.) This is an example, though still a simple one, of how recognition and interpretation of a metaphor may require attention to the *particular circumstances* of its utterance.

It is especially noteworthy that there are, in general, no standard rules for the degree of *weight* or *emphasis* to be attached to a particular use of an expression. To know what the user of a metaphor means, we need to know how "seriously" he treats the metaphorical focus. (Would he be just as content to have some rough synonym, or would only *that* word serve? Are we to take the word lightly, attending only to its most obvious implications – or should we dwell upon its less immediate associations?) In speech we can use emphasis and phrasing as clues. But in written or printed discourse, even these rudimentary aids are absent. Yet this somewhat elusive "weight" of a (suspected or detected[3]) metaphor is of great practical importance in exegesis.

To take a philosophical example. Whether the expression "logical form" should be treated in a particular frame as having a metaphorical sense will depend upon the extent to which its user is taken to be conscious of some supposed analogy between arguments and other things (vases, clouds, battles, jokes) that are also said to have "form". Still more will it depend upon whether the writer wishes the analogy to be active in the minds of his readers; and how much his own thought depends upon and is nourished by the supposed analogy. We must not expect the "rules of language" to be of much help in such inquiries. (There is accordingly a sense of "metaphor" that belongs to "pragmatics", rather than to "semantics" – and this sense may be the one most deserving of attention.)

3

Let us try the simplest possible account that can be given of the meaning of "The chairman ploughed through the discussion", to see how far it will take us. A plausible commentary (for those presumably too literal-minded to understand the original) might run somewhat as follows:

"A speaker who uses the sentence in question is taken to want to say *something* about a chairman and his behaviour in some meeting. Instead of saying, plainly or *directly*, that the chairman dealt summarily with objections, or ruthlessly suppressed irrelevance, or something of the sort, the speaker chose to use a word ('ploughed') which, strictly speaking, means something else. But an intelligent hearer can easily guess what the speaker had in mind."[4]

This account treats the metaphorical expression (let us call it "*M*") as a substitute for some other literal expression ("*L*", say) which would have expressed the same meaning, had it been used instead. On this view, the meaning of *M*, in its metaphorical occurrence, is just the *literal* meaning of *L*. The metaphorical use of an expression consists, on this view, of the use of that expression in other than its proper or normal sense, in some context that allows the improper or abnormal sense to be detected and appropriately transformed. (The reasons adduced for so remarkable a performance will be discussed later.)

Any view which holds that a metaphorical expression is used in place of some equivalent *literal*

Max Black

expression, I shall call a *substitution view of metaphor.* [. . .]

According to a substitution view, the focus of a metaphor, the word or expression having a distinctively metaphorical use within a literal frame, is used to communicate a meaning that might have been expressed literally. The author substitutes M for L; it is the reader's task to invert the substitution, by using the literal meaning of M as a clue to the intended literal meaning of L. Understanding a metaphor is like deciphering a code or unravelling a riddle.

If we now ask why, on this view, the writer should set his reader the task of solving a puzzle, we shall be offered two types of answer. The first is that there may, in fact, be no literal equivalent, L, available in the language in question. Mathematicians spoke of the "leg" of an angle because there was no brief literal expression for a bounding line; we say "cherry lips", because there is no form of words half as convenient for saying quickly what the lips are like. Metaphor plugs the gaps in the literal vocabulary (or, at least, supplies the want of convenient abbreviations). So viewed, metaphor is a species of *catachresis*, which I shall define as the use of a word in some new sense in order to remedy a gap in the vocabulary. Catachresis is the putting of new senses into old words.[5] But if a catachresis serves a genuine need, the new sense introduced will quickly become part of the *literal* sense. "Orange" may originally have been applied to the colour by catachresis; but the word is now applied to the colour just as "properly" (and unmetaphorically) as to the fruit. "Osculating" curves don't kiss for long, and quickly revert to a more prosaic mathematical contact. And similarly for other cases. It is the fate of catachresis to disappear when it is successful.

There are, however, many metaphors where the virtues ascribed to catachresis cannot apply, because there is, or there is supposed to be, some readily available and equally compendious literal equivalent. Thus in the somewhat unfortunate example,[6] "Richard is a lion," which modern writers have discussed with boring insistence, the literal meaning is taken to be the same as that of the sentence, "Richard is brave."[7] Here, the metaphor is not supposed to enrich the vocabulary.

When catachresis cannot be invoked, the reasons for substituting an indirect, metaphorical, expression are taken to be stylistic. We are told that the metaphorical expression may (in its literal use) refer to a more concrete object than would its literal

equivalent; and this is supposed to give pleasure to the reader (the pleasure of having one's thoughts diverted from Richard to the irrelevant lion). Again, the reader is taken to enjoy problem-solving – or to delight in the author's skill at half-concealing, half-revealing his meaning. Or metaphors provide a shock of "agreeable surprise" – and so on. The principle behind these "explanations" seems to be: When in doubt about some peculiarity of language, attribute its existence to the pleasure it gives a reader. A principle that has the merit of working well in default of any evidence.[8]

Whatever the merits of such speculations about the reader's response, they agree in making metaphor a *decoration*. Except in cases where a metaphor is a catachresis that remedies some temporary imperfection of literal language, the purpose of metaphor is to entertain and divert. Its use, on this view, always constitutes a deviation from the "plain and strictly appropriate style" (Whately).[9] So, if philosophers have something more important to do than give pleasure to their readers, metaphor can have no serious place in philosophical discussion.

4

The view that a metaphorical expression has a meaning that is some transform of its normal literal meaning is a special case of a more general view about "figurative" language. This holds that any figure of speech involving semantic change (and not merely syntactic change, like inversion of normal word order) consists in some transformation of a *literal* meaning. The author provides, not his intended meaning, m, but some function thereof, $f(m)$; the reader's task is to apply the inverse function, f^{-1}, and so to obtain $f^{-1}(f(m))$, i.e., m, the original meaning. When different functions are used, different tropes result. Thus, in irony, the author says the *opposite* of what he means; in hyperbole, he *exaggerates* his meaning; and so on.

What, then, is the characteristic transforming function involved in metaphor? To this the answer has been made: either *analogy* or *similarity*. M is either similar or analogous in meaning to its literal equivalent L. Once the reader has detected the ground of the intended analogy or simile (with the help of the frame, or clues drawn from the wider context) he can retrace the author's path and so reach the original literal meaning (the meaning of L).

If a writer holds that a metaphor consists in the *presentation* of the underlying analogy or similarity, he will be taking what I shall call a *comparison view* of metaphor. When Schopenhauer called a geometrical proof a mousetrap, he was, according to such a view, *saying* (though not explicitly): "A geometrical proof is *like* a mousetrap, since both offer a delusive reward, entice their victims by degrees, lead to disagreeable surprise, etc." This is a view of metaphor as a condensed or elliptical *simile*. It will be noticed that a "comparison view" is a special case of a "substitution view." For it holds that the metaphorical statement might be replaced by an equivalent literal *comparison*. [...]

The chief difference between a substitution view (of the sort previously considered) and the special form of it that I have called a comparison view may be illustrated by the stock example of "Richard is a lion." On the first view, the sentence means approximately the same as "Richard is brave"; on the second, approximately the same as "Richard is *like* a lion (in being brave)," the added words in brackets being understood but not explicitly stated. In the second translation, as in the first, the metaphorical statement is taken to be standing in place of some *literal* equivalent. But the comparison view provides a more elaborate paraphrase, inasmuch as the original statement is interpreted as being about lions as well as about Richard.[10]

The main objection against a comparison view is that it suffers from a vagueness that borders upon vacuity. We are supposed to be puzzled as to how some expression (M), used metaphorically, can function in place of some literal expression (L) that is held to be an approximate synonym; and the answer offered is that what M stands for (in its literal use) is *similar* to what L stands for. But how informative is this? There is some temptation to think of similarities as "objectively given", so that a question of the form, "Is A like B in respect of P?" has a definite and predetermined answer. If this were so, similes might be governed by rules as strict as those controlling the statements of physics. But likeness always admits of degrees, so that a truly "objective" question would need to take some such form as "Is A more like B than like C in respect of P?" – or, perhaps, "Is A closer to B than to C on such and such a scale of degrees of P?" Yet, in proportion as we approach such forms, metaphorical statements lose their effectiveness and their point. We need the metaphors in just the cases when there can be no question as yet of the precision of scientific statement. Metaphorical state-

ment is not a substitute for a formal comparison or any other kind of literal statement, but has its own *distinctive* capacities and achievements. Often we say, "X is M", evoking some imputed connexion between M and an imputed L (or, rather, to an indefinite system, L_1, L_2, L_3, ...) in cases where, prior to the construction of the metaphor, we would have been hard put to it to find any *literal* resemblance between M and L. It would be more illuminating in some of these cases to say that the metaphor *creates* the similarity than to say that it formulates some similarity antecedently existing.[11]

5

I turn now to consider a type of analysis which I shall call an *interaction view* of metaphor. This seems to me to be free from the main defects of substitution and comparison views and to offer some important insight into the uses and limitations of metaphor.[12]

Let us begin with the following statement: "In the simplest formulation, when we use a metaphor we have two thoughts of different things active together and supported by a single word, or phrase, whose meaning is a resultant of their interaction."[13]

We may discover what is here intended by applying Richards's remark to our earlier example, "The poor are the negroes of Europe." The substitution view, at its crudest, tells us that something is being *indirectly* said about the poor of Europe. (But what? That they are an oppressed class, a standing reproach to the community's official ideals, that poverty is inherited and indelible?) The comparison view claims that the epigram *presents* some comparison between the poor and the negroes. In opposition to both, Richards says that our "thoughts" about European poor and (American) negroes are "active together" and "interact" to produce a meaning that is a resultant of that interaction.

I think this must mean that in the given context the focal word "negroes" obtains a *new* meaning, which is *not* quite its meaning in literal uses, nor quite the meaning which any literal substitute would have. The new context (the "frame" of the metaphor, in my terminology) imposes *extension* of meaning upon the focal word. And I take Richards to be saying that for the metaphor to work the reader must remain aware of the extension of meaning – must attend to both the old and the new meanings together.[14]

But how is this extension or change of meaning brought about? At one point, Richards speaks of the "common characteristics" of the two terms (the poor and negroes) as "the ground of the metaphor" (*The Philosophy of Rhetoric*, p. 117), so that in its metaphorical use a word or expression must connote only a *selection* from the characteristics connoted in its literal uses. This, however, seems a rare lapse into the older and less sophisticated analyses he is trying to supersede.[15] He is on firmer ground when he says that the reader is forced to "connect" the two ideas (p. 125). In this "connexion" resides the secret and the mystery of metaphor. To speak of the "interaction" of two thoughts "active together" (or, again, of their "interillumination" or "co-operation") is to *use* a metaphor emphasizing the dynamic aspects of a good reader's response to a non-trivial metaphor. I have no quarrel with the use of metaphors (if they are good ones) in talking about metaphor. But it may be as well to use several, lest we are misled by the adventitious charms of our favourites.

Let us try, for instance, to think of a metaphor as a *filter*. Consider the statement, "Man is a wolf". Here, we may say, are *two* subjects – the *principal subject*, Man (or: men) and the *subsidiary subject*, Wolf (or: wolves). Now the metaphorical sentence in question will not convey its intended meaning to a reader sufficiently ignorant about wolves. What is needed is not so much that the reader shall know the standard dictionary meaning of "wolf" – or be able to use that word in literal senses – as that he shall know what I will call the *system of associated commonplaces*. Imagine some layman required to say, without taking special thought, those things he held to be true about wolves; the set of statements resulting would approximate to what I am here calling the system of commonplaces associated with the word "wolf". I am assuming that in any given culture the responses made by different persons to the test suggested would agree rather closely, and that even the occasional expert, who might have unusual knowledge of the subject, would still know "what the man in the street thinks about the matter". From the expert's standpoint, the system of commonplaces may include half-truths or downright mistakes (as when a whale is classified as a fish); but the important thing for the metaphor's effectiveness is not that the commonplaces shall be true, but that they should be readily and freely evoked.

(Because this is so, a metaphor that works in one society may seem preposterous in another. Men who take wolves to be reincarnations of dead humans will give the statement "Man is a wolf" an interpretation different from the one I have been assuming.)

To put the matter in another way: Literal uses of the word "wolf" are governed by syntactical and semantical rules, violation of which produces nonsense or self-contradiction. In addition, I am suggesting, literal uses of the word normally commit the speaker to acceptance of a set of standard beliefs about wolves (current platitudes) that are the common possession of the members of some speech community. To deny any such piece of accepted commonplace (e.g., by saying that wolves are vegetarians – or easily domesticated) is to produce an effect of paradox and provoke a demand for justification. A speaker who says "wolf" is normally taken to be implying in some sense of that word that he is referring to something fierce, carnivorous, treacherous, and so on. The idea of a wolf is part of a system of ideas, not sharply delineated, and yet sufficiently definite to admit of detailed enumeration.

The effect, then, of (metaphorically) calling a man a "wolf" is to evoke the wolf-system of related commonplaces. If the man is a wolf, he preys upon other animals, is fierce, hungry, engaged in constant struggle, a scavenger, and so on. Each of these implied assertions has now be made to fit the principal subject (the man) either in normal or in abnormal senses. If the metaphor is at all appropriate, this can be done – up to a point at least. A suitable hearer will be led by the wolf-system of implications to construct a corresponding system of implications about the principal subject. But these implications will *not* be those comprised in the commonplaces *normally* implied by literal uses of "man". The new implications must be determined by the pattern of implications associated with literal uses of the word "wolf". Any human traits that can without undue strain be talked about in "wolf-language" will be rendered prominent, and any that cannot will be pushed into the background. The wolf-metaphor suppresses some details, emphasizes others – in short, *organizes* our view of man.

Suppose I look at the night sky through a piece of heavily smoked glass on which certain lines have been left clear. Then I shall see only the stars that can be made to lie on the lines previously prepared upon the screen, and the stars I do see will be seen as organized by the screen's structure. We can think of a metaphor as such a screen, and the system of "associated commonplaces" of the focal word as the network of lines upon the screen. We can say that the principal subject is "seen through" the metaphorical expression – or, if we prefer, that the principal subject is "projected upon" the field of the subsidiary subject. (In the latter analogy, the implication-system of the focal expression must be taken to determine the "law of projection".)

Or take another example. Suppose I am set the task of describing a battle in words drawn as largely as possible from the vocabulary of chess. These latter terms determine a system of implications which will proceed to control my description of the battle. The enforced choice of the chess vocabulary will lead some aspects of the battle to be emphasized, others to be neglected, and all to be organized in a way that would cause much more strain in other modes of description. The chess vocabulary filters and transforms: it not only selects, it brings forward aspects of the battle that might not be seen at all through another medium. (Stars that cannot be seen at all, except through telescopes.)

Nor must we neglect the shifts in attitude that regularly result from the use of metaphorical language. A wolf is (conventionally) a hateful and alarming object; so, to call a man a wolf is to imply that he too is hateful and alarming (and thus to support and reinforce dislogistic attitudes). Again, the vocabulary of chess has its primary uses in a highly artificial setting, where all expression of feeling is formally excluded: to describe a battle as if it were a game of chess is accordingly to exclude, by the choice of language, all the more emotionally disturbing aspects of warfare. (Similar bye-products are not rare in philosophical uses of metaphor.) [. . .]

But the preceding account of metaphor needs correction, if it is to be reasonably adequate. Reference to "associated commonplaces" will fit the commonest cases where the author simply plays upon the stock of common knowledge (and common misinformation) presumably shared by the reader and himself. But in a poem, or a piece of sustained prose, the writer can establish a novel pattern of implications for the literal uses of the key expressions, prior to using them as vehicles for his metaphors. (An author can do much to suppress unwanted implications of the word "contract"; by explicit discussion of its intended meaning, before he proceeds to develop a contract

theory of sovereignty. Or a naturalist who really knows wolves may tell us so much about them that *his* description of man as a wolf diverges quite markedly from the stock uses of that figure.) Metaphors can be supported by specially constructed systems of implications, as well as by accepted commonplaces; they can be made to measure and need not be reach-me-downs.

It was a simplification, again, to speak as if the implication-system of the metaphorical expression remains unaltered by the metaphorical statement. The nature of the intended application helps to determine the character of the system to be applied (as though the stars could partly determine the character of the observation-screen by which we looked at them). If to call a man a wolf is to put him in a special light, we must not forget that the metaphor makes the wolf seem more human than he otherwise would.

I hope such complications as these can be accommodated within the outline of an "interaction view" that I have tried to present.

6

Since I have been making so much use of example and illustration, it may be as well to state explicitly (and by way of summary) some of the chief respects in which the "interaction" view recommended differs from a "substitution" or a "comparison" view.

In the form in which I have been expounding it, the "interaction view" is committed to the following seven claims:

(1) A metaphorical statement has *two* distinct subjects – a "principal" subject and a "subsidiary" one.[16]

(2) These subjects are often best regarded as "*systems* of things", rather than "things".

(3) The metaphor works by applying to the principal subject a system of "associated implications" characteristic of the subsidiary subject.

(4) These implications usually consist of "commonplaces" about the subsidiary subject, but may, in suitable cases, consist of deviant implications established *ad hoc* by the writer.

(5) The metaphor selects, emphasizes, suppresses, and organizes features of

the principal subject by *implying* statements about it that normally apply to
the subsidiary subject.

(6) This involves shifts in meaning of
words belonging to the same family
or system as the metaphorical expression; and some of these shifts, though
not all, may be metaphorical transfers.
(The subordinate metaphors are, however, to be read less "emphatically".)

(7) There is, in general, no simple
"ground" for the necessary shifts of
meaning – no blanket reason why
some metaphors work and others fail.

Notes

1 *Any* part of speech can be used metaphorically
(though the results are meagre and uninteresting in
the case of conjunctions); any form of verbal expression may contain a metaphorical focus.

2 Here I am using language appropriate to the "interaction view" of metaphor that is discussed later in
this paper.

3 Here, I wish these words to be read with as little
"weight" as possible!

4 Notice how this type of paraphrase naturally conveys
some implication of *fault* on the part of the metaphor's author. There is a strong suggestion that he
ought to have made up his mind as to what he really
wanted to say – the metaphor is depicted as a way of
glossing over unclarity and vagueness.

5 The *OED* defines catachresis as: "Improper use of
words; application of a term to a thing which it does
not properly denote; abuse or perversion of a trope or
metaphor." I wish to exclude the pejorative suggestions. There is nothing perverse or abusive in stretch-
ing old words to fit new situations. Catachresis is
merely a striking case of the transformation of meaning that is constantly occurring in any living language.

6 Can we imagine anybody saying this nowadays and
seriously meaning anything? I find it hard to do so.
But in default of an authentic context of use, any
analysis is liable to be thin, obvious and unprofitable.

7 A full discussion of this example, complete with dia-
grams, will be found in Gustaf Stern's *Meaning and
Change of Meaning* (Göteborgs Högskolas Arsskrift,
vol. 38, 1932, part 1), pp. 300 ff. Stern's account tries
to show how the reader is led by the context to *select*
from the connotation of "lion" the attribute (bravery)
that will fit Richard the man. I take him to be
defending a form of the substitution view.

8 Aristotle ascribes the use of metaphor to delight in
learning; Cicero traces delight in metaphor to the
enjoyment of the author's ingenuity in overpassing

the immediate, or in the vivid presentation of the
principal subject. For references to these and other
traditional views, see E. M. Cope, *An Introduction to
Aristotle's Rhetoric* (London, 1867), "Appendix B to
Book III. ch. II: *On Metaphor*".

9 Thus Stern, *Meaning* says of all figures of speech
that "they are intended to serve the expressive and
purposive functions of speech better than the 'plain
statement'" (p. 296). A metaphor produces an "en-
hancement" (*Steigerung*) of the subject, but the
factors leading to its use "involve the expressive
and effective (purposive) functions of speech, not
the symbolic and communicative functions"
(p. 290). That is to say, metaphors may evince
feelings or predispose others to act and feel in various ways – but they don't typically *say* anything.

10 Comparison views probably derive from Aristotle's
brief statement in the *Poetics:* "Metaphor consists in
giving the thing a name that belongs to something
else; the transference being either from genus to
species, or from species to genus, or from species
to species, or on grounds of analogy" (1457*b*). I have
no space to give Aristotle's discussion the detailed
examination it deserves. An able defence of a view
based on Aristotle will be found in S. J. Brown's *The
World of Imagery* (London, 1927), especially pp.
67 ff).

11 Much more would need to be said in a thorough
examination of the comparison view. It would be
revealing, for instance, to consider the contrasting
types of case in which a formal comparison is preferred to a metaphor. A comparison is often a prelude to an explicit statement of the grounds of
resemblance; whereas we do not expect a metaphor
to explain itself. (Cf. the difference between *comparing* a man's face with a wolf mask, by looking for
points of resemblance – and seeing the human face
as vulpine.) But no doubt the line between *some*
metaphors and *some* similes is not a sharp one.

12 The best sources are the writings of I. A. Richards,
especially Chapter 5 ("Metaphor") and Chapter 6
("Command of Metaphor") of his *The Philosophy of
Rhetoric* (Oxford, 1936). Chapters 7 and 8 of his
Interpretation in Teaching (London, 1938) cover much
the same ground. W. Bedell Stanford's *Greek Metaphor* (Oxford, 1936) defends what he calls an "integration theory" (see especially pp. 101 ff) with much
learning and skill. Unfortunately, both writers have
great trouble in making clear the nature of the positions they are defending. Chapter 18 of W. Empson's
The Structure of Complex Words (London, 1951) is a
useful discussion of Richards's views on metaphor.

13 *The Philosophy of Rhetoric*, p. 93. Richards also says
that metaphor is "fundamentally a borrowing between and intercourse of *thoughts*, a transaction between contexts" (p. 94). Metaphor, he says, requires
two ideas "which co-operate in an inclusive meaning" (p. 119).

14   It is this, perhaps, that leads Richards to say that "talk about the identification or fusion that a metaphor effects is nearly always misleading and pernicious" (*The Philosophy of Rhetoric*, p. 127).

15   Usually, Richards tries to show that similarity between the two terms is at best *part* of the basis for the interaction of meanings in a metaphor.

16   This point has often been made. *E.g.:* – "As to metaphorical expression, that is a great excellence in style, when it is used with propriety, for it gives you two ideas for one." (Samuel Johnson, quoted by Richards, p. 93) *The Philosophy of Rhetoric*. The choice of labels for the "subjects" is troublesome.

30

What Metaphors Mean

Donald Davidson

Metaphor is the dreamwork of language and, like all dreamwork, its interpretation reflects as much on the interpreter as on the originator. The interpretation of dreams requires collaboration between a dreamer and a waker, even if they be the same person; and the act of interpretation is itself a work of the imagination. So too understanding a metaphor is as much a creative endeavor as making a metaphor, and as little guided by rules.

These remarks do not, except in matters of degree, distinguish metaphor from more routine linguistic transactions: all communication by speech assumes the interplay of inventive construction and inventive construal. What metaphor adds to the ordinary is an achievement that uses no semantic resources beyond the resources on which the ordinary depends. There are no instructions for devising metaphors; there is no manual for determining what a metaphor "means" or "says"; there is no test for metaphor that does not call for taste.[1] A metaphor implies a kind and degree of artistic success; there are no unsuccessful metaphors, just as there are no unfunny jokes. There are tasteless metaphors, but these are turns that nevertheless have brought something off, even if it were not worth bringing off or could have been brought off better.

This paper is concerned with what metaphors mean, and its thesis is that metaphors mean what the words, in their most literal interpretation, mean, and nothing more. Since this thesis flies in the face of contemporary views with which I am familiar, much of what I have to say is critical. But I think the picture of metaphor that emerges when error and confusion are cleared away makes metaphor a more, not a less, interesting phenomenon.

The central mistake against which I shall be inveighing is the idea that a metaphor has, in addition to its literal sense or meaning, another sense or meaning. This idea is common to many who have written about metaphor: it is found in the works of literary critics like Richards, Empson, and Winters; philosophers from Aristotle to Max Black; psychologists from Freud and earlier to Skinner and later; and linguists from Plato to Uriel Weinreich and George Lakoff. The idea takes many forms, from the relatively simple in Aristotle to the relatively complex in Black. The idea appears in writings which maintain that a literal paraphrase of a metaphor can be produced, but it is also shared by those who hold that typically no literal paraphrase can be found. Some stress the special insight metaphor can inspire and make much of the fact that ordinary language, in its usual functioning, yields no such insight. Yet this view too sees metaphor as a form of communication alongside ordinary communication; it conveys truths or falsehoods about the world much as plainer language does, though the message may be considered more exotic, profound, or cunningly garbed.

From *Critical Inquiry* 5 (1978), pp. 31–47. Reprinted by permission of the author.

The concept of metaphor as primarily a vehicle for conveying ideas, even if unusual ones, seems to me as wrong as the parent idea that a metaphor has a special meaning. I agree with the view that metaphors cannot be paraphrased, but I think this is not because metaphors say something too novel for literal expression but because there is nothing there to paraphrase. Paraphrase, whether possible or not, is appropriate to what is *said*: we try, in paraphrase, to say it another way. But if I am right, a metaphor doesn't say anything beyond its literal meaning (nor does its maker say anything, in using the metaphor, beyond the literal). This is not, of course, to deny that a metaphor has a point, nor that that point can be brought out by using further words.

In the past those who have denied that metaphor has a cognitive content in addition to the literal have often been out to show that metaphor is confusing, merely emotive, unsuited to serious, scientific, or philosophic discourse. My views should not be associated with this tradition. Metaphor is a legitimate device not only in literature but in science, philosophy, and the law; it is effective in praise and abuse, prayer and promotion, description and prescription. For the most part I don't disagree with Max Black, Paul Henle, Nelson Goodman, Monroe Beardsley, and the rest in their accounts of what metaphor accomplishes, except that I think it accomplishes more and that what is additional is different in kind.

My disagreement is with the explanation of how metaphor works its wonders. To anticipate: I depend on the distinction between what words mean and what they are used to do. I think metaphor belongs exclusively to the domain of use. It is something brought off by the imaginative employment of words and sentences and depends entirely on the ordinary meanings of those words and hence on the ordinary meanings of the sentences they comprise.

It is no help in explaining how words work in metaphor to posit metaphorical or figurative meanings, or special kinds of poetic or metaphorical truth. These ideas don't explain metaphor, metaphor explains them. Once we understand a metaphor we can call what we grasp the "metaphorical truth" and (up to a point) say what the "metaphorical meaning" is. But simply to lodge this meaning in the metaphor is like explaining why a pill puts you to sleep by saying it has a dormitive power. Literal meaning and literal truth conditions can be assigned to words and sentences apart from par-

ticular contexts of use. This is why adverting to them has genuine explanatory power.

I shall try to establish my negative views about what metaphors mean and introduce my limited positive claims by examining some false theories of the nature of metaphor.

A metaphor makes us attend to some likeness, often a novel or surprising likeness, between two or more things. This trite and true observation leads, or seems to lead, to a conclusion concerning the meaning of metaphors. Consider ordinary likeness or similarity: two roses are similar because they share the property of being a rose; two infants are similar by virtue of their infanthood. Or, more simply, roses are similar because each is a rose, infants, because each is an infant.

Suppose someone says "Tolstoy was once an infant." How is the infant Tolstoy like other infants? The answer comes pat: by virtue of exhibiting the property of infanthood, that is, leaving out some of the wind, by virtue of being an infant. If we tire of the phrase "by virtue of," we can, it seems, be plainer still by saying the infant Tolstoy shares with other infants the fact that the predicate "is an infant" applies to him; given the word "infant," we have no trouble saying exactly how the infant Tolstoy resembles other infants. We could do it without the word "infant"; all we need is other words that mean the same. The end result is the same. Ordinary similarity depends on groupings established by the ordinary meanings of words. Such similarity is natural and unsurprising to the extent that familiar ways of grouping objects are tied to usual meanings of usual words.

A famous critic said that Tolstoy was "a great moralizing infant." The Tolstoy referred to here is obviously not the infant Tolstoy but Tolstoy the adult writer; this is metaphor. Now in what sense is Tolstoy the writer similar to an infant? What we are to do, perhaps, is think of the class of objects which includes all ordinary infants and, in addition, the adult Tolstoy and then ask ourselves what special, surprising property the members of this class have in common. The appealing thought is that given patience we could come as close as need be to specifying the appropriate property. In any case, we could do the job perfectly if we found words that meant exactly what the metaphorical "infant" means. The important point, from my perspective, is not whether we can find the perfect other words but the assumption that there is something to be attempted, a metaphorical meaning to be matched. So far I have been doing no more than crudely sketching how the concept of meaning may have crept into the analysis of metaphor, and the answer I have suggested is that since what we think of as garden variety similarity goes with what we think of as garden variety meanings, it is natural to posit unusual or metaphorical meanings to help explain the similarities metaphor promotes.

The idea, then, is that in metaphor certain words take on new, or what are often called "extended," meanings. When we read, for example, that "the Spirit of God moved upon the face of the waters," we are to regard the word "face" as having an extended meaning (I disregard further metaphor in the passage). The extension applies, as it happens, to what philosophers call the extension of the word, that is, the class of entities to which it refers. Here the word "face" applies to ordinary faces, and to waters in addition.

This account cannot, at any rate, be complete, for if in these contexts the words "face" and "infant" apply correctly to waters and to the adult Tolstoy, then waters really do have faces and Tolstoy literally was an infant, and all sense of metaphor evaporates. If we are to think of words in metaphors as directly going about their business of applying to what they properly do apply to, there is no difference between metaphor and the introduction of a new term into our vocabulary: to make a metaphor is to murder it.

What has been left out is any appeal to the original meaning of the word. Whether or not metaphor depends on new or extended meanings, it certainly depends in some way on the original meanings; an adequate account of metaphor must allow that the primary or original meanings of words remain active in their metaphorical setting.

Perhaps, then, we can explain metaphor as a kind of ambiguity: in the context of a metaphor, certain words have either a new or an original meaning, and the force of the metaphor depends on our uncertainty as we waver between the two meanings. Thus when Melville writes that "Christ was a chronometer," the effect of metaphor is produced by our taking "chronometer" first in its ordinary sense and then in some extraordinary or metaphorical sense.

It is hard to see how this theory can be correct. For the ambiguity in the word, if there is any, is due to the fact that in ordinary contexts it means one thing and in the metaphorical context it means something else; but in the metaphorical context we do not necessarily hesitate over its meaning. When

we do hesitate, it is usually to decide which of a number of metaphorical interpretations we shall accept; we are seldom in doubt that what we have is a metaphor. At any rate, the effectiveness of the metaphor easily outlasts the end of uncertainty over the interpretation of the metaphorical passage. Metaphor cannot, therefore, owe its effect to ambiguity of this sort.[2]

Another brand of ambiguity may appear to offer a better suggestion. Sometimes a word will, in a single context, bear two meanings where we are meant to remember and to use both. Or, if we think of wordhood as implying sameness of meaning, then we may describe the situation as one in which what appears as a single word is in fact two. When Shakespeare's Cressida is welcomed bawdily into the Grecian camp, Nestor says, "Our general doth salute you with a kiss." Here we are to take "general" two ways: once as applying to Agamemnon, who is the general; and once, since she is kissing everyone, as applying to no one in particular, but everyone in general. We really have a conjunction of two sentences: our general, Agamemnon, salutes you with a kiss; and everyone in general is saluting you with a kiss.

This is a legitimate device, a pun, but it is not the same device as metaphor. For in metaphor there is no essential need of reiteration; whatever meanings we assign the words, they keep through every correct reading of the passage.

A plausible modification of the last suggestion would be to consider the key word (or words) in a metaphor as having two different kinds of meaning at once, a literal and a figurative meaning. Imagine the literal meaning as latent, something that we are aware of, that can work on us without working in the context, while the figurative meaning carries the direct load. And finally, there must be a rule which connects the two meanings, for otherwise the explanation lapses into a form of the ambiguity theory. The rule, at least for many typical cases of metaphor, says that in its metaphorical role the word applies to everything that it applies to in its literal role, and then some.[3]

This theory may seem complex, but it is strikingly similar to what Frege proposed to account for the behavior of referring terms in modal sentences and sentences about propositional attitudes like belief and desire. According to Frege, each referring term has two (or more) meanings, one which fixes its reference in ordinary contexts and another which fixes its reference in the special contexts created by modal operators or psychological verbs. The rule connecting the two meanings may be put like this: the meaning of the word in the special contexts makes the reference in those contexts to be identical with the meaning in ordinary contexts.

Here is the whole picture, putting Frege together with a Fregean view of metaphor: we are to think of a word as having, in addition to its mundane field of application or reference, two special or supermundane fields of application, one for metaphor and the other for modal contexts and the like. In both cases the original meaning remains to do its work by virtue of a rule which relates the various meanings.

Having stressed the possible analogy between metaphorical meaning and the Fregean meanings for oblique contexts, I turn to an imposing difficulty in maintaining the analogy. You are entertaining a visitor from Saturn by trying to teach him how to use the word "floor." You go through the familiar dodges, leading him from floor to floor, pointing and stamping and repeating the word. You prompt him to make experiments, tapping objects tentatively with his tentacle while rewarding his right and wrong tries. You want him to come out knowing not only that these particular objects or surfaces are floors but also how to tell a floor when one is in sight or touch. The skit you are putting on doesn't *tell* him what he needs to know, but with luck it helps him to learn it.

Should we call this process learning something about the world or learning something about language? An odd question, since what is learned is that a bit of language refers to a bit of the world. Still, it is easy to distinguish between the business of learning the meaning of a word and using the word once the meaning is learned. Comparing these two activities, it is natural to say that the first concerns learning something about language, while the second is typically learning something about the world. If your Saturnian has learned how to use the word "floor," you may try telling him something new, that *here* is a floor. If he has mastered the word trick, you have told him something about the world.

Your friend from Saturn now transports you through space to his home sphere, and looking back remotely at earth you say to him, nodding at the earth, "floor." Perhaps he will think this is still part of the lesson and assume that the word "floor" applies properly to the earth, at least as seen from Saturn. But what if you thought he already knew the meaning of "floor," and you

were remembering how Dante, from a similar place in the heavens, saw the inhabited earth as "the small round floor that makes us passionate"? Your purpose was metaphor, not drill in the use of language. What difference would it make to your friend which way he took it? With the theory of metaphor under consideration, very little difference, for according to that theory a word has a new meaning in a metaphorical context; the occasion of the metaphor would, therefore, be the occasion for learning the new meaning. We should agree that in some ways it makes relatively little difference whether, in a given context, we think a word is being used metaphorically or in a previously unknown, but literal way. Empson, in *Some Versions of Pastoral*, quotes these lines from Donne: "As our blood labours to beget / Spirits, as like souls as it can, ... / So must pure lover's soules descend...." The modern reader is almost certain, Empson points out, to take the word "spirits" in this passage metaphorically, as applying only by extension to something spiritual. But for Donne there was no metaphor. He writes in his *Sermons*, "The spirits ... are the thin and active part of the blood, and are a kind of middle nature, between soul and body." Learning this does not matter much; Empson is right when he says, "It is curious how the change in the word [that is, in what we think it means] leaves the poetry unaffected."[4]

The change may be, in some cases at least, hard to appreciate, but unless there is a change, most of what is thought to be interesting about metaphor is lost. I have been making the point by contrasting learning a new use for an old word with using a word already understood; in one case, I said, our attention is directed to language, in the other, to what language is about. Metaphor, I suggested, belongs in the second category. This can also be seen by considering dead metaphors. Once upon a time, I suppose, rivers and bottles did not, as they do now, literally have mouths. Thinking of present usage, it doesn't matter whether we take the word "mouth" to be ambiguous because it applies to entrances to rivers and openings of bottles as well as to animal apertures, or we think there is a single wide field of application that embraces both. What does matter is that when "mouth" applied only metaphorically to bottles, the application made the hearer *notice* a likeness between animal and bottle openings. (Consider Homer's reference to wounds as mouths.) Once one has the present use of the word, with literal application to bottles, there is nothing left to notice. There is no similarity to seek because it consists simply in being referred to by the same word.

Novelty is not the issue. In its context a word once taken for a metaphor remains a metaphor on the hundredth hearing, while a word may easily be appreciated in a new literal role on a first encounter. What we call the element of novelty or surprise in a metaphor is a built-in aesthetic feature we can experience again and again, like the surprise in Haydn's Symphony no. 94, or a familiar deceptive cadence.

If metaphor involved a second meaning, as ambiguity does, we might expect to be able to specify the special meaning of a word in a metaphorical setting by waiting until the metaphor dies. The figurative meaning of the living metaphor should be immortalized in the literal meaning of the dead. But although some philosophers have suggested this idea, it seems plainly wrong. "He was burned up" is genuinely ambiguous (since it may be true in one sense and false in another), but although the slangish idiom is no doubt the corpse of a metaphor, "He was burned up" now suggests no more than that he was very angry. When the metaphor was active, we would have pictured fire in the eyes or smoke coming out of the ears.

We can learn much about what metaphors mean by comparing them with similes, for a simile tells us, in part, what a metaphor merely nudges us into noting. Suppose Goneril had said, thinking of Lear, "Old fools are like babes again"; then she would have used the words to assert a similarity between old fools and babes. What she did say, of course, was "Old fools are babes again," thus using the words to intimate what the simile declared. Thinking along these lines may inspire another theory of the figurative or special meaning of metaphors: the figurative meaning of a metaphor is the literal meaning of the corresponding simile. Thus "Christ was a chronometer" in its figurative sense is synonymous with "Christ was like a chronometer," and the metaphorical meaning once locked up in "He was burned up" is released in "He was like someone who was burned up" (or perhaps "He was like burned up").

There is, to be sure, the difficulty of identifying the simile that corresponds to a given metaphor. Virginia Woolf said that a highbrow is "a man or woman of thoroughbred intelligence who rides his mind at a gallop across country in pursuit of an idea." What simile corresponds? Something like this, perhaps: "A highbrow is a man or woman whose intelligence is like a thoroughbred horse and

who persists in thinking about an idea like a rider galloping across country in pursuit of ... well, something."

The view that the special meaning of a metaphor is identical with the literal meaning of a corresponding simile (however "corresponding" is spelled out) should not be confused with the common theory that a metaphor is an elliptical simile.[5] This theory makes no distinction in meaning between a metaphor and some related simile and does not provide any ground for speaking of figurative, metaphorical, or special meanings. It is a theory that wins hands down so far as simplicity is concerned, but it also seems too simple to work. For if we make the literal meaning of the metaphor to be the literal meaning of a matching simile, we deny access to what we originally took to be the literal meaning of the metaphor, and we agreed almost from the start that *this* meaning was essential to the working of the metaphor, whatever else might have to be brought in in the way of a nonliteral meaning.

Both the elliptical simile theory of metaphor and its more sophisticated variant, which equates the figurative meaning of the metaphor with the literal meaning of a simile, share a fatal defect. They make the hidden meaning of the metaphor all too obvious and accessible. In each case the hidden meaning is to be found simply by looking to the literal meaning of what is usually a painfully trivial simile. This is like that – Tolstoy like an infant, the earth like a floor. It is trivial because everything is like everything, and in endless ways. Metaphors are often very difficult to interpret and, so it is said, impossible to paraphrase. But with this theory, interpretation and paraphrase typically are ready to the hand of the most callow.

These simile theories have been found acceptable, I think, only because they have been confused with a quite different theory. Consider this remark by Max Black:

> When Schopenhauer called a geometrical proof a mousetrap, he was, according to such a view, *saying* (though not explicitly): "A geometrical proof is *like* a mousetrap, since both offer a delusive reward, entice their victims by degrees, lead to disagreeable surprise, etc." This is a view of metaphor as a condensed or elliptical *simile*.[6]

Here I discern two confusions. First, if metaphors are elliptical similes, they say *explicitly* what similes say, for ellipsis is a form of abbreviation, not of paraphrase or indirection. But, and this is the more important matter, Black's statement of what the metaphor says goes far beyond anything given by the corresponding simile. The simile simply says a geometrical proof is like a mousetrap. It no more *tells* us what similarities we are to notice than the metaphor does. Black mentions three similarities, and of course we could go on adding to the list forever. But is this list, when revised and supplemented in the right way, supposed to give the *literal* meaning of the simile? Surely not, since the simile declared no more than the similarity. If the list is supposed to provide the figurative meaning of the simile, then we learn nothing about metaphor from the comparison with simile – only that both have the same figurative meaning. Nelson Goodman does indeed claim that "the difference between simile and metaphor is negligible," and he continues, "Whether the locution be 'is like' or 'is,' the figure *likens* picture to person by picking out a certain common feature. . . ."[7] Goodman is considering the difference between saying a picture is sad and saying it is like a sad person. It is clearly true that both sayings liken picture to person, but it seems to me a mistake to claim that either way of talking "picks out" a common feature. The simile says there is a likeness and leaves it to us to pick out some common feature or features; the metaphor does not explicitly assert a likeness, but if we accept it as a metaphor, we are again led to seek common features (not necessarily the same features the associated simile suggests; but that is another matter).

Just because a simile wears a declaration of similitude on its sleeve, it is, I think, far less plausible than in the case of metaphor to maintain that there is a hidden second meaning. In the case of simile, we note what it literally says, that two things resemble one another; we then regard the objects and consider what similarity would, in the context, be to the point. Having decided, we might then say the author of the simile intended us – that is, meant us – to notice that similarity. But having appreciated the difference between what the words meant and what the author accomplished by using those words, we should feel little temptation to explain what has happened by endowing the words themselves with a second, or figurative, meaning. The point of the concept of linguistic meaning is to explain what can be done with words. But the supposed figurative meaning of a simile explains nothing; it is not a feature of the word that the word has prior to and independent of the context of use,

and it rests upon no linguistic customs except those that govern ordinary meaning.

What words do do with their literal meaning in simile must be possible for them to do in metaphor. A metaphor directs attention to the same sorts of similarity, if not the same similarities, as the corresponding simile. But then the unexpected or subtle parallels and analogies it is the business of metaphor to promote need not depend, for their promotion, on more than the literal meanings of words.

Metaphor and simile are merely two among endless devices that serve to alert us to aspects of the world by inviting us to make comparisons. I quote a few stanzas of T. S. Eliot's "The Hippopotamus":

> The broad-backed hippopotamus
> Rests on his belly in the mud;
> Although he seems so firm to us
> He is merely flesh and blood.
>
> Flesh and blood is weak and frail,
> Susceptible to nervous shock;
> While the True Church can never fail
> For it is based upon a rock.
>
> The hippo's feeble steps may err
> In compassing material ends,
> While the True Church need never stir
> To gather in its dividends.
>
> The 'potamus can never reach
> The mango on the mango-tree;
> But fruits of pomegranate and peach
> Refresh the Church from over sea.

Here we are neither told that the Church resembles a hippopotamus (as in simile) nor bullied into making this comparison (as in metaphor), but there can be no doubt the words are being used to direct our attention to similarities between the two. Nor should there be much inclination, in this case, to posit figurative meanings, for in what words or sentences would we lodge them? The hippopotamus really does rest on his belly in the mud; the True Church, the poem says literally, never can fail. The poem does, of course, intimate much that goes beyond the literal meanings of the words. But intimation is not meaning.

The argument so far has led to the conclusion that as much of metaphor as can be explained in terms of meaning may, and indeed must, be explained by appeal to the literal meanings of words. A consequence is that the sentences in which metaphors occur are true or false in a normal, literal way, for if the words in them don't have special meanings, sentences don't have special truth. This is not to deny that there is such a thing as metaphorical truth, only to deny it of sentences. Metaphor does lead us to notice what might not otherwise be noticed, and there is no reason, I suppose, not to say these visions, thoughts, and feelings inspired by the metaphor, are true or false.

If a sentence used metaphorically is true or false in the ordinary sense, then it is clear that it is usually false. The most obvious semantic difference between simile and metaphor is that all similes are true and most metaphors are false. The earth is like a floor, the Assyrian did come down like a wolf on the fold, because everything is like everything. But turn these sentences into metaphors, and you turn them false; the earth is like a floor, but it is not a floor; Tolstoy, grown up, was like an infant, but he wasn't one. We use a simile ordinarily only when we know the corresponding metaphor to be false. We say Mr. S. is like a pig because we know he isn't one. If we had used a metaphor and said he was a pig, this would not be because we changed our mind about the facts but because we chose to get the idea across a different way.

What matters is not actual falsehood but that the sentence be taken to be false. Notice what happens when a sentence we use as a metaphor, believing it false, comes to be thought true because of a change in what is believed about the world. When it was reported that Hemingway's plane had been sighted, wrecked, in Africa, the New York *Mirror* ran a headline saying, "Hemingway Lost in Africa," the word "lost" being used to suggest he was dead. When it turned out he was alive, the *Mirror* left the headline to be taken literally. Or consider this case: a woman sees herself in a beautiful dress and says, "What a dream of a dress!" – and then wakes up. The point of the metaphor is that the dress is like a dress one would dream of and therefore isn't a dream-dress. Henle provides a good example from *Antony and Cleopatra* (2.2):

> The barge she sat in, like a burnish'd throne
> Burn'd on the water

Here simile and metaphor interact strangely, but the metaphor would vanish if a literal conflagration were imagined. In much the same way the usual effect of a simile can be sabotaged by taking the comparison too earnestly. Woody Allen writes, "The trial, which took place over the following weeks, was like a circus, although there was some difficulty getting the elephants into the courtroom."[8]

Generally it is only when a sentence is taken to be false that we accept it as a metaphor and start to hunt out the hidden implication. It is probably for this reason that most metaphorical sentences are *patently* false, just as all similes are trivially true. Absurdity or contradiction in a metaphorical sentence guarantees we won't believe it and invites us, under proper circumstances, to take the sentence metaphorically.

Patent falsity is the usual case with metaphor, but on occasion patent truth will do as well. "Business is business" is too obvious in its literal meaning to be taken as having been uttered to convey information, so we look for another use; Ted Cohen reminds us, in the same connection, that no man is an island.[9] The point is the same. The ordinary meaning in the context of use is odd enough to prompt us to disregard the question of literal truth.

Now let me raise a somewhat Platonic issue by comparing the making of a metaphor with telling a lie. The comparison is apt because lying, like making a metaphor, concerns not the meaning of words but their use. It is sometimes said that telling a lie entails saying what is false; but this is wrong. Telling a lie requires not that what you say be false but that you think it false. Since we usually believe true sentences and disbelieve false, most lies are falsehoods; but in any particular case this is an accident. The parallel between making a metaphor and telling a lie is emphasized by the fact that the same sentence can be used, with meaning unchanged, for either purpose. So a woman who believed in witches but did not think her neighbor a witch might say, "She's a witch," meaning it metaphorically; the same woman, still believing the same of witches and her neighbor but intending to deceive, might use the same words to very different effect. Since sentence and meaning are the same in both cases, it is sometimes hard to prove which intention lay behind the saying of it; thus a man who says "Lattimore's a Communist" and means to lie can always try to beg off by pleading a metaphor.

What makes the difference between a lie and a metaphor is not a difference in the words used or what they mean (in any strict sense of meaning) but in how the words are used. Using a sentence to tell a lie and using it to make a metaphor are, of course, totally different uses, so different that they do not interfere with one another, as say, acting and lying do. In lying, one must make an assertion so as to represent oneself as believing what one does not; in acting, assertion is excluded. Metaphor is careless to the difference. It can be an insult, and so be an assertion, to say to a man "You are a pig." But no metaphor was involved when (let us suppose) Odysseus addressed the same words to his companions in Circe's palace; a story, to be sure, and so no assertion – but the word, for once, was used literally of men.

No theory of metaphorical meaning or metaphorical truth can help explain how metaphor works. Metaphor runs on the same familiar linguistic tracks that the plainest sentences do; this we saw from considering simile. What distinguishes metaphor is not meaning but use – in this it is like assertion, hinting, lying, promising, or criticizing. And the special use to which we put language in metaphor is not – cannot be – to "say something" special, no matter how indirectly. For a metaphor *says* only what shows on its face – usually a patent falsehood or an absurd truth. And this plain truth or falsehood needs no paraphrase – it is given in the literal meaning of the words.

What are we to make, then, of the endless energy that has been, and is being, spent on methods and devices for drawing out the content of a metaphor? The psychologists Robert Verbrugge and Nancy McCarrell tell us that:

> Many metaphors draw attention to common systems of relationships or common transformations, in which the identity of the participants is secondary. For example, consider the sentences: *A car is like an animal, Tree trunks are straws for thirsty leaves and branches*. The first sentence directs attention to systems of relationships among energy consumption, respiration, self-induced motion, sensory systems, and, possibly, a homunculus. In the second sentence, the resemblance is a more constrained type of transformation: suction of fluid through a vertically oriented cylindrical space from a source of fluid to a destination.[10]

Verbrugge and McCarrell don't believe there is any sharp line between the literal and metaphorical uses of words; they think many words have a "fuzzy" meaning that gets fixed, if fixed at all, by a context. But surely this fuzziness, however it is illustrated and explained, cannot erase the line between what a sentence literally means (given its context) and what it "draws our attention to" (given its literal meaning as fixed by the context). The passage I have quoted is not employing such a distinction: what it says the sample sentences direct our attention to are facts expressed by paraphrases of the sentences. Verbrugge and McCarrell simply want to insist that a correct paraphrase may emphasize "systems of relationships" rather than resemblances between objects.

According to Black's interaction theory, a metaphor makes us apply a "system of commonplaces" associated with the metaphorical word to the subject of the metaphor: in "Man is a wolf" we apply commonplace attributes (stereotypes) of the wolf to man. The metaphor, Black says, thus "selects, emphasizes, suppresses, and organizes features of the principal subject by implying statements about it that normally apply to the subsidiary subject."[11] If paraphrase fails, according to Black, it is not because the metaphor does not have a special cognitive content, but because the paraphrase "will not have the same power to inform and enlighten as the original.... One of the points I most wish to stress is that the loss in such cases is a loss in cognitive content; the relevant weakness of the literal paraphrase is not that it may be tiresomely prolix or boringly explicit; it fails to be a translation because it fails to give the insight that the metaphor did."[12]

How can this be right? If a metaphor has a special cognitive content, why should it be so difficult or impossible to set it out? If, as Owen Barfield claims, a metaphor "says one thing and means another," why should it be that when we try to get explicit about what it means, the effect is so much weaker – "put it that way," Barfield says, "and nearly all the tarning, and with it half the poetry, is lost."[13] Why does Black think a literal paraphrase "inevitably says too much – and with the wrong emphasis"? Why inevitably? Can't we, if we are clever enough, come as close as we please?

For that matter, how is it that a simile gets along without a special intermediate meaning? In general, critics do not suggest that a simile says one thing and means another – they do not suppose it *means* anything but what lies on the surface of the words. It may make us think deep thoughts, just as a metaphor does; how come, then, no one appeals to the "special cognitive content" of the simile?

Donald Davidson

And remember Eliot's hippopotamus; there there
was neither simile nor metaphor, but what seemed
to get done was just like what gets done by similes
and metaphors. Does anyone suggest that the
words in Eliot's poem have special meanings?

Finally, if words in metaphor bear a coded meaning, how can this meaning differ from the meaning
those same words bear in the case where the metaphor *dies* – that is, when it comes to be part of the
language? Why doesn't "He was burned up" as
now used and meant mean *exactly* what the fresh
metaphor once meant? Yet all that the dead metaphor means is that he was very angry – a notion not
very difficult to make explicit.

There is, then, a tension in the usual view of
metaphor. For on the one hand, the usual view
wants to hold that a metaphor does something no
plain prose can possibly do and, on the other hand,
it wants to explain what a metaphor does by
appealing to a cognitive content – just the sort of
thing plain prose is designed to express. As long as
we are in this frame of mind, we must harbor the
suspicion that it *can* be done, at least up to a point.

There is a simple way out of the impasse. We
must give up the idea that a metaphor carries a
message, that it has a content or meaning (except,
of course, its literal meaning). The various theories
we have been considering mistake their goal.
Where they think they provide a method for deciphering an encoded content, they actually tell us
(or try to tell us) something about the *effects* metaphors have on us. The common error is to fasten
on the contents of the thoughts a metaphor provokes and to read these contents into the metaphor
itself. No doubt metaphors often make us notice
aspects of things we did not notice before; no
doubt they bring surprising analogies and similarities to our attention; they do provide a kind of lens
or lattice, as Black says, through which we view
the relevant phenomena. The issue does not lie
here but in the question of how the metaphor is
related to what it makes us see.

It may be remarked with justice that the claim that
a metaphor provokes or invites a certain view of its
subject rather than saying it straight out is a commonplace; so it is. Thus Aristotle says metaphor
leads to a "perception of resemblances." Black,
following Richards, says a metaphor "evokes" a
certain response: "a suitable hearer will be led by a
metaphor to construct a . . . system."[14] This view is
neatly summed up by what Heraclitus said of the
Delphic oracle: "It does not say and it does not hide,
it intimates."[15]

I have no quarrel with these descriptions of the
effects of metaphor, only with the associated views
as to *how* metaphor is supposed to produce them.
What I deny is that metaphor does its work by
having a special meaning, a specific cognitive content. I do not think, as Richards does, that metaphor produces its result by having a meaning
which results from the interaction of two ideas; it
is wrong, in my view, to say, with Owen Barfield,
that a metaphor "says one thing and means another"; or with Black that a metaphor asserts or
implies certain complex things by dint of a special
meaning and *thus* accomplishes its job of yielding
an "insight." A metaphor does its work through
other intermediaries – to suppose it can be effective only by conveying a coded message is like
thinking a joke or a dream makes some statement
which a clever interpreter can restate in plain
prose. Joke or dream or metaphor can, like a picture or a bump on the head, make us appreciate
some fact – but not by standing for, or expressing,
the fact.

If this is right, what we attempt in "paraphras-
ing" a metaphor cannot be to give its meaning, for
that lies on the surface; rather we attempt to evoke
what the metaphor brings to our attention. I can
imagine someone granting this and shrugging it off
as no more than an insistence on restraint in using
the word "meaning." This would be wrong. The
central error about metaphor is most easily attacked
when it takes the form of a theory of metaphorical
meaning, but behind that theory, and statable independently, is the thesis that associated with a
metaphor is a cognitive content that its author
wishes to convey and that the interpreter must
grasp if he is to get the message. This theory is
false, whether or not we call the purported cognitive content a meaning.

It should make us suspect the theory that it is so
hard to decide, even in the case of the simplest
metaphors, exactly what the content is supposed to
be. The reason it is often so hard to decide is, I
think, that we imagine there is a content to be
captured when all the while we are in fact focusing
on what the metaphor makes us notice. If what the
metaphor makes us notice were finite in scope and
propositional in nature, this would not in itself
make trouble; we would simply project the content
the metaphor brought to mind onto the metaphor.
But in fact there is no limit to what a metaphor
calls to our attention, and much of what we are
caused to notice is not propositional in character.
When we try to say what a metaphor "means," we

soon realize there is no end to what we want to mention.[16] If someone draws his finger along a coastline on a map, or mentions the beauty and deftness of a line in a Picasso etching, how many things are drawn to your attention? You might list a great many, but you could not finish since the idea of finishing would have no clear application. How many facts or propositions are conveyed by a photograph? None, an infinity, or one great un-stable fact? Bad question. A picture is not worth a thousand words, or any other number. Words are the wrong currency to exchange for a picture.

It's not only that we can't provide an exhaustive catalogue of what has been attended to when we are led to see something in a new light; the difficulty is more fundamental. What we notice or see is not, in general, propositional in character. Of course it *may* be, and when it is, it usually may be stated in fairly plain words. But if I show you Wittgenstein's duck-rabbit, and I say, "It's a duck," then with luck you see it as a duck; if I say, "It's a rabbit," you see it as a rabbit. But no proposition expresses what I have led you to see. Perhaps you have come to realize that the drawing can be seen as a duck or as a rabbit. But one could come to know this with-out ever seeing the drawing as a duck or as a rabbit. Seeing as is not seeing that. Metaphor makes us see one thing as another by making some literal state-ment that inspires or prompts the insight. Since in most cases what the metaphor prompts or inspires is not entirely, or even at all, recognition of some truth or fact, the attempt to give literal expression to the content of the metaphor is simply misguided.

The theorist who tries to explain a metaphor by appealing to a hidden message, like the critic who attempts to state the message, is then fundamen-tally confused. No such explanation or statement can be forthcoming because no such message exists.

Not, of course, that interpretation and elucida-tion of a metaphor are not in order. Many of us need help if we are to see what the author of a metaphor wanted us to see and what a more sensi-tive or educated reader grasps. The legitimate function of so-called paraphrase is to make the lazy or ignorant reader have a vision like that of the skilled critic. The critic is, so to speak, in benign competition with the metaphor maker. The critic tries to make his own art easier or more transparent in some respects than the original, but at the same time he tries to reproduce in others some of the effects the original had on him. In doing this the critic also, and perhaps by the best method at his

command, calls attention to the beauty or aptness, the hidden power, of the metaphor itself.

Notes

1   I think Max Black is wrong when he says, "The rules of our language determine that some expres-sions must count as metaphors." He allows, how-ever, that what a metaphor "means" depends on much more: the speaker's intention, tone of voice, verbal setting, etc. "Metaphor," in his *Models and Metaphors* (Ithaca, NY, 1962), p. 29.

2   Nelson Goodman says metaphor and ambiguity differ chiefly "in that the several uses of a merely ambiguous term are coeval and independent" while in metaphor "a term with an extension established by habit is applied elsewhere under the influence of that habit"; he suggests that as our sense of the history of the "two uses" in metaphor fades, the metaphorical word becomes merely ambiguous (*Languages of Art* [Indianapolis, 1968], p. 71). In fact in many cases of ambiguity, one use springs from the other (as Goodman says) and so cannot be coeval. But the basic error, which Goodman shares with others, is the idea that two "uses" are involved in metaphor in anything like the way they are in ambiguity.

3   The theory described is essentially that of Paul Henle, "Metaphor," in *Language, Thought, and Cul-ture*, ed. Henle (Ann Arbor, Mich., 1958).

4   William Empson, *Some Versions of Pastoral* (London, 1935), p. 133.

5   J. Middleton Murry says a metaphor is a "com-pressed simile," *Countries of the Mind*, 2nd ser. (Oxford, 1931), p. 3. Max Black attributes a similar view to Alexander Bain, *English Composition and Rhetoric*, enl. edn. (London, 1887).

6   Black, *Models and Metaphors*, p. 35.

7   Goodman, *Languages of Art*, pp. 77–8.

8   Woody Allen, *New Yorker*, 21 November 1977, p. 59.

9   Ted Cohen, "Figurative Speech and Figurative Acts," *Journal of Philosophy* 72 (1975): 671. Since the negation of a metaphor seems always to be a potential metaphor, there may be as many platitudes among the potential metaphors as there are absurds among the actuals.

10 Robert R. Verbrugge and Nancy S. McCarrell, "Metaphoric Comprehension: Studies in Reminding and Resembling," *Cognitive Psychology* 9 (1977): 499.

11 Black, *Models and Metaphors*, pp. 44–5.

12 Ibid., p. 46.

13 Owen Barfield, "Poetic Diction and Legal Fiction," in *The Importance of Language*, ed. Max Black (Eng-lewood Cliffs, NJ, 1962), p. 55.

14 Black, *Models and Metaphors*, p. 41.

15 I use Hannah Arendt's attractive translation of "σημαίνει": it clearly should not be rendered as "mean" in this context.

16 Stanley Cavell mentions the fact that most attempts at paraphrase end with "and so on" and refers to Empson's remark that metaphors are "pregnant" (*Must We Mean What We Say?* [New York, 1969], p. 79). But Cavell doesn't explain the endlessness of paraphrase as I do, as can be learned from the fact that he thinks it distinguishes metaphor from some ("but perhaps not all") literal discourse. I hold that the endless character of what we call the paraphrase of a metaphor springs from the fact that it attempts to spell out what the metaphor makes us notice, and to this there is no clear end. I would say the same for any use of language.

31

Metaphor, Feeling, and Narrative

Ted Cohen

I

This essay rests on at least four assumptions, none of which will be defended. I begin by setting out these four as clearly as I can, along with some explanation of why I offer no defense of them.

(1) *There is no infallible sign that any given expression, spoken or written, is a metaphor.* Until about twenty years ago it was commonly supposed that a necessary condition of something's being a metaphor is that if taken literally it be absurd or self-contradictory or at least blatantly false. This would not have been a sufficient condition, of course, but it was thought to be necessary. It was my privilege to note that a metaphor need display no logical or semantic anomaly, and that indeed a metaphor taken literally need not even be false.[1] I promptly went on to the mistaken assertion that there must be *some* way in which metaphors are recognized, that every metaphorical expression must exhibit some anomaly if taken literally, although the oddity might be only pragmatic. I concluded that every metaphor taken literally must be something that, in the circumstances, the speaker or writer could not mean. Thus if the metaphor were a literal truth, like "Sydney is a warm city" or "No man is an island," the literal truth would be so obvious in the circumstances that one could not suppose the author to have intended to communi-

cate that truth, and one would be induced to look for another, metaphorical content.[2] That was a mistake.

I made this mistake because I took this for granted: "In understanding a metaphor, one must put together two or more elements in some novel way. The need for some novel construction is signaled by the impossibility of assembling the elements in the usual (literal) way." And that is a compound mistake. It seems a neat congruence between the mechanism of a metaphor and the signal that it is a metaphor, but it's a mistake because there need be no signal. Generally, of course, one does find an obstacle to taking a metaphor literally, either within the sentence itself, or within the more complex entity which is the utterance of the sentence within a certain context (that is, within what Austin called "the total speech act in the total speech situation"); but there need be no obstacle. A sentence might support both literal and metaphorical understandings, and if so, one might just miss the metaphor. One finds the literal construction significant, and then does not go on to attempt a metaphorical construction even though a metaphor is there for the taking. Some people are better than others at understanding metaphors, and some people are better than others at finding them.

(2) *There is a difference between expressions that are metaphorical and expressions that are not, that are*

From *Philosophy and Literature* 21 (1997), pp. 223–5, 227–37, 239, and notes. Copyright © The Johns Hopkins University Press.

literal. This is true despite the fact that there is no general reliable sign to indicate a metaphor, and also despite the fact that there may be no serviceable formula for defining "metaphor." Understanding a metaphor requires something more, something other than understanding a literal expression. Generally speaking, all who know a language can understand the language's literal expressions. This understanding sometimes fails because of the syntactic or semantic difficulty of a given literal expression – for instance, because of the presence of unfamiliar words; but knowledge of a language is the capacity, potentially, to understand the language's literal expressions. Those who know a language usually are able to understand metaphorical expressions in the language as well, but this understanding seems different. It requires wit, imagination, flexibility – a kind of initiative. And this initiating understanding is built on one's capacity for literal understanding. One must be able to deal with an expression literally, and then go on to do more with it. Thus literal expressions, and all expressions regarded literally have a settled fixity – at least relative to metaphorical expressions and all expressions (that can be) regarded metaphorically.

The idea that there is no difference between the literal and the metaphorical is a foolish idea, especially when advanced as a consequence of the fact that all language is "symbolic." Symbols can be deployed literally or, sometimes, metaphorically. To grasp a metaphor, one must have control of the literal use of the terms. If you do not understand "Macbeth doth murder Duncan," you cannot possibly understand "Macbeth doth murder sleep." Thus the metaphorical depends upon the literal, and the literal is independent of the metaphorical. When a metaphor ceases to be dependent, it ceases to be a metaphor.

(3) *At least some metaphors have no literal equivalents.* By this I mean the maker of a metaphor intends to get across something besides the literal meaning of the sentence he produces. Let us, for a moment, call that something the upshot or the point of the metaphor, its *content*. There is no function, no rule, no transformations, semantic, pragmatic, or otherwise, which will compute the content from the literal meaning.

By this I do not mean that some metaphors have *meanings* which are not the meanings of any literal expressions. This may be true, but I will not defend or even investigate this proposition. I will

avoid the topic for the simple but perfect reason that I come to you with no theory of meaning. With no theory of meaning, one has no systematic way of determining what the meaning of an expression is, whether an expression has more than one meaning, whether two meanings in fact are the same, or any of the other matters needing to be settled by anyone wishing to defend or attack any thesis about the existence of "metaphorical meaning." This does not seem to me an issue to be settled with reference to intuitive or ordinary senses of what to call "a meaning." Perhaps there is nothing to count as a metaphorical meaning (as Donald Davidson contends), or nothing to count as any kind of meaning at all, metaphorical or literal (as Nelson Goodman has it), or perhaps there are both literal and metaphorical meanings (as Josef Stern has been arguing with great ingenuity);[3] but in the context of this discussion, I do not care. . . .

(4) *The metaphorical content of a metaphorical expression is more or less specific.* Here is a wonderful crux in the topic of metaphor. On the one hand, as just noted in the previous assumption, there is no function that will calculate the metaphorical content of an expression from its literal meaning. But on the other hand, there *is* a content that it is correct to take from the expression. It is right to take Romeo's "Juliet is the sun" as Romeo's declaration that Juliet warms him and brightens his life; it is wrong to take it as a complaint that when Juliet is near, Romeo's skin breaks out in a rash.

Even if there were nothing accomplished in the use of metaphor besides the expression of feeling, this accomplishment would still be specific: not just any feeling is expressed by any metaphor. Perhaps some epithets are rather unspecific, like "son of a bitch," "bastard," and "asshole," and these may be examples of relatively unspecific expressions of feeling; but it is not obvious that their use is now metaphorical, if ever it was. When Churchill called Mussolini a utensil, however, although he undoubtedly expressed a feeling about Mussolini, the feeling was particular, and the same feeling would not be carried by "Mussolini is a pig" or "Mussolini is a dog." When you are inspired to deep, negative feelings (or positive feelings) about someone, and you choose to express those feelings in a metaphor, it requires facility to determine just what metaphor you should choose.

This communication of feeling in the use of metaphor is a remarkably subtle business, and I will note here one subtlety in need of explanation, and return to it much later in this essay. Suppose x is an A, and is not a B. It is a metaphor to say of x that it is B (or a B). The effect of this is to express feelings – say negative feelings – about x. In the more straightforward, seemingly simple case, the maker of the metaphor already has negative feelings about B, and these feelings are somehow transferred to x. But sometimes there are no particularly strong negative feelings about B held by the maker of the metaphor or by anyone else. And yet it is a negative thing to say about x that he is a B. Many of us feel negatively about maggots, and so it seems relatively straightforwardly a negative thing to say about someone that he is a maggot. Most of us do not have negative feelings about dogs, and yet it is typically a negative thing to say about someone that he is a dog. That is, even when it is not a bad thing about a B to be a B, it may still be a bad thing about an A to be thought of as a B. And it should be noted that the seemingly easier case is not so easy. It may be bad of a maggot to be a maggot, but it is differently bad of a person to be a maggot. The whole matter of seeing a person as something else, or of seeing anything as something else, and then discovering that seen this way, the person excites feelings is a wonderful mystery. I will take it up later, admitting more fully that I cannot explain it.

When feelings are not at the center of one's thoughts about metaphor, it is even easier to persuade oneself of the specificity of metaphorical designations. A quick and entertaining way to do it is by considering – or better, by playing – a parlor game taught to me many years ago.[4] It is played this way:

Each player takes a turn being someone whose identity the other players try to guess. When choosing an identity to assume, one's only constraint is that the mystery person be someone likely to be known by the other players. The mystery person can be fictional or real, alive or dead. The guessing players, in turn, ask one question of the impersonator, and the question must be of this form: "If you were a C, which C would you be?"; and the impersonator must answer truthfully. Thus the question might be "If you were a piece of furniture, which piece of furniture would you be?," or the category C might be vegetables, or academic disciplines, or mammals, or subatomic particles, or. . . .

I confess that when I learned this game I was doubtful that it would work well, or even that it

would work at all. It does work, and it has two extraordinary features that amazed me. First, the guessing players will indeed guess the mystery player within a short time, using only a few questions. Second, there will be arguments about the accuracy of answers given by the impersonator, with strong opinions being held on all sides, and sometimes people will persuade one another of what the right answer should have been. I recall a game in which the impersonator was Ho Chi Minh, and when he had been guessed, all the guessing players objected to the answer given to the question "If you were a metal, which metal would you be?" The impersonator had said "iron," and we all insisted that iron is too rigid, too blunt, too solid to be Ho Chi Minh. We thought tempered steel might have been right, with a few speaking up for aluminum. What do you think? I bet you have a thought, and that is significant. It means that one has a sense of the aptness of figures of speech, however well one can explain what makes one figure better than another, and even though one surely cannot *prove* anything.

No doubt these metaphors, or analogies, are understood as choices among alternatives, the alternatives being set by the choice of category C, and thus there is a certain artificiality in their use in this game. But all descriptions are understood as choices among possible descriptions, and, as Nelson Goodman has insisted, metaphors, too, are made in this way, as a selection within categories.[5] How else can we explain the suggestive power of metaphors? If Ho Chi Minh is tempered steel, then what is General Westmoreland? What kind of metal were the Viet Cong, the North Vietnamese regular army, the French army, the American army?

Not only is it impossible to identify the content as a function of the literal meaning, but neither can it be identified with the import grasped by competent users of the language. One might characterize, say, grammatical sentences of English as those acceptable to competent English speakers and, perhaps, understand the meanings of those sentences in terms of how they are taken by those competent speakers; but it is different with metaphorical content exactly because metaphors outrun (or flout) the normal constraints of the language, and not all competent users of the language are competent in dealing with such extravagances.

Grasping a metaphor is much like interpreting a work of art, and the assessment of either achievement is confused by too casual a use of the idea of "interpretation." You say to me "Don't go out-doors." I take you to have ordered me, or advised me, or pleaded with me not to go outdoors. It is misleading to say that this is how I have *interpreted* your utterance. Better to say that this is how I have understood you, and to leave "interpretation" as the name for something else I might do with your remark. Dylan Thomas says, "Do not go gentle into that good night," and interpretation is in order. A reader (or Thomas's father) may take this as a plea or advice not to go complacently outdoors after dark. That would be to understand an English expression. But one must do more. One must find in the utterance an admonitory plea not to acquiesce calmly in one's own death. That find-ing is an interpretation.

If one thinks of literal and metaphorical com-prehensions indifferently as understandings or in-terpretations, one is led to think of them as the same kind of semantic achievement. This leads to describing metaphor as a species of ambiguity (as in fact texts in grammar and linguistics did de-scribe metaphor until about 25 years ago), and this is a mistake. Whether or not there is metaphorical meaning, it is not simply an *other* meaning, on a par with some literal meaning. If I say "My money is in the bank," perhaps my money is on deposit in Hyde Park Bank & Trust, and perhaps it is buried beside the Mississippi. What I say is ambiguous: there are two literal meanings to be understood. If I say "My money has run aground," it is not another meaning you have found when you take it that my money is invested in ever lower-yielding stocks and bonds. Literal content is there to be understood. Metaphorical content is carried by a so-called figure of speech. It has to be figured out.

II

As everyone knows, Wittgenstein said, "Whereof we cannot speak, thereof we must be silent."[6] If this were true, and if speaking properly were speaking literally, then when we cannot speak lit-erally, we should stay silent. But perhaps we have things to do that cannot be done by speaking literally, and we cannot do these things remaining silent.

As almost everyone knows, Frank Ramsey is supposed to have responded to Wittgenstein's "Whereof we cannot speak, thereof we must be silent" by observing, "And we can't whistle it, either."[7] Perhaps that's true, too. And yet – per-haps there are times when one cannot speak liter-ally, and yet one must do something, and the thing available to do, exactly, is to whistle. What times would these be, and just what is this whistling?

Stanley Cavell has said, "We don't know when to speak and when to be quiet. First this ruins language, and then it ruins the world."[8] When should we speak, when remain silent? When liter-ality fails us, sometimes we should sit still, and sometimes we may try (whistling) a metaphor. But how do we know when is when? I think there is no formula to tell us when to speak, when not. We are all alone, deciding, figuring it out every time.

I will consider two examples in which individ-uals speak whereas others might have stayed silent. In each case I give the example briefly, along with a few questions that have occurred to me. They are not both obvious examples of metaphorical speak-ing, but they are examples of speaking when there is nothing literal to say, and this makes them instructive in thinking about metaphor. With the examples given I will try to understand what happens in them. If I fail, and say nothing useful, then I should have left the examples to speak for themselves, and kept quiet.

First, a Yom Kippur poem. A central doctrine in one strain of classical Judaism is that we know nothing about God. For Jews who hold this doc-trine there are no literal truths to be said or written about God. And yet in a Yom Kippur liturgy read and said by Jews of many different persuasions is this:

> We are Your people
> You are our King.
> We are Your children
> You are our Father.
> We are your possession
> You are our Portion.
> We are your flock
> You are our Shepherd.
> We are Your vineyard
> You are our Keeper.
> We are Your beloved
> You are our Friend.[9]

None of these six pairs of assertions is literally true. In fact each is literally a double falsehood.

Why do we say these things? Why do we say anything? And why so many things?

Next, Nathan and David, in a passage from the second book of Samuel.[10] King David is reported to have remained at home, in his palace, while his army was away besieging an Ammonite city, Rabbah. One morning as he is walking on the roof of the palace, David sees a young woman in her bath in a courtyard next door. David learns that she is Bathsheba, wife of Uriah, who is one of his soldiers. Struck by her beauty, David summons Bathsheba to him at the palace and sleeps with her. When she becomes pregnant, David sends a message to his military commander Joab, telling him to send Uriah to David. When Uriah returns from the war and makes a report to David, David urges him to spend the night with his wife Bathsheba. But Uriah spends the night alone, sleeping outdoors, and when David asks why, Uriah says he should not go home and be with his wife when Joab, the armies of Judah and Israel, and the ark are campaigning in the field. David keeps Uriah in Jerusalem one more night, wining and dining him, and indeed getting him drunk, but Uriah again abstains from going home. Then David sends an instruction to Joab. Joab is to set Uriah among a group of soldiers engaged in fierce fighting near the wall of Rabbah. When the fighting becomes especially dangerous, Joab is to withdraw from behind Uriah. Joab follows these instructions, Uriah is left unsupported and he is killed, and Joab reports the events to David. David then summons the widowed Bathsheba to live in the palace. The Lord is displeased with what David has done:

And the Lord sent Nathan unto David. And he came unto him, and said unto him, There were two men in one city, the one rich, and the other poor.

The rich man had exceeding many flocks and herds.

But the poor man had nothing, save one little ewe lamb, which he had bought and nourished up: and it grew up together with him, and with his children; it did eat of his own meat, and drank of his own cup, and lay in his bosom, and was unto him as a daughter. And there came a traveler unto the rich man, and he spared to take of his own flock and of his own herd, to dress for the wayfaring man that was come unto him; but took the poor man's lamb, and dressed it for the man that was come to him.

And David's anger was greatly kindled against the man; and he said to Nathan, As the Lord liveth, the man that hath done this thing shall surely die.

And he shall restore the lamb fourfold, because he did this thing, and because he had no pity.

And Nathan said to David, Thou art the man.[11]

What has happened here between Nathan the prophet and David the king? Two fundamental controlling points seem clear: (1) Nathan has not told David anything David did not already know, (2) When Nathan has finished speaking, David has new feelings and thoughts about something he has already known. How does Nathan bring this about?

III

According to Arnold Isenberg, in what he calls "critical communication," the customary relation of meaning to truth is reversed.[12] In ordinary communication, a sentence S is produced, the recipient understands S and then looks to the world to discover whether S is true. That is, the meaning of S is grasped in independence of the world and whatever is alleged of the world by S. Thus the meaning of S precedes the truth (or falsity) of S.

In critical communication, the recipient of S cannot fully grasp the meaning of S without turning to S's referent. Why not? Because, according to Isenberg, in critical communication the author of S is trying to show its recipient why the author *feels* the way he does. No sheerly descriptive S can do this if it is taken in the ordinary way. I want you to understand why I like x, and perhaps to like it, too, for the same reason why I like it. So I say "S," asserting that x has some property P. If you take S as an ordinary description, then my project is hopeless. You will understand S to say that x has P, and when you investigate x, you will find that indeed it has this property (and so S is true) – but you will not take this as a reason for liking x. It is not even a reason for *me* to like x, for no more than you do I subscribe to the general proposition that I like everything that has this property.

I do like x because of P, but it is because of this specific, peculiar occurrence of P, here in x. Thus I must get you to see P in x the way I do, which is a way of seeing x that carries a feeling about x. Isenberg puts this by saying you do not really grasp the meaning of my S until and unless you turn to *x* to fill in or complete my meaning. Isenberg's way of speaking about meaning is problematic, but his thought about the conveyance of feeling is irresistible. A principal ambition in the use of metaphor (although not the only one, nor one always present) is to induce others to feel as we do, and to do this by describing the objects of our feelings in a way which requires a special effort at comprehension on the part of others. When I offer you a metaphor I invite your attempt to join a community with me, an intimate community whose bond is our common feeling about something. Arnold Isenberg's "critical communication" is not concerned with metaphor, but it is concerned throughout with the connection between special descriptions and the feelings they aim to inspire. If I am right in thinking this is a characteristic enterprise of metaphor, then Isenberg's sense of the enterprise is a promising tool. I will adapt it, especially in trying to understand Nathan's instruction of David, but first in thinking of the import of the beautiful Yom Kippur poem.

IV

I find this example particularly useful because it comes with two stipulated assumptions, both given and neither open to question. The first is that there is nothing literal to be said, and the second is that something must be said.

The need to speak is given by God, who has directed the people to assemble at this time and account for themselves. Thus they must speak, they must address their God, and although in parts of the liturgy they speak the words God has given them to say, they must also speak for themselves, in their own words. What are they to say?

With nothing literal possible to say, the author of this poem has suggested a brilliant address. He will speak a metaphor. But he will not leave it at that, for there is the perilous possibility that the metaphor will be taken literally, or that it will be taken to exhaust what is to be said about God and God's relation to the people. And so he goes on, with metaphor after metaphor, each of them compelling *and each of them unsettling the others*. The search for more than one figure acknowledges the inadequacy of any one to exhaust what is to be said, and the multiplicity makes it impossible to fix on any one or two. The speaker has an impossible task: to speak comprehensibly about something incomprehensible. His response is to speak in every apt way he can conceive. The people cannot be both a vineyard and a flock; indeed literally they cannot be either. But they are both, somehow, in their relation to the unknowable God. And that God cannot be both our Father and our Shepherd. But he is, somehow, as our God.

To think of God – to see God – as my King, my Friend, my Keeper, my Portion, and so forth, is a staggering achievement (probably seldom managed, if ever); but a signal event of this awesome day is the attempt to do it. I am to think of God, of God's relation to me and that of me to Him, of what He has required of me and how I have failed the requirement. How am I to do this? One way is through these metaphors, thought deeply, imagined as intensely and vividly as I can find it in myself to do. I doubt that I succeed. But if I did, what then? Would I have attained a conception I might then record in some literal description? No. I cannot escape the figuration, I cannot dispense with the metaphors for they have no literal equivalent. I must continue, always, to speak to God and to think of God in figures, and, therefore, thanks again to God for giving me the power not only of literal language but of metaphorical extravagance and ecstasy.

I have written the last paragraph in terms of what *I* do, of how I address God, articulating in these figures my relation to God and how I feel that relation; but the liturgical poem is intended to be said and thought by a *community*. One may find it mysterious and awesome to recite these words, reaching for a felt conception during the already heightened felt awareness the High Holy Days are meant to bring, but there is an added intensity of feeling carried by one's sense that everyone else in the assembly is bent to this task. As one attempts this declaration of oneself, one feels oneself at one with a community of declarers, hoping for a consensus of feeling and indeed believing in one. The intimacy of community is felt during literal portions of the liturgy as well, when the assembly confesses its sins, when it engages in literal prayer, and when it asks for forgiveness, for instance. But here, at this point, in this metaphorical declaration, another dimension of community is sought, in a determination to express the inexpressible *together*, and thus to one another, and for one another, as well as to the unfathomable God to whom it is grammatically addressed. I think there is genius in this corporate enterprise. I wish I could explain it better, but then, again, I may flatter myself in thinking it is impossible to *explain*.

V

How can David not have known that he was rich in wives while Uriah had only Bathsheba? But David took Bathsheba anyway, and he has shown no contrition. What has Nathan done about this?

Of course Nathan has told David about the rich man and the poor man's ewe lamb, but that is not something known to Nathan or David because that story is not true. Even if it were true, it would make no difference, because the efficacy of the story does not depend upon the story's being true. That depends only upon David's entertaining the story sufficiently to begin to have feelings about the poor man and the rich man.

What has happened is something like this. David's anger and moral outrage at the rich man have been transferred to himself. Nathan says "You are the man," which is essentially "You, David, are the rich man who has taken a poor man's only ewe lamb," and David *connects*.

If Nathan's story tells David nothing new, then how does it work its effect? Perhaps we should say that Nathan does tell something new to David. He tells David that it is possible to see – that indeed Nathan does see – David in his treatment of Uriah and Bathsheba as a rich man taking a poor man's only ewe lamb; and when the story has been told, David himself sees David in that way. When David sees himself in this way, his sense of himself is changed: feelings about himself arise that had not arisen before. How does this happen? We should not settle for an easy answer: it is not a simple matter of similarity. No doubt David "is like" the rich man in the story. But that itself leads to nothing. What matters is that some specific feeling attached to David's sense of the rich man is provoked in David's sense of himself, to which it had not previously been attached. This is not achieved simply by drawing David's attention to the fact that he and the rich man share membership in some similarity class. Nathan needs the absolute particularity of the rich man. That is what arouses David's feelings. Nathan does not effect the transfer of feeling by saying "You resemble people whom you dislike." David might accept the proposition that he is like these disagreeable people and yet not be moved to anger at himself. After all, any group can be judged similar in some respect or other, and the question will remain, why should David identify himself as such a person with respect to his feelings? Nathan does not permit this way out.

Instead of telling David that he resembles people who make him angry, Nathan says, with absolute specificity and particularity, that David *is the rich man*, exactly the man at whom he is angry. And David responds at once.

Nathan's success is an Isenbergian achievement. Nathan achieves a community of feeling (between himself and David) by inducing in David a sameness of vision (with Nathan himself, a sameness in the way they now see David's treatment of Uriah). Indeed there is a kind of double community created. First, David and Nathan now both feel the same about David's treatment of Uriah, and, second, David now feels about himself as he feels about the rich man. I do not know how to analyze the proposition that, after the story, David sees himself as the rich man of the story, and I am not sure that any analysis is to be given. That David *does* now see in this way is proved, in the only way these things can be proved, by the fact that he now *feels* about himself as he already felt about the rich man. It is the feeling that anchors the metaphor and signals its success. And this similarity of feeling (the similarity between David's feeling about the rich man, and his newly arisen feeling about himself) is the only similarity that matters, and it might be as well to say that this is not a similarity of feeling, but an identity. Nathan says "You are the rich man," and David's implicit response is "Yes, and I loathe myself as I loathe the rich man."

In this similarity, a similarity in feeling, there may be an opportunity to credit a well-known remark of Black's: "It would be more illuminating in some of these cases to say that the metaphor *creates* the similarity than to say that it formulates some similarity antecedently existing."[13] This remark has appealed to many authors, including Nelson Goodman, and many have endorsed it; but it is difficult to make it plausible if the similarity in question is one between properties of two objects (as Black intended it). If we are concerned with feelings, however, then the remark is entirely sensible, because the second feeling (in this case, David's feeling about his own actions) is called into existence by the metaphor, and therewith its similarity to the original feeling (in this case, David's feeling about the actions of the rich man). [. . .]

VI

In summary: One motive to metaphor is the desire to communicate how one feels and why one feels that way. The use of metaphor certainly is not the only way to do this. Joke-telling is another way of doing it, and so is the use of sheerly literal remarks. What metaphor-making and joke-telling have in common is their solicitation of a complicity in the person to whom they are directed. They aim to induce intimacy and they do this in part by requiring an engagement of the hearer at the outset, just in order to understand what has been said. I suppose they are used in a kind of coercion, forcing the hearer to a special effort. The hearer is induced to join the speaker in a particular intimacy, probably a selective intimacy, not available to everyone; and already thus engaged, the hearer is nudged into the further intimacy of joining the speaker in feeling.

I want you to understand how I feel about A, and why, and to do this I must give you an experience in which you too sense the natural rising of this feeling about A. I choose B, something I know you have feelings about, and I assert $A = B$, which strikes me as an apt metaphor, hoping that you too will find it apt. Even if you do not then have the relevant feeling, I still hope that you will *understand* why I have the feeling, and your understanding will be based on your ability to imagine what it would be to be me, to be someone for whom $A = B$ is compelling. I do not know how to describe this feat of imagination, save to say that it is the ability to see A as B (whatever that may mean); but I do know that the successful use of metaphor is pervasive, and I think I have found one reason why.

Notes

1   Ted Cohen, "Notes on Metaphor," *Journal of Aesthetics and Art Criticism* 34 (1976): 249–59.
2   I made the mistake in "Notes on Metaphor" and continued making it in "Metaphor and the Cultivation of Intimacy," *Critical Inquiry* 5 (1978): 1–13.
3   Donald Davidson, "What Metaphors Mean," *Critical Inquiry* 5 (1978): 31–47; Nelson Goodman, *Languages of Art* (Indianapolis: Bobbs-Merrill, 1968), ch. 2, and "Metaphor as Moonlighting," in *On Metaphor*, ed. Sheldon Sacks (Chicago: University of Chicago Press, 1979), pp. 175–80; Josef Stern, "What Metaphors

Do Not Mean," in *Philosophy and the Arts*, ed. Peter French et al. *Midwest Studies in Philosophy*, vol. 16 (Notre Dame: Notre Dame University Press, 1991), pp. 13–52.
4   My teacher was my then colleague Professor Lars Svenonius. He called it "The Game of Analogies," taking that title, I think, from whoever had taught the game to him. It does not seem to me to matter whether one thinks of the game as one of analogies or of metaphors.
5   Goodman, *Languages of Art*, especially sections 6–8 of ch. 2.
6   This is the last line of Wittgenstein's *Tractatus Logico-Philosophicus: Wovon man nicht sprechen kann, darüber muss man schweigen.*
7   Although this quip is widely known and almost always attributed to Ramsey, I have been unable to locate any formal attribution.
8   I wrote this in a notebook when I thought I heard Cavell say it at Stanford in 1986. Sometime later I asked Cavell for the exact line and also asked whether it had by then been published. He replied that he did not remember delivering the line, but, he said, "I'd like to buy it from you." I do not like to dispute Cavell, but I think he already owns it.
9   These lines were composed in medieval France, in Hebrew. This translation is from the American edition of *Gates of Repentance* (New York: Central Conference of American Rabbis, 1978).
10 I am no biblical scholar. What limited confidence I have in dealing with this text I owe to Ms. Adrien Bledstein, the best Bible teacher I know. It was my luck and privilege to spend many years in her Bible class, a place where I learned to respect and confront the Torah, and where I also witnessed the miracle of a great teacher at work with a great book and students of every age, background, and description. Of late I have learned most studying with Amos Cohen, my son, who not only knows this material far better than I, but also shows me that at its best reading is a moral struggle.
11 Quoted from 2 Samuel 12 in the King James translation. The precedent events are recounted in chapter 11.
12 Arnold Isenberg, "Critical Communication," *Philosophical Review* 58 (1949): 330–44, and widely reprinted.
13 Max Black, "Metaphor," *Proceedings of the Aristotelian Society* 55 (1954–5) pp. 284–5. See also p. 152 in this book.

32

Metaphor and Prop Oriented Make-Believe

Kendall Walton

Dolls and hobby horses are valuable for their contributions to make-believe. The same is true of paintings and novels. These and other props stimulate our imaginations and provide for exciting or pleasurable or interesting engagements with fictional worlds. A doll, in itself just a bundle of rags or a piece of moulded plastic, comes alive in a game of make-believe, providing the participant with a (fictional) baby. What in real life is a mere stick enables a child fictionally to ride around on a horse, the better to chase bandits or stray cattle. Paint on canvas and print on paper lead us into exciting worlds of mystery, romance, and adventure and guide our travels through them.[1]

But props are not always tools in the service of make-believe. Sometimes make-believe is a means for understanding props. The props themselves may be the focus of our attention, and the point of regarding them as props in (actual or potential) games of make-believe may be to provide useful or illuminating ways of describing or thinking about them. Participating in the game may not be especially fun it itself and we may have little interest in the content of the make-believe world or the subject matter of our imaginings. A game may be cooked up simply to clarify or expose features of the props, simply so we can observe their role in it. This is make-believe in the service of the cognition of props. I call it *prop oriented* make-believe, and I contrast it to *content oriented* make-believe, whose

interest lies in the content of the make-believe, in the fictional world. In *Mimesis as Make-Believe* I emphasized the latter, exploring the ways in which props of various kinds contribute to make-believe activities.[2] I will focus now on prop oriented make-believe.

Paper airplanes, like hobby horses and toy trucks, serve as props in games of make-believe. They make it fictional, i.e. true-in-the-world-of-make-believe, that they are airplanes flying through the air, climbing, diving, landing on a runway, crashing.[3] But the fun of making and playing with paper airplanes does not derive entirely, maybe not even primarily, from their role in make-believe. Children who know nothing of actual airplanes and who think of what we call paper airplanes merely as folded pieces of paper that behave interestingly when thrown, might enjoy throwing them, watching them glide, experimenting with the effects of different folds on their flight, and so on. One's interest may be in the paper constructions themselves, apart from any make-believe. Frisbees suggest a game in which fictionally they are flying saucers. But most frisbee enthusiasts seem to be interested in throwing, catching, and watching the plastic disks themselves, not in fantasies about space travel.

There is nevertheless a point in calling the paper constructions *airplanes* and the plastic disks

From *European Journal of Philosophy* 1 (1993), pp. 39–42, 45–9, 51–7. Reprinted by permission of Blackwell Publishing Ltd.

flying saucers. These are convenient ways of indicating, for those who know about airplanes and flying saucers, what these toys are and how they work. The make-believe looks back toward the props themselves, rather than forward to the fictional truths the props generate; it is *prop oriented.*

Paper airplanes and frisbees thus differ from such props as hobby horses, non-flying airplane models (e.g. a model of the Wright brothers' airplane), and the kind of toy trucks that a child pushes around the floor. Merely manipulating or looking at *these* things is likely not to be much fun. One's interest is in the make-believe to which they contribute, in fictionally riding a horse or observing the Wright brothers' airplane or driving a truck.[4] In these cases make-believe looks forward to the content of the make-believe; it is *content oriented.*

Where in Italy is the town of Crotone?, I ask. You explain that it is on the arch of the Italian boot. "See that thundercloud over there – the big angry face near the horizon," you say, "it is headed this way." Plumbers and electricians distinguish between "male" and "female" plumbing and electrical connections. We speak of the saddle of a mountain and the shoulder of a highway.

All of these cases are linked to make-believe. We think of Italy and the thundercloud as something like pictures. Italy (or a map of Italy) depicts a boot. The cloud is a prop which makes it fictional that there is an angry face. Male and female plumbing or electrical connections are understood to be, fictionally, male and female sexual organs. The saddle of a mountain is, fictionally, a horse's saddle. But our interest, in these instances, is not in the make-believe itself, and it is not for the sake of games of make-believe that we regard these things as props. Our participation is minimal at best.[5] Imagining a boot, while seeing a map of Italy or seeing it in my mind's eye, may help me to understand your explanation of the location of Crotone. But I don't contemplate the Italian boot in the way one might contemplate Van Gogh's *Pair of Shoes* or even René Magritte's *The Red Model I.* Clouds *can* support extensive participation; one might, on a dreamy summer afternoon, fictionally examine the furrows of an angry face, wonder what it is angry about, and so on. One might be caught up emotionally in the fictional world the clouds present. But such involvement is unnecessary if the purpose is to identify which cloud you mean to point out. All this requires is to recognize which cloud can best be understood to

be an angry-face-picture. To do that it may be helpful to have the experience of, fictionally, recognizing an angry face, but no further participation is called for; there is no need to be caught up emotionally in the fiction. The plumbing and electrical connections invite scarcely any participation in the game in which they are understood to be props, despite its sexy subject matter. The conscientious plumber does his job without, fictionally, leering at the fixtures. (This plumbing terminology can be vaguely titillating, however, and it might cause embarrassment, especially when one comes across it for the first time. These reactions suggest that a certain perhaps implicit participation in the game may be likely, perhaps even inevitable, whether or not such participation helps the plumber to keep track of which fixtures can be connected to which others.) We may speak of saddles of mountains and shoulders of highways without even thinking of make-believe, let alone participating in it, although no doubt such thoughts were present when these expressions were first introduced or learned.

Make-believe – recognition of the possibility of make-believe, at least – is useful in these cases, even if it is not exciting or pleasurable or edifying in ways games of dolls and games with paintings and novels are. It is useful for articulating, remembering, and communicating facts about the props – about the geography of Italy, or the identity of the storm cloud, or functional properties of plumbing and electrical fixtures, or mountain topography. It is by thinking of Italy or the thundercloud or plumbing connections as potential if not actual props that I understand where Crotone is, which cloud is the one being talked about, or whether one pipe can be connected to another. The purpose is cognitive, but what I learn is not about boots, angry faces (or anger), or sex. The subject matter of the (potential) make-believe is merely useful.

There is nothing profound about the cognitive role of make-believe in these examples. The facts it helps us to grasp and remember and communicate are mundane, and the make-believe is dispensable, a mere convenience. There are other ways of locating Crotone; we don't have to think of Italy as a boot. But make-believe, we shall see later, plays a more essential and extensive role in our understanding of props than is apparent from these examples.

Appreciation of visual and literary representations typically involves participation in prop oriented games of make-believe, especially when the appreciation includes the experience of being "caught up in the story" or "emotionally involved" in the fictional world. But people sometimes find it convenient to devise *ad hoc* prop oriented games, often modifications of the standard content oriented ones, in describing the props themselves, the visual or literary representations, and their surroundings.[6] One might remark, for instance, that the author of a forthcoming novel murdered several of his characters with a pencil; this may be a way of pointing out that the author revised the novel so as to exclude those characters. The remark indicates a (possible) game of make-believe in which revising a novel in that manner makes it fictional that one kills characters with a pencil.

If the Metropolitan Museum borrows a portrait of Napoleon from the Louvre for a special exhibit and has it shipped to New York on the *Queen Mary*, one might observe that Napoleon is a "passenger" on the *Queen Mary*, thus invoking a (possible) game in which the presence of a portrait on a ship makes it fictional that the subject of the portrait is a passenger. I don't know whether anyone else has thought of games like this, let alone participated in them. But there is nothing exotic about them, and it takes only the remark that Napoleon is a passenger on the Queen Mary, in a suitable context, to call the possibility of such games to mind. There is no need for anyone to explain them.

Here are some other comments that can be taken in similar ways:

This statue isn't the original one. The Germans took the first Flaubert away in 1941, along with the railings and doorknockers. Perhaps he was processed into cap-badges.[7]

Christopher Robin had spent the morning indoors going to Africa and back [i.e. reading about Africa], and he had just got off the boat and was wondering what it was like outside, when who should come knocking at the door but Eeyore.[8]

The chair behind the couch is not the stationary object it seems. I have traveled all over the world on it, and back and forth in time. Without moving from my easy seat I have met important personages and witnessed great events. But it remained for Kirk Allen to take me out of this world when he transformed the couch in my con-

sulting room into a space ship that roved the galaxies.[9]

These examples illustrate the pervasiveness of make-believe in thought and conversation, the prevalence of hints of, allusions to potential and often fragmentary games, in addition to sustained engagement with full fledged, established games when we appreciate works of art. They also illustrate how little it takes to introduce even rather novel games. The quotation from Lindner suffices to introduce an unusual game in which a patient's exotic tales of other-worldly events make it fictional that the psychiatrist's chair is a space ship. We are constantly inventing new games of make-believe and communicating them to each other. This doesn't mean that we actively participate in these games. Many of them are prop rather than content oriented, our interest being not in the make-believe itself, but in the props. Thinking of the props as props in potential games of make-believe is a device for understanding them. [. . .]

It will have been evident that some of my examples are instances of metaphor. "Saddle" applied to mountains and "male" applied to plumbing fixtures are metaphors in anyone's book, dead ones anyway. My other examples may be less comfortably thought of as metaphors: "Napoleon is a passenger on the *Queen Mary*," "Crotone is on the arch of the Italian boot," "The ugly face in the sky is headed this way," and "There is a man" said while pointing toward a men's room sign. The ground of the distinction is unclear, however. To speak of the saddle of a mountain is to think of the topography in question as though it is a representational sculpture, but one whose make-believe is oriented to the prop. "It has been Grand Central Station around here all day" is a metaphor that involves thinking of the household in question as a kind of unwitting theatrical portrayal of Grand Central Station; one in which, again, the make-believe is prop oriented. The cases of the Italian boot, the angry face in the sky, and the rest room icons consist in regarding something as a representational picture whose make-believe is prop oriented. If "saddle" and "Grand Central Station" in these contexts are metaphors, why not also "The ugly face in the sky is headed this way" and "There is a man" said while pointing toward a men's room sign?

I am not going to propose a theory of metaphor. This is because I am very unsure what to count as metaphors, and because I am skeptical about whether anything like the class of what people call metaphors is a unified one, whether a single account will work for any reasonable refinement of that class. But I do want to explore the applicability of the notion of make-believe to some acknowledged metaphors, and to sketch some advantages of understanding these metaphors, at least, in terms of make-believe.

Other metaphors that plausibly involve prop oriented make-believe are easy to come by. "Argument is war" and the family of metaphors subsidiary to it, including talk of claims being indefensible, criticisms being on target, winning and losing arguments, shooting down arguments, attacking and defending positions, and so on,[10] suggest a game in which what people say in the course of an argument generates fictional truths about acts of war. The arguers or observers of an argument participate in the game if they take argumentative behavior to prescribe imagining acts of war, and imagine accordingly. But participation is not necessary for using and understanding the metaphors; it is enough to recognize or be aware of the game. The metaphors can work even if no one has ever participated in the game. The make-believe is prop oriented in that (or insofar as) it is the argument that one is interested in, and the make-believe war is thought of as a device for describing or understanding the argument.

In this case a single game or kind of game crops up intermittently but persistently in many different metaphorical utterances. Other metaphors of this sort include those deriving from the thought that "time is money,"[11] war metaphors applied to sports, and sports metaphors applied to war. More localized metaphors which also might be thought of as involving prop oriented make-believe include: "Man is the cancer of the earth," "Politician Jones started prairie fires on his campaign trip in the midwest," "an orgy of eating," and (at least before they died) "bottle neck," "traffic jam," "waves of immigrants," "chair leg," and "mouth of a river." (Metaphors that strike me as less plausibly amenable to this treatment include "Time flies," "Her spirits are rising," "She always took the high road in business dealings." "He knows which side his bread is buttered on," and "Happiness is a warm puppy." Perhaps not all of these are metaphors?)

The general idea is this: The metaphorical statement (in its context) implies or suggests or introduces or calls to mind a (possible) game of make-

believe. The utterance may be an act of verbal participation in the implied game, or it may be merely the utterance of a sentence that *could* be used in participating in the game. In saying what she does, the speaker describes things that are or would be props in the implied game. It may be possible in favorable cases to paraphrase what she says about them with reasonable fidelity. Typically, the paraphrase will specify features of the props by virtue of which it would be fictional in the implied game that the speaker speaks truly, if her utterance is an act of verbal participation in it.

There are many variations on the theme, and many differences among metaphors. The example of rest room signs suggests that some metaphorical utterances are not paraphrasable, at least not in the way I mentioned, although they may still amount to descriptions of the (potential) props. Some metaphorical utterances may not be assertions at all, even if they are declarative in form. And metaphorical sentences are not always ones that might be used in acts of verbal participation in the implied games. Nevertheless, we are now in a position to clarify and explain much that has been said about metaphor. Then we can look at some of the variations.

Many have taken metaphor to involve the bringing together of two distinct *categories* or *realms* or *domains*. Nelson Goodman speaks of the (literal) use of predicates in one realm guiding their (metaphorical) application in another.[12] We can think of the two realms as (a) that of the props and the generating facts, and (b) that of the propositional content of the implied make-believe. The latter is the home realm of the predicates that are used metaphorically, the realm in which they have literal application (I. A. Richards' *vehicle*). The former is the new or target or foreign realm (Richards' *tenor*).

Goodman says little about how the predicates from one realm organize another. My suggestion is that (in the case of some metaphors anyway) the mechanism involves our thinking of objects of the new realm as props, as generating the fictionality of propositions concerning the home realm. The predicates "male" and "female" get applied to plumbing fixtures by means of our thinking of plumbing fixtures as props which generate fictional truths about sexual identities. "Male" applies metaphorically to plumbing connections which make it fictional, in the implied game, that they are male.

This gives some content to talk of seeing or thinking of one kind of thing "in terms of" another, under the influence of metaphors, or of metaphors "yoking" different kinds of things together. Richard Moran speaks of metaphors getting us to adopt a perspective, to see one thing as *framed* by another.[13] This framing effect of metaphors is independent of and prior to the use metaphors sometimes have in making assertions. It will be present even when the metaphor is embedded in a context in which it is not asserted, when it is merely a question rather than an assertion, and when it is denied or negated.

All of this is accounted for if we think of the new perspective, the framing effect, as consisting in the metaphor's implication or introduction or reminder of a game of make-believe. "The health of General Motors is improving" implies a game of make-believe; it gets us to think of corporations as props in a game (even if we don't participate in the game). It also serves to assert something about General Motors. But approximately the same game of make-believe is implied equally by the following: "If General Motors' health is improving, unemployment will drop," "I wonder if General Motors' health is improving," "Is the health of General Motors improving?," "General Motors' health is not improving." All of these statements have the same "framing effect"; all of them introduce essentially the same game of make-believe. Probably "Caterpiller is in robust good health" and "Xerox has a slight cold" do so as well.

This account of the framing effect of metaphors, of their capacity to get us to see one kind of thing in terms of another, contrasts with two other tempting proposals. One is that it is a matter of seeing similarities. But regarding things (or states of affairs) of one realm as generating fictional truths, as prescribing imaginings, concerning another realm, is not essentially a matter of seeing similarities. Some principles of generation[14] are more or less conventional, and to the extent that they are, they are likely not to depend on similarities. (For example, halos on figures in Christian art make it fictional that they are saints.) One might have thought that "metaphors" based on conventions cannot be metaphors. Granted, if there are simply conventions that "slide" means one thing in photographic contexts and another in connection with children's playground equipment, the conventions merely define distinct literal meanings of the terms. But if there is a convention to the effect that a ridge connecting two higher

elevations makes it fictional that there is a saddle, we still have a metaphor. Calling a topographic feature a saddle is not *simply* to say that it is a ridge connecting two higher elevations. Calling it this implies the game of make-believe in which the conventional principle of generation just mentioned holds. In this sense the speaker gets us to see or think of such ridges as saddles. (Not for the first time, of course; the convention is a familiar one. But the metaphor reminds us of the game.) The freshest, most lively metaphors may be ones that introduce games, principles of generation, that are new to us. But metaphors like *saddle* (of a mountain) are not dead in a sense that ought to make us deny that they are metaphors, so long as they invoke, remind us of, the game of make-believe, familiar though it is. So long as they do this, their use as applied to mountains is parasitic on their original literal senses, and it is their use in the home realm, their application to riding equipment, that guides their application to mountain topography.

It seems unlikely that metaphors like "high" and "low" pitches, and "rising" and "falling" melodies, are grounded in similarities between pitch relations and spatial relations, although they may be not merely conventional but in some way natural. I speculate that the association has a lot to do with the fact that more energy is usually needed to produce higher pitched sounds than lower pitched ones, just as upward movement requires more energy than downward movement. To sound a higher note on a wind or string instrument one blows harder or stretches the string tighter. But in order to understand metaphors like "rising melodies" and "low tones" we needn't know how they came about, how it happens that we associate pitches and spatial positions as we do. The utterance is not an assertion of a similarity or natural connection, or a pointing out of one. All that matters is that these metaphors do pick out for us a game of a certain sort. (Notice, incidentally, that, if age and familiarity are any indications, these metaphors are as dead as doornails. Yet they remain metaphors. Their make-believe is active – indeed it is content as well as prop oriented, as we shall see.)

Many metaphors are not reversible.[15] "Life is hell" is very different from "Hell is life." But similarity is presumably symmetrical. Life resembles hell in exactly the respects that hell resembles life. This should make us wary of construing metaphor in terms of similarity. My proposal explains this irreversibility nicely. *Generates fictional truths about* is not symmetrical. A ridge between two higher elevations makes it fictional that there is a saddle, but the reverse does not hold (not in the same game anyway).

A second tempting account of what it is to see one kind of thing in terms of another is that this is a matter of imagining things of the one kind to be of the other kind.[16] This is not my view. On my view it is a matter of taking things of one kind to prescribe imaginings about things of another kind, not (in general) imagining things of the first kind to be of the second. Understanding the dotted lines of a balloon in a cartoon to prescribe imagining that the words in the balloon are thought but not spoken, is not to imagine that the dotted lines have anything to do with unspoken thought; it is not to imagine anything of the dotted lines at all. The lines merely prompt and prescribe certain imaginings, imaginings about the character whose portrayal the balloon's stem points to.

Some props do prescribe and prompt imaginings about themselves, however. An actor playing Hamlet probably makes it fictional not only that a prince of Denmark hesitates, but that he himself (the actor) is a hesitating prince of Denmark. So we are to imagine something about the actor, the prop – that he is a prince of Denmark and hesitates. It may be that the props in the plumbing case and in the case of the mountain saddle are also objects. Probably participants in the game are not merely to imagine a saddle, this imagining being prescribed by features of the mountain, but are to imagine of the ridge that it is a saddle.

It is less clear in other cases that props in games implied by metaphorical utterances are also objects. Consider "rising melody," "broken chord," "moving to a new key," "wistful melody," a "mountain of debt," a "healthy" (or "sick") corporation, and "the sea is laughing." If one were to participate in the game implied by "moving to a new key," what would one imagine to be moving? The piece, the musical work? Perhaps one would just imagine something's moving, an instance of something moving, as one listens to the modulation. It is not easy to see how one might imagine a corporation to be (literally) healthy or sick. (Nevertheless, the corporation is the object of *interest*. It is a prop if not an object of prop oriented make-believe.)

I should mention, again, that understanding and appreciating a metaphor need not involve any actual imagining in any case. It is enough to recognize the implied game, to be aware of prescriptions

to imagine in certain ways, without actually so imagining.[. . .]

In what sense does a person, on hearing a metaphor or any utterance implying a prop oriented game of make-believe, become aware of the implied game? In what sense does the metaphor introduce one to or remind one of a game of make-believe? In the simplest cases one is made aware of and can articulate the game's principles of generation. Perhaps the game introduced by talk of mountain saddles consists entirely in the single principle that ridges connecting higher elevations make it fictional that they are saddles. Such talk may make us fully aware of this principle. [. . .]

We do need to be prodded to engage in or even to recognize many other games, however. This is what metaphorical utterances do. Even very familiar games may not automatically come to mind when I experience things that would be props in them. On observing a ridge between higher elevations, I do not always imagine a saddle, nor does it always occur to me that the ridge might be understood to make it fictional that there is a saddle – unless someone reminds me of the game by saying "That is a saddle." I might come across an instance of a "weighty" argument, an "under the table" payment, someone's coming "out of the closet," a writing style with "punch," or an "unfolding" melody without the game of make-believe the metaphor implies occurring to me. I may need someone to remind me of the game by using the metaphor.

What metaphors do, in many cases, is to activate relevant dispositions or abilities, rather than to make us aware of the principles of generation. When someone describes a writing style as having punch or a melody as unfolding, I cannot say very well what characteristics of a writing style or a melody make these metaphorical attributions appropriate, which ones generate fictional truths about punches or about something's unfolding. But I may be prepared to recognize writing styles or melodies as having "punch" or as "unfolding."

The dispositions that metaphors activate are often far more extensive than these, and may involve whole families of predicates, not just the one or ones originally used metaphorically. A comment that a computer remembers a phone number may prepare me to think of computers behaving so as to make it fictional that they forget things, that they calculate, make decisions, and even lose patience or complain about their handlers or give up on a task. Your describing your household as Grand

Central Station might dispose me to describe mine as Coney Island, or as a cathedral on a Wednesday at midnight. Once someone establishes the precedent of describing people as animals by calling Jones a skunk, we may think of other people as, fictionally, being other animals (a tiger, beaver, pig, mouse, dinosaur). The remark that we are all in the same boat easily leads to a recommendation that we all row in the same direction. Metaphors often function something like the stipulative launching of a (content oriented) game of make-believe, which then grows naturally beyond the original stipulation. In suggesting "Let's let stumps be bears," or pointing toward a stump and declaring, "Watch out for the bear," a child may establish a game in which the presence of the stump makes it fictional that a bear is there. But the game is bound to be far richer than this. It may be understood, more or less automatically, that larger stumps count as larger bears and smaller ones as smaller bears, that an appropriately shaped stump makes it fictional that a bear is rearing on its hind legs; seeing a stump through the undergrowth will make it fictional that one sees a bear through the undergrowth, and children can behave in obvious ways so as to make it fictional that they run away from a bear in terror, or face it bravely, or offer it a blueberry ice cream cone. Such extensions of the game the child introduced are more or less inevitable, but it took an introduced to get it started.

Metaphorical utterances, like stipulated launches of games of make-believe, enable us to *go on* in new ways, to apply the predicates used in the original metaphor to new cases, and to apply related predicates metaphorically. If possessing a concept consists in such abilities or dispositions to go on, as some have suggested, metaphorical utterances expand our repertoire of concepts. The new concepts are concepts of properties we might describe as those of being *metaphorically Ø* – metaphorically unfolding, or metaphorically having punch, or being metaphorically under the table.

In uttering a metaphor one may assert that some such concept applies in a certain instance. But the introduction of the concept, the metaphor's role in enabling hearers to acquire it, is independent of the assertion. It is part of, or a result of, Moran's "framing effect," which a given metaphor and its negation, as well as the same metaphor in nonassertive contexts, may possess equally. Insofar as we are unable to specify the features of props by virtue of which a predicate applies metaphorically to them, insofar as we just go on, we are likely to consider purported paraphrases of the assertions in terms of such features inadequate.[17]

Many metaphors, especially the more interesting ones, do not enable us to go on with assurance. They leave us uncertain or perplexed or in disagreement about applications of the original metaphorical predicate and others in its family. It is very unclear what games are introduced by "Juliet is the sun," or by the description of a musical passage as a "rainbow."[18] Not only can we not specify the principles of generation, we are not prepared to identify with any assurance which people are metaphorically the sun and which are not (no matter how well we know them), or what musical passages are rainbows. Here is another example:

> Art is dead. Its present moments are not at all indications of vitality; they are not even the convulsions of agony prior to death; they are the mechanical reflex actions of a corpse submitted to a galvanic force.[19]

What do moments of art have to be like to be (metaphorically) reflexes of a corpse, as opposed to convulsions of a person not yet dead? We can neither say with any confidence, nor can we very well recognize which description is appropriate for the present moment of art, or for other moments of art in this or another culture. To the extent that the concept a metaphor introduces is unclear, it will be unclear what (if anything) the speaker is asserting. But that may not be the point of the metaphor. Its point may be, in part, to provoke us to think about what sorts of games along suggested lines might be reasonable or natural or intriguing.

Even if the nature of the game implied by a metaphor is fairly definite and a fairly definite assertion is made, the metaphor's interest may lie neither in the assertion, nor in the introduction of new concepts. Consider "There was anger in the rays of the sun."[20] Perhaps the game this metaphor introduces is one in which all sunlight contains anger, in which sunlight always makes it fictional that there is anger (although one might choose not to participate in or think about the game in which this is so). If this is right, the metaphor seems not to introduce any interestingly new concept, any new way of classifying things of the sort that might serve as props in the game. And the assertion (if there is one) is trivially true. What is of interest is the game of make-believe itself, but not simply the content of the make-believe, the fictional truth(s) generated by the sun's rays (roughly, the fact that fictionally there is anger). The make-believe may be content oriented, but it is prop oriented also. And the interest lies in the combination of the two views, in the sunlight's role as a prop in the envisioned game (not just a classification of sunlight that thinking of it as a prop might enable us to make). The metaphor shows us a way of regarding sunlight – as making it fictional that there is anger.

Many other metaphors would appear to be like this one. "The sea is laughing" seems likely to be more significant as an expression of a way of regarding the sea or some manifestations of it – regarding it as a prop in the implied game – than as introducing a way of classifying states of the sea or as asserting something about the sea on the occasion of utterance.

Metaphors thus make such things as sunlight and the sea into something like representational works of art. A Japanese brush painting of a flower may be interesting not (or not merely) because of what it makes fictional, but because of how it makes it fictional, because of the manner in which the brush strokes work to generate the fictional truths. To see how they do is to regard them in a special way, and regarding them in this special way is an important part of one's aesthetic experience of the painting. It is the *function* of pictures such as the Japanese painting to serve as props in games of make-believe. This is not in general the function of sunlight and the sea. In particular social contexts metaphorical utterances accord them this function. Sunlight and the sea are "found objects." Metaphors do the finding.

Notes

1 This is the second of three Carl G. Hampel Lectures presented at Princeton University in May, 1991. I gratefully acknowledge many helpful observations by the audience on that occasion, and by David Hills and Gideon Rosen.
2 Walton (1990).
3 To be *fictional* is to be (as we say) true-in-a-fictional-world, the world of a game of make-believe or a representational work of art, for instance. Features of props are understood to make propositions fictional, to generate fictional truths. It is because a folded piece of paper falls to the ground that it is fictional that an airplane crashes. What is fictional in a game of make-believe is what participants in the game are to imagine to be true. Propositions that are

fictional can be true as well. It is both true and fictional that something flies through the air, although it is only fictional, not true, that the flying object is an airplane. Participants in the game with the paper airplanes are to imagine that an airplane crashes, when the folded paper falls to the ground. See Walton (1990), Chapter 1.
4 One "fictionally rides a horse" when one behaves so as to make it fictional, true-in-the-world-of-make-believe, that one rides a horse, e.g. when one prances around the house straddling a hobby horse, imagining oneself riding a (real) horse.
5 Compare *ornamental* representations, which involve thinking about a game of make-believe without participating in it. See Walton (1990), §7.6.
6 I have in mind what I called "unofficial" games of make-believe, in Walton (1990), §10.4.
7 Barnes (1984), p. 1.
8 Milne (1928), p. 9.
9 Lindner (1954), p. 223.
10 Lakoff and Johnson (1980).
11 Lakoff and Johnson (1980).
12 Goodman (1968), pp. 74–80.
13 See Lakoff and Johnson (1980), p. 36; Davidson (1984); Moran (1989), pp. 87–112.
14 "Principles of generation" are principles specifying what features of props make what propositions fictional (i.e., true-in-the-fictional-world).
15 As Richard Moran (1989) points out, p. 93.
16 I. A. Richards (1936) speaks of imagining the tenor to be the vehicle, pp. 100–1 and elsewhere. Richards seems to associate this view closely with the idea that metaphors involve resemblance.
17 The metaphorical assertion that X is Ø might, however, admit of a paraphrase of the following form: "X is such as to make it fictional in game G that something (possibly X itself) is Ø." "Jones is a squirrel" might be paraphrased as "Jones has whatever it takes to make it fictional in game G that he is a squirrel." This paraphrase is literal, I presume. But it is not the kind of paraphrase people look for. It does not get rid of the predicates that are metaphorical in the original.
18 Pablo Casals so described a passage of Beethoven's A Major sonata for cello and piano, during a master class at Berkeley.
19 Marius de Zayas (1912). Quoted in Danto (1986), p. 81.
20 Mishima (1966).

References

Barnes, J. 1984. *Flaubert's Parrot*. New York: McGraw Hill.
Danto, A. C. 1986. *The Philosophical Disenfranchisement of Art*. New York: Columbia University Press.

de Zayas, M. 1912. "The Sun Has Set," in *Camera Work* 39: 17.

Lakoff, G. and Johnson, M. 1980, *Metaphors We Live By*. Chicago: University of Chicago Press.

Lindner, R. 1954. "The Jet-Propelled Couch," in Lindner, *The Fifty Minute Hour: A Collection of True Psychoanalytic Tales*. New York: Holt, Rinehart, and Winston.

Milne, A. A. 1928. *The House at Pooh Corner*. New York: Dutton.

Mishima, Y. 1966. *Death in Midsummer*. New York: New Directions.

Moran, R. 1989. "Seeing and Believing: Metaphor, Image and Force," in *Critical Inquiry* 16.

Richards, I. A. 1936. *The Philosophy of Rhetoric*. Oxford: Oxford University Press.

Walton, K. L. 1990. *Mimesis as Make-Believe: On the Foundations of the Representational Arts*. Cambridge, Mass.: Harvard University Press.

PART VII

Interpretation

Introduction

What is it about? What does it mean? These questions, and ones like them, frequently provoke hard thinking about works of literature. In Jane Austen's *Pride and Prejudice*, the questions press gently since they appear straightforwardly answerable. They are most urgent when they seem hardest, as in Franz Kafka's *Metamorphosis*, and their urgency may lead us to ask what counts as answering them. *Metamorphosis* is about a man who awakens one morning transformed into a giant bug; but this, far from answering our questions, is just what gets them going. What more do we want to know, then? What is interpretation?

An interpretation of a work is not the same as a description of it. A description of a musical work lists its directly audible properties – the sound of the music; an interpretation of it is inferred from these. Likewise, a description of a literary work mentions, for example, the text or the standard meanings of the words that make it up (see Part III). An interpretation of a work is something inferred from and thus constrained by its description. But not any inference from a work of art is an interpretation of it: an inference that produces an evaluation of a work is a critical judgment, not an interpretation (you do not interpret a poem when you infer from a description of it that it is shoddy in sentiment). An interpretation is a special kind of inference from a description of a work: it is one that explains the work.

Students of literature will be familiar with several models of literary interpretation or explanation. Some critics believe that it is enough to dissect the structure of the work so as to lay bare how it produces its effects. Others view interpretations as placing a work within a literary tradition or within some framework, such as psychoanalysis or post-colonialism. Richard Wollheim proposes an alternative to both of these conceptions, arguing that interpretation (which he calls "criticism") is the retrieval or reconstruction of the creative process, where this process is viewed as made up of intentional actions in a certain social and artistic setting.

These models of interpretation are not only different in form; they also generate interpretations with different contents. A formalist, a Marxist critic, and a retrievalist like Wollheim may fashion incompatible interpretations of *Metamorphosis*. Is this good or is it worrisome? Pluralists hold that a work may have multiple incompatible interpretations that are equally correct. Monists contend that a work may have only one correct interpretation, so that multiple interpretations are in competition with each other.

Many (so-called post-structuralist) arguments for pluralism follow this schema: interpretations are inferences from descriptions of works and are constrained only by those descriptions; but literary works have no single, correct description; so there can be multiple, correct interpretations of works of literature. Alexander Nehamas criticizes some instances of this argument schema and gives an argument for monism. Robert Stecker endorses monism but argues that it is compatible with many versions of pluralism, so long as interpretations may serve many purposes. Different models of interpretation are not in competition with one another if they serve different interpretive aims.

Nehamas and Stecker agree that one aim of interpretation is to descry the meaning of a work and that this is to be attributed to an author. Artworks are the products of intentional actions, and in the case of literary works some of these intentions are semantic. In ordinary linguistic situations, semantic intentions help fix what an utterance means in its context – for example, if I say "I am going to the bank," my semantic intentions determine whether I am saying that I am going to a financial institution or a riverside. Some philosophers have argued that the author's semantic intentions are irrelevant in literary interpretation. Following an examination of the best arguments for anti-intentionalism, Noël Carroll proposes that interpretation shares common ground with ordinary conversational communication.

For Carroll, interpretation requires attributing semantic intentions to the actual author of the work interpreted. An alternative advanced by Nehamas and also by Jerrold Levinson is that semantic intentions are to be attributed to a hypothetical or postulated author. The hypothetical author is a fictional creation of the interpreter, a being postulated as the owner of just those intentions whose realization best explains the work. Hypothetical author intentionalism undercuts some of the arguments for anti-intentionalism and at the same time enjoys explanatory benefits of its own.

An interpretation is not concerned exclusively with a work's meaning; it must also explain the work's non-semantic features. Jenefer Robinson argues that some non-semantic features of a story or poem can be attributed to a hypothetical author. Robinson is particularly interested in stylistic features, which are as much an expression of the character of a work's hypothetical author as your choice of music is an expression of your style.

The monism–pluralism debate is orthogonal to the actual–hypothetical author debate. Actual and hypothetical author intentionalism are consistent with both monism and pluralism; and monism, like pluralism, is consistent with anti-intentionalism. But intentionalism, if true, constrains the task of interpretation. As Wayne Booth puts the point, it gives readers obligations to hypothetical or actual authors.

33

Who Is Responsible in Ethical Criticism, and for What?

Wayne C. Booth

Whenever we read or listen to any story, whether it claims to be historical or fictional, we do not meet and respond to the single, simple voice that is often implied by current theories of "communication": a "sender" or "source" who transfers bits of information to a receiver. Even the most naive listener attending with total concentration to the simplest tale can be seen, on analysis, to be re-creating and responding to at least three different voices: that of the immediate teller, or narrator, who takes the whole tale straight and who expects the listener to do the same (the "time" in "once upon a time" is real time); that of the implied author, who knows that the telling is in one sense an artificial construct but who takes responsibility for it, for whatever values or norms it implies, and for the suggestion that "in responding to *me* you respond to a real person"; and the inferable voice of the flesh-and-blood person for whom this telling is only one concentrated moment selected from the infinite complexities of "real" life.

Similarly, every listener, no matter how unsophisticated or opposed to analysis, maintains at least three roles while listening: that of the immediate believer, who pretends that this story is happening and that it is all that is happening; that of one who "knows," even if only unconsciously, that he or she is dwelling in a selected, concentrated, and hence in some sense "unreal" or

"artificial" world; and that of the flesh-and-blood person whose extra-narrative life, though perhaps forgotten for the duration of the listening, impinges on it in myriad untraceable ways. Indeed, for some purposes we can trace even more than these three.

Though most listeners most of the time are not conscious of these complexities, they will come as no surprise to anyone who has followed criticism of fiction during the past quarter-century. They cannot be ignored in ethical criticism, because each of these authors and readers, tellers and listeners, has a different character from all the others and each will *respond to*, and thus be *responsible to*,[1] a richer set of characters than is suggested by most ethical criticism. [. . .]

What Are the Reader's Responsibilities to the Writer—the Flesh-and-Blood Author or Career Author?

Writers live precarious lives, lives threatened by despair, frustrated hopes, lonely anxiety. They feel neglected, misunderstood, useless. Though I obviously cannot make the care and feeding of artists my direct business in this book, it surely should be one part of every ethical critic's concern – yet it is almost entirely ignored in current discussions. Both reviewers and critics claim to serve a higher value than the cosseting of helpless writers:

From *The Company We Keep* (Berkeley: University of California Press, 1988), pp. 125–6, 134–5. Reprinted by permission of the University of California Press.

strict justice to the work itself, regardless of consequences for the author. It is assumed that to intrude concern for the author's personal fate would itself be unethical. Although in practice very few critics can claim never to have pulled punches (or punched harder) for "personal" reasons, I know of no serious discussion of how to think about such matters.

Is it enough to say that a reader should simply tell the cold truth about a work, in total disregard for the author's career? Quite aside from reviewing and formal criticism, might there not be, especially in a society in which writers feel misunderstood and neglected, an obligation to write the occasional carefully wrought fan letter? To buy, read, and teach books by neglected living authors along with the classics? To *buy* the books of authors we admire, rather than borrowing copies or xeroxing? To respect *famous* authors' privacy rather than hounding them with demands for publicity and conference appearances? All of this is reduced, in our usual talk about responsibility to the author, to one simple demand: thou shalt not plagiarize. Thus the whole rich range of possibilities for fruitful exchange between writers and authors is turned to the service of an unthinking individualism: what's mine is mine and what's yours is yours, and I fill my responsibility to you if I resist the impulse to steal from you. It is as if intellectual and artistic property were so much capital goods. Surely to borrow an author's work is not the worst imaginable mistreatment.

What Are the Reader's Responsibilities to the Work of Art—Which Is to Say, to the Implied Author?

At last we come, in our sorting, to a topic that will be central to us here: Do I as reader have any obligation to that elusive creature, the creating character whom I myself re-create as I read the work? If so, how am I to express it? What is the relation between taking *my* pleasure with a work and attempting to discover the pleasures that the author intends to share? Is Sartre in any sense right when he says that the writer requires of the reader "the gift of his whole person, with his passions, his prepossessions, his sympathies, his sexual temperament, and his scale of values"? What can it mean to say, with him, that the reader must "give himself generously"?

If I am to give myself generously, must I not also accept the responsibility to enter into serious dialogue with the author about how his or her values join or conflict with mine? To decline the gambit, to remain passive in the face of the author's strongest passions and deepest convictions is surely condescending, insulting, and finally irresponsible.

Note

1 As I have tried to dramatize in this introduction, to respond at all is already to be in a sense *response-able:* the word which we unfortunately tend to use only to cover duties is from the Latin *responsus*, past participle of *respondere*, from *re* ("back") and *spondere* ("to pledge").

34

Criticism as Retrieval

Richard Wollheim

It is a deficiency of at least the English language that there is no single word, applicable over all the arts, for the process of coming to understand a particular work of art. To make good this deficiency I shall appropriate the word "criticism", but in doing so I know that, though this concurs with the way the word is normally used in connection with, say, literature, it violates usage in, at any rate, the domain of the visual arts, where "criticism" is the name of a purely evaluative activity.

The central question to be asked of criticism is, What does it do? How is a piece of criticism to be assessed, and what determines whether it is adequate? To my mind the best brief answer, of which this essay will offer an exposition and a limited defence, is, Criticism is *retrieval*. The task of criticism is the reconstruction of the creative process, where the creative process must in turn be thought of as something not stopping short of, but terminating on, the work of art itself. The creative process reconstructed, or retrieval complete, the work is then open to understanding.

To the view advanced, that criticism is retrieval, several objections are raised.

1. The first objection is that, by and large, this view makes criticism impossible: and this is so because, except in exceptional circumstances, it is beyond the bounds of practical possibility to reconstruct the creative process.

Any argument to any such conclusion makes use of further premisses – either about the nature of knowledge and its limits, or about the nature of the mind and its inaccessibility – and the character of these further premisses comes out in the precise way the conclusion is formulated or how it is qualified. For, though an extreme form of the objection would be that the creative process can never be reconstructed, the conclusion is likelier to take some such form as that criticism is impossible unless the critic and the artist are one and the same person, or the work was created in the ambience of the critic, or the creative process was fully, unambiguously, and contemporaneously documented by the artist. This is not the place to assess the general philosophical theses of scepticism or solipsism, or their variants, but it is worth observing that these theses ought not to be credited with greater force outside general philosophy than they are inside it. The observation is called for, because traditionally philosophers of art permit the creative process, or, more broadly, the mental life of artists, to give rise to epistemological problems of an order that they would not sanction in inquiry generally.

These difficulties apart, the objection in its present form offers a persuasive rather than a conclusive argument against the retrieval view. For maybe the truth is that criticism *is* a practical impossibility, or is so outside very favoured circumstances. But sometimes the objection is stated to stronger effect,

From *Art and Its Objects*, 2nd edn. (Cambridge: Cambridge University Press, 1980), pp. 185–96, 199–204. Reprinted by permission of the publisher and author.

and then an incompatibility is asserted between the sceptical or solipsistic premises, however framed, and not just the practice of criticism as retrieval but the view that criticism is retrieval.

A step further, and it is asserted that from these same premises an alternative view of criticism follows. This alternative view may be expressed as, Criticism is *revision*, and it holds that the task of criticism is so to interpret the work that it says most to the critic there and then. Assuming the critical role, we must make the work of art speak "to us, today".

It is clear that this derivation too must require further premises, though less clear what they would be. One thing seems certain, though it is often ignored by adherents of the revisionary view, and that is this: If criticism is justifiably revision when we lack the necessary evidence for reconstructing the creative process, then it must also be revision when we have, if we ever do, adequate evidence for retrieval. We cannot as critics be entitled to make the work of art relate to us when we are in a state of ignorance about its history without our having an obligation to do so, and this obligation must continue to hold in the face of knowledge. Otherwise revision is never a critical undertaking: it is only, sometimes, a *pis-aller*, or a second best to criticism. Indeed, the strongest case for the revisionary view of criticism draws support from a thesis which appears to dispense with scepticism or, at any rate, cuts across it.

The thesis I have in mind, which is generally called "radical historicism" and is best known through the advocacy of Eliot, holds that works of art actually change their meaning over history. On this thesis the task of the critic at any given historical moment is not so much to impose a new meaning upon, as to extract the new meaning from, the work of art. That works of art are semantically mobile in this way is to be explained not simply – to take the case of a literary work – by reference to linguistic change or to shifts in the meaning of words and idioms, but, more fundamentally, more radically, by appeal to the way in which every new work of art rewrites to some degree or other every related, or maybe every known, work of art in the same tradition. To this central contention the thesis adds the corollary that, as some particular meaning of a work of art becomes invalid or obsolete, it also becomes inaccessible: it ceases to be a possible object of knowledge.

Radical historicism is a doctrine, like the Whorfian thesis about the non-intertranslatability of nat-

ural languages, with which indeed it has much in common, that has its greatest appeal when it gets us to imagine something which on reflection turns out to be just what it asserts is unimaginable. So, for instance, under the influence of radical historicism (or so it seems) we start to imagine how a contemporary of Shakespeare's would find the inherited reading of Chaucer's *Troilus* dull or dead, and we find ourselves readily sympathizing with his preference for a new revitalized reading inspired by *Troilus and Cressida*. And then we reflect that, if radical historicism is indeed true, just such a comparison was not open to one of Shakespeare's contemporaries, and is even less so to us. To him only one term to the comparison was accessible: to us neither is.

2. A second objection to the retrieval view of criticism goes deeper in that it concentrates upon the view itself and not merely upon its consequences. According to this objection, retrieval is, from the critical point of view, on any given occasion either misleading or otiose. From the outset the objection contrasts retrieval with its own favoured view of criticism, which may be expressed as, Criticism is *scrutiny* – scrutiny of the literary text, of the musical score, of the painted surface – and it holds that retrieval is misleading when its results deviate from the findings of scrutiny and it is otiose when its results concur with the findings of scrutiny. In this latter case it is (note) retrieval that is reckoned otiose, not scrutiny, and the reason given is that reliance upon retrieval presupposes scrutiny but not *vice versa*. Scrutiny is presupposed because it is only with the findings of scrutiny also before us that we can be certain that we are dealing with a case where the results of retrieval merely reduplicate those of scrutiny, and hence that retrieval is not misleading. So, overall, retrieval can never do better than scrutiny, sometimes it can do worse, and which is the case cannot be determined without the benefit of scrutiny.

But how does this objection characterize the difference between the cases where retrieval does no worse than, and those where it does worse than, scrutiny? The cases are distinguished in that, given a work of art and the creative process that terminates on it, there are two possibilities. One is that the creative process realizes itself in the work of art: the other is that it fails to. Now it is in the latter case that retrieval is misleading, whereas in the former case it is merely otiose. In the former case, scrutiny will show the critic that the work is as retrieval laboriously allows him to infer that it is: in the latter case, retrieval will lead him to infer that the work is as scrutiny will soon reveal it not to be.

This objection to the retrieval view shows itself vulnerable on a number of counts.

In the first place, though it is indubitably true that the creative process either is or is not realized in the work of art, nevertheless, if "realized" means (as it presumably does) "fully realized", this is not, from the point of view of criticism, the best way of setting out the alternatives. For critically it is a highly relevant fact that the creative process may be realized in the work of art to varying degrees. (There are, indeed, theoretical reasons of some strength, which I shall not assess, for thinking that the creative process is never realized in a work of art either to degree 1 or to degree 0: realization must always be to some intermediate degree.) But, it might be thought, this presents no real problem. For the objection can surely concede that the creative process may be realized to varying degrees, and can then further concede that sometimes, even when the creative process has not been fully realized, retrieval may not be misleading. All that it has to insist upon, surely, is that, if the creative process may be harmlessly, though otiosely, reconstructed up to the point to which it was realized in the work of art, retrieval is misleading if, and as soon as, it is carried beyond this point. However, as we shall see, this concession brings its difficulties in train.

Secondly: Suppose we confine ourselves (as the objection says) to that part of the creative process which is realized in the work of art. It becomes clear that there is something that reconstruction of this part of the process can bring to light which scrutiny of the corresponding part of the work cannot. It can show that that part of the work which came about through design did indeed come about through design and not through accident or error. Scrutiny, which *ex hypothesi* limits itself to the outcome, cannot show this. (A parallel in the philosophy of action: If an action is intentional, then, it might be thought, reconstruction of the agent's mental process will not tell us more about it than we could learn from observation of the action: but we can learn this from observation of the action only if we already or independently know that the action is intentional.) Accordingly – and as yet the point can be made only hypothetically – if criticism is concerned to find out not just what the work of art is like but what the work is like by design, then,

contrary to what the objection asserts, scrutiny, to be a source of knowledge, must presuppose retrieval.

Thirdly: The objection, as emended, states that that part of the creative process which is not realized in the work of art is not to be reconstructed. But how is this part of the process to be identified? There are two distinct grounds on which the distinction could be effected, and they give different results. We could exclude from critical consideration any part of the creative process in which the work of art is not more or less directly prefigured: alternatively, we might exclude only that part of the creative process which has no bearing at all upon the character of the work. Two kinds of case show how crucial it is which way the distinction is effected. The first case is where the artist changes his mind. Rodin's *Monument to Balzac* started off as a nude sculpture. Is the critically relevant part of the creative process only that which includes Rodin's change of mind to, and his subsequent concentration upon, the draped Balzac: or should it also embrace his concentration upon, and his subsequent change of mind from, the naked Balzac? The second case is where an artist sticks to his intention but fails in it. In writing *The Idiot* Dostoievsky set out to portray a totally good man. Prince Myshkin is not a totally good man, but Dostoievsky's depiction of him is clearly not unaffected by the original aim: it is the failed depiction of a totally good man. Should we, or should we not, regard Dostoievsky's original aim, unsuccessfully realized though it is in the work of art, as a critically relevant part of the creative process?

In the light of the next, or fourth, point, the previous two points can be sharpened. For the objection, in claiming that scrutiny can establish everything that at one and the same time is critically relevant and can be established by retrieval, totally misconceives the nature of the interest that criticism might take in the creative process and, therefore, what it stands to gain from reconstructing it. For the objection appears to assume that, if the critic is interested in the creative process, this is because, or is to be accounted for by the degree to which, it provides him with good evidence for the character of the work. The critic seeks to infer from how the work was brought about how it is. Now, of course, if this were so, then there would, on the face of it at any rate, be reason to think that retrieval was at best a detour to a destination to which scrutiny could be a short cut. But that this is a misconception is revealed by the fact that the critic committed to retrieval is not committed to any assumptions about the likely degree of match between the creative process and the resultant work and he will continue to be interested in the creative process even in the case when he knows that there is a mismatch between the two. The critic who tries to reconstruct the creative process has a quite different aim from that which the objection to the retrieval view assumes. He does so in order to understand the work of art – though it would be wrong to say, as some philosophers of art tend to, that he seeks understanding rather than description. Understanding is reached through description, but through profound description, or description profounder than scrutiny can provide, and such description may be expected to include such issues as how much of the character of the work is by design, how much has come about through changes of intention, and what were the ambitions that went to its making but were not realized in the final product.

But, fifthly, and finally, the objection, in opposing scrutiny to retrieval presents scrutiny as though it were itself quite unproblematic: or as though, given a work of art, there would be no difficulty, or at any rate no theoretical difficulty, in dividing its properties into those which are accessible and those which are inaccessible to scrutiny. In considering the objection I have gone along with this, particularly in the second point I raise. However, in the main body of *Art and its Objects* I rejected this traditional assumption, though I preferred to make my point by considering specific properties that resisted the dichotomy. Here I shall consider the matter more directly.

Crucially the view that criticism is scrutiny is seriously under-defined until an answer is given to the question, Scrutiny by whom? The following cases illustrate the problem: The listener who is ignorant of the mission of Christ will miss much of the pathos in the St Matthew Passion: a viewer who has not gathered that Bernini's mature sculpture requires a frontal point of view, as opposed to the multiple viewpoint against which it reacted, will fail to discern the emotional immediacy it aims at: a reader's response to Hardy's "At Castle Boterel" will be modified when he learns that the poet's wife had just died, and then it will be modified again as he learns how unhappy the marriage had been: the spectator who is made aware that in the relevant panel of the S. Francesco altarpiece Sassetta uses to paint the cloak that the Saint discards, thereby renouncing his inheritance, the most expensive and most difficult pigment available will come to recognize a drama first in the gesture, then in the picture as a whole, of which he had been previously ignorant. With any form of perception – and scrutiny is a form of perception – what is perceptible is always dependent not only upon such physical factors as the nature of the stimulus, the state of the organism, and the prevailing local conditions, but also upon cognitive factors. Accordingly, the scrutiny view needs to be filled out by a definition of the person whose scrutiny is authoritative, or "the ideal critic", and any such definition must be partly in terms of the cognitive stock upon which the critic can draw. There are a number of possible definitions, for each of which the appeal of the scrutiny view, as well as its right to go by that name, will vary.

A heroic proposal, deriving from Kant, the aim of which is to ensure the democracy of art, is to define the ideal critic as one whose cognitive stock is empty, or who brings to bear upon the work of art zero knowledge, beliefs, and concepts. The proposal has, however, little to recommend it except its aim. It is all but impossible to put into practice, and, if it could be, it would lead to critical judgments that would be universally unacceptable.

Another proposal is to define the cognitive stock on which scrutiny is based as consisting solely of beliefs that could themselves have been derived – though in practice they may not have been derived – from scrutiny of the work of art concerned. But this takes us round in a circle: for what requirement is placed upon the cognitive stock on which the scrutiny that gives rise to these beliefs itself depends?

A third proposal is to define the cognitive stock on which the ideal critic is entitled to draw by reference not to its source of origin but to its function. Whether or not the beliefs have been derived, or could have been derived, from scrutiny is now reckoned immaterial, and the requirement is only that they should contribute to scrutiny. Now, it is true that most beliefs capable of modifying our perception of a work of art are beliefs that, given appropriate background beliefs, could have been derived from perception of the work – or, at any rate, of some other related work by the same artist. Nevertheless, there are some beliefs of this kind that could not have been, they need to be acquired independently, and the novelty of the present proposal is that it says that these too are available to the ideal critic. Examples of beliefs that could not be gleaned from, yet could contribute to, perception of works of art are the following: That Palladio believed that the ancient temple evolved from the ancient house and therefore thought temple fronts appropriate façades for private villas; that Mozart's favourite instruments were the clarinet and the viola; that Franz Hals was destitute and in a state of total dependence upon the Regents and Regentesses of the Old Men's Almshouses in Haarlem when he painted their two great group-portraits; that the Athenian Geometric vase-painters who introduced lions on to their pots could never have seen such an animal; and that Titian painted the altar piece of *St Peter Martyr* in competition with Pordenone and wanted to outdo him in dramatic gesture.

However, it is important to see that a shift has just occurred in the argument. It is not plausible to regard the new proposal as, like the first two, operating within the scope of the scrutiny view in that it imposes a substantive restriction upon the cognitive stock that the critic may draw upon in scrutiny. For that a belief on which criticism is based should be capable of modifying perception is a minimal condition if the resultant criticism is to count as scrutiny. Accordingly, we need another way of taking the proposal, and one that suggests itself is to see it as proposing scrutiny as a restriction upon retrieval. In other words, reconstruction of the creative process is admitted as the, or at least a, central task of criticism, but it must have a purpose in mind, and that purpose is that its findings should be put to use in scrutinizing the work. Retrieval is legitimate because, but only in so far as, through its findings it contributes to perception. [. . .]

3. A third objection to the retrieval view, which is open to adherents of both the revisionary view and the scrutiny view and also to others, is that it confuses the meaning of the work of art and the meaning of the artist, and it encourages the critic to pursue the second at the expense of the first. The distinction upon which this objection rests is initially not hard to grasp. Eliot has pointed out the mistake that Poe evidently made when he wrote "My most immemorial year", and in *Crome Yellow* Aldous Huxley describes a young poet who is inordinately satisfied with the line "Carminative as wine" until the next morning he looks up the first word in a dictionary. Neither poet meant what his words mean. But these are very simple cases, and problems arise as soon as we try to project the distinction into areas of interest.

The basic problem is this: In order to determine the meaning of a work of art we have first to determine what the meaning-bearing properties of the work are, and it is only on a very naïve view of the matter that we can do this without invoking the creative process itself and thus losing the clarity of the distinction which the simple cases promised. A typical naïve view would be one that equated the meaning-bearing properties of a poem with the ordered and aligned words, or the "text". I have argued that, if we take this view, absurd consequences follow even as far as the identity of poems is concerned, and something similar goes for similar views. Nevertheless to say that we have to invoke the creative process in order to fix the meaning-bearing properties of the work of art does not commit us to the view, already dismissed, that every work of art has every meaning-bearing property that the artist wished it to have. The retrieval view concedes that an artist may fail. The objection then misfires. The retrieval view has no difficulty in distinguishing − in principle, that is − between the meaning of the work of art and the meaning of the artist, and it identifies the former as the proper object of critical attention.

All objections apart, and I shall consider no more, the retrieval view invites, in one significant respect, clarification. For the arguments that I have been considering for and against the view that the creative process is the proper critical object bear a close resemblance to arguments advanced of recent years for and against the critical relevance of the artist's intentions. It, therefore, seems appropriate to ask, How are the creative process (as I have introduced it) and the artist's intention (as it figures in recent debate) related?

The creative process, as I envisage it, is a more inclusive phenomenon than the artist's intentions, and in two ways. In the first place, the creative process includes the various vicissitudes to which the artist's intentions are subject. Some of these will be themselves intentional − change of mind − but some will be chance or uncontrolled. Secondly, the creative process includes the many background beliefs, conventions, and modes of artistic production against which the artist forms his intentions: amongst these will be current aesthetic norms, innovations in the medium, rules of decorum, ideological or scientific world-pictures, current systems of symbolism or prosody, physiognomic conventions, and the state of the tradition.

A consequence follows which is of major importance for the process of retrieval. In recording an artist's intention the critic must state it from the artist's point of view or in terms to which the artist could give conscious or unconscious recognition. The critic must concur with the artist's intentionality. But the reconstruction of the creative process is not in general similarly restrained. The critic must certainly respect the artist's intentionality, but he does not have to concur with it. On the contrary he is justified in using both theory and hindsight unavailable to the artist if thereby he can arrive at an account of what the artist was doing that is maximally explanatory. Retrieval, like archaeology, and archaeology provides many of the metaphors in which retrieval is best thought about, is simultaneously an investigation into past reality and an exploitation of present resources. Anachronism arises not when the critic characterizes the past in terms of his own day, but only when in doing so he falsifies it. There is no anachronism involved in tracing the *Virgin and Child with St Anne* to Leonardo's Oedipal strivings, or in describing Adolf Loos as bridging the gap between C. F. A. Voysey and Le Corbusier – if, that is, both these statements are true. In the main text I have said that the constant possibility of reinterpretation is one of the sources of art's continuing interest for us, and I stand by this.

On a related point, however, I expressed myself obscurely, when I talked about the ineliminability of interpretation, and I should like to clarify this point. For any discussion of the issue ought to be prefaced – as that in the text was not – by a simple but all-important distinction between different ways in which interpretations of the same work of art may be related. They may be compatible: they may be incommensurable: they may be incompatible. The first kind of case presents no problem, the third is clearly unacceptable, so it is only the second that need detain us, though not the least of our problems is that of identifying such cases. Indeed, whether incommensurability is a real feature of sets of interpretations, or whether it is only an epistemic mirage induced by our inability to see just how the interpretations fit together, is a fundamental question. Ultimately it relates to the limits of our cognitive powers. In the present state of the problem the best that can be done for aesthetics is to point out that the very same difficulties break out in the domain of psychological explanation. We are given explanations of others in terms, on the one hand, of moral inadequacy, and, on the other hand, of early

experience, or, again, in terms of social roles and of self-interest, and our knowledge of human nature is such, and may always remain such, that we do not know how to accommodate these pairs of explanations or how to emphasize each member of the pair appropriately.

A question remains: Is a limit set to retrieval? Obviously where evidence is lacking, our understanding stops short. The 30,000 years or so of Palaeolithic art must remain ultimately a mystery to us, short of a landslide victory for archaeology. We shall probably never know the authentic rhythm or phrasing of medieval plainsong. But are there cases where both retrieval is impossible (or barely possible – for it must be conceded that, like the creative process itself, reconstruction of the creative process is realizable to varying degrees) and the explanation lies in a radical difference of perspective between the artist and us, the interpreters?

I suspect that there are, and an analogy gives us an insight into the situation. For an outward parallel to the reconstruction of the creative process is provided, at any rate in the case of the visual arts, by the physical restoration of the work of art. Admirers of French romanesque architecture, well aware that originally a great deal of the sculpture that adorns such buildings would have been brightly painted, are nevertheless likely, when confronted with attempts to restore it to its original condition – for instance, the historiated capitals at Issoire – to deplore the result. The heavy hand of the restorer is partly to blame, but not totally. For the modern spectator there seems to be no way of getting anything like the original colours to make anything like the intended impact upon him. We might restate the point in terms of the present discussion and say that he seems powerless to reconstruct the creative process in a way that at once meets the demands of internal coherence and seems naturally to terminate on the work before him. Maybe he can do so computationally but he cannot internalize the result, and the consequence is that here we may have reached the limits of retrieval.

In such an eventuality the restorer may resort to a compromise. He may hit on a colour scheme that is acceptable to our eyes and is functionally equivalent to the original scheme. Similarly a musicologist may orchestrate Monteverdi's madrigals for modern instruments and we may listen to them in a comfortable concert hall. Or a clever modern producer may present Antigone as a political drama about women's rights, or relate *The Merchant of Venice* to twentieth-century central European anti-Semitic rhetoric. Any such attempt will be to varying degrees anachronistic. Some of the great art of the past is accessible to us, some is not.

When it is accessible, we should, surely, wish to retrieve it. But when it is not, or when it is retrievable only to an inadequate degree, we may be wise to settle for a counterpart. Either way round, it is better that we know what we are doing.

35

The Postulated Author: Critical Monism as a Regulative Ideal

Alexander Nehamas

Il n'y a pas une parole qu'on puisse com-
prendre, si l'on va au fond.

—*Paul Valéry*

Critical pluralism, broadly stated, is the view that literary texts, unlike natural phenomena, for which there is only one correct explanation, can be given many equally acceptable, even though incompatible, interpretations. But the thesis that, in contrast to science, "the use . . . of diverse but complementary vantages [is] not only rationally justifiable, but necessary to the understanding of art, and indeed of any subject of humanistic inquiry" seems to me to make a virtue out of necessity and a necessity out of fact.[1]

Such a fact is that within sixty years of its publication, a fiction like Kafka's *Metamorphosis* had already provoked 148 studies, of an astonishing variety.[2] This fact has been transformed into a virtue by Stanley Corngold, who accounts for this flood of criticism by attributing it to the very point of the story and, ultimately, to the very nature of literature. Corngold interprets Samsa's change into what is an essentially vague, incomplete, and indescribable monster as an allegory for writing itself – an activity which, according to many recent literary theorists, is bound to result in imperfect communication, unavoidable misunderstanding, and inevitable misreading: "The negativity of the vermin has to be seen as rooted . . . in the literary

enterprise itself . . . The creature . . . is . . . language itself (*parole*) – a word broken loose from the context of language (*langage*), fallen into a void of meaning which it cannot signify, near others who cannot understand it" (*Commentator's Despair*, pp. 26, 27). If this is so, why should we be surprised that the story, like all literature, will not yield itself to a definitive interpretation?

But of course Corngold's view is reached through an interpretation which must be itself correct if it is to explain why there cannot be a correct interpretation of the story. And this paradox of method is parallel to a paradox of content. *The Metamorphosis*, on this view, concerns the inability of literature to achieve perfect communication and so to receive final interpretation. This is what the story communicates. But if it succeeds in communicating it, it communicates that it fails to communicate; and if it fails, since this failure is what it communicates, it succeeds!

The claim that literature can ultimately communicate only that it cannot ultimately communicate is not uncommon in recent literary theory.[3] I suspect that it is reached by illegitimately extending the thesis that words are polysemous or radically ambiguous. The extension is made by assuming that if a text has a property (if, in particular, a word is ambiguous), then it refers to that property (the word signifies ambiguity). Thus, for example, given the fact that the sentence "The green is

From *Critical Inquiry* 8 (1981), pp. 133–49. Reprinted by permission of the University of Chicago Press and Alexander Nehamas.

either" is ungrammatical, Jacques Derrida infers that "it signifies an example of ungrammaticality."[4] To offer another example, J. Hillis Miller assumes that the history of words is essential to their meaning and writes:

> The effect of etymological retracing is not to ground the word solidly but to render it unstable, equivocal, wavering, abysmal. All etymology is false etymology, both in the sense that there is always some bend or discontinuity in the etymological line, and in the sense that etymology always fails to find an *etymon*, a true literal meaning at the origin.[5]

If texts indeed consist of words so construed, it may seem to follow that "a text never has a single meaning, but is the crossroads of multiple ambiguous meanings"[6] and that therefore every text "is 'unreadable', if by 'readable' one means open to a single, definitive, univocal interpretation."[7] This raises two questions. The first, which I shall not try to answer here, is why we must assume that a word must have had an original literal use in order to be univocal now and why we need to accept the "Rousseauistic or Condillacian law that all words were originally metaphors."[8] The second, to which I shall pay close attention, is why we must agree that to be "readable," a text must have a definitive interpretation – if by "definitive" we mean "unrevisable." For though the absence of an unrevisable interpretation implies that we can change our mind about what a text means, it does not imply that what a text means changes along with our mind.

Deconstructive critics begin with the realization that written texts are enormously independent of their writers and then proceed to sever altogether, at least in theory, the connection between author and text. Since writing remains "when the author of the writing no longer answers for what he has written," Derrida argues, "the text is cut off from all absolute responsibility, from *consciousness* as the ultimate authority, orphaned and separated at birth."[9] Geoffrey Hartman traces the idea of recovering authors' intentions to the Renaissance, with its concern for establishing original texts, and argues that "the more learning and scholarship we bring to an author, with the aim of defining his difference or individual contribution, the less certainty there seems to be of succeeding in this." Hartman concludes that "the notion of unique works of art, certified by the personal name of the author, fades away into nostalgia."[10] Michel Fou-

cault goes even further and claims that the author is a fiction created, more or less, by Saint Jerome, now moribund and an object of indifference: "What matter who's talking?"[11] In a work otherwise unsympathetic to post-structuralism, Jonathan Culler accepts this view when he writes, "The meaning of a sentence, one might say, is not a form or an essence, present at the moment of its production and lying behind it as a truth to be recovered, but the series of developments to which it gives rise, as determined by past and future relations between words and the conventions of semiotic systems."[12] The object of criticism cannot therefore be what the author meant by a text but what a text means in itself. Since in itself a text means what its constituents have ever meant, and since (according to deconstruction) no constituent is univocal, the text turns out to be the "crossroads" of all of its constituents' incompatible senses.

This radical pluralism is thus grounded on a view about the nature of texts, some of the many meanings of which are exhibited, with equal plausibility, by different interpretations. But interpretations, too, are written texts, and they also need to but cannot be read. Just as every reading is a misreading, so it will be in turn misread. As Miller says,

> The new turn in criticism involves an interrogation of the notion of the self-enclosed literary work and of the idea that any work has a fixed, identifiable meaning. The literary work is seen in various ways as open and unpredictably productive. The reading of a poem is part of the poem. This reading is productive in its turn. It produces multiple interpretations, further language about the poem's language, in an interminable activity without necessary closure.[13]

But we, at least, have now been brought to the closure of the exposition which opened with our paradoxical reading of *The Metamorphosis*. According to this reading, writing cannot communicate; every text is misread since a reading is just an effort to impose a single coherent meaning on the text and thus presupposes that communication has succeeded. Itself an instance of this law, *The Metamorphosis* has generated a large number of readings; yet, "any reading can be shown to be a misreading on evidence drawn from the text itself."[14] Every reading will thus be replaced, and every new reading will be in turn misread, all circling continually around a nonexistent center, each an effort to isolate an imaginary "literal meaning at the origin," each a falcon without a falconer.

Appalled by the anarchy he takes this view to lead into, E. D. Hirsch has insisted that one of each text's many interpretations, the author's own, must be taken as canonical: "If the meaning of the text is not the author's, then no interpretation can possibly correspond to *the* meaning of a text, since the text can have no determinate or determinable meaning."[15] Behind this view lies a theory of meaning which is ultimately derived from the work of I. A. Richards, who wrote that

[the] logical use of words with constant senses that are the same for each occurrence ... is an extremely artificial sort of behavior.... And the fluidity, the incessant delicate variation of the meaning of our words ... is the virtue of language for our other purposes. [It is not true] that if a passage means one thing it cannot mean another and an incompatible thing.[16]

Hirsch maintains his monism in the light of, or perhaps despite, his theory about the meaning of texts: "The nature of the text is to have no meaning except that which an interpreter wills into existence.... A text [is] only an occasion for meaning, in itself an ambiguous form devoid of the consciousness where meaning abides."[17]

To this view, which bears important similarities to the approach of Hirsch's opponents, one can make, with the King in *Alice in Wonderland*, an easy reply: "If there's no meaning in it ... that saves a lot of trouble, you know, as we needn't try to find any." But the witticism and its wording only serve to raise the crucial question: Is a text's meaning found, or is it made? Both sides initially agree that meaning is made, that a text means just what it is taken to mean by its interpreters.[18] Deconstruction infers that critics should therefore do self-consciously what they do in any case, which is to make their own meaning out of every text. Hirsch, by contrast, claims that critics ought now to go on to discover the meaning which a text was made to have by its author.

There is a large gap between the monism advocated by Hirsch and the radical pluralism which follows from the writing of some deconstructive critics. Within this gap are located some recent writers who argue that the meaning of a text is partly found and partly made. This argument is the basis for the limited pluralism of M. H. Abrams, Peter Jones, and Jack Meiland, according to which the "rules of the language" to which a text belongs determine a fundamental level of meaning, independent of all points of view, given to and found by the interpreter.[19] But just as the locutionary content of a sentence does not by itself determine what illocution that sentence is being used to perform in a particular case, so this "central core," though it limits the legitimate overall interpretations of a text, does not exhaust its meaning. Meiland, for example, calls this fundamental level the "textual meaning" and distinguishes it from the "literary meaning," over which critical disagreement occurs. He writes that "the agreed-upon textual meaning can serve as a criterion of validity for interpretations at the level of literary meaning. ... Any literary interpretation which does not cohere with basic agreed-upon textual meaning can be ruled out as an invalid interpretation" ("Interpretation," p. 36).

The central difficulty with this view is that, in my opinion, it simply tends to reify whatever it is that a text's interpreters do and do not, at some particular time, agree about. Textually, Meiland writes, "*Romeo and Juliet* is about a man and a woman who are in love with one another, whose families prevent their marrying, and who die due to a tragic misunderstanding" ("Interpretation," p. 35). But is this obvious because it is determined solely by the rules of English, or is it because it constitutes such a minimal interpretation, chosen just because the critics of the text are likely to agree about it?[20]

The existence of a well-defined notion of literal or dictionary meaning which can be of use to this view is itself problematic. Do dictionaries give us what words must essentially mean in all their uses, or do they simply supply us with a rough guess, a coarse grid against which, but not necessarily within which, to locate individual words and phrases? Whatever the answer to this question, even if we assume that the notion of a word's literal meaning is well defined, the difficulties of this theory are far from over. The main problem is that it is not possible to identify "textual meaning" with the literal meaning of the words of which a text consists. The words' literal meaning is specified through a set of roughly synonymous words supplied by the dictionary. But the textual meaning is a summary or paraphrase, that is, an interpretation (however minimal) of what these words, *given their literal meaning*, are being used to do on this particular occasion.

If textual meaning is a minimal interpretation of a text, then it is not surprising that it is compatible with a number of "literary" meanings, since these now turn out to be more specific interpretations of the text. For it is clear that a number of more particular specifications of any object are compatible with a more general specification of that object, even if they conflict with one another. Something can be an item of furniture and also a chair, a chaise, or a sofa; it can be any of these and also Louis XVI, Empire, or Directory style. None of this shows that it *is* all of these things. Similarly, though the textual meaning of *Romeo and Juliet* fails to determine a single overall reading of the play, this does not show that the play does have the many literary meanings that have been attributed to it. Compatibility with textual meaning is at best a necessary condition for validity, but this trivial fact offers no support for any sort of pluralism.

Such compatibility is *at best* necessary for validity because in fact we can both disagree about and revise our views of textual meaning. The object we were just imagining may turn out not to be an item of furniture at all but a strange machine; just so, we may revise our minimal interpretation of *Romeo and Juliet*. Though we are likely to agree about textual meaning, we cannot take this agreement for granted; textual meaning depends on substantive as well as on linguistic considerations. Are Romeo and Juliet, for example, a man and a woman or a boy and a girl? But more importantly, in many cases where our minimal and more specific interpretations are in conflict, we may choose to modify the former rather than to reject the latter. Our construal of Romeo's scream, "The time and my intent is savage-wild/More fierce and inexorable far/Than empty tigers and the roaring sea" has serious consequences for the nature of the misunderstanding which leads to his death.

But if textual meaning is not given, if it is also, like literary meaning, the product of revisable interpretation, have we not granted deconstruction all that it wanted in the first place?[21] Derrida is describing a view not unlike Meiland's when he writes that "the concept of a centered structure is in fact the concept of a free-play based on a fundamental ground, a freeplay which is constituted upon a fundamental immobility and a reassuring certitude, which is itself beyond the reach of the free-play.[22] The "center" is for Derrida the obvi-

ous or intuitive reading of a text, Meiland's textual meaning. Derrida argues that even the most obvious reading is the result of interpretation and can therefore be questioned, revised, or displaced.[23]

This is, I think, correct. Just as in scientific explanation there are no data immune to revision, so in literary criticism there are no readings impervious to question. But the fact about science does not show that apparently competing scientific theories are incommensurable and that therefore we cannot judge between them or that each such theory concerns its own distinct world.[24] Similarly, the point about criticism does not show that different interpretations of a text are, even if apparently incompatible, equally acceptable or that a text has as many meanings as there are interpretations of it. Readings are neither arbitrary nor self-validating simply because they are all subject to revision. Newer readings are always guided by the strengths and weaknesses of those which already exist; and though this process may never stop, it is not for that very reason blind.

Jones has tried to supply stronger support for the pluralist thesis. He claims that interpretation, "the business of making sense of the text, of rendering it coherent," is necessarily "aspectival"; he understands aspect as both "the point of view from which something is seen, and the appearance or face of the object perused" (*Philosophy and the Novel*, pp. 182, 181). His conclusion is that since every interpretation involves a viewpoint, and since no viewpoint (biographical, Marxist, psychoanalytical, etc.) is privileged, different readings of a text, even if apparently incompatible, can be equally acceptable.

Now consider the following case. In *The Metamorphosis*, there is a picture of a woman on the wall of Samsa's bedroom. A number of widely diverse readings of the story all take the picture as an object of Samsa's sexual interest. This unexciting fact is sufficient to show that though the activity of interpretation can proceed from different viewpoints, its results need not therefore be themselves different. Nor is it easy to show that if the results of different approaches are indeed different, then they are equally plausible. For we can, I think, produce a better (not simply a different) interpretation of the role this picture plays in Kafka's story. The text speaks of a glossy-magazine picture of "a lady done up in a fur hat and a fur boa, sitting upright and raising against the viewer a heavy fur muff in which her whole forearm has disappeared." Now Heinz Politzer describes this picture as "vulgar ...

animallike"; Robert Adams thinks that it is of an "impudent salacity"; Hellmuth Kaiser claims that it portrays an "erotically active, aggressive woman"; and Peter Dow Webster takes this woman as an "earth-mother."[25] These descriptions do not correspond to anything in the text, but once they are casually introduced, they tend to become, for some, parts of the story itself, and the picture thus acquires an erotic content. It is a short step from this to finding sexual significance in the insect's covering the picture with his body in order to protect it from being taken from his room along with the rest of his furniture. But what we do know about the picture is that it comes from a magazine and that it is of no one in particular (which accounts, incidentally, for its sketchy description). It is an object of no character and no individuality. If anything about it is interesting, it is that while it seems to be a picture of no interest, Gregor has made a frame for it himself: this is the only productive work we know him to have done, the only thing he has actually made. What he is protecting from being taken away, by assuming a position dictated to him more by his anatomy than by his desires, is his only real creation, his only real possession. That his most expressive action has been devoted to framing and bringing into prominence an object which is not so vulgar as it is banal underscores the shallowness of Gregor's relationship to the world and the depth of his attachment to that shallowness.

Interpretation is therefore in one sense aspectival, but criticism is not for this reason less than "objective." Different *ways* of trying to understand a text may well be equally legitimate: there probably isn't a general argument to the effect that psychoanalytic criticism, for example, should not be practiced. But simply because an activity can be pursued in different ways, it does not follow that different results must be reached; nor that if they are, then they must be equally plausible.

Jones draws this stronger conclusion when he slips into considering interpretation no longer as an activity but as that activity's very product: "The background against which, or the viewpoint from which, we interpret a text generally provides the most interesting differences between interpretations, between the patterns of coherence different critics determine" (*Philosophy and the Novel*, p. 186). Just as "aspect" covered both viewpoints and what is seen from them, so "interpretation" covers both the "business" of finding a pattern of coherence in a text and that pattern itself. Yet

though it is necessarily true that to peruse an object we must (geometrically, so to speak) do so through one of its appearances, faces, or aspects, what we peruse is not the appearance but the object. We cannot simply appeal to the different methods critics use in order to justify their different readings, though we sometimes think we can because we take what is true of the process of interpretation to be true of its product.

We are concerned with a pluralism of contents, not of modes or methods, with the view that the results of different approaches to a text, even if apparently incompatible, can be equally plausible parts or aspects of what the text means.[26] This would be, for example, the view that Gregor's metamorphosis stands as much for his alienation from a world of unproductive labor as for his regression to the anal stage because of an unresolved Oedipal conflict. Both views, so stated, seem plausible, and so does the pluralist position which tries to account for this appearance. But if we look at the texture of these interpretations, their plausibility ceases to be striking. The psychoanalytic reading, for example, must construe Gregor's father's kicking the vermin when it is stuck in a doorway as an act of pure aggression; Gregor, by contrast, and quite correctly, sees it as his "salvation." The Marxist reading fails to account for the effect his sister's music has on Gregor just before his death. Interesting difficulties facing interpretation are usually found on this specific level; we often grant a particular reading plausibility by not looking enough at its details.[27]

Actually, the proliferation of difficulties on this specific level may make it seem again as though the deconstructive view that every reading is a misreading is correct. And, in a way, it is, since every reading can be confronted with contrary evidence. But the absence of a reading which cannot be improved, which accounts for every feature, does not make a text "unreadable": it only indicates that there is more to understand. There is no definite description, explanation, or theory of anything. And though replacement may not proceed from worse to better in every individual case, it tends on the whole to preserve good readings in order to supplant them with others that are better.

This implies that we understand *The Metamorphosis* better today than it was understood in the past and that we will come to understand it better in the future. And though no aspect of our understanding of the story is given, we can on each occasion agree on the significance of some of its elements in a way which allows us to compare and evaluate, even if only tentatively, alternative readings.[28] This is not obvious as long as we try to compare in general terms a Marxist, say, and a psychoanalytic reading of *The Metamorphosis*: on this level, to ask "Which is better?" is to ask a silly question. But the point begins to appear if we turn to the specific, if less exciting, issues which we have been discussing here.

Miller writes, correctly, that "the 'obvious or univocal reading' of a [text] is not identical to the [text] itself"[29] – no reading ever is. Readings, interpretations, do not re-create or duplicate a text's meaning, they describe it.[30] To understand a text at all is to have an interpretation of it, and it is only in the light of one interpretation that we come to see, if and when we do, that a text can be read differently, that another interpretation is better. Thus from the point of view of a particular reading, the meaning which a later interpretation will attribute to a text does not exist. Nevertheless, the later interpretation does not, in absolute terms, create that meaning: it finds a meaning which, from its own point of view, had always been there. This is so, of course, only from its own point of view. But we cannot coherently describe this as "only a point of view" unless we produce yet another interpretation attributing to the text yet another meaning from yet another point of view (to be specified as such only by means of a further interpretation).

Meaning does not therefore reside in texts independently of all interpretation, there to be discovered once and for all or, if we are not lucky, to be forever lost; but this is not to say that it is fabricated. The critical monism which I advocate is a regulative ideal and identifies the meaning of a text with whatever is specified by that text's ideal interpretation. Such an interpretation would account for all of the text's features, though we can never reach it since it is unlikely that we can even understand what it is to speak of "all the features" of anything. What we do have (and that is what we need) is the notion of one interpretation answering more questions about a text than another and thus being closer to that hypothetical ideal which would answer all questions. The direction in which this ideal lies may change as new interpretations reveal features of a text previously unnoticed, rearrange the significance of those already accounted for, or even cause us to change some of our general critical canons. And though, in this way, there may not be a single ideal interpretation of a text toward which all of our actual interpretations in fact lead,

the transition from one interpretation to another can still be rational and justified. To interpret a text is to place it in a context which accounts for as many of its features as possible; but which features to account for, which are more significant than others, is itself a question conditioned by those interpretations of the text which already exist.[31]

To interpret a text is to place it in a context, and this is to construe it as someone's production, directed at certain purposes. A purpose is neither the end toward which motives aim, nor a text's "perlocutionary" effects, nor again a message lying behind the surface.[32] Meaning is a symbolic relation, and what an object symbolizes depends partly on which of many systems it can be construed as an element of.[33] At least the choice of symbol system is an intentional act, and to appeal to intention is to appeal to a particular explanation of why a text, or one of its features, is as it is. The picture of the woman is used in *The Metamorphosis* to show the banality of Gregor's life. This account is intentional in that it is teleological. But it is not thereby vulnerable to those sound arguments against appealing to intention construed as "design or plan in the author's mind" or as the efficient cause of that feature.[34]

To interpret a text is to consider it as its author's production.[35] Literary texts are produced by agents and must be understood as such. This seems to me self-evident; even deconstructive criticism generally accepts it, though it insists that the choice of agent is conventional and arbitrary. And since texts are products of expressive actions, understanding them is inseparably tied to understanding their agents. But just as the author is not identical with a text's fictional narrator, so he is also distinct from its historical writer. The author is postulated as the agent whose actions account for the text's features; he is a character, a hypothesis which is accepted provisionally, guides interpretation, and is in turn modified in its light. The author, unlike the writer, is not a text's efficient cause but, so to speak, its formal cause, manifested in thought not identical with it.[36]

A methodological constraint on this view is that the postulated author be historically plausible; the principle is that a text does not mean what its writer could not, historically, have meant by it. For example, we cannot attribute to particular words meanings which they came to have only after the writer's death.[37] What a writer could mean can be determined by linguistic or biographical considerations but also by facts about the history of literature and the world, psychology, anthropology, and much else besides, a change in our understanding of any of which can cause us to change our understanding of the text.

Meaning therefore depends on an author's intentions even if a writer is not aware of it. Since the author's intentions depend on what the writer could have meant, a text's meaning is to that extent a thing of the past, though its understanding is itself a thing of the future. Without Freud we would not have seen the sexual elements which are now part and parcel of *Oedipus Rex*. But if the Oedipal conflict is as basic to behavior as Freud thought, then the historical Sophocles, unaware of it as he may have been, could have considered it an issue. And we can argue from this that the character Sophocles, the play's author, did consider it an issue; it is then part of the play's meaning even if we could not have realized it until this century.

We must not, by contrast, accept a view of *The Metamorphosis* which holds that hours on the clock correspond to years in Gregor's life and that he

> should have caught the five o'clock train for work, that is, a psychic change should have occurred at the normal age of five, . . . [that is,] the formation of the superego. . . . But here it is, already six-thirty (Gregor is six and a half years old); he has missed the train or psychic energy necessary for progression.[38]

Kafka could not have known this highly technical, and highly doubtful, theory of development. Even if the theory were true, it simply lacks the power and generality of the Oedipal conflict which might convince us that Kafka could have come by it on his own and that it therefore belongs to the story.

The principle of the postulated author is not sheer invention. We can find it reflected in the practice of a critic like Quentin Skinner, who refuses to read some seventeenth-century legal texts as concerned with the doctrine of the judicial review of statute because the concept of judicial review did not arise until the next century.[39] Adams, to cite a clearly literary case, interprets the number three in *The Metamorphosis* as a symbol for masculinity, on the grounds that "Kafka might have learned of the association through any of several channels" though there is no evidence that he did.[40] Finally, Miller supports his view that Stevens' rock, in the poem of that title, stands for literal language partly because "Stevens might even have known (why should he not have known?) the world 'curiologic' . . . [from the] Greek *kuriologia*, the use of literal expressions."[41]

Now in one sense there is something arbitrary about constructing a historically plausible figure as a text's author. In principle we could always construct a different context and a different author and so give an unhistorical reading. This is not unlike the arbitrariness of our interpreting representational paintings as projections of familiar Euclidean space, since any two-dimensional figure can be construed as the projection of indefinitely many alternative worlds. Just as the effort to construct such worlds could be worth making, we could always try to read a text differently, postulating a different author and progressively refining our conception as new readings come to affect those from which they emerged. Progress in this direction would show a text to be, in a genuine and valuable sense, polysemous. But what we actually find in criticism is a number of self-consciously partial alternatives, directed only at some of the text's features in the expectation that many more partial, non-competing readings will emerge. This can no more support the view that each text, as a whole, has many meanings than can the claim that, given any interpretation of a text, a different one could always be constructed. What we need in both cases is an actual reading at least as general and powerful as the reading whose uniqueness is being questioned and with which it is incompatible.[42]

The monism I have presented is not threatened by the existence of many partial readings of a text since it can exploit discoveries made through such readings in pursuing a more complete understanding of the text. Methodological pluralism is compatible with a monism of content. The regulative end is to construct, for each text, a complete historically plausible author – a character who may not coincide with the actual writer's self-understanding, fragmentary and incomplete as it probably is. What a writer takes a text to mean is relevant but not telling evidence in literary criticism. Further, our construction will never be complete: in constructing the author of *The Metamorphosis*, we shall have to consider his close relation, perhaps his identity, with the author of *The Castle*, whose precursor is Kierkegaard (another character who may appear different through this connection) and who is in turn the precursor of Jorge Luis Borges and other future authors. Changes in literature and in everything that is relevant to it (in everything, that is) will change the constraints imposed upon the postulated author. And there is no reason to think that we shall ever abandon this construction, except perhaps that our interest may one day be exhausted.

Critical pluralists sometimes argue as Jones does that all interpretations are necessarily partial, that criticism "is always ... of a selection of properties" (*Philosophy and the Novel*, p. 193). If different critics were in fact necessarily concerned with different textual features, it might follow that different readings, being nonoverlapping, were equally acceptable.[43] But this is no more true than the claim, often made in this connection, that to see a feature differently is to see a different feature.[44] Like all theorizing, interpretation is based on some features of a text but is of the text as a whole. It is therefore partial only in the trivial sense that no reading can ever account for all of a text's features, not because distinct readings are directed at distinct features. Being partial in this sense means simply that there is no final, unrevisable interpretation of any text; but then why should we want such a reading?

The aim of interpretation is to capture the past in the future: to capture – not to recapture – first, because the iterative prefix suggests that meaning, which was once manifest, must now be found again. But the postulated author dispenses with this assumption. Literary texts are produced by very complicated actions, while the significance of even our simplest acts is often far from clear. Parts of the meaning of a text may become clear only because of developments occurring long after its composition. And though the fact that an author means something may be equivalent to the fact that a writer could have meant it, this is not to say that the writer did, on whatever level, actually mean it.

Second, the notion of recapturing the past suggests the repetition of an earlier act of consciousness and generates the hermeneutic problem of how we can put ourselves in the position of another epoch or culture, how we can see the world as they saw it, "from within."[45] Skirting most of the issues, I will simply deny that the aim of criticism is to re-create the original understanding of a text – particularly if by this we mean the experience of an original audience. It is quite true that we can never recreate the experience of the original audience of, say, *The Clouds*. It is not even clear whose experience we should pursue: the common experience of all the spectators of the comedy's first performance? that of an "average" member? the experience of Socrates or of Anytus? It is equally true that we

cannot hope to re-create even our contemporaries' experience of a text. And if it is claimed that my experience of *The Clouds* is more similar to yours than it is to Anytus', I will agree only if you can show that our interpretations are more similar. But if this is how we construe "understanding," then capturing the Athenians' understanding of *The Clouds* presents no theoretical difficulties. We must find what they thought, said, and wrote about it. This is in principle public information whose loss, even if it is final, poses no logical or hermeneutical problems.[46]

Still, criticism does not aim to capture what a text's original audience actually took it to mean but to find what the text means. We want to develop an interpretation which will be consistent with what we know about a text's language, its writer, its original audience, its genre, the possibilities of writing, history, psychology, anthropology, and much else. What a text means is what it could mean to its writer. But this is not what it did mean to the writer and to the text's original audience, nor need they have been able to understand it given only the articulated knowledge of human affairs which they then had. The meaning of a text, like the significance of an action, may take forever to become manifest.

Some critics believe that many texts, or parts of texts, have been correctly interpreted once and for all.[47] This, I have tried to suggest, is unlikely. Others, fearing perhaps that a final interpretation will make the text itself dispensable, deny this possibility on the grounds that all texts are essentially ambiguous and thus always open to new readings.[48] I have tried to show that we do not need to accept this latter view in order to justify what is, after all, the most basic consequence of the openendedness of all knowledge.

As I stated earlier, though texts belong to the past, their understanding belongs to the future. To do just what I have said we shouldn't, let me quote, quite out of context, Sidney's "The poet ... doth grow in effect another nature." Consider this nature not as the world the text represents but as the text itself. Each text is to our many interpretations what nature is to our many theories, and each is inexhaustible. Understanding a text is, in two ways, a historical enterprise: not only does it employ history but it also unfolds in time and depends on everything we now do and will come to know about the world, which includes ourselves. Understanding a text is as easy, or as difficult, as that. In interpreting a text we must come to understand an action, and so we must understand an agent and therefore other actions and other agents as well and what they took for granted, what they meant, believed, and what they wanted. For this reason, each text is inexhaustible: its context is the world.

Notes

1 M. H. Abrams, "A Note on Wittgenstein and Literary Criticism," *English Literary History* 41 (Winter 1974): 552.

2 These studies are listed and discussed in Stanley Corngold, *The Commentator's Despair: The Interpretation of Kafka's "Metamorphosis"* (Port Washington, NY, and London, 1973); all further references to this work will be included in the text. Many more interpretations of the story have, of course, been offered since.

3 Jacques Derrida, for example, forcefully defends this view in *Speech and Phenomena* (Evanston, Ill., 1973); *Of Grammatology* (Baltimore, 1974); and *Writing and Difference* (Chicago, 1976). See also *La Dissémination* (Paris, 1972).

4 Derrida, "Signature Event Context," *Glyph*, 1 (1977): 185. See also J. Hillis Miller, "The Critic as Host," in *Deconstruction and Criticism*, ed. Harold Bloom et al. (New York, 1979), p. 225. In another, brilliant essay, Miller relies heavily on the principle that if an artwork employs certain conventions, then it is also about those conventions ("The Fiction of Realism: *Sketches by Boz, Oliver Twist*, and Cruickshank's Illustrations," in *Dickens Centennial Essays*, ed. Ada Nisbet and Blake Nevius [Berkeley, 1971], pp. 85–153).

5 Miller, "Ariadne's Thread: Repetition and the Narrative Line," *Critical Inquiry* 3 (Autumn 1976): 70. See also "Critic as Host," pp. 218–20.

6 Miller, "Tradition and Difference," *Diacritics* 2 (1972): 12.

7 Miller, "Critic as Host," p. 226. See also Paul de Man, "Nietzsche's Theory of Rhetoric," *Symposium* 28 (Spring 1974): 44, and Geoffrey Hartman, "Literary Criticism and Its Discontents," *Critical Inquiry* 3 (Winter 1976): 205.

8 Miller, "Ariadne's Thread," p. 70; cf. "Tradition and Difference," p. 11. The same claim has been made at length by Derrida, "White Mythology: Metaphor in the Text of Philosophy," *New Literary History*, 6 (Autumn 1974): 5–74. For a criticism of this view, as exhibited in the early work of Nietzsche, see Arthur Danto, *Nietzsche as Philosopher* (New York, 1965), pp. 37–47.

9 Derrida, "Signature Event Context," p. 181.

10 Hartman, "Criticism and Its Discontents," pp. 204–5; all further references to this essay will be included in the text.

11 Michel Foucault, "What Is an Author?" *Language, Counter-Memory, Practice*, ed. Donald F. Bouchard, trans. Bouchard and Sherry Simon (Ithaca, NY, 1977), pp. 113–38.

12 Jonathan Culler, *Structuralist Poetics* (Ithaca, NY, 1975), p. 132. This view, as I suggest below, ultimately derives from New Criticism; see n. 16 below.

13 Miller, "Stevens' Rock and Criticism as Cure, II," *Georgia Review* 30 (Summer 1976): 333.

14 Ibid.

15 E. D. Hirsch, *Validity in Interpretation* (New Haven, Conn., 1967), p. 5. On the prescriptive nature of Hirsch's view, see Jack Meiland, "Interpretation as a Cognitive Discipline," *Philosophy and Literature* 2 (Spring 1978): 24–8.

16 I. A. Richards, *Interpretation in Teaching* (New York, 1938), p. 256. New Criticism assumed that "words ... include at least potentially, within their appearance in a given setting, (all) the meanings they have had ... in previous contexts" (Richard Strier, "The Poetics of Surrender: An Exposition and Critique of New Critical Poetics," *Critical Inquiry* 2 [Autumn 1975]: 173–4). Monroe Beardsley accepts this principle in *The Possibility of Criticism* (Detroit, 1970), pp. 19–20. If so, however, what reason is there to think that the changing meanings of the words of a text will be subject to a single univocal interpretation, as Beardsley believes? It is this monism which deconstruction has abandoned in its claim that words actually possess, in every appearance, all the meanings they have ever had, that every passage does mean "another and an incompatible thing."

17 Hirsch, "Three Dimensions of Hermeneutics," *New Literary History* 3 (Winter 1972): 246. Despite some evidence to the contrary (e.g., p. 256), Hirsch generally seems to accept this radical thesis of textual indeterminacy. For considerations weighing against this thesis, see Meiland, "Interpretation" (n. 15 above), pp. 32–3, and Beardsley, *Possibility of Criticism*, pp. 24–6.

18 See Hirsch, "Three Dimensions of Hermeneutics," p. 247: "If an ancient text has been interpreted as a Christian allegory, that is unanswerable proof that it can be so interpreted." But is this proof that the text has been *legitimately* so interpreted? Hirsch seems to presuppose that *in some sense* such a reading is accurate to the text; but this seems to beg the question at issue.

19 See Abrams, "Note on Wittgenstein"; "Rationality and Imagination in Cultural History: A Reply to Wayne Booth," *Critical Inquiry* 2 (Spring 1976): 447–64, esp. 457; "What's the Use of Theorizing about the Arts?" in *In Search of Literary History*, ed. Morton Bloomfield (Ithaca, NY, 1972), pp. 3–54, and "The Deconstructive Angel," *Critical Inquiry* 3 (Spring 1977): 425–38; Peter Jones, *Philosophy and the Novel* (Oxford, 1975), ch. 5, esp. pp. 182–3; all

further references to this book will be included in the text; Meiland, "Interpretation," esp. pp. 29–31 and 35–7; all further references to this essay will be included in the text. See also Quentin Skinner, "Motives, Intentions, and the Interpretation of Texts," *New Literary History* 3 (Winter 1972): 393–408.

20 Meiland is, in any case, correct that such agreement as does exist is a sufficient objection to Hirsch's thesis of the radical indeterminacy of textual meaning.

21 Meiland is clear on the dependence of textual meaning upon interpretation (see "Interpretation," p. 36), but he thinks that it results simply from the interpretation of physical marks as words and thus attributes to it a privileged status.

22 Derrida, "Structure, Sign, and Play in the Discourse of the Human Sciences," in *The Structuralist Controversy*, ed. Richard Macksey and Eugenio Donato (Baltimore, 1970), p. 248; rpt. in *Writing and Difference*, pp. 278–93. Cf. Miller, "Critic as Host," p. 218: "Is the 'obvious' reading, though, so 'obvious' or even so 'univocal'? ... Is not the obvious reading perhaps equivocal rather than univocal, most equivocal in its intimate familiarity and in its ability to have got itself taken for granted as 'obvious' and single-voiced?"

23 See Culler, *Structuralist Poetics*, pp. 244–5, for an elaboration of Derrida's position. The view that no part of the meaning of a text is given, which I have been supporting, bears close affinities to the approach of Stanley Fish. See, for example, "Interpreting the *Variorum*" (*Critical Inquiry* 2 [Spring 1976]: 473), where Fish attacks "the assumption that there *is* a sense, that is embedded or encoded in the text, and that can be taken in at a single glance." I diverge from Fish in his inferring that meaning cannot be located in the text but in its readers' experiences. See also his "Literature in the Reader: Affective Stylistics," *Self-Consuming Artifacts: The Experience of Seventeenth-Century Literature* (Berkeley, 1972), pp. 382–427.

24 On this point, see Hilary Putnam, "Meaning and Reference," in *Naming, Necessity, and Natural Kinds*, ed. Stephen Schwartz (Ithaca, NY, 1977), pp. 119–32, and "The Meaning of 'Meaning,'" *Mind, Language, and Reality* (Cambridge, 1975), pp. 215–72. For a different argument to this conclusion, see Larry Laudan, *Progress and Its Problems* (Berkeley, 1977), p. 141 ff.

25 Heinz Politzer, *Franz Kafka: Parable and Paradox* (Ithaca, NY, 1966), p. 72; Robert M. Adams, *Strains of Discord: Studies in Literary Openness* (Ithaca, NY, 1958), p. 152; Hellmuth Kaiser, "Kafka's Fantasy of Punishment," Peter Dow Webster, "Franz Kafka's 'Metamorphosis' as Death and Resurrection Fantasy," and Corngold, "Metamorphosis of the Metaphor," in *The Metamorphosis*, trans. and ed.

Corngold (New York, 1972), pp. 153, 158, and 11, respectively. I quote from Corngold's translation.

26 Wayne Booth deals with issues generated by methodological pluralism in *Critical Understanding* (Chicago, 1979), but his discussion, especially pp. 284–301, extends to pluralism of contents.

27 For the Marxist argument, see Bluma Goldstein, "Bachelors and Work: Social and Economic Conditions in 'The Judgment,' 'The Metamorphosis' and *The Trial*," in *The Kafka Debate*, ed. Angel Flores (New York, 1977), pp. 147–75 and 3–5. For the Freudian view, see Kaiser, "Kafka's Fantasy of Punishment," esp. p. 152.

28 Monroe Beardsley makes a similar point in his review of Booth's *Critical Understanding* in *Philosophy and Literature* 4 (Fall 1980): 257–65.

29 Miller, "Critic as Host," p. 224.

30 Stanley Cavell provides an excellent discussion of this issue in "Aesthetic Problems of Modern Philosophy," *Must We Mean What We Say?* (New York, 1969), p. 74 ff.

31 Putnam discusses such a view in relation to the philosophy of science and epistemology in "Realism and Reason," *Meaning and the Moral Sciences* (London, 1978), pp. 123–40.

32 The first view is held by Skinner, "Motives," pp. 401–2. For the perlocution view, see Meiland, "Interpretation," p. 39 ff, and Skinner, "Motives," p. 403. For the meaning-as-message view, see, e.g., Richard Kuhns, "Criticism and the Problem of Intention," *Journal of Philosophy* 57 (January 1960): for Kuhns, interpretation is the activity of "getting at the message which may go beyond the plain literal sense" (p. 7). The notion of meaning as message has recently been criticized by Wolfgang Iser in *The Act of Reading* (Baltimore, 1978), though he seems to me to conclude too quickly that meaning is "imagistic in character" (p. 8).

33 This is one of the central theses in Nelson Goodman's *Languages of Art* (Indianapolis, 1968), though Goodman avoids any discussion of intention.

34 See W. K. Wimsatt, Jr., and Beardsley, "The Intentional Fallacy," in Wimsatt, *The Verbal Icon* (Lexington, Ky., 1954), for the source of most of those arguments. Cavell ("A Matter of Meaning It," *Must We Mean What We Say?*, pp. 234–7) disagrees with Beardsley but offers a different account of intention.

35 This position may seem to transgress against the original New Criticism, structuralism (e.g., Roland Barthes, *Sur Racine* [Paris, 1963]), more recent theory sympathetic to the New Critics (e.g., John Ellis, *The Theory of Literary Criticism: A Logical Analysis* [Berkeley, 1974]), deconstruction, and approaches to interpretation via the activity of reading (e.g., Iser, *The Act of Reading*, and Fish, "Literature in the Reader" [n. 23 above]).

36 My postulated author is not unrelated to Booth's "implied author," to whom he appeals both in

Critical Understanding and in *The Rhetoric of Fiction* (Chicago, 1961), and to Kendall Walton's "apparent artist," discussed in his "Style and the Products and Processes of Art," in *The Concept of Style*, ed. Berel Lang (Philadelphia, 1979), pp. 45–66. I discuss this issue in more detail in another paper, "What an Author Is" (to be presented at the MLA convention, December 1981).

37 Beardsley argues that we can attribute such meanings to texts; see *Possibility of Criticism*, p. 19.

38 Webster, " 'Metamorphosis' as Death and Resurrection Fantasy" (n. 25 above), pp. 161–2.

39 Skinner, "Motives," pp. 406–7 and n. 41.

40 Adams, *Strains of Discord* (n. 25 above), p. 173.

41 Miller, "Stevens' Rock and Criticism as Cure," *Georgia Review* 30 (Spring 1976): 10.

42 Booth makes a similar point in more detail in *Critical Understanding*, pp. 168–9.

43 Though, strictly speaking, what would follow is that distinct parts of a text have distinct meanings, not that the text *as a whole* has more than one meaning.

44 Jones sometimes suggests this with his notion of the "interpreted-text"; see *Philosophy and the Novel*, p. 193.

45 For a discussion of problems connected with the hermeneutic circle, see Anthony Savile, "Historicity and the Hermeneutic Circle," *New Literary History* 10 (Autumn 1978): 49–70, and "Tradition and Interpretation," *Journal of Aesthetics and Art Criticism* 36 (Spring 1978): 303 and 315.

46 If it is now argued that even if we had the Athenians' interpretation, we could never really understand it, we can again apply the previous dilemma. We cannot understand their views because we cannot experience things as they did (which applies to any communication whatever) or because we lack background knowledge which they possessed (and which raises no problems in principle).

47 See Savile, "Tradition and Interpretation," p. 307; Abrams, "Rationality and Imagination" (n. 19 above), p. 457; and Hirsch, *Validity in Interpretation*, p. 171.

48 Iser, for example, seems to think that the dispensability of the text is a danger which taking meaning as "imagistic" avoids; see *The Act of Reading*, p. 4 ff. But this fear is widespread; see Cavell's discussion of Cleanth Brooks and Yvor Winters on paraphrase in "Aesthetic Problems." Claims to the effect that what is important about literary texts is not what they mean but their "emotional impact" are prompted by such a fear.

36

Art Interpretation

Robert Stecker

The concept of interpretation is one of the key concepts of our century. More and more objects of experience, including works of art and literature, have become objects of interpretation, where to speak this way signifies the uncertainty we feel about the nature or "meaning" of these objects. To speak of something being a matter of interpretation is sometimes to imply that (like matters of taste) there are many ways to look at that thing, no one of which is objectively right. Whatever interpretation actually is, it is these associations with uncertainty, multiplicity of perspective, and lack of objective rightness that have made it recently preeminent. Bearing this in mind, it is not surprising that there is considerable debate over the nature of interpretation itself, part of which involves the question whether the common associations are really part of the concept. Can questions of interpretation ever be given correct answers? Need there always be a multiplicity of equally good answers? Must we always be in a state of uncertainty about these answers?

In this paper, I will argue (a) that questions about the interpretations of artworks[1] not only can have correct answers but a single, comprehensive, correct answer, but (b) that this does not undermine the intuition that it is appropriate to bring a multiplicity of perspectives to art which produces many equally good, equally acceptable interpretations of the same work that cannot be

synthesized into a single comprehensive interpretation. I will argue that (a) and (b) are compatible and try to give reasons to accept both as true.

I Critical Pluralism and Critical Monism

Critical Pluralism is the view that there are many acceptable interpretations of many artworks that cannot be conjoined into a single correct interpretation.[2] Critical Pluralism is a philosophical doctrine about interpretation that reformulates those common associations from which we started. According to this view, there are *many* acceptable interpretations of many artworks. Hence Critical Pluralism affirms the idea that it is appropriate to bring a multiplicity of perspectives to the interpretation of a work. Furthermore, Critical Pluralism promotes the idea that there are *unacceptable* interpretations of a work (else there would be nothing with which to contrast acceptable interpretations) and, hence, can account for the uncertainty we feel about interpretive matters. Finally, Critical Pluralism denies that the search for a single *correct* interpretation is what interpretation is all about. At the very least, interpreters can have other legitimate aims.

It might also seem that Critical Pluralism denies *Critical Monism*. Critical Monism is the view that

From *Journal of Aesthetics and Art Criticism* 52 (1994), pp. 193–9, 205. Reprinted by permission of Blackwell Publishing Ltd.

there is a single, comprehensive, true (correct) interpretation for each work of art. (A true, comprehensive, interpretation of a work is one that is true, conjoins all true interpretations of the work, and one that comprehends the whole work.)[3]

Perhaps a full endorsement of the associations with which we began would lead to a denial of Critical Monism. Furthermore, there are many *versions* of Critical Pluralism that are incompatible with Critical Monism. I will critically evaluate some of these in the next section. What I want to show now is that Critical Pluralism *per se* is compatible with Critical Monism. One can consistently hold both views. Later, I will argue that (when Critical Monism is slightly modified) one *should* hold both views.

The reason why Critical Pluralism and Critical Monism are compatible turns on the distinction between truth or correctness and acceptability. It is important to realize that the notions of correctness and acceptability are not the same. To evaluate an interpretation for correctness and to evaluate it for acceptability are two different ways of assessing interpretations. To say that an interpretation is incorrect is to say it is untrue. Some interpretations may be unacceptable because they are untrue. But there are other reasons why interpretations can be unacceptable.[4] An interpretation can be unacceptable because, though it only makes true statements, it doesn't explain what puzzles us about a work. It gets bogged down in matters we regard as trivial rather than getting to the heart of the matter. Or, it may be unacceptable (to us) because it just isn't doing what we want an interpretation of a particular work to do. We may have heard that such and such is a great work of literature, but we have never been able to appreciate it. What we may be looking for is an interpretation that will enable us to do this. An interpretation that doesn't do this just won't do the job; it won't be an acceptable interpretation relative to our purposes. Whether an interpretation is acceptable varies according to the aim of those who produce or receive it. It varies depending on what it is for. (For the sake of brevity, I will confine myself to the interpreter's aim in what follows.) The correctness of an interpretation does not vary in this way.

What is needed to show that Critical Pluralism and Critical Monism are compatible is a logically possible *scenario* in which the defining conditions of both views are satisfied. So, for the sake of demonstrating the compatibility of these positions, let us suppose that some interpretations really are correct

(true), others are incorrect (false). To make this plausible, consider one interpretive project that Richard Wollheim has dubbed "retrieval."[5] Retrieval is the project of understanding a work as the product, for the most part, of design by its historical creator. This involves attempting to understand the writer's intentions and the vicissitudes they undergo. It involves as well understanding background conditions such as "aesthetic norms, innovations in the medium, rules of decorum, ideological or scientific world views, ... systems of symbolism, the state of the tradition"[6] current when the artist made the work. It is plausible that retrievals (this project as a whole or one of its proper parts), if they are possible at all, make factual claims. If so, such interpretations are true or false and are to be assessed as such. This is not to say they are the only interpretations that can be assessed for truth.

Now here, in a nutshell, is the scenario. We shall suppose that all correct interpretations about a given work are conjoinable into a single true interpretation, thus satisfying the defining conditions of Critical Monism. This assumption, by the way, is not implausible because it is a law of standard logic that the conjunction of true propositions is itself a true proposition. It can still be true that there are *other* acceptable interpretations, interpretations which are *not* true. Such interpretations are acceptable because they satisfy criteria of acceptability which have nothing to do with the truth of these interpretations. Such interpretations may aim at enhancing the aesthetic value of a work, or at making the work more relevant to the interpreter's contemporaries, or at just offering an interesting way of reading the work. (In general, such interpretations aim at enhancing appreciation of a work.) It shouldn't be supposed such interpretations proceed without any ground rules at all. To be acceptable, they must be consistent with *some* facts about the work. For example, it would not be acceptable, in the case of literary works, to ask readers to suppose that the words of a work were different from those actually constituting the text of a work. (On the other hand, it might be acceptable to attach unusual meanings to certain words in a text, e.g., archaic or obsolete meanings or to argue that a particular copy of a work does not contain the correct text.) However, the purpose of these ground rules is not to lead to true interpretations but interpretations that are *of* the work in question and that will enhance appreciation of it.

These acceptable but not true interpretations are not necessarily *false*. I prefer to think of them as *neither* true nor false. I think of *some* of these interpretations as asking us to imagine the work in certain ways, e.g., as the product of an apparent author or from the point of view of a system of beliefs, a "myth," an ideology, of contemporary interest. Such interpretations ask us to understand a fiction in terms of a further fiction.

Let me flesh out this idea with an illustration. In 1964, Jan Kott published a collection of essays entitled *Shakespeare Our Contemporary*.[7] In these essays, Kott interpreted many of Shakespeare's plays in such a way as to suggest resemblances, both thematic and stylistic, with contemporary theater. Thus in one of the best known of the essays, Kott suggested that we think of *King Lear* as an instance of theater of the absurd, comparing it with the plays of Samuel Beckett.

Now it may be that Kott was *asserting*, in these interpretations, that the plays actually represent characters and situations in these modern ways, that they really have the themes Kott finds, perhaps even that Shakespeare intended all this. Kott himself is not explicit about his own intentions. However, this is not how Martin Esslin takes Kott's essays. In the "Introduction" to the essays, Esslin makes it clear that he takes Kott to be aiming at giving us a way of reading the plays – a way of imagining the characters and the scenes in which they are represented – that makes the plays especially relevant to a contemporary audience. "Great works of art have an autonomous existence, independent of the intention and personality of their creators and independent also of the circumstances of the time of their creation. . . . The writing of . . . literary criticism can . . . be understood as an attempt to find in the past aspects of human experience that can shed light on the meaning of our own times."[8] The question of the truth of these interpretations does not seem to arise for Esslin. Relative to such an aim, Kott's interpretation of *King Lear* is not only acceptable but highly successful.

We can now complete the demonstration of the compatibility of Critical Pluralism and Critical Monism. It is *possible* that there are true interpretations of literary works and that all such true interpretations can be conjoined into a single, comprehensive, true interpretation. Still, there could be other acceptable interpretations of the same work which are *not* true. They are either false or, as I have suggested, neither true nor

false. Conjoining a false interpretation with a true one cannot result in a truth, let alone a true interpretation. Similarly, if we can make sense of a conjunction of a true interpretation with truth valueless ones, such a "conjunction" would not be true. I suspect that it would frequently not make much sense. So the truth of Critical Pluralism is preserved even on the assumption that Critical Monism is true. There are (or could be) many acceptable interpretations of the same literary work that are not conjoinable into a single correct interpretation even though all the true interpretations of that work are so conjoinable. Critical Pluralism is compatible with Critical Monism.

II Some Versions of Critical Pluralism Incompatible with Critical Monism

Although Critical Pluralism per se is compatible with Critical Monism, most proponents of Pluralism reject Monism. They are not being inconsistent. They hold *versions* of Critical Pluralism incompatible with Critical Monism. It is the purpose of this section to set out some of these versions of Critical Pluralism and evaluate their plausibility. I will be concerned with two general strategies for rejecting Monism. The first admits that there are true interpretations but claims, for one reason or another, that not all true interpretations can be conjoined into a more comprehensive true interpretation. I will call proponents of this strategy relativists. The second strategy denies that there are true interpretations. I will call proponents of this strategy anti-descriptivists. [. . .]

A. Relativism

[. . .] When we interpret a work, we interact with it. The literary work offers up to us a text produced by a certain individual in a particular historical context. We come to the work with certain beliefs or assumptions, reading according to certain conventions or rules.

Many of the people I am calling relativists are particularly impressed by the contribution of what we bring to the work through its interpretation. They claim that the truth of an interpretation is *relative* to the beliefs or assumptions, conventions, or rules that we bring to reading.[9] If we apply different conventions of reading to the same work, we get results that look incompatible: based on these conventions and the evidence, interpretation p is true; based on those conventions and the evidence, not-p is true. In fact, these interpretations are not incompatible since they are both true at the same time, but it is not clear how they can be combined into a single interpretation.

Some illustrations of interpretations based on different assumptions or conventions of reading will both help us to become clearer about what the relativist is claiming and to evaluate this claim. A famous Freudian interpretation of *Hamlet* claims that Hamlet's hesitation to revenge his father's murder is explained by the "fact" that Hamlet suffered from an "Oedipus Complex." That is, (put crudely), Hamlet subconsciously desired to do just what his uncle Claudius did do, and he is held back from revenge by his subconscious guilt about this. Opposed to this interpretation are many other "explanations" of Hamlet's hesitation. One among the many alternatives is to claim that Hamlet does not vacillate. The only thing that stands in the way of revenging his father's death is his scrupulous honesty. "Ghosts," after all, are not the most reliable sources of information. Hamlet must ascertain the facts, and, once he does this, he does not hesitate, or rather he would not, except that various unfortunate events beyond his control postpone action.

The Freudian interpreter is bringing the following "assumptions" to interpreting the play: first, that there are such things as the Oedipus Complex and they are among the fundamental motivators of human behavior; second, that this was as true in Shakespeare's day as it is now; third, that artists are capable of expressing such truths in their works even though these truths are not fully articulated until hundreds of years later in psychoanalytic theory. The proponent of the alternative interpretation simply lacks these assumptions but operates with a different set which I shall leave unarticulated.

Relativism, as I have described it, is committed to the claim that these interpretations are to be (and can only be) evaluated as true or false relative to the assumptions from which they start. In this example, at least, this claim is implausible. It is true that one interpreter may take for granted propositions that the other does not. But the assumptions are not held arbitrarily and are not immune to criticism. Freudians may not defend the propositions I have labeled "assumptions" when interpreting a text like *Hamlet*, but they do so at length elsewhere. Furthermore, there is no

lack of criticism of these Freudian claims. So there is no reason why both Freudians and their opponents cannot (re)evaluate Freudian assumptions as part of the evaluation of the Freudian interpretation of *Hamlet*. If this is possible, there is no reason why we cannot regard the Freudian interpretation and the rival mentioned above as competing, possibly incompatible alternatives. One interpretation does *not* exist in a conceptual universe unavailable to the other.

A relativist might reply that I have chosen the wrong kinds of assumptions in the preceding paragraph. The Freudian at least supposes that his assumptions are empirically testable. But critics make assumptions of a more normative character which are not empirical. These, it might be claimed, must simply be accepted or rejected, and interpretations which are based on such normative assumptions can only be evaluated relative to them.

For example, some schools of criticism (e.g., New Criticism) seem to require that an interpretation that exhibits a greater unity or coherence in a work is to be preferred to one that exhibits a comparatively lesser coherence or unity in that work. Other schools of criticism (e.g., deconstruction) might omit this requirement or even replace it with the requirement that we should expect a certain degree of incoherence or disunity in a work so that an interpretation which exhibits some degree of disunity in a work should be preferred to one that does not. It might be thought just inappropriate to bring New Critical standards to a deconstructive interpretation and vice versa.

However, barring the implausible supposition that this difference between New Criticism and deconstruction is a matter of sheer personal preference, it is unclear why the appropriateness of these standards cannot be evaluated. The first question that needs asking concerns the purpose of placing these requirements on interpretations. Is it being claimed that following the preferred requirement makes it more likely that the interpretation will be true? Or is it being claimed that following the preferred requirement makes an interpretation better for reasons independent of its truth? For example, a New Critic could plausibly claim that interpreting a work in such a way as to attribute to it great coherence and unity will enhance appreciation of the work. I will only be concerned with the first kind of claim for these requirements below.

Deconstructionists, as far as I can make out, believe that there is something about the nature of language, or of writing, that makes incoherence or disunity in a given text very likely. More commonsensically, someone could support the New Critical position by pointing out that most writers would want to produce a coherent and unified work, and the very good writers that critics usually talk about have the skill to accomplish this. Notice these positions no longer look so different in epistemic status from the Freudian position discussed above. Proponents of the respective positions have reasons to support their views, and both parties can examine and evaluate these reasons.

So far, I have argued that there is no need, nor is it desirable, to confine ourselves to making assessments of the truth of interpretations only relative to the assumptions or conventions of reading accepted by those who produce the interpretation. We need not stop with the question: taking these assumptions for granted, is the interpretation (likely to be) true? We can ask for a justification of the assumptions (conventions), and this can be presented in a way accessible to those who share the assumptions and to those who do not.

The relativist still need not admit defeat. He could admit that we can always *ask* for the justification of competing assumptions, conventions, or rules. What the relativist will deny is that non-arbitrary *answers* will always be forthcoming. It is when they are not that we are forced to accept relativism with regard to the competing assumptions, conventions, or rules.

A recent discussion, by Kendall Walton, of the principles that determine what is fictional in a work might be taken to support relativism.[10] (A proposition is fictional in a work if the proposition is true in the world of the work.) How do we decide what is fictional in a work of literature? Sometimes we seem to decide as follows: given that we already know that a set of propositions $p1 \ldots pn$ is fictional in a work, we infer that q is also fictional because we would infer q if we believed that $p1 \ldots pn$ were true in the real world. For example, we assume that fictional people have psychological traits because real people have psychological traits. (When we decide this way, we use the reality principle.) Very often, however, we don't use the reality principle. Sometimes we decide that q is fictional in a work because it was *mutually believed* by the author and his contemporary audience that q follows from $p1 \ldots pn$, and $p1 \ldots pn$ is fictional in the work. (When we decide this way, we use the mutual belief principle.)

Sometimes we use neither principle. The fact that certain fictional truths are salient in various ways leads us to make inferences that violate both principles. How do these facts help out the relativist?

It is often an *interpretive* question whether a proposition is fictional in a work. We have just seen that there are different rules (principles) we can follow in trying to answer this question. Often these rules yield different results, and different interpreters might opt for different rules in such cases. We can certainly ask: which rule should we follow? But Walton's discussion suggests that there won't always be grounds for choosing one rule over another. Following different rules has advantages and disadvantages which (might) pretty much balance out. In such a case, isn't it plausible to say that the truth of these different interpretations is relative to the rules that generate them?

These considerations do not *force* us to accept relativism. Walton himself suggests the view that if we have equally legitimate grounds for using different rules, and using these different rules yields incompatible results as to what is fictional in a work, then there is no fact of the matter about what is fictional in the work. Rather than say the truth is relative, Walton suggests the truth is, in these cases, indeterminate.

Another possibility – the one I favor – is that the truth is multiple without its being relative. That is, using different rules may indeed result in different, true interpretations. But when we understand the aims of these different interpretations and precisely what they assert, their collective acceptance does not require accepting relativism. One interpretation may aim at retrieval and make assertions about what the author successfully intended to do in the work. (Here we would expect an interpreter to use the mutual belief principle modified by salient facts about the work.) Other interpreters may be asserting no more than that the text of a work *can* have a certain meaning. Even if the some of the propositions that compose this meaning are incompatible with the propositions that compose the retrievalist's interpretation, what these two interpreters assert is not incompatible. (A work can be successfully intended to mean, in part, *p*, and at the same time, the text of the work can be construable as meaning not-*p*.)[11]

We can conclude that relativism still is not established. One might wonder, however, if the indeterminacy, that Walton suggests *sometimes* holds, is not a *pervasive* fact about interpretations. We will now turn to a discussion of this possibility.

B. *Anti-descriptivism*

An alternative to saying that there are many true interpretations of a work, but some of these are not combinable into a more comprehensive true interpretation (relativism), is to take the seemingly simpler line that there just are no true interpretations. This view obviously does not face the problem of explaining why pairs of true interpretations cannot be conjoined to make another true interpretation. However, it has its own explaining to do. First it has to explain why interpretations are never true. Second, it has to tell us how we *should* think of interpretations if we are not to think of them as true.

In section I above, I already pointed out a general strategy for accomplishing the second of these explanatory tasks. There, I distinguished between true and acceptable interpretations. The anti-descriptivist is going to propose that we think of interpretations as acceptable or unacceptable in ways that do not presuppose their being true. There are any number of possible ways of filling out this claim. Some claim that, though interpretations do not have the property of having the bivalent truth values true/false, they have *truthlike* values. For example, it is sometimes claimed that interpretations can be evaluated for plausibility even though they cannot be evaluated for truth.[12] Some claim that interpretations should be treated as prescriptions, which are incapable of truth or falsity, rather than as statements. Some suggest that interpretations are fictions, thus having the same status as the works of (fictional) literature being interpreted.

Since we should admit that interpretations can be acceptable without being true (and without having a [bivalent] truth value), the crucial question is why we should suppose interpretations of literature and art are *never* true.

There are a number of arguments for this conclusion which fail because they presuppose a one-sided or overly simple conception of literary interpretation.

Robert Matthews argues that interpretations of literature are typically neither true nor false because they are typically underdetermined by all possible evidence capable of establishing their truth.[13] Let us assume that such underdetermination implies that literary interpretations lack truth

value. Why does Matthews say that these interpretations are underdetermined? His first premise is that external evidence (facts external to the work) are irrelevant to determining the truth of interpretations. Matthews's second premise is that critics typically know all the relevant internal evidence in support of their interpretations. Matthews's final premise is that it is a conceptual truth that interpretations are not known to be true at the time they are proposed. It follows that, since interpreters of literary works know all the relevant evidence in favor of their interpretations, but this is insufficient to give them knowledge that their interpretations are true, the evidence for these interpretations underdetermines their truth.

I doubt that any of Matthews's premises is true. Matthews offers no justification of the first premise. What he does do is identify "external evidence" with evidence regarding author's intention and then denies that "art critical questions" are ever properly construed as about such intentions. This, however, simply legislates what an "art critical question" is and does so contrary to the practice of many critics. Certainly, *one* thing that could be understood by the expression "the meaning of a work" is what the author successfully intended in it. Furthermore, the distinction between internal and external evidence (if it can be made out at all) cuts across the distinction between meanings intended and not intended by an author. Assuming the internal/external distinction holds, there are both kinds of evidence for both kinds of meaning. There can be plenty of internal evidence of intended meaning. On the other hand, passages of a work can mean things not intended by authors in virtue of facts external to the works, such as linguistic or literary conventions, or in virtue of myths, ideologies, or perspectives interpreters bring to works.

Matthews's second premise is equally questionable. Literary works are neither simple nor transparent. They may not even be unchanging in ways relevant to their interpretation. It is not at all evident that a critic will ever discover all the relevant evidence for an interpretation, even if this is confined to internal evidence.

Finally, I see no reason to accept the conceptual claim made by the last premise. I can interpret a work for myself or for others. When I do the latter, I may have knowledge my audience lacks. Even when I interpret for myself, knowledge of my interpretation is not (conceptually) impossible. Commonly, when I set out to interpret a work, I don't know which interpretation is true. However, by the time I am ready to offer my interpretation to others, I may be certain of it. I am still interpreting the work.

Notes

1 The reader may find useful, at the very start, some indication of what I count as an interpretation of an artwork. I start from the intuition that one seeks an interpretation of an artwork when one finds one doesn't understand it and wants to make sense of it. I think there are basically two different ways this desire for understanding can be satisfied. One is the way we normally, I suppose, approach products of intentional human action. We try to figure out what the actual maker of the thing was trying to do, and in fact did, in making it. Such interpretations are historical explanations. They require the making of statements about the maker, her historical context, and, of course, the work. The other way one can try to satisfy a desire for understanding is to seek *an* understanding of a work: *a* way of taking a work that makes sense of its different parts as parts of a whole. Interpretations that seek to satisfy the desire for understanding in this second way may, but need not, dispense with statement making. They can be expressed as imaginative fictions, as prescriptions, as reports of personal experience. They can also be expressed as statements that assert that a work can be *taken* in a certain way, that a meaning can be *put upon* it. It might be better to have different names for these different ways of satisfying a desire for understanding, but the fact is that critical practice does not segregate them.

2 Some recent defenses of Pluralism include Stanley Fish, *Is There a Text in this Class? The Authority of Interpretive Communities* (Harvard University Press, 1980), Peter Jones, *Philosophy and the Novel* (Oxford: Clarendon Press, 1975), Joseph Margolis, *Art and Philosophy* (Atlantic Highlands: Humanities Press, 1980), Alan Goldman, "Interpreting Art And Literature," *Journal of Aesthetics and Art Criticism* 48 (1990): 205–14. Robert Kraut criticizes some arguments for Critical Pluralism but also attempts a plausible rendering of this view in "On Pluralism and Indeterminacy," in Peter A. French et al., *Midwest Studies in Philosophy* 16 (1991): 209–25. Critical Pluralism comes in different versions. For a specification of these and further references, see part II below.

3 Among the best defenses of Critical Monism are: Monroe Beardsley, *The Possibility of Criticism* (Wayne State University Press, 1979), pp. 238–61, P. D. Juhl, *Interpretation: an Essay in the Philosophy of Literary Criticism* (Princeton University Press, 1980), pp. 196–238, Alexander Nehamas, "The Postulated Author: Critical Monism as a Regulative Ideal," *Critical Inquiry* 8 (1981): 133–9. As with Pluralism, Monism has different versions, some of which are discussed in part III below, which should be seen for further references. The specification of a comprehensive, true interpretation given here needs modification to avoid generating an infinite regress. The qualified version of Critical Monism given in part III is such a modification.

4 For more on the idea that there are different criteria of acceptability, see Annette Barnes, *On Interpretation: A Critical Analysis* (Oxford: Basil Blackwell, 1988), pp. 42–62.

5 Richard Wolheim, *Art and its Objects: An Introduction to Aesthetics*, second edition (Cambridge University Press, 1980), pp. 185–201.

6 Ibid., pp. 200–1.

7 Jan Kott, *Shakespeare Our Contemporary* (Garden City: Doubleday, 1964).

8 Ibid., xi.

9 One version of this argument is found in Fish, *Is There a Text in this Class?* I criticize Fish's version of the argument in "Fish's Argument for the Relativity of Interpretive Truth," *Journal of Aesthetics and Art Criticism* 48 (1990): 221–30.

10 Kendall Walton, *Mimesis as Make-Believe: On the Foundations of the Representational Arts* (Harvard University Press, 1990), pp. 138–87.

11 For a more fully worked out version of this suggestion, see my "Incompatible Interpretations," *Journal of Aesthetics and Art Criticism* 50 (1992): 291–8.

12 This is frequently expressed in the writings of Joseph Margolis. For the idea that the criterion of acceptability for interpretations is plausibility, see Margolis, *Art and Philosophy*. More recently, Margolis has moved to the idea that interpretations have non-bivalent truth conditions in such writings as *The Truth about Relativism* (Oxford: Basil Blackwell, 1991).

13 Robert Matthews, "Describing and Interpreting Works of Art," *Journal of Aesthetics and Art Criticism* 36 (1977): 5–14.

37

Art, Intention, and Conversation

Noël Carroll

I

In the normal course of affairs, when confronted with an utterance, our standard cognitive goal is to figure out what the speaker intends to say. And, on one very plausible theory of language, the meaning of an utterance is explicated in terms of the speaker's intention to reveal to an auditor that the speaker intends the auditor to respond in a certain way.[1] That is, the meaning of a particular language token is explained by means of certain of a speaker's intentions.

Likewise, in interpreting or explaining nonverbal behavior, we typically advert to the agent's intentions. This is not to say that we may not be concerned with the unintended consequences of an action; but even in order to explain unintended consequences, one will need a conception of the agent's intentions. Nor is this reliance on intention something that is relevant only to living people; historians spend a great deal of their professional activity attempting to establish what historical agents intended by their words and their deeds, with the aim of rendering the past intelligible. Furthermore, we generally presume that they can succeed in their attempts even with respect to authors and agents who lived long ago and about whom the documentary record is scant.

Nevertheless, though it seems natural to interpret words and actions in terms of authorial intention, arguments of many sorts have been advanced for nearly fifty years to deny the relevance of authorial intention to the interpretation of works of art in general and to works of literature in particular. Call this anti-intentionalism. Whereas ordinarily we interpret for intentions, anti-intentionalism maintains that art and literature either cannot or should not be treated in this way. Likewise, where characteristically we may use what we know of a person – her biography, if you will – to supply clues to, or, at least, constraints on our hypotheses about her meanings,[2] many theorists of art and literature regard reference to an author's biography as either illegitimate or superfluous.

The realm of art and literature, on the anti-intentionalist view, is or should be sufficiently different from other domains of human intercourse so that the difference mandates a different form of interpretation, one in which authorial intent is irrelevant. In this essay, I scrutinize some of the grounds for drawing distinctions between art and life that advance the thought that authorial intent is irrelevant; and, in contrast, I also try to suggest some hitherto neglected continuities between art and life that might motivate a concern for authorial intention in the interpretation of art and literature.

II

Historically speaking, anti-intentionalism, under the title of "the intentional fallacy,"[3] arose in a context where biographical criticism flourished – that is, the interpretation of such things as novels as allegories of their authors' lives. Authors were geniuses whose remarkable personalities we came to know and appreciate all the more by treating their fictions as oblique biographies.[4] Undoubtedly, this sort of criticism promoted distorted interpretations – as any intentionalist would agree, insofar as it is not likely that Kafka intended to speak of his father in writing *The Metamorphosis*. But in banishing all reference to authorial intention, to authorial reports of intention, and to the author's biography,[5] anti-intentionalism was an exercise in overkill. That is, in performing the useful service of disposing of what might be better called "the biographer's fallacy," anti-intentionalists embraced a number of philosophical commitments that went far beyond their own purposes, as well as beyond plausibility.

Indeed, anti-intentionalism is often promoted as a means for rejecting critical practices that most of us would agree are misguided. It is generally unclear, however, whether one has to go all the way to anti-intentionalism in order to avoid the errors in question.

For example, anti-intentionalism was advocated as a principle that could dispense with taking outlandish authorial pronouncements seriously. Monroe Beardsley writes "if a sculptor tells us that his statue was intended to be smooth and blue, but our senses tell us it is rough and pink, we go by our senses."[6] This example is meant to serve as an "intuition-pump"; if we agree that a sculptor cannot make a pink statue blue by reporting that it was his intention to make a blue sculpture, then it must be the case that we regard such intentions – and such reports of intention – as irrelevant.

This solution to the case is too hasty, however, and the example need not force the intentionalist into anti-intentionalism. For with cases where the authorial pronouncement is so arbitrary, we may discount it, not because we think that authorial intentions are irrelevant, but because we think that the report is insincere. That is, we do not

believe that the sculptor in Beardsley's example really had the intention of making a blue statue by painting it pink.

Intentions are constituted, in part, of beliefs, on Beardsley's own view,[7] and we can resist attributing the belief to an artist that one makes something blue by painting it pink. We need not resort to the hypothesis of anti-intentionalism in such a case, but can instead suspect that the artist was putting us on, perhaps for the purpose of notoriety. That is, competent language users, especially trained artists, are presumed to know the difference between blue and pink. Flouting this distinction leads to the suspicion of irony.

For an actual literary example of the sort of problem that Beardsley has in mind, we could consider Andrew Greeley's sensational novel *Ascent into Hell*. Like many of Greeley's works, this story is a titillating tale of Catholic priests and sex, a kind of soft-core pornography, spiced with religious taboos. Greeley, however, has a note preceding the text of the novel entitled "Passover," in which he offers a symbolic reading of that ceremony, thereby perhaps insinuating that we should take the text of *Ascent into Hell* as an allegory of Passover.

Needless to say, it is difficult to regard the sexual escapades in the book as a serious Passover allegory. But the intentionalist is not forced to accept Greeley's implied intention at face value. One can simply, on the basis of the novel, note that Greeley could not genuinely have the belief that it could be read as that allegory, nor would he have written the text as he did if he had the desire – another component of intentions on Beardsley's view[8] – to render a modern-day Passover theme. In fact, one may hypothesize that Greeley included the red herring about Passover in order to reassure his Catholic readership that his book was not irreligious.

But, in any event, the intentionalist can reject the "Passover" interpretation of *Ascent to Hell* in the face of Greeley's implied intentions by denying that it is plausible to accept the authenticity of Greeley's ostensible intent. Thus the problem of aberrant authorial pronouncements need not drive us toward anti-intentionalism.[9]

Another frequent intuition-pump, employed in early arguments against intentionalism, argues that commending poems insofar as they realize authorial intentions is usually circular. For in many (most?) instances, including those of Shakespeare and Homer, we have no evidence of authorial intention other than their poems. Consequently, if we commend such a poem on the basis of its realization of intentions, and our sole evidence for that intention is the poem itself, then our commendation is tantamount to the assertion that the poem succeeds because it is the way it is because it is the way it is.

We cannot, in these instances, have grounds for discerning failed authorial intentions because the way the artwork is provides our only access to the intention. If it appears muddled, then that is evidence that the artist intended it to be muddled and, therefore, that it succeeded in realizing his intention. That is, commending works of art for realizing authorial intentions when the way work is is our only evidence of intentions threatens to force us to the counterintuitive conclusion that all works of art are commendable.[10]

The unwarranted presupposition here, of course, is that the artwork cannot provide evidence of failed intentions. In the introduction to his *The Structure of Scientific Revolutions*, Thomas Kuhn writes at one point that "having been weaned on these distinctions [the 'context of discovery' versus 'context of justification'] and others like them, I could scarcely be more aware of their import and force."[11] Clearly, any alert reader will note that Kuhn has said the opposite of what he meant to say. He intended to communicate that he had been *nurtured* on these distinctions, and not that he had been *weaned* on them.[12]

The text itself, in terms of the entire direction of what is being said, makes evident what Kuhn has in mind. Also, we know that the confusion over the dictionary meaning of *weaned*, like the meanings of such words as *fulsome* and *sleek*, is quite common among contemporary English speakers; so it is easy to recognize that Kuhn should not have written what he, in fact, wrote, given his intentions. From the text itself and our knowledge of language usage, we can infer that the sentence failed to realize Kuhn's intentions and that, from his own viewpoint, it is not a great sentence. And, similarly, with artworks – given their genre, their style, their historical context, and their overall aesthetic direction – one can say by looking at a given work that the author's intention has misfired, whether or not we go on to commend or criticize it.

Undoubtedly, as the preceding discussion indicates, one of the deepest commitments of early anti-intentionalism was the notion that authorial intention is somehow *outside* the artwork and that attempts to invoke it on the basis of the artwork

itself are epistemologically suspect. Underlying this view is a conception of authorial intentions as private, episodic mental events that are logically independent of the artworks they give rise to in the way that Humean causes are logically independent of effects. What we have access to, in general, for purposes of evaluation and interpretation is the work itself. The authorial intention is an external cause of the artwork of dubious availability.

However, this view of authorial intention gradually came to be challenged by another view – call it the neo-Wittgensteinian view[13] – according to which an intention is thought to be a purpose, manifest in the artwork, which regulates the way the artwork is. Authorial intention, then, is discoverable by the inspection and contemplation of the work itself.[14] Indeed, the artwork is criterial to attributions of intention. [. . .]

Given the conception of authorial intention as external to and independent of the artwork, the anti-intentionalist claim of its irrelevance to the meaning of the work is eminently comprehensible. But with developments in the philosophies of action, mind, and language, the neo-Wittgensteinian picture of authorial intention seems more attractive. The persuasiveness of anti-intentionalism comes to hinge upon which view of intention in general theorists find more plausible. And to the extent that early anti-intentionalism was based upon a crude view of intention, its conclusions are questionable.[15] Moreover, the more attractive, neo-Wittgensteinian view of intention not only makes authorial intention relevant to the interpretation of artworks but implies that in interpretating an artwork, we are attempting to determine the author's intentions. Thus, at this point in the debate, if anti-intentionalism is to remain persuasive, it must do so not only without presupposing a crude view of intention but also must accommodate the neo-Wittgensteinian picture of intention. [. . .]

Monroe Beardsley writes:

What is the primary purpose of literary interpretation? It is, I would say, to help readers approach literary works from the aesthetic point of view, that is, with an interest in actualizing their (artistic) goodness. The work is an object, capable (presumably) of affording aesthetic satisfaction. The problem is to know what is there to be responded to; and the literary interpreter helps us to discern what is there so that we can enjoy it more fully.[16]

Here, the underlying idea is that an artistic object has a purpose: affording aesthetic satisfaction. This is why we attend to artworks. Our object is to derive as much aesthetic satisfaction as is possible from the object. The role of the interpreter is to show us what there is in the object that promotes aesthetic experience. Nevertheless, one can readily imagine that what an author intended to say by means of an artwork is less aesthetically provocative than alternative "readings" of the work. For Beardsley, these readings, with respect to literature, have to be constrained by what the words of the text mean conventionally. Even with this caveat, it is easy to imagine instances where what the author intended is less aesthetically exciting than an alternate, conventionally admissible reading.

Moreover, since the point of consuming art, and of interpretation as an adjunct to artistic consumption, is to maximize aesthetic satisfaction, we should always favor those interpretations that afford the best aesthetic experience that is compatible with established textual meaning conventions. Furthermore, since aesthetic richness is our overriding concern, we need only interpret with an eye to that which is most aesthetically satisfying and linguistically plausible. Whether or not the meanings we attribute to the text were authorially intended is irrelevant. The proof of the pudding is in the tasting.

Of course, the best reading of the text – the one that is most aesthetically satisfying and also at least linguistically plausible – may coincide with the author's intended meaning, but that is of accidental importance. What is essential for the purposes of aesthetic consumption is that it be the best interpretation – the one that points to the maximum available aesthetic enjoyment – conceivable within the constraints of linguistic plausibility. Thus, for aesthetic purposes, we may always forgo concern for authorial intent in favor of the best aesthetic interpretation.

Where authorial intention and the best interpretation coincide, the reason we accept the interpretation has to do with aesthetic richness rather than authorial intention. Where there may be divergences between authorial intentions and textual meanings (that are richer than the putative authorial ones), we go with the latter because maximizing aesthetic satisfaction is our goal. As a matter of aesthetic policy, the best procedure is always to regard authorial intention as irrelevant because it either adds nothing to our aesthetic satisfaction or it

may even stand in the way of arriving at the most enjoyable experience of the work.

On Beardsley's view, there is generally a determinate best interpretation. However, the aesthetic argument can also be mobilized by theorists who eschew determinate meanings, preferring the "play of signification of the text." Here, the argument might begin by recalling that a text can be interpreted either as the utterance of an author or as a word sequence.[17] Read as a word sequence, the text may have multiple meanings compatible with the conventions of language. Given this, the question becomes, What is the best way to read the text – authorially or, so to speak, textually?

In defense of reading the text as a word sequence, one can invoke the Kantian notion that aesthetic experience involves the play of understanding and imagination. That is, taking the text as a word sequence allows us to contemplate it for multiple, diverse meanings and their possible connections. It provides the best way for us to maximize our aesthetic experience of the text, permitting us to track the text for its play of meaning and alternative import. Reading for authorial intent, where the author intends a determinate meaning rather than an "open text,"[18] may obstruct the delectation of the various shifts in meaning that would otherwise be available to the reader who takes the text as a word sequence. Thus, for the purpose of maximizing our aesthetic experience – construed here to be a matter of cognitive play with meanings – the best policy is to attend to the work as a word sequence rather than as an authorial utterance.

The conservative version of this aesthetic argument might hold that texts could be read as word sequences or as authorial utterances and that there is no reason why the intentionalist preference for authorial utterance must be given priority over the possibility of reading the text as a word sequence. Both readings are possible, and neither recommendation is binding.[19] So, if a good reason – like the Kantian aesthetic invoked earlier – can be advanced for anti-intentionalist interpretive practices, then the claims of intentionalism can be suspended. This does not preclude intentionalist interpretation, but only denies that interpretation must always be constrained by intentionalist considerations.

A more radical version of the aesthetic argument would advocate that intentionalist considerations are *always* best bracketed because they stand in the way of, or are irrelevant to, maximizing interpretive play.[20] Concern for authorial intent "closes" down the text; it limits the artwork as a source of interpretive enjoyment; it restrains the imagination (of the audience) unduly. This recommendation may be accompanied by the vague and perhaps confusing cliché that artworks are inexhaustible, insofar as word sequences, ex hypothesi, will tend to have more meanings than authorial utterances. But the argument can proceed without claiming that artworks are literally inexhaustible; only to urge that, for the purpose of making literary experience more exciting, we should treat artworks that way, rather as Morris Zapp in David Lodge's *Changing Places* keeps reinterpreting Jane Austen in the light of every literary theory that comes down the pike. That is, keeping artworks interpretively open – for example, by reading for word sequence meaning rather than authorial meaning – makes for more zestful encounters with art. […]

Aesthetic arguments for anti-intentionalism are a subclass of the general view that interpretations are purpose-relative.[21] One could advance anti-intentionalism, then, for purposes other than aesthetic gratification under the banner of purpose-relative interpretation; one could, for example, maintain that anti-intentionalism best realizes some moral or ideological goal, which outweighs whatever aims intentionalism supports.[22] Since I believe that the purpose that critics most often presuppose anti-intentionalism serves best is aesthetic enrichment, however, I focus the discussion on this issue.

With aesthetic arguments, the anti-intentionalist admits, in my reconstruction of the debate, that one could read for authorial intent, but maintains that we have certain aims in pursuing artworks that, so to speak, trump our concerns with authorial meaning. These aims center on the maximization of aesthetic satisfaction. Aesthetic satisfaction is the overriding interest that we have in consuming artworks. So in order to secure said satisfaction, we are best advised to take it that the aesthetically most satisfying interpretation outranks all others, most notably where a competing view is an intentionalist interpretation.

In order to develop this argument fully, the anti-intentionalist needs to say something about aesthetic satisfaction. This may cause difficulties in several registers. The first is the long-standing problem of defining the way in which we are to understand "the aesthetic" in *aesthetic satisfaction*. Moreover, there may be rival views of what con-

stitutes aesthetic satisfaction – Beardsleyan determinate meaning of a certain sort, or the inexhaustible play of meaning in the text. Which of these views must the anti-intentionalist endorse? But even supposing these technical difficulties with characterizing aesthetic satisfaction can be met, I remain unconvinced by aesthetic arguments for anti-intentionalism.

The heart of my disagreement is that it seems unproven that we have overriding interests in maximizing aesthetic satisfaction with respect to artworks. My reason for reservations here have to do with my suspicion that in dealing with artworks we have more interests than aesthetic interests – as "aesthetic interests" are usually construed within the philosophical tradition – and that there is no reason to think that these interests are always trumped by aesthetic ones. Indeed, as I argue, these other-than-aesthetic interests may in fact mandate constraints on the pursuit of aesthetic interest in ways that count against anti-intentionalism and for intentionalism. I would not wish to deny that we have interests in securing aesthetic satisfaction from artworks. But that interest needs to be reconciled with other, potentially conflictive interests that we also bring to artworks.

What are these other interests or purposes? Broadly speaking, I would call them "conversational." When we read a literary text or contemplate a painting, we enter a relationship with its creator that is roughly analogous to a conversation. Obviously, it is not as interactive as an ordinary conversation, for we are not receiving spontaneous feedback concerning our own responses. But just as an ordinary conversation gives us a stake in understanding our interlocutor, so does interaction with an artwork.

We would not think that we had had a genuine conversation with someone whom we were not satisfied we understood. Conversations, rewarding ones at least, involve a sense of community or communion that itself rests on communication. A fulfilling conversation requires that we have the conviction of having grasped what our interlocutor meant or intended to say. This is evinced by the extent to which we struggle to clarify their meanings. A conversation that left us with only our own clever construals or educated guesses, no matter how aesthetically rich, would leave us with the sense that something was missing. That we had neither communed nor communicated.

Not all conversations involve both communion and communication. Probably many firings do not.

But what, for want of a better term, we might call serious conversations do have, as a constitutive value, the prospect of community. Likewise, I want to maintain, this prospect of community supplies a major impetus motivating our interest in engaging literary texts and artworks. We may read to be entertained, to learn, and to be moved, but we also seek out artworks in order to converse or commune with their makers. We want to understand the author, even if that will lead to rejecting his or her point of view.

An important part of why we are interested in art is that it affords not only an opportunity to reap aesthetic satisfaction but is an opportunity to exercise our interpretive abilities in the context of a genuine conversation. Clever construals, even if aesthetically dazzling, do not necessarily serve our desire to commune or communicate with another person. Insofar as our pursuit of art is underwritten by, and is an exemplary occasion for, a generic human interest in communicating with others, it is not clear that a concern with aesthetics alone serves our purposes best.

Moreover, in stressing our conversational interest in artworks in terms of understanding the artist, I am not reverting to the notion that we pursue art in order to commune with remarkable personalities. Instead, I am making the more modest claim that art is obviously in part a matter of communication and that we bring to it our ordinary human disposition to understand what another human being is saying to us.

The idea of the maximization of aesthetic satisfaction has a very "consumerist" ring to it. In Buberesque lingo, it reduces our relation to the text to an I/It relationship. What I am trying to defend is the idea that, with artworks, we are also interested in an I/Thou relation to the author of the text. This interest in communicating with others is perhaps so deeply a part of our motive in, for example, reading that we may not have it in the forefront of our attention. But when we pick up Tom Wolfe's *Bonfire of the Vanities*, surely one of our abiding interests is to learn what someone else, namely Tom Wolfe, thinks about contemporary New York. And, the extent to which we have this conversational interest in the text limits the range of aesthetically enhancing interpretations we can countenance. That is, the purpose of aesthetic maximization will have to be brought into line with our conversational interests, which interests are patently concerned with authorial intent.

Furthermore, if I am right about the conversational interests that we have in artworks and literary texts, then our concern with authorial intention will not simply issue from the mutual respect we have for our interlocutor; it will also be based on an interest in protecting our sense of self-respect in the process of conversation. In order to clarify this point, a somewhat extended example may be useful.

In contemporary film criticism, films are often commended because they *transgress* what are called the codes of Hollywood filmmaking, thereby striking this or that blow for emancipation. Within the context of recent film criticism, it is appropriate to regard disturbances of continuity editing, disorienting narrative ellipses, or disruptions of eyeline matches as subversions of a dominant and ideologically suspect form of filmmaking. And given the historical evolution of the language game in which avant-garde filmmaking is practiced, the attribution of such meanings to contemporary films is warranted, especially on intentionalist grounds.

Once interpretations of narrative incoherences in recent films as subversions or transgressions of Hollywood International were in place, however, film critics, such as J. Hoberman of the *Village Voice*, began to attempt to project those readings backward. That is, if a narrative incoherence or an editing discontinuity in a film in 1988 counts as a transgression, why not count a similar disturbance in a film of 1959 as equally transgressive? Thus a hack film by Edward Wood, *Plan 9 from Outer Space*, is celebrated as transgressive as if it were a postmodernist exercise in collage.[23]

Plan 9 from Outer Space is a cheap, slapdash attempt to make a feature film for very little, and in cutting corners to save money it violates – in outlandish ways – many of the decorums of Hollywood filmmaking that later avant-gardists also seek to affront. So insofar as the work of contemporary avant-gardists is aesthetically valued for its transgressiveness, why not appreciate *Plan 9 from Outer Space* under an analogous interpretation? Call it "unintentional modernism," but it is modernism nonetheless and appreciable as such.[24]

One reason to withhold such an interpretation from *Plan 9*, of course, is that transgression *is* an intentional concept, and all the evidence indicates that Edward Wood did not have the same intentions to subvert the Hollywood style of filmmaking that contemporary avant-gardists have. Indeed, given the venue Wood trafficked in, it seems that the best hypothesis about his intentions is that he was attempting to imitate the Hollywood style of filmmaking in the cheapest way possible. Given what we know of Edward Wood and the B-film world in which he practiced his trade, it is implausible to attribute to him the intention of attempting to subvert the Hollywood codes of filmmaking for the kinds of purposes endorsed by contemporary avant-gardists.

An intention is made up of beliefs and desires. It is incredible to attribute to Edward Wood the kinds of beliefs that contemporary avant-garde filmmakers have about the techniques, purposes, and effects of subverting Hollywood cinema. Those beliefs (and avant-garde desires) were not available in the film world Edward Wood inhabited, nor can we surmise that even if Wood could have formulated such beliefs, it would be plausible to attribute to him the intention to implement them. For it is at the least uncharitable to assign to Wood the belief that his audiences could have interpreted his narrative discontinuities and editing howlers as blows struck against a Hollywood aesthetic.[25] That is, it is virtually impossible that Wood could have had the intentions – the beliefs and the desires – that contemporary avant-gardists have about the meanings of disjunctive exposition or the effects of such exposition on audiences.

Historically, it is undoubtedly most accurate to regard Edward Wood's narrative non sequiturs and nonstandard editing as mistakes within the norms of Hollywood filmmaking. One would think that the critic interested in transgression would want to have a way to distinguish between mistakes and transgressions. And the most obvious way to make such a distinction is to require that transgressions be intentional, which requires that the filmmaker in question have the knowledge and the will to violate Hollywood norms of filmmaking as a form of artistic protest. Insofar as it is anachronistic to impute the requisite knowledge (of the discourse of avant-garde theory) or the desire to subvert Hollywood codes to Wood, it is better to regard his violations of certain norms as mistakes. And, in general, it would seem that connoisseurs of artistic transgression would have an interest in being able to distinguish mistakes from subversions – interests that should drive them toward intentionalism.

Nevertheless, it is at this point that an aesthetic argument for anti-intentionalism may be brought to bear. To wit: if a transgression interpretation of *Plan 9 from Outer Space* yields a more aesthetically satisfying encounter with the film, and our primary purpose in interpretation is in promoting maximum aesthetic satisfaction, why not suspend

qualms about intention and take *Plan 9 from Outer Space* as a masterpiece of postmodernist disjunction *à la lettre*? Here, the anti-intentionalist might agree that such an interpretation cannot be squared with what it is plausible to say of the film, given the possible intentions of the historical director. But why not sacrifice the distinction between mistakes and transgressions if in the long run it supplies us with more aesthetically satisfying experiences?

That is, the argument against taking *Plan 9* as a transgression rests on the supposition that it is not a reasonable hypothesis of what Wood could have meant in producing the film. But so what? If we drop a commitment to discerning authorial intent, and regard any norm violation as a transgression, would not that make *Plan 9* more aesthetically interesting, and if our premium is on aesthetic interest, would not anti-intentionalist criticism be our best bet?

But I submit that insofar as we have a conversational interest in artworks, we will want to reject this sort of aesthetic argument. For if we take ourselves to be aiming at a genuine conversation, ignoring Wood's palpable intentions, it seems to me, can only undermine our sense of ourselves as authentic participants in the conversation. For, from the point of view of genuine conversation, we are being willfully silly in regarding *Plan 9* as a transgression of Hollywood codes of filmmaking. We are behaving as if we believed that a randomly collected series of phrases, derived from turning the dial of our car radio at one-second intervals, harbored the message of an oracle, and simultaneously we agree that all forms of divination are preposterous.

In his *Concluding Unscientific Postscript*, Kierkegaard notes that a comic moment arises when "a sober man engages in sympathetic and confidential conversation with one whom he does not know is intoxicated, while the observer knows of the condition. The contradiction lies in the mutuality presupposed by the conversation, that it is not there, and that the sober man has not noticed its absence."[26] By analogy, in supposing that Wood is a kind of Godard, we are acting as if a stream of drunken incoherencies constitute an enigmatic code. Indeed, we are placing ourselves in an even more ridiculous position than the butt of Kierkegaard's mishap, for we have voluntarily entered this situation.

In Kosinski's *Being There*, the naïf Chance utters all sorts of remarks about his garden, which other characters take to be of great gnomic significance. Since they are unaware that Chance is a simpleton, they are, in effect, applying something like Culler's anti-intentionalist rule of significance[27] to the sayings of a fool. The result, as with Kierkegaard's imagined conversation with the drunk, is comic. Taking something like *Plan 9* to be a radical transgression of Hollywood International seems to me to be a matter of willingly adopting the ludicrous position that those characters suffer inadvertently. It undermines any self-respecting view we could have of ourselves as participants in a conversation. Whatever aesthetic satisfaction we could claim of such an exchange would have to be bought at the conversational cost of making ourselves rather obtuse.

Aesthetic arguments for anti-intentionalism proceed as if aesthetic satisfaction were the only important interest we could have with respect to artworks. Thus, wherever other putative interests impede aesthetic interests, they must give way. But aesthetic satisfaction is not the only major source of value that we have in interacting with artworks; the interaction is also a matter of a conversation between the artist and us – a human encounter – in which we have a desire to know what the artist intends, not only out of respect for the artist, but also because we have a personal interest in being a capable respondent. In endorsing the anti-intentionalist view that aesthetic satisfaction trumps all other interests, we seem to be willing to go for aesthetic pleasure at all costs, including, most notably, any value we might place on having a genuine conversational exchange with another human being. For, as the *Plan 9* example suggests, we are willing to act as if we had encountered a profound, reflexive meditation on the dominant cinema, when, in fact, it is readily apparent that we are dealing with a botched and virtually incoherent atrocity.

Aesthetic arguments in favor of anti-intentionalism presume a species of aesthetic hedonism. They presuppose that aesthetic pleasure or satisfaction is our only legitimate interest with regard to artworks. Here it is useful to recall Robert Nozick's very provocative, antihedonistic thought experiment – the experience machine.

Suppose there were an experience machine that would give you any experience you desired. Super-duper neuropsychologists could stimulate your brain so that you would think and feel you were writing a great novel, or making a friend, or reading an interesting book. All the time you would be floating in a tank, with electrodes attached to your brain. Should you plug into the machine for life, preprogramming your life's experiences?[28]

Nozick thinks that our answer here will be obviously no, and part of the reason is that we wish to be a certain kind of person and do various things and not just have experiences as if we were such a person and as if we were doing those things. In other words, the pleasure of these simulated experiences is not enough; we have a stake in actually having the experiences in question. Applied to the aesthetic case, what I am trying to defend in the name of conversational interests is the claim that we have an investment in really encountering interesting and brilliant authors, not simply in counterfeiting such encounters. Knowing that *Plan 9* is a schlock quickie, but responding to it as if it were superbly transgressive, is akin to knowingly taking the heroics performed in Nozick's experience machine as if they were actual adventures. It is a matter of sacrificing genuine conversational experiences for aesthetic pleasures. And in doing so, one is willing to lower one's self-esteem for the sake of an aesthetic high.[29]

Of course, the problem I have raised with the use and abuse of the concept of transgression by contemporary film critics brings up general problems with aesthetic arguments in favor of anti-intentionalism. For example, the pervasive problems of allusion and irony are strictly analogous to the problems that we have sketched with respect to transgression. One could render both Richard Bach's *Jonathan Livingston Seagull*[30] and Heinrich Anacker's anti-Semitic, pro-Nazi "Exodus of the Parasites"[31] more aesthetically satisfying by regarding them as ironic. Yet I suspect that we resist this kind of interpretive temptation. And this resistance, I think, can be explained by our conversational interests in artworks. We have every justification for believing that these works are tawdry but sincere, and behaving as though they were ironic – whatever aesthetic satisfaction that might promote – would place us in what we recognize to be an ersatz conversation. We would be, respectively, laughing *with* what we know we should be laughing *at*, and appalled *along with* what we know we should be appalled *at*. Our conversation would not be authentic in either event, and whatever aesthetic satisfaction we secured would be purchased by making ourselves conversationally incompetent. Insofar as one of the abiding values we pursue in encounters with artworks is conversational, we are not willing to turn these particular pig's ears into silk purses.

Stanley Cavell has argued that one of the audience's major preoccupations with modern art is whether it is sincere. Given the dadaist tendencies of contemporary art, the spectator cares whether he or she is being fooled by the artist.[32] The encounter with the artwork is a human situation in which our self-esteem may be felt to be at risk. Likewise, I want to stress that insofar as the artistic context is a kind of conversation, we also may be concerned not only that the artist is given his or her due but that we carry through our end of the conversation. In terms of self-esteem, we have an interest not only in not being gulled by the artist but also in not fooling ourselves. And this interest gives us reason to reject interpretations of artworks that, however aesthetically satisfying they may be, cannot sensibly be connected to the intentions of their authors. The simulacrum of a brilliant conversation cannot be willfully substituted for a brilliant conversation and be a genuinely rewarding experience.

If these thoughts about our conversational interests in works of art are convincing, then they indicate that it is not true that the prospect of aesthetic satisfaction trumps every other desideratum when it comes to interpretation. Aesthetic satisfaction does not obviate our conversational interests in artworks. Moreover, our conversational interest in artworks is best served by intentionalism. Thus, in order to coordinate our aesthetic interests and our conversational interests, the best policy would not appear to be anti-intentionalism but the pursuit of aesthetic satisfaction constrained by our best hypotheses about authorial intent.

These hypotheses, moreover, will often depend on facts available to us about the biography of the artist. That the artist lived in fifteenth-century Italy, for example, will constrain attribution of his supposed intent to explore the themes of Greenbergian modernism in his canvases. Biographical data, in other words, can play a role in hypothesizing the artist's intention, while the recognition of the artist's intention, in turn, constrains the kinds of satisfactions, and, correspondingly, the kinds of interpretations we may advance with respect to artworks.[33] Not only is authorial intention derivable from artworks; authorial intention – and biographical information – are relevant to the realization of the aims, particularly the conversational aims, we bring to artworks. Aesthetic arguments do not show that anti-intentionalism is the best interpretive policy to endorse given our purposes with respect

to artworks. For we are interested in art as an occasion for communication with others as well as a source of aesthetic pleasure. And to the extent that communication or communion is among the leading purposes of art, authorial intention must always figure in interpretation, at least as a constraint on whatever other purposes we seek.

Notes

1 H. P. Grice, "Meaning," *Philosophical Review* 66 (1957). See also Grice's *Studies in the Way of Words* (Cambridge, Mass.: Harvard University Press, 1989).

2 The idea of interpretations as *hypotheses* about authorial intentions is derived from William Tolhurst, "On What a Text Is and How It Means," *British Journal of Aesthetics* 19 (1979).

3 See W. K. Wimsatt, Jr., and Monroe C. Beardsley, "The Intentional Fallacy," *Swanee Review* 54 (1946). This is an expansion of their "Intention," in *Dictionary of World Literature*, ed. J. T. Shipley (New York: Philosophical Library, 1943).

4 See, for example, E. M. W. Tillyard and C. S. Lewis, *The Personal Heresy: A Controversy* (London: Oxford University Press, 1939). Stein Haugom Olsen makes the very interesting claim that the intentional fallacy evolved from the personal heresy but that the shift to intention talk also changed the debate in fateful ways. See Stein Haugom Olsen, *The End of Literary Theory* (Cambridge: Cambridge University Press, 1987), pp. 27–8.

5 Anti-intentionalists have not always been careful to keep the issues of authorial intention, reports of authorial intention, and biography apart. But one should. For example, one may believe that authorial intent is relevant to interpretation and at the same time maintain strong reservations about the authority of authorial pronouncements about the meaning of their artworks. On the distinction between intention and biography, see Colin Lyas, "Personal Qualities and the Intentional Fallacy," *Philosophy and the Arts: Royal Institute of Philosophy Lectures*, vol. 6 (New York: St. Martin's Press, 1973).

6 Monroe C. Beardsley, *Aesthetics* (New York: Harcourt, Brace and World, 1958), p. 20.

7 Monroe C. Beardsley, "An Aesthetic Definition of Art" in *What Is Art?* ed. Hugh Curtler (New York: Haven, 1984); and Monroe C. Beardsley, "Intending," in *Values and Morals*, ed. Alvin I. Goldman and Jaegwon Kim (Dordrecht: Reidel, 1978).

8 Beardsley, "Intending."

9 For related arguments dealing with the problem of arbitrary authorial pronouncements, see P. D. Juhl, *Interpretation: An Essay in the Philosophy of Literary Criticism* (Princeton: Princeton University Press, 1980), esp. ch. 7, sec. 4.

10 Beardsley, *Aesthetics*, p. 458.

11 Thomas Kuhn, *The Structure of Scientific Revolutions* (Chicago: University of Chicago Press, 1970), p. 9.

12 If Kuhn had really meant "weaned" here, he should have written "weaned from," not "weaned on."

13 The *locus classicus* of this view of intention is G. E. M. Anscombe's *Intention* (Oxford: Blackwell, 1959). Mary Mothersill provides a brief but useful sketch of the history of these countervailing views of intention in her *Beauty Restored* (Oxford: Oxford University Press, 1984), pp. 15–21.

14 See, for example, Stanley Cavell, "Music Discomposed," in his *Must We Mean What We Say?* (Cambridge: Cambridge University Press, 1976), p. 181. Also see "A Matter of Meaning It" in the same volume. These originally appeared in *Art, Mind and Religion*, ed. W. H. Capitan and D. D. Merrill (Pittsburgh: University of Pittsburgh Press, 1967). Also relevant is Richard Kuhns, "Criticism and the Problem of Intention," *Journal of Philosophy* 57 (1960). Other arguments in the neo-Wittgensteinian vein include Frank Cioffi "Intention and Interpretation in Criticism," *Proceedings of the Aristotelian Society* 64 (1963–4); and A. J. Close, "Don Quixote and the 'Intentionalist Fallacy,'" in *On Literary Intention: Critical Essays*, ed. David Newton-de Molina (Edinburgh: Edinburgh University Press, 1976).

15 Monroe Beardsley himself seems to have agreed that the earlier view of intention upon which his arguments were based is inadequate – which is one reason why he developed what I call the ontological argument for anti-intentionalism that is examined later in this essay. See Monroe C. Beardsley, "Intentions and Interpretations: A Fallacy Revived," in *The Aesthetic Point of View*, ed. Michael J. Wreen and Donald M. Callen (Ithaca, NY: Cornell University Press, 1982), p. 189.

16 Monroe C. Beardsley, *The Possibility of Criticism* (Detroit: Wayne State University Press, 1970), p. 34.

17 For elaborations of this distinction, see Tolhurst, "On What a Text Is," and Jack W. Meiland, "The Meanings of a Text," *British Journal of Aesthetics* 21 (1981).

18 This notion is elaborated on by Umberto Eco in his *The Open Work* (Cambridge, Mass.: Harvard University Press, 1989).

19 I take this to be the point of Jack Meiland's "The Meanings of a Text."

20 It stands in the way of maximizing interpretive play if the authorial intent is determinate; it is irrelevant because if we adopt anti-intentionalist interpretive practices, then whether or not the author intended an "open text," we will read it in that like anyway.

21 This position has been defended by Laurent Stern in his "On Interpreting," *Journal of Aesthetics and*

Art Criticism 39 (1980); and Laurent Stern's "Facts and Interpretations," address to the Pacific Division meetings of the American Philosophical Association, Spring 1988.

22 A moral purpose that anti-intentionalism might be thought to advance is the emancipation of the spectator, a view with respect to interpretation that parallels the aspiration of many modern artists. But one wonders here whether the freedom of the reader here is genuinely moral or whether it is merely a strained moralization of the *free* play of cognition enjoined by Kantian aestheticism.

Or it might be felt that opening the artwork to interpretative play affords some kind of consciousness-raising heuristic; Jonathan Culler seems to have this view at the end of *Structuralist Poetics* where engaging the nonauthorially constrained play of textual signs teaches the reader something about the process of semiosis in general (p. 264). This claim would depend on a very controversial view of how language, in general, functions.

As well, one could imagine a literary theorist defending anti-intentionalism as securing an institutional purpose. That is, since the literary-critical institution is predicated on the production of interpretations, anti-intentionalism is facilitating because it keeps more interpretive options open. Nevertheless, the job security of literary critics hardly seems like the kind of overriding purpose that would move the rest of us.

Interestingly, intentionalism has also been defended for what might be thought of as institutional purposes. E. D. Hirsch, for example, wants to defend literary criticism as a cognitive discipline, and he believes that this requires determinate meaning, a commitment best served, on his account, by authorial intention. In this respect, Hirsch, unlike P. D. Juhl, is advancing intentionalism as a means to secure an end of the literary institution rather than as a thesis about the nature of meaning. See E. D. Hirsch, Jr., *Validity in Interpretation* (New Haven: Yale University Press, 1967); and E. D. Hirsch, Jr., *The Aims of Interpretation* (Chicago: University of Chicago Press, 1976).

23 This is not an invented example. See J. Hoberman, "Bad Movies," *Film Comment*, July–August 1980. Similar arguments appear in Hoberman's "Vulgar Modernism," *Artforum*, February 1982.

Moreover, I should stress that the issue raised by Hoberman's critical practice is not isolated. For it is often the case that the developments of avant-garde art are projected or read backward with respect to earlier works in the tradition. Thus, previously we saw Barthes's tendency to regard Mallarmé's modernist aspiration to efface authorship as a feature of all antecedent writing.

24 Hoberman, "Bad Movies."

25 Intentionalist criticism is guided by what a given text or artwork could have meant to the work's

contemporary informed audience. Reference to what the audience could have understood is not to be taken as an alternative to intentionalist criticism, however, but as a means of identifying authorial intent. For, *ex hypothesi*, we begin by attributing to the author the intention of communicating – of getting her audience to recognize her intention. Thus, what we conjecture as the intention of the author, charitably, is something that the author could reasonably believe the audience – that is, the informed audience – could recognize. It should also be noted that included under the rubric of intentionalist criticism is the elucidation of the author's presuppositions, especially the elucidation of the stylistic choice structure through which the author's intentional activity takes place. And again, what an informed audience could perceive as a stylistic option guides our hypotheses about the author's intentions for the reasons already given.

26 Søren Kierkegaard, *Concluding Unscientific Postscript* (Princeton: Princeton University Press, 1941), p. 466.
27 Culler, *Structuralist Poetics*, p. 115.
28 Robert Nozick, *Anarchy, State, and Utopia* (New York: Basic Books, 1974), p. 42.
29 Why, it might be asked, if this analysis is correct, do so many critics seem willing to indulge anti-inten-

tionalist criticism? One hypothesis is that by means of theoretical devices like unconscious or ideological motivation, they believe that they are getting at the author's actual intentions.
30 This example comes from Denis Dutton, "Why Intentionalism Won't Go Away," in *Literature and the Question of Philosophy*, ed. Anthony Cascardi (Baltimore: Johns Hopkins University Press, 1987).
31 Juhl, *Interpretation*, pp. 121–4.
32 Cavell, "Music Discomposed."
33 Daniel Nathan has argued that intentionalist arguments often depend on having access to contextual information about the text – rather than biographical evidence – and that the anti-intentionalist also may, in principle, have access to contextual information. I think, however, that an example like Edward Wood indicates that biographical information may also be required. For Wood was a contemporary of the Surrealist filmmaker Buñuel, someone who had the intellectual resources and the will to make a transgressive film. Thus, knowing that the filmmaker was Wood, and knowing something about Wood, and that the filmmaker was not Buñuel, is crucial to our dismissal of *Plan 9* as a mistake. See Daniel O. Nathan, "Irony and the Artist's Intentions," *British Journal of Aesthetics* 23 (1982).

38

Intention and Interpretation

Jerrold Levinson

II

When we ask ourselves, What do literary texts mean, and how do they embody such meaning as they have? I think there are only four models to choose from in answer. One is that such meaning is akin to word-sequence (e.g., sentence) meaning *simpliciter*. Another is that it is akin to the utterer's (author's) meaning on a given occasion. A third assimilates it to the utterance meaning generated on a given occasion in specific circumstances.[1] And a last model pictures it, most liberally, in terms of what may be called ludic meaning.[2]

Word-sequence meaning, roughly, is "dictionary" meaning – the meaning (or, usually, meanings) attachable to a sequence of words taken in the abstract in virtue of the operative syntactic and semantic (including connotative) rules of the specific, time-indexed, language in which those words are taken to occur. *Utterer's meaning* is the meaning an intentional agent (speaker, writer) has in mind or in view to convey by the use of a given verbal vehicle. *Utterance meaning*, in contrast, is the meaning that such a vehicle ends up conveying in its context of utterance – which context includes its being uttered by such-and-such agent. *Ludic meaning*, finally, comprises any meanings that can

be attributed to either a brute text (a word sequence in a language), or a text-as-utterance, in virtue of interpretive play constrained by only the loosest requirements of plausibility, intelligibility, or interest.

Literary meaning cannot be equated simply with untethered word-sequence (or sentence) meaning, because it is crucial to the task of interpretation that the sentences of a literary text be presumed to issue from a single mind,[3] to have a purpose, and to be the vehicle of a specific act of communication, widely construed. We do not treat literary texts the way we would random collections of sentences, such as might be formed in the sands of a beach or spewed out by computer programs. The sentences that make up a literary work, on a primary level, are not merely a collection or assemblage but the body and substance of what we assume to be a unitary act of expression.

Equally clearly, though, literary meaning cannot be equated *tout court* with utterer's meaning, since that would dissolve the distinction between normal practical linguistic activity – where the paramount object is to communicate what the speaker or writer is thinking or wanting to say – and communication in a literary mode, where the text is held to have a certain amount of autonomy,

From Gary Iseminger (ed.), *Intention and Interpretation* (Philadelphia: Temple University Press, 1992), pp. 222–32, 240–4, 252–3, 255. © 1992 by Temple University. All rights reserved. Reprinted by permission of Temple University Press.

to be something we interpret, to some extent, for its own sake, and thus not jettisonable in principle if we could get more directly at what the author had in mind to tell us. When a poet vouchsafes us, in plain language, what some enigmatic poem of his might mean, we do not react by then discarding the poem in favor of the offered precis. In ordinary verbal intercourse, what a person means takes precedence over, or overrides, what the person's language as uttered may end up meaning to a suitably grounded interlocutor; this seems not clearly so in the sphere of literary production. Finally, what I have labeled ludic meaning – which is akin to what Arthur Danto posits as the object or outcome of "deep" interpretation – is an inappropriate candidate for at least the fundamental meaning of literary texts, if only because it presupposes such in order to get off the ground.[4]

This leaves only utterance meaning – the meaning a linguistic vehicle has in a given context of presentation or projection, which context arguably includes, in addition to directly observable features of the act of utterance, something of the characteristics of the author who projects the text, something of the text's place in a surrounding oeuvre and culture, and possibly other elements as well. But what does such meaning amount to, for a typically complex work of literature? How do we get at it, and what are we aiming at in seeking it? To these questions, William Tolhurst has given an instructive answer:

> Utterance meaning is best understood as the intention which a member of the intended audience would be most justified in attributing to the author based on the knowledge and attitudes which he possesses in virtue of being a member of the intended audience. Thus utterance meaning is to be construed as that hypothesis of utterer's meaning which is most justified on the basis of those beliefs and attitudes which one possesses qua intended hearer or intended reader.[5]

> In understanding an utterance one constructs a hypothesis as to the intention which that utterance is best viewed as fulfilling.[6]

So utterance meaning is logically distinct from utterer's meaning and at the same time is necessarily related to it conceptually: we arrive at utterance meaning by aiming at utterer's meaning in the most comprehensive and informed manner we

can muster as the utterance's intended recipients. Actual utterer's intention, then, is not what is determinative of the meaning of a literary offering (or other linguistic discourse) but such intention as optimally *hypothesized*, given all the resources available to us in the work's internal structure and the relevant surrounding context of creation, in all its legitimately invoked specificity.[7] The core of utterance meaning can be conceived of analytically as our best appropriately informed projection of author's intended meaning from our positions as intended interpreters.

The compromise between intentionalism and anti-intentionalism suggested by Tolhurst's approach is thus that the core of literary meaning, as with any piece of discourse publicly presented, is not the meaning (the many meanings) of the words and sentences taken in abstraction from the author, or precisely of necessity the meaning that the author actually intended to put across, but our best hypothetical attribution of such, formed from the position of intended audience. This latter will tend often (e.g., in successful cases) to coincide with actually intended meaning, but the principled distinction between them remains important, both for seeing clearly what we are about when we strive to pin down with some degree of definiteness the meanings – possibly manifold – of a work of literature and for the light it casts on interpretive disputes in difficult cases.

This is a good point to remark how the idea of a best hypothetical attribution of intention to an author is itself best understood. I have in mind that this be done with a certain duality. Principally, a "best" attribution is one that is epistemically best – that has the most likelihood of being correct, given the total evidence available to one in the position of ideal reader. But secondarily, a "best" attribution of intention to an author might involve, in accord with a principle of critical charity, choosing a construal that makes the work artistically better, where there is room for choice, so long as plausibly ascribed to the author given the full context of writing. In other words, if we can, in a given case, make the author out to have created a cleverer or more striking or more imaginative piece, without violating the image of his work as an artist that is underpinned by the total available textual and contextual evidence, we should perhaps do so. That is then our best projection of intent – "best" in two senses – as informed and sympathetic readers. This does not, however, license our viewing a work under an interpretation on which it comes off well artistically if such is not one we could on good grounds epistemically associate with or impute to the historical author as we in the main grasp him.

Such is the view of literary meaning that guides my reflections throughout this essay. Before proceeding, though, we must address certain problems inherent in Tolhurst's formulation of the view and consider ways of meeting them.

III

The notion of a literary work's meaning, and thus of correct interpretations of it, is properly tied, as I have said, not to actual – even successfully realized – artist's intent,[8] but to our best construction, given the evidence of the work and appropriately possessed background information, of the artist's intent to mean such and such for his or her intended audience. In short this is because literature making (and art making generally) is closely analogous to a speech-act, that is, it is an act of attempted communication in a broad sense, one of an oblique sort. As such, its products – works of literature – should have the sort of meaning that the products or upshots of speech-acts – utterances – centrally have, namely, utterance meaning. And it can further be argued, as Tolhurst has done, that utterance meaning is capturable through the idea of the best contextually informed hypothesis of what a speaker–writer is attempting to communicate to the intended audience.

Tolhurst's proposal, however, was criticized a few years back by Daniel Nathan, on a number of grounds.[9] I first address those I regard as less troubling and then proceed to the one that strikes me as more weighty. Nathan begins by criticizing Tolhurst for having too narrow a notion of word-sequence meaning, one that abstracts unnecessarily from the "connotative characteristics of words."[10] I think this charge is unfounded. Tolhurst could allow all the general, language-wide, time-bound connotations of words to be comprised in word-sequence meaning and yet insist that the full meaning of an utterance in many cases is still determinately different from what the denotative and connotative meanings of the words involved will themselves underwrite and is instead finally fixed by features of the individual, pragmatic context of utterance.

Nathan next holds that Tolhurst's examples, in particular his appeal to Swift's *A Modest Proposal*, depend essentially on ignoring the complete texts of which his extracts are a part. But surely the theoretical point that Tolhurst is after still holds – that there easily could be literary texts that in their completeness justified either an ironic or literal reading, leaving context of utterance aside, but that, given such context, we would judge as clearly either ironic or nonironic. Consider as an example the following, which also illustrates the dependence of utterance meaning on activated context and its independence of speaker's actual meaning.

Emilia is a graduate student in history, whose adviser, Basil Bushwacker, is leaving to take a post at another university. As is well-known among her friends, Emilia harbors ambivalent and resentful feelings toward her rather egoistic and unavailable mentor, though he, fortunately, is oblivious to this. She will, however, continue to require his support in external ways for the near future. After a farewell presentation in his honor, she writes him a short note, whose purpose is to ensure his continued goodwill toward her in the coming years:

> Dear Dr. Bushwacker:
> I was delighted to be present at your valedictory event last week; the tributes, although impressive, did not do you justice. We will all be immeasurably sad to lose you, and hope you will find many opportunities to visit the friends and colleagues you leave behind at Wunderwelt U.
> Sincerely,
> Emilia Edelweiss

The meaning of the above, as a letter sent (or to be sent) to Dr. B., is roughly one of appreciation, praise, and gentle entreaty. That is the utterance meaning of the text employed in that fashion – it is how Dr. B., or a similarly placed recipient of a letter from a seemingly respectful charge, would naturally take it. Label this Open Letter. On the other hand, as a text circulated (or to be circulated) among the student's circle of friends, with the knowledge they are privy to and rightly bring to bear, the phrases of the text acquire ironic content that they did not possess as part of a letter written openly to the salutee: the "tributes" do not do justice because insufficiently upbraiding, the "sadness" will be immeasurable because minuscule, and so on. The utterance meaning of this entity –

label it Private Epistle – is quite different from that of Open Letter. It is one of blame, relief, and excoriation, for that is the authorial intention that would most naturally be projected on the words by Private Epistle's intended or appropriate audience. The texts – the complete texts – of both Open Letter and Private Epistle, however, are absolutely identical.[11]

I come now to Nathan's more worrisome charge. Tolhurst's proposal, he notes, is motivated by the desire to escape from strong intentionalism and its attendant problems, appealing instead only to a hypothesized author's intention. But Tolhurst has failed to notice that his proposal is still anchored in the author's actual intentions, through that intention, namely, that picks out a certain class or kind of reader as charged with the justifiable projection of intended authorial meaning definitive of work meaning. This reference to author's intention, claims Nathan, is both pernicious and ineliminable.

> Tolhurst allows cases where identifying the intended audience is not possible on public grounds, that is, the intended audience is different from the one the author is in fact addressing.... Further, given no limits to the narrowness of the intended audience, the author may be speaking a language the meaning of which is known only to himself and his family.... Tolhurst claims that the author is not in a privileged position vis-à-vis what he has written, that any member of that audience shares access to that meaning. But the determination of the intended audience is in principle a private matter, hence ultimately so is meaning.[12]

How should a hypothetical intentionalist respond to this? I think there are two options. One is to try to show that an author's intentional identification of an intended *audience* is significantly different from, and less troubling than, an author's intentional determination of the meaning of his text, as endorsed by full-fledged intentionalists. The other is to abandon the notion of an intended audience in favor of that of an *appropriate* audience, where this is not up to authorial determination.

Taking the first tack, we may note that the content of an audience-identifying intention is at least less problematic than the content of a semantic intention, especially one that would govern a complex work of literature as a whole. Dostoyevsky's intended audience in writing *The Brothers Karamazov*, if we could ascertain it, would be something on this order: competent readers of Russian, practiced in narrative fiction, aware of Russian history, familiar with Russian religious traditions, and so on. But Dostoyevsky's comprehensive meaning intention for *The Brothers Karamazov* has as object something hardly even imaginable apart from the novel itself and an exhaustive interpretation of it. Given this great difference in level between the two, then, it might seem to represent some progress that an analysis would, if not wholly avoiding intentions whose accessibility is in question, at least substitute for one whose scope is rather mind-boggling another that is more down to earth, in the role of anchoring a work's otherwise indeterminate meaning.

Note, next, that the nature of the audience intentionally targeted by an author is not, after all, particularly opaque to us. Consider my partial sketch of the audience at which *The Brothers Karamazov* was undoubtedly aimed. I consulted no oracle for it, neither did I study Dostoyevsky's diaries or the records left by his physician. I merely considered the novel itself, the demands of comprehension inherent in it, and the novel's context of creation (e.g., nineteenth-century Russia). This observation, however, shifts us toward the second option, that of an appropriate, as opposed to authorially intended, audience, in that it in effect invokes a hypothesization of the intended audience; that is, as that audience we would be most justified in assuming the author was aiming at – where "we" are now understood as just rational judges possessed of all relevant contextual information. But if this is the pass to which we come, it might be better simply to drop reference to intended audiences, even reasonably hypothesizable intended audiences, and just speak of an audience that is an *appropriate* (or *ideal*) one for a given work, as judged by what it would appear to take to understand such a work properly. Let us pursue that idea.

I suggest we may be guided in identifying an appropriate audience for a given work, whose best projection of authorial intention will, as before, be constitutive of basic work meaning, by certain norms and conventions understood to define the sphere of literary production and reception.[13] Thus, an appropriate reader, for anything presented in the framework of literature, might be profiled generally as one versed in and cognizant of the tradition out of which the work arises, acquainted with the rest of the author's oeuvre, and perhaps familiar as well with the author's public literary and intellectual identity or persona. These are ground rules, as it were, of the literary enterprise, of the implicit contract between writer and reader, and it is not clear that an author can unilaterally abrogate such an understanding in favor of a specified audience whose information or capacities are significantly at variance with those involved in the profile just sketched.

Thus the best response to Nathan's criticism of the residual actual intentionalism in Tolhurst's conception, as embodied in the idea of the author's intended audience, may be to excise that residue and rely instead on a notion of an appropriate reader, where the meaning of that is filled in both by what can be seen, from the work itself, as incontrovertibly required for textual understanding – for example, competence in the language (including dialects) employed and knowledge of the references and allusions embedded in the text – and certain givens of the cultural "language game" in which writer and reader are bound, involving a presumption of shared knowledge of traditions, oeuvres, writerly identities, and the like.[14]

Finally, to emphasize the fact that the central meaning of a literary work should be thought of as akin to that of an utterance in a context, as opposed to either what a text means apart from its quite specific context of issuance or what the author–utterer intends to convey, but to foreground more clearly its written condition and more formal mode of presentation, we could coin the term *literance* for what literary works are. Poems, novels, short stories are literances – texts presented and projected in literary contexts, whose meaning, it is understood by both author and audience, will be a function of and constrained by – though in ways neither might clearly predict – the potentialities of the text per se together with the generative matrix provided by its issuing forth from individual A, with public persona B, at time C, against cultural background D, in light of predecessors E, in the shadow of contemporary events F, in relation to the remainder of A's artistic oeuvre G, and so on.

IV

As an illustration of the hypothetical–intentionalist position on interpretation I am advocating, consider Kafka's story, *A Country Doctor*. In this

singular fiction the doctor of the title is awakened suddenly at night and summoned to the bedside of a boy suffering from a horrible wound, leaving his house servant at the mercy of his menacing groom. Though the boy is beyond help, the doctor is induced to attempt a curious cure, which involves getting into bed with the patient; the cure is, naturally, futile, and the doctor can scarcely extricate himself from the situation to return to what he fears are only the shambles of home and hearth he left behind just hours before. The relevant background information, or author-specific context of understanding, for an interpretation of this enigmatic narrative would surely include the following: Kafka regularly worked at night; Kafka thought of writing as "medicinal," "therapeutic," "a calling"; Kafka did not separate his writing and his life; Kafka was familiar with Freud's *Interpretation of Dreams*; and the content of Kafka's "A Hunger Artist," written five years after *A Country Doctor*, about a man who starves himself publicly as both an artistic performance and an admission that ordinary food had no appeal for him.

Given that as background, and given the intrinsic matter of the text, one might readily come up with this interpretation: *A Country Doctor* is a stylized dream report. Its content is basically the conflict between ordinary, sensual life, as represented by the servant girl Rose and the doctor's comfortable home, and one's calling: to heal, edify, spiritually succor. The doctor is in effect an artist, as is, more transparently, the Hunger Artist of Kafka's later tale. He is caught betwixt and between, naked and disoriented, as was Kafka between his literary and his domestic duties and desires. And the sick boy is like the doctor's younger self – through art (*Arzt*), one primarily tries to heal oneself, and only secondarily others.[15]

Thus our best informed-reader construction of what this specific writer, Kafka, was aiming to convey – was engaged in communicating – in writing *A Country Doctor*, may be something like the one just given. It makes sense to attribute such a meaning or content to the author as he is available to us – his appropriate, contextually sensitized, readers.

Still, we might just find out – from Kafka's secret diary, say, or a close informant, or even advanced aliens who were scanning Kafka's thought processes at the time – that Kafka's immediate, explicit intent in writing *A Country Doctor* was in fact to critique rural medical practices, to lampoon their typical unpreparedness and lack of materials, and to expose the deep-seated ignorance of the Czech peasantry. The text could just barely support such a meaning, much as "my car ran out of gas" can just manage to be the vehicle of a meaning in mind involving cabooses and clouds of chlorine.[16] Still, this would not supplant the interpretation just given as what the work, in a reader-accessible, Kafka-specific context, means. Our best construction, in a dual sense,[17] of what Kafka the writer is communicating in *A Country Doctor* would trump our discovery of what Kafka the person might oddly have been intending to mean on the occasion of penning the story. Admittedly the possibility of divergence between specific actual intent and best hypothesized intent given all appropriate reader data is a fairly thin one, but it is not therefore zero. And theoretically the difference is important for the philosophy of literary criticism.

V

We must briefly confront yet another problem for any hypothetical-intentionalist conception of literary meaning. Let us assume that the core meaning of a literary work is utterance meaning, that is, what a text says in an author-specific context of presentation to an appropriate, or suitably backgrounded, reader. Even if we agree that such meaning is given by a reader's best projection-in-context of what its author intended to mean, this still seems to leave aspects of utterance meaning – of what is said in a work – that go beyond that. There are, it can be fairly held, unenvisaged and not plausibly envisageable implications, unforeseen and not plausibly foreseeable resonances, hidden significations, and the like, of a given text, which are yet properly comprised in literary meaning as just defined. These can seem part of what is conveyed literarily even while not reasonably attributable to the author as we have hypothesized him on the basis of our relevantly engaged background knowledge.

Three strategies suggest themselves for dealing with unintended meanings properly ascribed to a literary work, from the point of view of hypothetical intentionalism. The first is to acknowledge them straightforwardly, but to qualify them as secondary; primary or central literary meaning, it

could be held, must still be in line with reasonably projectible intention, even though secondary meanings, ascribable to a work once it is centrally interpreted, need not conform to that standard of projectibility. The second is to propose a broader notion of the author's intended meaning, as hypothesizable by an appropriate reader, one that takes the existence of discoverable but unintended (and not reasonably ascribable) specific meanings in a literary utterance to be reasonably ascribable to the author as a class, or collectively, in virtue of his entry into the literary domain and implicit acceptance of a principle roughly licensing discerning of not explicitly intended, though possible-for-the-author[18] meanings that directly emerge from or are implied by a text centrally interpreted in line with reasonably projected intent, even when such meanings are not individually ascribable to the author as likely to have been meant.[19]

A third strategy, going beyond even a broadened notion of author's intended meaning, would be to appeal to what I have elsewhere called perspectives *justified* with respect to a given historically positioned work, although not *accessible* to its author (and therefore not plausibly projectible by him). Such perspectives might be considered justified, and thus the aspects of the work they revealed part of its literary content, if they can be shown to be rooted, abstractly or embryonically, in the concerns of the historically constructible author.[20]

Since my main concern in this essay is primary or central literary meaning, and since I think hypothetical intentionalism gives the best account of that, I will not attempt here definitively to settle this issue of aptly-ascribed-to-work-yet-improbably-ascribable-to-author unintended meanings, but will assume that a treatment along one or another of the lines just sketched would ultimately be adequate. [...]

X

A main thrust of Noël Carroll's engaging essay[21] is to undercut opposition to intentionalism that derives from the belief that the context of literary discourse is significantly different from that of ordinary conversation so that the intentionalism that is an exceedingly natural perspective in the latter case is not appropriate in the former. I am in partial agreement with that thrust, since I would hold, with Carroll, that a rather more absolute disjunction between the two contexts than is warranted is a characteristic of a number of recent influential theories of literary meaning, for example, Beardsleyan "New Criticism" and Barthesian "death-of-author-ism." But, *contra* Carroll, I think there are residual differences between the contexts and the rules and procedures of decipherment that hold sway in them. One difference, it seems to me, between literary and conversational situations is that utterer's meaning is virtually *all important* in the latter, while the meaning of the vehicle itself, if opposed to the former, counts for virtually nothing. I agree that when an author proffers a text as literature to a literary audience, just as when he or she speaks to others in the ordinary setting, he or she is entering a public language game, a communicative arena, but suggest that it is one with different aims and understandings than apply in normal, one-on-one (or even many-on-many) conversational settings. Although in informative discourse we rightly look for intended meaning first, foremost, and hindmost, in literary art we are licensed, if I am right, to consider what meanings the verbal text before us, viewed in context, *could* be being used to convey and then to form, if we can, in accord with the practice of literary communication to which both author and reader have implicitly subscribed, our best hypothesis of what it is being used to convey, ultimately identifying that with the meaning of the work. What distinguishes our forming that hypothesis in regard to a literary work, as opposed to a piece of conversation, is that we do so for its own sake, the contextually embedded vehicle of meaning in literature being indispensable, not something to be bypassed in favor of more direct access to personal meaning when or if that is available.

So here I would agree with Shusterman, as against Carroll, that literary and practical linguistic communication *are* to be distinguished: Carroll errs in denying or minimizing any difference in the operative conditions and criteria of the two. But I am very far from anchoring such distinctness, as Shusterman does, by ascribing historically unconstrained and reader-driven interpretability to the former. We may admit various modes of literary interpretation, answering to interests other

than those of truth, expression, and communication, but still hold it possible to locate among them what I have called basic interpretation, and to characterize in a fairly stable manner what that must orient itself toward. Only in relation to the results of basic, author-and-history respecting, interpretation, can such further modes of interpretation have a proper foothold and warrant. Shusterman claims that even if textual meaning (what Iseminger and I would call work meaning) is, as Knapp and Michaels (and Hirsch and Juhl) insist, ineluctably intentional, there is no reason to think it must always be authors' intentions that are at issue. Textual meaning is inseparable from intention, Shusterman allows, but perhaps readers' intentions are as relevant to determining, or contributing to, textual meaning as those of authors. This enfranchising of readers' intentions (purposes, perspectives), unconstrained by the goal of hypothetically reconstructing best authorial intention, is a good illustration of what I earlier labeled the ludic model of interpretation taken as paramount. By contrast, a virtue of hypothetical intentionalism stands out clearly, which is to mediate between a position, actual intentionalism, which gives just a little too much to authors as persons, and a ludic position such as that of Barthes or Derrida or Rorty or Shusterman, which gives altogether too much to readers and threatens to undermine the motivations of authors for upholding their end of the implicit literary contract.[22] Lest I be misunderstood, let me remark that I regard ludic interpretation, about which I have no more to say in this essay, as potentially an exciting and rewarding exercise in its own right, and a harmless one – as long as it does not displace the primary project of discerning fundamental, authorially anchored, if not authorially determined, literary meaning.

But to return to Carroll's essay, there is much I find congenial in it. Carroll rightly observes that, having tentatively accepted the basic relevance of authorial intention, one can avoid being driven back into anti-intentionalism by the problem of aberrant authorial pronouncements, for these need not be taken at face value: the finished work will often make incredible certain stated intents. And Carroll generally agrees with Lyas, sensibly enough, that the intentions most relevant to literary (or cinematic) works are ones that are largely evident in the works themselves, including both successful and failed intentions, and that these should not be conceived after the fashion of private mental episodes, but instead in neo–Wittgensteinian fashion, as fully embodied in behavior and its products.

It is the next step in the dialectic that worries me:

> Insofar as the intention is identified as the purposive structure of the work, this intention is the focus of our interest in and attention to the artwork ... tracking the intention – the purposive structure of the work – is the very point of appreciation ... the more attractive, neo–Wittgensteinian view of intention not only makes authorial intention relevant to the interpretation of artworks, but implies that in interpreting an artwork, we are attempting to determine the author's intentions.[23]

I am strongly inclined to concur with what is said here – but only if transposed into the key of hypothetical intentionalism, or if taken, charitably, as having a sense compatible with that already. The discernible purposive structure of the work can only be identified with the author's intention, I would say, if by this last one really means an optimal construction of authorial intention from the viewpoint of an ideal reader, imbued with the sorts of background information sketched earlier. For, Wittgenstein or no Wittgenstein, it is still possible for an author's semantic intentions in regard to a work, in whole or in part, not to be fully embodied in that work plus its ideal-reader accessible context of production.[24] And though it is true that "in interpreting an artwork we are attempting to determine the author's intentions," the (actual) author's intentions function here mainly as a heuristic goal, and success in this attempt is to be measured, not by correctly arriving at that actual intention, which may still, despite Lyas's and Carroll's confident internalism, be grounded in matters external to the total literary context, but by the process of constructing (projecting, hypothesizing) a most plausible authorial intention, in the light of both the text and the literature-germane circumstances of its issuance, having come to an end or achieved reflective equilibrium.

Perhaps Carroll's most striking example of an artwork whose correct interpretation putatively requires us to advert to the author's actual intentions, even though we can, by ignoring such intentions, arrive at an interpretation that makes the work more rewarding aesthetically, concerns a grade B (or C) science-fiction movie of 1959, Edward Wood's *Plan 9 from Outer Space*. Carroll claims that Wood's film, which contains narrative incoherence and editing discontinuities, is not properly seen as "boldly and provocatively transgressing Hollywood codes" (as *Village Voice* film critic J. Hoberman has suggested) because Wood did not have the intentions in filmmaking that avant-gardists of the 1970s or 1980s had, with whom Wood is being ranged by this suggestion. I certainly agree with Carroll in rejecting Hoberman's interpretation as a correct one – as opposed to a practical recommendation for dealing with schlock most enjoyably – but am not convinced that Wood's *actual* semantic intentions need be called to account. For can we not say that such expressive intent as Hoberman ascribes to Wood is simply not our best *hypothesis* of such intent, given all appropriate internal and external evidence (e.g., Wood's solid track record of earlier hack films)? Indeed, if we read him closely, this is precisely what Carroll does say:

> All the evidence indicates that Edward Wood did not have the same intentions to subvert the Hollywood style of filmmaking that contemporary avant-gardists have. Indeed, given the venue Wood trafficked in, it seems that the best hypothesis about his intentions is that he was attempting to imitate the Hollywood style of filmmaking in the cheapest way possible. Given what we know of Edward Wood and the B-film world in which he practiced his trade, it is implausible to attribute to him the intention of attempting to subvert the Hollywood codes of filmmaking.[25]

Thus, hypotheticized authorial (or, in this case, directorial) intent is perfectly adequate to handle the case of Wood's movie, that is, to avoid attributing avant-garde meaning and merit to it. Though we take aim at directorial intent, in our hypothetical construction of cinematic meaning, this doesn't entail that a director's actual semantic intent, whether plausibly hypothesizable or not, is determinant of such meaning.[26]

Notes

The author wishes to note that he has responded to a number of objections that have been made to the view of literary interpretation defended in this essay. See his "Hypothetical Intentionalism: Statement, Objections, and Replies," in M. Krausz (ed.), *Is There a Single Right Interpretation?* (University Park: Penn State Press, 2002), 309–18.

1 The distinction of word-sequence meaning, utterer's meaning, and utterance meaning is clearly set out in Tolhurst, "On What a Text Is and How It Means," *British Journal of Aesthetics* 19 (1979). It is also usefully reviewed in Jack Meiland, "The Meanings of a Text," *British Journal of Aesthetics* 21 (1981).

2 From the Latin for "play" or "game."

3 Or several working in tandem, as with coauthored works.

4 Arthur Danto, "Deep Interpretation," *Journal of Philosophy* 78 (1987).

5 Tolhurst, "On What a Text Is," p. 11. I previously invoked Tolhurst's ideas on literary interpretation in "Artworks and the Future," reprinted in Jerrold Levinson, *Music, Art, and Metaphysics* (Ithaca, NY: Cornell University Press, 1990).

6 Tolhurst, "On What a Text Is," p. 13; emphasis added.

7 As we see later, this is really the crux of the issue as I conceive it: what is the scope of specific author-based contextual factors in the genesis of a literary work that are legitimately appealed to in constructing our best hypothesis of intended meaning? The answer to this, I suggest, lies somewhere between narrowing such scope, on the one hand, to nothing more than the language and century of composition, and widening it, on the other hand, so far as to encompass the expressed intentions of the author to mean such and such as recorded in external sources (e.g., private diaries, taped interviews). As players in the literary language game, readers are expected and entitled to take into account much more than the former, while stopping short of the latter. The question is where exactly, along this continuum, to stop.

8 Tying literary meaning to successfully realized authorial intent is central to Annette Barnes's theory of interpretation in her book *On Interpretation* (Oxford: Basil Blackwell, 1988). I think such a strategy is problematic because there is no way of cashing out what such success amounts to without an independent notion of what a work means or when it is being correctly understood.

9 Daniel O. Nathan, "Irony and the Artist's Intentions," *British Journal of Aesthetics* 23 (1982).

10 Ibid., p. 248.

11 It is almost, but not quite, the case that the utterance meaning of Private Epistle is equatable with the utterer's meaning of its predecessor, Open Letter. Although the student undoubtedly had the ironic content in mind while penning Open Letter, she does not intend to convey that to her aimed-at audience – that is, Dr. Bushwacker.

12 Ibid., p. 250.

13 The note of sympathy here with Fish's notion of interpretive communities is intended but does not extend so far as to embrace the idea that it is the evolving consensus of such communities that fixes, through preferred strategies of interpretation, the meanings of works. Instead, such communities serve only to embody and exemplify the kinds of background assumptions and knowledge relevant to attempting to ascertain literary meanings generally.

14 The degree of knowledge, however, is not expected to be the same between authors and readers. Obviously, in most cases, an author will be in "possession" of his own oeuvre, tradition, and public persona to a much higher degree than the average well-disposed appropriate reader.

15 The substance of this interpretation owes to Walter Sokel, *Franz Kafka* (New York: Columbia University Press, 1966).

16 I have substituted chlorine for the argon of Hirsch's original example because the latter, being invisible, is narratively less apt.

17 See note 7.

18 I mean by this phrase to exclude such things as anachronistic meanings. An anachronistic meaning is one that is not just unlikely for an informed reader to attribute to a given author, it is one the author could not, in a strong sense, have meant. I mean to suggest also a stronger condition, namely, that such meanings, though unintended, would not be ones that would clearly be repudiated by the author of a text whose primary meaning is such as we have justifiably projected in context.

19 Hirsch's attempt to address this problem by appeal to the notion of an intentional *horizon* is in the spirit of this second strategy.

20 I proposed such a strategy in "Artworks and the Future," as a way of dealing with the possible Oedipal content of *Hamlet* from a Freudian perspective, despite the impossibility of Shakespeare's assuming any such point of view.

21 See Chapter 37 in this book.

22 By contrast, one recent influential continental view of interpretation, Jauss's Reception theory, seems on my limited knowledge of it to aim at the kind of balance between author and reader that hypothetical intentionalism represents.

23 See Chapter 37, p. 282 in this book.

24 This is not to deny that such intentions must be embodied somewhere in the physical situation of the author and his lived world, but only to insist that they may in some (unfortunate) cases be embodied in ways that are not open to discovery even by appropriate readers of the publicly available work.

25 See Chapter 37, pp. 285–6; emphases added.

26 Carroll comes closest to displaying his intentionalism as really of the hypothetical type defended in this essay, in his note 25, with which I find nothing to disagree.

39

Style and Personality in the Literary Work

Jenefer Robinson

In this paper I want to describe and defend a certain conception of literary style. If we look at literary style in the way I shall suggest, it will explain many of the problems that surround this elusive concept such as why something can be an element of style in the work of one author and not in another, what the difference is between individual style and general style, and how style differs from "signature." The ordinary conception of style is that it consists of nothing but a set of verbal elements such as a certain kind of vocabulary, imagery, sentence structure and so on. On my conception, however, a literary style is rather a way of *doing* certain things, such as describing characters, commenting on the action and manipulating the plot. I shall claim that an author's way of doing these things is an expression of her personality, or, more accurately, of the personality she seems to have. The verbal elements of style gain their stylistic significance by contributing to the expression of this personality, and they cannot be identified as *stylistic* elements independently of the personality they help to express. [...]

I Style as the Expression of Personality

In this first section I shall argue that style is essentially a way of doing something and that it is expressive of personality. Further, I shall sug-

gest that what count as the verbal elements of style are precisely those elements which contribute to the expression of personality.

Intuitively, my style of dress, work, speech, decision-making and so on is the mode or manner or way in which I dress, work, speak and make decisions. In short it is the way I *do* these things. In ordinary contexts, then, a style is always a way of *doing* something. No less intuitively, my style of dressing, working, speaking and making decisions is typically an *expression* of (some features of) my personality, character, mind or sensibility. Thus my vulgar way of dressing is likely to be an expression of my vulgar sensibility, my witty, intellectual way of speaking an expression of my witty, intellectual mind, and my uncompromisingly courageous way of making decisions an expression of my uncompromisingly courageous character.

In saying that a person's way of doing things is an *expression* of that person's traits of mind, character or personality, I am saying (1) that the person's way of doing things exhibits or manifests these traits, and (2) that it is these traits which cause the person to do things in the way they do. Thus these traits leave a matching imprint or trace upon the actions which express them. If my timid way of behaving at parties is an expression of my timid character, then (1) my behavior exhibits or manifests timidity – I behave in a manifestly timid fashion, blushing, refusing to talk to strangers,

From *Philosophical Review* 94 (1985), pp. 227–47. Copyright © 1985 Cornell University. Reprinted by permission of the publisher and author.

hiding in the washrooms, etc. – and (2) my timid behavior is caused by my timid character, i.e., it is not due to the fact that (say) I am pretending to be timid, imitating a timid person or acting the part of a timid person in a play, nor is it the result of secret arrogance and contempt for parties. In general, if a person's actions are an expression of her personality, then those actions have the character that they have – compassionate, timid, courageous or whatever – in virtue of the fact that they are caused by the corresponding trait of mind or character in that person, compassion, timidity or courage. In expression, as the word itself suggests, an "inner" state is expressed or forced out into "outer" behavior. An "inner" quality of mind, character or personality causes the "outer" behavior to be the way it is, and also leaves its "trace" upon that behavior. A timid or compassionate character leaves a "trace" of timidity or compassion upon the actions which express it.[1]

Just as a person's style of dressing, working and speaking is the mode or manner or way in which she dresses, works and speaks, so an author's style of description, character delineation and treatment of a theme is the mode or manner or way in which she describes things, delineates character and treats her theme. In other words, it is her way of *doing* certain things, such as describing or characterizing a setting, delineating character, treating or presenting a theme, and commenting on the action. Moreover, the writer's way of describing, delineating, commenting and so on is typically an *expression* of (some features of) her personality, character, mind or sensibility. Thus James' humorous yet compassionate way of describing Strether's bewilderment expresses the writer's own humorous yet compassionate attitude. Jane Austen's ironic way of describing social pretension expresses her ironic attitude to social pretension.

Now, a style is not simply a way of doing something. We do not say that a person has a *style* of doing so-and-so unless that person does so-and-so in a relatively consistent fashion. Thus we say I have a vulgar and flamboyant *style* of dressing only if I consistently dress in a vulgar and flamboyant way. It may be, of course, that my way of dressing differs considerably from one day to the next: yesterday I wore a purple silk pyjama suit, today I am wearing a frilly scarlet mini-dress and tomorrow it will be leather dungarees and a transparent blouse. Despite these differences, however, we still say that I have a consistent way of dressing, because all my outfits are consistently vulgar and

flamboyant. Moreover, my style of dressing is expressive of a particular feature of my personality, namely vulgarity and flamboyance. In an exactly similar way, we say that Jane Austen has a *style* of describing social pretension, because she consistently describes social pretension in an *ironic* way and the way she describes social pretension is expressive of a particular feature of her outlook, namely her irony.

So far I have talked only about a person's style of doing a particular thing, such as dressing. By contrast, when we say that a person has "a style," we normally mean that he or she has the same style of doing a number of different things. Thus when we accuse John of having a vulgar and flamboyant style, we may be referring to the vulgar and flamboyant way in which John not only dresses but also talks and entertains his dinner guests. Again, in characterizing Mary's style as generous, open, casual and easy-going, we may mean that Mary is generous, open, casual and easy-going in almost everything that she does. In this case Mary's style is expressive not of a single trait but of a number of traits which together "sum up" Mary's personality.

In just the same way, a person's literary style is their style of performing a wide range of (literary) activities. Thus, clearly, Jane Austen's style is not simply her style of doing any one thing, such as describing social pretension, but rather her style of doing a number of things, such as *describing*, *portraying* and *treating* her characters, theme and social setting, *commenting* on the action, *presenting* various points of view, and so on. In short, to borrow a concept from Guy Sircello, it is the way in which she performs the various "artistic acts"[2] which constitute the writing of a literary work. Now, a style of doing a wide range of things is just like a style of doing a particular thing in that it consistently expresses certain features of the mind, personality, etc., of the agent. We say that Mary has "a style" in virtue of the consistently generous, open, casual and easy-going way in which she does a number of different things. Similarly, a writer has a literary style in virtue of the fact that her style of performing a wide variety of artistic acts expresses the same qualities of (her) mind and temperament. For example, James' style of *treating* Strether, of *portraying* the difference between what Strether thinks of Waymarsh and what he thinks he thinks, of *emphasizing* the abstract and the timeless, of *commenting* on Strether's bewilderment and so on together constitute what we call

"James' style." And this style owes its coherence to the fact that all these artistic acts express the same set of attitudes, interests and qualities of mind.

Of course, not every artistic act of a writer in a particular work expresses exactly the same qualities of mind, character or personality. In *Emma*, for example, Jane Austen portrays Mrs. Elton in a quite different way from Jane Fairfax. This is because Jane Austen's attitude to Mrs. Elton is quite different from her attitude to Jane Fairfax. In the one portrayal she expresses (among other things) her love of the ridiculous, and in the other she expresses (among other things) her compassion for suffering sensibility. But Jane Austen's way of portraying Mrs. Elton and her way of portraying Jane Fairfax, as well as her way of portraying the other characters in the novel, her way of describing their personal relationships, her way of developing the plot, and all the other innumerable artistic acts which go into writing the novel *Emma* together add up to the style in which *Emma* is written, a style which expresses all those attitudes that together form the personality of the author of *Emma*.

If a writer has an individual style, then the way she writes has a certain consistency: the same traits of mind, character and personality are expressed throughout her work. Now, at a particular point in a novel, the writer may seem to express anxiety about, anger at or contempt towards a particular character, event or idea, although the writer does not seem to be a chronically anxious, angry or contemptuous sort of person. However, such "occasional" properties should not be thought of as properties of style. Only those properties which are "standing" or long-term properties can be considered stylistic. Thus stylistic qualities are likely to be qualities of mind, moral qualities and deep-seated character traits, rather than mood or emotional qualities such as "angry," "joyful," and "afraid." In the same way, we do not treat every angry, joyful or fearful action performed in real life as an expression of basic character or personality; it is only when someone consistently acts in a choleric or a cheerful way, that we infer to her essentially choleric or cheerful nature.

I have argued that a literary style is a way of performing "artistic acts," describing a setting, portraying character, manipulating plot and so on, and it is the writer's way of performing these acts which is expressive of all those standing traits, attitudes, qualities of mind and so on that together form her personality. What, then, is the relation

between the performance of these acts and what have traditionally been thought of as the verbal elements of style, such as a certain vocabulary, imagery and sentence structure? When a writer describes a setting and portrays character, she uses words, and the kind of word she uses, the sort of sentence structure she forms and so on together constitute the elements of verbal style. If a writer manipulates his theme from the point of view of one whose main interest is in thought and the development of consciousness (James) or if she portrays her characters with a judicious mixture of irony and compassion (Austen), then he or she does so by using language in certain ways.

Obviously the presence of certain verbal elements does not *entail* that a particular personality is being expressed.[3] If, however, (on a reasonable interpretation) those verbal elements are being used by a writer to perform artistic acts in a particular way, then we can infer from the way the acts are performed to characteristics of the writer's mind, character and personality. For example, Henry James uses negatives, abstract nouns, etc., in order to describe Strether's state of consciousness, to comment on Strether's bewilderment and to characterize Strether's attitude to Waymarsh, and he thereby expresses qualities of his own mind and personality.

Moreover, negatives, abstract nouns, non-transitive verbs, elegant variation and so on are verbal elements which at first sight seem to have nothing in common. What links them all together, however, as elements of "James' style" is their use in the artistic acts James performs: they are all elements of his style because they all contribute to the expression of his personality and attitudes. For example, using these particular verbal elements, James thereby describes Strether's state of consciousness in a particular judicious, abstractive, expository way and thereby expresses his own "subjective and abstractive tendency,"[4] his interest in the relations between minds (Strether's, the narrator's, the reader's), his moral sensitivity and his cool and judicious intellect.

II The Personality of the Implied Author

So far in this essay I have written as if the personality expressed by the style of a work were that of the writer herself. I have suggested that we infer from the way in which the writer performs the artistic acts in a work to the presence of personality traits and so on *in the writer* which cause her to perform those acts in the way that she does. But this is an oversimplification. What is more typically expressed by the style of a work is not the personality of the actual author, but of what, following Wayne Booth, we might call the "implied author,"[5] that is, the author as she seems to be from the evidence of the work. Thus however querulous and intolerant the actual Tolstoy may have been in real life, the implied author of *Anna Karenin* is full of compassionate understanding. [. . .]

Some literary works deliberately exploit a number of different styles. A good example is James Joyce's *Ulysses*. In this case the style of at least some of the different episodes of the book should be identified with the style not of the implied author "James Joyce" but of the narrator of that episode. The personality expressed by the style of the Cyclops episode, for example, is not the personality which the author seems to have; the coarse and unpleasant personality expressed belongs only to the nameless narrator of the episode. Notice, however, that this kind of case is parasitic upon the normal case: it is because a style is normally an expression of the personality of the writer that we infer from the style of the Cyclops episode to the presence of a coarse and unpleasant person writing or narrating it.[6]

Does it make sense to talk about "the style" of *Ulysses*? In a way it does not, because *Ulysses* contains so many different styles (some of which are not even "individual" styles).[7] Nevertheless, we can identify an implied author of *Ulysses* and detect the way in which he appears to *manipulate* the narrative point of view, *treat* the *Ulysses* theme, *characterize* Molly Bloom, etc. The way these artistic acts are performed is part of *the style of Ulysses*. For example, the presence of many different narrators with different styles is itself a feature of *Joyce*'s style and it is expressive of certain traits that Joyce seems to have, such as a boisterous creativity, a delight in the expressive capacities of language and an interest in the way reality can be viewed and reported from so many different points of view.[8] [. . .]

III   An Objection Considered

My thesis has been that the defining feature of a literary work which has an individual style is that the work is an expression of the personality of the implied author,[9] and that what links the diverse verbal elements of style together into a coherent whole is that they all contribute to the expression of this particular personality. One objection to this thesis is that there are many qualities of a work which *prima facie* are qualities of its style but which do not seem to express any qualities of mind or personality in the implied author. In particular, there are formal qualities (euphonious, Latinate, colloquial, ornate) and expressive qualities (dramatic, heroic, violent) which may be attributed to the style of a work but which are not (or need not be) qualities of the implied author's mind or personality.

In this section of the paper I shall argue that such formal and expressive qualities are not always qualities of the individual style of a work, and that when they are it is only because they contribute to the expression of qualities of mind, personality, etc. in the implied author. Among works which possess striking formal or expressive qualities (euphony, violence, etc.), I distinguish three sorts of case: (1) works which have such properties but lack style altogether, (2) works which have such properties and also belong to a general style category but which lack individual style, and (3) works which have such properties and which also possess individual style.

(1)   Intuitively, there could be a piece of characterless prose which nevertheless happens to be *euphonious*, i.e., the words it contains make a pleasing musical sound. Imagine, for example, an incompetent Freshman English paper in which the ideas are unclearly expressed, the sentence structure confused and the choice of words unimaginative. No one reading the paper would attribute to it an individual style. Yet, quite by chance, the ill-chosen words are euphonious: l's, m's and n's predominate, there are only a few plosives or fricatives, and the vowel sounds fit together in a melodious way. To say that this work is in a "euphonious style," however, is at best misleading, since intuitively it is not in a style at all. The possession of just one striking formal quality, such as euphony, is not normally sufficient to endow a work with style. Indeed even a string of nonsense syllables may be euphonious, although presumably they cannot be in a style. Hence euphony does not always contribute to individual style, just because it may be a quality of a work that lacks style altogether. On my view, of course, a euphonious work that lacks individual style is a euphonious work which fails to express any individual personality in the implied author.

(2) A more interesting situation arises when a work is in a "euphonious style" in the sense that it belongs to what Wollheim calls a "general" style category, although it does not possess *individual* style. General style categories, such as period or school styles, group together writers, painters or other artists who seem to the critic and historian to have important characteristics in common, for example, the Elizabethan pastoral lyric style or the style of the school of Donne (the Metaphysical style). To belong to a general category of literary style often involves obeying certain conventions and using certain techniques. Thus the style of Elizabethan pastoral love lyrics demands a certain stylized way of referring to the lover and the beloved, of describing their surroundings and so on. The imagery and the poetic forms employed all fall within a fairly narrow and predictable range. More importantly for my present argument, membership in a particular general style category often requires a work to have certain formal and expressive qualities. Thus the style of an Elizabethan pastoral love lyric is supposed to be charming and euphonious, the Metaphysical style colloquial and dramatic, and the Miltonic epic style (i.e., the style of works which imitate *Paradise Lost*) Latinate and heroic.

Now, intuitively, there is a distinction between merely belonging to a general style category and having a formed individual style. For example, although a poem must be (somewhat) colloquial and (somewhat) dramatic in order to count as a Metaphysical poem at all, it does not follow that every minor lyric by Carew or Suckling has an individual style. Indeed we may often be hard-pressed to distinguish between the lesser works of Carew and Suckling, just because they do lack "indivduality." Similarly, many of the poems in the collection *England's Helicon* obey all the requirements of the Elizabethan pastoral lyric style and yet remain "characterless." They are charming and euphonious but they have an anonymous air about them: they do not seem to have been written by anyone in particular. In short, a work which belongs to a general style category may have certain striking formal or expressive qualities even though it lacks individual style. An Elizabethan love lyric may be euphonious, a Metaphysical poem dramatic, a Miltonic epic Latinate without necessarily being in an individual style.

One of the merits of my theory of style is that it allows us to define and explain this intuitive distinction between individual and general style. On my view, the crucial difference is that whereas having an individual style necessarily involves the expression of personality in the implied author, belonging to a general style category has no such implications. Elsewhere[10] I have argued for this position in much greater detail than is either possible or appropriate here. If I am right, however, it follows that there can be works belonging to a general style category which possess the formal and expressive qualities characteristic of that style but which do not express any individual personality in the implied author. Hence these formal and expressive qualities, although qualities of general style, do not contribute to any individual style in the work just because they do not contribute to the expression of an individual personality in the implied author of the work.

(3) Finally, formal and expressive qualities such as "Latinate," "euphonious" and "dramatic" may be qualities that are present in works of individual style and which do contribute to the expression of personality in those works. It does not follow, however, that the implied author is a Latinate, euphonious or dramatic sort of fellow. These qualities in themselves do not express any particular trait in the implied author. Rather they can help to express many diverse traits, depending upon the artistic acts to which they contribute. In a similar way, Henry James' fondness for negatives does not in itself express any feature of "his" personality; it is the way the negatives are used in the performance of artistic acts, such as describing Strether's state of mind, which gives this feature of James' work its stylistic significance.

The quality of euphony, for example, may indeed contribute to individual style, but it does so by contributing to the expression of individual personality in a work. Consequently the contribution it makes is very different in different works. Both Swinburne's "Garden of Proserpine" and large passages of Milton's "Paradise Lost" can be described as euphonious, but the personalities expressed in the individual style of these two works are very different. In the Swinburne poem the gentle, musical sounds help to express the implied author's sense of world-weariness, melancholy and resignation,[11] whereas the famous Miltonic melody generally serves to help express the implied author's sense of the dignity and grandeur of his theme. To say that both works are in a "euphonious style" means simply that euphony is a formal quality of both works, which in both cases contributes to individual style. The way it contributes, however, is quite different in the two cases. Similarly it could be argued that both Jane Austen and Donne have *dramatic* styles, but clearly the dramatic qualities in each help to express quite different personalities and hence contribute quite differently to the styles of each.[12]

In summary then, the formal and expressive qualities I have been discussing are not always qualities of the individual style of a work: they may be present in works lacking any style at all or in works which belong to a general style category but do not have individual style. Moreover, even when such qualities contribute to the individual style of a work, they do so in very different ways. The "same" quality in two different works may contribute to the expression of quite different traits of mind and personality in the implied authors of those works.

There are two interesting corollaries of my discussion. First, it would seem to follow that no verbal element or formal or expressive quality in a work is always and inevitably an element or quality of individual style. Even such qualities as "euphonious" and "Latinate" do not contribute to individual style wherever they appear, and even when they do contribute to individual style, they do so in virtue of how they are used in the artistic acts in the work. Secondly, it would also seem to follow that *any* verbal element or formal or expressive quality in a work *can* be an element or quality of individual style, provided it contributes in the appropriate way to the expression of personality in the implied author.

In short, if my thesis is correct, then there is no "taxonomy" or checklist of style elements, that is, elements which contribute to individual style wherever they appear.[13] Euphony, Latinate diction, and the presence of many negatives are elements of individual style only if they are used in such a way as to contribute to the expression of traits of mind and personality in the implied author.

We cannot, therefore, identify the elements of individual style merely as the most striking or salient features of a work. On the one hand there are striking features which do not invariably contribute to individual style. I have argued that euphony, for example, may be a striking feature of works which lack individual style. Again, it would be a striking feature of a work if all the proper names in it began with the letter 'X', yet intuitively this would not be a feature of its *style* (although it could be if, for example, it were used to express the implied author's sense of fun).

On the other hand, moreover, there are many elements which are not particularly salient but which contribute to individual style. Thus a certain writer who has a formed individual style may have a preference for the indefinite article over the definite which contributes in a small way to the expression of her generalizing imagination and tendency to abstraction. Again, any careful, sensitive reader of *The Ambassadors* can tell that James tends to "interpolate" elements in his sentences, but we may not notice that the interpolations typically occur between verb or adjective and complement, or between auxiliary and main verb, and that they cluster towards the center of a sentence.[14] Yet it is non-salient elements such as these which contribute significantly to James' style, because they all help to express "James'" characteristic attitudes, interests and qualities of mind and personality.

IV Some Problems Resolved

I have argued that if a literary work has an individual style, the artistic acts in the work are performed in such a way as to express qualities of mind, attitudes, personality traits, etc., which make up the individual personality of the implied author of the work. The verbal elements of (individual) style are those elements which contribute to the expression of this personality. There is no "checklist" of elements or qualities which inherently or intrinsically contribute to individual style, no matter where they appear.

So far I have merely tried to make my thesis seem reasonable and to forestall some possible objections to it. In this final section I should like to make some more positive remarks in its favor. The best reason for accepting my theory is that it answers an array of difficult questions surrounding the concept of style.

(1) First, my theory explains why a correct description of a writer's style mentions some of its verbal characteristics but not others. On my view, what count as the elements of a style are precisely those verbal elements which contribute to the expression of the implied author's personality. In Henry James, for example, the relevant verbal elements include the recurrent use of nontransitive verbs, abstract nouns, negatives and the word "that." These all help to contribute to the expression of "James'" personality. But we could, no doubt, if we searched for them, discover many

recurrent elements in James' work which are not stylistically significant. Thus perhaps it would turn out that James had a penchant for nouns beginning with the letter 'f' or that his sentences invariably had an even number of words in them. A description of James' style would not mention these elements, however, precisely because they do not contribute to the expression of the personality of the implied author. In short, many quite diverse and seemingly unrelated verbal elements belong to the same style in virtue of the fact that they all contribute to the expression of the same personality. It is only if the frequent use of nouns beginning with the letter "f" can be shown to contribute to this personality that this particular verbal characteristic would be an element of style.

(2) For similar reasons, my theory explains why it is that the same verbal element may have stylistic significance in one work or author and no stylistic significance, or a different significance, in another work or author. For the same stylistic element may play no expressive role in the one case and an important role in the other. Alternatively, it may simply play different expressive roles in the two cases. Suppose, for example, that two writers tend to use the indefinite article rather than the definite. In one writer, who has a formed individual style, this may contribute to the expression of her generalizing imagination and tendency to abstraction. In the other writer, it may be an accident and it may have no expressive effect in the work, or perhaps it indicates a lack of strength and precision in the style. In the first writer we have located the presence of a stylistic element; in the second writer the same element has no stylistic significance or a different one. If we were to view a person's style as consisting of a set of elements which we can check off on a checklist, then it would make no sense to say that a particular element is sometimes stylistic and sometimes not. But if we view style as a function of the literary personality expressed by a work in the way I have suggested, then the problem dissolves.

(3) It is commonly believed that if a writer or a work has an individual style, this implies that the various stylistic elements have a certain unity. Yet there are no intrinsic connections among the features of James' style, for example: why should negatives, abstract nouns and "elegant variation" go together to form a unified style? My theory explains in a clear way what stylistic unity amounts to: a style has a unity because it is the expression of the personality of the implied author. Just as we

see the way a person performs the various actions of daily life as expressive of different facets of her personality, so we see the way in which a writer seems to perform the various artistic acts in a literary work as expressive of different facets of "her" personality. The many disparate elements of verbal style fit together only because they are being used to express the "same" personality: the writer uses the elements of verbal style to describe her characters, treat her theme, etc., thereby seeming to reveal a set of personality traits, qualities of mind, attitudes and so forth which "makes sense" out of (unifies) this multitude of artistic acts.

The question arises as to whether this set of "standing" traits forms a coherent personality. The concept of a "unified" or coherent personality is admittedly somewhat vague, since the most disparate and apparently inconsistent psychological traits seem capable of coexisting in normal, rational people. All I need to insist on, however, is that if a work has an individual style then the different traits expressed by the various artistic acts in the work (portraying Jane Fairfax, characterizing Emma's treatment of her father, etc.) coexist in a way which is consistent with our knowledge of persons and human nature. Moreover, the same traits must be consistently expressed throughout a work. Thus the implied author of *Le Rouge et le Noir* both admires and despises the aristocratic world to which Julien Sorel aspires, but because he does so consistently and because the conflict in his attitudes is one which we recognize as possible in a basically rational person, his admiration and scorn are both part of the personality expressed by the style of the work.[15] If however, a work expresses no individual personality at all or if the personality expressed is a confusion of different traits which do not fit together in an intelligible way, then it follows from my thesis that the work in question lacks individual style.[16] [...]

(6) Finally, as I have already remarked, one of the virtues of my theory is that it allows me to clarify the distinction between general and individual style.[17] If a work belongs to a general style category, then, although it may have formal and expressive qualities that are distinctive of that style, it may nevertheless remain "characterless": no personality "informs" the work. Alternatively, there may be personality traits expressed but they do not seem to belong to any particular individual. The work has an "anonymous" air about it,

because the artistic acts are performed in a way which is common to a large number of different writers.[18] By contrast, as I have argued throughout this paper, the defining quality of an individual style is that it expresses a coherent set of attitudes, qualities of mind and so on which seem to belong to the individual writer of the work: a work which has an individual style expresses the personality of the implied author of that work.[19]

Notes

1 See especially Richard Wollheim, "Expression," in Royal Institute of Philosophy Lectures, vol. I, 1966–7, *The Human Agent* (New York: St. Martin's Press, 1968), and *Art and its Objects* (2nd edn; Cambridge: Cambridge University Press, 1980), sections 15–19. See also Guy Sircello, *Mind and Art* (Princeton: Princeton University Press, 1972).

2 Guy Sircello, *Mind and Art* (Princeton: Princeton University Press, 1972), Chapter 1. I am not sure whether Sircello would approve of the use to which I put the concept of artistic acts.

3 See Frank Sibley, "Aesthetic Concepts", in *Philosophy Looks at the Arts*, ed. Joseph Margolis (New York: Scribner, 1962), and a large subsequent literature.

4 Ian Watt, "The first paragraph of *The Ambassadors*," reprinted in *Henry James*, ed. Tony Tanner (London: Macmillan, 1968), p. 291.

5 Wayne Booth, *The Rhetoric of Fiction* (Chicago: University of Chicago Press, 1961), especially pp. 70–7.

6 Compare *Tristram Shandy* which is written in Tristram's (the narrator's) style. The implied author seems to have a personality much like that of Tristram, but he is distinct from Tristram and appears from time to time to correct Tristram's opinions in helpful footnotes.

7 See, for example, *The Oxen of the Sun* episode.

8 Notice that plays can have individual style despite the fact that they contain many different "voices."

9 From now on I shall write as if the personality expressed by the style of a work were that of the implied author, because typically this is the case. However, the implied author may sometimes have all his or her properties in common with the actual author. Moreover, as I have already noticed, in some cases the personality expressed is that of the narrator.

10 "General and Individual Style in Literature," *Journal of Aesthetics and Art Criticism* 43 (1984). I argue there that if a work belongs to a general style category, such as a school or period style, then it obeys certain rules and observes certain conven-

tions, some of which undoubtedly foster certain kinds of formal and expressive properties. However, it is possible to write works which belong to a general style category and succeed to some extent in achieving the formal and expressive goals of that category without thereby expressing an individual personality in the implied author.

11 There go the loves that wither,
   The old loves with wearier wings;
And all dead years draw thither,
   And all disastrous things; …

12 Sometimes a writer performs the artistic act of "expressing" some quality in the external world, as when she, for example, "expresses" the violence of a battle or the fragility of an elf. Again, however, it is not the violence or fragility themselves which contribute to style, but the way in which violence or fragility is "expressed" (in this sense) by the writer. Thus one woman may "express" the violence of a battle with gusto, thereby expressing "her" enjoyment of fast-moving action and enthusiasm for heroic exploits, whereas another may "express" the violence with cool detachment, thereby expressing "her" ironic awareness of human folly. For further discussion of this issue, see Guy Sircello, *Mind and Art*, Chapter 4, and my "Expressing the Way the World Is," *Journal of Aesthetic Education* 13 (1979), pp. 29–44.

13 Cf. Richard Wollheim, "Pictorial Style: Two Views." It is possible that there are taxonomies for *general* style categories, unlike individual style.

14 See Seymour Chatman, *The Later Style of Henry James* (Oxford: Blackwell, 1972), pp. 126–7.

15 Lee Brown brought this example to my attention.

16 If for example, *for no apparent reason*, an author describes a certain character with unqualified approval in chapters 1, 3 and 5 and with a certain kind of qualified disapproval in chapters 2, 4 and 6, then it might be that the implied author is schizophrenic or, more likely, simply a confused creation.

17 See also my "General and Individual Style in Literature."

18 There are some general style categories such as the heroic epic, in which individual style is rarely found and might even be deemed inappropriate. The Homeric epics, however, do seem to contain passages that have individual style. It is interesting to note that the argument over the authorship of the *Iliad* is partly an argument about style and personality in the work. Those parts of the *Iliad* which have individual style provide a strong argument for scholars who wish to argue that there was one central author of the *Iliad* (call him "Homer") even though parts of it had been handed down by an oral tradition. By contrast, scholars who argue that there were a number of bards who contributed importantly to the creation of the *Iliad* point to the fact that there is no individual style to the *Iliad* as a whole.

Interestingly, both sets of experts seem implicitly to grant the connection between individual style and an individual personality which is expressed in the style. For an introduction to the problem of multiple authorship in the *Iliad*, see E. R. Dodds, "Homer" in *The Language and Background of Homer*, ed. G. S. Kirk (Cambridge: Cambridge University Press, 1964), pp. 1–21.

19 Many people have helped to improve this paper. I am particularly indebted to Lee Brown, Ann Clark, John Martin, Francis Sparshott, Kendall Walton, Richard Wollheim and the editors and referees of the *Philosophical Review*. I am also grateful to Berel Lang whose NEH Seminar on the Concept of Style aroused my interest in this topic.

PART VIII

Literary Values

Introduction

What do we value literature for? If we admit to seeing something of ourselves in "Xingu," Edith Wharton's depiction of a painfully shallow reading group, we may grant that we seek out literature in part to earn respectable social standing in our culture. Reading the right books helps us both to fit into desired social circles and to participate in the unfolding cultural moment. Perhaps we also identify with Wharton's Mrs. Roby, the character who shamelessly admits to reading for amusement: we value literature because it is enjoyable to read, without necessarily having clear views on why it is so enjoyable.

Philosophers in the analytic tradition have generally not pursued the idea that the value of literature might lie primarily in its extrinsic value as a kind of social currency, but have rather assumed that literature and our experiences with it have features that ground its value and explain the pleasure we take in it in some interesting way. There is general agreement that literature is valued in part as other art forms are, on straightforward aesthetic grounds: a phrase can be graceful, a sentence rhythmically engaging, a plot well-structured, or a character elegantly sketched.

But aesthetic value, construed as depending relatively directly on the experience of formal features of a work, has struck many as missing or misunderstanding crucial aspects of the value of literature. Literature seems to insist on attention to what it says or what it is about, and we seem intuitively to enjoy literature at least in part for the ideas and feelings it summons up. So it seems necessary to consider content as relevant to literature's value. Debate has focused in particular on cognitivism, which holds that literature is a viable and valuable source of knowledge, and on literature's moral or ethical content. The essays selected here collectively address the following questions: Can literature provide knowledge? If so, what kind of knowledge? And would providing knowledge count toward a work's value as literature? Does literature convey specifically ethical truth or have other ethically important consequences? And similarly, would being on the right side of ethical value count toward a work's value as literature?

Jerome Stolnitz offers a sustained challenge to cognitivism about art in general and literature in particular. He argues that works of literature do not provide justification for knowledge claims, and that the likely candidates for truths gleaned from literature, when stated in general terms, turn out to be trivial. Catherine Wilson takes issue with the focus on propositional knowledge that helps drive critiques offered by Stolnitz and others. She argues for a form of cognitivism in which literature provides conceptual knowledge, whose acquisition effects fairly profound but difficult to articulate changes in conceptions, recognitional habits, and judgments. Martha Nussbaum defends literature as a source of specifically moral knowledge and training in moral perception. She argues that its inextricable relation of form and content can both convey substantive moral truth and be an exemplar of the attentive care for particulars that is required for responsible moral agency.

In response to Wilson, Nussbaum, and other cognitivists, Peter Lamarque and Stein Haugom Olsen offer an array of arguments to undermine the view that literary experience meets the criteria necessary for status as a legitimate practice of inquiry and knowledge-gathering. They nonetheless want to give full weight to the humanistic content of literature, making exploration of the ideas and feelings presented in works central to the practice of literature. In their view this content can matter to the interpretation and appreciation of literature, without requiring its application and confirmation in relation to extra-literary reality.

Lamarque and Olsen are in part worried about philosophers trying to evaluate literature on philosophy's terms, as if literary value hung on serving the goals of philosophy rather than literature's distinctive goals as an art form. Nussbaum rejects this worry most explicitly, suggesting that the goals of the novelist and the moral philosopher can converge, and that a novel's philosophical achievements do contribute to its value as a novel. Berys Gaut takes up a related issue concern-ing evaluation of art, by asking how the ethical content of a work contributes to its aesthetic value. Gaut supports a view he calls "ethicism," which integrates evaluation of ethical content into aesthetic evaluation of a work: to the extent that a work manifests ethically worthy attitudes, this counts in favor of its aesthetic value. Gaut's ethicism explicitly broadens the domain of literary aesthetic value.

The readings in this section follow up in many ways on issues raised in previous sections. Certainly these contemporary thinkers are addressing questions that concerned Plato, Aristotle, Nietzsche, and Freud as they developed broad conceptions of how literature functions in human life. These readings also make numerous claims with implications for the project of defining literature. But the way one conceives of the values inherent in and promoted by literature may also influence one's approach to a variety of more specialized questions, such as the cognitive status of metaphor, the importance of emotional response to literature, and what is at stake in literary interpretation.

40

Xingu

Edith Wharton

I

Mrs. Ballinger is one of the ladies who pursue Culture in bands, as though it were dangerous to meet alone. To this end she had founded the Lunch Club, an association composed of herself and several other indomitable huntresses of erudition. The Lunch Club, after three or four winters of lunching and debate, had acquired such local distinction that the entertainment of distinguished strangers became one of its accepted functions; in recognition of which it duly extended to the celebrated "Osric Dane," on the day of her arrival in Hillbridge, an invitation to be present at the next meeting. [...]

The dimensions of Miss Van Vluyck's dining-room having restricted the membership of the club to six, the non-conductiveness of one member was a serious obstacle to the exchange of ideas, and some wonder had already been expressed that Mrs. Roby should care to live, as it were, on the intellectual bounty of the others. This feeling was increased by the discovery that she had not yet read "The Wings of Death." She owned to having heard the name of Osric Dane; but that – incredible as it appeared – was the extent of her acquaintance with the celebrated novelist. [...]

She had meant, she owned, to glance through the book; but she had been so absorbed in a novel of Trollope's that –

"No one reads Trollope now," Mrs. Ballinger interrupted.

Mrs. Roby looked pained. "I'm only just beginning," she confessed.

"And does he interest you?" Mrs. Plinth enquired.

"He amuses me."

"Amusement," said Mrs. Plinth, "is hardly what I look for in my choice of books."

"Oh, certainly, 'The Wings of Death' is not amusing," ventured Mrs. Leveret, whose manner of putting forth an opinion was like that of an obliging salesman with a variety of other styles to submit if his first selection does not suit.

"Was it *meant* to be?" enquired Mrs. Plinth, who was fond of asking questions that she permitted no one but herself to answer. "Assuredly not."

"Assuredly not – that is what I was going to say," assented Mrs. Leveret, hastily rolling up her opinion and reaching for another. "It was meant to – to elevate."

Miss Van Vluyck adjusted her spectacles as though they were the black cap of condemnation. "I hardly see," she interposed, "how a book steeped in the bitterest pessimism can be said to elevate, however much it may instruct."

"I meant, of course, to instruct," said Mrs. Leveret, flurried by the unexpected distinction between two terms which she had supposed to be synonymous. [...]

From *Xingu and Other Stories* (New York: Scribner, 1916), pp. 3, 5–11. Public domain.

"I was about to say," Miss Van Vluyck resumed, "that it must always be a question whether a book *can* instruct unless it elevates."

"Oh –" murmured Mrs. Leveret, now feeling herself hopelessly astray. [. . .]

"Oh, but don't you see," exclaimed Laura Glyde, "that it's just the dark hopelessness of it all – the wonderful tone-scheme of black on black – that makes it such an artistic achievement? It reminded me when I read it of Prince Rupert's *manière noire* . . . the book is etched, not painted, yet one feels the colour-values so intensely. . . . "

"Who is *he?*" Mrs. Leveret whispered to her neighbour. "Some one she's met abroad?"

"The wonderful part of the book," Mrs. Ballinger conceded, "is that it may be looked at from so many points of view. I hear that as a study of determinism Professor Lupton ranks it with 'The Data of Ethics.' "

"I'm told that Osric Dane spent ten years in preparatory studies before beginning to write it," said Mrs. Plinth. "She looks up everything – verifies everything. It has always been my principle, as you know. Nothing would induce me, now, to put aside a book before I'd finished it, just because I can buy as many more as I want."

"And what do *you* think of 'The Wings of Death'?" Mrs. Roby abruptly asked her.

It was the kind of question that might be termed out of order, and the ladies glanced at each other as though disclaiming any share in such a breach of discipline. They all knew there was nothing Mrs. Plinth so much disliked as being asked her opinion of a book. Books were written to read; if one read them what more could be expected? To be questioned in detail regarding the contents of a volume seemed to her as great an outrage as being searched for smuggled laces at the Custom House. . . . The meeting therefore closed with an increased sense, on the part of the other ladies, of Mrs. Roby's hopeless unfitness to be one of them.

41

On the Cognitive Triviality of Art

Jerome Stolnitz

ALREADY IN Hesiod, the founding document of Western aesthetics, the poet is said to speak truths, and yet already here, for the first, not the last time, the cognitivist affirmation is qualified or warped, by the Muses previously telling the shepherd that they impart to him lies that only seem like truth.[1] Plato had his own use for "lies" or "fictions", but he did not hesitate to charge the poets with truths or truth-claims about the gods or how to wage warfare.[2] So far as one can characterize the vast succeeding literature, the cognitivists have predominated against the sceptics, though we must always bear in mind their profound intra-mural differences over the nature of artistic truth, the vehicles of embodying and communicating such truths, and indeed the appropriate and therefore unorthodox meaning of "truth". Not only acknowledging but insisting upon these departures from a staple correspondence theory, they disparage Plato's obtuse literalism. Their celebrations of the distinctive nature of artistic truth have frequently been resonantly uplifting, though it will not be disputed that they have been almost as often manifestly vague and sometimes, one fears, quite gaseous.

Now, or any other time, is a good time to reconsider the issue. Further, should my argument for the cognitive triviality of fine art pass muster, it will go some way to explain why art's influence on social structure and historical change has been fairly inconsequential.[3] It may also afford a less hieratic defence of the currently popular view that the work of art has no reference beyond itself.

It is prudent to approach so volatile a concept as "artistic truth" by identifying truths that are, by contrast, beyond dispute. Scientific truths, for one. We have a relatively clear and firm conception of how science arrives at its truths. It will be protested that the once unquestioned belief in "scientific method" has recently been brought under fire and rejected. It continues to dominate the scientific community, however, and is still espoused by more traditionalist philosophers of science. In any event, both this conception and its challengers occupy positions of shared, partisan agreement within philosophy of science. But a "method of artistic truth" is not matter for debate and hardly makes sense. Secondly, scientific truths, once arrived at, are truths about the great world. Evidence, in the face of recent philosophers of science, is to be found in those who have thought so and continue to think so – scientists, many other philosophers of science, and in those humans in all the continents who, because of its successes, like no other way of knowing, have turned to science to control their environments and improve their lives. Philosophers' theories have little force against the palpable reduction in infant mortality and increase in longevity. Do the arts give us truths about the great world? This

From *British Journal of Aesthetics* 32 (1992), pp. 191–200. Reprinted by permission of Oxford University Press.

question we take up presently. Short of that discussion, we can give clear instances of scientific truth, the inverse square law, for example. But art?

History, for all its ignorance, disagreements, biases, and falsifications, has, unearthing documents, artefacts, and other evidence, attained undoubted truths about man's past, e.g., Caesar was assassinated in 44 BC.

A vast number of other truths about the great world have been gained by all human beings, not by any method, but simply by living and learning, e.g., summer is warmer than winter.

The models of science and history are relaxed even further if we turn to religious truths. Though talk of "method" is again inappropriate, there are a number of putative ways of knowing, such as revelation and priestly authority. The second criterion is the rub, since there is weighty reason to doubt that religious beliefs are indisputably true of the great world. But though your materialist will deny the truth and may question the meaningfulness of "Man is the creature of God," he will unhesitatingly accept that it is a recognizably religious truth-claim. The devout have sometimes thought to contend with such scepticism by abandoning "truth" as unfitted to and even unworthy of their beliefs. The articles of faith are beyond "truth", even beyond logical consistency, and though they are not amenable to the verification of scientific or historical truth, are more precious. They give "wisdom".

We may now be nearing a model more congenial to artistic truth. For where is it written, save in Philistia, that artistic truth must be subject to the same criteria as are satisfied by such prosaic truths as the inverse square law and the date of Caesar's assassination? This importunate demand will not be countenanced by those theorists who contend that the truths conveyed by art can be achieved in no other way. Artistic truths are truths broad and deep, too acute and suggestive, perhaps too tremulous, to be caught in the grosser nets of science, history, or garden variety experience, but no worse, indeed, all the better for that. But then they are also unlike religious truth-claims, being less doctrinaire, less parochial – freer. Did not Freud take more seriously the poets and novelists than virtually all of the academic psychology written up to his time?[4]

Thus urged, we go on to look for other reasons why artistic truth is *sui generis* and so to a linguistic oddity, or several such. Philosophers, critics, and others speak often enough of artistic truth. Con-

siderably less often do they speak of artistic knowledge. How should there be truth without knowledge? We have scientific truth and scientific knowledge, historical truth and historical knowledge. Understandably, for once truth has been established as that and therefore accepted by a judging mind, it is knowledge. Why do we hear so little of artistic knowledge? In religion, there are, in part because of the uncertainties remarked a moment ago, recurrent references to the state of mind of the believer – *Credo quia impossibile*, "I know that my Redeemer liveth," etc. There are, the phrase attests, religious believers; there are those who believe the findings of science and those who distrust them, those who accept history and those who think it "bunk". Whereas we have never heard of artistic believers. Why not? What would they believe, if they existed? There are also those who believe *in* science, in its capacity to yield more truths in future; so, similarly, those who believe in history and religion. Theorists aside, where are their counterparts in the arts? (There are certainly those who "believe in" art in the sense of "esteem highly" or "take very seriously".) Thus artistic truth moves still further away from religious truth as well as the other kinds of truth-*cum*-knowledge.

It is time now to consider some likely candidates for artistic truth. The Muses and their followers hold that truth is found in all the arts, including music, but novels and plays are in general closer than any of the others to the great world, the actualities of man in society. A comedy of manners, renowned for its deft psychological insights and thus propitious, gives us:

Stubborn pride and ignorant prejudice keep apart two attractive people living in Hertfordshire in Regency England.

This is, as far as it goes, a summary, reasonably accurate and thus true, of the story, of the fiction. So this is not what we want. Those who espouse artistic truth are not after the fiction. They will not, consequently, settle for other truths, of which there are a great many, about Elizabeth Bennet and Mr Darcy. They have much bigger game in mind – the truths that are, in some manner, created by the fiction – and so therefore do we. "Lies like truth" might be fictions so plausible that the audience takes them to be truths. But neither are the cognitivists after *als ob* truths. Many of them have insisted that art brings to light, above all, human character – the hidden, unvoiced, perhaps, apart from art, the unknown impulses and affects that stir and move our inner and then outer beings. They will settle for nothing less than psychological truths about people in the great world, truths universal, more or less, nor, therefore, will we.

Hence: Stubborn pride and ignorant prejudice keep attractive people apart.

We are compelled to abandon the setting of the novel in order to arrive at psychological truth. Yet in abandoning Hertfordshire in Regency England, we give up the manners and morals that influenced the sayings and doings of the hero and heroine. A greater influence is that of their personal relationships to other characters – the feather-brained family members, the ne'er-do-well soldiers and priggish parsons. Their motivations and behaviour respond to and are thus largely shaped by these other people, fictional all, and to each other, of course, fictional too. These interactions are integral to the finely detailed delineation of their characters which is, the critics are as one in holding, a major ground of the novel's excellence. Finally, we abandon their individuality in all of its complexity and depth. My statement of the psychological truth to be gained from the novel is pitifully meagre by contrast. Necessarily, since the psychologies of Miss Bennet and Mr Darcy are fleshed out and specified within the fiction only. Once we divest ourselves of the diverse, singular forces at work in its psychological field, as we must, in getting from the fiction to the truth, the latter must seem, and is, distressingly impoverished.

Can this be all there is? From one of the world's great novels?

Think of the infinitely more detailed and determinate exfoliations of the psychologies of Miss Bennet and Mr Darcy that have been carried out by literary critics. Think, if you will, of the countless critiques of other novels and plays that have revealed the motivations and feelings of their characters with a subtlety and refinement to which a good deal of academic psychology hardly aspires. These critiques enthusiastically promise and would deliver the deepest truths of human nature. They presuppose and endorse artistic cognitivism. They become the subjects of vigorous study and lively debate within literary criticism. Then think, finally, that they do all this without so much as creating a ripple extra-murally, in professional psychology or anywhere else.

None the less, my formulation of this novel's truth may well be unduly skimpy and it is a mistake, for anyone, of any persuasion, to generalize from a single case. Let us therefore move to more stable ground, Greek tragedy, which, since Aristotle, a grandsire of cognitivism, has been put forth as stellar evidence of its soundness. Thus the familiar

His *hybris* destroys the tragic hero.

Hybris is not best translated "pride" but rather "overweening arrogance". There are knottier problems in deciding what the psychological truth–claim asserts exactly. We identify the tragic hero just by reading the tragedy. How shall we identify the tragic hero in a sense of "tragic" that is not tied to the dramatic form? Possibly something like "a great man in history, not wholly evil, who is suddenly brought low" will do. Alcibiades? Bismarck? Sir Winston? This raises the larger problem, endemic to all derivations of truth from literature, that of quantification. The initial statements refer to Miss Bennet and Mr Darcy, or Ajax and Creon. Do the statements of psychological truth refer to all or most or a few of the flesh-and-blood beings they designate? How can we know? The drama or novel will not tell us. Praises of its "universality" must do more than beg the question or blur it. The difficulty is complicated in the instant case because *hybris*, to the Greeks, was inevitably destructive. Should we be sceptical of divine retribution, we would put it, "*Hybris* may destroy . . ." All these tergiversations, tedious, but unavoidable and thus instructive, finally yield:

His *hybris* must destroy/may destroy a great man in history [some great men?] [all great men?] who. . . .

A messy statement, which is not its chief weakness. A biographer of Napoleon might use it, tidied up, as a classical tag, to add some tone to his prose. It would be little more than a tag. He explains the hero's downfall by the Continental System and the invasion of Russia. These might be taken to be acts of *hybris* or they might be described as strategic miscalculations or in yet other ways. Any more strict application of the literary model would be profoundly misleading. The compactness and lucidity of the Greek tragedies make out sharply the predominance of *hybris* in the behaviour of Ajax and Creon, and its consequences in their madness or misery. Was *hybris*, as in the dramas, the sole cause or the primary cause of Napoleon's downfall? Can we ever achieve, have we ever achieved, the same tightly knit, luminous concatenation of character, action, and consequence concerning a historical figure that the tragedy brilliantly achieves in the epiphanic two hours of its life, and its hero's?

Given that his over-reaching contributed, in some measure, to Napoleon's downfall, did it play the same role as in the tragedies? The contingencies of the great world, the British bulldog, intestinal troubles, and Blücher's late arrival, leave behind the fictions and the inevitability of their unfolding. What remains of the truth(s) inferred from classical tragedy? We might as well settle for "Pride goeth before a fall". For such rewards, who needs great art?

Oedipus Tyrannus has been, since Aristotle, among the best evidence for those who think that tragedy teaches us about life. Now we are spared the tedium of formulating its truth because the play itself announces it. The Chorus, anguished by the calamities it has witnessed, would redeem some meaning from them:

"I will call no mortal happy... Till... all his hours have passed away."[5] For life can suddenly afflict any man, even at times of his happy prosperity. (The author of an autobiography I happen to be reading learned early that "unexpected things happen in life, one never knows what will happen."[6]) There are numerous other truths gleaned from *Oedipus* by literary critics and scholars. A thoughtful and informed study of the play arrives briefly, at one point, at its universal truth:

> In Oedipus' extreme case we recognize our common case, in which action and understanding never entirely cohere.... Oedipus' fate opens our eyes to the gaps between being and doing and understanding.[7]

Oedipus certainly acted without understanding and came to realize it. So have we all, much of the time. It is less certain that those who have read the play – leave out those who have never heard of *Oedipus Tyrannus* – had not previously learned this truth, at the cost of their own less dramatic pain.

We have been trafficking in banalities but only so can the large sagacities dear to cognitivism be put to rest. The truths disclosed or suggested by art now resemble less religious truths. They come more and more to resemble garden variety truths. They are, indeed, in other respects, even flimsier.

There are contradictions within science, history, and religion – the nature of light, that Germany was solely responsible for the Great War, the Trinity. The contradictions are acknowledged. Then efforts are made to overcome them or else, in religion, they are, with some difficulty, absorbed by faith. The quotidian saws, "Look before you leap" and "He who hesitates is lost" might be thought, by some pedantic person, to contradict each other. Even he will not think that another well-known truth from *Oedipus*, Man can never control his fate, and

> I am the master of my fate,
> I am the captain of my soul,

contradict each other. The words are formal contradictories. The utterances are so distinct, so discrete, come from universes of discourse so unrelated to each other, that it would be silliness worse than pedantry to make the logical point. We may contrast the truths derived from works of literature. We never say that they are terms in a contradiction. How should there be truth without the possibility of contradiction?

The possibility of contradiction and the necessity of confirmation. There are organized bodies of evidence that confirm or go to confirm the inverse square law, the date of Caesar's assassination, that man is created by God. We could also adduce meteorological data to establish that summer is warmer than winter, though this is not how people gain this truth. They do so by living and learning. Art, uniquely, never confirms its truths. If we find that stubborn pride and ignorant prejudice sometimes keep attractive men and women apart, we find the evidence for this truth about the great world in the great world. The fiction does not and cannot provide the evidence. Mr and Mrs Darcy would doubtless be more than willing to confirm the truth but they are, alas, unable to do so.

Bleak House is the source of a truth more easily elicited and, because it is much less ambitious, much more exact than those we have previously considered: Estate litigation in the Court of Chancery in mid-nineteenth-century England moved very slowly.

This statement affirms that there was a Court of Chancery in London at the time of which the novel speaks. There was, but not because the novel says so. We have other, necessary and sufficient reasons. If we do not accept the existence of the Court of Chancery despite the novel's sometimes realistic description, we surely do not accept what the novel alleges about the pace of estate litigation despite its vivid, humorous, and touching account of Jarndyce and Jarndyce. The author knew this. From his Preface to the novel:

"...everything set forth in these pages concerning the Court of Chancery is substantially true, and within the truth." He points to cases of record which equal or exceed in notoriety that of Jarndyce and assures the reader that "If I wanted other authorities for JARNDYCE and JARNDYCE, I could rain them on these pages."[8]

By curious coincidence, it was in the same year, 1853, that Harriet Beecher Stowe did just the same thing. Beecher Stowe, indeed, went Dickens something better, since she devoted an entire book of several hundred pages to confirming documentation. Her novel's description of slavery, published a year earlier, had been found powerfully persuasive by a large audience, though other readers were incredulous. The fiction was not enough. The fiction had to be shown to be true, a constraint not peculiar to mid-nineteenth-century novels in English: "It is *treated* as a reality [by the public] and therefore as a reality it may be proper that it should be defended." Thus: *A Key to Uncle Tom's Cabin; presenting the original facts and documents upon which the story is founded. Together with corroborative statements verifying the truth of the work.*[9]

In both instances, the truth was knowable and known before the fictions appeared.

In science, history, and religion, confirmation of a statement also counts as evidence for other, logically related statements. Thus truths, notably in the cumulative advances of science, support and build on each other. Out of them and epistemic auxiliaries, theories are constructed. There are no theories, strictly, in garden variety cognition. Even there, however, truths attach themselves to other truths and make up crudely defined but substantial nodes of knowledge. That summer is warmer than winter is built up from small experiences and sustains a host of related beliefs concerning dress, festivals, and other behaviours appropriate to each. Art is unlike any of these kinds of knowing. The truth derived from one work of art never confirms that derived from another work of art, though the truths are related to or resemble one another, not even if they should be identical. They are truths about the great world. Yet who has ever said or thought that *Antigone* confirms *Ajax*, though they are both Greek tragedies, by the same dramatist? Hardy does not confirm *Oedipus* any more than *Invictus* refutes it. The very speculation is silly, though remarking that it is is, again, instructive.

Science, history, and religion deal with a certain sector or stratum of reality or, alternatively, reality viewed from a certain perspective. These studies are carried on by specialists, who are knowledgeable and possess unusual abilities of thought and research. Garden variety knowledge is made up chiefly of truths not reserved to any one field of study, e.g., summer is warmer than winter, parents love their children. There are no specialists because almost anyone can learn these truths.

Art is quite extraordinary. It enters upon each of the above sectors of knowledge and any and all others besides. Its truths range from expansive pronouncements on man's fate to middle-sized assertions about the workings of pride in human nature to small-scale accounts of one period in the history of an English court. It is replete with epigrammatic observations hardly distinguishable from folk sayings. Like Terence's busybody, nothing human is alien to it, nor anything non-human either. It now falls out why there was, when we began, no trouble in finding clear cases of scientific, historical, religious, and garden variety truths, whereas no clear examples of artistic truth came to mind. None of its truths are peculiar to art. All are proper to some extra-artistic sphere of the great world. So considered, there are no artistic truths. Not one.

The metaphysicians and theologians have mulled over man's freedom from fate, the psychologists have studied pride along with other traits of character, the legal historians examine the cases to which Dickens only alludes in his Preface, the legal issues involved, and other cases as well. They have done so in elaborating complex theories of human destiny or human nature, or the centuries-long history of the Court, perhaps of the English judicial system. The metaphysician does not have to spend a good deal of his time, indeed most of his time, trying to find the cause of the plague on Thebes; there is no diverting dialogue of feather-brained family members or priggish parsons in the psychological studies, or any sub-plots or irrelevant though funny characters in the legal history.

Because novels and plays do spend most of their time on these other matters, the truths elicited from them are generally tangential, inchoate, vague, which may explain, in part, why they often seem to enjoy a weight of suggestiveness greater than they are entitled to. Such truths do not require specialists. The artist may chance to have first-hand knowledge – Dickens was a law reporter; most often, as Plato, an arch-cognitivist complained, he does not. But it is not by virtue of such knowledge that he is an artist. And even when such knowledge shapes the work of art, it is not, we have seen, the work of art that confirms. We may see why, for all the talk of artistic truth, there has been fairly little talk of artistic knowledge.

The immediate exception to the foregoing conclusions would be knowledge of art itself, which is another sector of the great world. Art might speak authoritatively in dealing with art. There are, of course, distinctive truths *about* art. They are mostly amassed by art historians, musicologists, etc., who are not, it is sometimes deplored, themselves artists. A work of art may suggest truths or truth-claims concerning art. But these are assertions, once they have been disengaged, that fall within the philosophy or, perhaps more usually, the psychology or sociology of art. Then they are taken over, if they have not already been arrived at independently, by the specialists who, as before, specify, expand and, where possible, confirm them. There are also works of art, probably too many in recent decades, that insinuate or trumpet truths about themselves.

The remoteness of artistic truth even from garden variety knowledge is more apparent than ever. There are no specialists either in art or garden variety knowing because none are needed. In everyday cognition, however, experiences available to all support relatively well-founded truths. There, too, these truths merge into bodies of knowledge. So as one can believe and believe in science and other ways of knowing, one accepts the deliverances of ordinary experience and trusts to them in the future. "That's just common sense," we say in knockdown tones; "that's just art" bears a quite different intonation. There are no "artistic believers" or people who "believe in art".

Finally, take the artistic truth that has as good a claim as any to be a breakthrough, a disclosure not previously known to science. The statement wrested from the novel is, once more, hopelessly unwieldy:

The criminal [some criminals?] [all criminals?] [criminals in St Petersburg?] [criminals who kill old moneylenders?] [criminals who kill old moneylenders and come under the influence of saintly prostitutes?] desires to be caught and punished.

It happens that the artist has formulated a more tractable statement in a letter sketching the prospective novel (the editor's brackets enclose Dostoevsky's additions to the letter): "[In addition] I hint at this thought in the novel, that [legal] punishment for a crime frightens a criminal much less than we think [the lawmakers in part] because the criminal himself [morally] demands it."[10]

Twentieth-century psychologists acclaim Dostoevsky, particularly for his understanding of the criminal, as "one of the greatest psychologists".[11] His "hint" has been taken up. It is therefore, of necessity, placed within a psychological theory. Dostoevsky's reference to moral compunction is psychologized into the dominance of the superego over the ego. Raskolnikov is considered along with a number of psychoanalytic patients who have manifested "the compulsion to confess". Dostoevsky's "a criminal" is replaced by a class of criminals.[12] A viable truth-claim, perhaps also a truth, is now established. Whereas the "hint" occupies one sentence in the letter, as something of an afterthought ("in addition"), the letter consists of an extensive outline of the story of Raskolnikov: "This is a psychological account of a crime. A young man expelled from the university . . . " and so on. Even so, it omits important elements of the plot, e.g., Sonia, that later appear in the finished work. Dostoevsky wrote a fiction. A supreme psychologist among novelists, he was a novelist, not a psychologist.

The proponents of artistic truth, justifiably reluctant to see it forced into the model of science or some other alien model, have typically insisted that it is *sui generis*. So it proves to be. Paradoxically, to start with, because there are no distinctively artistic truths. Generally, the truth is unvoiced. If so, it needs to be disentangled from the elements that enmesh it in the fiction. The uncertainty of their pertinence to the great world leads to a clumsy and ambiguous truth-claim. Only occasionally is the truth set out explicitly as a moral or *envoi*. In either case, the truth is one proper to some independent inquiry, usually psychology, and could probably have been arrived at otherwise. Only there is it developed systematically. In either case, there is no method of arriving at it in art and no confirmation or possibility of confirmation in art. Artistic truths, like the works of art that give rise to them, are discretely unrelated and therefore form no corpus either of belief or knowledge. Hence formal contradictions are tolerated effortlessly, if they are ever remarked. Only rarely does an artistic truth point to a genuine advance in knowledge. Artistic truths are, preponderantly, distinctly banal. Compared to science, above all, but also to history, religion, and garden variety knowing, artistic truth is a sport, stunted, hardly to be compared. These are the slight, dull, obvious realities which have been obscured by the grandiose pieties of cognitivism, the most lyrical, the very ecstasy of which is

"Beauty is truth, truth beauty" – that is all
Ye know on earth, and all ye need to know.

References

1   Hesiod, *Theogony*, ls. 27–8.
2   *Rep.* 377 ff., 600.
3   See Jerome Stolnitz, "On the Historical Triviality of Art," *British Journal of Aesthetics*, 31 (1991), 195–202.
4   See Peter Gay, *Freud* (New York, 1988), 159.
5   *Sophocles*, tr. Campbell (London, 1930), 128.
6   Felix Gilbert, *A European Past* (New York, 1988), 12.
7   Adrian Poole, *Tragedy* (New York, 1987), 91.
8   Charles Dickens, *Bleak House*, ed. Ford and Monod (New York, 1977), 3.
9   London, 1853. The foregoing quotation is from p. 1, italics in original.
10   Letter to M. N. Katkov, in Fyodor Dostoevsky, *The Notebooks for Crime and Punishment*, ed. Wasiolek (Chicago, 1967), 172.
11   Theodor Reik, *The Compulsion to Confess* (New York, 1959), 275. See Sigmund Freud, *Character and Culture* (New York, 1963), ch. XXIV; Heinz Kohut, *Self Psychology and the Humanities* (New York, 1985), 41.
12   See Reik, *The Compulsion to Confess*, 258 ff., 309–12.

42

Literature and Knowledge

Catherine Wilson

There is probably no subject in the philosophy of art which has prompted more impassioned theorizing than the question of the "cognitive value" of works of art. "In the end," one influential critic has stated, "I do not distinguish between science and art except as regards method. Both provide us with a view of reality and both are indispensable to a complete understanding of the universe."[1] If a man is not prepared to distinguish between science and art one may well wonder what he is prepared to distinguish between, but in all fairness it should be pointed out that the writings of anti-cognitivists contain equally strenuous statements of doctrine. For I. A. Richards, poetry consists of "pseudo-statements" which are "true" if they "suit and serve some attitude or link together attitudes which on other grounds are desirable".[2]

Here I defend the view that literary art can be said to be a source of knowledge. At the same time, I argue that much previous discussion has missed the point. In order to show that one can learn from a novel, or a poem, or a play, it is not sufficient to show that the work contains propositions of a general or philosophical nature, or again that it furnishes vicarious experiences which could not be attained in any other way. And in order to show that literature does not contribute to a person's intellectual understanding of the world, it is not sufficient to show that the knowledge it is said to impart could not be found in the pages of a textbook suitable for instruction in any established

discipline. The view I should like ultimately to defend should be viewed as an alternative to one which has found much favour among partisans of the cognitive value of literature, namely, the view that literary works contain or imply propositions which the reader is led to accept. The "proposition-theory", as I shall call it, is thoroughly indefensible for a number of reasons.

The most noted proposition-theorist, Morris Weitz, claims to find in Proust the revelation that "there are no essences to our emotions": "that jealousy, love and suffering manifest themselves in different ways and are recognized according to different criteria".[3] For Peter Jones, *Middlemarch* contains the implication that past desires and present hopes govern our interpretation of present sensory experience.[4] According to John Hospers, *Paradise Lost* implies that "man's state after the Fall is much better, in that he has free-will in a sense which he lacked before."[5] And finally, Coleridge claims that in writing *Hamlet*, "Shakespeare wished to impress upon us the truth, that action is the chief end of existence."[6] Philosophers who claim that it is possible to learn from a literary work, then, typically imply that the kinds of things one learns are that man's state before the Fall left something to be desired, that love has no single essence, that desires and hopes alter the very character of experience, and so on.

Such a claim is simply unacceptable from the start for the anti-cognitivist. Richards, Ayer, and

From *Philosophy* 58 (1983), pp. 489–96. Reprinted by permission of the publisher and author.

Carnap presumably never intended to deny that novels, poetry and plays contain implicit and explicit statements. What they wished to argue was that propositions like those listed above are incapable of communicating knowledge; they make no contribution to our understanding of the world, and it is in *this* sense that they are to be regarded as "meaningless" or as "pseudo-statements". When Weitz, then, argues against the "positivists" that *Native Son* "reveals a truth about the world which has not been revealed by any other novelist, sociologist, or philosopher" namely, that "the only freedom left to modern man is the freedom to destroy, first others about you and finally yourself,"[7] his claim is vitiated by an important ambiguity. If Weitz means that no sociologist and no philosopher could, in principle, establish this conclusion because of the inherent limitations of sociology and philosophy as disciplines, one is left wondering what sort of truth it is which is established neither by empirical observation nor by reasoning from a set of established or immediately plausible assumptions. If, on the other hand, Weitz means that Richard Wright has already anticipated what sociology or philosophy can, and so eventually will reveal, one is justified in wondering what the difference is between anticipation of this sort and mere conjecture. Whichever way his claim is interpreted, it plays directly into the hands of his sceptical opponent.

There are two further objections to the proposition-theory which are worth noting. First of all, even if it were true that Milton, Proust, Eliot, and Shakespeare all believed themselves to have valid sociological or philosophical demonstrations of the propositions their works may be read as implying, this would not provide the reader with any reason for belief. No matter how broad their presumed experience of humanity, they cannot be supposed to speak with any particular authority. And secondly, if what one learned from literature were the propositions which are contained in particular works, a wider acquaintance with literature would paradoxically result in a *constriction* of knowledge since, for many literary works, a work can be found which implies the opposite. Hospers himself admits that *Paradise Lost* also implies that "man's fall is a dire catastrophe, a work of Satan in defiance of God." Greek tragedy reveals the existence of an immutable order in the world which is independent of human hopes and wishes. Beckett's *Molloy* may be said to imply that action is absurd, motivation unintelligible.

Unfortunately, the anti-cognitivist's claim is no more coherent at bottom. It is the philosopher's responsibility, after all, to unmask, or to give an account of the ordinary sense in which we speak of works of art as "illuminating" or "edifying" or "revealing". If these descriptions are used speciously in connection with works of art, the philosopher is in a position to locate the source of the error and to unravel the confusion. Richards alone has struggled to explain why poetry is believed to be a source of knowledge. His explanation of the illusion of intellectual significance went as follows: in reading a poem a person may be struck with an impression of deep import. As a result of a mental habit of association between learning a fact of deep theoretical importance and similar feelings of significance, he concludes that he must have learned something. In fact, what he has experienced is simply a revision of his attitudes, the sum total of his emotional responses to the world. He regards with awe, or fear, or tenderness, presumably, what he hitherto regarded with indifference, mild interest, or repulsion. This account is altogether unconvincing. It is unclear how a moderately aware reader could ever confuse the acquisition of information with the reorganization of his attitudes if the two things are, as Richards insists, really poles apart. It is difficult to give a philosophically adequate explanation of how one might get the illusion of learning from a novel as it is to explain how one might actually succeed in doing so. As a result, it is clear that although the proposition theory is untenable, the theory of "emotive discourse" which is supposed to replace it is equally so.

In an influential book, Dorothy Walsh has attempted to locate the cognitive value of literature in an altogether different area by arguing that the philosophical classification of knowledge into "knowledge how" and "knowledge that" is radically incomplete.[8] A person may be said not only to know, e.g. *how* to play chess or ride a bicycle, and *that*, e.g. the War of the Roses began in 1456, but also *what it is like* to, e.g. fall suddenly in love, lose a child to death, or undergo religious conversion. According to Walsh, "knowing what" rounds out the complete picture of knowledge, and it is knowledge of this sort that literature provides. In the course of reading a novel, a person may acquire "knowledge in the form of realization; the realization of what anything might come to as a form of lived experience".

A view rather similar to Walsh's, to the effect that literature and art in general provide "intuitive" knowledge or "knowledge of essences", has been criticized on the ground that merely having the experience of x, or living through x is only a precondition of knowledge and not knowledge itself. For Monroe Beardsley, "Acquaintance ... does not become knowledge in the strict sense until the data are combined and connected by reasoning."[9] Walsh's defence against this line of attack consists in pointing out that we recognize a difference between the case of the man of whom it is simply *true* that he has been poor and lonely in the big city, and the case of the man who knows *what it is like* to have been so. There is something which the latter possesses which the former does not, although it is not to be identified with anything like the capacity to say "what it was like". "Knowing beyond saying," she argues, "is acceptable in such a case, not because saying is impossible but because the kind of saying that would be relevant is a saying that requires literary talent."[10] It is appropriate to ask the person who claims to know how to extract gold from common table salt for proof of his expertise, just as it is appropriate to ask the person who claims to know that there are people living in the centre of the earth for proof of his assertion. But in the case of "knowing what it is like to x" the demand for proof is altogether inappropriate, and the lack of such proofs does not impugn the claim to know.

It might appear that Walsh's theory meets the objections of the positivists while at the same time justifying the application of the term "knowledge" to something other than a body of doctrine. However, she does not take the trouble to interpret any particular knowledge claim in the light of her theory, and when an attempt is made, the theory reveals its underlying weakness. I shall try to illustrate this by considering a claim made by D. Z. Phillips concerning Edith Wharton's novel, *The Age of Innocence*.[11]

The novel in question is set in New York of the 1880s. The hero, Newland Archer, is a member of the convention-bound upper-middle class, and the story concerns his love for, and eventual renunciation of the brilliant, eccentric Ellen Olenska in favour of his mild, conforming, and altogether appropriate fiancée, May Welland. While many critics have seen in the novel an indictment of old New York and its spiritual values, Phillips argues that the significance of the novel is precisely the reverse:

"That it has all been a waste" is a not infrequent reaction on completing a reading of *The Age of Innocence*. In making such a judgment high priority is given to the importance of satisfying genuine love, talking out difficulties in frank, open discussion, making up one's own mind on moral issues and not paying too much attention to what one's parents or one's family have to say ... what I am protesting against is the equation of these beliefs with intelligence as such.[12]

He goes on to quote with approval Louis Auchincloss's remark that "This is the climax of the message; that under the thick glass of convention blooms the fine, fragile flower of patient suffering and denial."[13] "The philosophical consequences," Phillips continues, "of waiting on Edith Wharton's novel are that the artificiality of an abstract concept of reasonableness is revealed."[14] What the novel has revealed to him, he claims, is first, that the "reasonable man" of much of contemporary moral philosophy is a kind of phantom, and secondly, that "the question of what we mean by 'allegiance and change in morality' does not admit of a general answer."

Phillips's interpretation of the novel is, as he goes to a good deal of trouble to point out, idiosyncratic. However, I am not concerned here with the justifiability of his interpretation, but with his claim that the novel provides a counterexample to certain theses in philosophy. Any attempt to slough off such a claim as the report of a simple change in attitude is impossible to take seriously, for it is impossible to say in this case what attitude it is that is supposed to have changed, or to have gone through a process of reorganization. The claim is, after all, that contemporary moral philosophers are *mistaken*. At the same time, it would be wrong to suppose that the novel in any sense implies and justifies the propositions "Renunciation is a fine thing" or "Old values may be the best values." Unlike a philosophical treatise on reasonableness, the novel fails altogether to lay out the practical and spiritual advantages which might accrue from renunciation. It simply tells the story of a man who, as a matter of fact, chooses one woman over another whom he might have chosen without physical or legal consequences. We do not even see Archer prospering as a result.

What then of Walsh's claim? Can we interpret Phillips's alleged learning as simply the experience of coming to know "what it is like" to be a man of Newland Archer's type, in his situation? I think not. There is a wide logical gap between the realization of what it would be like to have Newland Archer's experiences and the realization that a certain popular philosophical conception of reasonable action is, in a certain sense, fraudulent. This is not, as it might seem, an accidental feature of the case. We are told that John Stuart Mill, the man brought up to be "a mere reasoning machine", was brought out of his nearly suicidal depression by a reading of Wordsworth. It might seem tempting to characterize Mill's transformation as the reorganization of his attitudes, but such a characterization would capture only part of the story. A change in attitude may, and typically does, come about as a result of something one has learned. Again, though, there is a logical gap between the realization, in Walsh's sense, of, for example, what it is like to live at one with Nature, and the realization that suicide is unwarranted.

One might make an effort to fill in the gap by arguing as follows: if the reader *really* understands what it would be like to have been Newland Archer, or to feel about Nature as Wordsworth did, that reader cannot help but abandon a shallow conception of reasonableness, and he cannot help but perceive the value of being alive. In the long run, I think this argument is successful. In the short run, it points up a serious ambiguity in Walsh's formulation.

The examples originally given to fix the concept of "knowing what *x* is like" were purposely chosen for their simplicity. In an effort to elucidate the concept of "knowing how", Ryle offered as examples the activities of fly-tying, chess-playing, and so on, and in an effort to elucidate the concept of "knowing what", Walsh offered us the experiences of losing a child to death, being lost in a forest, etc. It now appears, though, that there is both a "deep" way and a "shallow" way of "knowing what *x* is like". A reader may understand "what it is like" to be Newland Archer in the shallow sense, and his philosophical convictions may undergo no revision. But on the version of the theory we are now considering, *if* he understands what it is like to be Newland Archer in the "strong sense", his philosophical conceptions will necessarily be affected. The theoretical resources of Walsh's theory give out at just this point, for the mundane examples which were used to fix the concept of "knowing what *x* is like" are of no help in understanding the stronger concept. The person who knows what it is like to be poor and lonely in the big city has not necessarily been forced to alter his conceptions of poverty, or loneliness, or anonymity.

The positive account I have to offer at this point will be somewhat brief. Nevertheless, I think it comes closest to the "autobiographical" accounts of Mill and Phillips, and escapes the theoretical objections to which the "proposition theory" and the "knowing what" theory are subject. A person may learn from a novel, I want to argue, if he is forced to revise or modify, e.g. his concept of "reasonable action" through a recognition of an alternative as presented in the novel. Such a view can account for the impression of writers like Weitz that particular works can reveal such things as that the only freedom left in the world is the freedom to destroy yourself. But to insist that what has been learned here is that a certain statement is true is to truncate, in a radically unacceptable way, the more complex process. I want now to argue briefly that the term "learning" applies primarily to a modification of a person's concepts, which is in turn capable of altering his thought or conduct, and not primarily to an increased disposition to utter factually correct statements or to display technical prowess.

Let us take as unarguably central the case of the person who has learned the principles of civil engineering or who has successfully studied medieval history. Such a person should be able to state facts and theorems, and it would be reasonable to expect of the civil engineer that he could actually build. But we should expect the engineer to be able as well to solve engineering problems of a novel sort, and to be able to evaluate and criticize novel engineering proposals. We should expect the historian to be able to extrapolate from what he has learned to more general conclusions about authority, rebellion, social change, reform, and so on. The ability to go beyond what has actually been fed in in the teaching process stems, in each case, from a more fundamental – and perhaps even radical – alteration in the way in which the learner perceives, in one case, the physical environment, in the other, a period of history. The engineer must come to see buildings and materials in terms of their potential for integrity and stability. The historian must revise the way in which he once thought of war, class structure, religion, and so forth. These changes may lie, in one sense, behind the scenes: a person may be quite incapable of explaining *how* he perceives things now. But his learning must amount to *some* difference in what he is prepared to do or say under certain conditions; his new knowledge must be expressible in some way even if not in the form of one of the

Catherine Wilson

grander pronouncements of the proposition-theorists.

It is tempting, although I think ultimately a mistake, to raise questions at this point about the mechanics of the influence of literary works. One person, let us say, reads a Japanese novel in which alien and remote conceptions of honour or sacrifice are depicted. (There should ultimately be no more of a problem about how a novel can depict "honour" than about how a portrait can depict "gentleness", or a film "horror".) He later claims to have learned something from it. Another person reads the same novel, either notes or fails to note the themes of honour and sacrifice, but claims that he learned nothing from it. What is the difference between the two? What happens when the first person (a) recognizes the conception presented in the novel as superior to his own and (b) adopts it, in recognition of its superiority, so that it comes to serve as a kind of standard by which he reviews his own conduct and that of others?

The spuriousness of these questions can be seen as soon as they are shifted out of the realm of fiction. Consider the case of the young man who learns about kindness from his aged aunt. There need be no moment when the young man realizes that there is something defective about his conception of kindness; he need not even think of himself as possessing such a conception. Nor need there be a moment when he weighs the behaviour of his aunt against his own and decides in favour of his aunt. The difference between the young man who learns from the example of his aunt and a similarly situated young man who does not, does not amount to a kind of mechanical failure in the latter case, but to a difference *in the way they regard their aunts.* For the second man, she is "too kind" or "impossibly kind" or "kindness isn't everything" – or he may have failed to be struck by her kindness in the first place. The essentials are no different in the case of the reader who is left unmoved by, e.g., Japanese or Existentialist literature.

There is a good deal that remains to be filled in in the above account, notably the very idea of a person's possessing a concept of honour, kindness,

reasonableness, or even of "causal influence". Nevertheless, it suggests one way of preserving the insights of both proposition-theorists and their emotivist opponents without reproducing their incoherencies. The kind of understanding which literature affords cannot be represented as a body of statements occupying a particular location in the nexus of historical and scientific doctrine. But, as I have tried to show, by "knowledge" we do not mean that body of doctrine.

Notes

1 Herbert Read, *Education Through Art.* Quoted in M. Rader and B. Jessup, *Art and Human Values* (Englewood Cliffs, NJ: Prentice Hall, 1976), 254.
2 I. A. Richards, "Poetry and Beliefs" in Weitz (ed.), *Problems in Aesthetics*, 2nd edn (New York: Macmillan, 1970), 569.
3 Morris Weitz, *Philosophy in Literature* (Detroit: Wayne State University Press, 1963), 78–84.
4 Peter Jones, *Philosophy and the Novel* (Oxford: Clarendon Press, 1975), 47–9.
5 John Hospers, "Implied Truths in Literature", in Levich (ed.), *Aesthetics and the Philosophy of Criticism* (New York: Random House, 1963), 367.
6 S. T. Coleridge, *Shakespearean Criticism* quoted in Weitz, op. cit., 59.
7 Morris Weitz, "Does Art Tell the Truth?", *Philosophy and Phenomenological Research* III, no. 3 (March 1943), 345.
8 Dorothy Walsh, *Literature and Knowledge* (Middletown, Conn.: Wesleyan University Press, 1969), 96.
9 Monroe Beardsley, *Aesthetics* (New York: Harcourt Brace, 1958), 383.
10 Walsh, *Literature and Knowledge*, 104.
11 Edith Wharton, *The Age of Innocence* (New York: D. Appleton, 1920).
12 D. Z. Phillips, "Allegiance and Change in Morality" in *Philosophy and the Arts* VI (Royal Institute of Philosophy Lectures) (New York: St Martin's, 1973), 54–8.
13 L. Auchincloss, "Edith Wharton and her New Yorks" in *Edith Wharton: A Collection of Critical Essays*, ed. I. Howe. Quoted in Phillips, "Allegiance," 56.
14 Phillips, "Allegiance," 58.

43

"Finely Aware and Richly Responsible"

Martha Nussbaum

"The effort really to see and really to represent is no idle business in face of the constant force that makes for muddlement."[1] So Henry James on the task of the moral imagination. We live amid bewildering complexities. Obtuseness and refusal of vision are our besetting vices. Responsible lucidity can be wrested from that darkness only by painful, vigilant effort, the intense scrutiny of particulars. Our highest and hardest task is to make ourselves people "on whom nothing is lost."[2]

This is a claim about our ethical task, as people who are trying to live well. In its context it is at the same time a claim about the task of the literary artist. James often stresses this analogy: the work of the moral imagination is in some manner like the work of the creative imagination, especially that of the novelist. I want to study this analogy and to see how it is more than analogy: why this conception of moral attention and moral vision finds in novels its most appropriate articulation. More: why, according to this conception, the novel is itself a moral achievement, and the well-lived life is a work of literary art.

Although the moral conception according to which James's novels have this value will be elicited here from James's work, my aim is to commend it as of more than parochial interest – as, in fact, the best account I know of these matters. But if I succeed only in establishing the weaker claim that it is a major candidate for truth,

deserving of our most serious scrutiny when we do moral philosophy, this will be reason enough to include inside moral philosophy those texts in which it receives its most appropriate presentation. I shall argue that James's novels are such texts. So I shall provide further support for my contention that certain novels are, irreplaceably, works of moral philosophy. But I shall go further. I shall try to articulate and define the claim that the novel can be a paradigm of moral activity. I confine myself to *The Golden Bowl*,[3] so as to build on my previous interpretation.

I begin by examining the nature of moral attention and insight in one episode, in which two people perform acts of altruism without reliance on rules of duty, improvising what is required. This leads to some reflection about the interaction of rules and perceptions in moral judging and learning: about the value of "plainness," about the "mystic lake" of perceptual bewilderment, about "getting the tip" and finding a "basis." Finally I probe James's analogy (and more) between moral attention and our attention to works of art. In short: I begin assessing the moral contribution of texts that narrate the experiences of beings committed to value, using that "immense array of terms, perceptional and expressional, that . . . in sentence, passage and page, simply looked over the heads of the standing terms – or perhaps rather, like alert winged creatures, perched on

Excerpted version of chapter 5 from *Love's Knowledge* (Oxford: Oxford University Press, 1990), pp. 148–65. Reprinted by permission of Oxford University Press and Oxford University Press, Inc.

those diminished summits and aspired to a clearer air" (*GB*, pref., I. xvi–xvii).

I

How can we hope to confront these characters and their predicament, if not in these words and sentences, whose very ellipses and circumnavigations rightly convey the lucidity of their bewilderment, the precision of their indefiniteness? Any pretense that we could paraphrase this scene without losing its moral quality would belie the argument that I am about to make. I presuppose, then, the quotation of Book Fifth, Chapter III of *The Golden Bowl*. Indeed, honoring its "chains of relation and responsibility," I presuppose the quotation of the entire novel. What follows is a commentary.

This daughter and this father must give one another up. Before this "they *had*, after all, whatever happened, always and ever each other . . . to do exactly what they would with: a provision full of possibilities" (II.255). But not all possibilities are, in fact, compatible with this provision. He must let her go, loving her, so that she can live with her husband as a real wife; loving him, she must discover a way to let him go as a "great and deep and high" man and not a failure, his dignity intact. In the "golden air" of these "massed Kentish woods" (II.256) they "beat against the wind" and "cross the bar" (II.264): they reach, through a mutual and sustained moral effort, a resolution and an end. It is, moreover (in this Tennysonian image), their confrontation with death: her acceptance of the death of her own childhood and an all-enveloping love (her movement out of Eden into the place of birth and death); his acceptance of a life that will be from now on, without her, a place of death. She, bearing the guilt that her birth as a woman has killed him; he, "*offering* himself, pressing himself upon her, as a sacrifice – he had read his way so into her best possibility" (II.269). It is a reasonable place for us to begin our investigation; for the acts to be recorded can be said to be paradigmatic of the moral: his sacrifice, her preservation of his dignity, his recognition of her separate and autonomous life.

The scene begins with evasion, a flight from dilemma into the lost innocence of childhood. For "it was wonderfully like their having got together into some boat and paddled off from the shore where husbands and wives, luxuriant complications, made the air too tropical" (II.255).

They "slope" off together as "of old" (II.253); they rest "on a sequestered bench," far from the "strain long felt but never named" (II.254), the conflicts imposed by other relations. They might have been again the only man and woman in the garden. They immerse themselves in "the inward felicity of their being once more, perhaps only for half an hour, simply daughter and father" (254–5). Their task will be to depart from this felicity without altogether defiling its beauty.

The difficulty is real enough. Could it be anything but a matter of the most serious pain, and guilt, for her to give up, even for a man whom she loves passionately, this father who has raised her, protected her, loved her, enveloped her, who really does love only her and who depends on her for help of future happiness? In these circumstances she cannot love her husband except by banishing her father. But if she banishes her father he will live unhappy and die alone. (And won't she, as well, have to see him as a failure, his life as debased, as well as empty?) It is no wonder, then, that Maggie finds herself wishing "to keep him with her for remounting the stream of time and dipping again, for the softness of the water, into the contracted basin of the past" (II.258). To dare to be and do what she passionately desires appears, and is, too monstrous, a cruel refusal of loyalty. And what has her whole world been built on, if not on loyalty and the keen image of his greatness? It is no wonder that the feeling of desire for her husband is, in this crisis, felt as a numbing chill, and she accuses it: "I'm at this very moment . . . frozen stiff with selfishness" (II.265).

This is moral anguish, not simply girlish fear. Keeping down her old childish sense of his omnipotence exacerbates and does not remove her problem; for seeing him as limited and merely human (as Adam, not the creator) she sees, too, all the things he cannot have without her. And in her anguish she has serious thought of regression and return: "Why . . . couldn't they always live, so far as they lived together, in a boat?" (II.255). In pursuit of that idea she calls upon her ability to speak in universal terms, about what "one must always do." The narrator says of this "sententious(ness)" that it "was doubtless too often even now her danger" (II.258) – linking the propensity for abstractness and the use of "standing terms" with her past and present refusals to confront the unique and conflict-engendering nature of her own particular context.

I say this to show the moral difficulty of what is going on here, the remarkable moral achievement, therefore, in his act of sacrifice which resolves it. The general sacrificial idea – that he will go off to America with Charlotte – is in itself no solution. For it to become a solution it has to be offered in the right way at the right time in the right tone, in such a way that she can take it; offered without pressing any of the hidden springs of guilt and loyalty in her that he knows so clearly how to press; offered so that he gives her up with greatness, with beauty, in a way that she can love and find wonderful. To give her up he must, then, really give her up; he must wholeheartedly *wish* to give her up, so that she sees that he *has* "read his way so into her best possibility."

Maggie has spoken of her passion for Amerigo, saying that when you love in the deepest way you are beyond jealousy – "You're beyond everything, and nothing can pull you down" (II.262). What happens next is that her father perceives her in a certain way:

> The mere fine pulse of passion in it, the suggestion as of a creature consciously floating and shining in a warm summer sea, some element of dazzling sapphire and silver, a creature cradled upon depths, buoyant among dangers, in which fear or folly or sinking otherwise than in play was impossible – something of all this might have been making once more present to him, with his discreet, his half shy assent to it, her probable enjoyment of a rapture that he, in his day, had presumably convinced no great number of persons either of his giving or of his receiving. He sat awhile as if he knew himself hushed, almost admonished, and not for the first time; yet it was an effect that might have brought before him rather what she had gained than what he had missed . . . It could pass further for knowing – for knowing that without him nothing might have been: which would have been missing least of all. "I guess I've never been jealous," he finally remarked.

And she takes it: "Oh it's you, father, who are what I call beyond everything. Nothing can pull *you* down." (II.263–4).

This passage records a moral achievement of deep significance. Adam acknowledges, in an image of delicate beauty and lyricism, his daughter's sexuality and free maturity. More: he wishes that she be free, that the suggestion of passion in

her voice be translated into, fulfilled in a life of sparkling playfulness. He assents to her pleasure and wishes to be its approving spectator, not its impediment. He renounces, at the same time, his own personal gain – renounces even the putting of the question as to what he might or might not gain. (For even the presence of a jealous or anxious question would produce a sinking otherwise than in play.) The significance of his image resonates the more for us if we recall that he used to see Maggie (and wish her to be) like "some slight, slim draped 'antique' of Vatican or Capitoline hills, late and refined, rare as a note and immortal as a link, . . . keeping still the quality, the perfect felicity, of the statue" (I.187). That image denied (with her evident collusion) her active womanliness; it also denied her status as a separate, autonomous center of choice. It expressed the wish to collect and keep her always, keep her far from the dangers so often expressed, in the thought of these characters, by the imagery of water and its motion. Now he wishes her moving and alive, swimming freely in the sea – not even confined to his boat, or to the past's "contracted basin." Not "frozen stiff" with guilt, either.

We can say several things about the moral significance of this picture. First, that, as a picture, it *is* significant – not only in its causal relation to his subsequent speeches and acts, but as a moral achievement in its own right. It is, of course, of enormous causal significance; his speeches and acts, here and later, flow forth from it and take from it the rightness of their tone. But suppose that we rewrote the scene so as to give him the same speeches and acts (even, *per impossibile*, their exact tonal rightness), with a different image – perhaps one expressing conflict, or a wish to swim alongside her, or even a wish for her drowning – in any of these cases, our assessment of him would be altered. Furthermore, the picture has a pivotal role in his moral activity here that would not be captured by regarding it as a mere precondition for action. We want to say, *here* is where his sacrifice, his essential moral choice, takes place. Here, in his ability to picture her as a sea creature, is the act of renunciation that moves us to pain and admiration. "He had read his way so into her best possibility" – here James tells us that sacrifice *is* an act of imaginative interpretation; it is a perception of her situation as that of a free woman who is not bound by his wish. As such it is of a piece with the character of his overt speech, which succeeds as it does because of his rare power to take the sense and nuance of her speeches and "read himself into" them in the highest way.

The image is, then, morally salient. I need to say more about what is salient in it. What strikes us about it first is its sheer gleaming beauty. Adam sees his daughter's sexuality in a way that can be captured linguistically only in language of lyrical splendor. This tells us a great deal about the quality of his moral imagination – that it is subtle and high rather than simple and coarse; precise rather than gross; richly colored rather than monochromatic; exuberant rather than reluctant; generous rather than stingy; suffused with loving emotion rather than mired in depression. To this moral assessment the full specificity of the image is relevant. If we had read, "He thought of her as an autonomous being," or "He acknowledged his daughter's mature sexuality," or even "He thought of his daughter as a sea creature dipping in the sea," we would miss the sense of lucidity, expressive feeling, and generous lyricism that so move us here. It is relevant that his image was not a flat thing but a fine work of art; that it had all the detail, tone, and color that James captures in these words. It could not be captured in any paraphrase that was not itself a work of art.

The passage suggests something further. "It could pass, further, for knowing – for knowing that without him nothing might have been." To perceive her as a sea creature, in just this way, is precisely, to know her, to know their situation, not to miss anything in it – to be, in short, "a person on whom nothing is lost." Moral knowledge, James suggests, is not simply intellectual grasp of propositions; it is not even simply intellectual grasp of particular facts; it is perception. It is seeing a complex, concrete reality in a highly lucid and richly responsive way; it is taking in what is there, with imagination and feeling. To know Maggie is to see and feel her separateness, her felicity; to recognize all this is to miss least of all. If he had grasped the same general facts without these responses and these images, in all their specificity, he would not really have known her.

Her moral achievement, later, is parallel to his. She holds herself in a terrible tension, close to the complexities of his need, anxiously protecting the "thin wall" (II.267) of silence that stands between them both and the words of explicit disclosure that would have destroyed his dignity and blocked their "best possibility." Her vigilance, her silent attention, the intensity of her regard, are put before us as moral acts: "She might have been for the time, in all her conscious person, the very form of the equilibrium they were, in their different ways, equally trying to save" (II.268). She measures her moral adequacy by the fullness and richness of her imaginings: "So much was crowded into so short a space that she knew already she was keeping her head" (II.268). And her imagination, like his, achieves its moral goal in the finding of the right way of seeing. Like an artist whose labor produces, at last, a wonderful achieved form, she finds, "as the result, for the present occasion, of an admirable traceable effort" (II.273), a thought of her father "that placed him in her eyes as no precious work of art probably had ever been placed in his own" (II.273). To see Adam as a being more precious than his precious works of art becomes, for her, after a moment, to see him as "a great and deep and high little man" (II.274) – as great *in*, not in spite of, his difficulty and his limitation and his effort, great because he is Adam, a little man, and not the omnipotent father. In short, it is to see that "to love him with tenderness was not to be distinguished a whit, from loving him with pride" (II.274). Pride in, belief in the dignity of, another human being is not opposed to tenderness toward human limits. By finding a way to perceive him, to imagine him not as father and law and world but as a finite human being whose dignity is in and not opposed to his finitude, Maggie achieves an adult love for him and a basis of equality. "His strength was her strength, her pride was his, and they were decent and competent together" (II.274–5). Her perceptions are necessary to her effort to give him up and to preserve his dignity. They are also moral achievements in their own right: expressions of love, protections of the loved, creations of a new and richer bond between them. [. . .]

I have said that these picturings, describings, feelings, and communications – actions in their own right – have a moral value that is not reducible to that of the overt acts they engender. I have begun, on this basis, to build a case for saying that the morally valuable aspects of this exchange could not be captured in a summary or paraphrase. Now I shall begin to close the gap between action and description from the other side, showing a responsible action, as James conceives it, is a highly context-specific and nuanced and responsive thing whose rightness could not be captured in a description that fell short of the artistic. Again, I quote the passage:

"I believe in you more than anyone."
    "Than anyone at all?"

She hesitated for all it might mean; but there was – oh a thousand times! – no doubt of it. "Than anyone at all." She kept nothing of it back now, met his eyes over it, let him have the whole of it; after which she went on: "And that's the way, I think, you believe in me."

He looked at her a minute longer, but his tone at last was right. "About the way – yes."

"Well, then – ?" She spoke as for the end and for other matters – for anything, everything else there might be. They would never return to it.

"Well then – !" His hands came out, and while her own took them he drew her to his breast and held her. He held her hard and kept her long, and she let herself go; but it was an embrace that, august and almost stern, produced for its intimacy no revulsion and broke into no inconsequence of tears. (II.275)

We know, again, that the overt items, the speeches and the embrace, are not the only morally relevant exchange. There are, we are told, thoughts and responses behind her "Well then" – thoughts of ending, feelings of immeasurable love, without which the brief utterance would be empty of moral meaning. But we can now also see that even where the overt items are concerned, nuance and fine detail of tone are everything. "His tone at last was right": that is, if he had said the same words in a different tone of voice, less controlled, more stricken, less accepting, the whole rightness of the act, of his entire pattern of action here, would have been undone. He would not have loved her as well had he not spoken so well, with these words at this time and in this tone of voice. (His very tentativeness and his silences are a part of his achievement.) Again, what makes their embrace a wonderful achievement of love and mutual altruism is not the bare fact that it is an embrace; it is the precise tonality and quality of that embrace: that it is hard and long, expressive of deep passion on his side, yielding acceptance of that love on hers; yet dignified and austere, refusing the easy yielding to tears that might have cheapened it.

We can say, first, that no description less specific than this could convey the rightness of this action; second, that any change in the description, even at the same level of specificity, seems to risk producing a different act – or at least requires us to question the sameness of the act. (For example, my substitution of "austere" for "august" arguably changes things for the worse, suggesting inhibition of deep feeling rather than fullness of dignity.) Furthermore, a paraphrase such as the one I have produced, even when reasonably accurate, does not ever succeed in displacing the original prose; for it is, not being a high work of literary art, devoid of a richness of feeling and a rightness of tone and rhythm that characterize the original, whose cadences stamp themselves inexorably on the heart. A good action is not flat and toneless and lifeless like my paraphrase – whose use of the "standing terms" of moral discourse, words like "mutual sacrifice," makes it too blunt for the highest value. It is an "alert winged creature," soaring above these terms in flexibility and lucidity of vision. The only way to paraphrase this passage without loss of value would be to write another work of art.

II

In all their fine-tuned perceiving, these two are responsible to standing obligations, some particular and some general. Perceptions "perch on the heads of" the standing terms: they do not displace them. This needs to be emphasized, since it can easily be thought that the morality of these hypersensitive beings is an artwork embroidered for its own intrinsic aesthetic character, without regard to principle and commitment. James, indeed, sees this as its besetting danger; in the characters of Bob and Fanny Assingham, he shows us how perception without responsibility is dangerously free-floating, even as duty without perception is blunt and blind. The right "basis" for action is found in the loving dialogue of the two. Here, Maggie's standing obligations to Adam (and also those of a daughter in general to fathers in general) pull her (in thought and feeling both) toward the right perception, helping to articulate the scene, constraining the responses she can make. Her sense of a profound obligation to respect his dignity is crucial in causing her to reject other possible images and to search until she finds the image of the work of art with which she ends (II.273). Adam's image of the sea creature, too, satisfies, is right, in part because it fulfills his sense of what a father owes an adult daughter.

So, if we think of the perception as a created work of art, we must at the same time remember that artists, as James sees it, are not free simply to create anything they like. Their obligation is to render reality, precisely and faithfully; in this task they are very much assisted by general principles and by the habits and attachments that are their internalization. (In this sense the image of a perception as a child is better, showing that you can have the right sort of creativity only within the constraints of natural reality.) If their sense of the occasion is, as often in James, one of improvisation, if Maggie sees herself as an actress improvising her role, we must remember, too, that the actress who improvises well is *not* free to do anything at all. She must at every moment – far more than one who goes by an external script – be responsively alive and committed to the other actors, to the evolving narrative, to the laws and constraints of the genre and its history. [. . .]

How, then, are concrete perceptions prior? (In what sense are the descriptions of the novelist higher, more alert, than the standing terms?) We can see, first, that without the ability to respond to and resourcefully interpret the concrete particulars of their context, Maggie and Adam could not begin to figure out which rules and standing commitments are operative here. Situations are all highly concrete, and they do not present themselves with duty labels on them. Without the abilities of perception, duty is blind and therefore powerless. (Bob Assingham has no connection with the moral realities about him until he seeks the help of his wife's too fanciful but indispensable eyes.)

Second, a person armed only with the standing terms – armed only with general principles and rules – would, even if she managed to apply them to the concrete case, be insufficiently equipped by them to act rightly in it. It is not just that the standing terms need to be rendered more precise in their application to a concrete text. It is that, all by themselves, they might get it all wrong; they do not suffice to make the difference between right and wrong. Here, to sacrifice in the wrong words with the wrong tone of voice at the wrong time would be worse, perhaps, than not sacrificing at all. And I do not mean wrong as judged by some fortuitous and unforeseeable consequences for which we could not hold Adam responsible. I mean wrong in itself, wrong of him. He is responsible here for getting the detail of his context for the context it is, for making sure that nothing is lost on him, for feeling fully, for getting the tone right. Obtuseness is a moral failing; its opposite

can be cultivated. By themselves, trusted for and in themselves, the standing terms are a recipe for obtuseness. To respond "at the right times, with reference to the right objects, towards the right people, with the right aim, and in the right way, is what is appropriate and best, and this is characteristic of excellence" (Aristotle, *EN* 1106b21–3).

Finally, there are elements in their good action that cannot even in principle be captured in antecedent "standing" formulations, however right and precise – either because they are surprising and new, or because they are irreducibly particular. The fine Jamesian perceiver employs general terms and conceptions in an open-ended, evolving way, prepared to see and respond to any new feature that the scene brings forward. Maggie sees the way Adam is transforming their relationship and responds to it as the heroic piece of moral creation it is – like an improvising actress taking what the other actor gives and going with it. All this she could not have done had she viewed the new situation simply as the scene for the application of antecedent rules. Nor can we omit the fact that the particularity of this pair and their history enter into their thought as of the highest moral relevance. We could not rewrite the scene, omitting the particularity of Maggie and Adam, without finding ourselves (appropriately) at sea as to who should do what. Again, to confine ourselves to the universal is a recipe for obtuseness. (Even the good use of rules themselves cannot be seen in isolation from their relation to perceptions.)

If this view of morality is taken seriously and if we wish to have texts that represent it at its best (in order to anticipate or supplement experience or to assess this norm against others), it seems difficult not to conclude that we will need to turn to texts no less elaborate, no less linguistically fine-tuned, concrete, and intensely focused, no less metaphorically resourceful, than this novel.

III

The dialogue between perception and rule is evidently a subject to which James devoted much thought in designing *The Golden Bowl*. For he places between us and "the deeply involved and immersed and more or less bleeding participants" (I.vi) two characters who perform the function, more or less, of a Greek tragic chorus. "Participators by a fond attention" (*AN* 62) just as we are (Fanny alone of all the characters is referred to as "our friend" (II.162)), they perform, together, an activity of attending and judging and interpreting that is parallel to ours, if even more deeply immersed and implicated. James has selected for his "chorus" neither a large group nor a solitary consciousness but a married couple, profoundly different in their approaches to ethical problems but joined by affection into a common effort of vision. In his depiction of their effort to see truly, he allows us to see more deeply into the relationship between the fine-tuned perception of particulars and a rule-governed concern for general obligations: how each, taken by itself, is insufficient for moral accuracy; how (and why) the particular, if insufficient, is nonetheless prior; and how a dialogue between the two, prepared by love, can find a common "basis" for moral judgment.

Bob Assingham is a man devoted to rules and to general conceptions. He permits himself neither surprise nor bewilderment – in large part because he does not permit himself to see particularity:

> His wife accused him of a want alike of moral and intellectual reaction, or rather indeed of a complete incapacity for either.... The infirmities, the predicaments of men neither surprised nor shocked him, and indeed – which was perhaps his only real loss in a thrifty career – scarce even amused; he took them for granted without horror, classifying them after their kind and calculating results and chances. (I.67)

Because he allows himself to see only what can be classified beforehand under a general term, he cannot have any moral responsibilities – including amusement – that require recognition of nuance and idiosyncrasy. (By presenting him for *our* amusement, as a character idiosyncratic and unique, James reminds us of the difference between the novelist's sense of life and his.)

Fanny, on the other hand, takes fine-tuned perception to a dangerously rootless extreme. She refuses to such an extent the guidance of general rules that she is able to regard the complicated people and predicaments of her world with an aestheticizing love, as "her finest flower-beds" – across which he is, to her displeasure, always taking "short cuts" (I.367). She delights in the complexity of these particulars for its own sake, without sufficiently feeling the pull of a moral obligation to any. And because she denies herself the general classifications that are the whole of his vision, she lacks his

straight guidance from the past. Her imagination too freely strays, embroiders, embellishes. By showing us these two characters and the different inadequacies of their attempts to see and judge what stands before them, James asks hard questions about his own idea of fine awareness. He shows how, pressed in the wrong way, it can lead to self-indulgent fantasy; he acknowledges, in Bob, "the truth of his plain vision, the very plainness of which was its value" (I.284). So he suggests to us (what we also see in his protagonists, though less distinctly) that perception is not a self-sufficient form of practical reasoning, set above others by its style alone. Its moral value is not independent of its content, which should accurately connect itself with the agent's moral and social education. This content is frequently well preserved, at least in general outline, in the plain man's attachment to common-sense moral values, which will often thus give reasonable guidance as to where we might start looking for the right particular choice.

And in a scene of confrontation between Bob and Fanny, James shows us how a shared moral "basis," a responsible vision, can be constructed through the dialogue of perception and rule. Fanny has been led to the edge of realization that she has been willfully blind to the real relationship between Charlotte and the Prince. In this chapter (Book Third, Chapter X) she and her husband will acknowledge together what has happened and accept responsibility for nourishing the intrigue by their blindness. This preparation for real dialogue is announced by the contiguity of the metaphors in which they represent themselves to themselves. She, brooding, becomes a "speechless Sphinx"; he is "some old pilgrim of the desert camping at the foot of that monument" (I.364–5). As he stands waiting before her, we begin to sense "a suspension of their old custom of divergent discussion, that intercourse by misunderstanding which had grown so clumsy now" (I.365). She begins to perceive in him a "finer sense" of her moral pain (I.365); and this very sense of her trouble is, on his side, fostered by his old characteristic sense of duty. He imagines her as dangerously voyaging in a fragile boat; and he responds to this picture, true to his plain, blunt sense of an old soldier's requirement, with the thought that he must then wait for her on "the shore of the mystic lake; he had . . . stationed himself where she could signal to him at need" (I.366).

As the scene progresses, this very sense of duty brings him to a gradual acknowledgment of her risk and her trouble – and these elements of his old moral view combine with anxious love of her to keep him on the scene of her moral effort, working at a richer and more concrete attention. His sternness, on the other hand, prevents her from finding an evasive or self-deceptive reading of the situation, an easy exit; his questions keep her perceptions honest. Bob, while becoming more "finely aware," never ceases to be himself. Still the duty-bound plain man, but loving his wife concretely and therefore perceiving one particular troubled spot in the moral landscape, he begins to attend more lucidly to all of it; for only in this way (only by being willing to see the surprising and the new) can he love and help her: "he had spoken before in this light of a plain man's vision, but he must be something more than plain man now" (I.375) – something *more*, and not something *other:* for it is also true that he can help her in *her* effort to perceive well only by remaining true to the plainness of his vision. Because he sees himself as on the shore to help her, she cannot evade her presentiment of moral danger. He keeps her before the general issues, and thus before her own responsibility.

As they move thus toward each other, they begin to share each other's sentences, to fill, by an effort of imagination, each other's gaps (I.368). And they move from contiguity in images to the inhabiting of a shared picture that expresses a mutual involvement in moral confrontation and improvisation: they are now "worldly adventurers, driven for relief under sudden stress to some grim midnight reckoning in an odd corner" (I.371). A short time later she presents him with a picture into which he "could enter" (I.374). At the climactic moment, Fanny feels (as the result of *his* effort) a sharp pain of realized guilt; and Bob, responding with tenderness to her pain, opens himself fully to her moral adventure, to the concrete perception of their shared situation. She cries, and he embraces her,

> all with a patience that presently stilled her. Yet the effect of this small crisis, oddly enough, was not to close their colloquy, with the natural result of sending them to bed: what was between them had opened out further, had somehow, through the sharp show of her feeling, taken a positive stride, had entered, as it were, without more words, the region of the understood, shutting the door after it and bringing them so

still more nearly face to face. They remained for some minutes looking at it through the dim window which opened upon the world of human trouble in general and which let the vague light play here and there upon gilt and crystal and colour, the florid features, looming dimly, of Fanny's drawing-room. And the beauty of what thus passed between them, passed with her cry of pain, with her burst of tears, with his wonderment and his kindness and his comfort, with the moments of their silence, above all, which might have represented their sinking together, hand in hand, for a time, into the mystic lake where he had begun, as we have hinted, by seeing her paddle alone – the beauty of it was that they now could really talk better than before, because the basis had at last once for all defined itself.... He conveyed to her now, at all events, by refusing her no gentleness, that he had sufficiently got the tip and that the tip was all he had wanted. (I.378–9).

Both plainness and perception, both sternness and bewilderment, contribute to the found "basis." Perception is still, however, prior. They are, at the end, in the "mystic lake" together, not upon the dry shore. To bring himself to her he has had to immerse himself, to feel the mystery of the particular, leaving off his antecedent "classifying" and "editing." The "basis" itself is not a rule but a concrete way of seeing a concrete case. He could see nothing in this case until he learned her abilities; and he was able to learn them only because there was already something in him that went beyond the universal, namely, a loving, and therefore particular, vision of her. The dialogue between his rules and her perceptions is motivated and sustained by a love that is itself in the sphere of perception, that antecedes any moral agreement. James suggests that if, as members of moral communities, we are to achieve shared perceptions of the actual, we had better love one another first, in all our disagreements and our qualitative differences. Like Aristotle, he seems to say that civic love comes before, and nourishes, civic justice. And he reminds us, too, of Aristotle's idea that a child who is going to develop into a person capable of perception must begin life with a loving perception of its individual parents, and by receiving their highly individualized love. Perception seems to be prior even in time;

it motivates and sustains the whole enterprise of living by a shared general picture.

Finally, James's talk (or Bob's talk) of "getting the tip" shows us what moral exchange and moral learning can be, inside a morality based on perception. Progress comes not from the teaching of an abstract law but by leading the friend, or child, or loved one – by a word, by a story, by an image – to see some new aspect of the concrete case at hand, to see it as this or that. Giving a "tip" is to give a gentle hint about how one might see. The "tip," here, is given not in words at all but in a sudden show of feeling. It is concrete, and it prompts the recognition of the concrete.

I have already argued that Jamesian perceiving and correct acting require James's artful prose for their expression. Now I can go further, claiming that the moral role of rules themselves, in this conception, can only be shown inside a story that situates rules in their appropriate place vis-à-vis perceptions. If we are to assess the claim that correct judgment is the outcome of a dialogue between antecedent principle and new vision, we need to see the view embodied in prose that does not take away the very complexity and indeterminacy of choice that gives substance to the view. The moral work involved in giving and getting "the tip" could hardly be shown us in a work of formal decision theory; it could not be shown in any abstract philosophical prose, since it is so much a matter of learning the right sort of vision of the concrete. It could not be shown well even in a philosopher's example, inasmuch as an example would lack the full specificity, and also the indeterminacy, of the literary case, its rich metaphors and pictures, its ways of telling us how characters come to see one another as this or that and come to attend to new aspects of their situation. In the preface to this novel, James speaks of the "duty" of "responsible prose" to be, "while placed before us, good enough, interesting enough and, if the question be of picture, pictorial enough, above all *in itself*" (I.ix–x). The prose of *The Golden Bowl* fulfills this duty.

I say that this prose itself displays a view of moral attention. It is natural, then, to inquire about the status of my commentary, which supplements the text and claims to say why the text is philosophically important. Could I, in fact, have stopped with the quotation of these chapters, or the whole novel, dropping my commentary on it? Or: is there any room left here for a philosophical criticism of literature?

The text itself displays, and is, a high kind of moral activity. But, I think, it does not itself, self-sufficiently, set itself beside other conceptions of moral attention and explain its differences from them, explaining, for example, why a course in "moral reasoning" that relied only on abstract or technical materials, omitting texts like this one, would be missing a great part of our moral adventure. The philosophical explanation acts, here, as the ally of the literary text, sketching out its relation to other forms of moral writing. I find that the critical and distinction-making skills usually associated (not inaccurately) with philosophy do have a substantial role to play here – if they are willing to assume a posture of sufficient humility. As Aristotle tells us, a philosophical account that gives such importance to concrete particulars must be humble about itself, claiming only to offer an "outline" or a "sketch" that directs us to salient features of our moral life. The real content of that life is not found in that outline, except insofar as it quotes from or attentively reconstructs the literary text. And even to be the ally of literature – not to negate the very view of the moral life for which it is arguing – the philosopher's prose may have to diverge from some traditional philosophical styles, toward greater suggestiveness. And yet, so long as the temptation to avoid the insights of *The Golden Bowl* is with us – and it will, no doubt, be with us so long as we long for an end to surprise and bewilderment, for a life that is safer and simpler than life is – we will, I think, need to have such "outlines," which, by their greater explicitness, return us to our wonder before the complexities of the novel, and before our own active sense of life.

IV

We must now investigate more closely James's analogy between morality and art and its further implications for the moral status of this text. I speak first of the relationship between moral attention and attention to a work of art; then of the relationship between artistic creation and moral achievement.

Maggie begins, as I argued elsewhere, by viewing people as fine art objects in a way that distances her conveniently from their human and frequently conflicting demands. As she matures, however, she makes a more mature use of the analogy; she does not drop it. At the novel's end, her ability to view the other people as composing a kind of living, breathing painting, her attention to them as a response to this work (cf. II.236–8), expresses her commitment to several features of James's moral ideal which are by now familiar to us: a respect for the irreducibly particular character of a concrete moral context and the agents who are its components; a determination to scrutinize all aspects of this particular with intensely focused perception; a determination to care for it as a whole. We see, too, her determination to be guided by the tender and gentle emotions, rather than the blinding, blunt, and coarse – by impartial love for them all and not by "the vulgar heat of her wrong" (236).

But this conception of moral attention implies that the moral/aesthetic analogy is also more than analogy. For (as James frequently reminds us by his use of the author/reader "we") our own attention to his characters will itself, if we read well, be a high case of moral attention. "Participators by a fond attention" (*AN* 62) in the lives and dilemmas of his participants, we engage with them in a loving scrutiny of appearances. We actively care for their particularity, and we strain to be people on whom none of their subtleties are lost, in intellect and feeling. So if James is right about what moral attention is, then he can fairly claim that a novel such as this one not only shows it better than an abstract treatise, it also elicits it. It calls forth our "active sense of life," which is our moral faculty. The characters' "emotions, their stirred intelligence, their moral consciousness, become thus, by sufficiently charmed perusal, our own very adventure" (*AN* 70). By identifying with them and allowing ourselves to be surprised (an attitude of mind that storytelling fosters and develops), we become more responsive to our own life's adventure, more willing to see and to be touched by life.

But surely, we object, a person who is obtuse in life will also be an obtuse reader of James's text. How can literature show us or train us in anything, when, as we have said, the very moral abilities that make for good reading are the ones that are allegedly in need of development? James's artistic analogy has already, I think, shown us an answer to this question. When we examine our own lives, we have so many obstacles to correct vision, so many motives to blindness and stupidity. The "vulgar heat" of jealousy and personal interest comes between us and the loving perception of each particular. A novel, just because it is not our life,

places us in a moral position that is favorable for perception and it shows us what it would be like to take up that position in life. We find here love without possessiveness, attention without bias, involvement without panic. Our moral abilities must be developed to a certain degree, certainly, before we can approach this novel at all and see anything in it. But it does not seem far-fetched to claim that most of us can read James better than we can read ourselves.

The creation side of the analogy is succinctly expressed in James's claim that "to 'put' things is very exactly and responsibly and interminably to do them" (I.xxiv). The claim has, in turn, two aspects. First, it is a claim about the moral responsibility of the novelist, who is bound, drawing on his sense of life, to render the world of value with lucidity, alert and winged. To "put" things is to do an assessable action. The author's conduct is *like* moral conduct at its best, as we have begun to see. But it is more than like it. The artist's task *is* a moral task. By so much as the world is rendered well by some such artist, by so much do we "get the best there is of it, and by so much as it falls within the scope of a denser and duller, a more vulgar and more shallow capacity, do we get a picture dim and meagre" (*AN* 67). The whole moral content of the work expresses the artist's sense of life; and for the excellence of this the novelist is, in James's view, rightly held (morally) accountable:

> The question comes back thus, obviously, to the kind and the degree of the artist's prime sensibility, which is the soil out of which his subject springs. The quality and capacity of that soil, its ability to "grow" with due freshness and straightness any vision of life, represents, strongly or weakly, the projected morality. (*AN* 45)

On the other side, the most exact and responsible way of doing is, in fact, a "putting": an achievement of the precisely right description, the correct nuance of tone. Moral experience is an interpretation of the seen, "our apprehension and our measure of what happens to us as social creatures" (*AN* 64–5). Good moral experience is a lucid apprehension. Like the imaginings and doings of Maggie and Adam it has precision rather than flatness, sharpness rather than vagueness. It is "the union of whatever fulness with whatever clearness" (*AN* 240). Not that indeterminacy and mystery are not also there, when the context presents them, as so often in human life it does. But then the thing is to respond to that with the right "*quality* of bewilderment" (*AN* 66), intense and striving.

Again we can see that there is more than analogy here. Our whole moral task, whether it issues in the words of *The Golden Bowl* or in Maisie's less verbally articulated but no less responsive and intense imaginings, is to make a fine artistic creation. James does not give linguistic representation pride of place: he insists that there is something fine that Maisie's imagination creatively does, which is rightly rendered in his words, even though Maisie herself could not have found those words. Perceptions need not be verbal (*AN* 145). But he does insist that our whole conduct is *some* form of artistic "putting" and that its assessible virtues are also those for which we look to the novelist.

Two clarifications are in order. First, this is not an aestheticization of the moral; for the creative artist's task is, for James, above all moral, "the expression, the literal squeezing out of value" (*AN* 312). Second, to call conduct a creation in no way points toward a rootless relativism. For James's idea of creation (like Aristotle's idea of improvisation) is that it is thoroughly committed to the real. "Art deals with what we see . . . it plucks its material in the garden of life" (*AN* 312). The Jamesian artist does not feel free to create just anything at all: he imagines himself as straining to get it right, not to miss anything, to be keen rather than obtuse. He approaches the material of life armed with the moral and expressive skills that will allow him to "squeeze out" the value that is there.

This ideal makes room, then, for a norm or norms of rightness and for a substantial account of ethical objectivity. The objectivity in question is "internal" and human. It does not even attempt to approach the world as it might be in itself, uninterpreted, unhumanized. Its raw material is the history of human social experience, which is already an interpretation and a measure. But it is objectivity all the same. And that is what makes the person who does the artist's task well so important for others. In the war against moral obtuseness, the artist is our fellow fighter, frequently our guide. We can develop, here, the analogy with our sensory powers that the term *perception* already suggests. In seeing and hearing we are, I believe, seeing not the world as it is in itself, apart from

human beings and human conceptual schemes, but a world already interpreted and humanized by our faculties and our concepts. And yet, who could deny that there are some among us whose visual or auditory acuity is greater than that of others; some who have developed their faculties more finely, who can make discriminations of color and shape (of pitch and timbre) that are unavailable to the rest of us? who miss less, therefore, of what is to be heard or seen in a landscape, a symphony, a painting? Jamesian moral perception is, I think, like this: a fine development of our human capabilities to see and feel and judge; an ability to miss less, to be responsible to more.

V

Is this norm practical? Is there any sense to claiming that the consciousness of a Maggie Verver or a Strether can be paradigmatic of our own responsible conduct? In short (James reports a critic's question), "Where on earth, where roundabout us at this hour," has he found such "supersubtle fry" (*AN* 221)? And if they are not found, but "squeezed out" from coarser matter by the pressure of the artist's hand, how can they be exemplary for us? James's answer is complex. He grants, first, that he cannot easily cite such examples from daily life (*AN* 222). He insists, on the other hand, that these characters do not go so far beyond actual life that their lucidity makes them "spoiled for us," "knowing too much and feeling too much . . . for their remaining 'natural' and typical, for their having the needful communities with our own precious liability to fall into traps and be bewildered" (*AN* 63). Like Aristotle's tragic heroes, they are high but possible and available, so much so that they can be said to be "in *essence* an observed reality" (*AN* 223). And if the life around us today does not show us an abundance of such examples, "then so much the worse for that life" (222).

Here the opponent responds that it surely seems odd and oddly arrogant to suggest that the entire nation is dense and dull and that only Henry James and his characters are finely sensible enough to show us the way. Surely patterns for public life must be nearer to home, straightforwardly descriptive of something that is readily found. James has moved too far away; his sense of life has lost its connection with real life. James's answer is that there is no better way to show one's commitment to the fine possibilities of the actual than (in protest "against the rule of the cheap and easy") to create, in imagination, their actualization:

> to *create* the record, in default of any other enjoyment of it: to imagine, in a word, the honourable, the producible case. What better example than this of the high and the helpful public and, as it were, civic use of the imagination? . . . Where is the work of the intelligent painter of life if not precisely in some such aid given to true meanings to be born? He must bear up as he can if it be in consequence laid to him that the flat grows salient and the tangled clear, the common – worse of all! – even amusingly rare, by passing through his hands. (*AN* 223–4)

If he has done this – and I think he has – then these alert winged books are not just irreplaceable fine representations of moral achievement, they are moral achievements on behalf of our community. Like Adam Verver's sacrifice: altruism in the right way at the right time in the right images and the right tone, with the right precision of bewilderment.

Notes

1 Henry James, *The Art of the Novel* (New York, 1907), 149. In the citations that follow, individual preface titles will not be given. The title quotation is from *AN* 62.
2 Henry James, *The Princess Casamassima* (New York Edition) I.
3 All page references to *The Golden Bowl* (*GB*) are to the New York Edition (New York, 1909).

44

Literature, Truth, and Philosophy

Peter Lamarque and Stein Haugom Olsen

Let us recall the argument against the Propositional Theory of Literary Truth. It went roughly like this: if literary works are construed as having the constitutive aim of advancing truths about human concerns by means of general propositions implicitly or explicitly contained in them, then one should expect some kind of supporting argument, the more so since the purported truths are mostly controversial. However, there are no such arguments or debate either in the literary work itself, or in literary criticism. Literary works cannot therefore be construed simply as one among other discourses with the primary intention of advancing truths. This argument, along with the argument against the Theory of Novelistic Truth, is based on a conception of truth and truth-telling which is located within a nexus of activities such as making judgements, reasoning, providing evidence, questioning, debating, falsifying, and so forth: within a practice, as we have called it, of enquiry. There is clearly a conceptual link between this notion of truth and that of knowledge. What is known is true, and what is not true does not constitute knowledge but mere opinion. Knowledge is achieved by marshalling evidence supporting whatever truth-claim is being made. These conceptions of knowledge and truth are basic to the concept of science and they guarantee what may be called the *cognitive value* of the

insights achieved in science. This is so not merely in the natural sciences, but also in the social sciences and in history. The doubts that have been raised about the scientific status of these latter disciplines concern just the applicability in these disciplines of these notions of truth and knowledge. And what has been established so far in this discussion is that they cannot simply be presumed to explain the cognitive status of literature.

There are two possible ways out of this *impasse*. One is to redefine the concepts of knowledge and truth-seeking, at least loosening the connection with supportive evidence and argument. The other is a more radical redefinition of the whole notion of cognitive value, severing any necessary connection with the concepts of knowledge and truth. Supporters of the first alternative would attempt to retain the direct link between literature and truth and would insist that literary works yielded insights complementary to, yet as equally valid (in the same sense of "valid") as, the knowledge yielded by sciences of all descriptions. Supporters of the second alternative would be ready to abandon the notion that literature has a direct truth-seeking link with the world and instead settle for a different form of insight which lent itself to appraisal in terms other than those of knowledge and truth. We shall produce further

From *Truth, Fiction, and Literature* (Oxford: Oxford University Press, 1994), pp. 368–94. Reprinted by permission of Oxford University Press.

Peter Lamarque and Stein Haugom Olsen

arguments in favour of the second alternative. Here we shall deal with the first.

As a point of departure for the discussion of the first alternative, it is useful to return to Thomas Nagel's distinction between the external or objective and the internal or subjective point of view. We recall that Nagel identified in the sciences, and all knowledge-seeking enquiry, a striving for a kind of objectivity which

> allows us to transcend our particular viewpoint and develop an expanded consciousness that takes in the world more fully. All this applies to values and attitudes as well as to beliefs and theories.[1]

An ideal objectivity would provide what Nagel dubs a *view from nowhere*. Yet, he argues, such a view is unobtainable because each individual also has his own subjective nature which is

> an irreducible feature of reality – without which we couldn't do physics or anything else – and it must occupy as fundamental a place in any credible world view as matter, energy, space, time, and numbers.[2]

This subjective point of view is not only ineliminable, but "there are things about the world and life and ourselves that cannot be adequately understood from a maximally objective standpoint."[3]

Developing Nagel's notion of a subjective point of view, one might say that it has two aspects. There is what may be called the *experiential aspect*: everyone has mental experiences which are peculiarly their own. The character of these experiences "can be understood only from within or by subjective imagination".[4] There is also what may be called the *perspectival aspect*: the world is seen from a particular point of view, at a particular time and place, and under the influence of particular circumstances. The subjective point of view thus not only affords a unique quality of experience but also a unique location for the experience. It is the distinctive view of the world from somewhere in particular.

Those who want to argue that the cognitive value of literature can be identified with the help of redefined concepts of knowledge and truth could be taken as proposing a change in focus from the external, objective point of view from which generalizations of universal validity can be made, to an internal, subjective point of view. The

particular experience and particular situation are seen by the supporters of the first alternative as embodying a special kind of knowledge. One can come to share this knowledge through an act of "subjective imagination" in which one occupies in imagination the point of view of another self. Literature, according to this theory, is particularly suited to effecting this imaginative participation, by means of which practical wisdom is increased and moral knowledge expanded. On this view, although a literary work is held to yield the knowledge it does because of its distinctive literary features, nevertheless genuine knowledge and genuine truth are at stake and literature is seen to keep the same company with philosophy and even the sciences. Indeed inasmuch as one task of philosophy is to seek a better understanding of moral matters in its own terms, so literature, with a similar task, becomes a companion to philosophy or even a branch of philosophy.

Literature as a Source of Subjective Knowledge

Depending on whether the experiential or the perspectival aspect of the subjective point of view is taken as a point of departure, different theories of the cognitive value of literature result. The principal type of theory that makes the *subjective experience* central is that which presents a traditional humanistic view of literature as an instrument for training and extending our sympathetic understanding of other people. This type of theory might be labelled the Subjective Knowledge Theory of Cognitive Value. It faces three principal problems. First, it must justify the claim that "anything that might assist us to an imaginative participation can properly be said to extend the range of our humanistic understanding";[5] i.e. the claim that the subjective experience which a literary work induces represents a kind of *knowledge*. Second, it must give some sort of account of the difference between genuine and merely putative knowledge of this kind, including some means of distinguishing between the true and the false. And, finally, it must establish that literature *in virtue of being literature* promotes imaginative participation of the type that yields this kind of knowledge.

Drawing on Gilbert Ryle's distinction between "knowing how" and "knowing that" proponents of the Subjective Knowledge Theory argue that this distinction needs to be supplemented with a third type of knowledge, "knowing what it is like". "Knowing what it is like"

> is not the acquisition of information, or the inferential knowledge about something, as I might know that the cat is in the house on the basis of acquaintance with the cat-in-house situation, it is knowing in the sense of realizing by living through.[6]

Full recognition of the facts is compatible with failing to know what it is like to live through the situation made up of these facts:

> *Recognizing* that such and such is so with reference to some kind of human experience is not the same thing as *realizing* what this might be like as lived experience. Confession of failure to understand, in the sense of realize, is perfectly compatible with absence of doubt concerning matter-of-fact. For example, "I do not doubt that certain persons enjoy situations of physical danger and even seek them out, but I don't understand it." What the speaker does not understand is the lure, the fascination, of danger.[7]

Knowledge of the kind associated with "living through" is not amenable to evidential support (or any kind of reasons, or even proof). It is accepted on the authority of the person whom one knows to have lived through a situation. It attains its character of knowledge rather than mere awareness through being not just experience but an experience that one is self-consciously aware of having lived through, that is, by being "self-consciously recognized by the experiencer as his".[8] Knowledge of what it is like, for example, to fall suddenly in love, to lose a child to death, or undergo religious conversion, can only be attained and therefore shared by living through the experience personally or, derivatively, by reading an evocative description of the situation and the experience of living through it. Such a description would constitute an imaginative evocation of the experience.

Literature, so it is argued, is the mode of writing above all that can provide this type of evocative description for it presents to its readers a piece of "virtual experience, embodied, objectified, expressed, in the literary presentation".[9] This virtual experience embodied in the literary presentation "has a kind of 'public presence' and a kind of 'permanent presence' not possible in any case of

actual experience".[10] Through the presentation of an evocative description of this virtual experience literature offers the reader the opportunity of living through situations that he has never encountered in life. Moreover, since virtual experience can be elaborated and controlled by the artist, it is purer, focused on essentials in a way that everyday experience cannot be because of the contingencies of everyday life. "The importance of literary art, from the strictly cognitive point of view, is that it provides an enormous extension and elaboration of this kind of knowledge,"[11] i.e. the knowledge of subjective experience.

A claim to have experienced what it is like to live through a certain kind of situation is normally accepted even though the one making the claim may not be able to convey his knowledge of it:

> Knowing beyond saying is acceptable in such a case, not because saying is impossible, but because the only kind of saying that would be relevant is a saying that requires some degree of literary talent.[12]

This means that the question of truth arises only in connection with evocative descriptions. However, according to this theory, such a description is not true or false in an ordinary "correspondence" sense of true, but is instead authentic or inauthentic. The inauthentic evocation is "banal" or "pretentious",[13] the authentic evocation a powerful "imaginative enstatement".[14] Literary works therefore have to be true in the sense of being authentic in order to attain to the cognitive merit that the Subjective Knowledge Theory ascribes to them.

The Subjective Knowledge Theory has at its core experiential and psychological phenomena which are perfectly familiar to nearly all readers of literary as well as non-literary fictions. It is no part of our argument to deny that such responses are real or indeed that they are valuable and a source of much of the pleasure afforded by works of fiction. In Chapter 6 we offered an extended discussion of the potential values of imaginative involvement with fictive content. However, it is the further claims (1) that such involvement amounts to a kind of knowledge (and thus truth), and (2) that it lies at the heart of the cognitive values of literature, that we feel are not well substantiated. Our objections do not rely on the relatively trivial point that the terms "true" and "false" are used in an extended sense when equivalent to "authentic"

Peter Lamarque and Stein Haugom Olsen

and "inauthentic", though it is at least not obvious that authenticity as a mode of description is a cognitive value.

A more important issue is the cognitive status of an *experience*; it seems a much less acceptable extension of terminology to say that an experience as such can be a kind of knowledge (albeit "subjective" knowledge or "knowledge what it is like"). It is more plausible to suppose, not that the experience *is* the knowledge, but that knowledge arises as a *result* of the experience; the experience gives rise to the knowledge. In the literary case, we might say that as a result of reading the novel – and imaginatively engaging with its content – we now know better what it is like to be in a situation of a particular kind. This is not different in principle, though, from the knowledge we might gain about the town or country or culture where the novel is set, except that in the former case perhaps our knowledge rests more on imaginative involvement. It has been no part of the thesis of this book that knowledge of this kind is not derivable from reading works of fiction or literature. But as we saw in the case of metaphor what is prompted or stimulated or brought to mind by an imaginative turn of phrase is not necessarily to be projected back into the "cognitive content" of the phrase, nor grounds for assessing it as "true". Similarly in the literary context we cannot just take it for granted that any knowledge derived from an imaginative involvement with a work must be attributed to the artistic purpose of the work and serve as a yardstick for the value of the work.

This brings us to the principal objection to the Subjective Knowledge Theory which concerns its connection to literature *per se*. Can the idea of subjective knowledge illuminate what makes works of literature valuable within a culture? How does it relate to the kind of responses which are distinctive of a literary attention, or, as we have called it, the literary stance? One obvious problem is that many literary works simply do not provide the relevant kind of experience of "knowing what it is like" to live through a certain situation. It may make sense to say that Thomas Hardy's short lyrical poem "The Darkling Thrush" gives knowledge of what it is like to feel exhausted and burnt out yet nevertheless, inexplicably, to feel hope rise again for the future. It may even make sense to say that *Hamlet* gives knowledge of what it is like to be Hamlet or a person of that kind.

But let us consider a more sustained example, which we will develop through the remainder of this chapter, to see how engagement with the literary dimension of a work is something more than, and different from, subjective experience.

[*Within the room, Bolette is sitting on the sofa by the table, left, busy embroidering. Lyngstrand is sitting on a chair at the top end of the table. Down in the garden, Ballested is sitting painting. Hilde stands by him watching.*]

LYNGSTRAND [*his arms on the table, sits silently for a moment watching Bolette working*]. It must be awfully difficult to work a border like that, Miss Wangel.

BOLETTE. Oh, no! It isn't so difficult. As long as you remember to count.

LYNGSTRAND. Count? Do you have to count?

BOLETTE. Yes, the stitches. Look.

LYNGSTRAND. So you do! Fancy that! Why, it's almost like a form of art. Do you also design it?

BOLETTE. Yes, if I have a pattern.

LYNGSTRAND. Not otherwise?

BOLETTE. No, not otherwise.

LYNGSTRAND. Then it isn't really proper art after all.

BOLETTE. No, it's mostly what you might call ... handicraft.[15]

[Henrik Ibsen, *The Lady from the Sea*, Act V]

The scene from which this passage comes has all the subtlety of late Ibsen. Lyngstrand is the aspiring artist. His declared desire and aim is to become a sculptor, a profession for which he is singularly unsuited. He has a chest complaint which will ultimately kill him (though he does not know that himself), he has none of the physical strength that is needed to handle heavy materials, nor does he have any practical knowledge of the art. In this scene he is given the part of the spectator. He, like Hilde who watches Ballested painting, is the ignorant looker-on. Though he is the self-declared artist, the artist's role is in this scene given to Bolette and Ballested. Ballested, we know from the first act, like Bolette, needs a pattern or model. "What I am working on," he says to Lyngstrand at the beginning of Act I, "is that bit of the fjord over there between the islands." And he cannot finish his painting because "There isn't a model anywhere in town" for the figure he wants in the foreground. So, like Bolette, what he is producing will not, according to Lyngstrand, be really "proper art". And in the play he is not an artist, but a jack-of-all-trades who has acclimatized himself (to use his own word and one of the key concepts in the play) to the little coastal town where he was left behind when the theatre troupe to which he belonged broke up, seventeen or eighteen years before. However, the concept of "proper art" introduced here by Lyngstrand, is not one that Ibsen endorses. It is Bolette, whose handicraft requires an exactitude that demands that she counts, who does the creative work here.

Lyngstrand is in fact almost a parody of a class of characters in Ibsen's later plays (from *The Wild Duck* onwards) who in some way represent aesthetic as opposed to moral values, the values of "art" against the values of "life". It is a common feature of these characters that they are supremely egotistic and even vulgarly and pettily selfish. The scene round the quoted passage continues with a conversation between Lyngstrand and Bolette where Lyngstrand advances the view that marriage is "a kind of miracle" because of "the way a woman gradually comes to be more and more like her husband". To Bolette's suggestion that a man may also grow like his wife, Lyngstrand reacts with what today would be called male chauvinism, "A man? No, I never thought that." Lyngstrand, it turns out, is not talking about *men* in general either, but of the artist. The artist has a vocation which makes him superior to any woman. However, the artist, Lyngstrand maintains, needs a woman's attention as inspiration, and he proceeds to ask Bolette if, when he goes away "to become a famous sculptor", she will give her word that she will be faithful to him in her thoughts, will stay where she is, and think only of him, because this will help him in his art. Though Bolette gives Lyngstrand no indication that she takes his suggestion as anything but a further indication of his conceit, Lyngstrand firmly believes, as he reveals to Bolette's sister Hilde in Act V, that she has given him such a promise and that she will not accept the proposal of her former teacher, headmaster Arnholm, for that reason. As he admits to Hilde, he does not want to marry Bolette:

LYNGSTRAND. No, that wouldn't really work. I daren't think about anything like that for several years. And when I reach the point where I can, she'll be a bit too old for me then, I think.

HILDE. And yet you've asked her to think about you?

LYNGSTRAND. Yes, that can be of great assistance to me. As an artist, I mean. And it's something she can do very easily, since she hasn't any real vocation of her own. All the same, it's very nice of her.

HILDE. You think you'll be able to get on quicker with your sculpture if you know that Bolette is here thinking of you?

LYNGSTRAND. Yes, I think so. To know that somewhere in the world there is a lovely young woman sitting and silently dreaming about you... I think it must be so... so... Well, I don't really know what to call it.

HILDE. Perhaps you mean... exciting?

LYNGSTRAND. Exciting? Yes! Exciting is what I do mean. Or something like that. [*Looks at her for a moment.*] You are very clever, Miss Hilde. Really very clever indeed. When I come home again, you'll be about the same age as your sister is now. Perhaps you'll even look like her. You might even be of the same mind as she is now. As though you were both yourself and her... in one, so to speak.

[Act V]

Lyngstrand proposes to do what Hedda Gabler, Solness, Borkman, and Rubek actually do: feed on human life like a vampire to sustain their own aesthetic values. And when that life is used, he simply turns to another.

The theme of the egocentric artist who feeds on and destroys the values of life and love is a subsidiary but nevertheless important theme in *The Lady from the Sea* which links up obliquely with the main theme. However, the recognition and appreciation of this theme cannot really be described as going through an experience of what it is like to be such an artist or his victim. The reader or the audience notes the contrast between the ordinary, homely characters of Bolette and Ballested, who have acclimatized themselves to the backwater of the small, provincial, coastal town and who represent its values, and Lyngstrand who represents the destructive values of art. And the reader will note how they are evaluated through the way in which Ibsen presents them. This in itself, of course, constitutes an experience, but it is not at all of the same type as the experience of "falling suddenly in love, losing a child to death, or undergoing religious conversion", which the Subjective Knowledge Theory uses as its main examples. It may, perhaps, be described as the experience of what the characters of Bolette, Ballested, and Lyngstrand are like, but this is the experience of the spectator observing the interaction and behaviour of these characters. It would be to stretch the concept of "knowing what it is like" beyond any useful limit to insist that it could be applied to this experience.

An attempt has been made to strengthen the Subjective Knowledge Theory so as to take care of these objections; we shall look at this strong version in a moment and return to our example. However, the theory also runs into a more intractable problem relating to the nature of literature. It assumes that knowledge of what it is like can be acquired only by going through an experience oneself or by reading and being receptive to an evocative description, which is essentially a literary description. The problem arises because of the uniqueness and specificity of each individual literary work. Even literary works that deal with the same story present different visions of that story. The Orestes/Electra stories as presented by Aeschylus, Sophocles, and Euripides, are really different stories with different characters and different visions of the world. Equally, works dealing with the same themes, as perhaps do, say, Euripides' *Hippolytus* and Kingsley Amis's *Lucky Jim*, define these themes in totally different ways. Thus each literary work defines its own unique subjective experience *sui generis*. Moreover, although individual aspects, characters, or incidents abstracted from a work might yield an empathetic response in a reader it is most unlikely that literary works taken as a whole – as *works* – will present situations that could provide a coherent and unified experi-

ence describable as "knowing what it is like". A Hamlet-situation, for example, is far too complex and specific to give rise to any single and sustained experience of this kind, certainly not one that will be relevant to a reader's daily life. This does not mean that literature does not deal with "central human concerns", but it does imply that situations used to define these concerns and the manner of dealing with them are specific to literature, and consequently that the virtual experience offered by literature is specifically literary as well as unique. The view that "The importance of literary art, from the cognitive point of view, is that it provides an enormous extension and elaboration of this kind of knowledge [knowing what it is like]" thus seems to reduce to the near tautology that reading literature extends our knowledge of the kind of subjective experience offered by literary works.

Subjective Knowledge and Conceptual Enrichment

A stronger version of the theory defines a wider, more ambitious concept of subjective knowledge, and provides for this subjective knowledge affecting the reader's intellectual and moral life in a significant and positive way. This strong version of the theory emphasizes the capability of the subjective virtual experience offered by a literary work to enrich and modify the reader's concepts and conceptual scheme in such a way that his perception of, and his perspective on, his own life is changed. A literary work provides no new information, brings no new facts to light, but makes the reader perceive the facts he already recognizes "in a different light". Reading a literary work brings about "a modification of a person's concepts, which is in turn capable of altering his thought or conduct".[16] An example would be John Stuart Mill who was brought out of a near suicidal depression by reading Wordsworth. Through his reading of Wordsworth he came to see that what he felt before, that "life, to all who possess the good things of it, must necessarily be a vapid, uninteresting thing,"[17] was untrue, and he had gained a new perspective on life which conferred meaning where there was none before. Another example, used by proponents of the theory, is Wittgenstein suggesting to Norman Malcolm that he should read Tolstoy's *Hadshi Murat* in order to realize that war was not after all "boredom":

Malcolm might have found a new idea of how it is possible to think and speak of war and of its relationship to a host of other things, to love, to power, to fear, and to life and death. In this way, Malcolm's concept of war would have been enriched and extended, so that there would be new things which he would say about it, and things which he would no longer say – like perhaps that it was all boredom.[18]

This modification of a person's concepts implies that the reader

> (a) recognizes the conception [of a situation] presented in the novel as superior to his own [conception of the same type of situation] and (b) adopts it, in recognition of its superiority, so that it comes to serve as a kind of standard by which he reviews his own conduct and that of others.[19]

For example, Edith Wharton's *The Age of Innocence* can be read in such a way that if the reader adopts this reading, he can no longer

> believe, as the reasonable man does, in the unity of reason. Fundamental changes in moral perspectives need no longer be seen as the rejection and replacing of hypotheses or policies within a single framework within which moral beliefs must be determined. Old values do die, and new ones take their place. What separates Archer and his son is not a matter of different tentative beliefs within a common notion of reason but, rather, different ways of looking at the world, different conceptions of what is important in life.[20]

These philosophical consequences are not brought about through any normal argument, but by "*waiting on* the novel or story",[21] i.e. by being sensitive to what the literary work presents, by exploring the experience which the work offers. The philosophical consequence is logically tied to the literary work: "I have taken a good deal of time over the discussion of Tolstoy's story. There is no other way, I believe, of grasping the nature of the understanding Ivan attained on his deathbed."[22] Or put in general terms:

> though we may speak of a novel or a poem's bringing a man to see what is possible for

him, we can no longer conceive of these possibilities existing independently of the way in which he was brought to recognize them. If asked what he has learned from the novel or poem, the man may tell me to read it more carefully. Or he may read it himself, emphasizing what he takes to be the correct expression. But if this is unsuccessful, then he will not offer an alternative statement of the work. For what it has to tell us is internally related to the work itself.[23]

The strong version of the Subjective Knowledge Theory of the cognitive value of literature thus provides a strong justification for the claim that subjective experience represents knowledge. It also makes the relationship between the literary work and the imaginative participation in the subjective experience a logical one and thus ensures that the knowledge yielded by a literary work is specific to it as literature. What it does not provide, though, is an alternative account of the distinction between genuine and merely putative knowledge.[24] Both authentic and inauthentic literary works would seem to have the same capacity in principle to bring about "seeing things in a new light". Furthermore, although we acknowledged in discussing the fictive stance that entertaining propositions in works of fiction and engaging imaginatively with them might help to extend conceptual resources – thinking *of* things previously unthought in ways previously untried – there is not much beyond this that the distinctively literary qualities of a work can add; in other words there is no specific aesthetic contribution to the idea of conceptual enrichment which is not already present in any activity where new situations are brought to mind. Yet the Subjective Knowledge Theory claims some privileged cognitive value along these lines for works of literature. Otherwise, it is in the nature of the theory that such an account must proceed along the lines laid down by the weak version, albeit differing in detail, and therefore the same range of problems will also recur.

There are, moreover, two decisive objections against the strong version of the Subjective Knowledge Theory. First of all, the ambitious concept of subjective knowledge that includes philosophical consequences is incompatible with the view of the relationship between this subjective knowledge and the literary work as an internal or logical one. If one employs a concept of subjective knowledge that involves a modification of certain concepts which the reader has, i.e. a concept of subjective knowledge that entails consequences for the way in which the reader sees reality, then this new perspective on reality cannot *only* be available through one specific literary work. For even the modified or enriched conceptual scheme must, if it is applicable to the world, be *independent* of the work which modifies it. One can come to realize that war is not boredom in other ways than by reading *Hadshi Murat*, or that life after all must not necessarily be "a vapid, uninteresting thing" in other ways than by reading Wordsworth. To see exactly how this objection affects the strong version of the Subjective Knowledge Theory, it is illuminating to develop the example introduced earlier, bringing in references to other works by Ibsen.

In *The Lady from the Sea* a contrast is presented between Lyngstrand, the egocentric artist who feeds on and destroys the values of life and love, and the more homely characters of Bolette, Ballested, Arnholm, and Dr Wangel himself who represent these other values. However, in that play Lyngstrand is a subsidiary character and the values he represents die with him. In *When We Dead Awaken* when Arnold Rubek comes home "as a famous sculptor, prosperous and in good health", as Lyngstrand says *he* will do (*The Lady from the Sea*, Act IV), Rubek has created his masterwork and sucked the soul out of the woman who loved him. ("I gave you my young living soul," Irene says to him. "Then I was left standing there, all empty within. Soul-less. [*Looks fixedly at him.*] That's what I died of, Arnold" (Act I)). He let her remain his model and his inspiration but never touched her as a woman thus denying his own love for her and her love for him. "I was an artist, Irene," Rubek says when after many years they meet again at the beginning of Act I, "Above all else an artist." And to this explanation she responds, "[*with a hint of scorn*] The work of art first ... the human being second." Irene is then slowly recovering from a period of madness, walking around as a living dead, constantly watched over by a nun in black, an ominous figure who never speaks but whose presence oppresses Irene all through the play until the last act. Irene herself is also a powerful dramatic presence with her stiff bearing and her floor-length creamy white dress: a ghost out of the past that is to lead Rubek to his death among the snow and ice at the top of the mountain.

Rubek pays for his art with his and Irene's life and happiness. Art usurps life. Rubek's artist's role is incompatible with his life as a man. An artist lives in a house but does not have a *home*. *Home* and the values associated with it, love, companionship, loyalty, compassion, are values which the artist cannot realize in his life for himself or others. "Think", says Maja, Rubek's wife,

> how happy and comfortable we could be down there in our nice new house ...
> RUBEK [*smiles indulgently*]. Shouldn't one rather say "our nice new home"?
> MAJA [*curtly*]. I prefer to say "house". Let us keep it at that. [Act I]

The point is made even more strongly in *The Master Builder* where Solness has built his whole career on the fire that destroyed his wife Aline's ancestral home and his own possibility of ever having one:

> To be able to build homes for other people, I have had to renounce ... for ever renounce ... any hope of having a home of my own. I mean a home with children. Or even with a father and mother. [Act II]

> Everything I've managed to achieve, everything I've built and created ... all the beauty and security, the comfort and the good cheer ... all the magnificence, even ... [*Clenches his hands*] Oh, the very thought of it is terrible ...! [Act III]

> All this I somehow have to make up for. Pay for. Not in money. But in human happiness. And not with my own happiness alone. But also with others'. Don't you see that, Hilde! That's the price my status as an artist has cost me – and others. And every single day I have to stand by and watch this price being paid for me anew. Over and over again – endlessly! [Act II]

Aline Solness in *The Master Builder* is, like Irene, a living dead. For Solness to be able to build, her talent for "building children's souls" and "So building their souls that they might grow straight and fine, nobly and beautifully formed" (Act II) had to be wasted. And if we go to Ibsen's second-last play, *John Gabriel Borkman*, there is Borkman with his single-minded pursuit of his vision to *build*, who lays not only his own life waste but also those of the twin sisters Ella and Gunhild.

"You are guilty of a double murder," Ella Rentheim says to him, "The murder of your own soul and of mine" (Act II).

In *The Master Builder* the price paid for "the status of an artist" is defined almost exclusively in negative terms. Solness has crushed everyone in his egotism and there is no alternative to the Solness ethos. However, this price is also positively defined in various ways in Ibsen's later plays. In *The Lady from the Sea*, the values of life and home are given content by Dr Wangel and Arnholm and what they have to offer the women. In *Hedda Gabler* the Tesman family provides a set of moral and homely values which are beyond Hedda's recognition. In *John Gabriel Borkman* the marriage of the divorcée Mrs Wilton and student Borkman provides an alternative, though an ill-defined and thin one, to the death and destruction Borkman has brought over himself and his home. And in *When We Dead Awaken* Maja and Squire Ulfheim provide the contrast of the full-blooded couple to the now bloodless Rubek and Irene.

With the exception of *John Gabriel Borkman* it is characteristic of these late plays that the values of life and home are presented forcefully. They are well defined and come to life on stage. Even where they are ironically treated, as they are in *Hedda Gabler*, and even where their limitations are clearly brought out, as in *The Lady from the Sea*, they appear attractive. Art, on the other hand, becomes a prison of the soul, a threat to the homely values, a road to death or death-in-life. One does wonder whether the repetition of Maja's song which stands at the very end of everything Ibsen wrote, is not also his own song:

> I am free! I am free! I am free!
> No longer this prison for me!
> I'm free as a bird! I am free!
> [*The sound of Maja's song is heard still further down the mountain.*]

All of Ibsen's plays after *The Wild Duck* arguably present a situation where art and the artist are conceived as destructive and this is contrasted with the values of life and love. If one retained the idiom of "enriching or modifying the reader's concepts", one could say that each of the plays enriched or modified the reader's concepts of art and the artist in the *same way*. Each of them presents Ibsen's mature view of his own vocation and in the light of the parallels between the plays developed above, it would be unreasonable to insist that this view was unique and idiosyncratic in each of the plays. One might argue that each of the late plays offered a different *interpretation* of the view, but that would not imply that one learnt something different or that the reader's concepts were differently enriched or modified by each of the plays. The *same* modification or enrichment of a reader's concepts can consequently be brought about by *different* literary works. Furthermore, there is nothing in the modification or enrichment of these concepts which attaches it logically to reading a literary work and excludes other possible ways in which a reader could be brought to revise his concepts of art and the artist.

The second objection is that the strong version of the Subjective Knowledge Theory fails to make a distinction important in any theory that assumes cognitive consequences, i.e. between recognizing a conception of a situation and adopting that conception. A reader is not constrained to adopt a conception of reality which a literary work realizes for him through a subjective experience. The idiom of "enriching and modifying the reader's concepts" tends to obscure this distinction. What the reader learns from Ibsen's late plays is *Ibsen's* view of art (or at least that developed in his plays) and to the extent that he comes to see what Ibsen's concepts were, we might say that the reader's concepts have been modified or enriched. However, they are not enriched in the sense that he necessarily adopts the view of art and the artist developed by Ibsen. Moreover, the same logical constraint applies here as to the Propositional Theory. Reading a literary work a reader does not construe the work as *requiring* or *inviting* him to modify his concepts. These plays may bring some readers to adopt the conception of art and the artist which Ibsen, on the proposed interpretation, presents. But this is not something a reader will expect the plays, as literary works, to bring about. They are not read as treatises on art. The reader will work through interpretation to recognize the concepts the author uses to organize the presented situations, but there is no demand that he should accept or reject the authorial perspective. As will have become clear, there is a strong parallel between the philosophical consequences of "waiting on a story", i.e. the modification or enrichment of the concepts through which a reader understands a type of situation, which the strong version of the Subjective Knowledge Theory introduces, and the propositions of the

Propositional Theory of Literary Truth; and most of the arguments against the Propositional Theory apply equally to the strong version of the Subjective Knowledge Theory.

The problem is that once one takes the step from the weak to the strong version of this theory, literature ceases to be a source of insight into the subjective sphere of human existence *paralleling* philosophy as a source of insight into the external aspects, and becomes *subordinated* to philosophy. The strong version of the Subjective Knowledge Theory is not a theory of the cognitive value of literature at all, but represents a view of how to do philosophy, ultimately deriving from Wittgenstein. According to this view philosophy should shun general theories and concentrate on the particular situation. Literature is then naturally seen as a source of descriptions of particular situations which can be used to illuminate a philosophical problem. Literature is "a source of reminders (not examples) from which philosophy can benefit in wrestling with issues concerning the firm or slackening hold of various perspectives in human life".[25] Ignoring such particularity and detail as literature has to offer can not only "lead to an obscuring generality in philosophical theories about morality, but ... it can also lead to blindness with regard to certain perspectives on human life".[26] Trying to turn this view of a possible use of literature into a theory of the mimetic aspect of literature is necessarily problematic since this use is neither a *constitutive* nor even a *characteristic* function of literature. Literary works can be used as eyeopeners or as reminders in philosophy, and it is possible to discuss the effectiveness of literary works in these uses. But that discussion is not about the cognitive value of literature that defines or explains the high cultural value accorded to literature.

Literature as Moral Philosophy

Those theorists who are impressed by the perspectival aspect of the subjective point of view develop a different theory of the cognitive value of literature from those emphasizing the subjective experience. These theorists argue that the cognitive value of literature consists in the contribution it makes to moral reasoning. Literature presents to the reader various attempts to work through prominent alternative views of an ethical problem,[27] it aids him in the imaginative re-creation of moral problems,[28] presents "the mystery, conflict, and riskiness of the lived deliberative situation",[29] and is therefore a part of or a necessary adjunct to "moral reasoning":

A novel, just because it is not our life, places us in a moral position that is favorable for perception and it shows us what it would be like to take up that position in life. We find here love without possessiveness, attention without bias, involvement without panic. Our moral abilities must be developed to a certain degree, certainly, before we can approach this novel at all and see anything in it. But it does not seem far-fetched to claim that most of us can read James better than we can read ourselves.[30]

Literature does not, or does not often, depict *solutions*. What especially the novel does is aid us in the imaginative re-creation of moral perplexities, in the widest sense. (I don't contend that this is what is aesthetically valuable about novels; indeed I shall not deal with questions of aesthetic value at all. But I contend that this is an important fact about the novel as it has developed in the last few centuries.) Sometimes it is said that literature describes "the human predicament", which is perhaps a way of referring to this. But the pomposity of the phrase obscures the point. The important point is not that there is some *one* predicament which is *the* human predicament, and which literature sometimes describes; the point is that for *many* reasons it seems increasingly difficult to imagine *any* way of life which is both at all ideal and feasible; and literature often puts before us both extremely vividly and in extremely rich emotional detail why and how this seems to be so in different societies, in different times, and from different perspectives. I want to suggest that if moral reasoning, at the reflective level, is the conscious criticism of ways of life, then the sensitive appreciation in the imagination of predicaments and perplexities must be essential to sensitive moral reasoning. Novels and plays do not set moral knowledge before us, that is true. But they do (frequently) do something for us that must be done for us if we are to gain any moral knowledge.[31]

What literature supplies in moral reasoning is the working-out of a moral choice from a subjective point of view. This is important, according to these theorists, since a significant proportion of moral choices do not consist in the application of general rules, but in the exercise of moral judgment in given circumstances. Many moral judgments cannot, in other words, be made if one adopts the "view from nowhere" because they need to take into account the individual, subjective perspective on a situation.

In order to see exactly what this argument amounts to, and to assess it, it is useful to make a number of distinctions. First, a distinction needs to be made between the traditional humanist view that literature is valuable because it educates the reader's moral awareness by presenting situations of moral conflict and choice in all their complexity and with all their emotional implications, and the claim that literature because it presents such situations is an integral part of or necessary adjunct to *moral reasoning* and therefore to *moral philosophy*. Both Nussbaum and Putnam tend to run these two claims together: literature becomes an integral part of *moral argument* because it involves the reader in a process of discrimination and perception which develops his moral awareness, something which ordinary philosophical texts fail to do:

> For this novel [Henry James's *The Golden Bowl*] calls upon and also develops our ability to confront mystery with the cognitive engagement both of thought and feeling. To work through these sentences and these chapters is to become involved in an activity of exploration and unravelling that uses abilities, especially abilities of emotion and imagination, rarely tapped by philosophical texts.[32]

> What I am suggesting is that if we want to reason rationally about feminism, communism, liberalism, or just about life in the twentieth century, then what Doris Lessing does for our sensibility [in *The Golden Notebook*] is enormously important.[33]

The view that literature is an integral part of or necessary adjunct to moral argument and therefore to moral philosophy is, however, logically independent of the view that literature is educative of the reader's moral awareness. The former does not entail the latter in any way, and there is nothing contradictory in holding the latter while denying the former. This, indeed, was the position taken

up by F. R. Leavis who spent considerable energy and space defending both the moral importance of literature and the independence of both literature and criticism from philosophy.[34]

A further distinction has to be made between a strong and a weak thesis about the relationship between moral philosophy and literature. The strong thesis would be universal and essentialist, analogous to the claim that "All literature aspires to the condition of music." That is, it would claim that all literary works aspire to be part of or a necessary adjunct to moral philosophy and that it is in so far as they succeed in fulfilling this aspiration that they become good or great literary works. This thesis is implausible for two important reasons, one concerning its universalist, the other its essentialist aspect. First, there is the same objection as against the Subjective Knowledge Theory that it fails to account for all types of literary works: not all literary works present situations of moral conflict and choice. Indeed, there are major genres of literature, such as the lyric poem, that cannot very well be said to be occupied with "the sensitive appreciation in the imagination of predicaments and perplexities ... essential to sensitive moral reasoning".[35] And there are particular literary works that would not fall under the thesis, such as the Ibsen plays discussed earlier which, on the interpretation given there, concern themselves with the role of art and aesthetic value.

Secondly, it is a consequence of the strong thesis that a reader must ascribe value to a literary work on the basis of a judgment about the truth of the moral position involved. Moral reasoning is concerned with truth, with "getting it right", whether the nature of moral reasoning is thought of as the application of general rules or as discriminating between conflicting moral claims in a complex situation and balancing them against each other. However, as was argued at length in connection with the Propositional Theory, appreciation of a literary work can proceed independently of judgments about the truth of the work (or its content). In the case of Ibsen's plays as conceived under the interpretation given, it is arguable that the situation presented in the later plays (where the values of life are separated from the values of art and, even where ironically treated, represent a preferred alternative to the values of art) is "truer to life" and also more complex than the situation presented in the early plays (where the values of art and life are identical, but where "daily life" appears as conventional and constricting). However, to conclude on

Peter Lamarque and Stein Haugom Olsen

the basis of this that, for example, *The Lady from the Sea* is a better play than *Peer Gynt*, would be eccentric indeed, placing the highly competent above the truly excellent.

The thesis may also be given a weak form: some literary works incidentally have the feature that they contribute to moral reasoning. In this case, the fact that these were literary works would be of no special significance. There would be little reason to object to such a thesis, but it would be uninteresting from the point of view of literary aesthetics since it makes no claims about any systematic relationship between literature and philosophy. Again the philosophers who insist on a close relationship between moral philosophy and literature do not distinguish between the strong and the weak thesis. Nussbaum implies that her thesis will have consequences for "our conventional distinction between philosophy and literature", but she explicitly makes her claim with reference to one novel in particular, James's *The Golden Bowl*, adding that the claim holds good for "other related novels" and "tragic drama",[36] and elsewhere she makes it with particular reference to Greek tragic drama.[37] Putnam makes his claims with reference "especially" to the novel.[38] With regard to the *nature* of the relationship between philosophy and literature Putnam explicitly avoids making the claim that the contribution of the literary work to moral reasoning is part of its aesthetic value though he apparently believes that it is a property in particular of *good* novels. Nussbaum, on her part, insists that this contribution is made by virtue of the fact that the literary work is the sort of work that it is:

> But it is, in fact, not possible to speak about the moral view revealed within this text without speaking at the same time of the created text, which exemplifies and expresses the responses of an imagination that means to care for and to put itself there for us.... I claim that the views uncovered in this text derive their power from the way in which they emerge as the ruminations of such a high and fine mind concerning the tangled mysteries of these imaginary lives. And we could hardly begin to see whether such views were or were not exemplary for us if this mind simply stated its conclusions flatly, if it did not unfold before us the richness of its reflection, allowing us to follow and to share its adventures.[39]

But Nussbaum too avoids the question whether the moral value of this novel is (in part) *constitutive* of its aesthetic value. What appears then, is the following mixed thesis: *Some literary works make a contribution to moral reasoning and must therefore be considered as an integral part of or necessary adjunct to moral philosophy. The features of these works that make them valuable as moral philosophy are identical in part with those features that make them valuable as imaginative creations, i.e. as literary works. The function they serve in moral philosophy could not therefore be served by any other kind of text.* The question whether their moral value is part of, or integral to, their aesthetic value is simply not raised or not considered.

One final distinction, useful in the evaluation of this thesis, may be made between two types of relationship between philosophy and literature, philosophy *through* literature and philosophy *in* literature.[40] Philosophy *in* literature is the sort of relationship brought out in the above analysis of Ibsen's plays: a theme that is also the object of philosophical deliberation is given literary interpretation in terms of an imaginative world artistically constructed. However, this imaginative working-out of the theme is incommensurable with philosophical deliberation on the theme: one cannot transfer insights from one sphere to another though it is quite possible that an insight in one field should *inspire* the development of an insight in the other. Philosophy *in* literature is a relation where philosophy is subordinated to the purpose and function of literature, and consequently the aspect identified as philosophical in a literary work can only be identified as an integral part of, or as partially constitutive of, aesthetic value. Philosophy *through* literature, on the other hand, refers to "the use of imaginative literary forms as devices of exposition, for the more effective communication of philosophical conceptions that have already been fully worked out".[41] In this relation literary works are subordinated to the function and purpose of philosophical argument, and the focus of interest is consequently on the way in which an imaginatively realized fictive situation can throw light on a moral problem and not on the way in which a literary work redefines and develops these conceptions in a fundamentally different *literary* way. The focus is on the features that make the situation representative rather than the features that make it unique. Philosophy *in* literature refers to an essential relationship between philosophy and literature. Philosophy

352

through literature names a contingent relationship: it is incidental to their philosophical function that the texts used also have a function as literary works. This would be so even if it were true that those features that made these texts valuable in moral argument coincided with the features that made them valuable literary works.

Typical examples of works where it is easy to identify the relation philosophy *through* literature are Pope's *An Essay on Man* which presents, Quinton maintains,[42] the philosophy of Boling-broke, and *An Essay on Criticism* which presents neo–classical poetic doctrine. However, works of literature are rarely expository in the way that Pope is, and more interesting examples would be Dante's *Divina Commedia* or Milton's *Paradise Lost*. Whether James's *The Golden Bowl* can be construed in such a way that an independent philo-sophical view can be identified in it, is a question to which there is no immediately obvious answer. What is clear is that philosophy *through* literature, just like philosophy *in* literature, is a relationship that has to be identified through an interpretation, though the logic of the interpretative argument in the two cases will not be the same.

The relationship which Putnam and Nussbaum assert to hold between a limited range of literary works and moral philosophy must be characterized as philosophy *through* literature. The thesis formu-lated above is nothing more than a special version of the weak thesis. It asserts neither a universal nor an essential link between literary works (*qua* literature) and philosophy. Consequently it does not say any-thing that is theoretically interesting about the way in which philosophy either as discourse or as a provider of concepts and themes enters into the reader's appreciation of literature. The thesis is in fact a thesis about the role of literary works in moral philosophy. The focus of interest for both Nuss-baum and Putnam is the nature of moral argument and moral philosophy. They are both concerned to extend the notion of moral argument to involve "not just the logical faculties, in the narrow sense, but our full capacity to imagine and feel, in short, our full sensibility".[43] And the capacity to imagine and feel is necessary in moral philosophy because moral reasoning is concerned with practical situ-ations which must be fully realized. However, when they are presented in literature, these situ-ations are always, as Nussbaum herself puts it in the quoted passage, "exemplary". Literary representa-tions provide particularized illustrations that fall under general descriptions and judgments.

It may still be argued that if it is true that certain literary works make a significant contribution to moral argument, this is a value of these literary works which necessarily must influence the reader's total (as opposed to his merely aesthetic) evaluation of these works. Their contribution to moral reasoning is an additional reason for reading these works and recommending others to read them. It is of little importance that this merit is not aesthetic merit. However, this argument fails because there is no such *total* evaluation of a literary work. A work is read for a purpose. If it is read as literature, it is read in a special way, with a special type of attention, the sort of attention given to Ibsen's *The Lady from the Sea* in the first sections of this chapter. The grouping of characters set up at the beginning of Act IV, with Bolette embroidering and Lyngstrand looking on, Ballested painting and Hilde looking on, is construed as full of meaning, as setting up a contrast between Lyngstrand and Ballested and Lyngstrand and Bolette. And from this point of departure was developed a whole network of char-acterizations of Lyngstrand and his relationship to the other characters in the play. *The Lady from the Sea* might have been read in other ways, for example as an attempt to present a picture of a small Norwe-gian coastal town in the late nineteenth century. In that case all the attention to the artistic significance of details would have been wasted. Reading is pur-poseful, directed towards a goal, towards seeing the work from a perspective, and evaluation is always evaluation in relation to this perspective.

If a work is read as a piece of moral reasoning, one does not take up the literary stance towards it and the standards for evaluation will be different, even if the features of the literary works that make it valuable as moral reasoning are in part identical with those that make it valuable as a literary work of art. One such standard that operates when a work is judged as moral reasoning is the standard of "truth". Céline's novel *Journey to the End of the Night* comes in for criticism from Putnam because he presents the reader with "a 'mere' possibility"[44] rather than with a presentation that would cohere better with the reader's actual experience. Henry James receives praise from Nussbaum because "there are candidates for moral truth which the plainness of traditional moral philosophy lacks the power to express, and which *The Golden Bowl* expresses wonderfully."[45] But moral or philosoph-ical truth is not a standard governing literary ap-preciation. One may find Ibsen's vision of the artist and aesthetic value unconvincing though this may not prevent one from recognizing the power of his vision.

Notes

1   Thomas Nagel, *The View from Nowhere* (Oxford: Oxford University Press, 1986), 5.
2   Ibid. 7–8.
3   Ibid. 7.
4   Ibid. 26.
5   Dorothy Walsh, *Literature and Knowledge* (Middletown: Wesleyan University Press, 1969), 104.
6   Walsh, *Literature and Knowledge*, 101.
7   Ibid. 104.
8   Ibid. 137.
9   Ibid. 91.
10 Ibid. 91.
11 Ibid. 137.
12 Ibid. 104.
13 Ibid. 121.
14 Ibid. 123.
15 Henrik Ibsen, *The Lady from the Sea*. All the translations are from *The Oxford Ibsen*.
16 Catherine Wilson, "Literature and Knowledge", *Philosophy*, 58 (1983), 495.
17 John Stuart Mill, *Autobiography* (Oxford, 1924), 124.
18 R. W. Beardsmore, *Art and Morality* (London, 1971), 74.
19 Wilson, "Literature and Knowledge", 495.
20 D. Z. Phillips, "Allegiance and Change in Morality: A Study in Contrasts" in *Through a Darkening Glass: Philosophy, Literature, and Cultural Change* (Oxford, 1982), 25. Originally in *Philosophy and the Arts*. Royal Institute of Philosophy Lectures, VI (1971–2) (London, 1973), 47–64.
21 In his analysis of Edith Wharton's *The Age of Innocence* as well as in an analysis of Tolstoy's "The Death of Ivan Ilych" ("Philosophizing and Reading a Story", *in Through a Darkening Glass*, 64–81) Phillips has a section "Waiting on the Novel" ("Waiting on the Story" in the case of Tolstoy) followed by a section entitled "Philosophical Consequences of Waiting on the Novel (Story)".
22 Ibid. 79.
23 Beardsmore, "Learning from a Novel", 31.
24 Ibid. 34 ff.
25 Phillips, "Introduction", in *Through a Darkening Glass*, 1.
26 Ibid. 4.
27 Nussbaum, *The Fragility of Goodness* (Cambridge: Cambridge University Press, 1986), 12.
28 Hilary Putnam, "Literature, Science, and Reflection", in *Meaning and the Moral Sciences* (London: Routledge and Kegan Paul, 1978), 83–94.
29 Martha C. Nussbaum, "Flawed Crystals: James's *The Golden Bowl* and Literature as Moral Philosophy", in *Love's Knowledge: Essays on Philosophy and Literature* (Oxford, 1990), 142. Originally in *New Literary History*, 15 (1983–4).
30 Martha C. Nussbaum, "'Finely Aware and Richly Responsible': Literature and the Moral Imagination", in *Love's Knowledge*, 162. Originally in Anthony J. Cascardi (ed.), *Literature and the Question of Philosophy* (Baltimore, 1989). See pp. 329–40 in this book.
31 Putnam, "Literature, Science, and Reflection", 86–7.
32 Nussbaum, "Flawed Crystals" in *Love's Knowledge*, 143.
33 Putnam, "Literature, Science, and Reflection", 91.
34 His most systematic development of this view is perhaps to be found in the first part of *The Living Principle: English as a Discipline of Thought* (London, 1975).
35 Putnam, *Literature, Science, and Reflection*, 87.
36 Nussbaum, "Flawed Crystals" in *Love's Knowledge*, 138.
37 Nussbaum, *The Fragility of Goodness*, 13.
38 Putnam, *Literature, Science, and Reflection*, 87.
39 Nussbaum, "Flawed Crystals" in *Love's Knowledge*, 140–1.
40 The distinction is borrowed from Anthony Quinton's lecture, *The Divergence of the Twain: Poet's Philosophy and Philosopher's Philosophy*, A Lecture to Mark the Official Opening of the Centre for Research in Philosophy and Literature, University of Warwick, 8 October 1985 (Centre for Research in Philosophy and Literature, University of Warwick, 1985), 1.
41 Quinton, *The Divergence of the Twain*, 1.
42 Ibid. 4.
43 Putnam, "Literature, Science, and Reflection", 86.
44 Putnam, "Literature, Science, and Reflection", 90.
45 Nussbaum, "Flawed Crystals" in *Love's Knowledge*, 142.

The Ethical Criticism of Art

Berys Gaut

Ethicism

This essay argues that the ethical criticism of art is a proper and legitimate aesthetic activity. More precisely, it defends a view I term *ethicism*. Ethicism is the thesis that the ethical assessment of attitudes manifested by works of art is a legitimate aspect of the aesthetic evaluation of those works, such that, if a work manifests ethically reprehensible attitudes, it is to that extent aesthetically defective, and if a work manifests ethically commendable attitudes, it is to that extent aesthetically meritorious.

This thesis needs elucidation. The ethicist principle is a pro tanto one: it holds that a work is aesthetically meritorious (or defective) *insofar as* it manifests ethically admirable (or reprehensible) attitudes. (The claim could also be put like this: manifesting ethically admirable attitudes *counts toward* the aesthetic merit of a work, and manifesting ethically reprehensible attitudes *counts against* its aesthetic merit.) The ethicist does not hold that manifesting ethically commendable attitudes is a necessary condition for a work to be aesthetically good: there can be good, even great, works of art that are ethically flawed. Examples include Wagner's Ring Cycle, which is marred by the anti-Semitism displayed in the portrayal of the *Nibelungen*; some of T. S. Eliot's poems, such as *Sweeney among the Nightingales*, which are similarly tainted by anti-Semitism; and Leni Riefen-stahl's striking propaganda film, *The Triumph of the Will*, deeply flawed by its craven adulation of Hitler. Nor does the ethicist thesis hold that manifesting ethically good attitudes is a sufficient condition for a work to be aesthetically good: there are works such as Harriet Beecher Stowe's *Uncle Tom's Cabin* which, though the ethical attitudes they display are admirable, are in many ways uninspired and disappointing. The ethicist can deny these necessity and sufficiency claims, because she holds that there are a plurality of aesthetic values, of which the ethical values of artworks are but a single kind. So, for instance, a work of art may be judged to be aesthetically good *insofar as* it is beautiful, is formally unified and strongly expressive, but aesthetically bad *insofar as* it trivializes the issues with which it deals and manifests ethically reprehensible attitudes. We then need to make an *all-things-considered* judgment, balancing these aesthetic merits and demerits one against another to determine whether the work is, all things considered, good. And we should not suppose that there is any mechanically applicable weighing method that could determine the truth of such a judgment: overall judgments are plausibly ones that resist any form of codification in terms of mechanically applicable principles. These kinds of pro tanto and all-things-considered judgments are common in other evaluative domains, notably the moral domain.

From Jerrold Levinson (ed.), *Aesthetics and Ethics: Essays at the Intersection* (Cambridge: Cambridge University Press, 1998), pp. 182–97, 199, 201, 202. Reprinted by permission of the publisher and author.

The notion of the aesthetic adopted here should be construed broadly. In the narrow sense of the term, aesthetic value properties are those that ground a certain kind of sensory or contemplative pleasure or displeasure. In this sense, beauty, elegance, gracefulness, and their contraries are aesthetic value properties. However, the sense adopted here is broader: I mean by "aesthetic value" the value of an object *qua* work of art, that is, its artistic value. This broader sense is required, since not all of the values of an object *qua* work of art are narrowly aesthetic. Besides a work's beauty, we may, for instance, aesthetically admire it for its cognitive insight (subject, as we shall see, to certain conditions), its articulated expression of joy, the fact that it is deeply moving, and so on. However, this broader sense of "aesthetic" does not mean that just any property of a work of art counts as aesthetic. Works of art have many other sorts of value properties that are not values of them *qua* works of art: they can have investment value, value as status symbols, and so forth.

The notion of manifesting an attitude should be construed in terms of a work's displaying pro or con attitudes toward some state of affairs or things, which the work may do in many ways besides explicitly stating an opinion about them. (Such attitudes can run the gamut from unmixed approval through neutrality to unmixed disapproval, and also include various complex and nuanced attitudes that display both approbatory and disapprobatory aspects, such as those revealed in jealous or conflicted attitudes.) What is relevant for ethicism are the attitudes *really* possessed by a work, not those it merely claims to possess: so the attitudes manifested may be correctly attributable only by subtle and informed critical judgment. A novel may state that it condemns the sexual activities it describes, but from the subtly lubricious and prying manner in which it dwells on them, it may be correct to attribute to it an attitude of titillation, not of moralistic disgust. Just as we can distinguish between the attitudes people really have and those they merely claim to have by looking at their behavior, so we can distinguish between real and claimed attitudes of works by looking at the detailed manner in which events are presented.

Ethicism does not entail the causal thesis that good art ethically improves people. Since the ethicist principle is a pro tanto one, it allows for the existence of great but ethically flawed works; and

even if all aesthetically good works were ethically sound, it would not follow that they improve people, any more than it follows that earnest ethical advice improves people, for they may be unmoved by even the most heartfelt exhortation. Much of the ethical discussion about art, particularly concerning the supposedly pernicious effects of some popular films and music genres, has been concerned with the question of whether such art morally corrupts. This is a version of the causal thesis and should be kept distinct from ethicism. Further, ethicism has nothing to say about the issue of censorship, nor does it give any grounds of support to either the friends or foes of artistic censorship. All that follows from ethicism is that if a work manifests morally bad attitudes it is to that extent aesthetically flawed, flawed as a work of art. The fact that a work of art is aesthetically flawed is not grounds for its censorship: if it were, the art museums of the world would suffer serious depletion.

Objections to Ethicism

1. Ethicism fails to distinguish sharply enough between ethical and aesthetic evaluation. There is an aesthetic attitude in terms of which we aesthetically evaluate works; this aesthetic attitude is distinct from the ethical attitude we may adopt toward works; and ethical assessment is never a concern of the aesthetic attitude. So the ethical criticism of works is irrelevant to their aesthetic value.

The existence of the aesthetic attitude has, of course, been much disputed. But, even if we accept its existence, its adoption is compatible with ethicism. To see why, we need to specify in more detail what the aesthetic attitude is. There are two basic ways of doing this: the aesthetic attitude may be individuated by some feature intrinsic to it or by its formal objects.

Consider the case in which the attitude is individuated by its formal objects: these may be understood in narrow aesthetic fashion, as beauty and its subspecies, such as grace and elegance, or characterized more broadly by the criteria to which formalists appeal, such as Beardsley's unity, complexity, and intensity. Since the presence of these properties arguably does not require, or suffice for, the presence of ethical properties, it may be held that ethical assessment is irrelevant to aesthetic evaluation. Yet this objection is unconvincing, for the list of properties deployed is too narrow to embrace all those of aesthetic relevance. In the assessment of art, appeal is made to such properties as raw expressive power and deep cognitive insight as well as to beauty, elegance, and grace; and the relevance of these expressive and cognitive values explains how there can be great works, such as *Les Demoiselles d'Avignon*, that are militantly ugly. So the narrow aesthetic view fails. In more sophisticated fashion, the formalist appeals to purely intrinsic properties of works as aesthetically relevant, an appeal motivated by a conception of the work of art as autonomous from its context. But that conception is flawed, for a work can be fully interpreted only by situating it within its generative context. There is reason, then, to spurn the restricted diet of aesthetically relevant properties offered by the narrow aesthetic and formalist views, and as yet no reason to exclude ethical properties from a heartier menu.

The alternative is to individuate the aesthetic attitude by some feature intrinsic to it, and for the opponent of ethicism the most promising feature is the detachment or disengagement we purportedly display toward fictional events. Since it is logically impossible to intervene in such events, the will is detached, practical concerns are quiescent, an attitude of contemplation is adopted. Given the practical character of morality, it follows that ethical assessment plays no role in aesthetic attitude and therefore no role in aesthetic evaluation. But the step from the claim that the will is disengaged and therefore that ethical assessment has no role to play does not follow: there is similarly no possibility of altering historical events, and we are in this sense forced to have a detached or contemplative attitude toward them, but we still ethically assess historical characters and actions. If it is objected that we are ethically engaged in history because we hope to draw from it lessons for our current practice, the same may be said of the lessons we can draw from fiction, such as the psychological insights that Freud discovered there.

The point about ethics and the will deserves elaboration, for it will be relevant to the position defended later. On what might be termed the *purely practical* conception of ethics, the ethical assessment of a person's character is determined only by what he does and by the motives that determine his actions. Any feelings or thoughts that play no role in motivating actions are ethically irrelevant: thoughts, fantasies, and desires, however gruesome, inappropriate, or corrupt we would

judge the actions they motivate to be, are not themselves ethically bad, unless they issue in actions that express these feelings and thoughts. So a person may be ethically good while having these feelings and thoughts, and his goodness may consist partly in his capacity to resist their influence on the will, for these feelings and thoughts may have arisen purely passively in him, and he is not to be held responsible for their occurrence. This view, as has just been noted, speedily runs into problems in historical cases where the will cannot be engaged, yet where ethical assessment is still appropriate. But it can be shown to be flawed on other grounds too. Much of our ethical assessment is directed at what people feel, even though these feelings do not motivate their actions. Suppose that Joe is praised for some deserved achievement by his friends, but he later discovers that they are secretly deeply jealous and resentful of him. Their feelings have not motivated their actions, yet we would properly regard these people as less ethically good were we to discover this about them. They are flawed because of what they feel, not because of what they did or their motives for doing it. Also, that people feel deep sympathy for us, even though they are completely unable to help us in our distress, is something that we care about and that properly makes us think better of them. In fact, much of our vocabulary of ethical assessment is directed wholly or in part at the assessment of feelings: we criticize people for being crude, insensitive, callous, or uncaring; we praise them for being warm, friendly, and sensitive. So for the ethical assessment of character an *affective-practical* conception of assessment is correct, a conception which holds that not just actions and motives, but also feelings that do not motivate, are ethically significant. Virtue of character is "concerned with feelings and actions," as Aristotle correctly observes.[1] Such an affective-practical conception of ethical assessment allows the ethical assessment of the feelings that people have when they respond to fictions, even though they cannot act toward the fictional events described.

2. A more radical objection holds that ethical assessment has no place in the assessment of art. Works of art can at best manifest attitudes toward those fictional characters and situations they describe, and such attitudes are not ethically assessable, since they are directed toward merely imagined objects – such objects cannot be harmed or hurt in reality, for they do not exist. What is

Berys Gaut

ethically assessable, in contrast, are attitudes directed toward real characters and situations, but works of art do not manifest attitudes toward such things, for they do not describe them. Hence, there is no place left for the ethical assessment of art.

Even at first blush, the objection is hyperbolic, since not all works of art are fictions: Riefenstahl's film is a documentary of the 1934 Nuremberg rally, and Hitler was not a fictional character. So, at best, the argument would apply only to a subclass of works of art. Second, attitudes directed toward only imagined states of affairs can in fact properly be ethically assessed. Consider a man whose sexual life consists entirely of rape fantasies, fantasies he has not about women he sees in real life, but about women he only imagines. Would we say that there is nothing to be said from an ethical point of view about the attitude he manifests in his imaginings about these fictional women? Clearly, what a person imagines and how he responds to those imaginings play an important part in the ethical assessment of his character. The mere fact that the women he imagines cannot be harmed does not bracket his inner life from ethical assessment, since what is at issue are the attitudes he manifests in his fantasy life. And nothing in our judgment about him requires us to assume that what is bad about his fantasies is that he may act on them – perhaps he is confined to prison for life. He stands ethically condemned for what and how he imagines, independently of how he acts or may act. (Here again, we return to the ethical importance of feelings, but see now that feelings toward merely imagined people can be ethically relevant too.) Further, the attitudes people (and works) manifest toward imagined scenarios have implications for their attitudes toward their real-life counterparts, for the attitudes are partly directed toward kinds, not just individuals. When the rape fantasist imagines his fictional women, he is imagining them *as women*, that is, as beings of a kind that also has instances in the real world; and that he imagines them as women is, of course, essential to his imaginative project. Thus, by virtue of adopting such an attitude toward his imagined women, he implicitly adopts that attitude toward their real-life counterparts – and so reveals something of his attitude toward real-life women. Indeed, it is inevitable that, however apparently exotic the fictional world, the kinds shared between it and the real world will be vast, given the limits on the human imagination, the interests we have in fiction (which include exploring possibilities that reorder the actual world), and interpretive constraints, which involve drawing on background information about the real world in the interpretation of fictions. So the attitudes manifested toward fictional entities will have many implications for attitudes manifested toward real entities.

3. Ethical assessment is relevant to a work's aesthetic merit, but ethicism gives the connection the wrong valence: works can be good precisely *because* they violate our sense of moral rectitude. Often the most fascinating characters in works are the evil ones, such as Satan in *Paradise Lost*. And recall the passage in *King Lear* in which blind Gloucester asks Lear, "Dost thou know me?" and Lear replies, "I remember thine eyes well enough. Dost thou squiny at me? / No, do thy worst, blind Cupid, I'll not love." As Lawrence Hyman writes, "The dramatic effect requires our moral disapproval," but Shakespeare manages to "transfigure that moral shock into aesthetic pleasure."[2]

It is important to distinguish between the evil or insensitive characters represented by a work and the attitude the work displays toward those characters. Only the latter is relevant to the ethicist thesis. Satan is indeed fascinating because evil, but the work represents him as such, showing the seductive power of evil, and does not approve of his actions. Milton was not a Satanist. And while the power of Lear's bad joke does rest on its hearty heartlessness, it is part of the point of *Lear* that the flamboyant insensitivity displayed by Lear in his derangement is of a piece with the gross egoism that leads to disaster, an egoism overcome only by grief and loss, and transmuted into a finer moral wisdom. Lear's attitude toward Gloucester is represented by the play, but not shared by it. It is true that some works, such as de Sade's *Juliette*, not merely represent evil, but also manifest approval toward that evil. If this work has indeed any serious aesthetic merit, it can in part be traced to the literary skill with which it represents the attitude of finding sexual torture erotically attractive: yet the ethicist can consistently and plausibly maintain that the novel's own espousal of this attitude is an aesthetic defect in it.

It may be objected that the novel's approbatory attitude toward evil is a reason why it is aesthetically good: evil arouses our curiosity, for the evil person may do and experience things we can scarcely imagine, let alone understand; and the novel's ability to satisfy this curiosity, to show us what it is like to engage in such actions, is a prime source of its aesthetic merit. Yet from the fact that we are fascinated by the attitudes manifested, we cannot conclude that our interest in them is aesthetic: our fascination with Adolf Hitler or Jeffrey Dahmer is not an aesthetic one, and our interest in de Sade's work may similarly stem from a curiosity about psychopathic states of mind. Suppose, however, that our interest in *Juliette* is aesthetic, perhaps because of the way that interest is inflected by a concern with the work's stylistic and rhetorical system. This still does not undermine ethicism. For our interest here is in being able to imagine what it is like to have evil attitudes, and so in coming to understand them, and this is satisfied by the vivid *representation* of an evil attitude. But, again, representation of an attitude by a work does not require the work itself to share that attitude: works may manifest disapproval toward characters or narrators who are represented as evil. Moreover, if, as the objection holds, it is our curiosity that is aroused, we have a cognitive interest in not seeing evil approved of, for such approval implies that there is something good about an attitude we know to be bad.

Some Arguments for Ethicism

There are, of course, further objections and elaborations open to the opponent of ethicism, some of which will be touched on later, but enough has been said to give rational hope that they may be laid to rest. The question remains as to why ethicism should be endorsed. Part of the answer is to be sought in its congruence with our considered aesthetic judgments; we do decry works for their insensitivity, their moral crudity, their lack of integrity, their celebration of cruelty, their slimy salaciousness. But it is the mark of an interesting philosophical thesis that, while some find it obviously true, others find it obviously false; and ethicism is, fortunately and unfortunately, an interesting philosophical thesis. So it would be good to have an argument for its truth.

1. George Dickie has advanced a simple argument for the truth of ethicism. A work of art's moral vision is an (essential) part of that work; any statement about an (essential) part of a work of art is an aesthetic statement about that work; so a statement about a work of art's moral vision is an aesthetic statement about the work.[3]

However, it is not true that any statement about an essential part of a work is an aesthetic statement about it. For instance, it is essential to a poem that it be composed of the particular words that comprise it. So it is essential to it that it have in it the particular letters that it has. So, if it is true of a particular poem that it has in it exactly as many letter *e*'s as it has letter *c*'s, then that is an essential feature of the poem. But that is not an *aesthetic* statement about the work, since it standardly plays no role in our appreciation of it. Likewise, consider a statue carved in limestone. It is essential to its being the particular statue which it is that it be composed of the crushed shells of ancient sea creatures. But whereas the statue's texture and color are generally relevant to its aesthetic merits, the mere fact that it is composed of crushed shells is not. For, again, this fact standardly plays no role in our appreciation of it as a work of art. So a premise on which Dickie's argument rests is false.

2. Perhaps the most influential opponents of ethicism have been formalists. However, David Pole not only has argued that ethicism is compatible with formalism, but has tried to derive ethicism from it. He holds that the immorality of a work is a formal defect in it, since it is a type of internal incoherence. For if a work of art presents a morally bad view, it will do so by distorting or glossing over something it presents. But then something is lacking within the work itself and so "some particular aspect [of the work] must jar with what – on the strength of the rest – we claim a right to demand." This jarring is an internal incoherence in the work and thus a defect that the formalist would acknowledge as such.[4]

If a work is morally corrupt, it follows that it distorts something and so jars with a truth about the world, but it does not follow that it has to jar with anything else in the work, for the work may be systematically immoral. *The Triumph of the Will*, for instance, is held together thematically by its offensive celebration of Nazism. So Pole's formalist derivation of ethicism fails.

3. An approach glanced at by Hume and elaborated by Wayne Booth holds that literary assessment is akin to an act of befriending, for one assesses the implied author of a work as a suitable friend. A good friend may possess a variety of merits (being intelligent, good company, lively, etc.), and some of these are ethical: she is trustworthy, sensitive, kind, and so on. So assessing someone as a friend involves among other things assessing her ethical character, a character

displayed in the case of the implied author in the literary work in which she is manifested.

The approach has its merits, and captures the pro tanto structure of ethicism well, but it is ill-equipped to cope with some Hollywood films whose impersonality and industrial-style production may give the audience little sense of an implied author or authors, but whose ethical stance may elicit their aesthetic condemnation. And the approach also runs afoul of one of the objections considered earlier: for the implied author is a fictional construct, albeit one implicit in, rather than described by, the text. If fictional characters, such as Satan and Lear, can be interesting because of their moral failings, the corrupt fictional character of an author can similarly be interesting, and the aesthetic merit of her work be accordingly enhanced. Appeal to the characters of fictional beings will not ground ethicism.

4. More promising is an argument that may be extrapolated from views defended by Richard Eldridge and Martha Nussbaum. For Eldridge a person's moral self-understanding cannot completely be captured by general theories, but must be developed and sustained by an awareness of the relation of her story to the stories of others, an awareness that literature is peculiarly well placed to articulate and extend: "all we can do is to attempt to find ourselves in cases, in narratives of the development of persons."[5] For Nussbaum, too, morality is a matter of the appreciation of particular cases, and literature can refine our awareness of moral particularities in a way that eludes the flailing grasp of philosophy: "To show forth the force and truth of the Aristotelian claim that 'the decision rests with perception,' we need, then – either side by side with a philosophical 'outline' or inside it – texts which display to us the complexity, the indeterminacy, the sheer *difficulty* of moral choice."[6] This conception of literature as moral philosophy naturally suggests a cognitivist argument for ethicism: it is an aesthetic merit in a work that it gives insight into some state of affairs, and literature can yield insights into moral reality of a depth and precision that no other cultural form is well placed to match; so the moral insights delivered by literary works enhance their aesthetic worth.

There is much here that should be retained and accounted for in any successful defense of ethicism, and an attempt will be made to do so in what follows. Yet the argument rests on a radically particularist account of morality, which denies

the existence of any general and informative moral principles. If that view be denied, as I believe it should, the idea of literature as the culmination of moral philosophy is rendered less compelling. And even if the claims of literature were rendered more modest, we would still require an explanation of why the insights literature can provide are aesthetically relevant. Works of art can be interesting and informative as social documents, but the fact that much can be learned from them about the attitudes and circumstances of their time does not ipso facto make them aesthetically better: one can learn much about Victorian agricultural politics from *Tess*, and on the subject of nineteenth-century whaling practices *Moby-Dick* is excruciatingly informative. Likewise, old photographs and films can have great value as documentary sources of their times, but these cognitive merits do not thereby improve these objects *qua* works of art. So the cognitivist approach must be supplemented in order to give an account of the conditions under which cognitive merits are aesthetically relevant.

The Merited-Response Argument

Ethicism is a thesis about a work's manifestation of certain attitudes, but in what does this manifestation of attitudes consist? It is obvious that works prescribe the imagining of certain events: a horror film may prescribe imagining teenagers being assaulted by a monster; *Juliette* prescribes imagining that acts of sexual torture occur. Perhaps less obviously, works also prescribe certain responses to these fictional events: the loud, atonal music of the horror film prescribes us to react to the represented events with fear, *Juliette* invites the reader to find sexual torture erotically attractive, to be aroused by it, to be amused by the contortions described, to admire the intricacy of their implementation, and so forth. The approbatory attitude that *Juliette* exhibits toward sexual torture, then, is manifested in the responses it prescribes its readers to have toward such torture. The attitudes of works are manifested in the responses they prescribe to their audiences.

It is important to construe this claim correctly to avoid an objection. Consider a novel that prescribes its readers to be amused at a character's undeserved suffering but that does so in order to show up the ease with which the reader can be seduced into callous responses. Then one response (amusement) is prescribed, but a very different attitude is manifested by the work (disapproval of the ease with which we can be morally seduced); hence, the manifestation of attitudes is wholly distinct from and independent of the prescription of responses. What this objection reveals is that prescriptions, like attitudes, come in a hierarchy, with higher-order prescriptions taking lower-order ones as their objects. Thus, my amusement at the character's suffering is prescribed, but there is a higher-order prescription that this amusement itself be regarded as callous and therefore as unmerited. So the complete set of prescriptions that a work makes must be examined in order to discover what attitudes it manifests: taking individual prescriptions out of context may mislead us about the work's attitudes. Here, as elsewhere, the application of the ethicist principle requires a grasp of interpretive subtleties and contextual factors. Talk of prescriptions from now on should be construed as involving the complete set of relevant prescriptions that a work makes toward fictional events.

The claim that works prescribe certain responses to the events described is widely applicable. *Jane Eyre*, for instance, prescribes the imagining of the course of a love affair between Jane and Rochester, and also prescribes us to admire Jane's fortitude, to want things to turn out well for her, to be moved by her plight, to be attracted to this relationship as an ideal of love, and so forth. Similar remarks apply to paintings, films, and other representational arts. Music without a text is also subject to ethical criticism if we can properly ascribe to the music a presented situation and a prescribed response to it. If Shostakovich's symphonies are a musical protest against the Stalinist regime, we can ethically assess them.

The notion of a response is to be understood broadly, covering a wide range of states directed at represented events and characters, including being pleased at something, feeling an emotion toward it, being amused about it, and desiring something with respect to it – wanting it to continue or stop, wanting to know what happens next. Such states are characteristically affective, some essentially so, such as pleasure and the emotions, while in the case of others, such as desires, there is no necessity that they be felt, although they generally are.

The responses are not simply imagined: we are prescribed by *Juliette* actually to find erotically attractive the fictional events, to be amused by them, to enjoy them, to admire this kind of activ-

ity. So the novel does not just present imagined events, it also presents a point of view on them, a perspective constituted in part by actual feelings, emotions, and desires that the reader is prescribed to have toward the merely imagined events. Given that the notion of a response covers such things as enjoyment and amusement, it is evident that some kinds of response are actual, not just imagined. Some philosophers have denied that we feel actual emotions toward fictional events, but there are, I believe, good reasons for holding this to be possible.

Though a work may prescribe a response, it does not follow that it succeeds in making this response merited: horror fictions may be unfrightening, comedies unamusing, thrillers unthrilling. This is not just to say that fear, amusement, and thrills are not produced in the audience; for people may respond in a way that is inappropriate. Rather, the question is whether the prescribed response is merited, whether it is appropriate or inappropriate to respond in the way the work prescribes. If I am afraid of a harmless victim in a horror movie because of her passing resemblance to an old tormentor of mine, my fear is inappropriate. And my admiration for a character in a novel can be criticized for being based on a misunderstanding of what he did in the story. So prescribed responses are subject to evaluative criteria.

Some of these criteria are ethical ones. As noted earlier, responses outside the context of art are subject to ethical evaluation. I can criticize someone for taking pleasure in others' pain, for being amused by sadistic cruelty, for being angry at someone when she has done no wrong, for desiring the bad. The same is true when responses are directed at fictional events, for these responses are actual, not just imagined ones. If we actually enjoy or are amused by some exhibition of sadistic cruelty in a novel, that shows us in a bad light, reflects ill on our ethical character, and we can properly be criticized for responding in this fashion.

If a work prescribes a response that is unmerited, it has failed in an aim internal to it, and that is a defect. But not all defects in works of art are aesthetic ones. From the point of view of shipping them to art exhibitions, many of Tintoretto's paintings are very bad, since they are so large and fragile that they can be moved only at great risk. But that is not an aesthetic defect. Is the failure of a prescribed response to be merited an *aesthetic* defect (i.e., is it a defect in the work *qua* work of art)? That this is so is evidently true of many artistic genres: thrillers that do not merit the audience being thrilled, tragedies that do not merit fear and pity for their protagonists, comedies that are not amusing, melodramas that do not merit sadness and pity are all aesthetic failures in these respects. Works outside these genres, which similarly prescribe a range of responses, are likewise aesthetic failures if the responses are unmerited. And in general it is a bad work of art that leaves us bored and offers no enjoyment at all. We are also concerned not just with whether a response occurs, but with the quality of that response: humor may be crude, unimaginative, or flat, or may be revelatory, profound, or inspiring. And the aesthetic criticism of a work as being manipulative, sentimental, insensible, or crude is founded on a mismatch between the response the work prescribes the reader to feel and the response actually merited by the work's presentation of the fictional situation.

The aesthetic relevance of prescribed responses wins further support from noting that much of the value of art derives from its deployment of an affective mode of cognition – derives from the way works teach us, not by giving us merely intellectual knowledge, but by bringing that knowledge home to us. This teaching is not just about how the world is, but can reveal new conceptions of the world in the light of which we can experience our situation, can teach us new ideals, can impart new concepts and discriminatory skills – having read Dickens, we can recognize the Micawbers of the world. And the way knowledge is brought home to us is by making it vividly present, so disposing us to reorder our thoughts, feelings, and motivations in the light of it. We all know we will die, but it may take a great work of art to drive that point fully home, to make it vividly present. We may think of the universe as devoid of transcendent meaning, but it may take *Waiting for Godot* to make that thought concrete and real. We may believe in the value of love, but it may take *Jane Eyre* to render that ideal unforgettably alluring. On the cognitive-affective view of the value of art, whether prescribed responses are merited will be of aesthetic significance, since such responses constitute a cognitive-affective perspective on the events recounted. For such responses not merely are affective, but include a cognitive component, being directed toward some state of affairs or thing, and bringing it under evaluative concepts. By prescribing us to be amused, to enjoy, to be aroused by scenes of sexual torture, *Juliette*

aims to get us to approve of the imagined events, to think of them as in some way desirable, and so to endorse an evaluation about events of that kind.

These observations can be assembled into an argument for ethicism. A work's manifestation of an attitude is a matter of the work's prescribing certain responses toward the events described. If these responses are unmerited, because unethical, we have reason not to respond in the way prescribed. Our having reason not to respond in the way prescribed is a failure of the work. What responses the work prescribes is of aesthetic relevance. So the fact that we have reason not to respond in the way prescribed is an *aesthetic* failure of the work, that is to say, is an aesthetic defect. So a work's manifestation of ethically bad attitudes is an aesthetic defect in it. Mutatis mutandis, a parallel argument shows that a work's manifestation of ethically commendable attitudes is an aesthetic merit in it, since we have reason to adopt a prescribed response that is ethically commendable. So ethicism is true.

To illustrate: a comedy presents certain events as funny (prescribes a humorous response to them), but if this involves being amused at heartless cruelty, we have reason not to be amused. Hence, the work's humor is flawed, and that is an aesthetic defect in it. If a work prescribes our enjoyment (as almost all art does to some extent), but if we are supposed to enjoy, say, gratuitous suffering, then we can properly refuse to enjoy it, and hence the work fails aesthetically. If a work seeks to get us to pity some characters, but they are unworthy of pity because of their vicious actions, we have reason not to pity them, and hence the work is aesthetically flawed. Conversely, if the comedy's humor is revelatory, emancipating us from the narrow bonds of prejudice, getting us to see a situation in a different and better moral light and respond accordingly, we have reason to adopt the response, and the work succeeds aesthetically in this respect. If the enjoyment it offers derives from this kind of revelatory humor, we have reason to enjoy the work. And if a work prescribes pity toward characters who suffer unfairly and through no fault of their own, we have reason to pity them, and the work succeeds aesthetically in this way. Similar remarks apply to the range of other responses prescribed by works, such as admiring characters, being angry on their behalf, wanting things for them, and so forth.

The merited-response argument for ethicism captures what is plausible in the last two of the arguments surveyed earlier, but sidesteps the pitfalls into which they stumble. If a work prescribes certain attitudes, these may be sufficiently patterned to justify crediting an implied author to it, and this explains why the befriending argument looks plausible. But the merited-response argument has the advantage of avoiding the problems that stem from taking the implied author as foundational in an argument for ethicism. And the cognitive argument is not so much rejected as incorporated into the current argument, which makes use of a cognitive-affective view of art. Art can teach us about what is ethically correct, but the aesthetic relevance of this teaching is guaranteed only when the work displays it in the responses it prescribes to story events. While tacking on to a novel a claim that a certain type of committed love is an ideal will not do much for its aesthetic worth, getting us to *feel* the attraction of that ideal as embodied in a particular relationship is the central and animating excellence of several novels, including *Jane Eyre*.

Notes

1 Aristotle, *Nicomachean Ethics* 2.6 1106b16, trans. Terence Irwin (Indianapolis: Hackett, 1985).

2 Lawrence Hyman, "Morality and Literature: The Necessary Conflict," *British Journal of Aesthetics* 24 (1984): 149–55, at 154–5.

3 George Dickie, "The Myth of the Aesthetic Attitude," in *Philosophy Looks at the Arts*, ed. Joseph Margolis (Philadelphia: Temple University Press, 1987), 113.

4 David Pole, "Morality and the Assessment of Literature," in his *Aesthetics, Form and Emotion* (London: Duckworth, 1983), 49–50.

5 Richard Eldridge, *On Moral Personhood: Philosophy, Literature, Criticism and Self-Knowledge* (Chicago: University of Chicago Press, 1989), 20.

6 Martha Nussbaum, "Flawed Crystals: James's *The Golden Bowl* and Literature as Moral Philosophy," *New Literary History* 15 (1983): 43.

Index

Printed in Great Britain
by Amazon